Expanding Cinemas

SUNY series in Latin American Cinema

Ignacio M. Sánchez Prado and Leslie L. Marsh, editors

Expanding Cinemas

Experimental Filmmaking across the
Luso-Hispanic Atlantic since 1960

EDUARDO LEDESMA

Published by State University of New York Press, Albany

© 2024 State University of New York

All rights reserved

Printed in the United States of America

No part of this book may be used or reproduced in any manner whatsoever without written permission. No part of this book may be stored in a retrieval system or transmitted in any form or by any means including electronic, electrostatic, magnetic tape, mechanical, photocopying, recording, or otherwise without the prior permission in writing of the publisher.

Links to third-party websites are provided as a convenience and for informational purposes only. They do not constitute an endorsement or an approval of any of the products, services, or opinions of the organization, companies, or individuals. SUNY Press bears no responsibility for the accuracy, legality, or content of a URL, the external website, or for that of subsequent websites.

For information, contact State University of New York Press, Albany, NY
www.sunypress.edu

Library of Congress Cataloging-in-Publication Data

Name: Ledesma, Eduardo, 1972– author.
Title: Expanding cinemas : experimental filmmaking across the Luso-Hispanic Atlantic since 1960 / Eduardo Ledesma.
Description: Albany : State University of New York Press, [2024]. | Series: SUNY series in Latin American cinema | Includes bibliographical references and index.
Identifiers: LCCN 2024019518 | ISBN 9798855800500 (hardcover : alk. paper) | ISBN 9798855800524 (ebook) | ISBN 9798855800517 (pbk. : alk. paper)
Subjects: LCSH: Experimental films—Spain—History and criticism. | Experimental films—Portugal—History and criticism. | Experimental films—Brazil—History and criticism. | Experimental films—Latin America—History and criticism. | Motion pictures—Production and direction. | Motion pictures—Technological innovations.
Classification: LCC PN1995.9.E96 L34 2024 | DDC 791.43/611—dc23/eng/20240722
LC record available at https://lccn.loc.gov/2024019518

Contents

List of Illustrations		vii
Acknowledgments		xi
Introduction	Border Crossings in Intermedial and Transnational (Luso-Hispanic) Film Studies	1
Chapter 1	Transatlantic Exchanges in 1960s Militant Cinemas: Helena Lumbreras's Debt to the Cinema of Fernando Solanas and Santiago Álvarez	33
Chapter 2	Brazilian Cinema Novo and the Iberian Escuela de Barcelona: Art Cinema under Authoritarianism	87
Chapter 3	Remediating Past Filmic Technologies: The Return of Super 8 and Video in the Era of Global Digital Cinema	173
Chapter 4	Cell Phone Cinema and Amateur Genre Film in the Luso-Hispanic Atlantic	241
Chapter 5	Expanded and Immersive Cinema: VR, AR, and MR Film in Latin America, Latinx US, and Spain	299
Coda	Future Trends in Experimental Cinema and Audiovisual Technology across the Luso-Hispanic Atlantic	351

Notes 383

Works Cited 403

Index 431

Illustrations

1.1 Brechtian moment (04:57). 74
1.2 "Remapping" Spain (04:59). 74
1.3 Detail from Ramón Casas's *La carga* (1899) (09:55). 79
1.4 Asturian Revolution, 1934. Civil Guards repressing miners (09:59). 80
1.5 The labyrinth of the *sindicato* (23:07). 83
1.6 Escher meets Kafka (23:18). 83
2.1 Poetry on-screen in *Terra em transe* (8:36). 109
2.2 Photography and photo collage within *Terra em transe* (19:21). 115
2.3 *Fata Morgana*, pre-credits sequence by comic book artist Pelayo Izquierdo (00:33). 129
2.4 *Fata Morgana*, title sequence and moving script (01:36). 132
2.5 *Sexperiencias*, image from collage-montage opening sequence (02:01). 138
2.6 *Sexperiencias*, symbolic representation and metalepsis of global violence (37:00). 140
2.7 *Nocturno 29*, visual-object poem by Joan Brossa within film (08:52). 145
2.8 *Nocturno 29*, the enigmatic Pierrot (08:44). 147
2.9 *Cabeças cortadas*, Diaz II phones Eldorado (06:05). 165

3.1 *Esto no es un recuerdo* (2006), playing with pigeons in Plaza Catalunya (00:28). 183

3.2 *Esto no es un recuerdo* (2006), stop-action sequence with toys (00:53). 184

3.3 *Come Out* (1971), a film by Narcisa Hirsch (08:25). 194

3.4 *pneurosis* (2001) and the aesthetic of attraction (01:08). 201

3.5 *pneurosis* (2001) and digital postproduction effects (04:31). 201

3.6 *This Is Just to Say I—Nro 21: (Projects: 02—The Kiss)* (2012). Denegri returns to Val del Omar's kiss sequence (02:43). 217

3.7 *This Is Just to Say III—Nro 6: Oh, the Golden Days of Video Making I* (2016). Bars and tone (00:01). 217

3.8 *This is Just to Say III—Nro 6: Oh, the Golden Days of Video Making I* (2016). Lego structure assembly, out of focus (00:29). 227

3.9 *This is Just to Say III—Nro 6: Oh, the Golden Days of Video Making I* (2016). Lego structure or contemporary art? (00:43). 228

4.1 Early Latin American cell phone fiction film, *Checklist* (2004) (01:11). 246

4.2 Opening establishing shot from *Rojo en el bosque sangriento* (00:26). 262

4.3 A meta-reflexive moment as the phone rings in *Rojo en el bosque sangriento* (01:50). 264

4.4 Inspecting the ghoulish bakers in *Sangre y levadura* (01:22). 270

4.5 Employees react to supervisor's speech (00:56). 272

4.6 Meta-reflexive shot captures the filming process in *09*. YouTube trailer (00:43). 278

4.7 Carolina's confessional: a classic transnational found footage shot. YouTube trailer (02:00). 280

4.8 *iMedium* promotional poster: the haunting of our cell phone technology. IMDB website. 286

4.9 *iMedium* the application (00:13). 288

5.1	Lola arrives to La Habana in *Madrid Noir*.	318
5.2	Photography as intermedia in *Madrid Noir*.	320
5.3	*Pájaros de papel* narrative focus on music, disability, and inspiration.	323
5.4	*Pájaros de papel*, interactivity, synesthesia, and musical improvisation.	327
5.5	*Use of Force*, empathy or distance?	332
5.6	*Carne y Arena*, this book's author in front of Dallas exhibit.	341
5.7	*Carne y Arena* material signs of immigrant tragedies.	343
5.8	HD video testimonial by migrants.	346

Acknowledgments

This book has represented a lengthy and sustained major effort over the last decade, and owes a debt of gratitude to many, many individuals—family, friends, colleagues—and institutions, chief among them the University of Illinois at Urbana-Champaign, my alma mater and academic home. I still owe much, of course, to my formative years as a graduate student at the University of Illinois-Chicago and at Harvard University and to the many mentors and lifelong friends I met at both of these other academic homes, far too many to name.

But first and foremost, I am indebted to my wife, Jill, an amazing scholar, friend, and partner in every sense, who makes all these efforts worthwhile and who reminds me of my real priorities. To my family, my mother Rosario, my sister Carolina, and my niece Ana, for all their love and support over the years—thank you! To my dearest and oldest friends Eugenio DiStefano, Emilio Sauri, Ana Martín Sagredo, Susana Domingo Amestoy, Tara Toscano, Steve Buttes, Beth Bouloukos, and many others, including everyone still in Spain. To my many running friends throughout the years—you have helped me maintain my sanity. Especially to my old crew in Chicago—John, Chris, Rick, Matt, Brian—and the 4PTC running friends in Champaign-Urbana, my unofficial mentors during so many noon runs.

A special note of thanks to Rebecca Colesworthy at SUNY Press, for her patience while waiting for the book manuscript and for advocating for my project. And, of course, to the wonderful series editors who also believed in this project and offered useful feedback at its outset, Ignacio Sánchez Prado and Leslie Marsh for including the text in their Series in Latin American Cinema. I would also like to thank the generous anonymous readers for SUNY Press, who, with their insightful comments, were instrumental in making this the best book it could be.

Likewise, I have benefited from many valuable interlocutors in our field of Spanish and Latin American film studies (or film studies more broadly) over the years, and it would be impossible to mention them all. Chief among them, however, are Steven Marsh, Matthew Marr, Sam Amago, Susan Larson, Sarah Thomas, Ignacio Sánchez Prado, Ernesto Livón-Grosman, David Rodowick, Salomé Aguilera Skvirsky, Susana Domingo, Eugenio DiStefano, and, as I said, many others.

I gratefully acknowledge the generosity of various journals and presses in granting permission to include modified extracts, extensively revised, of some of my articles previously published in their venues. These include, in chapter 1, "Helena Lumbreras's *Field for Men* (1973): Midway between Latin American Third Cinema and the Barcelona School," *Studies in Spanish and Latin American Cinemas*, vol. 11, no. 3, Fall 2014, 271–88, reproduced with permission of Intellect Limited through PLSclear; in chapter 2, "Intermediality and Spanish Experimental Cinema: Text and Image Interactions in the Lyrical Films of the Barcelona School," *Journal of Spanish Cultural Studies*, vol. 14, no. 3, Fall 2013, 254–74, reprinted by permission of Taylor & Francis; in chapter 3, "Intermediality and Hispano-Argentine Experimental Film: Subverting Media, Transgressing Borders with Super 8," *Revista Hispánica Moderna*, vol. 70, no. 2, Dec. 2017, 117–41; in chapter 4, "Cell Phone Cinema: Latin American Horror Flicks in the Post-digital Age," *Revista de Estudios Hispánicos*, vol. 53, no. 3, Oct. 2019, 821–54; and in the coda, "Do Androids Dream of Electric Llamas? AI Generated Cinema in Latin America," *FORMA: A Journal of Latin American Criticism and Theory*, vol. 3, no. 1, 2023, 77–105. I have also acknowledged the specific use of these articles in the appropriate chapters. Along these lines, I would like to thank several filmmakers and artists who made their work available, and in some cases patiently answered my questions via email or otherwise, especially Mariano Lisa (lifelong partner of the late Helena Lumbreras), Andrés Denegri, Gustavo Caprín, Daniela Cugliandolo, and Albert Alcoz. Almost all images used in the text are screen captures from various films and works available on the internet, and their reproduction is covered under fair use. In all cases every effort has been made to obtain permission to reprint or use any material found herein.

I have also received much institutional support over the last few years for the completion of this book. The University of Illinois at Urbana-Champaign's Conrad Humanities Scholar Award provided me with valuable funding that has been instrumental for the book's completion. The Humanities Research Institute Faculty Fellowship and the Unit for

Criticism & Interpretive Theory Senior Faculty Fellowship also facilitated invaluable teaching releases. The Hispanex Program from the Ministry of Culture and Education in Spain provided funding for a 2019 research trip to the Filmoteca de Catalunya in Barcelona.

I would be remiss not to thank my amazingly supportive colleagues and friends in the Department of Spanish and Portuguese at the University of Illinois at Urbana-Champaign, especially my mentor Mariselle Meléndez for her continued faith in me, our department chair, Melissa Bowles, and also my literature colleagues Mónica García-Blizzard, Javier Irigoyen-García, Anna Torres-Cacoullos, John Karam, Joyce Tolliver, Alejandro Ramírez Méndez, Pilar Martínez-Quiroga, Carolyn Fornoff (now at Cornell University), and all the other colleagues and graduate students at Illinois, too many to list individually. A special mention to my dear colleague Elena Delgado, who passed away in March 2024 and with whom I was working closely on another book. Elena was an unofficial mentor since I arrived at Illinois, and I will miss her. And thanks also to our late colleague and friend Dara Goldman, whose lovely laughter still echoes in the department's hallways.

Introduction

Border Crossings in Intermedial and Transnational (Luso-Hispanic) Film Studies

Does it make sense to think about national cinemas anymore?[1] And what even constitutes cinema today, after the supposed disappearance of film (celluloid), the arrival of video (analog and digital), and the emergence of online streaming and other forms of post-cinema, expanded cinema, virtual reality (VR), and installation art? What becomes of the spectator, or what does the spectator *become*, with the astonishing prospects for interactivity and immersion in this brave new audiovisual mediascape?

These and similar questions were on my mind on April 2022 as I entered the dark exhibition space in Dallas's Nasher Sculpture Center that housed Mexican filmmaker Alejandro González Iñárritu's VR cinematic installation *Carne y Arena: Virtually Present, Physically Invisible* (2017) [Flesh and Sand]. Admittedly, these abstract considerations about nation, medium, and spectatorship were less pressing than the real life-or-death tragedies that motivated González Iñárritu and also drew me to his exhibit, chief among these the almost one thousand migrant deaths in 2022 at the US-Mexico border. The constant news drumbeat about the plight of immigrants and refugees under "zero tolerance" policies was equally distressing. Our nation's inhumane immigration enforcement was exemplified by the Trump administration's child separation policy in 2018 or, more recently, by the instrumentalizing of Title 42 and the COVID-19 pandemic to bar entry to legitimate asylum seekers. At the center of these issues was (and is) a lack of public empathy coupled with the political right's fearmongering about a perceived migrant "invasion."

The stated purpose of González Iñárritu's VR exhibit was to bring its visitors closer to the lives and suffering of others, approximating privileged individuals like myself, a middle-class academic, to the embodied experience of a forced migrant or a refugee asylum seeker crossing into the country illegally—to make me *feel* powerless, cold, and frightened as if *physically there*, walking through the desert in the dead of night toward an uncertain future or no future at all. Traversing the exhibit, I moved through several interconnected spaces, from an initial installation displaying shoes and other personal belongings found in the Sonoran Desert—the material traces of ill-fated migrant journeys—to a ten-minute VR experience aimed at placing me (virtually) in the midst of a border crossing to a final section containing testimonial videos of migrants telling their harrowing first-person stories.[2]

The exhibit's overall effect was emotionally and intellectually impactful. In addition to triggering an affective reaction, the piece raised many theoretical questions for me. For instance, I was unsure about how *Carne y Arena* might be categorized within an expanding media landscape, or how the work related to the "cinema." Did I have a kind of cinematic experience, a VR one? Had I partaken of an elaborate art installation or something entirely different? Protean by nature, perhaps *Carne y Arena* could be provisionally described as a mixed reality work, one that combined 3D virtual content with multiple physical spaces. But considering its multifaceted nature, *Carne y Arena* can be associated with all the aforementioned media arts and many others, including conceptual art, ethnographic documentary, testimonial narrative, even first-person video games. In addition to being disconcerted by the heterogeneity of its media, I was also puzzled about *Carne y Arena*'s national origin, speculating whether it was created and funded by a US production company, by a Mexican one, or, as was the case, by a transnational conglomerate. These questions about media, form, and nation appeared interrelated and, I began to surmise, could serve as a theoretical lens to recast past and present experimental audiovisual works in a different light, providing a neoteric paradigm to study the cinematic arts.

Carne y Arena and the other experimental works I research in this book adumbrate compelling concerns about the changing essence of cinema today. As cinema increasingly incorporates assorted materials and media, both analog and digital, and as it repositions the spectator as active participant or protagonist, it prompts critics to ask epistemological questions such as, How might we study and categorize these types of expanded cinema, as well as other works created with emergent technologies? What is the place of these rising technologies within a book about experimental cinema and alternative formats? Or perhaps, how might we untangle the relationship of VR, cell phone cinema, or video installations not only to cinema but to other audiovisual media such as video games, vlogs, and the like?

Not coincidentally, the difficulty to neatly align *Carne y Arena* and other contemporary pieces with traditional media categories is often matched by the slipperiness of attributing a single stable national affiliation to these same works. For example, González Iñárritu's cinematic VR is a co-production between several international companies, including the US-based mass media giant Legendary Entertainment, the Canadian expanded reality production company PHI Studio, and the US advocacy and impact philanthropy company Emerson Collective—a complicated mix of for-profit and nonprofit interests. This itinerant installation also received local support from various galleries, museums, and art centers in cities where it was shown, such as the Milan-based art institution Fondazione Prada or in Mexico City the UNAM-affiliated Centro Cultural Universitario Tlatelolco.[3] To this same point, *Carne y Arena* premiered at the 2017 Cannes Festival and has been exhibited throughout Europe, Mexico, Canada, and the United States. The production team epitomizes the same transnational ethos: directed by a Mexican filmmaker recognized as a global auteur, backed by an international film unit that included Mexican cinematographer Emmanuel Lubezki, and designed by a pluri-national group of VR specialists, and, crucially, featuring Mexican and Central American migrants as "actors" who played themselves—but were later transformed into 3D CGI-animated characters.

Set in the borderlands between the United States and Mexico, *Carne y Arena* depicts an all too familiar immigration journey composited from various testimonial accounts. It broaches hot-button issues including the brutal reality of economically driven migration, the ongoing refugee crisis, and the policing of bodies and borders, matters that are central to US-Latin American relations. These same issues, however, exceed hemispheric concerns and have implications throughout and beyond the Luso-Hispanic Atlantic. Underscoring its geographical translatability, *Carne y Arena* circulated globally by appealing to a claim of universality justified by its affinity with the multiple migrant and refugee crises worldwide: one need only consider the incessant arrival of *pateras* in Spain, the detention centers in Lampedusa, the more than fourteen million Syrian refuges resettled globally, those fleeing Russia's war of aggression in Ukraine, or the recently displaced Palestinians fleeing that calamitous conflict.

I derived the academic motivation for this book in part from a desire to understand how *Carne y Arena*'s recourse to combining media and mobilizing transnational affiliations inflected its potent emotional impact and ability to communicate weighty subjects to increasingly detached spectators. This remarkable piece of VR cinema encapsulates the primary areas of interest for *Expanding Cinemas*. Primarily, *Carne y Arena* brings to our attention key concerns present in many contemporary experiments in the cinematic arts, including the two most salient strands of inquiry in this book: first, questions about the limits of nation and transnationalism as categories through which to study film and audiovisual media; second, issues related to the hybridization of media, that is, media mixing and intermediality in moving image arts—including the many ways the concept of cinema continues to expand beyond its own media borders. Patently, the VR piece's political force resides in its desire to bring attention and a sense of immediacy to border and immigration issues and to bridge the perceived empathy gap of US public opinion toward the plight of Central American and Mexican migrants, and by extension, to other migrants and refugees elsewhere. The effectiveness of this political imperative is predicated not only on the work's radical recourse to mixing media but also on its collaboration across national boundaries and its demand for *global* social justice.

To that end, González Iñárritu's piece was advertised as offering possibilities for embodiment that placed spectators into the scene of the action, within the cinematic VR diegesis, and, in a best-case scenario, would transform them into empathetic co-participants. *Carne y Arena* intended to provide these spectator-participants with a kind of presence or sense of being there, replicating the experience of being one of the migrants, if briefly and in a limited sense. This shift in the role of the spectator came with the acknowledgment that once they removed the VR glasses, the (putative) participants' privilege and safety would be restored—really, they were never at risk in the first place. In consequence, while a positive appraisal of *Carne y Arena*'s political dimension might focus on its empathetic and transformative possibilities, a more cynical one would cast the exercise as an example of (unintentional) 3D misery porn. Critics also validly charged that the prohibitive price of admission, ranging from fifty-five to seventy dollars depending on ticketing fees, denied access to those of modest means. Finally, the promotion of *Carne y Arena* reflected the work's pro-immigrant stance, likely attracting a self-selected audience already predisposed toward empathy and fully appraised as to the dire conditions at the border so that its actual impact on public opinion was minimal.

Successful or not, there is little doubt that the materiality of the exhibition and its mixing of multiple media is at the core of *Carne y Arena*'s political impetus and that the ontology of borders, their legitimacy, and the question of nation and transnationalism similarly anchors the work's intent. Although, according to detractors such as Julie Ward, *Carne y Arena*'s recourse to a facile notion of empathy—one that calls for a more compassionate enforcement of the law—obscures precisely those greater questions about the legal status of migrants and the legitimacy of borders, indeed, the lawfulness of the law itself. The piece, Ward argues, allows for a continuation of the oppressive power imbalance in US-Mexico-Central American relations so that its "opresión compasiva se plantea como una solución, en lugar de poner en evidencia a las fronteras nacionales como construcciones temporales y caprichosas cuyos efectos generan violencia y sufrimiento innecesario para millones de personas" [compassionate oppression is offered as a solution, instead of questioning national borders as temporary and arbitrary constructions whose effects generate unnecessary violence and suffering for millions] (54).

Ward's implication to abolish borders and allow the free flow of people across nations appears unfeasible at a time when the US electorate bristles at any suggestion to ameliorate the situation at the Rio Grande (*Río Bravo* in Mexico), as the post-Brexit European Union project teeters, and while "big," "beautiful" walls are being erected along various international demarcation lines. And yet that kind of radical transgression is what many of the works I examine perform on a different scale, as they deconstruct or disrupt various types of conceptual borders, perhaps as a necessary first step to one day abolishing them and as a precursor to moving from abolishing conceptual borders to eradicating physical ones. Interestingly, the concept of erasing, challenging, and undermining physical borders functions as a provocative correlative for crossing media and genre barriers (which may also be material) and signals the emergence of increasingly transient and negotiated cultural identities, identities that further complicate our traditional understanding of the distinctly national as that which is separated, made distinct, by borders. Transnationalism and intermediality, therefore, emerge as two primary critical lenses to understand cinema and post-cinema today.[4]

What, Then, Is This Book About?

In *Expanding Cinemas*, I argue that intermediality and transnationalism have had a continued presence in experimental film and other audiovisual formats. In fact, crossing media and/or national boundaries has been a filmic practice, in not only experimental but also documentary and commercial modalities, since the cinema's inception. That said, these tendencies to transgress borders, especially experimenting with media and genre, are more pronounced in noncommercial, self-referential works that are often preoccupied with their own form. This aesthetic preoccupation with media boundaries is at times also thematized on screen, as the films wrestle with cross-border political topics, practices, and identities. These border crossing practices have ebbed and flowed through time, intensifying during specific historical moments—I would argue we are in one such moment now. Interest in experimenting with intermedial and transnational approaches to filmmaking, I believe, increased notably after both the radical political shifts of the 1960s and following the vertiginous technological media developments of the 1990s and 2000s. As *Carne y Arena* makes evident, contemporary cinema, along with its post-cinematic and expanded variants, has been fundamentally transformed: the emergence of new technologies, formats, and platforms has accelerated the process of transnationalism and increased global exchanges between filmmakers, audiences, and films; those same technologies are expanding possibilities for amateur and experimental artists to create, distribute, and archive their own work, bypassing commercial production and distribution. Moreover, these same artists no longer may consider the national as their primary trait for personal identification, seeking instead shifting affiliations along ethnic, racial, ability, gender, sexual, or professional lines.

The notion of cinema, or the cinematic, as an "expanding" category has been gathering currency for quite some time. "Expanded cinema" is a protean and highly flexible or elastic term that has been considered since the 1960s and has returned with enhanced relevance in our time. For example, it features prominently in Jill Murphy and Laura Rascaroli's edited collection *Theorizing Film Through Contemporary Art: Expanding Cinema* (2020). In that book its authors assert that the "cinematic" in contemporary moving image art denotes work "that has to do with the activities, materialities, and processes of filmmaking" but is located beyond conventional understandings of the cinema and of filmic language (33). But where these authors think of cinema as expanding into other modalities and art forms primarily in the twenty-first century after the arrival of digital media, I examine the links between cinema and other arts since the 1960s.

Like Murphy and Rascaroli's own text, the title of my book is a direct reference to Gene Youngblood's influential treatise on (mainly North American) experimental filmmaking and its increasing intermediality in the '60s.

Youngblood's *Expanded Cinema* (1970) explored such (then) novel formats as cybernetic cinema and computer films, holographic movies, synesthetic cinema and other experiments that pushed the limits of the medium and dared to imagine what the next century would bring in terms of media mixing, new exhibition venues, immersive environments, participatory spectatorship, and more. Youngblood's exploration of the experimental genres also suggested that new forms of cinema triggered the potential "expansion" of the spectator's consciousness, as well as fostering an awakening sense of global unity, and, as such, his book was a hopeful exercise in mysticism, utopian thinking, and arguably, worldmaking. Fittingly, he concluded *Expanded Cinema* by optimistically asserting that "through the art and technology of expanded cinema we shall create heaven right here on earth" (419). While this utopian dream, so representative of its time, has not come to pass, experimental filmmakers and artists today are equally sanguine about the transformative possibilities of newly emerging cinematic arts, as these are constantly reformulated and continuously expanding, "restaging and re-presenting the cinematic medium's specific configuration of space, experience, presence/absence, production and consumption, technology, myth, perception, event, and temporality" (Murphy and Rascaroli 38).[5]

Of course, Youngblood, while highly influential, was not the only critic, theorist, or practitioner excited by the possibilities of expanding the cinema, far from it. Experimental cineaste Jonas Mekas wrote several pieces on the same subject in the '60s and '70s, as did independent filmmaker Stan VanDerBeek and visual experimental artist Carolee Schneemann, among others.[6] Among leading critics, Sheldon Renan, in his 1967 book *An Introduction to the American Underground Film*, dedicates a full chapter to expanded cinema. Renan began defining the concept of expanded cinema using a broad and "expanding" definition, including not only various technological formats (multiple projectors, computer generation, etc.) but also different forms of spectatorship. According to Renan, rather than a particular form or format, expanded cinema should be appraised as "a spirit of inquiry that is leading in many different directions," indeed, directions that might not even require "film" at all (227).

Another recent text that has engaged with the notion of the cinema as an expanding medium is Jonathan Walley's *Cinema Expanded: Avant-Garde Film in the Age of Intermedia* (2020). As I have done, Walley grounds the theoretical concept of expanded cinema in the experimental and avant-garde cinema of the 1960s, seeking to understand how the many forms and modalities practiced by filmmakers, including happenings, installation videos, live cinematic performances, light shows, multi-screen and other types of cinema, reflect the influence of various arts while remaining grounded on the cinematic. For Walley, expanded cinema is "moving image works that claim new territory for cinema, beyond the bounds of the familiar materials and practices of filmmaking and the traditional theatrical exhibition space" (10). But where Walley remains firmly anchored in an understanding of expanded cinema as a form that ultimately retains its medium specificity (its "filmic" ontology), I argue for the dissolution of "film" into a broad landscape of comingling media. Moreover, his book, otherwise an excellent treatise on the subject of the expanded nature of cinema, is focused mainly on North American and (Anglo) European films, leaving the Luso-Hispanic Atlantic open for investigation.

What is required now is a better understanding of these far-reaching shifts in the cinema and its technologies, in particular as it pertains to the Luso-Hispanic region. Until the transnational turn in film studies in the 2010s, most texts about the cinemas of Latin America and Spain focused mainly on the national and largely studied mainstream productions. This book, instead, examines overlooked genres from a broad region, the Luso-Hispanic Atlantic, a geographical construct that, in addition to the Iberian Peninsula and Latin America, expands to include Brazil. Through the analysis of often neglected militant, art house, amateur, and experimental films and formats, the book provides fresh perspectives that can help understand not only the cinema and the audiovisual media of the twenty-first century, but also, retrospectively, that of the twentieth. Grounded on close readings of individual films, and the comparative analysis of works from throughout the Luso-Hispanic Atlantic, this book problematizes the persistence of national discourses in an increasingly globalized world by framing these concerns around less studied genres that reveal the fissures in long-held national and medium-specific narratives.

Expanding Cinemas represents a necessary addition to the existing corpus on Luso-Hispanic film studies. Outside of a few scholars, mainly working in languages departments, and a handful of dedicated film series such as this one, research in this area has been lacking. With few exceptions, North American and European film scholarship based in film and media studies departments has largely neglected the cinema of the Spanish- and Portuguese-speaking world or has considered it a derivative cinema, an imperfect imitation of its Global North models. Films from Latin America, especially those that do not "perform" the conventional idea of national cinema, that do not faithfully reproduce Global North expectations about anticolonialist Third Cinema, or that do not rehash the well-trodden narratives of magical realism, are seen as exceptional curiosities when compared with the ubiquitously dominant Hollywood cinema. In addition, Luso-Hispanic films simply lack the cultural cache bestowed upon (some) Asian and European cinemas by critics. Regrettably, the preponderance of American mainstream cinema criticism also reflects and aligns with a reality in terms of the movies being screened globally.[7] Compounding this neglect, film critics writing from within Iberian and Latin American studies have seldom focused their attention on experimental formats—with a few notable exceptions, such as Cynthia Tompkins, Steven Marsh, Jesse Lerner, Ben Bollig, Josetxo Cerdán, Miguel Fernández Labayen, Román Gubern, Rosalind Galt, Masha Salazkina, Enrique Fibla-Gutiérrez, Udo Jacobsen, and Albert Alcoz, among a scant few others.

In this book I show how the "minor" cinemas—experimental and alternative genres and formats—from these "peripheral" regions have maintained an ongoing dialogue with key international film movements, not in a derivative but in an innovative capacity, and frequently, although not always, adopting oppositional stances against commercial cinema. One caveat here is that, as I also consider throughout the book, this narrative of resistance might obscure or distort a more nuanced but no less accurate account involving works that trouble the stark distinction between commercial and alternative or undermine the reductive binary assumption that experimental necessarily entails progressive values and mainstream always defaults to regressive positions. Indeed, I examine several works that undermine the narrative of resistance and cast "experimental" as a fraught category.

Nevertheless, even allowing space for nuance and counter-readings, a posture of opposition pervades many of the audiovisual texts I study, perhaps partly as a result of my own selection process but also explained by the region's lengthy heritage and association with militant and oppositional media. A majority of the cases I study reflect the myriad ways in which film can be used as a weapon for political, social, or artistic dissent against established power, whether through its form and content or how it circulates and is viewed. There are contextual, geopolitical, and historical reasons for these oppositional practices, which I examine throughout the book. To cite just one prominent example, the attitude of resistance against mainstream commercial cinema in Latin America, seen as complicit with US imperialism, was especially potent during the 1960s in the political milieu that followed the 1959 Cuban Revolution. This contestatory attitude also found its correlatives in other global regions, including the Iberian Peninsula, and would reverberate through later time periods.

The 1960s is precisely the period I examine in the first two chapters of the book—indeed, the period best known by critics from the Global North, although still underappreciated in its transnational and intermedial dimensions.[8] At this time, Luso-Hispanic cinema featured provocative alternatives to the standard Hollywood fare offered on most cinematic screens. Salient among these alternatives are the militant Third Cinema that sought to export revolutionary ideas and practices globally, the radical aesthetics of art cinema as exemplified by Brazil's Cinema Novo, and abstract experimental cinemas reinventing film form, such as the Argentine Grupo Goethe or the Barcelona School in Spain. Furthermore, as I explore in the last three chapters, these oppositional gestures, whether genuine or postured, have resurfaced today in a different guise. One distinction between then and now is that Latin American and Iberian experimental, avant-garde, and documentary creators are no longer exclusively filmmakers and can leverage digital tools to bypass large-scale commercial production and distribution, opting instead to distribute their work online as they (arguably) seek to democratize film practices.[9] Again, it is important to insert nuance into these assertions, as I do in these latter chapters: such democratization of access, once the shining promise of the internet and of new audiovisual media forms, is by no means a foregone conclusion or unproblematic. As popular media platforms become increasingly relevant for production and distribution of alternative forms of cinema and post-cinema, it is necessary to recognize that these platforms are owned by global megacorporations that surveil, data mine, and exploit their users, as well as influence content and viewing trends and reinforce biases. We must not reproduce the utopianism and unbridled optimism displayed by Youngblood's idea of the expanded cinema.

Another crucial distinction between the '60s and '70s and recent post-analog times is that relations to commercialism, to the negotiation between filmmakers' amateur and professional status, have become murkier, as the utopian militancy of the earlier period has been replaced with a messier relationship to global events, to capital and capitalism, to existential issues such as climate change and immigration, and to the flows of artists and their works across nations. No longer are the more radical films advocating, with a single-minded purpose, for an anti-capitalist, anti-colonial, or anti-establishment struggle as works did in the '60s, now filmmakers navigate a less distinct, perhaps less dogmatic, web of ambivalences and gray areas that are rarely ideologically clear-cut but instead are infinitely intricate and challenging to disambiguate and are often co-opted by shadowy "systems."

What Is/Are Experimental Cinema(s)?

Before we move forward it is necessary to raise the question of terminology, beginning with the meaning of the word "experimental," featured in the book's subtitle and closely allied to the idea of "expanded" or "expanding" cinema. A restrictive definition might narrowly consider only works that focus on film form and materiality, while avoiding those with narrative content and/or documentary functions. In this book, however, I argue for a broader concept of "experimental," one that denotes an "expanding" classification or category of alternative audiovisual forms of (re)presentation that are typically created outside of the mainstream film industry, usually by independent and amateur filmmakers with low budgets, and most often are entirely noncommercial, although not always. In fact, in this expanded understanding of the term, the experimental may at times include some exceptional feature films, as with the work of filmmakers like Carlos Reygadas, Pedro Costa, Lisandro Alonso, or Lucrecia Martel, who engage with narrative content even as they experiment with form and push against traditional notions of "story." For these and other filmmakers the separation between narrative and nonnarrative forms is more ambivalent; in fact, "narrative" is seen as one more cinematic dimension to experiment with, as a border to cross.

Experimental is at times also seen as synonymous with avant-garde, the terms used interchangeably, although this general meaning of "avant-garde" is not to be confused with the specific periods and movements of the historical or the neo-avant-gardes. That said, those historical movements were key to mixing media and experimenting with film form, to thinking of film as both an artistic and "scientific" practice. The experimental modality was also called "experimental" on account of its link to a scientific approach to making movies, involving stretching the limits of the cinematic format through trial and error and careful observation of the cinematic as a temporal art that could be finely calibrated and measured, as espoused by the first practitioners of the historic avant-garde, especially impressionist, constructivist, and formalist filmmakers—including the Soviet montage school—but also expressionists, surrealists, and others.

In short, experimental film displays a desire to constantly explore form and content and to reinvent itself, always pursuing ways to consider its own medium, and its intermedial possibilities. In this book's generous (and productive) interpretation of the term, experimentation might be found in one or more elements from these nonmainstream films, whether in the editing, cinematography, subject matter, and technologies and techniques used or in the way narrative is constructed, deconstructed, or dispensed with altogether. Some fiction films, full-length features, and even commercially viable works can, of course, still be considered experimental on some level, even though these cases are in the minority, as the experimental cinema label tends to privilege the marginal, underground, and noncommercially viable.

Experimental, when applied to the audiovisual arts and if broadly interpreted as I am proposing, comprises an eclectic variety of forms, formats, and genres, as well as filming approaches and technologies, including militant cinema, documentary and essayistic film; amateur film; home movies; 8 mm, 16 mm, and Super 8; cell phone videos; assorted types of expanded cinema; virtual and augmented reality cinema, audiovisual installations, artificial intelligence (AI)-generated films, and more. Other examples skirt the boundary between "home movies" and avant-garde art, freely playing with various filmic media in the spirit of Jonas Mekas, Bruce Conner, and Stan Brakhage or their counterparts from the Luso-Hispanic Atlantic, including Mario Peixoto, José Val del Omar, Claudio Caldini, Enrique Pineda Barnet, Silvestre Byrón, Narcisa Hirsch, or Carlos Reygadas, among countless others.[10] Yet far from restricting themselves to exploring aesthetic form, these alternative filmmakers and their "other" cinemas—experimental, regional, at times abstract—also delve into social and political concerns, especially when they hail from the margins of the Global North; "experimental," then, can incorporate a political dimension.

As such, this book is vested in discourses about the innovative and arguably democratizing impulse arising from film practices that are based on past and present emerging technologies. *Expanding Cinemas*, however, does not attempt to provide an all-comprehensive overview of the rich gamut of alternative film practices in the region, but instead it focuses on a circumscribed set of films and filmmakers that can be identified by the intermedial and transnational sensibilities they inscribe into their work, and that I trace back to their "experimental" spirit. These filmmakers and creators, who I briefly identify in the chapter overviews below, purposefully transgress marked geographical and aesthetic boundaries, sharing strategies and styles across the Atlantic and beyond in their efforts to create countercinemas aesthetically and politically oppositional to market-driven commercial filmmaking.

Admittedly and as previously mentioned, this clear-cut opposition between commercial and experimental does not always hold.[11] Not every "noncommercial" film deliberately avoids wider distribution and financial success; in many instances, even radically experimental films remain rooted in the market logic they purport to evade, performing their aesthetic "otherness" (i.e., deliberately flaunting their "experimental" difference from the commercial films of the Global North) to gain access to niche venues (cult circuits, art house festivals, museums and galleries, specialized streaming platforms, etc.). The tensions between commercialism and avant-gardism, between artist and technician, or between self-promoting amateur and professional are central to arguments about the status of militant, experimental, and documentary filmmaking in the region.

Why the Luso-Hispanic Atlantic?

The discussion now brings us to a geographic term that also merits further consideration. Spanning a broad period from the 1960s until today, this book is informed by current debates about contestatory form and politics in various types of experimental cinemas, including avant-garde, militant, and documentary films from throughout Latin America, Brazil, and the Iberian Peninsula, an expansive area I am calling the Luso-Hispanic Atlantic. I am extending the term "Hispanic Atlantic" that already has a lengthy use in cultural studies to include Lusophone nations as well. The Hispanic Atlantic is an imagined "region" framed around the notion of a shared "Hispanic transnational culture" and that represents a strategic challenge to established Anglo-centric perspectives on the Atlantic (D'Lugo 3). Following Joseba Gabilondo, I am considering the Hispanic Atlantic as "Latin America, Spain, and the Latino United States," a geographical construct, which is always in flux and should be expanded to comprise other locations, for instance Equatorial Guinea and Morocco (Gabilondo 91). Moreover, the filmmakers I study whittle away at these imaginary and/or material boundaries (Tordesillas, the US-Mexico border, national and regional *fronteras*, the Atlantic Ocean itself) so that at various times other nations and imagined affiliations (Portugal, Brazil, Latinx US), regions (the non-Hispanic Caribbean, diasporic communities), and less determinate and virtual spaces (digital environments and platforms) can be included within the purview of the Luso-Hispanic Atlantic.[12]

Selecting the geographic scope of the Luso-Hispanic Atlantic offers specific insights into the cinema, insights that differ from those obtained through the comparative study of other global regions (Africa, Asia, etc.). Latin American and Iberian alternative moving image formats and technologies provide a particular viewpoint into issues related to migration and diaspora, colonialism and imperialism, and hybrid identities and *mestizaje/mestiçagem*, among other concerns that are both highly localized and regionally relevant, rendering the study of cinematic representations of this set of transnational exchanges especially meaningful.

Simply put, the cultural transfers (while fraught and uneven), migratory flows, cultural hybridity, and shared imaginaries of the Luso-Hispanic Atlantic bind the region in ways that make the comparative study of its films necessary and productive, not only to grasp the development of its cinematic movements and industries but also to gain insight into the region's cultural and political history. By shedding light on the way these films and filmmakers relate and diverge, by "thinking about the transnational in Iberian and Latin American Cinemas in terms of a travelling cinema," we begin to see "the sounds and images of new syntheses of [shared] identities, subjective and collective" across the region (Perriam et al. 4). That said, there will be times in the book when I extend my comparisons and analysis to other films and regions, especially when discussing emerging formats and less-discussed contemporary phenomena. This allows me to create a comprehensive map, placing Ibero-American case studies in dialogue with relevant works from other places even as the focus remains on the Luso-Hispanic Atlantic.

Transnationalism and the Cinema

By now, it should be clear that *Expanding Cinemas* is written along two fundamental structuring axes that act as selecting, organizing, and theoretical principles applied to each film and audiovisual work I study. The first axis is the notion of cinema as a transnational phenomenon, with a special focus on its transatlantic dimension, including Latin America, Spain, and Latinx US. The second axis is the nature of cinema as an intermedial practice, as a consequence of the material and contextual situation within the region. While existing scholarship has not juxtaposed these strands explicitly,

I shall argue throughout the book that transnationalism and intermediality go hand in glove in the audiovisual works I study and function as inextricably interconnected and intersecting axes that are at times even mutually constitutive, as well as being fundamental aspects of contemporary and past cinemas from the region.

Let us consider the transnational axis first. By using a transatlantic/transnational paradigm, this book places emphasis on issues of human mobility—immigration, exile, diaspora—but also the mobility of ideas, art, and material objects—epistolary and video dialogues between artists, the international circulation of films, the global nature of new(er) media, the inherent mobility of camera phones and those who wield them, the embodied motion of VR cinema and its user experience—as well as cross-cultural identities and the continuous sharing of experimental and nontraditional film practices across borders.

I wish to anticipate that traversing the transnational axis also entails interrogating the close ties between concepts of medium and intermediality, that is, those exchanges and movements across media that often accompany transnational flows. These media concerns that are foregrounded by experimental cinema can be related to preoccupations with national origin, with the mobility of filmmakers, while also considering the malleability of nationalities and the national as imaginary constructs in constant renegotiation. This is not to say that transnationalism and intermediality are always necessarily intertwined, but rather that there are affinities between these analytical approaches to the cinema that make them a suitable pairing for productive study of films, in particular, of experimental ones. But I will return to "intermedial" in the next section, as the transnational warrants more work here.

Speaking of the transnational requires thinking first about the national. The concept of "national" cinema has been under deconstruction since at least the last decades of the twentieth century, although, as I and other critics sustain (Stephanie Dennison, Deborah Shaw, Marvin D'Lugo, Stephen Rawles, etc.), films have always been transnational products since the early days, if not in terms of their site of production then at least in terms of their exhibition, in the international nature of their crew and cast, and through the highly mobile lived experience of many filmmakers from Latin America and Spain. The globalization of the film industry, a condition that, according to Thomas Elsaesser, has always been a present reality, has been magnified lately, as evidenced by "the intensely networked character of contemporary cinema, which has sharpened our awareness of how such networks [function]—of personal contacts, professional exchanges, cross-border trade in artistically valorized assets, and flows of both finance and cultural capital" ("National, Transnational, and Intermedial" 26).

Despite these cross-border flows, the "national" seems to periodically reassert itself and is by no means a defunct category. This persistent presence of nation and national imaginaries is reflected in the global resurgence of nationalisms in the twenty-first century from both the left and right of the political spectrum, including its right-wing populist variants. Perhaps somewhat ironically, these new nationalisms are a kind of transnational phenomenon easily copied and exported as we have seen with the many echoes of Trumpian populism in places like Brazil, Hungary, and elsewhere. But despite the flaring of nationalist sentiments, the equally problematic forces of globalization have continued to diminish the potency of national categories and characteristics in the latest cinemas. Adding to these trends, audiences are increasingly formed and informed by international films, viewed mainly through online streaming platforms, a practice that responds more to genre choices—in particular horror, sci-fi, comedy, action, and hybrid genres—and serialized viewing preferences than to selection based solely on the national origin of the films as might have occurred in the past. These spectatorial tendencies are bolstered by a burgeoning transnational cooperation at every level of the industry, from commercial cinema to independent filmmaking and even amateur movies, distinctions that are also increasingly blurred.

The myriad competing claims as to who represents the "nation" in Latin American countries, or for that matter in the Spanish state, are equally contentious and difficult to untangle and are often reflected in the cinema of the region(s) in question. Whether indigenous claims that go beyond national boundaries, ethnic minorities within the confines of the nation, immigrants and refugees who identify with more than one country, the space of the nation and its defining characteristics are under pressure from multiple directions.

Nations today are a mosaic of languages, origins, and allegiances, giving way to a shifting panorama that can hardly be identified with a unified and stable notion of "the national," leaving a possibility for the transnational or supranational, as well as the hyperlocal and the regional, to replace, complement, or map onto the elusive construct of the national in the imaginary of the citizenry. In that sense, we can view and treat the national in cinema, as Elsaesser suggests, as "a subcategory of the transnational." I endorse

Elsaesser's bold assertion that "a transnational perspective on national cinema is . . . a theoretical necessity" ("National, Transnational, and Intermedial" 23). The critic casts doubt on the constructed idea of national cinema and defines a subset of the national which he calls the "performed national." The performed national would include a significant number of films that are created with foreign audiences in mind, films that stage a certain idea of the national by now dated if not fully defunct, an idea that is rooted in stereotypes, folkloric fantasies, tropes, and reductionist understandings of the national imaginary. These same films often cast highly recognizable global stars such as Gael García Bernal, Ricardo Darín, or Penélope Cruz, to name some recurring actors, and deploy established directors groomed for export by big financial interests, including such internationally recognizable auteurs as Walter Salles, Alejandro Amenábar, Guillermo del Toro, or the very same Alejandro González Iñárritu. These are filmmakers who have worked globally, with multinational budgets, casts, and crews and of course have a particular sensibility for and appeal to transnational audiences, often relying on narratives with a "universal" interest, as we saw with *Carne y Arena*. I am speaking of works, in other words, that acknowledge the existence of, and indeed specifically target, a certain market that, paradoxically, is itself transnational but at times retains a nostalgic appetite for outdated and falsified national narratives.

This type of transnationalism is present at every level of the film industry, even for films that do not fit within the mainstream. For instance, although the experimental, militant, and amateur films I study might not fall within the mega-multinational production spectrum, they are often just as global-facing in their thematic content, their distribution aspirations, or their artistic influences. As I stated above, even when such films seemingly adopt a posture that appears antithetical to commercial interests, they might recur to global genre trends or perform a certain idea of "independent" filmmaking for the sake of self-promotion, often straddling the line between the national and the global.

Our critical lens, to remain discerning, must encompass assorted geographies and read these films through their multiple affiliations, whether national, regional, or transnational, including studying how they relate to online communities and spaces, underground screenings, gallery and museum exhibitions, or global festival circuits. In short, all of these geopolitical categories are at work simultaneously so that as Elsaesser affirms, in addition to "adopting a transnational perspective" the critic must also recognize "the need for a new investment in the national—even as the national is mediated through the transnational, while also having a stake in the local or the regional" ("National, Transnational, and Intermedial" 26).

Stephanie Dennison has also written about the transnational turn in the cinema of the Luso-Hispanic Atlantic, examining its multidirectional flow of films and mutual influences across the ocean, in her edited volume *Contemporary Hispanic Cinema: Interrogating the Transnational in Spanish and Latin American Film* (2013). As she suggests, "for Latin American filmmakers and producers, the main impetus for collaborating with producers from Spain . . . is to increase a film's chance of entering both/either the Spanish TV market, and/or the European cinema circuit. And many of the transnational funding initiatives that Hispanic or Latin American films tap into are linked to international film festivals" ("National, Transnational, and Post-national" 14). Of course, the market and its financial incentives are more motivating for some filmmakers than for others, just as the motivation for a militant filmmaker is quite different from that of an art cinema auteur or an experimental artist, even as these divisions and their driving factors can blur and intersect.

While Dennison foregrounds the recent explosion in transnational Luso-Hispanic commercial cinema, she also reminds readers that the same could be said for militant and experimental genres from the 1960s, recalling that the period "witnessed a similar boom [to the one we are experiencing now], which lasted well into the 1970s, [and] that was categorized by a desire to see Latin American avant-garde cinema" (14–5). As previously intimated, throughout the book I will bridge both of these eras, from the New Latin American militant films to contemporary audiovisual experiments, by arguing that the specific form taken by transnationalism was quite different for each period. The move toward making film a transnational phenomenon was motivated by very dissimilar impulses; one, arguably, to spread leftist political ideas and models globally, and the other, to tap into international film circuits, alternative venues, and online distribution with various intents: political, artistic, commercial, and other. At the same time, I will consider how, despite vastly differing political and historical circumstances, there are various ways in which these cinematic eras overlap, including their related mechanisms of film circulation, filmmaker migration, and industry globalization.

Intermediality: A Constitutive Aspect of the Cinema

Until now I outlined some principles that define the first axis of the book, that is, transnationalism in the films of the Luso-Hispanic Atlantic, in particular as it applies to lesser formats and experimental genres. The second axis of the book is an examination of intermediality as it pertains to the cinema, both as a theoretical angle to study the films themselves, including the various audiovisual media that interact with or comprise them, and also considering the material consequences of intermediality in the cinema. While I delve into various definitions and implications of the "intermedial" in some depth in chapter 1, I want to establish a baseline understanding of the term in these opening pages.

As a multisensory expressive medium (or a compendium of assorted media), film has since its inception been bound up with other art forms, with photography, theater and performance, literature, painting, sculpture, and architecture, so that critics have often remarked on its hybrid nature. Intermediality can be defined as the relationships of different media (filmic in our case) within a work of art, but also as the interactions of different media exchanges between distinct works, or even the translation or transformation across media of a particular work, sometimes referred to as transmediation. The presence of photography within film is a constitutive reality for celluloid cinema, for example, but we can also think of the image of a photograph within a film as an intermedial presence or reference. The relationship between (moving) images and sound, or even text, within a film can typically be thought of as intermedial. The word "medium" itself implies an in-betweenness, so that intermedial becomes somewhat redundant as a term, or rather it expresses a radical and endlessly multiplying in-betweenness (Éric Méchoulan). While there is no generally agreed upon definition of "intermediality," and even the word "medium" remains highly contested, the way I choose to understand the term as it relates to the cinema is first as a combination or fusion of various media into a final amalgamation, which we might consider as a different "medium," and second as a set of references or intertexts situated within one medium but evoking or thematizing another.

As I anticipated earlier, as we grapple with "intermediality" I want to also consider the potentially intimate association between the transgressing of media separations and the concept of the transnational as a crossing of borders and as reflected in the cinema (by now this should be a familiar idea). In essence, intermediality and transnationalism are intertwined or coiled around each other in cinematic practice. Although not many critics have examined this connection between the intermedial and the transnational, there have been a handful of significant contributions that have broached the subject. For example, Lúcia Nagib and Anne Jerslev, examining the case of Brazil, have found parallels between media hybridization and cultural globalization. Their notion of "impure cinema," which I draw on throughout this book, argues for "cinema's very nature as a mixture of arts and media" even as they assert that "the impure or intermedial approach cannot rule out and indeed depends on the specifics of the medium" (intro. to *Impure Cinema* vi, xxii).[13]

Interestingly, we encounter in the theoretical notion of intermediality a paradox that in many respects echoes the tension that exists between the transnational and the national, that is, the oscillation between individual media and combined media, or between medium purity and medium hybridity. As theoretically troublesome as it may be, one cannot think of a combination of media, in other words, without at some point considering an individually distinct medium, which in turn would seem to again suggest the pernicious argument for medium specificity, indeed much like the national returns once and again. Nagib and Jerslev attempt to resolve this seeming contradiction, at least with regard to film, by considering the cinema as a "method" rather than an "object." This distinction rings true in the aftermath of the rise of digital media, when the separation of "arts" from "media" has become, as Nagib and Jerslev argue, essentially impossible and when the ontology of the cinema as "film" has been abandoned in favor of a broader understanding of cinema as an art with a long history comprising hybrid media, of which digital film is just the latest instantiation.

That is not to say that those intermedial methods and practices we call the "cinema" are not rooted in materials and media objects at their most fundamental level. However, the intermedial methodology involves considering and adopting an "impure" assemblage of methods and materials, and today's practitioners of intermedial arts—including cinema and also other (often performative) arts such as theater, opera, or mixed media painting—do not usually concern themselves with debates about medium specificity, and even if they do, they still adopt intermediality as a preferred and de facto practice. Medium specificity as a theoretical and practical idea is all but abandoned, and as Christopher Townsend observes, was a founding myth of modernism that mainly privileged "nonrepresentational painting," although filmmakers also pursued this chimera (80).

Regarding media in contemporary art, Irina Rajewsky has remarked on the way intermedial studies have "heightened awareness of the materiality and mediality of artistic practices and of cultural practices" ("Intermediality" 44). Like Nagib and Jerslev, Rajewsky connects her broad definition of the term "intermediality" to the crossing of both cultural and media borders, stating that she freely applies the term to "all those phenomena that (as indicated by the prefix inter) in some way take place between media. 'Intermedial' therefore designates those configurations which have to do with a crossing of borders between media, and which thereby can be differentiated from intramedial phenomena" ("Intermediality" 46). Again, the crossing of material borders can also function, at least metaphorically, as a reminder of the crossing of national borders, and although not many critics beyond Nagib and Jerslev have made this point explicitly, some have connected the combination of media to the movement across space, to translation. Translation, from the Latin *trasnlatio*, "to carry across," and related to the Greek *metaphorá*, the trope of metaphor but also meaning "to transfer" or "to carry over," similarly gestures to migration, diaspora, and exile, translations that complicate the concept of "home" and by extension "nation" and "national." Moving away from the idea of pure media is in some ways like leaving the nation behind, leaving the safety of home and opening oneself up to the "impure."

Other scholars have examined the nexus between intermediality and transnationalism. In *An Accented Cinema: Exile and Diasporic Filmmaking* (2001), Hamid Naficy defines "accented cinema" as a type of radically deterritorialized and often artisanal filmmaking, meaning amateur and noncommercial. According to Naficy, these films traverse physical borders and fuse multiple media; accented films are "hybridized and experimental—characterized by multifocality, multilinguality, asynchronicity, critical distance, fragmented or multiple subjectivity, and transborder amphibolic characters" (32). The filmmakers that interest Naficy, much like the ones I include in my book, are displaced, exiled, never quite home anywhere, and often represent what he calls "accented," a descriptor that may apply to their language(s), their accent(s), their national disidentification, or the transgressive nature of their work. Thus their "accented" films, which by their multimedial and displaced logic, as films and filmmakers transition across cultures and nations with ease or difficulty, unsettle the supposed universality and un-accented-ness of Hollywood film and menace the very existence of reified nation states.

Again, while the opposition between Hollywood as the dominant production mode and all other cinema models is by now somewhat of a trope in film criticism, the concept of the "accented" film is nevertheless a useful category to think through the work of diasporic filmmakers. It is also closely allied to Third Cinema and to the Latin American works I discuss in the initial chapters, including Fernando Solanas and Octavio Getino's iconic 1968 masterpiece *La hora de los hornos* (released in English as *The Hour of the Furnaces*).[14] For Naficy, "in its formal practices, *The Hour of the Furnaces* is a clear progenitor of the accented style" (30). Underscoring what I have been proposing and echoing Naficy, Laura U. Marks argues in *The Skin of the Film: Intercultural Cinema, Embodiment, and the Senses* (2000) that "intercultural films" reflect "experimental styles that attempt to represent the experience of living between two or more cultural regimes of knowledge, or living as a minority in the still majority, white, Euro-American West" (1).

As critically troublesome and contradictory as they might seem, the terms transnational, intermedial, intercultural, accented, and hybrid not only apply to questions of national identification and the cinematic medium but also allude to a certain destabilization of genre categories. Associating the transnationalism of hybrid media experiments with other types of genre impurity, Nagib and Jerslev opine that "tearing down walls between fiction and life is indeed the aim of many intermedial and intercultural projects" (xxv). In *Moving Verses: Poetry on Screen in Argentine Cinema*, a study of the nexus between poetry and film in contemporary Argentine films, Ben Bollig endorses intermediality as a theoretical matrix to read film through but cautions against applying an intermedial methodology from a position of ahistorical and decontextualized techno-utopianism, asserting that "a simple celebration of intermediality as the mixing of forms or the blurring of generic boundaries risks obscuring the cultural and political networks in which genres and art forms exist, a properly political reading of intermedial artworks should be attentive to the subtle encounters that are at work—and the presuppositions and contexts behind them" (208). This is the type of nuanced reading of the intersection of media, culture, and form that I have sought to implement in *Expanding Cinemas*, applied to its various periods and cinematic formats and illustrated through close interpretations of specific works, while remaining attuned to the thematic and formal characteristics of these films and to the sociohistorical backdrops surrounding their production.

To sum things up, *Expanding Cinemas: Experimental Filmmaking across the Luso-Hispanic Atlantic since 1960* examines various types of noncommercial cinema—militant, art house, abstract, amateur, cellular films, VR formats—and how they relate to each other, asking questions such as, Do these "minor" cinemas oppose market demands and expectations and their homogenizing effect, and if so, how? How do visions of the Luso-Hispanic Atlantic, or individual nations therein, manufactured by counter-cinemas differ from those offered by mainstream narratives? How does the entrance of the "popular" through home movies and other do-it-yourself films democratize filmmaking, if at all? And how are the effects of diaspora, cultural relocation, and displacement reflected by the intermedial hybridity of these films?

New forms and venues of creation and reception are changing the materials and contents of cinema. As film production has already shifted from public theater screens to home computers, phones, and other portable devices, experimental approaches are becoming more readily available to a generation willing to mix media freely, old and new. At stake is determining not just how a shared transatlantic and transnational oppositional cinema arose in the 1960s and developed through later decades, but also understanding how its principles have been resurrected by today's digital counter-cinemas; it also demands gauging the latter's democratizing and political potential, in tension with commercializing tendencies inherent to globalization. By studying these works I wish to add to our understanding about noncommercial and emergent cinema from the Luso-Hispanic Atlantic, providing *nuestro cine* with greater visibility in cinema history.

Previous Scholarship and Critical Influences

While it is impossible to engage every single text in the pertinent secondary literature that has informed my thinking on these subjects, I acknowledge the more significant ones here and apologize for any omissions. Others can be found in the copious endnotes, and more are referenced in the works cited. I have paid homage to Youngblood's transformative concept of cinema as an ever-expanding art form, and to various subsequent texts that "expanded" his original idea for new times. I have already mentioned the meaningful contributions from authors like Lúcia Nagib and Anne Jerslev, or Hamid Naficy, in my previous discussion, which have been critical for my extension of the idea of associating transnationalism and intermediality. In the following sections I list other relevant scholarly works that partake of this discussion.

In this book I intervene into three scholarly areas: texts about Latin American and Iberian cinema, studies of experimental and documentary film, and works that investigate the impact of new media on the production, viewership, and archival practices of cinema. Mine is among a few texts to examine experimental genres across the Luso-Hispanic Atlantic and to place those cinemas in dialogue with intermediality and transnationalism. To date, most studies about Latin American and Iberian cinema have centered on either fiction or documentary film, including general texts that examine

Iberian and/or Latin American cinema in isolation or those that focus on a particular nation.[15]

Canonical works within Luso-Hispanic film studies rarely mention amateur and experimental genres, let alone analyze those films in detail. Few established works consider the mutual transnational influence between Latin American and Iberian cinema. In 2019, Antonio Gómez López-Quiñones stated that transatlantic film studies are not yet "coherently developed . . . methodologically defined and bureaucratically organized" (299–312) but identified them as a burgeoning field, to which this book contributes its specific focus on experimental cinema. In addition, not many texts within Luso-Hispanic film studies are recent enough to have covered the rise of digital media and streaming platforms. While some articles have been written about digital cinema in the region, many found in Josetxo Cerdán and Miguel Fernández Labayen's 2019 dossier on this subject for the *Journal of Latin American Cultural Studies*, there are no significant monographs. Some books have tackled transnationalism without linking it to intermediality, including Stephanie Dennison's aforementioned edited volume *Contemporary Hispanic Cinema* (2013). A handful of studies have considered intermediality in cinema but within a narrower national focus, for instance Ben Bollig's *Moving Verses* (2021).

Some texts have broached the interdependent nature of the national/transnational dynamic. Ignacio Sánchez Prado's *Screening Neoliberalism: Transforming Mexican Cinema, 1988–2012* (2014), which is primarily focused on performing an incisive analysis of neoliberalism's impact on Mexican national cinema, contains a chapter on transnational issues and the three global auteurs, Alejandro González Iñárritu, Alfonso Cuarón, and Guillermo del Toro.[16] Other scholars delving into the national/transnational include Leslie Marsh, whose *Branding Brazil: Transforming Citizenship on Screen* (2021) studies how Brazilian and other national film industries construct a singular brand by promoting an idea of the "national" for the consumption of international audiences. Others research the presence of the hyperlocal and the rural (a new ruralism) within contemporary film, for example Matt Losada's *The Projected Nation: Argentine Cinema and the Social Margins* (2018). Examining the classical period from the 1930s through the 1950s, Ana Laura Lusnich, Alicia Aisemberg, and Andrea Cuarterolo's edited volume *Pantallas transnacionales: El cine argentino y mexicano del período clásico* (2017) [Transnational Screens: Argentine and Mexican Cinema of the Classic Period] does pay close attention to questions of transnationalism focused on Argentina and Mexico. Singularly focused on the Mexico-US relationship, Laura Isabel Serna's *Making Cinelandia: American Films and Mexican Film Culture before the Golden Age* (2014) tackles Hollywood's influence on its neighbor to the south, and vice versa. Robert McKee Irwin and Maricruz Castro Ricalde's edited volume *Global Mexican Cinema: Its Golden Age* (2013) picks up where the two previous volumes left off and examines various global cinematic exchanges during the golden age. Nevertheless, although these books yield critical information about the interplay of national and global forces, as primarily "national" studies they seldom consider contemporary cinema that is created and imagined beyond the borders of the nation state and rarely engage in comparative study of films from across the Atlantic—or when they do, their readings remain centered on the country that anchors the study.[17]

On the Iberian side, while some newer studies have framed Spanish film within an international context, such as Sam Amago's *Spanish Cinema in the Global Context: Film on Film* (2013) or the earlier *Refiguring Spain: Cinema, Media, Representation* (1997) by Marsha Kinder, they seldom recognize the multidirectional exchanges across the Luso-Hispanic Atlantic, especially when it comes to alternative and "minor" cinemas.[18] Given the focus on experimentalism, in my book I chose not to focus on commercial co-productions dominated by Spanish media companies, exemplified by the Ibermedia Program covered by Tamara Falicov's publications on the cultural politics of co-productions; neither did I consider highly profitable co-productions involving the United States and/or Spain, with Latin American nations.[19]

There are two notable precursor books that do examine Latin American experimental cinema in-depth: first, a catalog to an exhibition titled *Ism, Ism, Ism/Ismo, Ismo, Ismo: Experimental Cinema in Latin America* (2017), edited by Jesse Lerner and Luciano Piazza; second, Cynthia Tompkins's *Experimental Latin American Cinema: History and Aesthetics* (2013). Lerner and Piazza's panoramic catalog collects short essays and filmmaker statements about films from throughout the region and includes the Latinx US as well. The book accompanied a traveling exhibition and film series that brought little-known movies and directors to the attention of Latin American and US audiences and critics. Tompkins's book is an excellent monograph that also adopts a generous definition of what constitutes "experimental," examining mainly narrative art films from recent decades.[20]

My own work departs from both of these excellent texts by providing a more in-depth reading of experimental works than Lerner and Piazza's broad overview and by exploring modalities and genres that Tompkins does not consider.[21] In addition, I bring into the discussion of Latin American and Iberian cinema aspects from what new media theory and digital film scholarship calls a "mobile aesthetic," as captured in texts such as Marsha Berry and Max Schleser's *Mobile Media Making in an Age of Smartphones* (2014), or in older works examining alternative storytelling, such as Janet Murray's *Hamlet on the Holodeck: The Future of Narrative in Cyberspace* (1998), books that emphasize the shift away from traditional screens to new modes of spectatorship. A couple of additional texts worth mentioning cover less typical ground, for example Patricia Zimmerman's classic study of home movies and amateur film, *Reel Families: A Social History of Amateur Film* (1995), which, although it has a global outlook, is mainly interested in US films. Also Masha Salazkina and Enrique Fibla-Gutiérrez's edited work *Global Perspectives on Amateur Film Histories and Cultures* (2020), which sheds light on questions of medium specificity and also considers formats such as Super 8 in Mexico, Spain, and beyond.

Hence, although my book establishes a conversation with the above-cited texts and others mentioned in the endnotes, its focus on the Luso-Hispanic Atlantic through a decidedly transnational perspective, its theoretical divergence from established accounts of the experimental through reliance on the concept of intermediality, its reconceptualizing of previous assertions about the connection between aesthetics and politics in the Latin American and Iberian context, and its historical account delineating trends in experimental cinema over the last fifty years all mark it as a significant departure from previous scholarship, and, I believe, a reframing of the existing critical literature. By the same token, the emphasis on new media approaches to filmmaking present in the last three chapters also suggest novel directions for Latin American and Iberian cinema and film scholarship not yet considered by others, including my study of the shift toward cell phone filmmaking and viewing on small screens, the emergence of VR cinemas throughout the Luso-Hispanic Atlantic, and, as I briefly consider in the coda, the far-reaching effects of AI on the art and industry of moving images.

Chapter Overviews: From the 1960s to the Present

Although every chapter in this book revisits the nexus between intermediality and transnationalism to study specific films, each one also focuses on a distinct genre, media type, and instance of the "experimental." The book's organization is chronological and moves along three differentiated stages. It begins in the 1960s during a period when the intermedial was less prominent although still present, as seen in the use of cinematic montage and collage, or in the integration of theater, music, and other arts into film. Then the book turns to a transitional period lasting from the 1970s through the turn of the century when concerns about media obsolescence and disappearing formats, including Super 8 and video, coincided with a nostalgia for a vanishing idea of the "nation." Finally, attention shifts toward a contemporary post-digital moment when the definition of what constitutes the "cinematic" has expanded to include emerging technologies and variants such as films shot with cell phones or experiments in VR that have redefined spectatorship and irrevocably altered viewing practices.

In chapter 1, "Transatlantic Exchanges in 1960s Militant Cinemas: Helena Lumbreras's Debt to the Cinema of Fernando Solanas and Santiago Álvarez," I open in the '60s as militant cinema became global, after the 1959 Cuban Revolution, when ideologies and formats that aligned with the Hollywood model came under increasing attack. Transnationalism and intermediality provide a fresh perspective to reappraise New Latin American and Iberian militant cinema by focusing on three filmmakers who, although united in their shared vision of a transnational socialist uprising, encountered dissimilar contexts in Argentina (Solanas), Cuba (Álvarez), and Spain (Lumbreras). The exchanges between these filmmakers were representative of a multidirectional flow of artistic and political influence in a militant scene that spread throughout the Luso-Hispanic Atlantic and beyond. As the United States and the Soviet Union vied for hegemony through proxy wars and cultural influence, Latin American militant cinema became a transnational phenomenon. For many filmmakers, practicing their craft was a matter of life or death, as their movies, whether documentaries or experimental fiction, became political and advocated for a revolution in form and content, functioning as direct irritants to US-backed dictatorial regimes. Simultaneously, these three filmmakers interrogated the specificity of film as a celluloid-based medium by using strategies borrowed from painting, advertising, and popular music. Their promiscuous media use aligned with their revolutionary goals, destabilizing all kinds of orthodoxy. Leaving a mark on cinematic history, their collaborative and transnational approaches to the cinema served as a model for contemporary cineastes, as discussed in later chapters.

Focusing on art house films, chapter 2, "Brazilian Cinema Novo and the Iberian Escuela de Barcelona: Art Cinema under Authoritarianism," contrasts Brazilian Cinema Novo through its *enfant terrible*, Glauber Rocha, with the lesser-known Barcelona School (1960–1970), an experimental cinema group originating from the Catalan capital. Shared contacts, common aesthetic traits, and akin political ideologies mark these schools as "reflections" of each other across the Luso-Hispanic Atlantic. Both movements were acclaimed by critics and generally misunderstood by mainstream audiences, both were at times oppositional and at times complicit with military rule, and both extended the limit of the possible in terms of incorporating a multiplicity of artistic media into their cinema.[22] The chapter opens with an analysis of Rocha's *Terra em transe* (released in English as *Entranced Earth*, also known as *Land in Anguish*, 1967) considered a tropicalist masterwork. In *Terra* Rocha juxtaposes hyper-theatrical, operatic scenes with documentary segments, upending genre and medium specificity. Read widely as a political allegory for Brazil's 1964 military coup, I argue it was Rocha's recourse to a chaotic intermediality that made *Terra* aesthetically and politically relevant for filmmakers across the Atlantic. The chapter analyzes how the Barcelona School, which emulated its Brazilian and French new wave counterparts, engaged with Franco's dictatorship through elliptical art house films rather than overt dissent. Specifically, I explore how text–image interactions activate anti-Francoist discourse in three films: Vicente Aranda's *Fata Morgana* (1965), José María Nunes's *Sexperiencias* (1968), and Pere Portabella's *Nocturno 29* (1968). I close the chapter by examining the collaboration between Cinema Novo and the Barcelona School, which materialized in Rocha's *Cabeças cortadas* (1970) [Severed Heads]. Arguably Rocha's most transnational film, *Cabeças cortadas* was a commercial and artistic failure but offers fascinating insights into the limitations of art house cinema as a tool for political transformation.

In chapter 3, "Remediating Past Filmic Technologies: The Return of Super 8 and Video in the Era of Global Digital Cinema," I spring forward to the 2000s to appraise the return of Super 8 and video as "vintage" media that are reemerging within experimental cinema. The focus is on understanding the materiality and limits of the cinematic medium as it disappears, as it combines with other media, first replaced by analog video and eventually subsumed into the digital. The films under consideration also represent a lengthy transatlantic dialogue between Argentine and Iberian experimental filmmakers, exchanges that are the product of a long history of diaspora, exile, and the transnational experience.[23] I analyze films by Daniela Cugliandolo, an Argentine expat now residing in Barcelona, placing them in conversation with works by Narcisa Hirsch, a leading experimental filmmaker from the 1960s still active in Buenos Aires. Cugliandolo is an heir to Hirsch and the '60s Goethe Group; her films represent a spatiotemporal nexus, straddling the Atlantic *and* retracing past avant-garde traditions. The expat Cugliandolo digitally manipulates Super 8 footage in a homage and parody of the work of her precursors in the Goethe Group. I analyze two films, *pneurosis* (2001), where Cugliandolo explores the interplay between subjective and objective perspective, and *Esto no es un recuerdo* (2006) [This Is Not a Memory], where she fabricates a nostalgic home movie to explore exile, memory, and time's passage. The second half of the chapter turns to analog video, as I study a transatlantic video dialogue entitled *This Is Just to Say* (2014–2016) between filmmaker Andrés Denegri and fellow artist Gustavo Caprín. The epistolary exchange between these Argentines living in Argentina and Spain, respectively, places the nostalgia for analog video within a conversation about transnational identity. Shot in analog and later digitized, their videos range from the radically abstract to the mundane, eliciting nostalgic evocations about the effect (and affect) of diaspora and exile.

In chapter 4, "Cell Phone Cinema and Amateur Genre Film in the Luso-Hispanic Atlantic," I consider the impact of mobile telephony on amateur and independent filmmaking across the Luso-Hispanic region. The cell phone has placed cameras within the reach of video makers, citizen journalists, and amateurs interested in recording their daily lives, in the best scenarios democratizing access. Home movies, selfie films, and short videos are cheaply and instantly shared through social media and mobile phone festivals, as national specificity erodes further. While spanning every genre and subject, there is a marked affinity toward horror in Luso-Hispanic cell phone films, in works that recall the unfinished, grainy, and pixelated aesthetic associated with found footage and surveillance feeds. Changing viewing practices slant toward a close-to-the-body experience, point and shoot filmmaking, vertical formats, and shorter works, providing a sense of immediacy and presence. I study a set of one Iberian and three Latin American films spanning various phases of cell phone cinema. These include *Rojo en el bosque sangriento* (Tetsuo Lumière, Argentina, 2006) [Red in the Bloody Forest], an early horror film and parody about struggling amateur filmmakers; *Sangre y levadura* (Juan Carlos Mazo, Colombia, 2016) [Blood and Yeast], a horror musical bridging amateur and professional production; and *09 La Película* (Javier Aguirrezábal, Chile, 2014) [09 The Film], a full-length found footage movie that managed a limited commercial release. I conclude with *iMedium* (Alfonso García López, Spain, 2018), a sci-fi short about a near future in which cell phones become the source for techno-terror.

The last chapter casts its regard toward other emerging formats. Chapter 5, "Expanded and Immersive Cinema: VR, AR, and MR Film in Latin America, Latinx US, and Spain," considers notions of immersion, empathy, and interactivity by investigating how VR narratives envelop the participant-spectator within synthetic environments to generate a sense of presence or "being there." As cinema abandons the 2D screen for embodied 3D experiences, it diffuses the separation between onscreen and real space.[24] In the Luso-Hispanic Atlantic we encounter a VR scene that varies vastly across the region, where affluent nations have access to experimenting with this technology while others lag behind, reestablishing certain regional and national differences.[25] After donning a VR headset and experiencing the works, including reading, viewing, listening, and moving through 3D spaces, I perform a close analysis of four case studies from across the Luso-Hispanic Atlantic. The first two examples are animation VR films, one from Spain entitled *Madrid Noir* (James Castillo, 2021) and another from Argentina entitled *Pájaros de papel* (*Paper Birds*, Federico Carlini and Germán Heller, 2019). In these works the user-viewer unlocks certain game-like aspects of VR, including assuming a first-person point of view, and both also emphasize the VR "experience" over their allusive political subtexts. In *Madrid Noir*, set in Francoist Spain, the user assumes the role of a detective gathering evidence to solve a case. In *Pájaros de papel*, an allegorical narrative about authoritarianism set in 1940s Argentina, the user directs a musical piece and its accompanying light show. The last two pieces I visit, one by the Latinx journalist Nonny de la Peña and one by the Mexican filmmaker Alejandro González Iñárritu, attempt to situate the user in the pain of others to mobilize empathy. Based on real events, they focus on urgent issues related to immigration and social justice. The first work, *Use of Force* by de la Peña, recreates the murder of an undocumented immigrant by US Border Patrol, inserting the user as an observer and documenter of the crime. The second work, by González Iñárritu, is the aforementioned installation *Carne y Arena: Virtually Present, Physically Invisible* (2017). Like de la Peña, González Iñárritu hopes to shift the minds of US citizens toward a pro-immigration stance. VR narratives offer a possibility, however tenuous, to understand the plight of others.

The closing, "Coda," considers emerging modes of creating and viewing audiovisual media across the Luso-Hispanic Atlantic, including 360-degree documentary, TikTok films, video game movies or machinima, and AI-generated cinema. Their influence is exploding the experimental cinema landscape in the region, and they form the basis for some final reflections on the nexus of intermedial and transnational approaches to filmmaking and film criticism, as the second half of the twenty-first century draws nearer.

Chapter 1

Transatlantic Exchanges in 1960s Militant Cinemas

Helena Lumbreras's Debt to the Cinema of Fernando Solanas and Santiago Álvarez

Setting the Stage for an Ibero-American Intermedial, Transnational Militant Cinema: The Centro Sperimentale as Nexus

In this chapter I group three 1960s militant filmmakers—Helena Lumbreras (Spain), Fernando "Pino" Solanas (Argentina) considered with his close collaborator Octavio Getino, and Santiago Álvarez (Cuba)—to establish productive transatlantic and transcontinental comparisons among a generation of young directors who shared a conviction in Marxism as a political system and a predilection toward experimental modes of representation, as well as a utopian vision and revolutionary praxis nourished by the atmosphere of the 1959 Cuban Revolution.[1] Beyond their unwavering commitment to radical politics and mutual aesthetic affinities, these three directors have a common cinematic lineage traceable to a singular institution in Rome. While this shared "family tree" is only one influence on their work (among many others), it provides a key to comprehend the transnational exchanges between Latin American and Iberian militant cinema in those turbulent years—exchanges that greatly benefited filmmakers from both sides of the ocean in developing a new aesthetic language in their anti-authoritarian battle. These three directors either studied at or were advised by close mentors and associates who spent time at the Italian state-run Centro Sperimentale di Cinematografia [Experimental Center for Cinematography] in Rome, where numerous prominent New Latin American filmmakers trained. The New Latin American Cinema movement of the 1960s and '70s was born amidst the postcolonial and anti-dependency struggles in the continent, spreading like wildfire and becoming a linchpin for cultural resistance against the rise of military regimes. Indeed, these three filmmakers (Lumbreras, Solanas, Álvarez) were among other towering figures that refashioned militant cinema who had links to the Centro (Laviosa et al. 176–82; Tompkins 10–2).

The Centro was the third oldest film school in the world, after the Moscow and Leningrad film academies established in 1919 after the Russian Revolution. In the immediate post–World War II era, Rome was prominent among only a handful of film schools—the others were in Berlin, Paris, Prague, and New York (Laviosa et al. 175). With a left-leaning ideology and the visibility provided by neorealism's success, Rome was an ideal destination for aspiring filmmakers with militant inclinations. The Centro directly trained one of the directors I examine (the Spanish Lumbreras) and indirectly formed the others (the Argentine Solanas and the Cuban Álvarez) through their close collaborations with former Rome students, providing all three with a common aesthetic base and a shared approach to militant documentary. Their style was grounded on experimental and avant-garde techniques and on repurposing a multiplicity of media, including photographs clipped from magazines and other periodicals, images from paintings, assorted found footage, television broadcasts, fragments taken from other films, and classical and popular music, in short, a mix of high and low cultural artifacts from eclectic sources. These film techniques were taught in Rome, where students learned every aspect of filmmaking from an intermedial perspective, attending courses in multiple specializations including "acting, directing, photography, set design, costume design, screenwriting, sound production, editing, [and] production" (Laviosa et al. 178).

The Centro was established in 1934 during Mussolini's fascist regime, and consequently the institution was initially framed around "an Italian film avant-garde movement caught between reactionary and revolutionary forces" (Mariani 30). Like its politics, the school's promotion of avant-garde versus realist aesthetics also fluctuated during the 1940s and '50s, but by the 1960s the Centro espoused unrestricted artistic freedom and the rupture of cinematic norms, and these progressive winds were soon reflected in the politics of the Centro and its faculty as well as its two publications, *Bianco e nero* and *Cinema*. As Italy progressed toward socialism in the aftermath of

May 1968, and with Roberto Rosellini's appointment as director, the Centro decidedly adopted a daring avant-garde ethos (Liehm 249). As the oldest film school in Western Europe, the Centro was a competitive institution that only admitted a handful of talented international students each year. In the aftermath of World War II, the Centro primarily taught its students the then ground-breaking aesthetic of neorealism, but also Soviet-montage and those practical techniques necessary to develop an agile, low-cost cinema ideally suited for agit-prop and clandestine filming, such as using lighter 16 mm handheld cameras to cite one specific tactic. Without fully discarding a commitment to documentary realism, the school's instructors, chief among them the Center's founder, teacher, and filmmaker Umberto Barbaro, taught Russian theory and techniques (Shiel 17). Indeed, Masha Salazkina has shown that there were many Soviet-Italian interactions going back to the 1920s, and by the '50s and '60s "Soviet films became the cornerstone of cinematic education, an integral part of the curriculum of the Centro" ("Soviet-Italian" 43).

Films made by Italian directors who studied at the Centro, such as Roberto Rosellini and Vittorio De Sica, circulated widely in Spain and Latin America and inspired emerging militant cineastes around the globe, eager to emulate, improve upon, and adapt the Italian examples to their own circumstances. Rachel Gabara underscores the relevance of the Centro and neorealist films to young Latin Americans, where "the self-titled 'New Cinema' arose in the late 1950s and 1960s in reaction to the state of affairs following the 1959 Revolution in Cuba and in the wake of neorealism. Several of the [Latin American] filmmakers at the forefront of the movement studied in Italy and many acknowledged the direct influence of neorealism on their work" (192). Making a powerful case for grouping many of the New Latin American cineastes as a transnational community of exiled and diasporic filmmakers, Libia Villazana asserts that "the transnational features of their work and of their careers as filmmakers are unequivocal. First, they have been actively engaged in aesthetic and production exchanges with Europe and the influence of European cinema trends is apparent in their work. Secondly, and departing from the first point, their theoretical formulations and empirical cinema exploration have in turn influenced other cinemas, most notably African and Asian but also European and Russian cinemas" (44). To Villazana's point on transnationalism, it is notable that not only Latin Americans (e.g., Fernando Birri [Argentine], Julio García Espinosa, Tomás Gutiérrez Alea, and Humberto Solás [Cubans], and Nelson Pereira dos Santos, later Gustavo Dahl and Paulo Cézar Saraceni [Brazilians]) and a few from Spain (e.g., Helena Lumbreras and Jorge Grau) but also numerous African and Asian filmmakers studied in Rome, in an atmosphere rife with leftist and postcolonial (largely Fanonian) thought.[2] Notable North African filmmakers who studied at the Centro addressed decolonization struggles in their work, including Souheil Ben-Barka (Morocco), Mousa Haddad (Algeria), and Ababacar Samb Makharam (Senegal), making the school an incandescent flame lighting the tricontinental revolutionary spirit (Burke 147).

As I already indicated, beyond neorealism, filmmakers trained in early Russian avant-garde methods (primarily montage), since, as Salazkina argues, "Soviet film theory and practice became a special reference point in critical debates about cinema's medium-specific properties among certain Italian artists engaged in the broader debates of European film circles" ("Moscow-Rome-Havana" 99). The Latin American and Iberian filmmakers, hailing from hybrid cultural backgrounds, often mixed media and film styles and did not perceive montage as antithetical to neorealism. Solanas and Lumbreras certainly drew aspects from both styles, and Álvarez was conversant with both but shifted from neorealism to a montage approach in later films. This impure cinema has been theorized by Hamid Naficy, who terms it "accented cinema" and describes it as relying on interstitial and artisanal modes of production, distribution, and consumption (40–62).[3] Such hybridity was also patent in most Cuban cinema, where "the pervasive influence of Italian Neorealism in the early sixties and the fascination with the French New Wave in mid-decade had, by the end of this period, given way to broad-based stylistic experimentation and characteristically Cuban eclecticism" (Burton, "Revolutionary").

Turning to Fernando "Pino" Solanas, it is straightforward to trace the Centro's lasting mark on his films. Although Solanas did not himself study there, he apprenticed his trade directly under one of the institution's first Latin American graduates, fellow Argentine Fernando Birri—the so-called father of New Latin American Cinema. In 1956, Birri returned from his studies in Rome and founded the Escuela Documental de Santa Fe [Santa Fe School of Documentary Film], fashioned after the Centro and a cradle for Latin American militant filmmaking. Solanas has recognized Birri's preeminent ascendancy on his own cinema, and through him, the impact of the Centro and neorealism. The Centro's and Birri's influence on Solanas's work is transmitted in various ways, through Birri's example of filming with small-gauge format, through the person of cameraman and filmmaker Gerardo Vallejo, who learned from Birri in Santa Fe and became an integral member of Solanas's group Cine Liberación, through the editors that worked for both Birri and Solanas (e.g., Antonio Ripoll and Juan Carlos Macías), or the inclusion of clips from Birri's 1960 documentary *Tire dié* [Throw Me a Dime] in Solanas's *La hora de los hornos* (1968), and so on. Solanas and Getino edited *La hora de los hornos* in Rome as well, where they could work safely and with access to better equipment. We can conclude that Birri's training at the Centro Sperimentale was instrumental in shaping Third Cinema trends in Argentina and throughout Latin America, a training Solanas understood as providing "a meeting ground of the political and avant-garde engaged in a common task which is enriching to both" (qtd. in Shohat and Stam 260).

Solanas and Getino therefore fashioned a filmmaking style that was indebted to Birri and his fellow graduates from the Centro, a style that combined Eisensteinian and Vertovian montage, Brechtian narrative theories, the financial backing and model of the ICAIC's cinema (Álvarez created the intertitles for *La hora*), French New Wave handheld camera techniques, and a neorealist reliance on non-actors and non-studio settings; they also drew heavily, as Cynthia Tompkins notes, on the British documentary movement (pioneered by John Grierson), "which contributed to the articulation of a national identity as it privileged social responsibility" (14).[4]

By the mid-1960s, Latin American militant cinema was a global phenomenon, garnering attention from critics, filmmakers, and audiences alike on both sides of the Atlantic. Solanas and Getino's best-known movie, the epic masterpiece *La hora de los hornos*, garnered the Critics' Award at the 1968 Mostra Internazionale del Cinema Nuovo in Pesaro, Italy. Like the Centro, since 1964 the festival at Pesaro had become a global focal point where radical leftist filmmakers showcased their cinematographic experiments and where Latin Americans, Europeans, and others shared ideas. In short, Pesaro was a key site for exchanges "among the various fractions of the European leftists and the Thirdworldist artists" (Rozsa and Salazkina 70). In 1967 the Viña del Mar festival (Chile) also became a focal point for Latin American directors, providing ferment for both aesthetic and political revolution, but Pesaro afforded greater global visibility for the films and, in turn, better funding opportunities. Viña del Mar may have been the place where the Latin Americans forged a united continental vision for their cinema, but Pesaro was the place where that vision went global, transatlantic, tricontinental. *Cinema Nuovo*, the magazine affiliated with the Pesaro festival and the new Italian left, was "one of the first journals to systematically include accounts of the New Latin American Cinema, and especially the Cuban film industry, playing an important role in its dissemination around

Europe" (Rozsa and Salazkina 70). As Julianne Burton accurately observes, virtually all the principal militant Latin American films were first screened in Pesaro ("Old and New" 33). The 1964 Pesaro session was a who's who of experimental, militant, and avant-garde filmmakers, counting among its participants the Italian neorealists Roberto Rossellini and Cesare Zavattini, the founder of Brazilian Cinema Novo Glauber Rocha, the originator of the French New Wave Jean-Luc Godard, and various North American experimentalists, most notably the great Jonas Mekas. Such cross-cultural exchanges among leading visionaries were yielding a thrilling new cinema that sought nothing short of world-making. Transnational collaborations and the cross-pollination of styles would lead to a transformation of global militant cinema. The revolution might not be televised, but it would surely be filmed, on film, and promoted by film.

Fernando Solanas's *La hora de los hornos* and Its Transatlantic Circulation

Amidst these vigorous transnational exchanges, Latin American cinema became an imitated referent for militant filmmakers worldwide, including in Europe. *La hora de los hornos*, to name one concrete example, was a must-see film in Spanish and Italian leftist circles, indisputably the preeminent militant Latin American documentary of its time. And *La hora*'s appeal was not restricted to cinema *cognoscenti*. After its premiere in Pesaro for an audience of filmmakers and leftist intelligentsia, Solanas's film was screened for Italian factory workers at the Centro Documentazione Cinema e Lotta di Classe [Center for Documentary Cinema and Class Struggle], and later was shown throughout working-class neighborhoods in Rome's gritty periphery, where, according to Mariano Mestman "allí no sólo trabajaban con materiales sobre conflictos gremiales del país o europeos, más cercanos a la experiencia de los asistentes, sino también con films latinoamericanos. Y entre éstos últimos *La hora de los hornos* fue uno de los más proyectados en esos años" [they did not only deal with national or European working-class conflicts, relatable to the viewers, but also with Latin American films. And *La hora* was among the most viewed in those years].

Mestman details the significance of the Argentine film for Spanish militants between 1969 and Franco's death in 1975, suggesting that *La hora* was screened by clandestine film organizations in Madrid, including the outlawed Communist trade union Comisiones Obreras, and throughout Spain, but most saliently in Barcelona where "ya en los primeros setenta fuese utilizada en proyecciones que acompañaban el trabajo político contra el régimen franquista" [since the early '70s it was deployed in film screenings that accompanied political action against Franco's regime]. Catalan film historian Román Gubern corroborates that the film was in great demand by militant organizations (*Viaje* 276). Speaking about the transnational adaptability of Solanas's documentary, Bruce Williams stipulates that "international readings reinterpreted and recontextualized *La hora de los hornos* in diverse ways, allowing non-Argentine audiences to translate the film transnationally. Whatever awareness these spectators lacked of the specific context of Argentina was compensated for by their ability to appropriate the film for their own purposes, or for those of international left-wing movements" (124).

In October 1969 Solanas and Getino published their reflections about their film in a politico-theoretical manifesto entitled "Hacia un tercer cine: Apuntes y experiencias para el desarrollo de un cine de liberación en el tercer mundo" ["Towards a Third Cinema: Notes and Experiences for the Development of a Cinema of Liberation in the Third World"], which was published in Cuba's *Tricontinental* journal, issue 13. Simplified to its basic tenets, the manifesto argues for the heroic imperative of fashioning a combative Third Cinema for the developing world, a cinema that will resist authoritarian, imperialist, capitalist, and colonial power structures and promote revolution, succeeding where First Cinema (commercial cinema including Hollywood, even if progressive) and Second Cinema (art cinema, European avant-garde cinema) have failed. It is fitting that this foundational Third Cinema document appears in *Tricontinental*. *Tricontinental* magazine, the periodical published by the Cuban Organization of Solidarity with the People of Asia, Africa, and Latin America was, as its wordy name indicates, part of the transnational vision of the Cuban Revolution to export its political ideology and support decolonial and anti-capitalist (or anti-imperialist) struggles in Africa, Asia, and (Latin) America. The concept "tricontinental" was born in Cuba during the 1966 Tricontinental Conference in Havana and aligned symbiotically with Third Cinema's stated objectives, that is, "to stake out a position, make a stand, display an evident commitment to causes and ideals and not be considered dogmatic and closed," and to export these values globally (Wayne 128).

Evidently films such as *La hora de los hotnos* had no viable commercial release in Spain, given the political climate under Francoism and the unpopularity of documentary with mainstream Spanish audiences. The films circulated among those who were politically motivated to seek them out in clandestine format. But as Elena and Mestman argue, even for those filmmakers who somehow missed *La hora,* the transformation in militant film brought about by the New Latin American Cinema "se había dejado ya sentir con fuerza en la importante labor desempeñada desde distintas publicaciones por un puñado de jóvenes críticos que encontraban al otro lado del Atlántico estímulos y referentes muy precisos de cara a la ansiada renovación del propio cine español" (81) [had been powerfully felt in the important work developed in various publications by a handful of young critics who found in the opposite shores of the Atlantic the precise referents needed to stimulate the longed-for renovation of Spanish cinema]. Through influential film publications from Italy, France, and Spain, through clandestine projections in Spain and festivals worldwide, arose a sphere of circulation that linked militant filmmakers from Spain to those in Latin America and beyond. To cite an illustrative example that captures New Latin American Cinema's impact on Iberian critics and filmmakers alike, consider that in Andrés Linares's *El cine militante* (1976) [Militant Film]—the first Spanish book about militant cinema, published shortly after Franco's death—nearly a third of its pages are devoted to Third Cinema from Latin America.

Even under severely adverse political conditions the transatlantic flow of filmmakers and films was unstoppable, so the road map of leftist film circulation that Salazkina schematically delineates as Moscow-Rome-Havana had, by the late 1960s, expanded to New York, Buenos Aires, Paris, Barcelona, Madrid, Rio de Janeiro, Santiago de Chile, Mexico City, and other urban centers throughout Europe and Latin America (97). By then the New Latin American Cinema was entirely transnational in terms of style, funding, and distribution. In the words of Javier de Taboada—echoing Hamid Naficy's concept of "accented cinema" as a reflection on the mobility of postcolonial filmmakers on account of exile, diaspora, migration, and so on—the new cinema was undermining "los límites de lo 'nacional' como categoría básica de clasificación para el cine producido en las distintas partes del mundo, y su puesta en cuestión a partir de la existencia de un cine transnacional, diaspórico, exiliado o acentuado" (38–39) [the limits of the "national" as a basic organizing principle for global cinema, and its upending by a transnational, diasporic, exiled, or accented cinema]. To be sure, cinema has always been at least partly transnational (certainly in terms of circulation), but these films simultaneously courted national and foreign audiences, as they sought to spread decolonial thought and insurgent militancy internationally and also secure funding from wealthier nations. Mestman recounts a telling anecdote from 1970 about *La hora de los hornos* that captures how Latin American Third Cinema, and more specifically Cine Liberación, was similarly instrumentalized for insurgent purposes in Argentina and across the Atlantic, showing the reach of global militant cinema distribution:

> While the *Unidad Móvil Rosario* (the Rosario Mobile Cinema Unit, one of the most active groups of *Cine Liberación* in the city of Rosario, Argentina) extracted and used the famous chapter of "The Factory Occupations" from the second part of the film for political work with workers in the area surrounding the Swift industrial plant outside Rosario where the confrontation with management was taking place, at the same time, on the other side of the Atlantic, the militant French filmmaker Marin Karmitz was incorporating this same chapter of "The Factory Occupations" for his fiction film *Camarades* (Comrades 1970) to show how the young French militants and workers were debating their own labor conflicts on the basis of the screening of the Argentinian film. (Mestman 40)

Militant Latin American and Iberian cinema was evidently transnational, but how was it also intermedial? Was there an interplay between intermediality and transnationality? And if so, was intermediality understood and applied in the same fashion on both sides of the Atlantic?

Intermediality, Transnationality, and Santiago Álvarez's ICAIC Films

As articulated by Lucy Mazdon, transnational cinema should be broadly conceptualized, and "[it] should not be reduced to international co-productions or an accumulation of national cinemas. Understanding cinema as transnational means being aware of its porosity, its intersections with others (including the national), its indeterminacy and its contingency" (qtd. in Fisher and Smith). Conceptualizing these militant films as transnational (and transatlantic) in addition to national allows for a productive comparison and a shift of focus, from a hegemonic single-culture perspective (Spanish, Argentine, Cuban) to one that negotiates several cultures and approaches to filmmaking, even as the films themselves are grouped under a shared rubric of 1960s and '70s militant cinema. The reality is that these filmmakers navigated very specific national cultural contexts but, as I show, were also immersed in regional, transatlantic, and transnational conversations and collaborations, so their films bore the stamp of what their fellow militant cineastes were doing throughout the Latin American continent and across the ocean.

This promiscuous filmmaking across borders, nations, and oceans brings to a head the question of intermediality as an equally promiscuous comingling of media and interrogates how, if at all, that practice relates to the transnational characteristics of 1960s and '70s militant cinema. Evidently, the flow of cultural material across borders as militant films (re)appropriate assorted audiovisual sources (newsreels, television, other films) taken from myriad national and international contexts is itself a hallmark of intermedial practice—at least if we generously accept intermedial to encompass citing, parodying, intertextuality, collage, montage, and other hybrid practices. Of course, a narrower understanding of the term might identify it strictly with relations in which one medium interpenetrates one or more other media (e.g., poetry or painting intermixed with the cinema, as in the work of Stan Brakhage or Pere Portabella), or the imitation of a medium's formal qualities or processes by another (as with Wassily Kandisnky's paintings as a reinterpretation of musical themes, rhythms, and compositions, or early cinematography's inclusion of theater and vaudeville). In a specifically cinematic definition of the term intermediality, Jonathan Mack states, "This is to say that within a single text of a particular medium, attention can be called to the artifice of that medium by re-creating (or attempting to re-create), referencing, imitating, or evoking the sense of another distinct medium" (25).[5]

The intertextual is often also intermedial. Since at least Mikhail Bakhtin, Julia Kristeva, and Roland Barthes we have known that texts are a layered quilt or mosaic of quotations, deliberate citations, unintended borrowings, plagiarism, and so on. Certain types of intertextuality (e.g., *ekphrasis*), might insert a recollection or evocation of a visual work into a written text. Although the ultimate product is amalgamated into a text-based description, this particular form of intertextuality can certainly be categorized as intermedial. Something similar occurs with collage. Whereas in painting collage involved the incorporation of found objects, readymades, and assorted items into a surface or canvas, the technique transferred to the cinema in other ways. For example, either items were glued, scratched, or painted directly onto the celluloid (again, Brakhage) or, more typically, images of photographs, paintings, and script hailing from various sources were included within the frame by filming them or assembled into the final product in some other way. Similarly, photomontage collated photographs, newspaper clippings, and drawings from various sources—either borrowed, found, or created for the purpose—to fashion a newer piece. This is somewhat analogous to cinematic montage. While montage is strictly a cinematic process or editing technique, given that the juxtaposition of shots is the basis of the medium itself, it can also be understood as intermedial. Especially if we consider Eisenstein's or Vertov's idea of montage (with its echoes of Cubism), we see that it entails placing disparate fragments of film adjacent to each other, to create a new idea or new synthesis of sorts, to fashion a pluriperspective. These shots can also be overlaid with sound, making montage an assemblage of image, sound, and at times even script. As in collage, shot sources can hail from different stock, color schemes, varying graininess, and so on. Even as all of these experiments and devices are subsumed into a digital mash-up (as happens today), specters of these other disappearing media remain. As such, these intermedial practices and techniques also prefigure the arrival of digital media, in what David Rodowick diagnosed as the unmooring of our old understanding of the cinema, once "we can no longer take for granted what 'film' is—its ontological anchors have come ungrounded—and thus we are compelled to revisit continually the question, What is cinema?" (93). Along with this recalibration of the cinema, it is practical to allow for the intermedial to become a useful theoretical tool to approach whatever remains of the old media, or to reassess the cinema of the past, still anchored to its celluloid roots. That is, our ideation of intermediality must be as porous and impure as our encompassing understanding of the transnational. That said, the intermedial as a theoretical category and as a praxis responds to a very specific moment of the here and now, is tethered to its particular historical juncture, and acquires different shades through time.

Jürgen E. Müller argues that "intermediality is closely intertwined with particular social and institutional practice" so that employing intermediality is not an aesthetic approach that exists in a vacuum, rather it responds to the political conditions of its time and place (17). For instance, montage, as well as collage, developed by and during the first avant-gardes in 1920s Europe, are paradigmatic intermedial practices that cross the borders of historically "separate" media—writing, painting, photography, film, music—in order to test those very limits, to push against the so-called material specificity of each historical medium. But these same intermedial strategies have been adapted time and again with different signification and political intent. In specific contexts, montage has been closely allied with politics for both the right (fascism) and the left (socialism), through its capacity to manipulate materials and emotions to influence ideas and subvert or reinforce particular ideologies. In sum, such questions about material media in relation to film and politics have not lost their relevance since the 1920s and 1960s, when they were hotly debated in artistic circles. Montage, collage, and other aesthetic experiments that transgress media boundaries have gained even greater currency after the advent of the digital (see chapters 4 and 5 in this text), as the issue moves beyond material considerations into a more diffuse notion of medium. But these material, theoretical, and political concerns were especially prominent in the 1960s when the term "intermedia" first made its appearance—when Dick Higgins published his essay "Intermedia" (1965).

Nowhere was the intermedial strategy more salient than in the work of Cuban filmmaker and director of the ICAIC's newsreel division, Santiago Álvarez (born to Spanish émigrés in Cuba). As I will argue, Álvarez had a profound impact on the cinema of Helena Lumbreras. Critics including Maria Chiara D'Argenio remark on the Cuban filmmaker's heterogeneous media mixing, stating that "Álvarez put together this 'intermedial' material through editing and collage, and constructed a documentary [style] that does not follow conventional narrative patterns" (128). In his writings about dialectical montage Eisenstein theorized that the way disparate cinematic fragments relate to each other creates the message the film wishes to impart—the juxtaposition of fragments is greater than the sum of the individual ones (as exemplified by the Kuleshov effect). Speaking about Iberian films, Sara Nadal-Melsió underscores the import of how fragments relate so that "militant cinema's aesthetic impurity constantly echoes its constitutive and relational heterogeneity" (335).

A radical intermediality, suffused with elements from Soviet-montage, is fundamental to Álvarez's 1960s cinema. Intermediality provided the aesthetic force behind his cinema's agit-prop political message, doing so quite effectively. Soon, Álvarez's influential precursor techniques became exemplary models for global militant cinema. According to film scholar D'Argenio, these techniques included the "use of different types of material and mass media, ideological montage, dynamic editing, collage, centrality of visual and aural rhythm, use of non-synchronized sound and non-conventional narration/narrative" (128). In Álvarez's films, the spectator plays an active role in what D'Argenio describes as "a dialogical relationship," one in which "the formal experiments induce the viewer to focus on the way the film is constructed; the montage of juxtapositions and associations, to create the actual meaning of the film; the performativity of the film, to participate in the revolutionary struggle" (129).

Overall, filmmaking conditions were vastly different for Álvarez, as compared to Solanas in Argentina and Lumbreras in Spain. If in Argentina and Spain militant documentary was out of necessity an underground endeavor without state support (state persecuted, actually), in Cuba the situation was nearly ideal for leftist filmmakers. There, cinema was institutionalized shortly after the triumph of the Revolution in 1959, through the state-controlled ICAIC (Instituto Cubano del Arte e Industria Cinematográficos [Cuban Institute for the Cinematic Art and Industry]). There is no doubt about the impact of the techniques promoted by the Centro Sperimentale on the ICAIC's filmmakers and on the Cuban institute's mission to promote revolutionary cinema, indeed, to foment an international cultural revolution, making its films and filmmakers ambassadors of the Cuban political model. While Álvarez himself did not go to Rome, several of his close collaborators at the ICAIC did. Tomás Gutiérrez Alea (aka "Titón"), with whom Álvarez co-directed his second film *Muerte al invasor* (1961) [Death to the Invader] studied in Rome, as did several of the ICAIC's other co-founders and principal filmmakers, including Julio García Espinosa, Humberto Solás, Humberto Delgado, and the Spanish-born cinematographer Néstor Almendros—although many others, including José Massip and Álvarez himself, were cinematic autodidacts. That said, Álvarez absorbed the techniques his fellow filmmakers brought back from Rome, as well as developing his own.

Álvarez, Gutiérrez Alea, and their ICAIC colleagues were charged by the revolutionary government with shaping the direction of the Cuban film institute, which they modeled on the Centro (Gazelas 308; Tompkins 12–13). The Cubans had been at the Centro during the last years of neorealism, and among the lessons they learned from that movement was the need to develop a style that would be suited to limited financial means and adequate to leftist political aspirations. According to the Colombian novelist Gabriel García Márquez, who also spent time at the Centro, neorealism was "the only type of cinema we could realize in our continent, a cinema taken straight from reality, needing practically no resources" (García Márquez 331). But neorealism, prominent in these filmmakers' earliest works—such as Alea and García Espinosa's short *El mégano* (1955) [The Charcoal Worker]—was soon complemented with a variety of other influences, many originating in Latin America, including Brazilian Cinema Novo and Argentine militant documentary. Even as it shifted away from neorealism the institute remained committed to "formal plurality in artistic practice," rejecting wholesale the Stalinist directives to adopt socialist realism, as the Cubans reacted "against the superficial attribution of class character to specific formal features in artistic expression" (Rozsa and Salazkina 75). Both the Argentines Solanas and Getino's "Towards a Third Cinema" manifesto and García Espinosa's "Toward an Imperfect Cinema" were "quite unambiguous" in their rejection "of Soviet socialist realism alongside Hollywood as examples of First Cinema" (Rozsa and Salazkina 75).

Besides being eminently transnational and formally daring, ICAIC films were notoriously heterogeneous from a material and stylistic standpoint, as they irreverently mixed and subverted their models, recycling past and present cinematic scraps. This cheeky recycling is famously thematized in a self-reflexive scene in Alea's *Memorias del subdesarrollo* (*Memories of Underdevelopment*, 1968) in which a fictional ICAIC filmmaker (played by Alea himself) creates a movie from discarded celluloid scraps cut out of Hollywood films by prudish Batista censors, on account of their sexually explicit content. The repurposing (and recycling) of these forbidden fragments aligned with Cuba's material reality and with the ICAIC's political intent: in an intermedial sense the approach collaged and reused assorted celluloid gauges at a time of scarcity (especially of new 35 mm stock), whereas politically it parodied Batista's censorship apparatus and ridiculed the bourgeois morality that these censored fragments represented, even as it critiqued the US consumer culture on display in the source Hollywood material. Using discarded or repurposed material became a defining trademark for Cuban militant filmmakers, and the approach was exported to Third Cinema practitioners worldwide who were eagerly emulating the Latin American films.

From the embers of neorealism, the lasting influence of Soviet-montage, the refreshing spontaneity of the French New Wave, and the brash defiance of Brazil's Cinema Novo arose a decidedly intermedial and inventive New Latin American Cinema that was at once local and global, a cinema that sought new forms, new materials, and new publics. To this point, in an article about Álvarez's aggressive Soviet-montage style, Kristi Wilson remarks that his "arsenal of artistic strategies includes violating copyright, remixing iconic images, and a unique use of song as argument that both evokes a particularly Cuban history of musical counterpoint and reaches out in a transcontinental way toward what he hoped would become a newly literate, reinvented, revolutionary public" (410). The technique of remixing assorted materials was by no means exclusive to Álvarez and Alea's films. Actually, Solanas's *La hora de los hornos* also borrows, repurposes, and quotes extensively from other films, newsreels, stock images, and publicity and explicitly recycles images taken directly from Álvarez's short *Now!* (1965). This detail attests that the Cuban filmmaker was having a resounding impact on the Latin American militant film scene and vice versa. These shared intermedial practices were parallel to a common political project uniting the continent against US imperialism. Amidst open hostilities with the neighbor to the north, the ICAIC sought to further an agenda that established alliances and solidarity with Third World armed struggles, whether in Vietnam, Bolivia, the Congo, or even the United States itself, by supporting the civil rights movement.

Furthermore, Álvarez's work on films such as *Now!*, *LBJ* (1968), or *79 primaveras* (*79 Springs*, 1969), and his innumerable newsreels for the ICAIC, had far-reaching influence not only in the American continent but also in European, Asian, and African militant circles, so that as Ignacio del Valle Dávila observes in regard to the newsreels, "a pesar de su surgimiento un tanto tardío, el Noticiero ICAIC Latinoamericano consiguió imponer un estilo de realización documental y convertirse en un referente cinematográfico ineludible en Cuba y América Latina, así como entre buena parte de los cineastas militantes de Europa" (45) [despite its late arrival, the ICAIC's Latin American Newscast imposed a documentary style and became an unavoidable cinematic referent in Cuba and Latin America, as well as among a significant number of European militant filmmakers]. Del Valle sustains that collage was Álvarez's preferred stylistic device, a technique inherently intermedial (in its use of cut-up sections from various footage sources), but also easily adaptable to film's material specificity (through the process of filming the assembled materials and subsuming them into a single celluloid negative). Álvarez skillfully integrated film from disparate footage, gauges, materials, and colors, as well as photographs from periodicals, title frames, and assorted images, editing all these scraps painstakingly with a Moviola. The collage fragments were assembled through a sophisticated dialectical montage, moving beyond merely juxtaposing images to include analysis and manipulation of facts and events, given that, according to the filmmaker himself, "el empleo de las estructuras de montaje permite que la noticia originalmente filmada se reelabore, se analice y se ubique en el contexto que la produce, otorgándole mayor alcance y una permanencia casi ilimitada"

(Álvarez qtd. in Del Valle 46) [through montage the original filmed news item can be reelaborated, analyzed, and placed in the context that produced it, granting it greater reach and almost unlimited permanence].

Álvarez was not the only ICAIC filmmaker adopting this particular montage style; in fact, everyone was experimenting with intermedial collage to some degree. But he employed these devices with more virtuosity than most, with the exception perhaps of the ICAIC's enfant terrible and its most radical cineaste, Nicolasito (Nicolás Guillén Landrián). The Europeans were taking note of the effervescent energy emanating from the Cuban film industry. In Spain, Lumbreras adapted collage techniques she likely saw in ICAIC films, probably in Álvarez's since they were broadly disseminated through clandestine screenings. Like Álvarez, she was fond of syncopating collage and photomontage images with a dubbed-in extradiegetic musical soundtrack that was meant either to emphasize or to undermine the visual track. Lumbreras was exposed to Cuban and Argentine militant films while studying in Italy, where they were frequently screened, during her extensive European travels, and in Spain via underground viewings. Later, she would view Latin American films in Barcelona's Central del Curt, which since its 1974 founding by Joan Martí Valls and Martí Rom screened marginal, amateur, avant-garde, and militant cinema and distributed films throughout Spain (García-Merás 31, 39). Furthermore, Lumbreras, her partner Mariano Lisa, and fellow filmmaker Llorenç Soler were all three active members of the Central del Curt and involved in programming. As early as 1967, despite ongoing censorship, many foreign films could be viewed "in their original uncut version" at theaters designated as *salas especiales* [special exhibition venues] (Cerdán et al. 399). Lumbreras read about Álvarez's latest films and techniques in the Italian and Spanish film journals and probably obtained clandestine copies of *Cine Cubano*, the ICAIC's periodical active since 1960. She was well versed in the intermedial aspects of the cinema of the ICAIC and Cine Liberación, and probably quite familiar with the manifestoes that also made the rounds in her world.

As further proof of the transnational appeal of Latin American documentaries in European film festivals, we can point to the wide circulation of Álvarez's films, some of which garnered awards in Spain. In 1963 his film *Ciclón*, which placed Cuban cinema "en el mapa del cine mundial" [on the map of world cinema], won first prize in the television documentary category in Bilbao's VII Certamen Internacional de Cine Documental Iberoamericano y Filipino [VII International Competition of Ibero-American and Philippine Documentary] (García Borrero 159). *Ciclón* represented the first film in which Álvarez departed from his initial realist style—an aesthetic that, according to the cineaste himself, imitated the "capitalist newsreels" (Rist). After that conventional phase, Álvarez decanted for an aggressive Soviet-style cinema fashioned on the early avant-garde films by Pudovkin, Eisenstein, and Vertov, and not on the more recent state-prescribed Socialist realism. He learned Soviet techniques by viewing films and from his colleagues who studied at the Centro in Rome and possibly directly from a handful of ICAIC collaborations with Soviet filmmakers working in Cuba, chief among them Mikhail Kalatozov and Vladimir Vajnstok (Rist; Matuskova 128).

In 1966, Álvarez's politically incendiary *Now!*—a film that galvanized militant filmmakers worldwide with its powerful indictment of racial injustice in the US and its call to revolutionary action—won the first prize at the Bilbao festival. Increasingly, mentions of Álvarez's political films appeared in Spain's leading cinema journal *Nuestro Cine* [Our Cinema], a combative magazine that since 1961 "ejercía como plataforma de las ideas marxistas en el campo de la crítica cinematográfica" (Fernández-Santos) [functioned as a platform for disseminating Marxist ideas within the discipline of film criticism]. From the journal's pages, critic Miguel Bilbatúa enthusiastically applauded Álvarez's work, vehemently proclaiming that "*Now!* es un documental que debía ser visto por todo el mundo. *Now!* es lúcido, sobrecogedor, necesario" (qtd. in Luciano Castillo) [*Now!* is a documentary that should be seen by all. *Now!* is lucid, overwhelming, necessary].

Examining the intermedia relationships in these films, as well as the transatlantic exchanges between Latin America and Iberian militant filmmakers, is of the utmost relevance to film studies as Nadal-Melsió argues in an issue of the *Spanish Journal of Cultural Studies* dedicated to militant cinema. Speaking specifically about Solanas and Getino's *La hora*, but more broadly about the embracing of Latin American cinema in Spain, she stipulates that the history of how *La hora* was received in Spanish militant and clandestine circles "could easily justify a special issue of its own. . . . The same would be true of the influence of figures like Fernando Birri or Oscar Masotta and their transatlantic trajectories, which. . . also merit critical reassessment" (338).[6] Reinforcing these associations through an in-depth analysis of Lumbreras's film *El campo para el hombre* (1975) [Field for Men] will be the thrust of the remainder of this chapter, while anchoring the discussion of the transatlantic flows of films (such as *La hora de los hornos* and *Now!*) on the question of media hybridity.

Helena Lumbreras in the Context of 1960s Counter-Cinema

In the opinion of film critic Annalisa Mirizio, the entirety of Helena Lumbreras's filmography is best comprehended through the lens of a Marxist militancy that was aligned with kindred ideological projects fermenting in Latin America in the 1960s and '70s. Mirizio sustains that, in addition to providing counter-information during a time of tumultuous political upheaval and seeking to transform spectators into militants for the working-class struggle, Lumbreras's long-term political project was "hacer del cine un instrumento para luchar en la sociedad: [para Lumbreras] no se trata de que el cine funcione como una acción política, sino que sea en sí mismo una acción política común" (432) [to fashion cinema itself into an instrument for societal conflict: for Lumbreras it is not about making film work as a political action, but that film itself should become a political action]. *El campo para el hombre* was directed by Lumbreras in the repressive milieu of Franco's dictatorship and must be evaluated with that context in mind. It is a work that bridges documentary and experimental genres while expressing the urgent need for economic, political, and formal freedom—the sort of liberation most people in Spain desperately yearned for in late Francoism. Lumbreras was a filmmaker with ties to many directors already mentioned: to Solanas, to the Italian neorealists, especially to Zavattini and Pasolini, and to a cadre of Iberian militant cineastes. I believe that Lumbreras's cinematic intermediality is a political maneuver that associates, on a formal level, the concepts of medium purity and specificity as socially alienating, while aligning medium hybridity and the heterogeneous mixing of materials with utopian aspirations for liberation. I will show in the following sections that her filmmaking style, while singularly distinctive, owed a considerable debt to Latin American cinema in general and to Solanas and Álvarez in particular.

In 1973, Barcelona-based filmmakers Helena (also Elena) Lumbreras Giménez (1935–1995) and Mariano Lisa Escaned (1945–) made a clandestine documentary called *El campo para el hombre*, which denounced the dismal conditions in rural Spain under the Franco dictatorship, foregrounding the dire need for agrarian reform and land redistribution. The film is executed in a cinematic style midway between the militant documentary prevalent in Third Cinema and the experimental film practiced by European art cinemas of the 1960s, such as the Barcelona School and the French New Wave.[7] As previously stated, Lumbreras had studied at the Centro Sperimentale in Rome where she received her degree as director and where she acquired experience as a scriptwriter, editor, and cinematographer. At the Centro she worked with a variety of media and learned multiple filmmaking styles. Lumbreras did not meet Birri, Espinosa, or Alea at the Centro since they preceded her in Rome by a decade—although she would have coincided with them at festivals and other film events. As Elena Blázquez points out, Lumbreras had met Álvarez at the Leipzig Film Festival, another venue that featured political and militant cinema, like the Festival of Oberhausen, the Festival of Solothurn, and the People's Festival in Florence. In any case, her films shared much with the Latin Americans' perspective and methodology, whether with Solanas and the Spanish-born Getino's powerful if overly didactic *La hora*, which left an indelible imprint on Lumbreras's work, or with the visual staccato of Álvarez's montage documentary style. During a question-and-answer session after a screening of *El campo* at the Madrid Film Forum "La Claqueta" (Nov. 24, 2018), the film's co-director Mariano Lisa spoke at length about Lumbreras's filmic influences. Lisa mentioned the importance of neorealism and specifically De Sica's *Ladri di biciclette* (*Bicycle Thieves*, 1948), as well as Pasolini and Antonioni's filmography, but also emphasized the immediate and key role played by Latin American militant cinema for the Colectivo, primarily Álvarez's documentaries, as well as other '60s underground and marginal cinemas (36:00–38:00).

Notable as well, according to Lisa, was the guidance from legendary Dutch documentary filmmaker Joris Ivens, a friend and mentor to Lumbreras who also shared a long history with Latin American cinema. When Lumbreras met him, Ivens was already a seasoned and well-respected veteran filmmaker associated with both anti-colonial struggles and leftist politics, having made prominent *engagé* films about the Spanish Civil War (*The Spanish Earth*, 1937), and the Vietnam War (*Far from Vietnam*, 1967).[8] Spending considerable time in Latin America, he made films for the ICAIC about the Cuban Revolution's popular militias (*Pueblo en armas* 1961 [People in Arms]) and two important works in Chile, *A Valparaiso* (1962) and a film about Salvador Allende's 1964 electoral defeat *El tren de la victoria* (1964) [The Train to Victory]. Everywhere he traveled in the continent, Ivens gave lectures that were attended by Latin American documentarians of the ilk of Álvarez, Patricio Guzmán, Raúl Ruiz, and Pedro Chaskel, among other luminaries, and later he shared his accumulated knowledge about making militant films with Lumbreras and her team (De la Puente).

At the same Madrid event, Lisa revealed that Luis Buñuel's 1933 pseudo-ethnographic documentary *Tierra sin pan* (*Land without Bread*), also known as *Las Hurdes*, was considered by Lumbreras as a counterexample not to be followed. Although Buñuel's film could, on account of its theme about an impoverished region abandoned by the state, be considered a key precedent, it became a foil for how not to portray the peasant working class in *El campo para el hombre*; the filmmaker found Buñuel's documentary too ironic and distanced from its subjects, too elitist. Absorbing the theoretical debates arriving from Latin America, Lumbreras believed the intellectual class had to integrate with its working-class film subjects in an effort to achieve class equality, and in turn, create a united front against Francoism and capitalism.

Lisa reminisced that, among many skills, Lumbreras acquired a fastidiously precise metrical editing style at the Centro from a Soviet-montage instructor (47:00–48:00). Such montage relied on a painstakingly measured assembly of heterogeneous media and materials gathered from archival sources and on-site filming. Since editing *El campo* in Francoist Spain was perilous, Lumbreras completed the final cut at the Cinecittà studios while living in Rome, prior to her definitive return to Spain in 1969 (50:00). As these revelations by her lifelong partner and fellow filmmaker confirm, for Lumbreras, the Latin American cinematic influence—whether received directly from those filmmakers at festivals or by studying their films, through Ivens's mentorship, or from her years at the Centro Sperimentale—was a salient component in an otherwise rich tapestry of filmic referents. It is also the case that her militancy through cinema was made possible by the thriving clandestine film scene in Spain's urban centers, but also by a transnational support system that included the parallel struggles and shared ideological vision with Third Cinema filmmakers, and the technical and financial support she received from the Italian left.

It should not be surprising that in 1960s Spain militant filmmakers would adopt strategies from Third Cinema. Despite notable divergences, there were many affinities between Spain and Latin America's cultural and political milieu in that period. The repressive conditions under the Franco regime were reminiscent, although less extreme, of political oppression in Brazil and Paraguay, and later in Argentina, Chile, Uruguay, Bolivia, and other Latin American countries under authoritarian military rule. The sole exception, as mentioned, was Cuba, where leftist filmmakers labored freely under the auspices of the revolutionary government, which nevertheless controlled the messaging through oversight of the ICAIC under the direction of Alfredo Guevara. While in Spain political prisoners did not habitually "disappear," and torture was less widespread than in the Southern Cone, the climate of censorship and fear was palpable. As Rosalind Galt observes,

"[I]ndividual filmmakers may or may not have personally feared for their lives, but it remains undeniable that the history, within a generation, of disappearance, torture and murder of democrats and leftists casts a shadow of violence over any form of political speech" ("Missed" 203). Roberto Arnau Roselló concurs that, despite the proximity of Italian and French cinemas, there was greater affinities between Iberian and Latin American militant film, given "el contexto de represión, marginalidad y clandestinidad en el que se desencadenan estas prácticas [fílmicas] en España, lo que las acerca más a las existentes en algunos países latinoamericanos (Argentina, Chile, Bolivia, etc.) que a los europeos" ("Los colectivos" 295) [the context of repression, marginality and clandestineness in which cinematic practices took place in Spain, which approximated them more closely to those in some Latin American countries (Argentina, Chile, Bolivia, etc.) than to European ones].

Although Spain was not engaged in processes of decolonization like much of the Third World, its status as a relatively impoverished peripheral nation in Southern Europe, and the backwardness of its film industry in the '60s and '70s encouraged opting for a Third Cinema aesthetic praxis that emphasized process over product. But as previously stated, Spanish underground filmmakers were keenly aware of European avant-garde cinematic trends (Russian montage, French New Wave, Italian neorealism), drawing on those lessons as well. Iberian militant cinema was, therefore, at a unique crossroads between the radical Latin American filmmakers and the European art house avant-garde. Indeed, I would suggest that, on account of her interstitial position between so-called European Second Cinema and Latin American Third Cinema, Lumbreras was able to articulate a hybridized counter-ideological cinema that coherently integrated experimentalism and political commitment. My interest in the following sections is to examine how Lumbreras's film *El campo para el hombre* bridges both documentary and experimental genres while expressing the need for economic, political, and formal liberation from the authoritarian constraints of late Francoism, and by extension from realist filmmaking styles exemplified by the state's newsreels Noticiarios y Documentales [Newsreels and Documentaries] (NO-DO). Additionally, I will contend that Lumbreras's promiscuous mixing of different media—her intermedial practice—is a political maneuver that associates, on a formal level, the concepts of medium specificity and medium purity as socially alienating, while aligning medium hybridity with utopian dreams of liberation from oppression—material, political, formal—thereby advocating a return to a utopian, holistic, and collective way of life. In the next section I will contextualize the historical and material conditions of film practice in Spain, the backdrop to Lumbreras's filmmaking possibilities; then I shall analyze some scenes from *El campo para el hombre* to illustrate Lumbreras's intermedial approach and its political goals. Throughout the rest of the chapter, I will continue to interweave a narrative about the influence on her filmmaking by Latin American cinema, more specifically as it pertains to Solanas and Álvarez's impact.

Lumbreras and Her Class Film Collective

Notwithstanding her relative obscurity and regrettable absence from many official film historiographies, Lumbreras's relevance as the most prominent among a handful of women making clandestine revolutionary films in the 1960s and 1970s in Spain (undeterred by Franco's repressive apparatus) cannot be overstated. Indeed, part of my intent with this chapter is to commemorate Lumbreras and frame her work considering the aesthetic and transformative possibilities of militant documentary film as a political praxis, or, as the well-known metaphor goes, of the deployment of the camera as a gun. While Lumbreras was all but neglected as a filmmaker for decades, there is increasing awareness, as of late, of her work. In October 2018 *El campo para el hombre* was featured at New York's MoMA as part of a series titled "Catalan Cinema's Radical Years, 1968–1978." More recently, in April 2022, the Center for Contemporary Culture Tabakalera (San Sebastian, Spain) featured a retrospective of her films as part of a cycle dedicated to feminist cinema. In 2020, the Filmoteca de Catalunya's Conservation and Restoration Center (2CR) restored and archived Lumbreras's more relevant films on YouTube to make them accessible to anyone interested. The growing interest about her films is a hopeful sign that her sacrifices on behalf of militancy and democracy are finally being recognized, and her skill as a filmmaker is being reappraised. What is still necessary as part of this recuperation is to credit those filmmakers from Latin America that inspired and left their indelible mark on her films, to understand, in other words, the cultural intertexts and intermedia that undergirded her oeuvre.

Lumbreras and her lifelong partner Mariano Lisa founded a filmmaking collective, which, in 1975, adopted the name Colectivo Cine de Clase [Class Film Collective], but which had been active since 1968. Colectivo was militantly opposed to the regime, as well as to the center-right government that followed it during Spain's transition to democracy (La Transición), a period now seen as a problematic compromise that left Francoist structures intact and many questions unresolved. At that time, Lumbreras's collective was among a handful of groups providing alternatives to both the low-quality, often sexist mainstream comedies (*españoladas*) and the socially committed Nuevo Cine Español (NCE) [New Spanish Cinema], categorized by critics as "a movement of political protest inspired by Italian Neorealism" (Faulkner 205).

In a Marxist vein, like many of its Latin American filmic counterparts concerned with the revolutionary ideal of *tierra y libertad* [land and liberty], *El campo para el hombre* presents the desperate plight of agriculture in two paradigmatic case studies: large Andalusian estates (*latifundios*) and small Galician sharecropping farms (*minifundios*). For each scenario, Lumbreras edits the material with great artistic and political sensibility. On the one hand, she creates a document that aims to mobilize the audience using the strategies of the provocateur: anonymity (there are no credits), flexibility (in the employ of different methods and media to communicate a message), and adaptability (to the onerous conditions of production and distribution). On the other hand, she experiments with form to inscribe the film within a post–May 1968 avant-garde aesthetic that grew increasingly suspicious of traditional narrative structures.

As we have seen, inspired by films from the ICAIC and elsewhere, Lumbreras pioneers in Spain an early type of intermediality by synthesizing an assortment of media and techniques into her film, including painting, folk music, advertisement, typography, and Soviet-style montage sequences. This intermedial orientation recalls, as previously stated, the earlier work by Álvarez in Cuba and by Solanas and Getino—as part of the collective Cine Liberación—in Argentina. Recalling the ICAIC's avant-garde aesthetics, Santiago Juan-Navarro could be describing Lumbreras's style, characterized by a "naturaleza vanguardista signado por el montaje frenético, el cine-collage y el contrapunto intermedial, que remedaba el estilo del primer Santiago Álvarez" (91) [its avant-garde nature marked by a frenetically paced montage, the use of film-collage and an intermedial counterpoint, which was reflected in Santiago Álvarez's style]. Intermediality and montage impart a one-two punch in Lumbreras's militant films, working synergistically to deliver their powerful political message. The effects of the intensified intermediality in Lumbreras's work are often jarring and even defamiliarizing; by juxtaposing filmed material from disparate sources, dynamically combining word and image to create visual dissonance and critical distance, or marshaling graphic discontinuities, Lumbreras and the Colectivo sought to shock spectators into awareness of Spain's political situation. As was the case with their Latin American counterparts, the filmmakers' conviction was that this awareness would translate into political action so that their cinema would become a direct operation on reality rather than its mere representation. As Lumbreras forcefully asserted, "No hacemos historia del cine sino que hacemos la historia con el cine" (qtd. in García-Merás 16) [We do not make film history but rather we make history with film].

Situating 1960s Iberian Oppositional Filmmakers: NCE, the Barcelona School, and Militant Cinema(s)

Although this chapter is primarily focused on exchanges between Latin American and Iberian militant cinemas, and in particular considers how Solanas and Álvarez informed Lumbreras's filmmaking, it is necessary to frame their influence in relation to the often-determinant sociopolitical factors affecting filmmakers in the Peninsula. Simply put, some filmic strategies that had proven incendiary in Latin America in terms of fomenting insurgency did not work in Spain, where there was little appetite or even likelihood for a generalized armed uprising. And in contrast with most of the Southern Cone, the specific conditions of late Francoism in the Peninsula at times permitted more flexibility, even a degree of artistic freedom, resulting in a less stark division between commercial and militant cinema. The ever-changing conditions of censorship that filmmakers encountered during the forty-year fascist dictatorship ranged widely from unyielding state control and severe penalties to periods of relative loosening (such as the so-called Fraga Spring's lessening of censorship), a panorama far too complex to outline here with the nuance it deserves.[9] Suffice it to say that the seesawing of the censorship apparatus resulted in a spectrum of cinematic responses, from those mainstream filmmakers who developed a flexible sense for how far they could proceed in questioning the system to more radical ones (like Lumbreras) who opted to reject the state's tenuous "relative freedom," embracing illegality as a means to liberate content choice and increase revolutionary potential, in a sense, adapting a kind of Guevarian *foquista* strategy to spark oppositional unrest and applying guerrilla tactics to the creation and distribution of films.

Within this broad panorama, while Lumbreras, Llorenç Soler, Andrés Linares, and other militant filmmakers went underground, others became prominent directors within the established industry. By late Francoism, mainstream filmmakers generally opposed the regime and wanted to bring about a new aesthetic for Spanish cinema, the most prominent among them opting for neorealism. Mainstream cinema's gradual turn toward an edgier, socially committed, and at times neorealist film style—a national alternative to the otherwise dominant Hollywood style—can be traced to the 1955 Salamanca Conversations, when a cadre of daring young directors including Basilio Martín Patino, Juan Antonio Bardem, and Luis García Berlanga launched what later became known as the Nuevo Cine Español (NCE), framing it around a set of progressive social and formal propositions. Many of the NCE's directors were members of the clandestine Spanish Communist Party and therefore committed to undermining the system's right-wing ideology from within, outsmarting the censors by using allegories and parables to critique Francoist society, which they successfully achieved in films such as Bardem's *Muerte de un ciclista* (*Death of a Cyclist*, 1955) or Berlanga's *El verdugo* (*The Executioner*, 1963).

There were other participants in this intricate cinema scene. The Barcelona School (Escuela de Barcelona [EdB]), another principal Iberian counter-cinema movement at that time, was producing avant-garde films that were successful in securing state funds by virtue of their artistic "special interest" (Galt, "Impossible" 493). Such was the case with Vicente Aranda's allegorical tale *Fata Morgana* (1965) or Jorge Grau's mediocre and wholly apolitical *Tuset Street* (1967), a film that counted with the collaboration of the Cuban-Spanish cameraman Néstor Almendros, who later participated in other EdB projects (I also will address collaborations between the EdB and Cinema Novo in chapter 2 when I focus on art cinema). Like the NCE directors, many of the EdB's filmmakers engaged in the "contradictory experiences of being opposed to the dictatorship yet accepting subsidies from the state and representing Franco's Spain at foreign film festivals" (Faulkner 206). Other members of the group, however, were less financially compromised and produced films that could not pass censorship because of their decidedly anti-regime content, as was the case with the Portuguese-born José María Nunes's revolutionary narrative *Sexperiencias* (1968), Jacinto Esteva's political documentary *Lejos de los árboles* (*Far from the Trees*, 1972), or Pere Portabella's *Nocturno 29*, which was subjected to significant cuts. Thus, while some EdB films were shown in Madrid and Barcelona's newly opened (1967) art houses (*salas de arte y ensayo*) without police intervention, others only accessed clandestine circulation, much like Lumbreras's films, in cine-clubs, private apartment screenings, and, occasionally, festivals abroad

(D'Lugo 1997). In that sense, although most of their work could not be rigorously considered as militant cinema, the EdB filmmakers did partake of an oppositional and at times clandestine atmosphere.

But, whereas the NCE's cinema of consciousness attempted to lay bare the hypocrisy and injustice of the regime from within by pushing against the limits of censorship with neorealist and often satirical films that "portrayed Spanish society as corrupt and complacent" (Higginbotham 11), and the EdB created an art cinema with "elliptical" narratives difficult for working-class audiences to relate to, there was also an underground film community working in the shadows of both commercial and art cinema, a community that was committed to a radical revolutionary politics of liberation. Taking advantage of the loosening of state control during *apertura* and a concomitant rise in civil society activism, these groups began a campaign of militant cinema whose main objective was to accelerate the regime's demise. This inevitable end was hoped to be at hand on account of the political concentration of power in an ailing and decrepit Franco, further hastened with the 1973 assassination (by the Basque separatist group ETA) of Admiral Luis Carrero Blanco, the *Caudillo*'s handpicked successor. In addition to Lumbreras's group there were other militant film groups operating as clandestine cells, including Cantabria's Cine Libre Santanderino [Santander Free Cinema], the Communist Party–affiliated Colectivo de Cine de Madrid [Madrid Film Collective] led by Andrés Linares, and others. As this broad panorama demonstrates, Iberian filmmakers labored under sundry conditions of legality and illegality to sabotage Francoist rule.

Formation and Ideology of Lumbreras's Class Film Collective

Helena Lumbreras's films must be appraised in the context of this effervescent proliferation of subversive and clandestine filmmaking in Spain, and in relation to the encouraging models of resistance provided by militant movements from throughout Latin America, including groups that were endorsing direct action through film or considered film as a form of direct action toward revolution. The Spanish filmmakers did not uncritically embrace the Latin American examples but adapted their tenets to local conditions. Nor did they always see eye to eye politically with their transatlantic counterparts. For instance, Mestman has shown that European Marxist filmmakers were suspicious of the populist resonance of the Peronist message in *La hora de los hornos*. Their distrust was reinforced by

Juan Perón's choice to cozily seek refuge in fascist Spain from 1960 until his return to Argentina in 1973, rather than opting for exile in Marxist Cuba. That choice and Peronism's right-leaning tendencies led the leftist European intelligentsia to suspect the Argentine leader's fascist proclivities. That did not, however, detract from the film's popularity among European militant circles. Filmmakers, misgivings aside, enthusiastically embraced the Argentine film's avant-garde format (exemplified by its intermedial montage) and its anti-colonial, anti-imperialist message but abandoned nationalist and populist discourses in favor of orthodox Marxist principles. Mestman observes in regard to the film's transnational appeal that it is "essential to think the history of this type of cinema beyond the definitions that have circulated concerning Third Cinema, for it dealt with a practice of intervention, of *cine-acción* [film-action] with *La hora de los hornos* that in its time transcended national borders to enter the catalogues of alternative distributors that supplied the parallel circuits of militant cinema in the United States, Great Britain, France, Italy, Spain, and many other countries" (40). What the film certainly tapped into in the Iberian militant imaginary was a growing sense of immediacy, of urgency, especially concerning working-class rights and the potential for a global leftist alliance for solidarity and mutual assistance in anti-authoritarian struggles.

In 1973, the members of the Colectivo Cine de Clase were cognizant of the political urgency to hasten the regime's collapse and to pave the way for greater class equality. The collective comprised Lumbreras as the principal filmmaker and de facto inspirational leader (notwithstanding the group's disavowal of hierarchy), her companion Mariano Lisa (a high school philosophy teacher), and on occasion the underground filmmaker Llorenç Soler and one or two other friends. A native of Cuenca, Lumbreras studied briefly at Madrid's Escuela Oficial de Cinematografía [Official Film School], founded in 1947 under a different name, but soon left for Rome, where while studying at the Centro she became politicized. After receiving her director's degree in 1964, she began working at the Radiotelevisione Italiana, Italy's national broadcasting company, making television documentaries about the working class and establishing ties with the Italian left, including creating films for the Italian Communist Party (Arnau Roselló, *La guerrilla* 516). In Italy, she acquired additional technical skills while working as assistant director for notable filmmakers, including Gillo Pontecorvo, Federico Fellini (with whom she worked on the filming of *Satyricon*, 1969), Cesare Zavattini, Francesco Rosi, and Pier Paolo Pasolini (Gómez Viñas). In 1968, moved by the international spirit of revolutionary unrest, and after turning down Pontecorvo's request to work on his film *Queimada* (*Burn!*, 1969), Lumbreras returned definitively to Spain to join the anti-Francoist struggle and make clandestine films.

With minimal equipment and some financial support from Pasolini, Lumbreras and her small crew, which included Soler, began filming a documentary entitled *España 68: El hoy es malo pero el mañana es mío* (1968) [Spain 68: Today It Is Bad, but Tomorrow Is Mine].[10] *España 68* documents student and worker strikes and protest marches in the fight against the regime. Interestingly, one of the protagonists is the folk singer (*cantautor*) Raimon; thus *España 68* established a cardinal connection between film and another medium deployed in the anti-Franco resistance: the protest music of the Nova Cançó (New Song). Later, Lumbreras drew on song as an effective device in *El campo para el hombre* by recruiting the participation of 1960s Spanish folk singer Julia León. This dependence on popular music paralleled similar instances in Álvarez's ICAIC documentaries, in Solanas and Getino's *La hora de los hornos*, and in Gerardo Vallejo's contemporary film *El camino hacia la muerte del viejo Reales* (1974) [The Journey toward Death of Old Man Reales].

Like their Argentine counterparts who filmed *La hora* at immense personal risk during General Onganía's dictatorship, the films that Lumbreras and Lisa made together in the following years also carried a significant danger, only somewhat mitigated by the anonymity afforded by the collective nature of the enterprise. Militant filmmakers believed that collectivity was both a way to emphasize the collaborative nature of the left's revolutionary project and to maintain its focus on social and class dynamics. Lumbreras, for instance, argued that her group aimed for "un cine colectivo, que niega la división social del trabajo, considerando igualitariamente a todos los que intervienen en cada uno de sus productos. Esta acción cinematográfica implica que las obras no se parcialicen, ni técnica ni intelectualmente" (qtd. in Martí Rom 69) [a collective cinema that negates the division of labor, considering equally everyone who participates in each of its products. This filmic action implies that the work is not subdivided, technically or intellectually]. The concern with relations and methods of production was also generally typical of Third Cinema, which "sought to break down the divisions of labor and hierarchies of command which the film industry, as a microcosm of the social totality, has institutionalized" (Wayne 47). For that reason, the roles of cameraperson/scriptwriter/director/worker were equally shared, and responsibilities shifted often among the members of Lumbreras's group. That said, it was her sociopolitical and artistic vision that permeated the Colectivo's philosophy and aesthetic, although nobody was directly credited in the films (also a precautionary measure against arrest). Emphasizing collectivity over concepts of leadership or auteurism served to evade police control by "helping to share the responsibilities among the members of the group in case of probable repressive actions" (Fernández Labayen and Souto 232). Thus, a belief in collective enterprise was inherent to the group's ideology: cooperative action, a denial of social division of labor, and equally shared risk and credit (232).

Although a similar emphasis on collectivity was present in Solanas's group Cine Liberación in Argentina, as well as Álvarez's ICAIC, as I stated, the Cuban reality was unique since those filmmakers did not work in opposition to the regime but alongside it. The exception was found among those few Cuban filmmakers who operated against the ICAIC's directives, chief among them "Nicolasito" (Nicolás Guillen Landrián). His films were banned as counter-revolutionary, eventually leading to Nicolasito's expulsion from the Cuban film institute and his forced exile from the island. The majority of ICAIC filmmakers, if they respected the Revolution's version of Marxist heterodoxy, were afforded the space to create and did not labor under politically adverse conditions, although they suffered from periodic material shortages. As a consequence of the triumph of the Revolution, according to Paulo Antonio Paranaguá, Cuban documentary lost some of its militant urgency while retaining its pedagogical mission and its cutting-edge aesthetic (45).

Both the philosophy of collectivity and a genuine concern for workers (rural and urban) prevalent in Latin American documentary were reflected in *El campo para el hombre* through its depiction of the agrarian struggle. The film's closing lyrics, accompanied by images of farm laborers returning from their fields, reinforce the spirit of collective fight: "que seamos dueños del campo, y en colectivo el trabajo, y la tierra agradecida, daría lo necesario" (56:55) [we shall be owners of the land, and our work shall be collective, and the land, thankful, will provide what is needed]. This optimistic refrain imagines the bountiful state supposedly attainable in a collectivized society, echoing Marx's oft-quoted phrase from the *Kritik des Gothaer Programms* (1875) [Critique of the Gotha Program], "from each according to his ability, to each according to his needs" (27), and evoking a 1960s utopian vision of the holistic and nurturing relation between a personified Mother Earth and her loving children, as represented by the farmers that are the idealized subjects of the film.

Financial and Political Obstacles during the Filming of *El campo para el hombre*

There were many hindrances associated with the film's production. Despite their precautions, Lumbreras and Lisa were arrested and imprisoned for several weeks, not on account of their filmmaking, which remained undetected, but for their labor activism and their suspected militancy in the clandestine Catalan Communist Party, an offense that carried a maximum sentence of twenty years—a risk routinely assumed by several filmmakers in those years, including Joaquim Jordà and others associated with the Barcelona School. As a result of their arrest, both Lisa and Lumbreras lost their high school teaching posts, finding themselves in a precarious financial situation.

Furthermore, the production of *El campo* coincided with the increased repression sparked by the 1973 Carrero Blanco assassination. As such, the conditions of filming were financially and politically hopeless; something to bear in mind when evaluating the final product, which reflected its complicated process. For instance, it was necessary to record sound and image separately, for security reasons—in case either should fall into the hands of the authorities—but also for practical, technical reasons since it was difficult to keep sound and image coupled in 16 mm film. In addition, the camera was a low-cost, hand-cranked Bolex Paillard, which could only film fifteen- to twenty-second segments but was easily portable and did not require an energy source—and it was the same type of small handheld camera being used by militants elsewhere, since most films were shot either in Super 8 or 16 mm. Indeed, the troubled process of creating the film was itself a reflection of the ethos of a political struggle that made-do with limited means. Gómez Viñas observes, "[L]ejos de convertirse en un obstáculo, las carencias materiales fueron asumidas con naturalidad por el Colectivo, adaptando el lenguaje visual a las posibilidades técnicas" [Far from being an obstacle, these material difficulties were absorbed by the Collective, who adapted their visual language to the available technical possibilities], an approach, once again, reminiscent of Third Cinema. In fact, these were very similar filming conditions and technical means to those experienced by Solanas and Getino in Argentina, with a small but highly mobile crew in which "everyone did everything," a 16 mm unmotorized spring-wound Bolex handheld camera without sync-sound, a wholly self-financed film, and perilous conditions for filming, transporting, distributing, and screening the movie (Rist 320–21).

Beyond sheer necessity and safety, there were compelling aesthetic reasons for Lumbreras to embrace such limitations; to mention one, the lack of synchronicity between image and sound (joined together in postproduction) added a sense of tension and urgency to the film's message. This aesthetic restriction, moreover, aligned with the notions of "imperfect cinema" and its subordination of quality and technique to messaging, as espoused by García Espinosa and adhered to by many Third Cinema filmmakers, Álvarez included. Nevertheless, for Lumbreras, technical quality remained a crucial concern, even if it sometimes took a back seat to revolutionary imperatives and to connecting with working-class audiences. Her meticulous attention to technique was undoubtedly a product of her training at the Centro Sperimentale and her work with the technically exacting Italian filmmakers; at the same time, Lumbreras stayed steadfastly allegiant to the Argentine Cine Liberación filmmakers' directive to "insertar la obra como hecho original en el proceso de liberación, ponerla antes que en función del arte en función de la vida misma, disolver la estética en la vida social" (Solanas and Getino, "Hacia un Tercer Cine" 64) [insert the work as an original fact in the process of liberation, place it first at the service of life itself, ahead of art; dissolve aesthetics in the life of society].

As widely documented, for Cine Liberación the practice of "inserting the film into life" included stopping the film to discuss it with the audience during screenings, for example to make the case for a Peronist revolution. According to Lisa, an identical approach was in effect with *El campo* and other films by Lumbreras—and, when the movie was not interrupted to open dialogue, there was at least an introduction at the beginning and a conversation at the end of the projection. This didactic maneuver served to both render spectators into active participants and to educate or indoctrinate them as to societal problems and their revolutionary solutions. So that, as Lisa recalls, they were producing "un cine que aparte de información, es de agitación" (Fernández Labayen and Souto, "Network of Affinities" 409–10) [a film that in addition to providing information, seeks to mobilize].

The esprit de corps espoused by Lumbreras and her team dovetailed with their desire to also involve the subjects of their documentaries in the filmmaking process. This empowering procedure was carried out not only by giving the subjects—agrarian laborers, factory workers, miners, and so on—a voice and allowing them to speak for themselves (off script), but also by considering their opinion about what the film should include. In later films, such as *O todos o ninguno* (1975) [All or None], a movie about a strike by Catalan steel workers, Lumbreras encouraged her subjects to handle the camera themselves, demonstrating that "through her creative process, Lumbreras intended to collaborate with the workers as equals, holding a vote, if necessary, to make decisions about film production" (Fernández Labayen and Souto, "Network of Affinities" 404). As per Fernández Labayen and Souto, the collective's films exemplified "Lumbreras and Lisa's dialogic process, which sought their subjects' active participation. They had used this methodology of actively involving the film's subjects in its production in *El campo para el hombre*" (403). These egalitarian practices, employed by Lumbreras's Colectivo Cine de Clase but also by the Argentine Cine Liberación and other militant film collectives, were primarily meant as anti-authoritarian measures but also sought to disregard class-based and other barriers between filmmakers and their subjects. The goal was to create a sense of a unified struggle (anti-dictatorial, anti-colonialist, anti-imperialist, anti-capitalist) and to place at its center the common people, rather than the intelligentsia. The same utopian egalitarian drive sought to abolish the division between the aesthetic realm and lived experience, thereby bringing film-art to the streets and the streets into film.

Leaving ideological chimeras of seamlessly blending art and life aside, the collective's documentaries at times exhibit a tension between aesthetics and practical reality. Simply put, Lumbreras had to balance her aesthetic aspirations with the serious difficulties posed by clandestine filmmaking. For instance, 16 mm film stock was scarce (and 35 mm was financially out of reach) and all major laboratories for developing film were under state control. Notwithstanding the challenge, Lumbreras planned and executed the film so that it retained a high degree of aesthetic value, as if willing to maintain its status as a work of art that also did political work. Even after Lumbreras's meticulous editing and postproduction, the film has a rushed and "unfinished" look that betrays its conditions of production. This rough aesthetic attests to how the crew had to keep moving, just barely ahead of the local Guardia Civil, Franco's repressive force. Filming conditions never allowed second takes, reenactments, or overly composed framings; therefore, as in Third Cinema, necessity and style became closely aligned. Concerning the collective's haphazard filming, fellow member Soler laments that "lo hacíamos porque teníamos una fe en lo que hacíamos, pero rodar bajo esas circunstancias era muy incómodo y desagradable. En aquella época, si te veían con una cámara, automáticamente aparecía un policía. Y pasábamos mucho rniedo" (qtd. in Camí-Vela, "Entre" 548) [we did it because we had faith in what we were doing but it was very uncomfortable and unpleasant to film under those conditions. At that time if anybody saw you with a camera, a policeman would appear immediately. And we were always very scared].

El campo: Between Realism and Experimentalism

As I stated, in *El campo para el hombre* Lumbreras did not merely pursue a set of political ends at the expense of aesthetic concerns. Indeed, Lumbreras and other Spanish clandestine filmmakers insisted that it was not sufficient to combat Francoist ideology with films that resembled the matter-of-fact, realist style of the state's main propaganda instrument, the infamous NO-DO. Rather, it was imperative to alter both form and style to effectively counter the message propagated by official regime discourses. Admittedly, the NO-DO's propagandistic voice-over and realist aesthetic was also characteristic of the initial phase (1960–1962) of the Cuban newsreel *Noticiero ICAIC Latinoamericano* directed by Álvarez. But this rather conventional aesthetic was replaced by Álvarez's more daring techniques in his documentary and experimental films, and in the later *noticieros* (García Borrero 159). This shift away from "realist" reportage was not atypical in other Third Cinema movements, and, as in Cuba, Iberian militant cinema praxis also evolved toward aligning political and artistic revolutionary goals rather than focusing on producing dry political tracts.

An anti-realist stance, however, presented a dilemma for militant filmmakers. On the one hand, narrative, linearity, and realism were to be avoided since they were seen to represent ideologically suspect forms derived from Renaissance perspective painting and its entanglement with empire, with rigid Cartesian concepts of subjectivity, and later with the nineteenth-century bourgeois novel and its link to capitalist modes of production. As Noël Burch argues, the dominant mode of film construction (the "institutional mode of representation"), perhaps best exemplified by Hollywood film (First Cinema), relies precisely on causality (including narrative, individualized characters, a continuous diegetic space, etc.) to contribute to institutional modes of oppression, and "developed into an ideological vehicle of unprecedented power" displaying "massive. . . political and social consequences" (Burch 84).[11] On the other hand, a degree of continuity, narrative, and causality was necessary to establish a logical argument for land redistribution and agrarian reform and, potentially, to convincingly instigate revolutionary action leading to change.

Today, Hollywood film and realist aesthetics are no longer considered as negatively as they were in the long 1960s by leftist filmmakers and critics, who judged them to be bourgeois art forms complicit with neocolonialism. There is greater awareness of oppositional filmmaking and filmmakers within the Hollywood system itself, as exemplified by the anti-establishment films of the so-called New Hollywood or American New Wave in the '60s and '70s, with classics such as *Midnight Cowboy* (1969), *The Graduate* (1967), *Easy Rider* (1969), and *Taxi Driver* (1976), to name but a few. But militant cineastes during Lumbreras's time routinely accused Hollywood of promoting and exporting capitalism, neocolonialism, and authoritarianism globally.

Lumbreras's film, however, sought a compromise between the opposing tendencies of realism and experimentalism, forging a middle ground facilitated and enhanced by the disruptive potential of the interplay between different media. By manipulating a heterogeneous body of media and their traditions, she managed to maintain a cogent and self-critical political argument while also engaging with aesthetic avant-garde practices, avoiding both the dangers of apolitical formalism and realism's putative complicity with dominant ideology. Although *El campo* does follow a set narrative pattern, and attempts to present the agrarian problem in a coherent and chronological fashion with the ultimate purpose of bringing about a revolutionary political change (establishing cause and effect in its argument), it does not rely on some didactic militant cinema practices such as the use of voice-over narration or the at times overly dogmatic style associated with Third Cinema mainstays, including Solanas and Getino's *La hora de los hornos* but also Fernando Birri's *Tire dié* (1962) [Throw Me a Dime] and Pedro Chaskel and Héctor Ríos's *Venceremos* (1970) [We Shall Triumph], among others.

This departure from realism does not imply that *El campo* does not owe a considerable debt to Third Cinema (this score should be evident by now), quite the contrary. The film, as mentioned, adopts its production, distribution, and exhibition tactics from Latin American militant cinema. Nor is this to suggest that militant Third Cinema did not itself display many aesthetic, even poetic, moments, as with the final take in Patricio Guzmán's *La batalla de Chile. Tercera parte* (*The Battle of Chile. Part Three*, 1979), which closes with a long tracking shot of the austere beauty of the Atacama Desert, as a *kena* (Andean flute) wistfully plays the socialist anthem "Venceremos" [We Shall Triumph]. I submit that by incorporating the influence from European avant-garde filmmaking and the ICAIC's experimental films, *El campo* overcame Third Cinema's worst didacticism. Lumbreras's film serves, but is not subservient to, its liberation goals; it is not instrumentalized by a revolutionary politics. It is, at least on this point, in opposition to Getino's definition of a staunchly militant cinema. The filmmaker from Cine Liberación was adamant that "cine militante es aquel cine que *se asume íntegramente como instrumento*, complemento o apoyatura de una determinada política, y de las organizaciones que la lleven a cabo al margen de la diversidad de objetivos que procure: contrainformar, desarrollar niveles de conciencia, agitar, formar cuadros" (Getino, "El cine" 129, my emphasis) [militant cinema is that cinema that is *taken entirely as instrument*, complement, or support of a specific political goal, and of the organizations that carry out any number of the diverse objectives that it seeks: counter-information, raising consciousness, agitation, training of cadres].

The Colectivo Cine de Clase thus created a style meant to appeal to society's working and popular sectors but linked to aesthetic vanguards, and therefore occupying a space between Third Cinema and European experimental and art house films. Consequently, a palpable tension exists at times in *El campo* between its aesthetic and political functions. Despite his unfortunate choice of the word *instrument* (echoing Getino), Arnau Roselló has noted this dialectic, observing that Lumbreras's radical filmmaking "cumpl[e] la función política concreta de convertirse en un instrumento de la liberación de los sectores oprimidos" ("La guerrilla" 372) [fulfills the concrete political function of being an instrument for the liberation of oppressed sectors], while also recognizing that it is located "a medio camino entre la contra-información y la transgresión formal" (374) [halfway between counter-information and formal transgression].

Combining formal parameters and political functionality, Lumbreras's film also takes cues from the Barcelona School's nuanced experimental approach to oppositional filmmaking, as seen in Portabella's *Nocturno 29* (1968) or Nunes's *Sexperiencias* (1968). Some critics sustain that even when the Barcelona School's art house films delved into the political their transgressive form rendered them unintelligible, or uninteresting, to working-class spectators. Nevertheless, Galt, who also locates the politics and aesthetics of the Barcelona School in the intersection of militancy and experimentalism, convincingly counters that all these tendencies were heterogeneously (impurely) intermingled, so that "theoretical debates on Marxism and culture linked the [Barcelona School's] project of engaged cinema to the contested direction of the European Left. And avant-gardist forms mixed uneasily with art cinema, exploitation genres and the global claims of Third Cinema" ("Impossible" 491).

As discussed, Lumbreras's cinema is eminently impure as well as intermedial in its own amalgamation of several European and Latin American militant film strains. An analogous catalog of impure, mixed media can be traced to Álvarez's cinema as well, as exemplified by his film *Now!*, which Santiago Juan-Navarro aptly describes as "la expresión más radical de este uso de un cine-*collage*" [the most radical expression of this kind of film-collage] (94). This six-minute film condemns racial injustice in the United States, using filmed static photographs, film fragments, and television footage of civil rights marches in the early '60s, police brutality, dogs attacking African Americans in Birmingham, Alabama, and disturbing images of lynchings, most of the photographs taken from popular magazines such as *Life* and *Newsweek*. The rapid-fire montage—most images are only on-screen for seconds—is accompanied by a Lena Horne song by the same urgent name. The song *Now!* was banned in the United States for its incendiary lyrics in support of the civil rights movement. Álvarez takes the political impact of the original song even further in his soundtrack as he adds the clear suggestion of the need for armed struggle. The film and the soundtrack famously close with the punctuating sound of a machine gun, accompanied by an image of bullet holes spelling the word "Now!" This skillful montage was not lost on Lumbreras, who applies some of the same rapid editing methods in *El campo* and other films.

If Lumbreras adopted elements from the ICAIC's rapid editing approach, "animating" press still photographs through cropping and collage, visual and aural rhythms, and an added nonsynchronous soundtrack, the Spanish filmmaker also derived a sense of political clarity and urgency from Cuban documentary. And Álvarez's imperative enjoiner to immediate action in *Now!* would also have suggested to Lumbreras the opening sequence of Solanas's *La hora*, which features a torch or fuse being lit and, in rapid montage, images of street fighting, explosions, and police repression. In essence, the opening of *La hora de los hornos* captures the initial moments of an epic and long struggle, displaying brief momentary flashes that echo the film's name ("the furnaces," conflagration, explosion) and, like the movie's title, directly refer to José Martí's quote "es la hora de los hornos y no se ha de ver más que la luz" [it is *the hour of the furnaces* and only their light shall be visible]. The Martí quote was famously included as an epigraph in Che Guevara's influential text "Crear dos, tres . . . muchos Vietnam" [Create two, three . . . many Vietnams] (1967), a political tract that made the rounds among European militants and was meant as an exhortation to guerrilla warfare on a global scale. In *La hora*, the visual idea of Guevarian *foquismo* is reinforced through sound, as a syncopated drumbeat by percussionist Domingo Cura grows gradually louder, suggesting the countdown to a universal impending conflagration of revolutionary violence, marking the beginning of the end of the capitalist order. That same unsettling drumbeat returns at the end of the first part of *La hora de los hornos*, accompanying an uncomfortably long (five-minute) tightly cropped close-up of the Christ-like face of the recently executed Che, a politico-aesthetic device that Lumbreras will occasionally emulate in her films.

To return this circle of filmic citations back to Lumbreras's militant cinema, it is noteworthy that the filmmaker adopts the spirit and techniques displayed in Álvarez and Solanas's documentaries, capturing the fatality and heroism attributed to revolutionary action. For example, in her 16 mm documentary film *España 68*, the Iberian filmmaker opens with a rhythmic montage of newsreel footage from the Spanish Civil War with the background music of the Republican Army's song "Los cuatro generales" [The Four Generals], which shortly thereafter transitions into scenes from 1960s university student pro-democracy marches and gatherings, set to the protest folk music of Catalan singer Raimon, himself featured as a participant in these student sit-ins.[12] In addition to establishing a continuity between Republican past and revolutionary present, the filmmaker highlights the international solidarity aspect of both Spain 1936 and Spain 1968. The filmed images of students and clipped photographs from student protests and police repression are now underscored by the Nova Cançó folk music in increasing crescendo. At a particular moment, Lumbreras includes in the sequence several images of students carrying banners with the famous Alberto Korda 1960 photograph of a defiant and heroic Che, at once a tribute to the Cuban icon and a citation of Solanas's film, and also a recognition of the transatlantic nature of the leftist fight (04:38).

For Lumbreras, the Christ-like photograph of the bearded Che functions as part of a revolutionary iconography that at once points to the repressive nature of the regimes these films condemn and serves as tribute to the heroism of those who oppose them, the symbolic figure operating at a transnational level—both the heroic Che and the martyred Che's photographs circulated globally and acquired tremendous symbolic value, affording the Argentine-Cuban a quasi-mythical status. In a lengthy meditation on both photographs of Che (heroic living Che and the martyred Che), which she also links to the famous 1936 staged image of the fallen Republican solider by Robert Capa, Libby Saxton concludes that "the stasis of the Bolex [film camera] and its subject during these moments unsettles the distinctions between film and photography and between the handheld shot and the icon made without human hands" (109). But Lumbreras's recourse to iconography does not rely on a purely naturalistic depiction, laden as it is with intertextuality, intermediality, and symbolic layers, and has as its ultimate goal—like Solanas's image of Che, or Álvarez's bullet-punctuated "Now!"—to ignite the spark of militancy in viewers, to rouse them into fueling the conflagration.

Lumbreras's partial rupture with conventional realist representation was a reaction against fascist propaganda films that preferred a newsreel style that strove for greater realism—it was a parallel (fascist) track to Stalinist socialist realism, from the opposite pole of the political spectrum, a "realism" that was no less contrived. Chief among the realist fascist filmmakers was José Luis Saenz de Heredia, who directed the infamous film *Raza* (1942) [Race], a fictional narrative based on an embarrassingly mediocre and ideologically repugnant novel and, later film script, written by Franco himself (and indebted to fascist ideas about racial "purity"); or Heredia's sycophantic and propaganda-laden documentary *Franco, ese hombre* (1964) [Franco, That Man]. In contrast, Lumbreras's heterogeneous style flies in the face of any concept of either "racial" or "material" purity. By mixing different media, from newsreel to her own filmed material to images of paintings to text, *El campo* transgresses categories of fiction and documentary to avoid duplicating the hegemonic discursive strategies of dominant cinema as exemplified by the heavy-handed style of the NO-DO documentaries. Naturally, this same move away from news-realism and toward avant-gardism had been anticipated by Álvarez in his capacity as head of the ICAIC's newsreel division.

In *El campo*, Lumbreras merges aesthetics and politics through the hybrid combination of material media and formal strategies: from the transparently didactic inclusion of landownership statistics to the experimental addition of superimposed text and montage. It is worth exploring some of the devices Lumbreras deploys to achieve a high degree of intermediality and hybridity, many of them inspired by Solanas's incendiary montage sequences and Álvarez's virtuoso filmic collages.

Intermedial and Hybrid Strategies in *El campo para el hombre*

As mentioned, Lumbreras spares no materials to include in her film, found footage, charts, folk paintings, still photographs, assorted music, and so on. These heterogeneous materials are assembled into a cinematic montage of discontinuous elements that jar the viewer's senses, provoking a Brechtian distancing effect. *El campo* traverses multiple discourse registers (drawing from base and superstructure, linking workers and intellectuals), from the simple statements by farm laborers who confront the camera in close-up, to the intercut "talking head" academic analysis by Xosé Manuel Beiras—an expert on agrarian issues and author of *O atraso económico de Galiza* (1972) [Galicia's Economic Backwardness]—to the plaintive song of a blind man (*cantar de ciego*) narrating Spain's history from a Marxist perspective. This plurality of voices is intensified by a proliferation of media that counters processes of media segregation and hierarchization that can be arguably traced to the Renaissance's ideological division of the arts and disciplines into separate social categories. Incorporating assorted media triggers a break with habituation necessary to awaken perception; as Marshall McLuhan wrote in *Understanding Media* (1965), "the moment of the meeting of media is a moment of freedom and release from the ordinary trance and numbness imposed by them on our senses" (55). In her film, Lumbreras also blurs the distinction between high and low art, between academic opinion and the experiential voice of laborers, to dissolve rigid categories and to fulfill Marxist (or given the emphasis on agrarian work, Maoist) hopes for a classless society.

The film opens with a sequence that draws on fairy tale discourses through a biting satire that mocks the totalizing narratives of National Catholicism. The storyline presents a beautiful rural utopia where peasants happily work the land and all children go to school, referring ominously to a dark past when *los rojos* [the reds, or communists], like sinister boogeymen, threatened the established social order:

> Existía un país que era diferente de todos los demás. En este país, lucía siempre el sol. Tenía unas costas maravillosas y el mar que las bañaba era del más limpio azul. Los habitantes de aquel país eran felices, alegres, cantaban y tocaban la guitarra. Además, eran valientes. Toreaban en las plazas nobles reses. Dios se enamoró de aquella tierra y la colmó de bendiciones. ¿Lo habéis adivinado ya? Esa tierra de ensueño era España. Pero no siempre había sido así. Hacía treinta años, unos hombres muy malos que eran los rojos habían querido sumir a este país en el mayor de los caos. Pretendían una reforma agraria. ¡Qué disparate! Quitar los campos a las nobles familias que los poseían desde tiempo inmemorial y en los que se criaban los toros más bravos para la fiesta nacional, y en donde paseaba la hermosa estampa del señorito andaluz. En este país maravilloso había

un pueblecito que se llamaba Villalba. Sus moradores vivían en paz y eran muy felices. Los labriegos madrugaban con el sol, se complacen con el alba, con los trinos de los pajarillos y con las flores, aún cubiertas de rocío. Pedro es uno de los labradores de la aldea que va a sacar los frutos de la tierra para alimentar a su familia. A Pedrito se le han pegado las sábanas. Su mamá lo despierta para ir a la escuela. En Villalba todos los niños son amigos y todos los niños van a la escuela. (01:05)

[There once was a country that was different from all the others. That country was always sunny. Its coastline was beautiful, and the sea was deep blue. The inhabitants of that country were happy and cheerful people who sang and played the guitar. They were also very brave. They were bullfighters. God fell in love with that land and blessed it. Have you guessed it yet? That dream land was Spain. But it had not always been that way. Thirty years earlier some evil men—the "reds"—tried to immerse this country in the most absolute chaos. They wanted to undertake land reform. What a crazy idea! They wanted to take the land away from the honorable families that had owned it since the beginning of time; those same fields where the fiercest bulls were grown for bullfighting and where the beautiful presence of the Andalusian nobleman was felt. In that breathtaking country there was a small village named Villalba. Its inhabitants lived peacefully and were very content. Farm workers awoke at sunrise; they found great pleasure in the sun, in birds' singing and flowers covered in morning dew. Pedro is one of the village farmers who extract the fruit from the land to feed his family. Pedrito (his son) overslept. His mom woke him up to go to school. In Villalba all the children are friends, and all children go to school.][13]

Lumbreras presents this homogeneous and non-pluralistic fascist fantasy with ironic overtones. The parodic use of the fairy tale form is an aesthetic tactic that aims to delegitimatize the regime's often-repeated narrative of technological and economic progress, while retaining a connection to folk traditions that speak directly to a popular audience. This valorization of the popular as the source of national strength was also an element of Third Cinema. Speaking about this narration, the film's co-director Lisa states that it also sought to ridicule the self-important voice-over present in institutionalized state media: "la anormalidad es la voz profesional que, en el comienzo de *El campo para el hombre*, lee la empalagosa narración oficial, alegórica e idílica, de la situación del campo y del campesinado español. Redactamos el texto recurriendo a una escritura hiperliteraturizada, que imita el canon que se empleaba en tal tipo de literatura en los medios de comunicación institucionales, fuera cine de ficción o documental o producto televisivo" (3) [abnormality is also present in the professional voice that, in the film's opening, reads the oleaginous official narrative, allegorical and idyllic, about the situation for the Spanish agrarian region and its labor force. We wrote that text using a hyper-literary language that imitates the canon of those types of narratives in institutional communication media, whether fiction cinema, documentary, or television program].

This same segment also calls to mind Buñuel's film *Las Hurdes* (also known as *Tierra sin pan*), which has been interpreted as a parody of the ethnographic documentary, and which served in its time as a harsh criticism of the state's neglect of Spain's rural regions and the resulting misery of its landless peasantry. Thus, *Tierra sin pan*, which abounds with surrealist elements, might also be seen as a precursor to Lumbreras's own use of ethnographic parody in this segment of *El campo*, with the significant difference that her ridicule is not directed against the film's landless subjects, whereas Buñuel shows little empathy toward the *hurdanos*. Even as she mocks the National Catholic fairy tale, Lumbreras proceeds to expose its mechanisms and institutions of indoctrination, in this case, present in the schoolhouse. Fascist ideology is made materially visible through its symbols, as an image of a unified and homogeneous Spain is made manifest by a crucifix, and by a map of the Iberian Peninsula whose regional borders are conspicuously absent. We are lulled to sleep, along with the children, as the schoolmaster tediously lectures about the wonders of Spain's agrarian system and the land's rich yield. Then, quite unexpectedly, the monotony of the lesson is shattered (see figs. 1.1 and 1.2).

In a Brechtian move meant to shock spectators, one of the students rises suddenly and throws an inkwell against the map of Spain prominently displayed in the front of the class. Red paint splatters on its pristine surface, disintegrating the myth of unity expressed by the fascist motto—*una, grande, libre* [one, great, free]. Serving as the symbolic destruction of the regime's conventional progress narratives, but also of didactic and univocal narrative forms (as exemplified by the boring lecture, by the NO-DO documentary format and arguably by much of Spanish mainstream cinema under

Figure 1.1. Brechtian moment (04:57). *Source: El campo para el hombre* (1975). Dir. Helena Lumbreras.

Figure 1.2. "Remapping" Spain (04:59). *Source: El campo para el hombre* (1975). Dir. Helena Lumbreras.

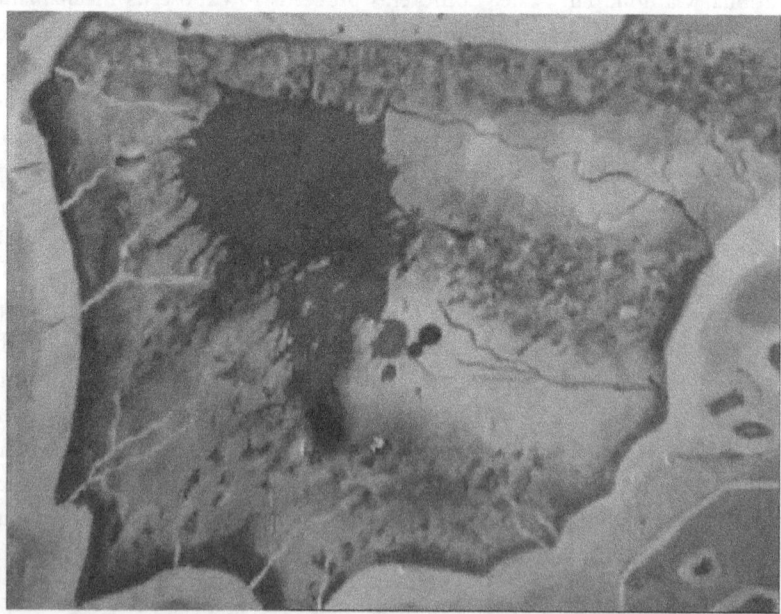

Franco), the map is splashed with a blood red stain that abruptly breaks the otherwise black-and-white filmstrip, bringing to it a painterly effect caused by hand-coloring the celluloid. Whereas realist cinema conceives of the screen as a window onto the world that draws the spectator into its diegesis, obscuring film's constructed nature, the sudden splash of red vividly foregrounds the presence of the camera and of the filmic material, raising awareness of the artifice behind the fiction, of its material nature and, consequently, of its conditions of production. These self-reflexive agit-prop techniques have a lengthy history in Third Cinema, and as Julianne Burton has observed, they affirm "the Brechtian paradox that dislocation and distancing, rather than unbroken identification, increase the conscious and critical participation of the spectator" ("Revolutionary"). The devices used, first by Álvarez and later by filmmakers like Solanas and Getino or Lumbreras, included showing glimpses of the filmmaking process, using parody and irony of established genres, presenting a disjunction between image and sound, and a "marked shift between lyricized and naturalistic visual styles" (Burton, "Revolutionary").

By using these intermedial, self-reflexive, and Brechtian techniques, Lumbreras undoubtedly hoped that spectators would see the lies concealed behind the progress fairy tale that Franco and his technocrat ministers had spun around the so-called economic miracle, product of the 1950s developmentalist policies encouraged by the International Monetary Fund. These soulless economic initiatives, which mainly benefited Madrid and Barcelona, led to tangible but unequal growth and left nonurban centers, including most of Andalusia and Galicia, in greater misery. In addition, Lumbreras's movie suggests her optimistic belief in the causal link between the form of an aesthetic intervention and its sought-after political effects. The ironic tone and the shock value managed, perhaps, to disrupt established patterns (habitus) and awakened the spectator to action, even as it engaged his or her affective reaction to the indoctrination of the school children. The rebellious schoolboy arguably stands in, through a *mise en abyme*, for the spectator, displaying the type of noncompliant reaction that Lumbreras hoped to elicit from the audience. Inevitably, the sudden explosion of red ink, which acts like a radical rewriting of the map toward socialism (making it "red"), also has its roots in Vertov's Soviet-style agit-prop montage. Juan-Navarro observes that Vertovian montage also forms the nucleus of Álvarez's filmmaking style, since "el impacto de los documentales de Álvarez se basa principalmente en la yuxtaposición violenta de imágenes que produce en el espectador un shock cognitivo y emocional" (94) [the impact of Álvarez's documentaries is based mainly on the juxtaposition of violent images that produce a cognitive and emotional shock for the spectator]. According to Lisa, Lumbreras shared with the Cubans the affinity for Vertov, since "Helena trajo de Italia varios filmes prohibidos en España, como *Tres cantos a Lenin* de Dziga Vertov y otros sobre luchas obreras en Italia y del movimiento radical japonés. También cine cubano. Por supuesto veíamos ese cine en proyecciones clandestinas" (Lisa, email with the author) [Helena brought from Italy several films that were forbidden in Spain, such as Vertov's *Three Songs About Lenin* (1934) and other movies about worker struggles in Italy and from the radical movement in Japan. Also Cuban film. Naturally, we watched those films in clandestine screenings].

Thus, bringing attention to the red ink and to the surface of the celluloid shifts focus from questions of realist representation (relation of signifier to signified) to questions of the material properties of the sign itself. These questions of materiality are not, however, a move toward abstraction, toward a formalist "pure" cinema as exemplified by the 1960s films of North American structuralists Paul Sharits, Michael Snow, and Hollis Frampton. Instead, the attention to materiality in *El campo* underscores the material relations of the art object and how it is made, and therefore reconnects its formal signifier with its signified, which is a message about production, labor, and (unfair) economic relations. Furthermore, by capturing the splatter of ink via the filmic medium, Lumbreras affiliates intermedial practices that disturb medium specificity with the Marxist ideal of a society without any division of labor, upending established codes of representation and conventions of social interaction, in accordance, once again, with one of García Espinosa's preeminent Third Cinema tenets that sought to abolish the specialized cultural worker—in essence making culture something everyone partakes in. Fervently believing that only the Revolution would free the masses and render their "presence," their lived experience, absolute, García Espinosa concludes that total and free presence of the masses will precipitate "the definitive disappearance of the rigid division of labor and of a society divided into sectors and classes. For us, then, the Revolution is the highest cultural expression because it will abolish artistic culture as a fragmentary human activity" ("For an Imperfect" 78).

The involvement of the spectator in the filmic process is achieved (in this scene) technically by building up to the climactic moment when the child throws the inkwell via a Vertovian rhythmic montage of shots (increasingly approaching close-ups of the boy's face) that rapidly decrease in duration, providing a sense of crescendo, anticipating an imminent explosion of revolutionary fury—again, following both Álvarez's and Solanas's examples.

The sense of identification with the boy's defiant action is further sealed by aligning the boy's, the camera's, and the spectator's point of view at the precise moment when the ink splatters on the map, thereby inserting us in the process and, as Lumbreras would have it, eliminating the gulf between filmmaker, filmed subject, and spectator. This overlapping of multiple subject positions—which parallels the layering of media—is not allowed to fully coalesce, however, or to erase critical thinking as might happen in realist cinema, since the estrangement produced by the ink splattering awakens the spectator back into an active analytical mode and away from mere unreflective sympathy. In that sense, the intermedial nature of the scene is the catalyst that triggers the viewer's cognitive reaction.

An analogous intermedial mechanism is at work during the iconic slaughterhouse scene in Solanas's *La hora de los hornos*. Robert Stam analyzes with precision how the sequence "fuses Eisenstein with Warhol by intercutting scenes from a slaughterhouse with pop-culture advertising icons." As the scene develops, "a shot of the exterior of a slaughterhouse coincides with an account of the police repression of its striking workers. The advertising/slaughter juxtaposition, meanwhile, evokes advertising itself as a kind of slaughter whose numbing effect is imaged by the mallet striking the ox unconscious." Stam further establishes how the filmmakers achieve the desired shock effect by confronting incompatible sounds and images: "The vapid accompanying music by the Swingle Singers (Bach grotesquely metamorphosed into Ray Conniff) counterpoints the brutality of the images, while underlining the shallowly plastic good cheer of the ads" ("Two Avant-Gardes" 278–79).

Lumbreras picks up on the effectiveness of this layering of media materials—the dynamic fragments from the slaughterhouse and the static advertising images; the mix of film, photographs, and advertising drawings; the overlay of the postproduced musical soundtrack—and she applies a similar procedure to her own film. Embracing intermediality came naturally for Lumbreras and her team, since, according to Lisa, the Colectivo understood cinema "como un medio inclusivo de las diferentes artes (pintura, literatura, música) y de los diferentes géneros (poesía, novela, historia, periodismo, ensayo, diseño) productos del pensamiento (filosofía, ciencia, tecnología)" (email with the author) [like a medium that encompassed various arts (painting, literature, music) and multiple genres (poetry, novel, history, journalism, essay, design) as well as intellectual products (philosophy, science technology)]. And although the "shock" delivered to the spectator by both Solanas's and Lumbreras's scenes comes in part through their paradoxical content (both scenes juxtapose official narratives of progress with a discordant and unblemished reality), it is also delivered through the clash of distinct media sources and their contrasting aesthetic styles.

Plurivocality, Intermediality, and Intertextual Referencing

It is worth noting that at times Lumbreras also departs from Solanas's strategies and opts for another take on militant techniques, one that approximates the later films from the ICAIC. For instance, Lumbreras substitutes the univocal, male, didactic voice-in-off—so characteristic, especially, of early Third Cinema films such as *Tire dié* or *La hora*—with a plurality of voices. Case in point, in one sequence rather than a narrator's voice we are confronted by a *cantar de ciego*, a medieval ballad (*romance*) that hails back to oral tradition and was usually performed by blind beggars who traveled from town to town singing about historical events, horrific crimes, or epic narratives. The syllabic rhythm of the *romance*, traditionally accompanied by popular music, is effectively mobilized by Lumbreras to retell Spain's historical past as a Marxist tale of the proletariat's exploitation by capital. By giving voice to a single anonymous narrator who represents the collective voice of the working class throughout history, Lumbreras mirrors within the film's structure the tactic of anonymity and collective responsibility so critical to the militant filmmaker's modus operandi.

Additionally, the visual montage sequence that accompanies the blind man's song adopts Eisenstein's dialectical editing techniques, also typical of Latin American Third Cinema as we have discussed. Salient visual features are emphasized both within each individual shot (where they act as dynamic elements in tense juxtaposition with each other) and between one shot and the next. These features might be strong opposing compositional lines, drastic color contrasts (seen in grayscale since the film is in black and white), abrupt sound changes, and so on. By intensifying the contrast between consecutive shots' salient graphic and aural features, Lumbreras triggers spectator reactions, forging (according to Eisenstein's theory) a meaning greater than the sum of the individual shots.

At the heart of this scene, Lumbreras performs an exercise of intertextuality, which is also a form of intermediality: the images she selects create a rich referential montage from variegated materials, many recognizable to Spanish viewers. Taken from well-known art historical (bourgeois) sources, the images encapsulate scenes of war, poverty, and destruction. There are fragments taken from medieval paintings depicting feudal modes of exploitation: royal courts and battles, castles, fortifications, and, in stark contrast, starving peasants toiling on the land. These are dynamically juxtaposed and offer a succession of events almost narrative in nature, depicting a logical cause and effect between exploitation, war, and human misery. Spectators can also appreciate Renaissance paintings, including representations of the conquest that inscribe the cycles of oppression within narratives of empire. The anti-colonial critique is further punctuated by an anti-capitalist and anti-imperialist discourse. These messages can be adduced from images depicting the Industrial Revolution and illustrating class warfare during early capitalism, such as a *modernista* painting by Catalan artist Ramón Casas titled *La carga* (1899) [The Charge] (fig. 1.3) that captures a common sight in fin-de-siècle urban life: mounted police breaking a strike, in this case, in Barcelona, a city with a long tradition of anarchist and socialist revolt (and, not coincidentally, the center of operations of the Colectivo Cine de Clase). There are many other visual media incorporated into this cinematic montage, including revolutionary posters, political cartoons, and

Figure 1.3. Detail from Ramón Casas's *La carga* (1899) (09:55). *Source: El campo para el hombre* (1975). Dir. Helena Lumbreras.

documentary photographs, and each contributes its own style and aesthetics to this striking sequence. Closer to Spain's recent history, one faded photograph depicts a man in working-class attire flanked by two grim-faced Civil Guards, recognizable by their *tricornios* [three-cornered hats]; another filmed photo shows a column of prisoners, also surrounded by the dreaded Civil Guard (fig. 1.4). This image gains additional currency if we place it in its historic context: it was taken during the 1934 Asturian Revolution, when union miners revolted against capital and took control of that province only to be brutally repressed by the Civil Guard and Moroccan colonial troops.[14] While this event took place during the Second Republic, it was a clear premonition of the war to come.

Regardless of their original context, the images are ironically quoted, re-semanticized, and integrated within the film's revolutionary narrative; thus, any older painting that had been subsumed by the market or co-opted by art's institutions is arguably redeployed in a new medium as combative imagery, much like Álvarez's repurposing of United States iconography or Solanas's use of advertising images or classical sculptures. Far from facilitating detached observation, these "resignified" paintings, in conjunction with

Figure 1.4. Asturian Revolution, 1934. Civil Guards repressing miners. (09:59). *Source: El campo para el hombre* (1975). Dir. Helena Lumbreras.

the other media that frame them—song and music, film, narrative—acquire political significance and a status of historical evidence. Here, Lumbreras is quite possibly also citing the section titled "The Models" (the eleventh chapter) in *La hora de los hornos*, a section that harshly criticizes the adoption of European high culture by Latin American nations, as revealing a type of dependency that entails surrendering to neocolonialist oppression by embracing the supposedly "superior" Western cultural models. In that scene, the spectator is treated to a rapid montage succession of art images (Greek and Roman statues, Renaissance paintings, abstract art) as the voice-over accuses, "copista, traductor, intérprete, cuando más espectador, el intelectual neocolonizado será siempre empujado a no asumir su posibilidad. Crece entonces la inhibición, el desarraigo, la evasión, el cosmopolitismo cultural, la imitación artística, los agobios metafísicos, la traición al país" (1:05:25; qtd. in "Hacia un Tercer Cine" 60) [copyist, translator, interpreter, at best a spectator, the neocolonized intellectual will always be reduced to not seizing his potential. That is when inhibition grows, as does uprootedness, escapism, cultural cosmopolitanism, artistic imitation, metaphysical anxiety, a betrayal of the nation]. The description of the alienated neocolonized intellectual will be one that Tomás Gutiérrez Alea explores in-depth in his now canonical ICAIC film *Memorias del subdesarrollo*. Lumbreras transposes this critique of models to a class critique, challenging the superiority of high art versus popular traditions. And by adopting Latin American Third Cinema models, she also (ironically) subverts or reverts the claims of superiority maintained by European and North American cinema.

Moreover, by repurposing images that represent other historical struggles beyond Spain, Lumbreras inserts the current fight for Spanish freedom into a universal and ongoing conflict in the context of Marxist historiography, reflecting a continuity of class exploitation that also denies bourgeois narratives of progress. The film's emphasis on a diachronic recounting of history once again falls in line with Solanas and Getino's *La hora*, exhibiting "a narrative structure that relies significantly upon the exposition of historical discourse in a diachronic fashion. This is not only an analytical tool for the examination of reality, but mainly a didactic resource whose aim is to reinforce the propositional content of the narrative" (Garibotto and Gómez 127). Furthermore, by alluding in the storyline to narratives of empire and colonization, the film also links to Fanonian discourses about decolonization struggles in Latin America, Africa, and Asia, in a transnational and tricontinental maneuver.

Inevitably, the montage process does violence to those images as it forces them to create new meaning. Indeed, the aesthetic of montage, according to Walter Benjamin in his famed essay "Das Kunstwerk im Zeitalter seiner technischen Reproduzierbarkeit" (1935) [The Work of Art in the Age of its Technological Reproducibility], was a process whose shock effect bore the trace of violence: the changes of scale and focus, the clash of lines, are an assault on the audience that ideally would result in the awakening of their class consciousness. Therefore, it can be argued that these posters, engravings, and paintings no longer function as decorative works that might adorn the walls of the wealthy, but rather represent carefully selected scenes laden with the kind of imagery that best contributes to the films' political aims. The narrative of oppression cuts across different media, represented by the paintings, the song, and the script, and is encapsulated by the film, which acts as a synthesizing stratum. Thus, the "essence" of the cinematic is revealed as manufactured from fragments of other media, and quite the opposite of "pure" cinema; what we have instead is an avant-garde, impure, and intermedial one. As Eunha Choi suggests, "An invariable condition of impure mixture remains the single specificity attributable to cinema since its emergence as a quintessentially modern art form" (4). I would argue that the revelation of impurity in fact mitigates the otherwise didactic element of narrative instigated by the necessary cause-and-effect Marxist analysis implemented in *El campo*.

Iconicity and Visual Abstraction

Another instance in Lumbreras's film where aesthetic form acquires revolutionary political purpose occurs during a stylized scene in which a Galician laborer is complaining about the inept and bureaucratic nature of the regime's vertical trade union, the *sindicato vertical* (23:05). The "vertical" was a reference to its hierarchical, non-egalitarian nature—it was a state-run institution created to quell worker unrest rather than to solve actual labor disputes—in sharp contrast to the illegal, worker-organized leftist trade unions such as Comisiones Obreras and Unión Sindical Obrera, which operated clandestinely in favor of class struggle and at times infiltrated the *sindicato vertical*. In this montage, abstract schematic shapes (figs. 1.5 and 1.6) accompany the Kafkaesque narrative as a frustrated agrarian laborer describes the futility of navigating the labyrinthine corridors of the *sindicato*'s bureaucracy:

> Nos mandan a los sindicatos. Y dicen, vaya usted a aquella puerta. Entonces, dicen, vaya usted a la otra. Entonces dicen,

Figure 1.5. The labyrinth of the *sindicato* (23:07). *Source: El campo para el hombre* (1975). Dir. Helena Lumbreras.

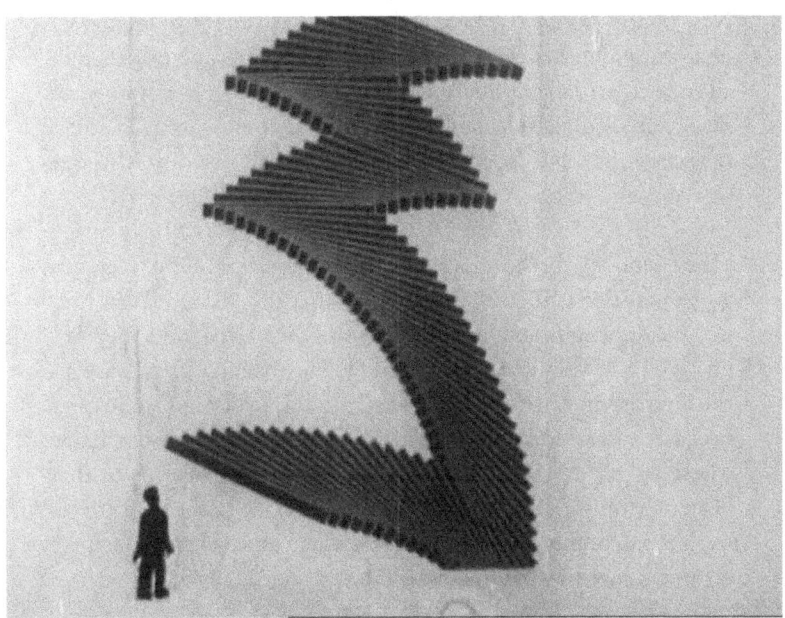

Figure 1.6. Escher meets Kafka (23:18). *Source: El campo para el hombre* (1975). Dir. Helena Lumbreras.

por favor, ¿quiere subir usted hasta el piso de arriba? Entonces venimos y dicen, no, no es esta puerta, debe usted ir al de abajo. Nos tienen de arriba para abajo, nos encontramos mudos en una, porque no tenemos preparación, en la otra que no sabemos adonde ir, en la otra que no hay quien vaya con nosotros a ese sitio verdadero donde tenemos que ir, nos encontramos solos. A veces cursis. No sabemos que decir, ni que nos digan, ni que nos apañen, ni que vayamos ni que hagamos. (23:03)

[They send us to the (government) trade union. And they say, go to that door. Then they say, go to that other door. Then they say, please, could you go upstairs? Then we arrive and they say, no, it is not this door, you must go downstairs. They have us running around, we find ourselves without a voice, in some cases because we are not educated, in others because we do not know where to go, in other cases because no one will take us to that place where we need to go, we find ourselves alone. Sometimes we feel ridiculous. We do not know what to say, how to act; we do not know how to ask, where to go, or what to do.]

As in Kafka's parable "Vor dem Gesetz" (1915) [Before the Law], where a man from the country awaits until death before a door that never opens, or in Mariano José de Larra's chronicle about Spain's frustrating bureaucratic institutions in "Vuelva usted mañana" (1833) [Come Back Tomorrow], the Galician laborer in *El campo* has no access to justice, at least not within the system. Stylistically, the sequence substitutes realist representation with a collage of semi-abstract and somewhat disorienting icons. The spectator is only able to decode their symbolic value with the aid of the verbal narrative that interprets them. Undifferentiated, stylized human stick figures, such as those used to signal restrooms, appear surrounded by equally schematic structures: Escherersque stairs and infinite mounds of paper. The human figures are dwarfed by the brutalist shapes. The shots alternate at varying speeds and increasing frequency, provoking an unsettling effect for spectators. The ensuing visual confusion allegorizes the loss of direction of the Galician working class, illustrating the need to find a way out of the bureaucratic labyrinth of the state-sponsored fascist trade union. The section also foregrounds the difference between the state-run trade union *sindicato único*, or *vertical*, and the aforementioned clandestine trade unions closely linked to political militancy and to progressive agendas. Using both iconic symbols and a verbal narrative within the same filmic sequence takes advantage of possible disjunctions between the two, mobilizing once again Eisenstein's concept of dialectical montage. But whereas for Eisenstein the conflict was between one shot and the next, with Lumbreras the contrast also lies within the intermedial elements of the shots (photographs, diagrams, maps, sketches, verbal description), between the realist narrative and the abstracted visual shapes and between its verbal and visual codes.

By Way of Closing: Intermediality as Political Praxis

As I have shown throughout this chapter, despite her interest in avant-garde aesthetics, Lumbreras remained firmly grounded in her role as committed filmmaker unwilling to sacrifice the clarity and expediency of her message for unnecessary stylistic effects. Her use of avant-garde techniques, whether adapted from Latin American cinema or European art cinema, were meant to induce spectatorial awareness and political change. She neither wholly rejected the utilitarian conception of filmic representation—*El campo* had a specific political objective, land redistribution and a general one, defeating the regime—nor did she embrace a position that placed instrumentalism above all aesthetic concerns. By maintaining a productive tension between both dimensions of militant filmmaking, her work asymptotically approximates the cinema of those filmmakers in the Barcelona School such as Jacinto Esteva, Pere Portabella, and José María Nunes, whose "political proclivities," as Galt argues, represent "a refusal of instrumentalized politics in favor of an aesthetic suspension of power" ("Impossible" 495). I say asymptotically because she remains solidly tethered to the politics of Third Cinema as well. As I have consistently shown, Lumbreras's impure style, like an alchemist's elixir, amalgamated components from myriad sources: from the early avant-gardes, from European art cinema, and, most saliently, from Latin American Third Cinema, in fact "admitting influence from all fields except the cultural institutions of realism and the Francoist state" (Galt, "Impossible" 498).

Lisa maintains about those heady days of political resistance that the Colectivo positioned itself as a group providing counter-information, that is, facilitating access to ideas that were not present, could not be present, in state-sanctioned media—in this and other aspects of their work they were closer to Solanas's own goals for *La hora*. But although they were concerned with documenting reality as it was, the Colectivo also wanted to create art through a rigorous approach to metrical montage, which brought them near the agit-prop filmic collages created by Álvarez, Espinosa, Alea, and other notable cineastes at the ICAIC. In Lisa's own inspiring words, "Considerábamos que en su base el cine documenta. . . . Que sea documento no quiere decir que no pueda convertirse en arte. El cine, como sucesión de fotogramas tiene un ritmo y ese ritmo, si está bien estructurado, produce poesía" (email with the author) [We believed that at its foundation film was meant to document . . . but the fact that it is a document does not preclude it from becoming art. Film, insofar as it is a succession of photograms, has a rhythm, and that rhythm, when it is well structured, produces poetry]. Lisa's lovely words proclaim an *ars poetica* for the Colectivo, one that impossibly anneals revolutionary fervor, artistic delight, and scientific rigor. This manifest will to structure, to experiment and mix media, to be impure and subversive formally as well as thematically, characterized Lumbreras's entire filmography. Critically, Lumbreras's intermedial style, so evocative of Álvarez's documentaries, intensified political commitment insofar as it challenged rigid disciplinary limits, questioning the subjugation of aesthetics to politics in militant film. The radicalness of *El campo* does not reside in its Marxist analysis alone but in the complex intermedial approach that imbricates that content with the form that renders it meaningful, ultimately locating the film in the convergence between art and the praxis of life. In coming chapters, we shall see the reverberations of this intermedial ethos throughout various other transatlantic media exchanges. In the next chapter, for example, we shall ponder how and why European and Latin American art cinemas from this same period commingled across oceans and media—more specifically by examining the to-and-fro vicissitude of Brazilian Cinema Novo and the Barcelona School as they associated in unexpected ways.

Chapter 2

Brazilian Cinema Novo and the Iberian Escuela de Barcelona

Art Cinema under Authoritarianism

Introduction: Cinema Novo and the EdB

This chapter places into dialogue the well-studied Brazilian Cinema Novo, through the films of its leading filmmaker Glauber Rocha, with the lesser-known Iberian, perhaps Catalan, experimental cinema movement known as the Barcelona School (Escuela de Barcelona [EdB], 1960–1970).[1] These 1960s new cinemas from opposite sides of the Atlantic have much in common: both movements represent variants of art cinema, which Solanas dubbed "Second Cinema" to distinguish it from the more militant "Third Cinema," a tenuous distinction at best, as we shall discuss. Both Cinema Novo and the EdB were formally innovative and rejected classical narrative structure, had more success in festivals and with critics than with mainstream audiences, operated under adverse political circumstances and authoritarian rule, and both movements identified as anti-establishment and anti-authoritarian broadly speaking but were not, with exceptions, directly oppositional as militant and clandestine film were. That stated, both Cinema Novo and the EdB pushed the limits of what was possible and presented various degrees of resistance to the authoritarian regimes they worked under. However, in sharp contrast with the filmmakers in chapter 1, whereas the militant cinemas practiced by Lumbreras, Solanas, and Álvarez represented a collective effort, the art cinemas and new waves of the 1960s emphasized the figure of the auteur's individual vision, often to the exclusion of the rest of the team. Arguably, the filmmakers of Cinema Novo and the EdB imagined themselves as cultural elites rather than part of the masses; even Rocha, initially a radical leftist who praised the popular classes, came from a middle-class background and identified primarily with the intelligentsia. One final and critical formal trait shared by Brazilian and Iberian art cinemas: they were vibrantly intermedial and closely associated with emerging postmodernist art forms, such as conceptual art, Pop Art, minimalism, performance art, comic books, electronic music, and so on. In terms of their intellectual and artistic affiliations, both groups partook of the same transnational film networks, attended the same festivals, screened films in similar venues, and used similar distribution channels.

Although much has been written about Rocha's cinema, a transatlantic comparative lens can shed new light on his innovative films by contextualizing them within broader artistic and political currents that shook the world during the tumultuous '60s. Like Cinema Novo, the EdB was part of a worldwide surge of "new waves" (including the French Nouvelle Vague, Czech New Wave, Novo Cinema Português, and the British Free Cinema) that became pivotal in the rise of art house theaters. On the political front, it is also worthwhile to revalorize how the undeservedly understudied EdB—at times labeled elitist—sought to resist or critique Franco's dictatorship through their avant-garde filmmaking. Juxtaposing Cinema Novo and the EdB can be justified on additional grounds, for instance, the professional associations between Rocha (and to a lesser extent Carlos Diegues) and several prominent EdB figures (Esteva, Portabella, Muñoz Suay), their stylistic affinities, and an analogous political milieu in Brazil and Spain.

Political conditions were akin, at least by some measures, as both countries endured authoritarian right-wing rule, in Brazil under Field Marshall Castello Branco and the Armed Forces Junta, which seized power after the 1964 US-backed coup (aka the "Brazilian Revolution") that deposed the legitimate leftist president João Goulart, and in Spain under the decades-long Franco regime that was equally undemocratic. Avant-garde filmmakers in both countries grappled with their respective situations by attempting a delicate balance between aesthetics and politics, between theory and revolutionary praxis—a praxis that perforce entailed a degree of possibilism, both in Brazil and Spain. Meaning that these cineastes, who, I insist, did not operate as clandestine militant filmmakers, nevertheless sought ways to create oppositional cinema within their respective censorship limitations. Rapidly shifting conditions led to ambiguous relations with the regimes in power both in Brazil and Spain, including considerable hand wringing about the use of self-censorship to circumvent official scrutiny, questioning whether to encode critique via allegory even if it risked becoming unintelligible, and wondering how to avoid having films exhibited as examples of a regime's tolerance to artistic freedom, and so on. Naturally, despite these parallel conditions, there were particularities for each movement to sort out, and further complicating matters, the national sociopolitical context in both countries was in constant flux, as was the commitment level of any individual filmmaker. As an example, in the 1960s Rocha's iconoclastic films upended cinematic norms and viewer expectations while (somewhat obliquely) opposing the recently installed military dictatorship. Later, Rocha's politics shifted, and by the late 1970s he tacitly acquiesced to military rule, to the chagrin of fellow leftists. Across the Atlantic, the EdB engaged in their own (subtle) opposition to Franco's reified dictatorship by encoding political critique within avant-garde filmmaking, attuned to the changing political winds and benefiting from state funding when possible.[2]

The two experimental film movements (EdB and Cinema Novo) maintained sporadic contacts throughout the 1960s and '70s, which eventually culminated in an ill-fated collaborative project between the EdB and Rocha on the film *Cabeças cortadas* (1970) [Severed Heads]. This was by no means Rocha's only collaborative work with European filmmakers, having worked for Godard that same year in *Le vent d'est* (*Wind from the East*, 1970), where he had a small part (Nagib, Preface xiv). Rocha, who during his lengthy exile from Brazil spent considerable time in both Europe and Cuba, became a nexus between Latin American (especially Brazilian and Cuban) and European avant-garde filmmakers. In Spain, mutual exchanges were both direct (filmmakers meeting at festivals and other events) and indirect (through the press), as both the EdB filmmakers and the *cinemanovistas* contributed regularly to the same European journals, most notably *Positif* and *Cahiers du Cinéma*, and translations from these articles were reprinted in Spanish journals such as *Nuestro Cine* and *Film Ideal* (Shaw and Dennison 86). Since 1961 *Film Ideal*, a magazine closely affiliated with the EdB, had printed translations of critical texts about the new Brazilian cinema, and by 1965 *Nuestro Cine* published the first extensive article on Cinema Novo, which the authors declared to be as influentially noteworthy as the Nouvelle Vague. This initial article was followed by others scattered through various Spanish journals, including insightful interviews with leading *cinemanovistas* (Elena 232–33; 237).

In the spirit of these transatlantic conversations, two journalists also affiliated with the EdB as script writers, Manuel Pérez Estremera and

Augusto Martínez Torres, published an extensive interview with Rocha in *Nuestro Cine*'s July 1967 issue, an opening salvo for future collaboration. Soon after, Rocha's manifesto "Eztetyka da Fome" (1965) [An Aesthetics of Hunger], appeared in translation in the same journal (Elena 237).[3] As Martínez Torres recalls, Iberian critics and filmmakers alike were enthralled by Rocha's cinematic style, and "queríamos hacer cine y aquella nos parecía una de las más validas salidas" (*Buñuel* 79) [we wanted to make films and Rocha's seemed like one of the most worthwhile approaches]. Rocha and fellow *cinemanovistas* shared with the French New Wave and the Catalan EdB a commitment not just to revolutionize form but to further a *politique des auteurs* that had been endorsed by *Cahiers* since the early 1950s. This pro-authorial stance granted absolute deference to the filmmaker's worldview and, as I mentioned, stood in stark contrast to the emphasis on collective values, shared labor, and lack of hierarchy espoused by militant cinemas, as exemplified by Argentina's Cine Liberación, Jorge Sanjinés's Ukamau group in Bolivia, or Lumbreras's Colectivo Cine de Clase in Spain.[4]

As a result of his rising status, Rocha's films and theoretical writings were enthusiastically promoted by EdB members and by critics from the various leftist film magazines, including *Nuestro Cine*—critics such as Estremera and Martínez Torres, but also Ángel Fernández Santos and Miguel Marías. These critics posed Rocha's films as examples to be followed by the newly emerging Spanish cinema, declaring his as a viable model for a freer, combative, and independent filmmaking in the anti-capitalist struggle, one that could be produced even under authoritarian rule. This new filmmaking practice, ideally, would be incorporated into "los frentes de resistencia cultural antifranquista" (Elena 237–38) [anti-Francoist cultural resistance fronts]. As the dictatorship's grasp loosened, Spanish cinema became increasingly daring, and the moment was sensed as ripe to welcome Rocha's guidance, so that as Elena astutely declares, "[E]n la hora del *aggiornamento* del cine español y la intensificación de la Resistencia contra la Dictadura, las enseñanzas de Rocha y el *Cinema Novo* no podían caer en saco roto" (239) [At the hour of Spanish cinema's rebirth and of intensifying resistance against the dictatorship, Rocha's lessons could not fall on deaf ears]. Iberian filmmakers took note, so that, in an interview with critic Beniamino Biondi, EdB director Antoni Padrós confirmed both Rocha's and Ruy Guerra's films were inspiration for his own and praised their exemplary revolutionary potential (Biondi 138). That revolutionary force was filtered through form and content, and, as I will discuss, intermediality played a vital role within it.

As an ongoing useful conceptual tool, this chapter continues to examine media theory's notion of intermediality to analyze how some of Cinema Novo's and the EdB's films mobilized political critique by engaging in "impure" media practices. Whereas chapter 1 focused almost exclusively on the use of montage and collage by militant filmmakers, this chapter pays close attention to relations between text and image, sound and image, and genre mixing, among other intermedial exchanges. These also include the EdB's deployment of collage, montage, and metalepsis and Cinema Novo's extensive use of musical intertexts and fragments from popular culture. The concept of cinematic "impurity," as charted in Lúcia Nagib and Anne Jerslev's edited volume *Impure Cinema* (2014) is read in terms of both a challenge to media specificity and as the insertion of the political into aesthetic concerns. Elsewhere, Nagib and Stefan Solomon advocate for the applicability of intermediality as a theoretical tool for cinema studies, promoting it as a far-reaching critical trend: "Given cinema's inherent hybridity, intermediality has increasingly been chosen to address it alongside, or even in lieu of, more established methods, such as comparative, intertextual, adaptation and genre-based studies, for its wider premise that keeps the interrogation on the properties of the medium constantly on the critic's horizon" (Nagib and Solomon "Intermediality" 122). As Nagib argues throughout her critical writings, intermediality also works particularly well when applied to transnational or transatlantic cinema studies, where impurity and heterogeneity refers to both media and national boundary blurring.

This chapter also traces the EdB's intermedial practices to the historic avant-gardes, as well as to the influence of contemporary movements from the 1960s, foremost among them Cinema Novo and Tropicália, but also Fluxus, the New York School, and the French New Wave. After exploring important affinities between Rocha and the EdB's films and situating both movements within their own historical and cultural contexts, the chapter continues by studying the uses of political allegories in the Brazilian filmmaker's 1967 *Terra em transe* (released in English as both *Entranced Earth* and *Land in Anguish*), placing special scrutiny on the interplay between sound, image, and text-based media and reflecting on Rocha's reception by, and influence on, the EdB and its cinematic work. While there is considerable research published about *Terra em transe* by Ismail Xavier, Robert Stam, and other notable critics, examining the film through the lens of intermediality and in the context of the poetry and politics of experimental cinema affords a fresh perspective. Then, shifting focus across the Atlantic, the chapter studies how text-image interactions and other intermedial devices activated anti-Francoist discourse in three strikingly different EdB films: Vicente Aranda's *Fata Morgana* (1965), José María Nunes's *Sexperiencias* (1968), and Pere Portabella's *Nocturno 29* (1968), establishing some parallels between these particular films and Rocha's, and with Cinema Novo more broadly. Finally, to analyze a tangible filmic exemplar of these art cinema transatlantic exchanges, the chapter turns to the singular collaborative project between Rocha and the EdB, *Cabeças cortadas*—a much maligned and cultish surrealist allegory about waning dictatorships and decadent dictators—to further scrutinize the affinities and tensions between these experimental schools and filmmakers. As I hope to show, by virtue of its location filming in Spain, in *Cabeças cortadas* Rocha seeks to invert the map of colonizer and colonized, reframing, extending, and upending the geography of the Third World to include the then (relatively) underdeveloped Iberian Peninsula. While this maneuver is problematic in many respects (not the least Spain's own complicity in colonialism, imperialism, and genocide in Latin America, Africa, and Asia), Rocha approaches the film with a great deal of irony and insists on minimizing differences between the Southern European marginalized periphery (Spain, Portugal, Italy, and Greece) and the Latin American continent (Martínez Torres, *Buñuel* 69). By doing so he repositions Brazil as a leading nation in cultural and cinematic production in the vanguard of art cinema.

Closing the chapter with a decidedly transnational and intermedial film also brings to the fore the potential of these collaborations to reinforce leftist political resistance across the Atlantic, much as we saw in the previous chapter with the example of militant films. In an interview Rocha stated that his intent in making *Cabeças cortadas* was to create a film that bridged political violence in the Old and New Worlds, as well as experimenting with mixing various media. *Cabeças cortadas*, Rocha assured, "is a film against the dictatorships, it is the funeral of the dictatorships. I deal with a character who might be the apocalyptic encounter of Perón and Franco in the ruins of the Latin American civilization. I filmed it at the rocks of Cadaqués, where Buñuel filmed *L'Âge d'or*. Spain is Europe's Bahia." And he goes on about the film's experimental elements, "*Cabeças cortadas* dismounts all the dramatic schemes of the theater and the cinema. The future of the cinema will be sound, light, delirium, that line interrupted since *L'Âge d'or*" (qtd. in Galt, "Mapping").

The multifaceted paradox that emerges, of course, is that Rocha's allegory (which fiercely resists the attempt to be read allegorically) presents an anti-colonial critique from within a former colonial empire (Spain), even as in true Buñuelian fashion it also seeks to undermine the very Enlightenment rationality that lies at the root of colonialism and capitalism. As with Rocha and other *cinemanovistas*, the EdB also endeavored to sabotage Western rationalism, considering Buñuel as their ideological and stylistic precursor. Pere Portabella, for example, worked as cameraman for the legendary surrealist *cineaste* on *Viridiana* (1961), and Glauber Rocha counted Buñuel among his strongest influences. In short, the chapter elucidates the numerous connections between Cinema Novo's heterogeneous filmmaking and the EdB's intermedial practices and examines their shared aesthetic grammar, as well as their political and/or countercultural resistance in Brazil and Spain, respectively, during the sociopolitical turmoil of the 1960s and '70s.

The Question of Intermediality and the 1960s Art Cinema Avant-Garde

Although we framed much of the theoretical discussion of the previous chapter around intermediality, it is appropriate to revisit the term in relation to art cinema. While it may seem anachronistic to apply media theory's notion of intermediality, which has only recently become common currency, to analyze how both Rocha and the EdB's films mobilized political critique by engaging in impure and contaminated media practices, especially in regard to relations between the verbal, the visual, and the aural, it is worth remembering that the '60s was the moment when the term "intermedia" itself was coined and when media mixing became a prominent strategy in the arts with the irruption of Fluxus onto the avant-garde art scene. Furthermore, the practice of "intermediality" predates the term's theoretical reemergence and proliferation in the 1990s, which becomes evident when studying "[the] unstable relations of various media to each other and the (historical) functions of these relations" (Müller 18).[5] As we have discussed, intermediality might be defined as the mixing of distinct media—such as poetry and film (the latter a sound and image composite, the former oral, written, and performative)—to create a single "text." By medium I mean simply a medium of artistic expression. As such, "[intermediality] is determined by the medial constellation constituting a given media product, which is to say the result or the very process of combining at least two conventionally distinct media or medial forms of articulation. These two media or medial forms of articulation are each present in their own materiality and contribute to the constitution and signification of the entire product in their own specific way" (Rajewsky 52). Intermediality paradoxically demands differentiating between source media, even as those media cross over and comingle, hybridize, and relate to each other in ways that radically confuse medium specificity and blur genre conventions.[6] We have, therefore, not a homogeneous totality but an interplay and negotiation of differences within temporarily stable composite media structures that shift, morph, group, and regroup in an increasingly dynamic and multilayered media landscape. These differences enact tensions at the formal level—for instance between word and image interactions—that, as argued by media theorist Ágnes Pethő, deconstruct "the unity of the image" so that the remediated filmic text ultimately subverts its own medium identity and authority (234).

Intermediality as a theoretical concept confronts the limitations of individual media (as well as their limits or liminal areas), and therefore it is ideal to conceptualize experimental artistic practices, such as Cinema Novo or the EdB's filmmaking, as approaches that inherently challenge media and genre categories. According to Jürgen Müller it has become "unacceptable to see 'media' as isolated monads" in light of contemporary media practices, a statement that is as applicable to the 1960s neo-avant-garde films of the EdB, Cinema Novo, or the Nouvelle Vague as to today's New Media arts (18).[7]

Devoted to a spirit of heterogeneity, 1960s counterculture mounted a systematic attack against race, gender, sexual, *and* medium purity or segregation, advocating for border transgressions that cannot be disengaged from intermedial art practices by Fluxus, Cinema Novo, or the EdB, which functioned "as a means of recognizing and challenging media in their normative uses so as to reconfigure awareness about them and to promote both aesthetic and social criticism" (Williams 47). Nevertheless, as Mary Ann Doane has pointedly theorized, dismantling the specificity of media by combining various media results in unresolved tensions and traces palpable in neo-avant-garde intermedial art, which betrays "a drama of identity and its loss and subsequent regeneration. As media converge, they do not simply accumulate, but generate new forms and possibilities that rely on the 'haunting' effect of earlier singular media" (148). Steven Marsh also expounds at length on the notion of haunting and spectrality regarding filmic media in his recent book about Spanish experimental cinema, *Spanish Cinema Against Itself* (2021), splendidly describing intermediality as "an encounter, often a discordant encounter, with and between different media that results in ill-fitting formulations rather than the telos of assimilation by one of the others" (40). According to David James, the'60s represents a special "flowering" of film's messy interdependence with other media, as shown by "the connections between the social relations produced by underground film and those produced by poetry and jazz; the importance for structural film of the social institutions of painting; and the way the social activities of political film were framed by the mass media" (*Allegories* 348).

My interest in this chapter is both to recognize the persistent haunting traces of material difference and explore how film's inherent, constitutive drive to assimilate other media attained a special intensity in the 1960s, as a product of transatlantic exchanges between the New and the Old World's art cinema scenes. It was at that precise historical juncture that movements such as Fluxus, Tropicália, the Nouvelle Vague, Cinema Novo, and the EdB embraced cinema's impurity, engaging with "not only its promiscuous borrowing from other arts and entertainment forms but also its constitutive combination of heterogeneous visual, graphic and acoustic materials of expression, each with its own registers of temporality and mobility, organized to varying degrees of integration, continuity, balance and closure or, conversely, tension, dissonance, disjunction, and openness" (Hansen 240). Film had indeed become messy, intricately tangled with other media-art forms, and germane to the chaotic politics of the times.

Glauber Rocha and the Famished Violence of Cinema Novo

Throughout the 1960s and '70s Cinema Novo became progressively politicized, as did its principal figure, leading theorist and enfant terrible Glauber Rocha, in response to the devolving political situation after the passage of Institutional Act Number 5 (AI-5) in 1968 and the unbridled repression, disappearances, and extrajudicial killings that ensued during the so-called years of lead (1968–1974). As the preeminent director of the new Brazilian cinema, among other well-respected names such as Leon Hirszman, Nelson Pereira dos Santos, Carlos "Caca" Diegues, and Ruy Guerra, Rocha had achieved international acclaim with his trilogy of revolutionary films: *Deus e o diabo na terra do sol* (*Black God, White Devil*, 1964) *Terra em transe* (1967), and *Antônio das Mortes* (1969) better known as *O dragão da maldade contra o santo guerreiro* (*The Dragon of Evil Against the Holy Warrior*). Although his work is perhaps best categorized as art cinema or "Second Cinema," some critics and audiences also considered Rocha as a leading proponent of Third Cinema who was at the forefront of the Latin American avant-garde on account of his experimental films and critical writings, including his influential manifesto "An Aesthetics of Hunger" (1965) and the lesser-known "An Aesthetics of Dreams" (1971). Along with Fernando Solanas and Santiago Álvarez, Rocha received high accolades at European and North American festivals. As I sustained in chapter 1, their respective approaches to cinema were emulated by filmmakers from other nations considered as "peripheral," including countries throughout Latin America, Africa, and Asia, but also in Southern Europe in places such as Spain, Portugal, and Greece, which Rocha considered as an extension of the underdeveloped world. This view of the Iberian Peninsula as a developing nation on the margins of European progress narratives was not unusual in the 1960s. Uneven development and a truncated modernity were characteristics of the Iberian Peninsula and had been aggravated by both Franco's and Salazar's economic and cultural policies. The perception, or perhaps myth, of Spain's backwardness was, in addition, greatly exaggerated from the perspective of foreign visitors who considered some of the local customs as folkloric, atavistic, or even backward, especially when compared with the forward-thinking ways of Northern European countries. This perception of Spain as closer to Africa than Europe in terms of development, Spain as a Third World nation, had a long history that lasted well into the 1980s. The stigma of "backwardness," real or exaggerated, was present not only in the popular imaginary but also in scholarly circles and was associated with every sphere of life, from the greater incidence of diseases to the lesser developed economy to the considerable waves of immigrants leaving for other Western European nations, either as temporary workers or as permanent exiles.[8]

For Rocha the inclusion of these European countries within the less developed nations meant the possibility to expand the range of the tricontinental struggle against capitalism and imperialism that we discussed in the previous chapter, to have insurgency gain a foothold in Europe. In a 1980 letter to the São Paulo Cinemateca, Rocha insisted on grouping together five of his films (*Deus e o diabo*, *Terra em transe*, *O Dragão*, *Cabeças cortadas*, and *Idade da Terra*) as part of a unified political-aesthetic discourse about decolonial struggles in the Third World (Glauber, *Mostra* 8). As we saw with Cine Liberación and the ICAIC, such revolutionary films did well in European festival circuits among primarily left-leaning audiences. European critics on the lookout for emerging styles wrote enthusiastically about Cinema Novo and other new Latin American cinemas in widely read journals such as *Cahiers du Cinéma* and *Positif* (France), *Cinema Nuovo* (Italy), and *Nuestro Cine* and *Film Ideal* (Spain). Brazilian filmmakers were generously represented in their articles, prompting Julianne Burton to write in a 1975 report about the Pesaro Film Festival that "First World critics have a fascination with Brazilian Cinema Novo. In both Europe and the U.S., the amount of critical material on the Brazilian film cycle rivals that which can be found on all other Latin American national film movements combined" ("Old and the New").

Decolonial filmmaking, however, was not looked upon kindly by the Brazilian military authorities, and Rocha found himself increasingly under threat of arrest during his first decade as a filmmaker, as did other artists and intellectuals. The filmmaker left Brazil for a "voluntary" exile in 1971 on account of the worsening censorship at home. During his decade-long absence Rocha lived through an intensely international phase in his career. This period resulted in various films made in Congo, Spain, Italy, and Cuba, as Rocha transformed into a transnational filmmaker, exporting strategies of Cinema Novo globally to any place undergoing decolonizing struggles or resistance against right-leaning authoritarianism. His filmography delineates at least two aesthetically distinct styles: the first period, which includes *Terra em transe* and ascribes fully to his 1965 manifesto "Estética da Fome" [An Aesthetics of Hunger] quasi-militant praxis (a kind of apology for violent resistance); and a later phase (including his work during and after exile) that embraces a surrealist turn in accordance with his esoteric and elliptical 1971 text "Eztetyka do Sonho" [An Aesthetics of Dreams], a sequel manifesto that places aesthetics on an equal or superior footing to politics, leading to a more ambiguous ideological stance.

In 1965 Rocha penned "Estética da Fome," where he argued that Cinema Novo's political and aesthetic force resided in its fundamental mandate to depict a justifiable revolutionary violence that stemmed from the unsatisfied hunger instigated by colonialism, neocolonialism, and underdevelopment so that "violence is normal behavior for the starving" (*On Cinema* 43). Such seemingly irrational and explosive violence by the famished, present in all of Rocha's films, was in the director's view quite logical given the history of virulent oppression and exploitation in Brazil, throughout Latin America, and throughout the Third World. As such, violence was a necessary instrument since "the moment of violence is the moment when the colonizer becomes aware of the existence of the colonized" (Rocha, *On Cinema* 43). Cinema needed to reflect social and structural violence at the level of both form and content. Brazilian filmmakers, argued Rocha, must wield the camera like a weapon, making formal and thematic violence paramount to their style. Rocha put his theories into practice, his style striking a definitive blow against narrative continuity and rationalism. Indeed, the Bahian filmmaker dove into a powerfully lyrical experimental aesthetic that located its center in expressive violent imagery and enigmatically elliptical plot lines. Michael Chanan relates Rocha's filmic style to both Pasolini's and Godard's, describing its "jagged and abrupt montage, constant play of shifting oppositions, and often theatrical *mise-en-scène*" (742). A violent irrational style, ideally suited for a violent irrational era.

Terra em transe, Populist Politics, and Brazilian Military Rule

Although the 1964 military coup in Brazil was immediately followed by arrests of union leaders, labor organizers, and leftist politicians, the newly installed regime did not immediately clamp down on the cultural field, although Rocha was briefly imprisoned in 1965 for publicly protesting the Junta (Pereira 64). The full-on repressive move against culture came somewhat later, first in 1967 with the investiture of a new authoritarian leader (Artur da Costa e Silva), a modified right-leaning constitution and the restrictive Lei da imprensa (Press Law). Cultural repression attained its full force by 1968, after the so-called coup within the coup, and the immediate promulgation of the aforementioned AI-5 decree (*Ato institucional nº 5*) [Institutional Act No. 5] that aggressively curtailed the cultural and political freedom and dissolved congress altogether. These changes in the political landscape ignited guerrilla activity, which in turn led to tightening censorship and savage control measures, as well as the forced and/or self-imposed exile of leading artists and intellectuals, Rocha included. As a result of this rout of the left by authoritarian forces, filmmakers became obsessed with analyzing the precipitous defeat of progressive sectors, and, as Stam observes, a number of *cineastes* "performed tortured autopsies of the debacle, in films whose veiled or explicit theme was the coup itself or the problems of the left" (*Tropical Multiculturalism* 233). *Terra em transe*, in some respects, partook of this type of self-examination.

While produced immediately before the hardening of censorship laws, and despite its elliptical narrative, *Terra em transe* was reportedly considered by government censors as dangerous Marxist propaganda that could aggravate simmering class conflicts. Stam appropriately identifies the film as Rocha's "baroque allegory about the coup d'état and its aftershocks," and there can be little doubt that Brazil's slide toward authoritarianism is at the heart of the movie's plot (*Tropical* 234). *Terra* is also a reprise of a short documentary filmed by Rocha in the Brazilian state of Maranhão in 1966, aptly called *Maranhão 66*, a film that chronicles José Sarney Costa's ascent to power as governor. At that time, Sarney was a young and idealistic populist leader, not unlike the ill-fated leftist president João Goulart deposed by the 1964 coup or his predecessor Juscelino Kubitschek. Sarney, like other Latin American populist leaders (indeed, much like Perón), eventually betrayed his commitment to progressive liberalism and social justice and fell into corruption, collaborating with the dictatorship for the sake of expediency and to ensure his own political survival.[9]

Wagner Cabral da Costa dubs this short film as "espetáculo político-carnavalesco" [a political-carnivalesque spectacle], and as the critic suggests many characteristics of Rocha's documentary prefigure the spectacular elements of *Terra em transe* (447–75). For example, the carnivalesque and popular ingredients in Sarney's investiture ceremony to the governorship included large crowds dancing samba and an interminable harangue by the rising politician full of empty promises, amidst a festive atmosphere punctuated by the sound of drums and fireworks. A large rally attendance by the working masses was assured with a mandatory state holiday and free public transportation for the day, a veritable case of bread and circuses as incentives and graft were harnessed to influence the polls. Rocha's camera meticulously captured the ensuing political carnival (Cabral da Costa 448). A friendship grew between Sarney and Rocha after the filming of this flattering documentary, which, although stylistically artful, was evidently propaganda. The coziness between politician and filmmaker was rewarded with financial assistance, through the *Banco do Estado do Maranhão*, for the creation of *Terra em transe* (Cabral da Costa 454; Pereira 65). The irony is not lost, given *Terra em transe*'s ferocious critique against both right-wing authoritarianism and left-wing populism and its depiction of political corruption. This auspicious beginning was not the only time Rocha would compromise his beliefs in favor of achieving (arguably) loftier ends and in some ways anticipates his later praise for the military regime in the 1970s.

But even in his initial phase, Rocha's genuine opposition to the dictatorship did not preclude him from working within the system to ensure Cinema Novo's survival, which placed him in an ambiguous, at times problematic and contradictory, political position. He shared this "flexible" political expediency with the EdB directors in Spain, and that would lead to analogous situational politics—a practice that in Spain was termed *posbilismo* and Pereira labels as *convivência* for the Brazilian case (65). This flexible, perhaps ethically compromised stance entailed working within the constraints of the political reality rather than going underground and/or making militant films, an alternative chosen by filmmakers like Solanas in Argentina and Lumbreras in Spain, at great personal risk. But such an "in-between" position was not necessarily an easy one to sustain either. The complexity of *convivência* meant an unpredictable arbitrariness; for instance, *Terra em transe* was initially prohibited under censorship rules and only after its selection by the Cannes Festival was the film released in Brazil (Pereira 66–67). If Rocha's movie was seen as transgressive from a formal standpoint, on a content-level it also raised the censors' suspicions, given the movie's marked anti-authoritarianism and thinly veiled allegories about national politics. Cabral da Costa believes it is not difficult to read the characters of *Terra em transe* as allegorical versions of specific protagonists of the real events in Maranhão and to then extrapolate that state as a microcosm of Brazil at-large, the most obvious parallel being the character Felipe Vieira as a stand-in for Sarney himself (454). Viewing *Maranhão 66* and *Terra em transe* comparatively supports this argument so that the later fiction film would be a "remediation" of the documentary, or if we consider fiction and documentary as discrete modes of representation that actually coexist within the same medium (film), then it would be an intertextual recycling.

Of course (political) allegorical readings of *Terra em transe* abound, arguably the most convincing and thorough being Ismail Xavier's analysis in *Allegories of Underdevelopment* (1997). The critic sees in the film a schematic and highly symbolic/oneiric representation of Brazilian politics right up to the 1964 coup, although for the sake of facilitating comprehension Rocha elides the nuanced complexity of the actual political forces at play. Thus, for Xavier, the parties involved in the struggle are personified by the individual characters. In his reading, "Diaz embodies the ascetic, conservative, Christian tradition. . . . Authoritarian and powerful . . . he personifies the ruling class which above everything preserves tradition and purity" (78). In other words, Diaz is the right-wing Latin American dictator per excellence, at the service of the oligarchy, in alliance with foreign capital (represented by the EXPLINT, or "international exploitation corporation"), and averse to both populism and leftist projects that seek to upend the status quo. Vieira, as we already stated, is the "populist leader of rural origin, a typical Latin American *caudillo*," who betrays his better instincts and is finally corrupted (78–79). Rocha's film condemns Brazil's chaotic politics, where the intelligentsia considered the common people (*o povo*) incapable of developing a class consciousness without their leadership, but also a situation in which those same leaders often switched their ideological allegiance for personal profit or convenience. Rocha wished to depict the lack of clarity and ethical commitment in the political scene, stating that "[En Brasil] había gente de izquierda que ahora está con la derecha. Este es otro tema que intento abordar en *Terra em transe*: en un estado en trance con gran complejidad entre las tendencias, los partidos, la formación ideológica, es muy difícil hablar con precisión del futuro" (qtd. in Martínez Torres, *Buñuel* 100) [In Brazil there were people from the left that now are with the right. This is another topic that I try to broach in *Entranced Earth*: it is a state in trance, with complex relations within political tendencies, within parties, in the ideological belief-system; therefore, it is quite difficult to speak about the future with any precision].

Despite its anti-authoritarian agenda, the film's most salient contributions are its lyrical style, its elliptical narrative, and its gestural handheld camera work, which approximates Rocha's filmmaking to EdB art house cinema rather than to a more dogmatic militant film like Solanas's *La hora de los hornos*. In my view, *Terra em transe* functions as a bridge between the "poetic" filmmaking of European art films by the likes of Pasolini, Godard, or Portabella and the militant praxis represented by the political wing of New Latin American Cinema. *Terra* embraces much of the allegorical elusiveness of the former (art cinema), while retaining the gritty documentary realism of the latter (militant film) but avoiding its more egregious pamphlet-propaganda aspects. Rocha explicitly turns his back on Solanas's style in the second Cinema Novo manifesto, "An Aesthetics of Dreams," judging the Argentine's epic masterpiece quite harshly. Echoing other uncharitable critics, Rocha reduces *La hora* to a mediocre political tract that subordinates aesthetics to its reductionist revolutionary message: "[*La hora*] is a 'pamphlet' of information, agitation and polemics of the kind that are currently being used in various parts of the world by political activists" (*On Cinema* 122).

In contrast, Rocha and the EdB filmmakers, without wholly excluding the political, appear to prioritize their interest in aesthetics and media experimentation over other concerns, saturating their films with an assortment of audiovisual media. Eminently intermedial, Rocha's films incorporate television footage, newspaper excerpts, literature, music, and a vast medley of mass and popular media forms. A true believer in the culture of the people, his films amalgamate ingredients from popular music (afro-Brazilian beats, samba, ballads from the northeast), popular narrative styles (*cordel* literature, oral traditions, sermons), and popular religious rituals and practices (mystic

Catholicism, *candomblé*) and effectively meld these disparate constituents into a digestibly coherent assembly. As with much of Cinema Novo, Rocha's films represent a drastic deviation from previous Brazilian cinema and from mainstream commercial Hollywood productions, bridging Second and Third Cinemas.

In the post–War World II period global art cinemas took various approaches to confronting the harsh reality and political fractures in the aftermath of the carnage; for example, Italian neorealism and associated movements like Nuevo Cine Español sought to capture life as it was, with simple narratives, minimal mediation, on-location filming, causal storylines, and non-actor performances. In contrast, Cinema Novo, like other "new waves" (EdB, French and Czech New Wave) abandoned narrative causality and verisimilitude in favor of more "poetic" styles. Various art house auteurs adopted lyrical filmmaking, among them Godard, Truffaut, Fellini, Pasolini, Bergman, Buñuel, Portabella, Nunes, and countless others. Not all these filmmakers were politically invested with a radical transformation of the social, although Godard, Rocha, and EdB filmmakers Nunes and Portabella stand out for their dedication to sociopolitical critique. Their political intervention, however, is layered under the distorting effect of the figurative elements, disconnected narratives, types rather than distinct protagonists, baroque sets, and enigmatic dialogue. Both Rocha and EdB filmmakers like Portabella, Nunes, or Aranda rely on archetypal characters, imbuing them with an air of mystery or even mysticism. But the Brazilian director's style is not purely lyrical; his films also reveal a tension between documentary realism (handheld camera, occasional location shooting, use of natural light, use of non-actors) with avant-garde techniques that court the lyric-oneiric (jump cuts, disjunction between sound and image, aggressively tilted camera angles, rapid montage editing, poetic dialogues). This tension plays out in *Terra em transe,* which bizarrely conjoins documentary fragments and realistically depicted violence with neobaroque surrealist moments, including the irruption of anachronistic objects or mysteriously illogical scenes, such as the suit and tie-clad Diaz's recreation of the New World's first Catholic mass or the use of poetic speech in everyday exchanges, as with much of Paulo Martins's dialogue.

Anachronistic and noncausal narration, elliptical dialogues, alienated characters who are incapable of communicating, and episodic, open-ended, ambiguous, and unresolved situations—these are some of the art elements that closely ally Rocha's films with the EdB, justifying a comparative analysis of directors who were, after all, quite familiar with each other's cinema. In this chapter the study of two paradigmatic Rocha films will bookend my analysis of several works by the Barcelona-based cineastes. Like the EdB, the *cinemanovistas* wrestled with how to join poetry and politics to achieve profound cultural and social transformation, including resisting autocracy. Xavier proposes that Rocha's entire cinematic oeuvre represents a desperate effort to reconcile these seemingly opposite forces, the lyrical-aesthetic with the realist-political:

> En este sentido, estuvo siempre aquel "compromiso en todos los frentes" que tantas veces convirtió al intelectual en una figura dilacerada. Y no es azaroso que éste sea un tema explícito en el cine de Glauber, particularmente en *Terra em transe*. Cuando oímos la frase que pronuncia el personaje de Sara, "la política y la poesía son demasiado para un solo hombre," una primera reacción consiste en ver allí, sobre todo, un gesto de consuelo para aliviar los dolores de Paulo Martins, el poeta. Finalmente, la misma película sería un ejemplo elocuente de negación de esa sentencia, al promover una notable conjunción de esos dos compromisos—una conjunción que, además, pautó toda la vida de Glauber Rocha. ("Glauber Rocha")
>
> [In this sense there was always a "commitment on all fronts" that often turned the intellectual into a figure torn apart (by conflict). And it is not coincidental that this is an explicit theme in Glauber's films, especially in *Entranced Earth*. When Sara's character utters the phrase "politics and poetry are too much for one man alone," our first reaction is to read it as a consoling gesture meant to alleviate the poet Paulo Martins's anguish. Ultimately, the movie itself is an eloquent example of negating Sara's sentence, since it promotes a notable conjunction of those two aspects (poetry and politics)—a lifelong directive for Glauber Rocha.]

In short, Xavier confirms the strained confluence of two opposed forces, poetry and politics, whose contentious coexistence is routinely thematized in 1960s avant-garde filmmaking, quite prominently in Rocha's. The antagonistic debate could also be mapped onto other binomial opposites such as fiction and documentary, or high and low art, that were under assault by progressive filmmakers. It is elucidating to analyze *Terra em transe* in depth to delineate how it forges an uneasy alliance between the metaphorical-fictional and the documentary-realist modes.

Intermedial Experimentation in *Terra em transe*

In *Terra em transe* dynamic exchanges between the aforementioned opposing tendencies, the lyrical (poetic) and the political (realist), or as Rocha articulates it, the interplay between the metaphorical-fictional and the documentary-realist modes, was achieved through an intermedial style that blended these polarities. By juxtaposing hyper-theatrical, operatic scenes with documentary segments, Rocha calls attention to, or frames, the tragic nature of reality itself. As the fictional world mirrors events in extradiegetic reality, the two become enmeshed in messy ways. A film about a fictional coup becomes a film about the Brazilian coup, and by extension about any Latin American coup. Arguably, the recourse to a chaotic intermediality that mixes genres and media increases the film's universal relevance. The question of politics is entangled with the question of intermediality and aesthetics. According to Nagib when a film incorporates other forms and media within its fabric, "diluting frontiers and genres," it also activates its capacity for political dissent so that "the recourse to different media within a film immediately suspends the pedagogical character of representational narratives by introducing a dilemma." So rather than "giving univocal lessons, [the intermedial film] multiplies the meanings of the referent" ("The Politics of Impurity" 31). A multivocal text can be read transnationally in various ways, as it speaks differently to each cultural milieu.

Beyond its own intermedial status, *Terra em transe* was instrumental in inspiring a broad array of Brazilian mixed-media arts, arguably becoming a seminal work that helped to spark the rise of the interdisciplinary art movement Tropicalism in the 1960s (in Portuguese known as both Tropicália and Tropicalismo), in addition to the lasting legacy of Oswald de Andrade's 1920s *Antropofagia*. *Terra em transe* directly motivated the musicians Caetano Veloso and Gilberto Gil, the visual artist-sculptor Hélio Oiticica, the poet Torquato Neto, and others into founding a movement that irreverently commingled art forms and genres, playfully mixing painting, graphic design, sculpture, music, poetry, and film, as well as combining elements from high art, folk art, and avant-garde and popular culture alike (Pereira 66–67). Rocha also associated media hybridity with popular and folk traditions, explaining that those intermedial practices guided his films:

"Brazil is a very colorful country. We have a tradition called the *reisados* in which the people dress up as Nativity figures; we have the tradition of popular engravings and the rural circuses. Since I believe that film is also linked to painting, I'm interested in that kind of visual integration of color with music and dance" (qtd. in Burton, *Cinema* 111).

Plausibly having triggered Tropicalism (at least in part), Rocha's conspicuous style and media mixing also drew the attention of EdB filmmakers. They eagerly absorbed emerging tendencies from beyond Spain, welcoming foreign influence amid a 1960s frenzy to learn from art that came from "outside." Luis Buñuel and prominent EdB filmmakers, such as Jacinto Esteva and Pere Portabella, saw *Terra em transe* at Venice, Pesaro, and other festivals, reinforcing their positive opinion toward Rocha after the resounding success of his first film, *Deus e o diabo na terra do sol*. Rocha personally met with EdB filmmakers at European festival venues, connecting with Esteva, who owned the production company Filmscontacto—which eventually led to the production of *Cabeças cortadas*, a collaboration between two Iberian companies, Filmscontacto and Profilms, with Rocha's company Mapa Films. According to John Sanderson, "[L]a coincidencia de la participación en el Festival de Pesaro de dicha película [*Dante no es únicamente severo* (1967) de Jacinto Esteva y Joaquim Jordà] y de *Terra em transe* supuso una primera toma de contacto entre la productora barcelonesa y [Glauber Rocha]" [The coincidence at the Pesaro Film Festival of Jacinto Esteva and Joaquim Jordà's *Dante Is Not Only Severe* (1967) with *Terra em transe* propitiated the first contact between the Barcelona production company and Glauber Rocha]. Shortly thereafter Esteva's production company extended an offer to Rocha to direct a film in Spain, which the Brazilian director promptly accepted. Augusto Martínez Torres, who worked with several EdB filmmakers, wrote the script for Rocha's Iberian film *Cabeças cortadas*.

Buñuel, who was close to Portabella and other EdB members, was another point of contact between Rocha and the Barcelona group. As Martínez Torres reports, in 1967 the Brazilian filmmaker held a private showing of *Terra em transe* for the Aragonese auteur, prior to the film's official premier at that year's Venice Mostra (66). Buñuel, whose experience as filmmaker was also bound up with a transnational perspective born of exile and dictatorship, shared Rocha's irreverent attitude against authority, a distrust toward realism, and a derisive take against facile conceptions of good and evil. Existing synergies between Buñuel's surrealist cinema and the EdB's forays into irrational plots also aligned with Rocha's cinematic project, especially after he adopted his "Estetyka do sonho" in 1971, which marked a departure from his more militant phase into a baroquely absurdist period. In addition to admiring Buñuel's work, Rocha also appreciated Portabella's films, especially *Nocturno 29*, and invited the Catalan director to participate in *Cabeças cortadas*. In an amusingly irreverent twist, in his brief cameo, Portabella's character is beheaded (Martínez Torres, "Cabezas Cortadas" 95).

Although these mutual influences were patently discernible in his work, as was the impact of the Nouvelle Vague, Rocha maintained that his films spearheaded the emergence of a novel style that might have been (unwittingly and unavoidably) informed by European cinemas, but that was not subservient to those models; rather, his filmmaking stripped them of their European self-absorption and refashioned them—devoured and regurgitated them, to flesh out the anthropophagic metaphor—with a uniquely Brazilian sensibility, one that represented the Latin American concerns and conditions more broadly:

> El verdadero arte, el importante para América Latina, es de ruptura, agitación, no puede ser de complacencia o de formalismo tradicional. Necesitamos una nueva estética. No me interesan las obras perfectas a niveles estilísticos, las obras complacientes de imitación, de repetición de los modelos tradicionales. Podremos tener un nuevo lenguaje y esta nueva estética debe partir de la ruptura, de no aceptar, porque si un intelectual sirve a una tradición cultural establecida por los países colonizadores, también les sirve desde un punto de vista político. . . . Lo que destaca del *Cinema Novo*, aunque tiene algunas relaciones con el cine europeo, porque es imposible librarse en un momento de la colonización, es que no le respeta, no le adora, porque a Godard le consideramos un gran cineasta, pero nadie lo imita. . . . En España no podrá hacerse un nuevo cine si los cineastas imitan a Fellini. Lo importante es Buñuel. (Qtd. in Martínez Torres, *Buñuel*, 101)

> [The true art, the important one for Latin America, is the art of rupture and agitation; it cannot be one of consensus or traditional formalism. We need a new aesthetic. I am not interested in stylistically perfect works, works that are pleased to imitate, to repeat traditional models. We can have a new language and that new aesthetic must begin with rupture, with nonacceptance,

because if an intellectual serves a cultural tradition established by the colonizers, then he also serves them politically . . . what stands out about Cinema Novo, although it has established some relations with European cinema because it is impossible to free ourselves instantly from colonization, is that it does not respect that cinema, it does not worship it, because although we consider Godard as a great filmmaker, nobody imitates him. . . . In Spain you cannot have a new cinema if filmmakers imitate Fellini. The important filmmaker is Buñuel.]

As to those European models, then, one could appreciate them but should not imitate them slavishly, to follow untrodden paths instead. Buñuel, however, was accorded a preferential status, not as a colonizer filmmaker but as a transnational one that, given his adoption by Mexico, could be claimed by Latin American cinema (both Second and Third). Regarding Buñuel, Rocha could not have been more enthusiastic, claiming in a 1987 interview that the filmmaker was both Iberian and Latin American in his outlook and aesthetic tendencies: "Es un cineasta personal, latinoamericano, español, ibérico, que tiene un lenguaje propio y una visión profundamente crítica del subdesarrollo de la gente, de la oposición psicológica, del moralismo de la clase media, de la alienación del pueblo; por eso creo que Buñuel es la máxima expresión de la cultura ibericolatinoamericana [*sic*] en el cine" (qtd. in Martínez Torres, *Buñuel* 60) [He is a personal filmmaker, Latin American, Spanish, Iberian, who has his own (cinematic) language and a profoundly critical vision of underdevelopment, of psychological opposition, of the moralism of the middle class, of the people's alienation; that is why I think that Buñuel is the maximum expression of Iberian-Latin American film culture]. The admiration between the Brazilian and Spanish-Mexican filmmakers was mutual, and in a coincidental mirroring of Portabella's later cameo in *Cabeças cortadas*, Rocha was accorded a role as an extra in Buñuel's last Mexican film and surrealist tour de force, *Simón del desierto* (*Simon of the Desert*, 1965) (Martínez Torres 62).

Having established this convoluted web of transatlantic interconnections and mutual creative stimuli, I would like to return to the analysis of Rocha's political allegory film. Despite its formal originality, *Terra em transe*'s plot is a straightforward and somewhat transparent national allegory. The film is set in the fictional Eldorado, a country whose name evokes colonial myths of gold, greed, and plunder and could stand for any Caribbean or Latin American nation—including, and perhaps especially, Brazil. The movie opens when a conservative leader named Porfirio Diaz—a reference to the nineteenth-century Mexican dictator and a gesture to the Pan-American and Ibero-American perspective adopted by Rocha—assumes absolute power in Eldorado through a coup d'état, squelching all opposition. Diaz's main political foe is the populist politician Felipe Vieira and his leftist allies, including the film's principal protagonist (and the consciousness through which we experience the action), poet-journalist Paulo Martins. Paulo, who is a representative of Brazil's bourgeois intelligentsia, wages armed resistance against the dictator Diaz with the encouragement of his militant lover Sara and dies gunned down by the police in the film's opening minutes. His drawn-out theatrical (nay, operatic) death scene contains a long flashback of the events that led to this tragic finale and to the collapse of a fledgling leftist revolution. In flashback, through a kind of revolutionary bildungsroman, Paulo recalls the years leading up to the calamitous present and his own political evolution: his original subservience to the strongman Diaz, his idealistic conversion to the communist cause, his support for the populist governor Vieira, his political disillusionment and numerous betrayals, and his overwhelming desire to attain a meaningful death.

The plot and its potential allegorical readings have been dissected in great detail by Xavier, Stam, and other critics, but what has not been carefully studied is how *Terra em transe* deploys intermediality to enhance its political message. In the following sections I examine how the film incorporates and synthesizes a heterogeneous mixture of media and materials from high, low, and popular culture, including poetry (and text-based materials more broadly), music, photography, and other media to promote its ideological subtext. Xavier believes the film's "poetic style" relies on a variety of sources to provide its lyrical impetus, including written poetry (at times overlaid on the screen), lyrical dialogues and monologues by Martins and other characters, and iconographic images and scenes that play into the spectator's lyrical sensibility.

I shall begin by discussing the most salient presence of poetry in the film, namely a set of frames displaying an actual poem on-screen (see fig. 2.1). During Paulo's dramatic death scene, the following text is superimposed on the moving images as if the film screen were a page (the white dunes and sky forming the background/surface, and Paulo's silhouette becoming one more textual signifier within the image):

Figure 2.1. Poetry on-screen in *Terra em transe* (8:36). *Source: Terra em transe* (1967). Dir. Glauber Rocha.

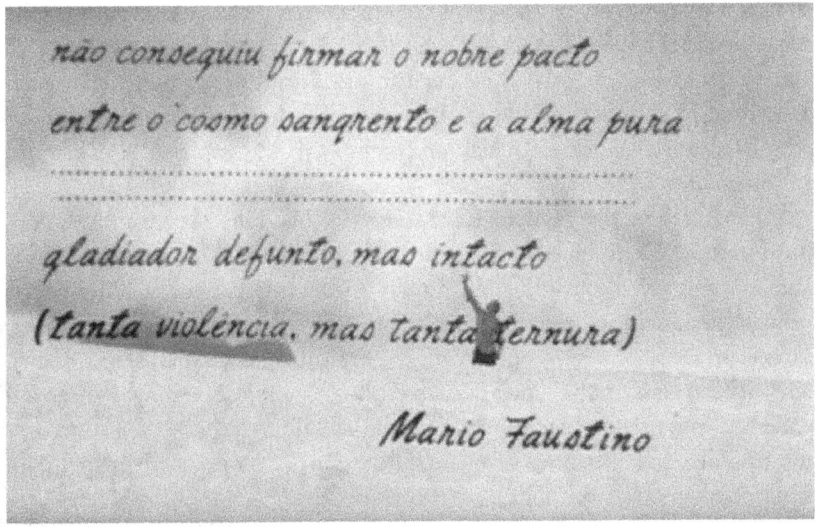

não conseguiu firmar o nobre pacto
entre o cosmos sangrento e a alma pura
. . .
gladiador defunto mas intacto
(tanta violência, mas tanta ternura)

—Mário Faustino

[He failed to sign the noble pact between the pure soul and the bloody cosmos, a defunct gladiator, but still intact—so much violence, yet so much tenderness.—Mário Faustino, "Epitaph of a Poet"]

Johnson and Stam's discussion on the film's employment of poetry does not consider the question of intermediality, focusing instead on poetry's political and aesthetic relevance. For them, these verses encapsulate the film's central dialectic, counterpoising "art on the one hand, and social reality on the other" (*Brazilian Cinema* 152). That is to say, Johnson and Stam see the conflict as one between idealism and the role of the artist on the one hand (the "pure soul"), and the stark reality of a messy and violent political situation (the "bloody cosmos") on the other. That dialectic also captures the very dilemma that Rocha faced as a film director in tumultuous times, which also characterized the existential anguish of Latin America's intellectual left as it tried to sort out its role in the wake of authoritarianism (when faced with a choice of whether to stay and fight with the gun or the camera or to retreat into exile).

Poetry is at the heart of Rocha's movie. The film is eminently lyrical, dream-like (or "entranced" as its title suggests), both in terms of its images and avant-garde filmmaking techniques and, as stated, through its poetic script. The highly stylized script makes its lyrical nature felt in Paulo's lines; in the presence of direct poetry quotes by Faustino, Castro Alves, Rocha, and others; and in its operatic dimension (grandiose settings, theatrical speeches, fantastic or anachronistic wardrobes, etc.). *Terra em transe*, according to Stam, partakes both of poetic and dramatic modes at the expense of conventional narrative modes:

> Paulo represents the poet, abroad in the world of class struggle and coups d'état. His habitual mode of speech, simultaneously frenetic and solemn, is poetic. The lava of his words repeatedly erupts into apostrophe, incantation, angry curses. His poetry, ubiquitous in *Terra em transe*, punctuates, interrupts, underlines and counterpoints the action. Most often, however, it expresses his inner voice, rather like the soliloquies in Hamlet. Paulo recurrently appears in close up with his voice off, in a technique reminiscent of the Orson Welles' adaptations of Shakespearean tragedies. ("*Land in Anguish*")

Illustrative of the accumulation of lyrical effects, in the operatic death scene the staccato rhythms established by the sound of the police gunshots are in perfect sync with Paulo's lyrical monologue (taken from a poem by Rocha) and work in tandem with other sounds and images: Faustino's poetic epitaph overlaid on-screen, Villa-Lobos's sublime (even transcendent) soundtrack, and the stylized black-and-white images played in slow motion. For Nagib this baroque accumulation of lyrical elements "expose intermediality as a key procedure in the director's [Rocha] mode of filmmaking. Poetry, in diegetic and extradiegetic form, is the language adopted by *Terra em transe*'s protagonist" ("Intermedial" 323). This is even more evident in the reprise of the death scene at the end of the film, when the machine-gun fire becomes increasingly intertwined with the police sirens and the music soundtrack, creating a sound palimpsest of operatic dimensions, as Paulo makes his dramatic last stand. And yet this palimpsest never quite attains a level of unity or seamless cohesion, rather it maintains a fragmentary quality typical of avant-garde compositions:

> In the best Brazilian films, hybridity is not just a property of the cultural objects portrayed, but rather inheres in the film's very processes of enunciation, its mode of constituting itself as a text. The final shot of *Terra em transe* exemplifies this process brilliantly. As we see the film's protagonist Paulo wielding a rifle in a Che-Guevara-like gesture of quixotic rebellion, we hear a soundtrack composed of Villa-Lobos, *candomblé* chants, samba, and machine-gun fire. The mix, in this feverish bricolage, is fundamentally unstable; the Villa-Lobos music never really synchronizes with the candomblé or the gunfire. . . [revealing] counterpoints where the tensions are never completely resolved or harmonized, where the cultural dialogue is tense, transgressive, not easily assimilated. (Stam, "Palimpsest Aesthetics" 68)

The same can be said about the hybrid mixing of media in these scenes, as poetry, collage, text, and image converge in a cacophonous assemblage with strong surrealist overtones, all of it suspended at the brink of chaotic disintegration. If anything binds the scenes together, however, it is their poetry or notion of the poetic, as the lyrical connects easily to music, to the sound of recited speech, to opera, to visual and aural rhythms, and to the evocative images on display. Such poetry is not a sign of elitism; rather it is profoundly egalitarian, since Rocha's films do not depend principally on high culture (poetry, classical music, opera) but counterpoise it with popular and folk traditions (oral storytelling, *cordel*, song). The recourse to practices and media originating in popular culture that we see not only in this scene but throughout the film, including *candomblé* music and rituals, samba, carnival, *cordel* literature and ballads, popular songs, and folk traditions, all seek to embody a certain élan vital of the people (*o povo*). In Rocha's own words, "I wanted to display the wealth of popular culture as a kind of challenge to oppressive cultural forms, since I am also interested in showing how the economically and politically oppressed have great creative strength in their music, clothing and choreography" (Burton, *Cinema and Social*

Change 111). It is in the unstable combination of these various genres and modes that intermediality gains a political dimension and creates a radical aesthetic, which as Nagib maintains, places "intermediality on a par with the cosmogonic impetus that propels the director's work" ("Intermediality" 324).

Poetry, however, retains a prominent centrality in this heterogeneous mix of modes, media, and materials. For Stam, this recourse to poetry serves to strike a contrast with the realist aspects of political violence, to show how the ideal inevitably degrades when confronted with real world problems. Thus, Rocha inserts poetry, whether through written form or in the voice-over, to destabilize realist filmic modes. In some cases, the film enlists poetry in an ironic clef, for example by quoting the poetry of Castro Alves, a nineteenth-century Romantic and icon of Brazil's nationalist causes, even as the film chronicles the destruction of Eldorado's national project as the fictional country is torn apart by the different factions. By the 1960s the vision of a unified Brazil was understood as a dangerous chimera, a fantasy promoted by the military to justify their rule and the eradication of difference and dissent. Part and parcel of Rocha's rejection of nationalism is his skepticism toward any grand narratives. His film is equally critical of fascism, populism, and communism, all of them failed totalizing projects, and poetry often serves to expose the political tensions that the artist-intellectual faces when demands are placed upon him by those same inadequate political models. This mechanism (the opposition between art and politics) is exposed in the film through the character of Sara, "who generally represents the best face of orthodox communism, [but] tells Paulo that poetry and politics are too much for one man" (Stam, "*Land in Anguish*"). The hope for Eldorado (and for Latin America), according to Rocha, is to be found in the *povo*, in the popular masses, which despite their capacity for brutality and uncontrollable violence have a vital strength that may form the basis for a (better) future society. But it is the intermedial recourse to poetry within the movie that negates Sara's assertion, since "the film itself not only 'includes' poetry but also proceeds poetically, constituting the cinematographic equivalent of poetry" ("*Land in Anguish*"). Interestingly, for the Brazilian critic, Rocha's "enthusiasm for poetry and his reservations about its social efficacy apply as well to cinema," as neither guarantees the triumph of the Revolution. Without using the word "intermediality," Stam transparently alludes to the film's use of transmedial and intermedial analogies within its visual and textual discourse. *Terra em transe* equates poetry and cinema during a supremely self-reflexive scene in which "we see Paulo aim his camera out of his apartment window and take a photograph, while his off-screen voice comments: 'I, for example, devote myself to the vain exercise of poetry'" (Stam, "*Land in Anguish*").

Poetic expression is therefore equated with photography and film in a thought-provoking intermedial analogy. This intermedial comparison echoes both Pasolini's theories postulating film as a kind of visual poetry and Stan Brakhage's conception of "poetic film" as a cinematic variant that rejects narrative in favor of visual experimentation and transcendence. In *Moving Verses*, a beautifully written monographic reflection on the intermedial relationship between Argentine film and poetry, Ben Bollig writes that "the connections between a sense of cinematic renewal or rebirth in Latin America in the 1960s and the winds of change in European art cinema are, of course, not mere coincidence. The 'cinema of poetry,' whose 'birth' Pasolini . . . identified around the time of the first Pesaro film festival in 1965 is a largely unexplored point of contact between the two continents' cinematic production" (25). Nagib has traced *Terra em transe*'s intermediality to theories on film and poetry by Pasolini and others, claiming that "the film performs a decisive intermedial leap to become the 'cinema of poetry' argued for by Pasolini and Eisenstein, both of whom ranked high in Rocha's pantheon" ("Intermedial" 342).

The presence of poetry in film, as with other text-image interactions, is nothing new; I will later delve into experiments in fusing these genres by the early avant-gardes. But in this case Rocha was also part of a tendency within Latin American experimental cinemas that, as Ben Bollig and David Wood argue, "from the 1960s onward [Rocha used poetry as] . . . a tool of resistance or critique, a way of seeking out spaces of artistic creation that evaded, transcended or openly denounced hegemonic narrative forms" (116). Nagib goes further, making the case for the Brazilian cineaste as a polymath, polyvalent artist who wished to turn the seventh art into a total work of art, since "Rocha was extremely proficient in poetry, fiction writing, theatre, drawing, journalism and television, all of which found expression in his cinema [so that] . . . Rocha's work could be seen as the fulfilment of Wagner's utopia of the *Gesamtkunstwerk*, or total artwork, which has often been discussed within the framework of intermediality" ("Intermediality" 325).

There are other instances within the film of using script as critique, including informative titles that also convey some other meaning through their font or placement, essentially standing out as extradiegetic inserts or elements that remit to other media forms. For instance, the overdetermined toponym "Alecrim," placed over an aerial shot of that fictitious province in

Eldorado, exudes colonialism by echoing the Portuguese geography (Algarve, Almada, Alentejo) with its Arabic inflected lexicon (marked by the prefix "al-"), but also signifies the "rosemary" bush with its Catholic overtones, and is additionally a signature street in Lisbon's historic harbor district (rua do Alecrim), the port from which ships sailed to the overseas colonies. The word itself is written in a vintage "Western"-style typeface that summons images of the frontier, a font type that he will revisit in *Cabeças cortadas*. Rocha's *nordestino* films (especially *Deus e o diabo* and *Antônio das Mortes*) are decidedly Westerns, set in the arid *sertão* badlands, so it is not strange to see this font in use here. The evocation of the frontier also points to a certain lawlessness present in Eldorado, a country very much at the margins of prosperity and civilization.

Text is again deployed in the film when Paulo walks into Viera's leftist newspaper, where he will work. Overlaid on-screen are the words "Aurora Livre: Jornal Independente e Noticioso" (18:01) [Free Dawn: Independent and News-Filled Journal]. The form and type of the text is reminiscent of newspaper headlines, its name "Aurora Livre" significantly recalls anarchist publications, and this intermedial insert generally functions to create the sense that we are in the presence of committed leftist journalism, but also of political propaganda for the populist leader—casting doubt on its "independent" label. So, the text both informs and undermines the legitimacy of the newspaper or of political newspapers in general. This delegitimizing maneuver is enhanced by yet another intermedial intrusion, as Sara, Viera's right-hand and Paulo's future lover, enters the newspaper office. In a disorienting scene filmed through a series of jump cuts that are eminently Godardian, Sara drops several photographs on Paulo's desk (18:40). The spectator can see these documentary photos of starving, sick, and impoverished children, images of reality that irrupt with accusatory force into the fiction, prompting Paulo to demand that something be done, one of many instances when Third Cinema elements enter this art film (Second Cinema) mode (see fig. 2.2).

It is through the violent intrusion of another medium, with its documentary capacity to puncture through the fictional narrative, that Rocha reminds the spectator of the very real questions posed by this fictional film. As Cory Hahn sees it, "[H]ere, material evidence, proof of the persisting conditions of inequality and poverty, propels the protagonist to return to politics" (27). The photograph is a frame within the filmic frame that confronts spectators in Brechtian fashion with the harsh reality behind the

Figure 2.2. Photography and photo collage within *Terra em transe* (19:21). *Source: Terra em transe* (1967). Dir. Glauber Rocha.

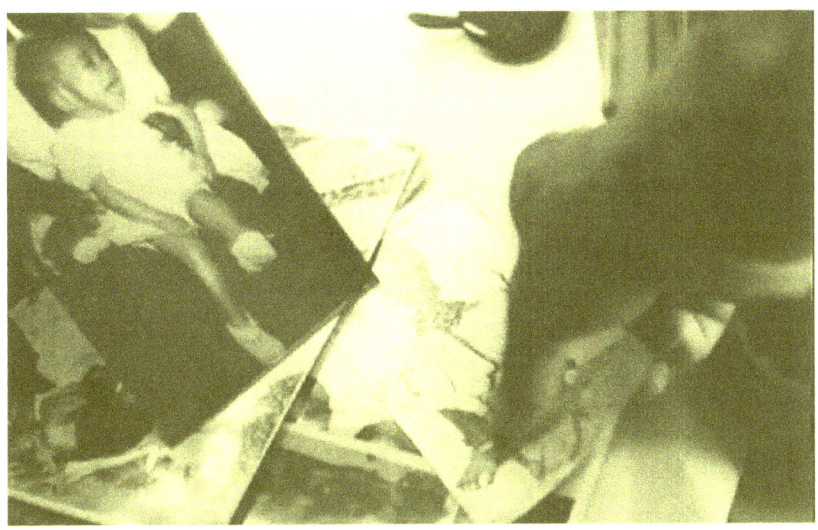

illusionistic fiction. In the context of the 1960s we can read that exhortation to action as yet another tricontinental (transnational) call for Pan-American unity, and for all developing nations, to join the anti-capitalist fight.

There are many other intermedial strategies present in *Terra em transe*. Among these we could mention the pervasive presence of opera, operetta, and many operatic scenes in the film, including Diaz's coronation (enhanced by the use of the Rio de Janeiro opera house as Diaz's palace), the insertion of documentary footage into the film (from Rocha's own *Maranhão 66* film [25:16]), the presence of television broadcasts, the short film within the film that Paulo creates to undermine Diaz, the deployment of carnival and samba, the use of Afro-Brazilian music—in the opening moments we hear African chanting and the sound of tall candomblé hand drums or atabaques; the presence of jazz, bossa nova, and rock 'n' roll; the reverberating echoes of *cordel* literature (inexpensive chapbooks sold for popular consumption in Brazil's northeast); and a long etcetera of other media and materials inscribed into the film to both foreground its cultural heterogeneity and further politicize it by introducing a desirable degree of "impurity."[10]

André Bazin pejoratively referred to "impure cinema" to decry a cinema that abandoned medium specificity and became "contaminated by other art forms, notably literature and theater" (Nagib, "The Politics of Impurity" 22). As Nagib has demonstrated in her scholarship on intermediality, Bazin's concept of cinematic "impurity" held, in addition to its reference to medium and material, certain negative connotations about race, gender, and ethnicity ("The Politics of Impurity" 22). Quite the opposite, Rocha's cinema of impurity is a celebration of hybridity and ambiguity in terms of race, gender, ethnicity, and even politics, questions central to a multiracial and ethnically heterogeneous Brazilian society. As Nagib astutely observes in her analysis of the political uses of media mixing in contemporary film form, "[T]he recourse to different media within a film immediately suspends the pedagogical character of representational narratives by introducing a dilemma . . . which, rather than giving univocal lessons, multiplies the meanings of the referent" ("The Politics of Impurity" 31). In *Terra em transe* the insertion of the various media does just that, by destabilizing European forms such as opera or classical music as well as traditional literary forms such as the epic or the lyric poem, with autochthonous elements such as *candomblé* or *cordel* literature. One can see how this politics of mixing and ambiguity opposed and arguably undermined the principles and practices of the military regime, which were aligned with the nationalist and traditionalist concepts best represented by the country's positivist motto, *ordem e progresso* [order and progress] and included a strict policing of boundaries (geographic, bodily, generic, racial, sexual). The obscenely overloaded, palimpsestic layering of media and cultural forms seen in Rocha's film, therefore, upends the stability and purity sought after by the regime and reaffirms that "the content of a film becomes impure insofar as its form incorporates other forms, thus diluting frontiers and genres, including those of sex and gender that lie at the core of cultural studies" (Nagib, "The Politics of Impurity" 31).

The overly dramatic, theatrical, and operatic is also prominent in much of Rocha's other work but seems to reach its apex in this particular film, in my assessment, and will be mirrored in a degraded form by his later Spanish film *Cabeças cortadas*. Of course, theater and opera are themselves already highly intermedial arts (integrating song, music, script, poetry, dance, acting, stage design, and more), so their inclusion in the film only magnifies an already predominant hypermediality. Stam and more recently Nagib have addressed in considerable detail the inclusion of opera (and opera buffa or operetta) in the film in terms that associate the genre with the aesthetic project of creating a heterogeneous, hybrid, and impure cinematic work, one that sought a radical break from realism:

> *Terra em transe* is linked to one of the least realistic of artistic genres—opera. Rocha has often expressed his fondness for the "cinema opera" of Welles and Eisenstein. Opera itself, especially Verdi and his Brazilian counterpart, Carlos Gomes, pervades the soundtrack. Paulo's death, coextensive with the film, recalls the protracted agonies of opera, where people die eloquently, interminably, and with poetry on their lips. As if to call attention to the operatic reference, the wounded Paulo twice declaims: "Eu preciso cantar!" (I must sing!) . . . The film also shares with opera its love of exalted, stylized speech. Although some of the dialogue is naturalistically rendered, the world of the film remains one where people speak naturally to each other in poetry. (Stam, "*Land in Anguish*")

The inclusion of theater and opera in the film is complicated by intermixing them with contemporary mass media, in the forms of documentary inserts, television, and the film within the film. All these genres, decontextualized and juxtaposed in unusual ways, function to defamiliarize perception in a Brechtian sense and seek to uplift the spectator into an elevated comprehension of the film's political urgency. This urgency does not (necessarily) represent a call for direct action, as it did in Lumbreras's or Solanas's militant films. It does not express an imperious command to pick up arms, like Paulo, against the encroachment of authoritarian rule. Instead, it merely suggests Rocha's desire to enhance the audience's critical awareness, to inoculate them against ideological manipulation regardless of its origin, an unorthodox position that likely was the product of his distrust of all political dogmatism.

The comparison between Rocha (specifically) and Cinema Novo (more generally) with EdB filmmakers and films is not gratuitous on my part. As I have observed the two movements shared many affinities, stylistically and politically, and, in some respects, they shared indirect ways of dealing with adverse sociohistorical conditions. There were also the many personal contacts between these filmmakers, all of whom viewed themselves as inscribed within a community of global, progressive, leftist artists on the verge of radical world-making. Rocha and several EdB filmmakers were directly aware of each other's films, and it was therefore not entirely surprising when the Brazilian accepted a commission to make a film in Spain in close collaboration with the EdB. The analysis of *Terra em transe* has provided an insight into Rocha's filmmaking, his use of other media, and his political stance. Prior to examining the collaborative project *Cabeças cortadas* it is necessary to acquire a notion of the EdB's own filmic tendencies and context. In the next sections I examine several EdB films and filmmakers to gauge how they responded to their historical juncture to interpret how they relate to and with Cinema Novo.

Understanding the relationship between the EdB and Cinema Novo also requires further elaboration of the question of intermediality by placing it within an older media history. To this end I will briefly examine some of the EdB's predecessors in intermedial word and image experiments, prior to situating it in the context of Spain's 1960s film scene. I will conclude this middle segment of the chapter by exploring how text-image interactions activate anti-Francoist discourse in three strikingly distinct but paradigmatic EdB films: Vicente Aranda's *Fata Morgana* (1965), José María Nunes's *Sexperiencias* (1968), and Pere Portabella's *Nocturno 29* (1968).[11] Concurrently I will argue for the strong connection between the EdB's intermedial practices and its efforts toward political and countercultural resistance, in ways that bring to mind Cinema Novo. All along I will point out these Iberian filmmakers' affinities with Rocha's style and where they diverge. In the chapter's concluding segment, I will return to the Brazilian director to study how *Cabeças cortadas* represents an ill-fated attempt at synthesis of EdB and Cinema Novo tendencies.

Historical Antecedents to 1960s Text-Image Intermediality

Although the proliferation of pop culture and mass media in the 1960s propitiated film's turn to greater intermediality, the cinema has been intermedial since its inception. Certainly we could look back to the pioneering work of Georges Méliès, who in the fin-de-siècle brought into early cinema elements as disparate as the circus, magic shows, theater, dance, and, as Brian Jacobson beautifully puts it, the "plasticity and fluidity, artificiality, and the manipulation of light" of nineteenth-century iron and glass architecture (189), and that is without delving into the hand-painted celluloid that characterized not only the Frenchman's cinema but also that of the Spanish filmmaker Segundo de Chomón. But the moment when the intermedial truly explodes within the cinematic is during the effervescent commingling of the arts in the 1920s and '30s avant-garde. The so-called historical avant-gardes experimented with media by mixing poetic script with visual images in films as innovative and stylistically disparate as Man Ray's surrealist *L'étoile de mer* (*The Starfish*, 1928) and *Les mystères de Château de Dé* (*The Mysteries of the Chateau of Dice,* 1929), Paul Strand and Charles Sheeler's cubist city symphony *Manhatta* (1921), Marcel Duchamp's abstract short *Anémic cinéma* (1928), and Luis Buñuel's groundbreaking *Un chien andalou* (*An Andalusian Dog,* 1929). In these filmic "poems" the interaction between text and image foregrounds cinema's dual time-based and spatial nature, which fluidly combines verbal and visual metaphors, allowing for different forms of inscription.

Nevertheless, although some early twentieth-century modernists adopted an aesthetic of fragmentation by marshaling collage, montage, and intermediality to violate rules of medium specificity, others demanded a *cinéma pur* free from the contamination of other media. The battlelines were drawn as avant-garde filmmakers such as Man Ray, Francis Picabia, and Marcel Duchamp argued against a narrowly circumscribed concept of medium, embracing cinema's inherent intermediality, while others—René Clair, Viking Eggeling, Hans Richter—sought the cinematic medium's "purification" (Beaver 23). Cubist and Surrealist filmmakers that chose to incorporate techniques from the visual (painting, photography, architecture) and script-based arts (poetry) were not pursuing a totalizing convergence of different media into film, but they wished to maintain productive intermedial states within the work of art. Thus, whereas proponents of medium specificity sought what was unique to each medium, intermedialists wanted to bring those media into overlapping contacts and novel relationships, allowing for impure commingling and unusual material combinations. The hope was that hybridizing older media into a new "medium" allowed for effects not achievable by the individual media that composed it. Medium, for these artists, was not narrowly reduced to "material" or production methods but to a negotiation between both that also took into account the "traces" or material remains, impressions, or influence of one medium in another. These "traces" could be as direct as paint or scratches applied to the surface of the celluloid's emulsion, or as "indirect" as the image of a newspaper's text captured on film, even the allusion or memory of an older technology such as the magic lantern or the panorama.

The historical avant-garde's interest in intermediality and text-image interaction was revitalized with zealous momentum in the 1960s by artist-filmmaker groups such as Fluxus, the Nouvelle Vague, the New York School, Cinema Novo and Tropicália in Brazil, and the EdB and its affiliated artists in Dau al set [Seventh Face of the Die] in Spain. However, unlike movements that evolved within democratic states and were (mainly) driven by aesthetic concerns, Cinema Novo's and EdB's intermediality also doubled as a strategic response toward the adverse sociopolitical circumstances present in Castelo-Branco's Brazil and Francoist Spain, respectively. The Nouvelle Vague, specifically Godard's counter-cinema, taught both Rocha and EdB filmmakers how to mobilize interruptions and alienating Brechtian devices—the inclusion of titles, solid frames and scratched film, discordant sound, and other aggressive breaks with diegetic conventions—that would awaken spectators' reflection and potentially activate their critique of the "system." This relationship with the French New Wave was true for Rocha, who had collaborated with Godard in *Le vent d'est* (1970), where he appeared in an often-cited cameo, but even more so for the Iberian filmmakers who were geographically proximate to France. As Galt observes, "[T]he engagement with French cinema is particularly close because the border, only a few hundred kilometers away, functions as a potent symbol of political freedom" ("Mapping"). EdB filmmakers were sympathetic to Godard's criticism of the industry and how capitalist financing shaped films ideologically (Lesage).[12] Singling him out as an intermedial filmmaker, Pethó refers to Godard's oeuvre as "the most intellectually challenging meditation upon the intermedial nature of the moving pictures" indeed, as a counter-cinematic attack on film's apparent "seamlessness," which the French director achieved through discontinuities, jump cuts, collage, and a free-associational narrative style (231). Acquainted with Godard's techniques, EdB directors such as Nunes and Portabella deployed collages of decontextualized text intermingled with images to protest world events (i.e., in Nunes's film *Sexperiencias* or Portabella's *Nocturno 29*).

Whereas EdB filmmakers, like Rocha, acquired ideological and cinematographic inspiration from Godard, from Fluxus they learned how to mobilize different media to achieve distancing effects, cross-pollinating film with mainstream commercial and popular forms (comics, advertisement, narrative cinema, pulp-fiction) and high culture, underground, or avant-garde forms (poetry, happenings, conceptual art). Since 1962 high-profile mixed-media Fluxus events (including Flux Films) were staged in the United States and Europe to articulate anti-commercial, anti-capitalist messages. For instance, in his short *The End* (1962), Dick Higgins disrupts a commercial ad's message by playing it backward, a tactic emulated by Aranda and Portabella's own subversion of commercials. Displaying another technique later repurposed by Nunes's *Sexperiencias*, in Wolf Vostell's short television décollage *Sun in Your Head* (1963) the Fluxus artist films, distorts, flickers, interferes with, and reedits images from television to foreground viewing mechanisms and the tube's hypnotic effects, as well as condemning militarism (the film features aerial bombardments and concludes with a nuclear explosion) in what could be called a glitch art piece ahead of its time. The anti-imperialist, anti-militarist vein promoted by Fluxus (the product of the younger generation's disgust with the aftermath of World War II, Korea, Vietnam, and other conflicts) would percolate into Cinema Novo and EdB filmmaking as well, indeed into most of the new cinematic movements of the era. In the EdB, these ideological debates were bound up with questions about how to renovate and reinvigorate a moribund Spanish cinema under a waning regime.

Many of these debates coalesced around the contentious 1967 "Jornadas de Sitges," a gathering of mainly avant-garde Iberian (mostly Catalan) filmmakers presided by the EdB's Román Gubern and heavily attended by EdB members and supporters, including Ricardo Muñoz Suay and Joaquim Jordà, both of whom would soon thereafter participate in Rocha's *Cabeças cortadas*. The meeting was fiery to say the least; after issuing declarations against the regime and Madrid's "cine mesetario" [flatland cinema], the group proposed a Marxist-Situationist cinema approximating "ciertas posiciones del grupo *Fluxus* y a ciertas corrientes estructurales" (Bonet and Palacio 62) [certain positions from the Fluxus group and certain structuralist tendencies].[13] The majority of the EdB filmmakers were not interested in taking things to the extreme of militant clandestine cinema, with the possible exceptions of Jordà and Nunes, whose films would often be censored or outright forbidden. Jordà would later be involved with militant filmmaking in Italy, including his co-direction with Gianni Totti of *Lenin vivo* (1970) [Lenin Alive] and his involvement in promoting the cause of the Uruguayan Tupamaro urban guerilla war (Aubert, *L'Ecole* 267).

It is evident that not only the European and Latin American new waves but also Fluxus and the Situationists inspired the EdB's films politically and formally, although the group's intermedial tendencies stemmed somewhat "naturally" from the interdisciplinary background of its filmmakers and collaborators, for example musician Carles Santos, poet Joan Brossa and painter Antoni Tàpies (both Brossa and Tàpies, like fellow painters Modest Cuixart, Joan Ponç, and Joan Josep Tharrats, were also members of the neo-Dadaist group Dau al set), architect Ricardo Bofill, writers Román Gubern and Gonzalo Suárez, painter-filmmaker Antoni Padrós (only distantly associated with the EdB), producer-filmmaker Pere Portabella, and so on. Without flattening regional distinctions and contextual particularities, the artistic exuberance of that moment in the '60s in Spain was not wholly dissimilar to what was happening in Brazil with the rise of Tropicalism, and indeed elsewhere throughout the globe one could find an artistic awakening parallel to that of the first avant-gardes.

As we have seen, significantly influenced by Fluxus, Tropicália, and other mixed-media artists, filmmakers in both Cinema Novo and the EdB made films deliberately intending to disrupt the essentialist notion of medium specificity and its claim that each art has exclusive properties that decisively determine its form and content. Defenders of the fixed and autonomous boundaries of media, modernist believers in the essence of each separate medium, forcefully opposed these impure films and art forms. Clement Greenberg, an ardent proponent of medium specificity in the '60s, stated in his polemic "Toward a New Lacoon" that "purity in art consists in the acceptance . . . of the limitations of the medium of the specific art. . . . It is by virtue of its medium that each art is unique and strictly itself" (32). The rejection of what James calls "Greenberg's Kantian modernism," the "proposal that the defining project of aesthetic modernism was each medium's search for its own, irreducible properties and the consequent elimination of what was not essential to it" began to take place as "micro-cinemas"—such as the EdB, Cinema Novo, the Nouvelle Vague, and so on—"recapitulated earlier avant-garde projects, Dada and Constructivism in particular, that turned against the theoretical and material institutions of art itself and the idea of aesthetic autonomy these maintained" (*The Most Typical* 11–13). James correctly identifies that such challenges to the modernist paradigm of medium specificity were characteristic of a 1960s wholesale attack against "boundaries between genres, between media, between art and non-art, and between art and life, and often in a way that called into question the fetishism of the commodity art-object" (*Allegories* 48). EdB and Cinema Novo films partook of this subversion of medium specificity by offering a cinema that was as impure as it was (paradoxically) fashionably stylized, influenced by the surface-quality of pop culture in all its manifestations. In the specific case of the EdB, the impurity and generic mélange they enacted through their filmmaking held added political significance if we believe, as Marsha Kinder argues in *Blood Cinema*, that "during the Francoist era, *any difference* in verbal or filmic language in the Catalan cinema carried subversive implications, even when the plot seemed more personal than political" (394). Fascism, ultra-nationalism, and other right-leaning authoritarian ideologies often aligned against concepts of heterogeneity, mixing, and impurity, whether in the context of the arts, of social policy, of immigration, race, and so on. In Brazil, especially during its populist years leading to military rule (1945–1964), "what came from outside was seen as impure, and therefore dangerous," so that an emphasis was placed on the national as a way to counter foreign cultural imperialism (Schelling 68). Rocha, however, was decidedly an internationalist, a firm believer in the tricontinental, and not afraid to allow for the "impure" commingling of local, regional, and transnational elements in his cinema—a cinema that he viewed as both distinctly Brazilian and also universal.

Through its departure from aesthetic norms, formal experimentation can become subversive, not just because "under dictatorship, any claim of difference is simultaneously an act of resistance" (Galt, "Missed Encounters" 201), but rather because a denial of medium specificity and the move toward intermediality, especially in the context of the 1960s, represented a critique against capitalism (and the commodification of art) and was counter to Spain's narrative of progress under Francoism or Brazil's own drive toward modernization and development at all costs. Fluxus's Higgins articulated his argument against medium specificity by denouncing the complicity of "pure media" with exploitative practices linked to specialization and the division of labor, making some of the points that I discussed in the previous chapter about militant cinema's political deployment of intermedia. In the '60s such sentiments were also evidenced by the proliferation of art forms that purposefully escaped medium specificity: art installation, happenings, performance art, experimental theater, and so on. What is difficult to gauge is whether the effect desired by these filmmakers—not only remaking the art world but also undermining the structures of authoritarianism—was indeed achievable through such cinematic strategies. James is skeptical, stating about the filmic avant-gardes that "although political significance was claimed for these formal developments . . . the actual political effect was ambiguous" (*Allegories* 99).

James's sobering skepticism notwithstanding, regarding the Spanish case other critics such as D'Lugo, Kinder, Besas, Higginbotham, and Galt have convincingly argued that the films of the EdB mobilize experimental form with radical political intent, namely pushing for democratic freedoms and for a reorientation of society toward the values of the left. The Brazilian case was, arguably, less successful in achieving practical results, when many of the Cinema Novo filmmakers eventually chose or were forced into exile and given that the country could not emerge from military rule until 1985. But in regard to the EdB, critics have not delved in sufficient detail into the specifics of how formal experimentation served filmmakers to achieve political results. In what follows I expand prior arguments for the

EdB's political relevance by examining how the school's opposition against the regime, its censorship, and the wanton consumerism it promoted was specifically achieved through an intermedial style that combined script and images using procedures (e.g., collage, montage, and metalepsis) that were genealogically traceable to the early avant-gardes.[14] I will also demonstrate that by challenging concepts of medium specificity the EdB performed a critique of the division of class and labor and of the capitalist progress narratives espoused by Franco's regime in its later phase (the period of political upheaval known as "tradofranquismo," late Francoism, roughly 1960–1975). The use of avant-garde form was part of a historical conjuncture—the '60s—in which artists throughout the globe were immersed in spirited debates as to how an ideological struggle might be enacted through cultural production, and in particular through film, exploring alternative methods of production, exhibition, and distribution. My point, therefore, is not that a critique of authoritarianism (whether Francoism, the Brazilian dictatorship, or similar ones elsewhere) could *only* have been enacted through avant-garde form (other approaches included realism as well as the gritty militant Third Cinema), rather I am interested in exploring *how* by conjoining political critique with avant-garde form the EdB enhanced both, thus mitigating some of the critiques levied against Second Cinema (art house) by Solanas, Gracía Espinosa, and others.[15]

Recovering the (Almost) Forgotten Project of the EdB

Although critics of avant-garde film outside of Hispanism and Latin American cultural studies, such as P. Adams Sitney, David James, or Scott MacDonald, seem by and large unaware of endeavors by experimental filmmakers in Spain and Latin America, they have usefully identified other contemporary schools of experimental cinema and poetry (such as the Lettrists, the Situationists, and Fluxus) that deployed text and image to mount a social critique of capitalism. And while Cinema Novo, or the new Latin American cinemas more broadly, have received well-deserved attention from Latin Americanist film critics (Michael Chanan, Julianne Burton, Randal Johnson, Robert Stam, Teshome Gabriel, and a long etc.), it is high time to recover the EdB's experimental practice that has been excluded both from film studies' counter-cinema histories and from scholarship on Hispanic cinema, as Rosalind Galt documents. Fortunately, a handful of Hispanists (Teresa Vilarós, Fèlix Fanés, Anna Cox, Sara Nadal-Melsió, David Vilaseca, and most notably Steven Marsh and Rosalind Galt) are overturning the deliberate "framework of overlooking" that results in the EdB's films being "'missed' by film history" (Galt, "Missed Encounters" 193–96). Although much remains to be done, these scholars are uncovering an astonishing variety of EdB films, from poet-filmmaker José María Nunes's overtly political works to Vicente Aranda's cryptic allegories and Pere Portabella's lyrical masterpieces. Not unlike Cinema Novo's films, the works of the EdB are located at the juncture of poetry and cinema; indeed they were, in their time, poised at the cutting edge of several media and art forms (film, photography, poetry, Pop Art, music, performance, high fashion). Despite, or perhaps by virtue of, being fully immersed in the tempestuous '60s cultural scene and created under the unfavorable conditions of late Francoism, the EdB represented a momentous thrust for cultural, social, and even political change within *and* arguably outside of the film industry.

Aesthetically the EdB has been typically posited as oppositional to the realist tendencies of the Madrid-based Nuevo Cine Español (NCE), best exemplified by Luis García Berlanga's and Juan Antonio Bardem's socially progressive but comparatively more formally conservative films. According to standard accounts, the EdB rejected conventional narrative content, replacing it with lyrical forms and episodic fragments, while the NCE remained grounded in a neorealist approach, enacting a familiar opposition traceable to debates between Soviet social realism and the avant-gardes as exemplified by the polarized stance between Adorno and Lukács, and as discussed in chapter 1.

Yet a more nuanced account should reflect that the division of realist versus avant-garde does not map neatly onto the NCE and the EdB. As Steven Marsh masterfully demonstrates in his *Spanish Cinema Against Itself*, there was much crossover, collaboration, and mutual contamination between these groups and further study should consider such mutual influences. For instance, there are NCE directors whose aesthetic is not easily categorized as neorealist, such as Basilio Martín Patino, Manuel Summers, and to an extent José Luis Borau. Patino, in particular, creates a remarkable ironic montage with found footage in *Canciones para después de una guerra* (*Songs for After a War*, 1971), which could undoubtedly be considered as "experimental." Similarly, despite learning from the work of François Truffaut, Eric Rohmer, Claude Chabrol, and other Nouvelle Vague filmmakers, Joaquim Jordà's cinematic debut was *Día de muertos* (1960) [Day of the Dead], a short film produced by Bardem and reminiscent of NCE films. Furthermore, Bardem's own *Muerte de un ciclista* (1955) draws on a variety of "experimental" visual devices and formal techniques to achieve its scathing critique of Franco's bourgeoisie, and Carlos Saura's hunting scenes in *La Caza* (*The Hunt*, 1965) marshal a Russian-style montage to allegorically evoke the Civil War. These are but a few among many NCE films that formulate approaches that might be categorized as formally avant-gardist. Despite these undeniable points of contact, however, one might still draw some distinctions between the EdB's penchant toward an unapologetically experimental, noncommercial cinema, and the NCE's somewhat firmer commitment to realist form and commercial distribution, understanding these as merely referential points of a spectrum along which individual films must be placed based on their own specific formal characteristics. Arguably the less nuanced, reified narrative espousing the EdB's formal radicalism against the NCE's realism also echoes the differentiation between Third and Second Cinema, and functions analogously to the oppositional "supplementarity" that Laura Mulvey saw in a "politically and aesthetically avant-garde" cinematic practice that could only exist in its antithetical relation to Hollywood cinema (James, *The Most Typical Avant-Garde* 12).[16] These oppositional comparisons, in other words, are only so useful as to identify the most extreme examples of various film schools, styles, or tendencies. Thus, the EdB and the NCE remain inextricably bound in 1960s Spanish cinematic accounts, just as militant and art cinema are associated in various ways.

Nonetheless, I sustain that differences of approach are evident between the two movements (EdB and NCE) and relevant to my argument on intermediality as a political intervention for resistance against authoritarianism. As early as 1952 with *Bienvenido, Mr. Marshall* (*Welcome, Mr. Marshall!*), the NCE critiqued the Francoist system from within, in fact, acting on a "possibilist" philosophy that included accepting state funding. The EdB's position was that by accepting state protection and money, the NCE had become a "mere instrument[s] of the regime" (somewhat hypocritical, since some EdB filmmakers also accepted state funds), thereby its critical stance was gradually becoming institutionalized and it was beneficiary of the very capitalism it once opposed (Faulkner, *A Cinema of Contradiction* 15). As the other oppositional cinema (i.e., without considering cinema operating illegally, like Lumbreras's Colectivo Cine de Clase), EdB filmmakers pursued subversive sociopolitical objectives, mounting a peripheral—and often quite subtle—assault on the regime's centralist bourgeois ideology. Arguably the EdB succeeded in undermining the regime even while working under the constraints of its rigid censorship and, like the NCE, while taking advantage when possible of state-sponsored subsidies for art films with "special interest," as facilitated by the Ley Fraga (1966).[17]

In brief, as Galt argues, it is through radical form that the political enters most forcefully into the works of the EdB. In the '60s Spain was in an economic boom that was the result of tourism and international trade fomented by the regime in its effort to open up the country and moderately liberalize, albeit without making significant changes to the political system. As Teresa Vilarós observes, Spain's opening to multinational corporations and to massive foreign investment, coming on the heels of twenty years of isolationism and autarky, stood in sharp contrast with its still repressive political landscape, a fact that the EdB desired to expose through its cinema. Consequently, the EdB arguably sought to produce films that avoided "commodification," functioning as countercultural criticism, with some notable exceptions. Director and enfant terrible Joaquiím Jordà defined the EdB's collaborative and countercultural spirit in a manifesto that, according to Galt, affirmed the essence of their film practice as grounded on "[a] formal concern for the structure of image and narrative, an experimental character, a co-operative system of production and . . . characters and situations different from those in the cinema of Madrid" ("Missed Encounters" 194). Despite this common project, the school's production is better defined by what it is not (neorealist social cinema) than by what it is (a palimpsestic, heterogeneous sampling of counter-cinematic strategies).

While a complete rendition of the EdB's far-ranging practices and their consequences is not possible here given my specific focus on intermediality as a vehicle for understanding the school's artistic radicalism, I hope to spark interest toward further research into the work of other notable directors such as Joaquim Jordà, Carlos Durán, Jacinto Esteva, Jaime Camino, Román Gubern, Ricardo Bofill, and Gonzalo Suárez, among others—work begun by Steven Marsh, Rosalind Galt, Esteve Riambau, Casimiro Torreiro, and others but is still incomplete. Suárez, for instance, wrote the script for *Fata Morgana* and later directed another EdB signature film, *Ditirambo* (1967), a detective story spoof that assembled modernist techniques in order to "a través de una fábula de alcance político, emprende[r] el camino de la rebeldía y de la acción" (Oliver 122) [through a fable with political reach, march down the road of rebellion and action]. A full accounting of the diverging trajectories of these filmmakers is needed, as well as further study into important precursors, such as the understudied film *Vida en sombras* (1947) [Life amidst Shadows] by Lorenzo Llobet Gràcia, a story about a man whose life is closely intertwined with the cinema, described as a "brilliant reflexive film . . . [that] quietly slipped into oblivion" (Kinder, *Blood Cinema* 456), or recent films by the EdB's many aesthetic descendants, such as Marc Recha, José Luis Guerin, Jaime Rosales, Mercedes Álvarez, and Isaki Lacuesta. This tight-knit group (which includes many of Portabella's students) associated with Barcelona's Universidad Pompeu Fabra has reclaimed the EdB's avant-garde mantle of formal innovation, setting themselves as the counter-cinematic alternative to today's mainstream cinema. Among their films we might point to the work of Álvarez—who collaborated with Guerin in *En Construcción* (*Under Construction*, 2001)—specifically her award-winning documentary *El cielo gira* (2004) [The World Turns], which depicts life's harsh conditions in a town near Soria and has been described as "un cine contemplativo deudor del estilo de Kiarostami" (Mourenza 10) [a contemplative cinema indebted to Kiarostami's style]. Much remains to be studied in regard to these new filmmakers' indebtedness to the EdB as well. Likewise, although I only examine three salient EdB filmmakers, the group as a whole warrants additional research since—true to their hallmark heterogeneity—their later careers took significantly different paths even while retaining the school's imprimatur.

What many EdB films do share (despite their diversity) is their semi-marginal status as art cinema and a keen sense of the poetic capabilities of film form, often placed at the service of a committed agenda. As Galt insists, "[I]n these films, an anti-Franco imperative was tied for the first time to avant-gardist form rather than to the compromised social progressivism of the New Spanish Cinema auteurs" ("Missed Encounters" 194). Such avant-garde form, as I hope to show, achieved its radicalism precisely by tapping into profoundly intermedial strategies. These strategies roughened film form—to defamiliarize, in a Shklovskian sense—to make the task of viewing and interpretation more difficult, collapsing semiotic regimes (verbal and visual) into each other, thereby actuating novel methodologies to "read" films. Let us now shift our attention to the three films I selected for closer analysis, Vicente Aranda's *Fata Morgana*, José María Nunes's *Sexperiencias*, and Pere Portabella's *Nocturno 29*.

Fata Morgana: The Politics of Comics and High Fashion

Conceivably the EdB's most emblematic film, Vicente Aranda's *Fata Morgana* (1965), employs a pop culture and advertising style that draws on collage and montage to ironically critique consumerism—and in the opinion of some critics could be said to have launched the EdB's cinematic prospects. Aranda himself was born in Barcelona to a humble family and had to emigrate to Venezuela for work in 1952. Upon his return in 1959, he failed to be admitted to Madrid's official film school but was soon thereafter accepted by a Barcelona-based group of artist-intellectuals that had not yet really coalesced as the EdB and included Román Gubern and Ricardo Bofill, as well as several other future EdB filmmakers. With the guidance and backing of these sons of the Catalan bourgeoisie, Aranda was able to fund his first film, *Brillante porvenir* (*Brilliant Future*, 1965), a neorealist tale set in Barcelona that loosely follows some of the plot line of Fitzgerald's *The Great Gatsby* (1925). *Fata Morgana* was Aranda's second film, and by this point the director had found his stride and was aiming for a decidedly avant-garde approach. Deemed as difficult on account of its "elliptical surrealist narrative" (Bentley 192), *Fata Morgana* revolves around an apocalyptic scenario that is never fully explained, requiring spectators to parse its absurdist plot. In truth *Fata Morgana* is best described as an anti-narrative, given its deliberate hermeticism, its resistance to exegesis, and its disregard for continuity; its characters lack transparent motivations, and time and place are ambiguously imprecise. Set in a modern city (likely Barcelona, although landmarks and toponyms are elided) that is being evacuated due to a mysterious, undisclosed threat, the film strongly resonates with the Cold War's climate of nuclear paranoia as well as with an oppressive sense of surveillance.

A stylized pre-credits comic book sequence drawn by Pelayo Izquierdo (see fig. 2.3) was quite possibly inspired by Guy Debord's use of comics in

Figure 2.3. *Fata Morgana*. Pre-credits sequence by comic book artist Pelayo Izquierdo (00:33). *Source: Fata Morgana* (1965). Dir. Vicente Aranda.

the Situationist short film *Critique de la separation* (*Critique of Separation*, 1961), and could also refer to Roy Lichtenstein's and Andy Warhol's comic-inspired Pop Art, or to paintings by the Valencian 1960s *Equipo Crónica*.[18] Whatever its inspirational sources, by including the comic book sequence Aranda underscores the EdB's disregard for medium specificity, "illustrating" the possibilities for political intervention afforded by compositing different media. As mentioned earlier, although source media (poetry, comic, music, etc.) retain some of their individual characteristics, once they become part of the celluloid they are integrated into a composite form that engulfs and modifies them. They are not, however, reduced to, or "converged" into a single medium, rather film both assimilates *and* represents the nuanced tensions, exchanges, and relations between component media. The malleability and hybrid nature of film—inherited from early technologies of the image: the panorama, the camera obscura, photography, performance—facilitates the mixing of different kinds of images and text. By emulating the refashioning of "impure" popular art forms (comics, advertisement, graffiti) so typical of Pop Art's reaction against Abstract Expressionism's "pure" painting, and by using intermedial techniques such as collage, assemblage, and word-image interactions, EdB films reinforce their genealogic link to early twentieth-century Dada and Surrealist movements also fond of intermedia explorations.

Fata Morgana's comic book opening also lays out the film's convoluted plot: spectators are informed that several years prior to the imprecise time when the "story" begins, a woman was murdered for no ostensible reason, and that Gim, a supermodel played by real-life model Teresa Gimpera, will be the next victim unless a James-Bond-esque special agent J. J. (Marcos Martí) saves her. In an absurdist twist, the murderer turns out to be an eccentric criminology professor (Antonio Ferrandis) who studies the sadomasochist attraction between assassins and their victims. The plot is as surrealist and absurd as it is elliptical and anti-causal, making the viewing experience a challenge even for habitual art house filmgoers.

In addition to introducing the word and image dynamic and schematically suggesting the film's hermetic plot, the comic book opening sequence also presents the world of high fashion that will constitute the film's diegetic backdrop. As it spirals into a vortex of death, sex, and consumer excess, Aranda deftly interweaves the high fashion and detective subplots into the labyrinthine narrative via a playful poetics of *eros* and *thanatos*. Doing further work, the first sequence's material heterogeneity with its enriching references to publicity, newspapers, and photography also begins to set up the film's political potential, even as it defines one of the principal characteristics of the EdB's pop aesthetic.

The purpose of the "intermedial" enrichment that constitutes the EdB's brand is to bring "textural" qualities drawn from other media into (the) film, to fortify its potential for critique (by "textural" I am nodding to "text," from the Latin *textus*, a tissue or fabric, and from the Greek *texere*, to weave, all of these terms associated with tactility, touch, fabric, writing, weaving). Moreover, the aesthetic branding featured in *Fata Morgana* is distinctive of EdB films and premised on the world of '60s high fashion and Pop Art as reflected in mass culture media such as television and advertising. EdB filmmakers were conversant with Adorno's critique of the culture industry's connection to fascism and aware of mass media's manipulation of society into passivity and overconsumption. As such, the EdB's recourse to frivolous mass culture elements should be read in an ironic clef, and at least presents itself as paradoxical given the school's subversive tendencies. The EdB decidedly produced films that raised spectator consciousness in relation to relevant issues—censorship, consumerism, tourism—potentially energizing dissenters who at this late period of the *dictadura* were starved for something new, both aesthetically and politically. In brief, the blend of formal abstraction and political protest that framed Aranda's film and much of the EdB's filmography was paradoxically inscribed within (and critical of) both the consumer mass culture and the countercultural tendencies of the period.

Sharply stylized scenes populated by languid models and chic minimalist sets—an aesthetic shared with Antonioni's films and with Saura's *Pepermint Frappé* (1967)—provide *Fata Morgana* with the slick appearance of an advertisement for luxury commodities, which coupled with the murder and sexploitation theme make it seem hedonistic, frivolously commercial, and decidedly apolitical. An attentive reading reveals its subtext of cultural critique against commercialism and unfettered capitalism that is historically quite significant, given the rapid and unequal growth in the 1950s resulting from the "economic miracle" engineered by Franco's technocrats. As images on television and in the public space became increasingly commercialized, the EdB set about repurposing the strategies of advertising with the intent to shock the public out of their media-dulled sensibilities, highlighting the incongruence between the "mediocre" economic gains of the middle class and the lack of political freedom. Precisely by its parodic remediation of commercial advertising, and through the transformation of models into actresses, *Fata Morgana* forces a confrontation between high and mass culture aimed at destabilizing arbitrary dividing boundaries between high and low, in a somewhat playful but also threatening gesture to established artistic norms and, in like fashion, to established political structures.[19]

Additionally, the case can be made that the presence of text, comic book sequences, and advertising throughout *Fata Morgana* is doubly political in that it represents a constant refashioning of both print media and photography within the confines of a film that strikes against medium "purity" and against the political status quo that encouraged realist norms. The comic book's intromission blurs the line between comic and film, two modalities that promiscuously combine word and image. For Vilaseca, inserting the comic book sequence into the film subverts "the traditional hierarchy between fictional creation and the 'real world' (the latter appearing as a mimetic supplement of the former)" ("Deleuze" 29). Vilaseca's point identifies Aranda's use of metalepsis (a term I will return to later): *Fata Morgana*'s layering of pseudo-reality upon pseudo-reality, of comic strip and advertising within its diegesis, completely destabilizes the cinematic norms of realism and verisimilitude prevalent in Francoist documentaries (Noticiarios y Documentales [NO-DO]) and in social-realist cinema. Aranda himself explains this introduction of diverse genres as a "move to distract the censors' attention from the [film's] covert political implications" (D'Lugo 139).

The comic book sequence is not the only use of textual script and moving image in tandem. In a kinetic credit sequence that warrants scrutiny, both title and cast credits are cleaved into their constitutive syllables, which then glide off-screen in multiple directions (see fig. 2.4), as if dramatizing

Figure 2.4. *Fata Morgana*, title sequence and moving script (01:36). *Source: Fata Morgana* (1965). Dir. Vicente Aranda.

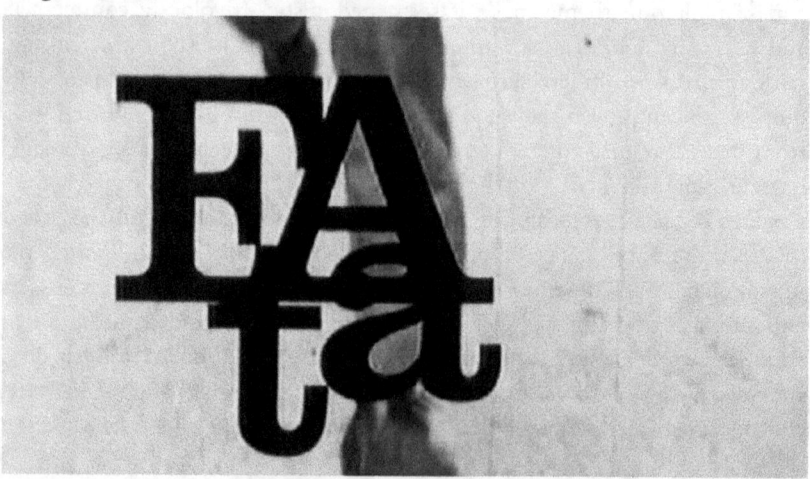

the film's pervasive form and content fragmentation. Also, this is what I would deem a Brossian moment, after Joan Brossa, the neo-Dadaist poet and visual artist that was closely affiliated with the EdB and famously fond of kinetic script and language games; here the letters are shaped like Brossa's letter poems and behave as if they had intent, as in the Catalan poet's lettrist works. A sobering intertitle follows the credits: "Note to the viewer: this film takes place after the events in London." Bookending the film with another intertitle, the last frame in *Fata Morgana* reads: "and then, the same thing happened as in London." These enigmatic references to some unexplained apocalyptic events add to the unease pervading the film. Critics contend that this evocation through words, not images, of some unknown cataclysm activates spectator memories of the unmentionable Spanish Civil War. *Fata Morgana* might therefore be read, as Galt speculates, in allegorical cue as "a traumatic text: one in which the historical experiences of Francoism cannot be spoken directly, and indeed are properly barred entirely from cognition. The film cannot speak about what happened in London, nor can it show what is to happen in Barcelona" ("Missed Encounters" 203). While allegorical interpretation risks oversimplification, decoding such hidden subtexts might also provide an entry point to understand the film contextually. In an astonishing self-reflexive move, *Fata Morgana*'s content mirrors its intermedial layering, as the unspeakable past (possibly the Civil War or its aftermath) supplements both Francoist oppression and 1960s fears of nuclear holocaust, rendering characters who, gripped by paralyzing anxieties, seem powerless to prevent impending doom (*fatum* or fate), whether the murder of the model-protagonist or some unnamable cataclysm. It is this paralysis, displayed by the characters and implicit in the spectator, that the film wishes to dislodge, like a mirage. The sense of unescapable fate refers indirectly to the film's title "Fata Morgana," a term that describes a mirage or optical illusion related to the refraction of light, one that makes objects seem closer than they are and has been reported at sea. A mirage, like propaganda, advertising, or audiovisual media.

In order to extricate a passive public drugged by advertising and by the regime-controlled television from their paralyzed state, Aranda's film arguably undermines the corporate tools that manipulate consumer society. As with Fluxus, the EdB's confrontational stance against television is paradoxically articulated through the strategies of both television and print advertising, revealing an aesthetic tension that negotiates between mass cultural and experimental modes, and that alternatively rejects and abandons itself to the inescapability of contemporary culture's mass media technologies.

Such tension productively reflects and problematizes the desire to possess and consume images. Thus, in one of the film's emblematic scenes, the elegant model Gim meanders through the desolate city and is accosted by male characters who have previously seen her in billboards and magazine advertisements, and therefore already view her physical body as a commodified extension of her graphic image, so that the model becomes for them an icon (to be worshipped), a mirage (to be dispelled), or an object (to be grasped) rather than an actual person. Multiplying this distancing effect, spectators are also first introduced to Gim through her photograph in the opening sequence and later see her in other publicity images before ever recognizing the "real" model on-screen. Yet the film also constantly recontextualizes and repurposes Gim's marketing image to deconstruct the insidious commercialism it represents by turning it into something quite different, a target for critique. For instance, in one scene Gim's sleek image (as it appears in a Cinzano vermouth billboard) becomes the fetishistic object of desire for some youths who steal it, parade it throughout the city, and ultimately enshrine it in their male clubhouse. The ritualistic fragmentation of the billboard—they only take the head and torso—is echoed elsewhere in the film by the photographs of murdered models depicted in impossibly twisted postures, thus establishing a nexus between commercialism, sadistic sexual desire, and death. By establishing the linkages "commercialism-desire-death," Gim's advertising image is resemantiziced to condemn the commodification of human beings in a world where bodies are routinely fragmented, consumed, and disposed of as waste. The fragmentation of images is formally paralleled by a fragmentation of text (as with the opening credits) and by discontinuities, non sequiturs, and nonsensical statements in the dialogue.

Dismembered in word and image, both the real Gim and her advertising effigy shuttle aimlessly between urban locations with no apparent purpose, as a kind of postmodern *flâneur*. For Nadal-Melsió, this nonlinear, illogical perambulation is tantamount to one more criticism of the political situation in Spain: "the global, cosmopolitan, and impossibly chic bodies that fill the screen bespeak an erasure of presence, as the characters in the film wander disoriented between the proliferation of an all-encompassing global capital and the silence and passivity imposed by Francoist rule" (467). Formal devices of text and image fragmentation underscore a political point, exposing the language of advertising as an empty, meaningless consumerism complicit with the regime's techno-capitalist fascism in the permanent deferral of the real. Granted, even considering the film's crypto-critique, the recourse to a fashion model (Gimpera) who had been featured in extradiegetic advertising campaigns, and the sleek advertising aesthetic, problematically renders an image of the EdB "productively sullied by commerce and consumerism" (Galt, "Mapping"). Nevertheless, the challenge to medium purity staged by the film reinforces, rather than detracts from, its critique of capitalism (so enthusiastically endorsed by Franco's regime as it touted its newly acquired, if modest, prosperity), and of the division of labor implied by material specificity. Indeed, the circulation of fragmented images of advertised commodities through an intermedial style of cinematic production that emphasizes process allows the filmmaker not only to critique capitalist modes of production, which insist on the whole, complete, and final "product," but also to question the unseen division of labor that manufactures both image and product. It seems evident that the fragmentation also poses a challenge to the "unity of the image" (Pethő 234), not just in a photographic but also a filmic sense, in fact narrativizing the deconstruction of the filmic medium in the act of "cutting-up" and editing text, images of models, advertising collages, and the very celluloid these assorted materials are inscribed into.

Furthermore, intermediality functions in *Fata Morgana* to critique artistic specialization and disunity (insofar as painters only paint, filmmakers only make films, etc.), promoting instead solidarity, cooperation, and combination within the arts in the spirit of the EdB and its followers. This artistic cooperation between filmmakers, poets, visual artists, and so on, even within the framework of an auteurist cinema that considers the director as the prime creator, recalls the practice by Lumbreras's Colectivo and other militant groups in taking turns at different roles within the creative collective, which they expressively did to avoid the trappings of class, hierarchy, and the division of labor according to capitalist models. As discussed in chapter 1, from a Marxist perspective, division of labor alienates the worker from her work, therefore, "the 'intermedia' discussion of the 1960s evidently interprets the concept in such a way that the 'specialization' into individual arts is a process comparable to the critique of the fact that people deem their work processes and the resulting products to be alien" (Schröter 120). Thus it is the case that Aranda's practice of an "impure" cinema functions on multiple levels as a counter-ideological art bent on undermining the Francoist system through its fragmented images, words, commodities, and landscapes.

Sexperiencias: Poetic Collage as Advertisement and/or Political Denunciation

Much like Vicente Aranda, and unlike many of their companions in the EdB, José María Nunes (1930–2010) came from a humble working-class family from Faro, Portugal. Emigrating with them to Barcelona at the age of twelve, the Nunes family lived in poverty in the shantytown at the foot of Montjuich. Nunes worked his way up from the most menial jobs in the film industry until his opportunity at a directorial debut with the film *Mañana . . .* (1957) [Tomorrow . . .], after which he joined the EdB group. *Sexperiencias*, his sixth film, is arguably his most successful work in terms of the interest it generated when it was (clandestinely) screened and on account of its long-lasting thematic relevance and enduring interest for film critics. It is arguably his most experimental piece, one in which intermediality is the paramount unifying aesthetic and political strategy aimed at rattling bourgeois sensibilities and condemning the sociopolitical status quo.

Like *Fata Morgana*, Nunes's *Sexperiencias* is set in an imprecise urban landscape (once again, a barely recognizable Barcelona stripped of landmarks), populated by nondescript cipher-like characters closer to types than to individuals and organized around a tenuous plot with no beginning or end. But unlike Aranda's movie, rather than presenting dismembered images of bodies or sobering yet ambiguous intertitles, *Sexperiencias* relies on text and image interactions in an overtly political intervention that strategically deploys newspaper headlines describing pivotal global events. As in Nunes's 1966 art film *Noche de vino tinto* (*Night of Red Wine*), *Sexperiencias* also revolves around two loners who are drawn to each other despite irreconcilable differences in age, sex, and social class. Schematically, *Sexperiencias* disjointedly "narrates" the impossible romance between María (Marta Mejías), a young idealistic woman, and Carlos (Portuguese actor Carlos Otero), a jaded older man, framed by the political happenings of 1968: the Prague Spring, the May 1968 student revolts, the assassinations of Martin Luther King Jr. and Robert F. Kennedy, the conflict in Biafra, the Vietnam War, and so on. The dialogue between the two protagonists is at times lyrically cryptic and at times highly referential and politically charged. The generational conflict is thematized through the couple's gestures and body language and made textually evident by the accusatory newspaper headlines charging the older generation with the dismal state of world affairs. The generation gap, reflecting a reality of the 1960s culture wars that pitted the young against their parents' generation, persists despite efforts by the two lovers to come together, romantically and ideologically, to overcome their significant age difference. Rapid cultural changes widen the distance between the young idealist played by María, representing the new left, and the cynical older man played by Carlos, representing an "old school" anarchist. As the film concludes, the woman protagonist marches off toward an unknown destination with the intention to do "something" to help bring about a change in the world, while the man stays behind, unwilling or afraid to cast his lot with her. Through María, Nunes foregrounds the freshness and enthusiasm of youth linked to a revolutionary collectivist spirit indebted to the 1959 Cuban Revolution. Through Carlos, he pays a nostalgic tribute to the Civil War–era anarchists, by 1968 in their fifties and sixties, who fought to preserve a utopian vision of the Republic (or for an even more utopian anarchist revolution) but were subsequently defeated and annulled by the lengthy dictatorship.

In this charged film intermedial strategies complement a tricontinental and transnational political perspective, the revolutionary media tactics making echo of the global winds of revolution. From its opening scenes *Sexperiencias* presents key international events through an intermedial collage of headlines and photos extracted from various newspapers (*Paris Match*, *L'Express*, *La Vanguardia*, *Mundo Obrero*) and read or commented by the protagonists' voice-over, often accompanied by the rebellious songs of the Nova Cançó or American folk music, including Bob Dylan (see fig. 2.5). In addition to these palimpsestic images, the film is full of posters and flyers on walls with everything from political slogans to photographs of cultural icons such as Che Guevara, Marilyn Monroe, President John F. Kennedy, and so on. Collage, produced by reassembling preexisting texts and images into a new work, draws some of its radical strength through its destruction of narrative discourse and its potential repurposing of the source material, as discussed in chapter 1 in relation to its use by militant filmmakers. That said, Nunes's approach is less dogmatic, in keeping with the art cinema nature of his film, closer to Rocha's insertion of photographs in *Terra em transe* than to the in-your-face collage by Santiago Álvarez, for instance. As we already saw in *Fata Morgana*, the fragmentation, repurposing, and remediation of the readymade elements of mass culture was an effective intermedial strategy mobilized by the EdB to subtly inscribe cultural and ideological critique in their films. Akin to Aranda's use of comics, Nunes's use of current event headlines introduces into the otherwise fictional narrative an element of metalepsis, defined as "any intrusion by the extradiegetic

138 | Expanding Cinemas

Figure 2.5. *Sexperiencias*, image from collage-montage opening sequence (02:01). *Source:* Filmed image from Feb. 12, 1968, issue of weekly French magazine (*L'Express*) *Sexperiencias* (1968). Dir. José María Nunes.

narrator or narratee into the diegetic universe (or by diegetic characters into a metadiegetic universe)" (Genette 234–35).

The sudden irruption into the diegesis of the extradiegetic "real"-world headlines (then still current and pressing in the spectators' consciousness) signals a narrative transgression that is matched by the formally transgressive intermediality and also underscores the film's political urgency. This is similar, again, to the use of the real photographs of starving children in Rocha's film. Breaking through the fictional border by providing the current event context shifts the film's positionality along the spectrum fiction-documentary, away from fictional narrative and toward the documentary pole, indeed toward an "experimental" and militant documentary form that seeks to transform the "real" world, although one that retains many aspects of the art film (its rejection of continuity editing, its elliptical narrative, characters that directly address the spectator, etc.). Moreover, the fragmented mixing of images and text—already present to a lesser degree in the source newspapers—connects the film with modernist art (Cubist, Dada, and Surrealist collage), and as in *Fata Morgana*, ironically mimics advertising's own promotion of consumerism through modernist collage. In that sense, *Sexperiencias* functions as a recuperation of the political possibilities of avant-garde collage techniques that had long been coopted by advertising, stripping the commercial message but keeping the sleek form. The characters read and comment on these world headlines, pondering what their course of action should be. Ultimately, the film provokes an unsettling dissonance between the urgency communicated by the troubling headlines and the political inaction of the characters, who gripped by anxiety (like in *Fata Morgana*), remain unable to take decisive measures.

In another instance of the metaleptic blend of real and fictional spaces, María and Carlos—in their role as stand-ins for the audience—repeat time and again that something *must* be done, as if explicitly exhorting passive spectators into militant action in the real world, presumably to do something against the Franco regime, although the words are never spoken. Another avant-garde tactic deployed by Nunes to raise spectator consciousness and disrupt realist narrative form through defamiliarization is his recourse to sound, often out of sync, at times silent, at times disconcertingly mismatched to the image. Granted, the film was dubbed, the actors recording their own voices over the silent images, which was a production necessity but also added to the sense of estrangement that Nunes deliberately sought. The incongruity and dissonant juxtaposition of text, image, and soundtrack disorients the spectator and augments anxiety, supplementing the extradiegetic tension caused by the sense of powerlessness in the face of political and cultural oppression. The film seems to be leading toward some resolution in a crescendo, but that tension is never fully released, transferring the unsatisfied desire for action to the spectator.

A key and oft-commented scene displays the film's complex palimpsestic layering of signs. In this scene, newspaper headlines and devastating photographs of the Vietnam War (recalling that in 1968 the war was in the midst of the fiercely bloody Tet offensive and constantly in the news) are jarringly overlaid with the off-screen sounds of a soccer match and interspersed with shots of the female protagonist's naked body covered with painted stick figures (see fig. 2.6). While the soccer match is easily interpreted as an example of the uses of spectacle for mass distraction within fascist regimes, the painted body resists deciphering. The schematic human figures might iconically represent the rising death toll in Southeast Asia,

Figure 2.6. *Sexperiencias* symbolic representation and metalepsis of global violence (37:00). *Source: Sexperiencias* (1968). Dir. José María Nunes.

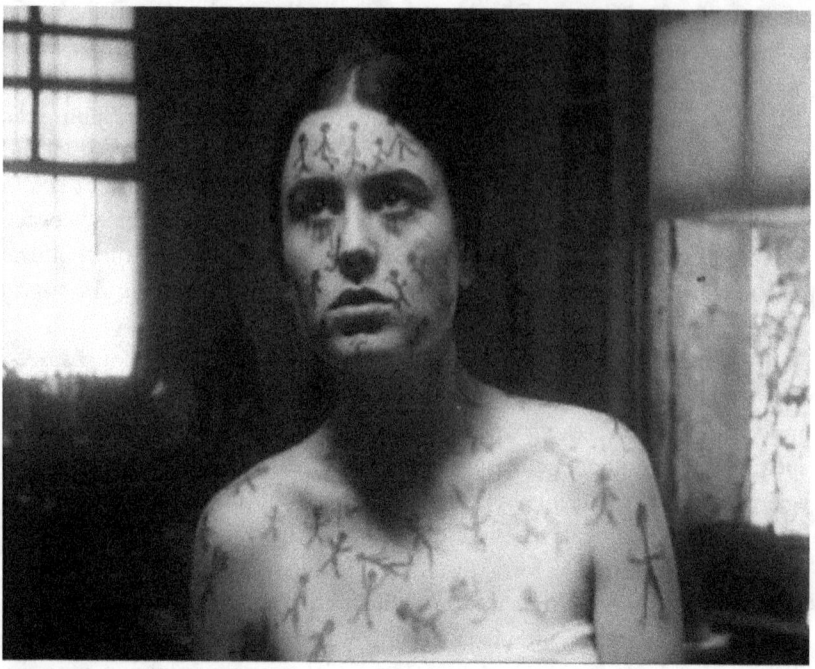

creating what Galt describes as "a surreal corporeality" ("Impossible" 497). Thus, the body art inscribes representational elements of the world onto María's flesh. Incongruously, María is a (fictional) character in the film, while the stick figures stand for (real) human deaths, thus the film engages a complex form of metaleptic transgression between fictive and real worlds, which as we have seen serves in EdB cinema to challenge both (realist) narrative and (capitalist) politics.

Nunes's aggressive editing further complicates the metaleptic amalgamation of reality and representation. The scene alternates in a rapid montage between glimpses of María's actual painted body and fragments from an equally decorated and somewhat uncanny mannequin's "body." María's nudity is only insinuated since we do not glimpse anything other than her arms, head, and uppermost torso, while the mannequin's anatomically inaccurate lower body only superficially simulates nudity. While cleverly resolving the impossibility of showing the naked body, or the dead corpses, and in so doing making a veiled reference to censorship, Nunes also uses the image of the fragmented mannequin to indict consumer society in a move evocative of Aranda's critical deployment of fashion models in *Fata Morgana*. Linking the mannequin to the models is only natural since in Spanish the word *maniquí* also means fashion model and has the negative connotation of being all surface and little substance. At any rate their connection to both consumer capitalism and death is clear: the role of the display mannequin is to lure consumers into making a purchase; at the same time they are inanimate, "dead" objects only performing "aliveness," a classic example of the Freudian uncanny. Furthermore, by covering both María's fragmented body and the dismembered mannequin with graphic marks that symbolize Vietnam's dead (and the dead in other global conflicts), Nunes makes palpable the connection between the upheavals in 1968 and capitalist exploitation, between high fashion in the First World and destruction in the Third. Viewed as such, the political stakes the film presents amount to nothing less than a demand for (universal) human rights and a condemnation of capitalism (although admittedly these projects might not always coincide).[20] This universal antiwar stance becomes a concrete accusation against Vietnam, but it also relates that US war of aggression to the Spanish conflagration of 1936—a strategy deployed by Nunes but also present in the next film I discuss, *Nocturno 29*, where "Como cineastas con afinidades comunistas, Joan Brossa y Pere Portabella sentían una necesidad ineludible de abordar el tema [Vietnam], y a tal fin ingeniaron un medio de referirse a todas las guerras, tanto a la Guerra antiimperialista del Vietnam como a la guerra civil (que había dado paso al régimen militar)" (Torrell 453) [As filmmakers with communist sympathies Joan Brossa and Pere Portabella felt a need to broach the Vietnam subject, so they devised a method to refer to all wars, whether the war of imperialist aggression in Vietnam or the Civil War that enabled the military regime].

I would argue that the disruptive and confrontational intrusion of collage-like newspaper clippings negates the "pure" materiality of the celluloid (by introducing a "trace" of newsprint even if only as an image on celluloid). Additionally, the newsprint fragments reference cinema's ontology as isolated still images stitched together and projected at twenty-four frames-per-second, foregrounding film's status as a constructed medium grounded in visual, textual, and aural traditions, and therefore exposing its supposed specificity as mere illusion (analogous to the effect of continuous motion produced by filmic persistence of vision). Film, in other words, is made of image (plus textual and aural) fragments collaged together through the photographic process. In this ingenious fashion—by "collaging" together political headlines into the film's fabric—Nunes fuses the ideological content with an aesthetic of intermediality. Not coincidentally Carlos is a printmaker (and a typographer, typesetters having traditionally been affiliated with the Spanish anarchist movement), often at work making posters whose content we are never allowed to see; we are left wondering if they are anti-Francoist flyers ("octavillas") or publicity images of svelte models selling some vapid beauty product—more likely, in an echo of the EdB's own duality, Carlos does publicity work for a living and creates the political flyers at night. Carlos unites the figure of the craftsman worker and the artist-intellectual all in one, unifying their class division much as Nunes himself did, from impoverished origins into the intelligentsia. In fact, Carlos's concern with the materiality of print (typesetting, headlines, protest flyers) is further complemented by his drawing skills and his guitar playing—in one scene he plays while singing a political song in Portuguese, establishing yet another nexus between his "intermedial" interests and an act of protest against the other Iberian fascist dictatorship (Antonio Salazar, who remained in power in Portugal until deposed by the 1970 Carnation Revolution).

Near the melancholic close of the film María leaves Carlos to go "do something," supposedly something political. Carlos has been a faithful mentor and lover, but he lacks the *élan vital* necessary to pursue this new fight, so María moves on. As stated before, her decision is emblematic of a general criticism presented by the film and present in 1960s counterculture, setting the young generation against the old, the new left against the old left. And just as the youth counterculture rejects their parents' materialism in a search for something better, so the film rejects pure cinema in favor of something else. Nevertheless, Nunes's film, despite its "experimental" art cinema status, also denies a cinema based only on the abstract image (such as American structuralist film), relying instead on some limited narrative (albeit lyrical and fragmented), on a surreptitious political (anti-Francoist) message, and on poetic dialogues.

Nunes's style addresses the spectator directly and in specific ways: his use of newspaper collage invites the audience to reflect upon worldwide events and by extension alludes to the untenable political situation posed by Francoism and by the cultural hegemony it forced on the Spanish people. At the core of the film's concerns are questions of material and materialism, in its critique of "the problematic duality of an economic liberalization which arrived hand in hand with a still significant degree of political repression" (Vilarós, "Cine y literatura" 203). The characters reject the mediocre economic gains and demand political transformation. Nunes's confrontational politics, a product of the 1960s zeitgeist, is integrally connected to his understanding of experimental cinema as filmmaking aimed at disrupting and stimulating the spectator into action (*against* the regime and the consumerist onslaught of capital), a cinema suffused by the angst and urgency to effect change despite the difficulties of radical action. Therefore, it is inscribed in a tradition of a cinema that wants to act upon reality, not just represent it, defying the facile categorization of Second Cinema as lacking in commitment, in fact, further eroding the division between Second and Third Cinemas that we have seen in other works.

Nocturno 29: Poetic Subversion of the Advertising *Filmlet*

Portabella's film *Nocturno 29* has been meticulously analyzed by a couple of critics. For instance, Josep Torrell has examined its political allegory, assigning various symbolic roles to the film's characters, which, as in Rocha's movies, approximate types rather than actual individuals. *Nocturno 29* is an episodic film whose narrative structure, according to Torrell, approximates poetry. Steven Marsh has performed an insightful formal reading, which without ignoring the political allegory subsumes it to questions of form and materiality, demonstrating that *Nocturno 29* is, "in its initial composition, an intermedial work, and that intermediality—that is, the film's formal properties—marks its relation to the political conjecture" (*Spanish Cinema* 46–47). My own reading will, like Marsh's, also straddle queries about intermediality and politics, more specifically considering the form of the "filmlet" and how it is deployed by Portabella to radicalize form and content alike.

Nocturno 29 (1968) was inherently intermedial and conceived as a mix of arts and genres, as one might expect from the product of a close collaboration between director Pere Portabella, neo-avant-garde poet Joan Brossa, and experimental pianist Carles Santos. In truth, all three of these artists are themselves polymaths that resist being defined as director, poet, and musician, respectively, considering themselves artisans in a larger sense. Case in point, Brossa, an accomplished visual poet, contributed to the creation of both the script and the cinematography of *Nocturno 29*. Brossa's central role in Portabella's films of the 1960s cannot be overstated since the poet was a living link between the 1930s and '40s Surrealist avant-garde movement and the 1960s neo-avant-garde's intermedial practices.[21] Portabella, who referred to Brossa as his "ideal interlocutor," recognized fully the influence the poet had on his filmmaking, stating that "during production, I respected the literary origin of some of his ideas and gave them a different treatment so as to highlight the interdisciplinary nature of the film's structure, but *Nocturno 29* was [also] the consolidation of our shared language—indicative of a system and an internal logic adapted to my purposes as a film director" (Portabella).

Portabella's filmmaking style, with its careful construction and interrelation of sight and sound, is characterized by interdisciplinarity and genre ambiguity. In Marsh's words, Portabella creates "an acoustic image and an image of the acoustic" ("Legacies" 552). For Portabella, an important part of sound is in fact silence, a concept with obvious aesthetic and political connotations in Franco's Spain. The only audible sound as *Nocturno 29* opens is the nostalgic whirring of a film projector. The initial images are a horizontal pan of a sparse landscape. A figure appears in the horizon, walking toward the camera. Once in close-up, the figure is shown as a long-haired young man, perhaps a hippy or beatnik, wearing a ratty fur coat. Then, presented in medium close-up through a series of defamiliarizing jump cuts, the man slowly turns around as the camera rotates around him in the opposite direction. This camera movement is evocative, quite possibly a citation, of a memorable scene in Glauber Rocha's 1964 *Deus e o diabo na terra do sol*. It is the iconic "kiss scene" between the outlaw *cangaçeiro* Corisco and Rosa, an embrace set to Heitor Villa-Lobos's *Bachiana Brasileira no. 5* (coincidentally sung by Catalan soprano Victoria de los Ángeles), in which the camera effectuates a similar rotation and set of jump cuts. Returning to *Nocturno 29*, the male character is soon joined by a woman, alone in the dessert-like landscape. In a surrealist moment that combines the sexually liberated, the revolting, and the bizarre to mock bourgeois sensibilities, the two nondescript beatniks remove some of their clothing, pick at bloody scabs with a safety pin, and get ready to make love. This oneiric sequence lasts several minutes but ends abruptly when the film "breaks," revealing as it unravels its material nature. Indeed, Portabella effectively mimics on-screen the visual effect of a torn filmstrip as it passes through the projector and follows that shocking instant of self-awareness with some rather astonishing images. Regarding this rather abrupt break Marsh observes that the sonorous undoes the visual, just as the experimental maneuver undermines the film's more "realistic" start: "the image is overtracked by the prosaic cranking rhythms of a film camera. Once more the process of naturalization is undone by the artificial mechanism of the apparatus, and the visual is subverted by the sonorous" (*Spanish Cinema* 53).

The next shots (which evoke Duchamp's readymades) are of a chair, which has been denaturalized as such (its back and seat canning removed) and is presented as a visual or object poem quite characteristic of Brossa's neosurrealist tendencies (see fig. 2.7). The chair is, in fact, very similar to an object poem that Brossa dedicated to the Spanish poet Miguel Hernández, a heroic icon of Spain's defeated Republic who died in a Francoist prison in 1942. Without a seat, bare boned, the chair might indeed symbolically stand for a skeleton, or perhaps for the bareness of trees during winter. This last interpretation seems to be supported by yet another object poem—also an installation piece—on display at the Brossa Foundation in Barcelona, consisting of a rocking chair without its seat and back caning and surrounded by dead leaves. The rocking chair can be allegorically read as a symbol of the Spanish people under the long Francoist winter, devoid of "leaves" (the soul) and always ready to utter a sycophantic "yes" with its rocking movement. This allegorical reading, of course, does not deny or contradict the formal and aesthetic impetus of the sequence (and the EdB's penchant for formalism more broadly). The scene pays direct homage to Surrealism and to the first avant-gardes, marking the EdB as a successor to the earlier movements. This connection is established through the neo-Dadaist Brossa, whose art embodied the new avant-garde spirit, but also, as Marsh has

Figure 2.7. *Nocturno 29* Visual-object poem by Joan Brossa within film (08:52). Source: *Nocturno 29* (1968). Dir. Pere Portabella.

suggested, because *Nocturno 29* is filmed in Port Lligat, where Dalí lived and worked, in the same landscape that the Surrealist artist captured in his paintings, nearby where he and Buñuel collaborated on films and also where Man Ray, Marcel Duchamp, and later Glauber Rocha would photograph, paint, and film, respectively (Marsh, *Spanish Cinema* 54).

Many of these geolocated traces of the past (situated in Northern Catalonia: Barcelona, Port Lligat, Cap de Creus, Cadaqués) are marked by intermedial culture and transnational flows of artists and artistic movements (Surrealism, Dada, neo-Dada, etc.) and they point back to Brossa as the nexus, the poet-painter-sculptor-entertainer-magician polymath, arguably Portabella's artistic confidant and lyrical muse. This brings us back to the radical role played by Brossa's poetry in Portabella's film. As a type of poetry that already pushes the limits of its own ontological status as poem (as a conventionally understood structure of rhymed script), destabilizing the notion that the lyrical is only present in written or oral form, Brossa's object poetry (*poema objeto*) acts subversively both against traditional poetic genres and as a poetic force within the cinematic image. In the opening sequence I am discussing, the chair proceeds to transform itself visually into a celluloid fragment, underscoring the film-poetry connection, and eventually links itself to the body of a mysterious, *commedia dell'arte* inspired harlequin (a *pierrot*), who enigmatically and militaristically marches off-screen in an uncertain direction (see fig. 2.8). The juxtaposition of the two unrelated segments and the abrupt celluloid break marks another instance of metalepsis: it might indicate a breach between the idyllic and seemingly "real" world of the young couple and another ontological level that remains unexplainable. Ambiguously, the sequence suggests that things are not quite as they appear (or should be), and, once again, the political connotations of this abrupt (Buñuelian) attack on vision, "ripping" the veil from the spectator's eyes, becomes quite evident. This sequence also confirms Brossa's obsessive interest in magic, already present in Portabella's previous short *No compteu amb els dits* (*Don't Count on Your Fingers*, 1967), a film that structures a series of fragmentary and disconnected pseudo-publicity spots, leaving it to the spectator to tease out a meaning from its surrealist, indeed magical logic. It is also no coincidence that both Portabella's films and Brossa's poems feature a recurring imagery of top hats, playing cards, and sleight-of-hand trickery, which served to denounce the Francoist system's own prestidigitation as it presented a superficially modernized Spain to the world, while a more sober reality reigned at home. Franco himself then might be allegorized as a sinister clown (such as *Nocturno*'s harlequin-*pierrot*) or evil warlock who

Figure 2.8. *Nocturno 29* the enigmatic *pierrot* figure (08:44). *Source: Nocturno 29* (1968). Dir. Pere Portabella.

hides, Oz-like, behind the curtain of his projected lies but whose cheap trickery could easily be exposed if only someone would "rip" through the veneer of the official discourse. This is the reading offered by Torrell, who interprets the opening as contrasting the younger generation's desire for freedom with the authoritarian pierrot who is unconcerned by demands for democracy. For Torrell, the scene shows that there is no place for the young in this Spain (453). Marsh, in contrast, is decidedly more interested in "how the politics of *Nocturno 29* emerge in the film's formal practice and via the interstices of filmic composition in ways that extend beyond the limits and limitations of a univocal interpretation as allegory, as *only* anti-Francoist discourse" (*Spanish Cinema* 46). Again, whether focusing on the admittedly transparent allegorical-political reading or centering on what is occurring formally as the driving mechanisms within the film, what is evident is that intermediality holds the key to both—and both form and content work together inextricably so as to make them inseparable in the analysis, whether using a somewhat rigid symbolic decoding or a lyrical exploration of form and what it evokes.

None of these aspects of style or substance are haphazard. Portabella has detailed how the superficially incoherent *Nocturno 29* is the product of a meticulously calculated narrative structure. For the Catalan director, the film's narrative structure is based on "una serie o suite de situaciones que, aunque aparentemente inconexas, giran siempre en torno a un desarrollo temático, que da 'cuerpo' y unidad a la historia sin recurrir para ello a la utilización de una anécdota como continuidad argumental" (Expósito 244) [a series of situations that, although seemingly unconnected, revolve around a thematic development that provides heft and cohesion to the story without needing to rely on the anecdote to provide plot continuity].

The intense lyrical nature of the opening sequence defines it as a kind of poetry, a genre that, like film, eludes medium specificity by resisting a tangible description of what its "materials" are. These can be oral, written, or as in the case of most of Brossa's work, visual and conceptual. Yet the film, which functions as a poetry-film hybrid, also negates traditional hierarchies that mark one media as superior to the other. For Portabella, both film and poetry (as well as music) function through images *and* through text and sound. In fact, his collaboration with Brossa was an equal partnership, which allowed Portabella to approach film from an essentially non-filmic perspective, as he himself stated: "no me interesaba ver el cine desde el cine" (Expósito 245) [I was not interested in understanding cinema from within cinema], meaning, he wanted to approach it eccentrically (or intermedialy), from the perspective of other arts, such as poetry or music.

Through its strange title *Nocturno 29* (which immediately signals a musical composition, or a nighttime themed lyrical poem, as Marsh and others have noted), the film establishes a crypto-political message that also demonstrates Portabella's highly structured, even fastidiously meticulous, approach to filmmaking. Twenty-nine (29) corresponds to the number of years from the end of the Spanish Civil War and defeat of the Republic in 1939 until the film's release in 1968, marking nearly three decades of darkness, silence, and political repression.[22] Twenty-nine is also the number of sequences in the film, short fragments that do not follow a traditional narrative development but rather work independently, episodically, as poems in an anthology or as television advertisements or *filmlets*, a concept I will return to in short.

Portabella's poetics of discontinuity becomes overtly political in a particularly provocative sequence. In fact, it is one of two sequences "mutilated" by the censors as a sine qua non condition for the film's theatrical release. In this sequence a man arrives to what we presume is his home, enters a room, turns on the television, and begins watching a military parade. Strictly controlled by the regime, television was, along with the NO-DO, the preferred method of state propaganda, arguably the most efficient mass medium for political indoctrination and the promotion of consumer capitalism. The televised event, possibly the yearly commemoration on July 18 of the "Glorioso Alzamiento" [Glorious Uprising] marking the outbreak of the fascist rebellion in 1936, seems to be taking place in Barcelona as identified by the Columbus statue at the end of the Ramblas (itself a colonialist symbol of the regime's nostalgia for empire), a rare geographical marker for an EdB film. The man sits down in a plush armchair and proceeds to pluck out his eyes, slowly, one at a time. This highly symbolic, Oedipal gesture, as Torrell suggests in his reading, likely signifies a refusal to look at the militarized image of the city, once an autonomous bastion of Republicanism, now subjugated to Madrid's centralist control; for Torrell the man is likely the symbolic embodiment of the clandestine opposition to the regime (453). Setting aside the interpretation of the sequence as a scenification of Oedipal desires to kill Franco as the putative father (or better yet, *padrastro*) of the nation—Kinder has already explored connections between Oedipality and politics in Spanish postwar cinema (*Blood Cinema* 13)—let us consider the tribute rendered to the first Surrealist avant-garde by the scene. Surely the Buñuelian overtones of this savage attack on vision cite the opening of *Un chien andalou*, which should not surprise us given Portabella's close ties to the Surrealist filmmaker whom he worked with as the producer of the controversial film *Viridiana* (1961).

Nonetheless, the eye-plucking sequence remains ambiguous enough to stand symbolically as opposition not just to the regime but by extension to all the other global conflicts already mentioned in the context of *Sexperiencias*. The outcry here echoes tricontinental discourses against right-leaning authoritarianism and US-backed wars of aggression in developing nations—marking a kind of orthodox communist response in line, for example, with discourses promoted by Cuba's *Tricontinental* magazine. The man's refusal to watch the "official" story might also be an exhortation to "open" one's eyes to the real political conditions, directed at the spectator, at the working class, or at other sectors opposed to Franco. But more broadly, it signifies a condemnation of First World capitalist accumulation and global inequality (as exemplified by later scenes located at the staunchly conservative private club Círculo Equestre [Equestrian Circle] and at the posh Banco Hispano Americano in the privileged Gràcia district). The eye-gouging scene is simultaneously a political and an aesthetic intervention, political since it decries the official discourse represented by the parade, aesthetic because it represents the act of resistance in a symbolic, nonnaturalistic, stylized fashion that rejects social realism: there is no blood and the eyes are patently fake, prosthetic, surreal (like the eyes of a mannequin), eyes that reappear in various other visual and object poems by Brossa. The self-mutilation remains concealed from spectators (obscene, from the Latin *obscaena*, offstage, as with Oedipus's act), filmed from behind the armchair in a somber high-key lighting that suffuses the scene with a neosurrealist aesthetic that intensifies its jarring effect. Thus, the victorious narrative shown on the television is disrupted, indeed dismembered, and replaced by a counternarrative of uncanny horror, of obscenity. The spectator, however, is censored from seeing the event directly, denied its autopsy so to speak (*autopsy*, from the Greek "to see with one's own eyes," as we would learn from Stan Brakhage's celebrated 1971 film *The Act of Seeing with One's Own Eyes*).

On a formal level, this eye-popping sequence denies medium specificity, not just through its connection to Brossa's impactful visual poetry but also through its incorporation of another medium, the television, which transmits the regime's propaganda in audiovisual form. Brossa, who undoubtedly inspired the cruel "visual" pun of the removal of the eyes, was himself no stranger to the disruption of mediatic boundaries. As Fèlix Fanés has observed: "although poetry was the central aspect of his creative corpus, [Brossa] had always diversified his creative efforts, taking them toward other territories such as theater and object art. (By abandoning medium specificity and embracing different [artistic] languages, Brossa internalized the surrealist and dada legacies" [472].)

Previously I argued that the EdB structured its opposition to both the regime and the irresponsibly apolitical commercialism of a newly prosperous Spain through its critique against *and* its incorporation/appropriation of the tools of advertising, fashion, and propaganda. In the case of *Nocturno 29*, this is reflected thematically through the negative depiction of bourgeois subjects and structurally through the use of *filmlets*, short commercial spots that were becoming prevalent in Spain at that time and from which Portabella "drained all its commercial purpose" (Fanés 474). According to Portabella:

> Apareció este nuevo espacio cinematográfico: los *filmlets*. . . . Partimos de una estructura que el espectador ya conocía y nuestro trabajo consistía en *extraer su significado y darle otro distinto*; siendo al mismo tiempo una forma de ruptura con la narrativa aristotélica. (Expósito 245–46, my emphasis)

> [This new cinematic space appeared: the filmlet. We began with a structure that the spectator was already familiar with, and our

job was to *extract its meaning and give it another*; it was a break with Aristotelian narrative.]

In Francoist Spain, *filmlets* were used by advertisers to bombard the captive spectator with ads prior to the screening of a feature film, taking advantage of reiterative name branding and seeking immediate impact through very intense, short pieces. Interestingly, the largest company to use these short spots in Spain, Movierecord, was owned by the pro-regime ultra-Catholic organization Opus Dei, demonstrating the unholy alliance between the fascist-capitalist state, religion, and advertising (Riambau 217). In *Nocturno 29* Portabella succeeds in subverting the original intention of the *filmlets* to fight against its mechanisms of control, that is, to awaken the spectators from their passive condition and release them from the grip of consumerism. Portabella unhinged viewer expectations and destabilized established patterns of spectatorship by exposing the ossified status quo of mainstream cinema and through his provocative reappropriations of the crassest and soulless forms of consumer capitalism present in Franco's "different" and "open" Spain. We could say that Portabella's Brechtian style of filmmaking, like Nunes's more overt political style and Aranda's enigmatically allegorical mode, successfully demystified Francoist discourse and exposed the problematic role of corporate advertising in propping up a moribund but in many ways still lethal regime. These films were not lost on Glauber Rocha, who seized the opportunity to ally himself with the EdB to produce a transnational film that ultimately exposed the synergies and dissonances between Cinema Novo and the EdB. Next, I turn to Rocha's Iberian film debacle, *Cabeças cortadas*, situating it within an anti-authoritarian vein considering what we have learned about the EdB's position against Francoist discourses, but also examining how the movie strayed into the at times nihilist irrationality of the most absurd Surrealist experiments. It is worthy of note that, irrespective of the failure that *Cabeças cortadas* became, both in terms of its aesthetic and political dimensions, Rocha was and remained highly respected by Buñuel and Portabella, the former stating that he wished to be half as talented a filmmaker as the Brazilian auteur (Casas 338).

Cabeças cortadas as (Failed) Transnational Allegory

It was an involute confluence of personal and historical events that brought Rocha to Spain in 1969 to make what would become his most obscure and reviled film, *Cabeças cortadas*, after he "voluntarily" exiled himself from

Brazil, seeking novel creative horizons and greater artistic freedom as well as dodging potential political persecution. *Cabeças* is a movie that neither critics nor spectators appreciated but that Rocha always defended as an imperfect but neoteric film, one that broke with many cinematic norms regarding plot and character and had been profoundly misunderstood and unfairly maligned (Pierre, *Glauber Rocha* 62). For Rocha, who was unwilling to admit the film's real shortcomings, its failure was merely a reflection of a lack of imagination by film critics and further proof of the repressive hold that Western rationalism exerted on creativity (perhaps he also credited some adversity in the production of the movie). The filmmaker declared that "la deconstrucción radical de *Cabeças cortadas* chocó a la crítica racionalista formalista occidental y el contra-discurso contracultural marginó un texto cinematográfico innovador que materializaba directamente la verdad histórica a través de una estructuración trascendente del inconsciente" (qtd. in Rocha, Asín and Pitarch) [the film's radical deconstruction shocked the rationalist-formalist Western critics, and (even) the countercultural counter-discourse marginalized an innovative cinematic text that materialized historical truth directly through a transcendent structuring of the subconscious]. With this rather convoluted statement, Rocha identifies several structuralist and post-structuralist currents that inform his work, including Marxism, deconstruction, Freudian psychoanalysis, and arguably surrealism, which the Brazilian filmmaker intimates as tools necessary to interpret his film, a film that Marsh describes in a single word, "chaotic" (*Spanish Cinema* 54). By the late 1960s and early 1970s Rocha was fully immersed in a surrealist phase, although arguably Surrealism had always been present in his films. Regrettably, Rocha's earnest attempt to capture the subconscious in moving images fell flat with audiences and (most) critics, but his film warrants some attention because it lives up to the vision of a truly transcontinental, transatlantic enterprise; because it enacts every intermedial strategy we have considered thus far; and because it brings together, albeit in self-destructive fashion, the threads of Latin American and European art cinema discourses.

The film, despite its obtuse ideological message, was originally censored in Brazil for unknown reasons but was released in 1978, precisely because censors thought it was so hermetical that any underlying political subtext would be unintelligible to audiences (Glauber, *Mostra* 38). Humberto Pereira da Silva writes that Rocha partly wished to make a film in Spain on account of the country's cultural and historical ties to Latin America, as well as its lengthy association with surrealist cinema through Buñuel and Dalí and more recently the EdB directors (79–118). Hence, Rocha decided to film in Cadaqués (in the Catalan region of Ampurias), the same place where Buñuel and Dalí had filmed *L'Âge d'or* (*The Golden Age*, 1930) and near where Portabella filmed various scenes of *Nocturno 29*. Thus he rendered *Cabeças cortadas* as a kind of surrealist homage to the Aragonese filmmaker (Buñuel had also recently returned from exile) and also inserted his movie into a longer tradition of irrational art (Pereira da Silva 88–89). Remarking on these pervading bonds between the EdB and Rocha to Surrealism and Dada, as well as their shared choices for filming locations, Marsh declares that "this trace structure—of personalities, films, paintings, and places—forms a locus around a surrealist genealogy" (*Spanish Cinema* 54). Rosalind Galt also makes a fair argument for this aesthetic association between Rocha-Buñuel and surrealism and stipulates how the legacy of the older Spanish-Mexican cineaste may have weighed on the choices of the young Brazilian, and may have served as inspiration to create a film with sweeping transnational import:

> For Rocha, as for Buñuel, the Barcelona School was part of what drew him to Franco's Spain. He encountered the group in Barcelona, and Ricardo Muñoz Suay became both executive producer and assistant director on *Cabeças cortadas*. Thus, while Spain was a seemingly unlikely destination for the Marxist director, Rocha found in Cadaqués both a past and present significance. The desolate landscape of Cap de Creus evokes *L'Âge d'or*, but, for Rocha, it also spoke of Brazil and Brazzaville, of anti-colonialism, exile, and displacement. *Cabeças cortadas* links the Barcelona School, Third Cinema and the historic avant-garde, locating the School firmly within a network of global cinematic engagement, a history of radical response to the violent injustices of the 20th century. While most critics, even those in Catalonia, tended to see their political situation as cordoned off from the world and the Barcelona School as marginal even to Catalan cinema, Cadaqués demonstrates the global centrality of this limit point of Spain. ("Mapping")

While possibly overstating the significance of *Cabeças*, Galt's point about the kinship between Rocha (and by extension Cinema Novo) and the EdB is accurate, as is her assessment of the avowedly transnational dimension of the project. Ironically, Buñuel, who admired Rocha's first three films, despised *Cabeças cortadas*, furiously shouting that it was nonsense when he first saw it at a Madrid screening (García Garzón 298). Nonsense was, in some respects, what the Brazilian sought in a film that was explicitly created to explore the irrational side of power and its corrosive potential, but the results were likely more nonsensical than anticipated.

Besides wishing to chart the irrational subconscious, Rocha also hoped to cement his status as a tricontinental filmmaker and expand anti-capitalist and anti-colonialist cinema beyond those three initial continents (Asia, Africa, and Latin America), into the very heart of capital and imperialism, Europe (although in its arguably less developed periphery). In a theoretical text where he defines the tricontinental filmmaker, Rocha includes both Buñuel and Godard in this category, making a case for reading "tricontinentality" beyond geographical borders, as the creation of a political transnational cinema: "The operative word is ideology, and it knows no geographical boundaries. When I speak of Tricontinental cinema and include Godard [or Buñuel] in this grouping, it is because his work opens a guerrilla-like operation in the cinema: he attacks suddenly and unexpectedly, with pitiless films. His cinema becomes political because it proposes a strategy, a valuable set of tactics, usable in any part of the world" (Rocha, "Tricontinental Filmmaker" 80). Rocha will try to apply these "guerilla-like" tactics in *Cabeças*, a film he intended as a crushing critique of coloniality from within a former colonial empire. Filming in Catalonia was an added tangible irony in a movie that recycles and ridicules imagery from imperial Spain and literally drags the symbols of empire (monarchy, colonial territory, chivalry) through the muck, as Rocha channels a kind of cinematic Cervantes espousing a critique of Western legacies.

Despite their transnational character and surrealist bent, Rocha's exile films did not render setting as trivial or national identity as irrelevant. As it happens, *Cabeças cortadas*'s loose plot is partly motivated by the choice of setting, since the now aging Diaz II (ostensibly the same dictator as his *Terra em transe* namesake, here played by the Spanish star Francisco Rabal), is now exiled in Spain, becoming increasingly unhinged and living out his latter days amidst his rancid memories, a Latin American King Lear with a significant dose of Macbeth, and at times even Don Quijote.[23] Densely referential, the film is a veritable palimpsest of literary, artistic, and musical intertexts. In addition to its nods to Shakespeare's *King Lear*, *Macbeth*, and *The Tempest*, the film contains myriad allusions, overt and subtle, to Goya's *Disasters of War* prints and Dalí's surrealist paintings, to Cervantes's *Don Quijote*,[24] to the medieval epics *Tirant lo Blanc* and *Romance del Mio Cid*, to the Spanish picaresque novel, to Valle Inclán's *Tirano Banderas* (1926), to the surrealist poetry and theater of Federico García Lorca, to a mediocre adaptation of *Macbeth* by León Felipe entitled *Macbeth o el asesino del sueño* (1954) [Macbeth or the Murderer of Sleep], to Borges's short stories, to Buñuel's cinematography (especially *L'Âge d'or* and *Simón del desierto*), and, as some critics have contended, to the magical realism of Gabriel García Márquez, who was present during the filming and was at that very moment writing *El otoño del patriarca* (*The Autumn of the Patriarch*, 1975) (Fuentes and Vera 265; Cardoso 113; Sanderson; Elduque, "O touro" 455–65; Gutierrez 97). Unfortunately, this mélange of references was much too muddled to be easily discernible by critics or spectators, who were left with the impression of a cacophony of ideas and tendencies, of voices and murmurs. This layered intertextuality, however, went in tandem with an intense commitment to intermediality, as I shall argue. First, a brief synopsis of the plot is helpful before proceeding with the analysis.

The film has a schematic plot, and like other surrealist films it loosely associates a series of oneiric, trance-like, and otherwise disconnected scenes around the figure of Emmanuel Diaz II. The main character's madness, modeled on King Lear's and Don Quixote's, is triggered by feelings of guilt and remorse about having enslaved, exploited, and murdered his subjects in Eldorado—we find this out from Diaz's telephone conversations with his henchmen and ex-lovers back home, and through his ravings, hallucinations, and delusional monologues. The decrepit ailing monarch (read an ailing Franco here) spends much of the film pursuing pleasures of the flesh or wallowing in abject degradation. He relives past glories, exiled in a ruinous medieval castle, while the modernized forces of rebellion plot against him. Meanwhile, Diaz interacts with his doctor and his priest, plays with tiny models of caravels (a mockery of discovery and conquest), and replicates colonialism by enslaving an indigenous peasant and a Mexican man, both of whom seem as anachronistic and out of place as the crumbling medieval fortifications and the brocade wardrobe worn by Diaz and his "court." In this film Rocha magnifies the Latin American baroque's use of anachronism (here overlaid, exaggerated, amplified) that collapses medieval, colonial, and contemporary times and that the filmmaker had already unleashed in *Terra em transe*. A mystical shepherd (played by Pierre Clémenti) roams the countryside carrying a scythe and performing miracles while he foments an uprising against Diaz, recalling of other messianic figures in Rocha films such as Sebastião.[25] An archetype and symbolic figure, the scythe-carrying shepherd is dressed entirely in white—the color of death in Islam. Fittingly, he is the harbinger of Diaz's eventual destruction. After the prophetic shepherd restores sight and mobility to a blind paralytic peasant, his mystical reputation grows and he is acclaimed as the messiah who will bring Diaz to justice. Accurately prophesied, the shepherd-reaper will ritualistically cut off the dictator's head in one of the final scenes, just one of many severed heads as the title indicates. Concurrently, leftist guerrilla revolutionaries arrive from Eldorado to overthrow Diaz. Diaz's queen, Doña Soledad, loosely modeled on Lady Macbeth, has three sons who dispute the right to Eldorado amongst them (echoes of King Lear and his three competing daughters). In a strange and surrealist twist, one of the sons is played by the same actor as the mystical shepherd, and this son-shepherd eventually murders his siblings. Doña Soledad kills herself after the murder of her sons, and like St. Agueda, ritualistically cuts off her breasts. Soon thereafter, Diaz is beheaded by the shepherd and his crown is then placed on the head of Dulcinea, a peasant farmer who Diaz had lecherously pursued in earlier scenes. This marks an inversion of the hierarchical order, although it presumably replaces one kind of tyranny with another. There are more twists in the "chaotic" plot (Marsh is correct in using this descriptor), and scenes often resist the chronological summary I have imposed on the film's slippery structure. Indeed, I have introduced a sense of linearity and clarity, but the viewing experience is rather more oneiric and trance-like, even intoxicating, hallucinogenic—as it undoubtedly was for the cast and crew as well.

Rocha truly believed that this "chaotic" story about a mad dictator had universal appeal, fitting many marginalized and underdeveloped countries that suffered under ruthless autocrats and were undergoing chaotic, nightmarish, and destructive political processes. Spain, as a country under totalitarian rule with an Iberian tradition, a country with uneven modernization and questionable development, and one with an established culture of irrationality in the arts, was easily integrated into Rocha's tricontinental geographical imaginary. In an interview Rocha attributes as a key parallel between Spain and other regions of the "underdeveloped" world the resilience of popular culture, stating that "el aspecto figurativo de la película está directamente inspirado en la tradición popular, lo que seguramente habría sido imposible en países europeos desarrollados e industrializados, en los que el arte popular campesino fue absorbido por la sociedad de consumo" (qtd. in Rocha, Asín and Pitarch) [the film's figurative element is directly inspired by popular traditions, which would have been impossible in developed and industrialized European countries, where popular peasant art has been engulfed by consumer society]. Gatti interprets the film as instilling a precarious balance between its transnational components and its national references, suggesting that *Cabeças* amplified a transnational dimension that had already been present in *Terra em transe*:

> No caso de *Cabeças cortadas* o contexto nacional se torna transcontinental; Diaz II incorporaria, portanto, o Caudilho ibero-americano, num arco que se estende de Porfirio Diaz a Franco a Perón. Glauber já havia criado uma diegese transnacional em *Terra em transe*: a Eldorado do filme tem elementos que a identificam com o Brasil e os diálogos são em português, mas o espanhol emerge tanto nos nomes dos personagens (Julio Fuentes, Porfirio Diaz) como nos poemas criados pelo personagem Paulo Martins, produzindo um ambiente poliglótico que remete a alegoria à problemática política de muitos países latino-americanos. (Gatti 116)

> [In the case of *Cabeças cortadas* the national context becomes transcontinental; Diaz II embodies, therefore, the Ibero-American *Caudillo*, in an arc that sweeps from Porfirio Diaz to Franco to Perón. Glauber had already created a transnational diegesis in *Terra em transe*: Eldorado has Brazilian elements, and the dialogue is in Portuguese, but Spanish emerges in the names of several characters (Julio Fuentes, Porfirio Diaz) and in Paulo Martins's poetry, fomenting a polyglot environment that connects this allegory to the political problems of many Latin American countries.]

Rocha was enthusiastic about making a film in Spain, and the EdB's filmmakers fervently desired a greater transnational projection for their own cinema, so both sides were initially enthusiastic about the project. EdB cineastes planned to foment, through Jacinto Esteva's production company Filmscontacto, numerous high-quality co-productions in collaboration with prominent filmmakers of the international "new waves," chief among them the Brazilians Rocha and Diegues (Martínez Torres, *Buñuel* 80). Diegues visited Rocha's set in Spain while negotiating potential projects with the EdB that never came to fruition, especially after the debacle that befell *Cabeças*. Close friends, both Brazilian filmmakers worked with their countryman Eduardo Escorel, who edited Rocha's *Cabeças cortadas* and Diegues's *Macunaíma* (Martínez Torres, *Glauber Rocha* 101). These were not the only Brazilians to visit Rocha in Spain and interact with the Catalan art scene.

Along with Diegues, Caetano Veloso toured Rocha's set, underscoring the ties between the Tropicalist musician and Cinema Novo (Torres, *Glauber Rocha* 101). While in Spain, Veloso met with counterculture icons like the folk singers Pau Riba and Joan Manuel Serrat, leading figures in the Nova Cançó. In turn, the EdB filmmakers and producers exchanged ideas and made plans with the Brazilians. In 1970, Muñoz Suay wrote in *Nuestro Cine* that he had great hopes that Cinema Novo was "un recurso ilimitado para resolver parte de nuestros graves problemas cinematográficos . . . un movimiento amplio, sólido y revulsivo" (qtd. in Elena 229) [an unlimited resource to resolve some of our grave cinematic problems . . . a broad, solid, and shocking movement]. Suay and other EdB producers hoped that collaborations with foreign filmmakers would situate Spain as a fulcrum of the new waves and perhaps open the Iberian public to innovative films, in contrast with the unimaginative mainstream fare. Given the EdB's stylistic affinities with Cinema Novo, it is not surprising that Rocha's radical project was the first to be produced, but after the film's resounding critical and box office failure, Filmscontato scrapped all international co-production projects (Martínez Torres, *Buñuel* 80). In that sense *Cabeças* represented the simultaneous zenith and nadir of the transcontinental phase of the EdB.[26]

Rocha's motivation to pursue this Iberian venture was partly ideological (a way to irritate two dictatorial regimes at once), artistic (to experiment working with EdB cast, crew, and methods), and also pecuniary (the Catalans were willing to reward his efforts generously). After viewing *Antônio das Mortes* in 1969, Pere I. Fages—an EdB film critic, reporter, and producer and a militant of the proscribed Catalan Communist Party—contacted Rocha with an offer of $100,000 and a guarantee of total artistic freedom to make a film in Spain (Torres, *Glauber Rocha* 68). Rocha accepted and wrote a rough draft of the script. The Spanish producers (including Juan Palomeras, Josefa Pruna, Esteva, Muñoz Suay, and Fages himself) were concerned that Rocha's script would be rejected by the censors, on account of either its leftist allegorical message (politics) or its radical experimentalism (aesthetics). The underlying political critique was still discernible within the surrealist and rambling text, as was the case with *Terra em transe*, which was censored in Brazil in 1968 (Elena 235). For *Cabeças*'s detractors the absurdist plot and muddled ideological message undermined both its politics and aesthetics. Some of the message's looseness likely stemmed from Rocha's attempt to make the allegorical content vague enough to function as an archetypal scenario with transnational readability. Nevertheless, it was unclear whether the film was "a deliberate appeal to international audiences that necessarily renders the allegory ambiguous and applicable in various contexts, or whether the film is simply open to interpretation due to the potential for transnational application of its narrative and its imagery" (Martin-Jones 186). A less charitable reading, such as Buñuel's, suggested that the film was just nonsensical. In any case, audiences were left scratching their heads at the film's abstruseness.

Fear of state intervention during the filming went far beyond concerns about censorship. In fact, while scouting locations, Rocha and the Spanish producers were harassed and briefly detained by the Civil Guard. This episode profoundly unsettled the filmmaker, resembling police repression in Brazil and reminding him that Spain was, in effect, also an autocratic regime. Fages, for example, was already politically compromised and shortly thereafter fled in exile to Paris, remaining there until Franco's death in 1975. The production team was overjoyed when, contrary to their worst fears, the censors approved the script. Moreover, in a move characteristic of this brief period of *abertura* in Spanish cultural policy, the government even offered a modest subsidy by granting the film "special interest" status (Martínez Torres, *Glauber Rocha* 69–71; Fuentes and Vera 264). In Brazil, however, the military censors considered *Cabeças cortadas* subversive as much as unintelligible, prohibiting its public screening until 1978 when they relented, now on account of the film's redeeming opacity (Fuentes and Vera 264). The final product, an awkward hybrid of the EdB and Rocha's most extreme surrealist and farcical tendencies, seemingly confirms Salomé Aguilera Skvirsky's assessment of Cinema Novo at-large, as filmmaking in which "anachronism was elevated to an aesthetic principle. Combined and uneven development were its topical substrate, and allegory its mode of signification. The result was grotesque, absurdist representations, which, according to its defenders, represented the total farce of modernization schemes from above" (73). Adding to Cinema Novo's penchant for the absurd and farcical (deployed with greater success and skill in Rocha's early films), the fragmentary script was completed on an ad hoc basis, as scenes were spontaneously altered, with poorly coordinated contributions from Suay, Torres, and Pruna as well as Rocha himself, likely too many cooks for this cinematic broth. A great deal of improvisation by the actors also guaranteed that no one adhered strictly to what was already a schematic dialogue, and the resulting brew was further seasoned with a significant amount of drug and alcohol consumption by the cast and crew. The result was tumultuous, enigmatic, and at times senseless. But paradoxically, for Rocha, who had wished to immerse his cinema fully in the realm of the irrational as a form of countercultural resistance, this chaotic senselessness was by design.

Irrationality was the project's defining characteristic and its point, perhaps appropriately given the theme of the mad dictator in winter, or in autumn, to align with García Márquez's novel. As Rocha had openly stated in his 1971 lecture-manifesto "An Aesthetics of Dreams," rationalism was that element in Western colonialism and imperialism that stifled the cultural production of the Third World and enslaved its denizens, espousing instead the liberating potential of the irrational, and specifically of irrational, sudden violence—the same violence that spurred Guevarian-style *foquismo* throughout Latin America. In turn, the irrational in film, according to José Carlos Avellar, was a reaction against the documentary impulse and the overwhelming influence of neorealism in Latin American cinema, a needed corrective swing of the pendulum from Rocha's perspective (*Glauber* 135). In contrast to dogmatic rationalism, irrationality was seen as a catalyst enabling the rise of popular culture, as a necessary destabilizing force that might facilitate the people's progression toward freedom, since Rocha upheld that "the encounter between revolutionaries detached from bourgeois reason and the most significant structures of this popular culture will be the first configuration of a new revolutionary sign" (*On Cinema* 124). Detractors felt that *Cabeças cortadas* had taken this directive toward the irrational to an extreme, rendering the film entirely absurd, arbitrary, confusing, and utterly meaningless, and these criticisms where not wholly misguided. Film critic Paulo Perdigão, a contemporary of Rocha's, opined that "O capricho espanhol de Glauber . . . constitui uma queda na mais completa irracionalidade. Protegido pela dimensão do sonho, Glauber Rocha pode permitir-se, desta vez, sem necessidade de maiores explicações, a criação de uma realidade arbitrária, que só vale na medida puramente simbólica e virtual, significante em si mesma" (qtd. in Gatti 119) [Rocha's Spanish dalliance . . . was a fall into the most absolute irrationality. Shielded by the dimension of dreams, Glauber Rocha was able to, without needing to explain himself, create an arbitrary reality, one whose only value was purely symbolic and virtual, a signifier onto itself]. Part of the film's disorganized nature is due to its indiscriminate mix of media and artistic modalities, arguably a case of intermediality carried too far, as well as its anachronistic mélange of historical periods so that the very elements that render it a remarkable intermedial phenomenon also disintegrate any possibility for transparent signification, for readability by any audience national or transnational, whether in Brazil, Spain, or elsewhere.

Messy Intermediality as Transnational Tropicalism in Rocha's Iberian Film

To clarify some of the questions that swirl around the film's unreadable "strangeness," I turn once again to the project's markedly intermedial nature. This intermedial dimension can be understood in the context of the 1960s art scene in Brazil, which was itself a reflection of wider global trends toward media mixing (Fluxus, Pop Art, etc.). *Cabeças cortadas* can be in part considered as a "happening" and in part as a cinematic offshoot of the Tropicália movement. Nagib argues that most late phase Cinema Novo films displayed "the strong inflections of Tropicália" ("Intermediality" 125). For Nagib, one of the defining characteristics of Tropicália and its cinematic output through Cinema Novo, as seen in films such as Rocha's *Terra em transe* or Carlos Diegues's *Macunaíma* (1969), was that "interventions recognized no frontiers between the established arts and media but circulated freely across them" ("Intermediality" 123). Rocha's *Cabeças* is a prime example of movement (translation) across media and national borders, so that in addition to its multilayered literary intertextuality, one can observe the copious amalgamation of popular music, theater, architecture, painting, and numerous artforms among a complex web of media technologies and formats referenced by, or included within, the film—elements adapted both from Tropicália and other Brazilian arts and popular culture but also from Catalan and Spanish sources (Nova Cançó, medieval oral traditions, Mexican boleros, ballads, flamenco, etc.). Along with media mixing, Tropicália was known to fuse avant-garde art and popular traditions, a practice that, not unlike similar ones by the EdB, sought to destabilize barriers between high and folk art, elite and popular culture, and upended reified notions of "good taste." In *Cabeças*, by drawing on an admittedly "messy" constellation of Iberian and Latin American referents, Rocha fashions a transnational variant of Tropicalism that is closely allied with the Spanish-speaking world, a pan-Hispanic offshoot of Brazilian Tropicália.

To see how Rocha enacts such a complex multilayering of cultural referents in the film, it is best to isolate one particular artistic modality and examine its presence in specific scenes. We might consider, for instance, the film's eclectic use of popular music, present in both its intradiegetic and extradiegetic forms (motivated and unmotivated by the plot), which includes Mexican *rancheras*, Spanish and Mexican *boleros*, Catalan *coblas*—which typically accompany the *sardana* folk dance—as well as flamenco, the folkloric music from Andalusia associated with the gypsy or Romani community and accompanied by *palmas* (rhythmic hand clapping). If that variegated mélange were not sufficient, there is a scene that includes a *pasodoble*, a militaristic music associated with bullfighting and with the traditionalist values originating in Castile, Spain's central region and the seat of authoritarian rule, colonialism, and empire. The film's musical score was selected through an arguably naive 1960s leftist perspective that automatically associated folk music with popular resistance. This idealization occurs with the flamenco music, present in scenes in which peasants and gypsies rise in revolt against Diaz II.[27] Other pieces, including the *pasodoble*, are meant ironically, to ridicule and undermine authoritarianism and traditionalist values. As evident from his filmography, Rocha preferred popular music (samba, *cordel* ballads, etc.), which he believed manifested the creativity and spirit of the people (*o povo*), and as such exuded revolutionary potential.

As I have suggested, the film's intermedial apparatus, including its heterogeneous mix of musical styles, is mobilized as a postcolonial critique that mocks the regime's colonial and imperialist discourse, a recurring trope in a fascist ideology whose smoldering embers still lingered in the waning years of Francoism. To comedic effect, in one scene the epic *pasodoble* plays as Diaz II drags himself along the filthy castle floor, gradually inching toward two diminutive model caravels held by his doctor and his priest. The tiny ships, a small-scale parody of Spain's past grandeur (signifying the Armada, the "Discovery," the Conquest, etc.) add to the scene's general irreverence. While the decrepit Diaz recalls how he usurped Eldorado's throne by murdering the previous king (in one of the film's many references to Shakespearean tragedy), the doctor examines his vital signs and the priest prays for his soul, foreshadowing the autocrat's looming demise. Just as the minuscule caravels and Diaz's undignified behavior ridicule notions of Spain's "glorious" history, the music drives home the very same point. Playing in the background, Antonio Amaya's *pasodoble* "Chamaco, Gran Torero" (1955) [Chamaco, Great Bullfighter], with its overblown nationalist and patriotic lyrics about the brave bullfighter Chamaco, strikes a contrast between the uber-masculine caricature of the Iberian *torero* and the balding and undignified Diaz, prostrate on the dirty floor. The *pasodoble*, a military-type march reliant on sonorous brass instruments, is mobilized in ironic tone, mocking delusions of Diaz's greatness or nobility. Other songs, in some cases performed off key by Diaz (Rabal) himself, also comment ironically on plot events. This musical meta-commentary includes Mexican classics like the *ranchera* "Fallaste corazón" (by Mexican singer-songwriter Cuco Sánchez, also the title of a Mexican melodrama film released in 1970 in which Cuco had a part), and the 1959 bolero "Sabor a mí" by Álvaro Carrillo, both tunes used to illustrate the dictator's failure as leader ("falláste" [you failed]) and to display his megalomania ("sabor a mí" [taste of me]). Thus, the contrast between this audio collage and the visuals, the layering of historical periods, and the multiplicity of referents from Spain, Brazil, Mexico, and beyond create a potpourri that is ultimately difficult to decode and in many respects muddies the waters, diluting the message in a case of sensory overload.

Regrettably, Rocha obsessively oversaturates the numerous material media and cultural referents so that the accumulated palimpsest overwhelms the senses. The film's thickened intermedial layering begins with the opening credits, which are worth discussing to better understand how Rocha overlays a pan-Hispanic sensibility onto Tropicalist techniques, even if the result is somewhat undigestible. A static establishing shot locates the action in a ruinous medieval castle seen in the distance, as the credits roll, and the extradiegetic soundtrack plays the Mexican *ranchera* "Allá en el Rancho Grande" [Out on the Big Ranch]. Once again, the juxtaposition of the medieval image and the twentieth-century Mexican soundtrack set up a shocking anachronism, as well as juxtaposing geographical discontinuities (Latin America and Spain). The castle is the medieval monastery of San Pedro de Roda (Catalonia), a structure dating from the tenth century and only partially restored. The mix of historical periods and geographical locales is wholly in accord with Rocha's intent to create an allegorical and structuralist film that functions on a symbolic rather than a realist level and plays into the irrationality factor, enhancing the tone of baroque surrealism. Motivated by his interest in structuralist theories, including the work of Lévi-Strauss and Lacan, as well as classical literary referents, Rocha meant to explore the abstract drives and mechanisms that underlie the operations of power under authoritarianism, as well as the workings of the irrational mind when moved by unconscious desire. Echoing Christian Metz and other psychoanalytic film theorists, Rocha insisted that the cinema allowed for a materialization of the subconscious mind on-screen, and *Cabeças cortadas* had to be read through an interpretation of its symbols. Rocha characterized his movie as a structuralist film:

> É um filme estruturalista. Reduzi toda a história ao significante. . . . Cada vez que vejo o filme encontro novas explicações. Há todo um arco de sugestões. Deixei que o trabalho seguisse a estrutura do sonho, tal como Borges e Shakespeare. . . . Sim, Shakespeare está presente em *Cabeças cortadas* de forma pouco shakespeariana. Antes de fazer o filme li todas as obras, especialmente *Macbeth* e *A tempestade*. Creio que também poderia definir o filme assim: uma viagem borgeana pela obra de Shakespeare. (qtd. in Pierre, *Textos e entrevistas* 259)

> [*Cabeças cortadas* is a structuralist film. I reduced all of history to a signifier. . . . Each time I see the film I find new interpretations. There is an arc of suggestions. I let the work follow the structure of a dream, like Borges and Shakespeare. . . . Yes, Shakespeare is present in *Cabeças cortadas* in a non-Shakespearean way. Before making the film, I read all his plays, especially *Macbeth* and *The Tempest*. I could also define the film thus: it is a Borgesian journey through the work of Shakespeare.]

As I have suggested, the anachronistic juxtaposition of the archaic and the contemporary is also part and parcel of the hybridity characterizing both Rocha's films and Tropicália at-large. But perhaps the leap between medieval Iberia and rural Mexico or badlands Brazil is not wholly irrational. The *ranchera* is a musical style developed during the Mexican Revolution and associated with rural Mexico, with folk traditions such as mariachi music and with the ranching lifestyle that also echoes the Western—a genre Rocha was fully conversant with. It was not difficult for Rocha to associate Mexican *charro* (cowboy) Westerns with the *cangaçeiro* (bandit) films about northeastern Brazil, and with Iberian (and Italian) spaghetti Westerns. In this case, the "Rancho Grande" is none other than Diaz's castle, thereby linking the origins of the conquest to the development of enormous landed estates (*latifundio*) in Latin America, which in turn resemble the oppressive conditions in northeastern Brazil's *sertão*, as seen in Rocha's *nordestino* films. This is added to the fact that the Mexican Revolution also entailed a kind of Western gun slinging ethos that was fueled by land reform demands, a violence from the underprivileged classes seeking redress, which renders these associations even more plausible. As if to confirm this point, the credit typography in *Cabeças cortadas* is patently shaped to suggest a Western, although the bright pink color of the letters immediately undermines the traditional Western and places us right back into a Tropicalist sense of colorful irreverence. The cinematic intertextuality of the credit scene also cites the iconic—but decidedly reactionary—1936 Mexican romantic comedy *Allá en el Rancho Grande* [There in the Big Ranch], the film that arguably launched Mexican golden era cinema and propelled it into the international stage (King 46–47). Rocha intended for *Cabeças cortadas* to become an equally influential film, a film that would generate a Spanish-language Tropicalist movement, and he was also making an ironic commentary on the obsolescence of "nationalist" cinemas exemplified by *Allá en el Rancho Grande*. The problem, however, was that the complexity of the intermedial and intertextual referencing, and the arcane nature of the message, was not easily decoded by spectators, and unlike his previous films, this movie did not transport viewers on a visceral level—except toward revulsion, that is. Sadly, what originated as an ambitious and intellectually sophisticated project devolved into a cacophony of theories, styles, media, and misplaced ideological directives.

The opening scene that follows the credit sequence further illuminates Rocha's fervent wish to create a pan-Hispanic Tropicália as evidenced by its jarring mix of disparate elements. The scene opens with a protracted traveling long to medium shot of Diaz II. The dictator, holding two phones and a poodle, is simultaneously speaking with two people from Eldorado, a former lover Alba Moreno and Diaz's legal representative Freddy Bull (see fig. 2.9).

Figure 2.9. *Cabeças cortadas* Diaz II phones Eldorado (06:05). *Source: Cabeças cortadas* (1970). Dir. Glauber Rocha.

While on the phone with Alba he reminisces about sentimental affairs, with Bull he directs the sale of assets needed to sanitize his image back home, proposing a foundation with his name and a statue of himself. Diaz also asks about the deteriorating political situation back in Eldorado and requests that large sums be deposited in his Swiss bank accounts. In a reference to Evita Perón, he speaks to Alba about the devotion the people of Eldorado had for his late wife, Beatriz, and asks if the masses still visit her pantheon. As death nears, Diaz is increasingly obsessed with his potential legacy. A large tapestry with religious motifs hangs behind the autocrat, who sits at an oversized desk. The ground is covered with old newspapers. The tapestry is reminiscent of the official decor found, for instance, in Franco's residence, the palace of El Pardo, often depicted in the NO-DO. But the opulence is completely lacking; in general Diaz's castle denotes shabby decadence and decrepitude and ruins, or as Rocha himself stated, the decaying architecture hints at the impending death of all dictatorships. There are many elements of Tropicália in this scene as well, including Diaz's psychedelic "medieval" tunic, which may be inspired by Hélio Oiticica's experiments with colored fabrics, his *parangoles*. Those brightly colored cloaks, which Oiticica designed to be wearable sculptures for dancing samba, were meant to inject color into the world. Diaz, however, seems weighed down by his colorful outfit, as if the robes represented the trappings of authoritarian power. As the scene ends, Diaz plays the recording of a 1930s Gardel tango, "Cuesta abajo" [downhill] for his poodle Gaucho, once again referencing Argentina, and indirectly its association with Perón, but also reinforcing the decadence of this has-been ruler, of an empire on its way down, *cuesta abajo*.

More could be said about Rocha's recourse to intermediality and intertextuality as instruments to unravel the decaying traditionalist values espoused by the right. There are various scenes in the film that directly cite Dalí's Surrealist paintings (and echo Surrealism's obsession with putrefaction and decay), most notably *La persistència de la memòria* (1931) [The Persistence of Memory], well known in popular culture for its "melting" or decomposing clocks signaling the disintegration of time itself. Symbolizing spaciotemporal relativity, the painting is evoked in a scene where Diaz II first raises a clock toward the sun, and afterward an egg, while standing on the beach in Cap de Creus (near Cadaqués) where Dalí set his famous painting—the irreverent scene actually resembles a deviant or inverted eucharist. Here, the intermedial reference to Dalí's painting also inscribes the film within a tradition of surrealist cinema dating to Buñuel and Dalí's *Un chien andalou* and *L'Âge d'or*, precedents for Rocha's own rejection of rationalism and logic in favor of an instinctual art. In several other scenes the unexplained presence of a bull signifies another intertextual reference to the Spanish visual arts. For instance, the mysterious animal appears during the death of Doña Soledad, consort of Diaz II, and her sons. In the context of a film about the death knell of dictatorships, the bull harkens back to Picasso's *Guernica* (1937), perhaps the Iberian artist's best-known anti-Fascist painting. As a multivalent symbol whether in the *Guernica* or in *Cabeças cortadas*, the bull might stand for Diaz, for Franco or any dictator, for the enduring values of traditional Spain, for fascism itself, and so on. Citing these well-known paintings—in essence remediating them—affiliates the canvas and the screen as parallel surfaces upon which to inscribe anti-authoritarian narratives. Considering the associations between avant-garde painters and filmmakers (and the many artists who were both, such as Man Ray, Duchamp, Léger, Warhol, etc.), these elements of media mixing are not merely "copies" of original visual artworks but rather interpretations or translations into the cinematic, integrated into the multilayered network of referents detailed previously. The purpose remains the same: to destabilize norms, to commingle the arts and eschew "purity" of media, to surrealistically juxtapose various unlikely sources in seemingly arbitrary but thought-provoking ways, to challenge reified cultural values, and to amalgamate high and low art forms within the film through the chance encounter of a Brazilian and a Catalan counterculture on a dissecting Moviola.

In time, *Cabeças cortadas* was classified as an experimental film lacking any chance for commercial success, even within art house circuits. It was steeped in Surrealism and was, perhaps accordingly, somewhat incoherent, too much even for Rocha cinephiles and art film devotees. Arguably, it was also a bit too haphazard, too spontaneous and unscripted, even "sloppy" in its execution. Rocha was concerned with the way his spontaneous filming was working out in this project, and Martínez Torres, a direct witness to the filmmaker's method, recalled that "hasta el momento anterior de rodar el primer plano de cada día no tiene la menor idea de lo que hará y teme que no se le ocurra absolutamente nada" (*Glauber* 98) [until the instant right before filming the day's first shot he does not have a clue of what he will do, and he is afraid that he will not be able to think of anything at all]. A joint venture that sought to usher in a radical new style, the film took Rocha's freewheeling filmic practices and the EdB's own eccentric tendencies to an extreme. Although that "rough" and improvisational style had worked exceedingly well with Rocha's Brazilian films, perhaps due to certain unfamiliarity with the popular traditions he was handling in *Cabeças* or because exile, or his drug and alcohol intake, had begun to take a toll on his health, this film failed to achieve its potential as a piece of revolutionary art. For Martínez Torres the film had strayed too far from the *cangaçeiro* Westerns that Rocha was best suited for (*Buñuel* 80–81). In the opinion of Avellar, improvisation was constitutive of Rocha's filmmaking from the early films; his freewheeling approach (never having a finalized script, developing scenes on the fly, asking actors to improvise, filming without storyboards) reached its successful high point during *Terra em transe*, and it spun out of control with *Cabeças*, like a calibrated instrument that had gone out of tune or a tightrope act that became unbalanced, losing its aesthetic equilibrium. Avellar considers that, at its height, this jazz-like improvisational approach was highly effective, as it was the product of a constant self-reflexive questioning of the moviemaking process itself, as a *becoming* rather than an end product. The critic convincingly proposes that it was the handheld camera shots and the improvisational and off-script approach to shooting that energized Rocha's style: "Actually, shooting like that, revealing the nervous presence of the camera rather than the actual scene, was a creative operation to make the cinematographic language more complex" ("ImagiNation" 76–77). Avellar goes a step further and links the aesthetics of the camera work not only to Rocha's own artistic sensibility but to a prevalent ethos of the times. Discussing a scene from *Terra em transe* he explains,

> [T]he scene is improvised, not because it was not thought about when writing the script, but because it was still being thought about during the shooting. The image was trembling not because the operator was lacking in camera skills, but because at that time reality was being discussed in this way, in a nervous, trembling discourse. Then [the] cinema thought about the script as a challenge to shooting, shooting as a challenge to editing and the film as a challenge to the way of seeing [the world]. Cinema was considered an expression that is finished, ready, on the screen, and at the same time unfinished; part of a process that does not end with shooting: image-provoking, rushes, work print so that the spectator can clean out and order everything in his imagination. ("ImagiNation" 76–77)

Rocha's film with the EdB, initially meant as a loose sequel to *Terra em transe*, became a delirious and out of control experiment that, in the Brazilian filmmaker's judgment, was unjustly treated by both the right and the left (qtd. in Bentes 372). Simply put, the film's labyrinthine experimental temporality (plot events did not follow any clear chronology) and its overreliance on allegory, character types, and symbolism rather than traditional narrative were just too puzzling for audiences and critics, and lacked the cohesion of his earlier films. Coupled with hasty editing and irregular filming, the overall effect was that of a jumbled, directionless work. Rocha always defended the approach, comparing the film's style to free-flowing poetry rather than a structured narrative (Avellar, *Glauber* 148). The filmmaker also qualified this style as "neosurrealism," the result of the Latin American intellectual's shifting position between rationalism and romanticism, as illustrated by Paulo Martins in *Terra em transe* or by Rocha himself (Avellar, *Glauber* 151). But in this case, Rocha was almost the lone voice in the desert. The film was all but forgotten soon after its disastrous 1970 premier in San Sebastian, and although it has been shown several times in festivals or retrospectives, it remains Rocha's least known and most reviled work, perhaps rightfully so. In retrospect, it is evident that although the film failed to create a transnational political allegory that could function irrespective of specificity of setting—to become truly tricontinental—it arguably succeeded in using intermediality as a creative source for political dissent and offered some novel techniques that might have succeeded had the craftsmanship been less haphazard. Despite its spectacular failure, it is precisely in the mix of genres and the hybrid crossover of local, national, and international styles that the film obtains a radical impurity that undermines any possible commercialism and inscribes it into the realm of the experimental and the neo-avant-garde, but also, perhaps, of the unreadable.

By Way of Closure:
Experimental Film and the Ethics of Intermediality

We have seen how the works of Cinema Novo, specifically Rocha's films, and the EdB exemplify the role experimental cinema can play in specific historical contexts to destabilize dominant aesthetic and political discourses. Not unlike the turn of the century avant-garde—especially Surrealism—and in dialogue with several of the new European and American cinemas of the '50s and '60s, both Cinema Novo and the EdB focused on a type of generic impurity and intermediality that negated medium specificity and subverted mainstream film practices with the goal of activating slumbering middle-class audiences into political action, or at least some form of ideological awakening. While these films did not always engage directly with politics as was the case with militant cinema, they did so allegorically, obliquely, and operating within strict censorship limitations. Whereas in Brazil these attempts at less overt political filmmaking were met by the regime's forceful counter-resistance, increased censorship, and the forced or voluntary exile of filmmakers, in Spain oppositional movies aligned more favorably with the waning years of the dictatorship and functioned as harbingers of its approaching demise. Rocha's *Cabeças cortadas* attempted to bridge these disjointed temporalities and separate geographies by creating a film that, by fusing both strands of art cinema (Catalan and Brazilian), functioned as a trigger for transatlantic revolt. But Rocha's film failed to rouse audiences in either nation, arguably undermined by its own extreme experimentalism and unreadability. Nevertheless, all these works represented a challenge to preconceived ideas about film form. The intrinsic material intermediality displayed by these remarkable films can be seen in how they fearlessly and freely mixed script and image, poetic imagery and referential political discourse, elite and mass culture (advertising, comics, fashion), music and theater, moving images and the painterly arts.

In the case of the EdB, its filmmaking stood clearly apart from other contemporary cinematic practices in Spain because of its bold stylistics—save for perhaps some of the more daring experiments within the NCE, such as Patino's work. EdB directors were not nearly as politically militant as their clandestine counterparts, the various collectives best exemplified by Lumbreras's group, and they certainly did not incur the same political risks. But they were at the vanguard of cinematic transgressions against established norms and embraced a spirit of freedom that eagerly anticipated the inevitable arrival of democratic rule. And they affiliated political liberation with artistic transgression. As Jean Paul Aubert observes, with their poetics of the "fragment" the EdB struck a blow at Greenberg's essentialist argument that located the nature of an artistic practice in either its material or its method (*Seremos Mallarmé* 231–33). Such use of fragmentation was closely linked, as in Rocha's case, with a profoundly intermedial conception of art. As Aubert sees it, the EdB's fragmentation of sound and image was manifold, including "asociaciones insólitas de imágenes, montaje de diálogos con largas citas incluidas, discursos polifónicos, acumulación de sonidos y de temas musicales, encuentros de los timbres vocales y de los acentos más diversos gracias a la presencia de actores y actrices de los países vecinos" (*Seremos Mallarmé* 182) [astonishing associations between images, montage of dialogue with lengthy inserted quotes, polyphonic speeches, an accumulation of sounds and musical themes, encounters of vocal chords and diverse accents traceable to the presence of actors from neighboring countries]. Fragmentation, argues Aubert, becomes a mandatory norm in these films, and discontinuity their defining characteristic, with the aim of subjecting the spectator to "la experiencia molesta de lo incompleto" (182) [uncomfortably experience the incomplete].

Ahead of its time in Spain, the EdB practiced a post-medium poetic that corresponds, *avant-la-lettre*, to Rosalind Kraus's redefinition of genre specificity in the post-medium age, as a self-reflexive practice aware of its past, which "through such contemplation [will] escape absorption into capitalist modes of production. Such reflection must involve an acknowledgement of the medium specific practices that are being replaced or combined, and an intent to use art as an exploration of the idea of art" (Bernstein). Indeed, the films analyzed in this chapter exemplify this post-medial condition by calling into question the cinematic medium's supposed limitations and reconfiguring experimental film as an "open field for the interplay of 'conventions' and 'possibilities'" (Bernstein). Through the interplay with poetry and other media, and a complex representation of word and image, the EdB and Cinema Novo refashioned film as a hybrid material that connected with past experimental artistic practices and anticipated contemporary intermedial and digital "convergence" as practiced on the web, as we shall see in the following chapters. No less importantly, the films of the EdB functioned as subtle political interventions registering protest, resisting Francoist Spain's hegemonic structures, and offering a radical alternative to realist (mainstream) film practices.

Even grittier and no less intermedial, Cinema Novo—especially the films of its preeminent genius and leading practitioner Glauber Rocha—tapped into the spirit of Tropicália to mix genres, styles, and materials to create a cinema that embraced impurity, drawing on the literary and poetic arts for its surrealist scripts, on painting for its symbolic referents, and on a complex musical mélange for its Brechtian distancing effects, all of these elements working together in unison. During its initial phase Cinema Novo represented an angry denunciation and challenge to neocolonialism, to underdevelopment (to "hunger"), to US imperialism, and to local corruption in Brazil, as a specifically evolved form that was claimed by both Second and Third Cinema, blurring the boundary between both. In its later phase, however, and especially after the repressive turn taken by the military government after 1968, Cinema Novo sought to abandon some of its nationalist impulses to become a transnational, global, and/or tricontinental cinema of anti-colonialism (Rocha, for example, would also film his more militant 1970 film *Der Leone have sept cabeças* [*The Lion Has Seven Heads*], a pro-guerilla insurgency film whose protagonist is loosely based on the figure of Che). *Cabeças cortadas* is a prime example of this tricontinental effort by Cinema Novo to expand beyond Brazil. Arguably, as the movement became more global and abandoned some of its national and regional themes and characteristics (the *cangaçeiro* film, the *favela* film), it lost some of its artistic clarity and political efficacy. Even as its experimentalism was becoming more marked, it became evident that some aspects of Rocha's filmmaking did not perform well in translation. That did not mean that the collaboration between the EdB and the preeminent filmmaker of Cinema Novo lacked any measure of success, for the film provided one more example (if fraught) of the potential transatlantic exchanges between Iberian and Latin American filmmakers and strengthened a sense of political unity and solidarity among left-leaning cineastes working under adverse conditions, whether at home or in exile. In the balance, the transatlantic affiliation between Cinema Novo and EdB was not founded on neoliberal commercial interests (as many such contemporary collaborations are) but on a shared aesthetic and ideological vision. It was an association that fomented alterity, intermediality, and cultural hybridity and represented the best intentions of filmmakers to transcend reductive nation-state-centered projects in favor of a global leftist solidarity cinema.

Chapter 3

Remediating Past Filmic Technologies

The Return of Super 8 and Video in the Era of Global Digital Cinema

Introduction: Yearning for Home and for Those Golden Days of Video Making

This chapter represents a transatlantic comparative reading of various so-called minor formats (Super 8 and analog video), straddling multiple chronologies (from the 1960s until today) and geographies (primarily Argentina and Spain).[1] The first two chapters in this book were anchored in the tumultuous 1960s (chapter 1) and the 1970s (chapter 2), and with this chapter we establish associations between that first phase of experimental cinema and its reverberations in the digital age. The chapter examines the continuity and discontinuity between the work of the 1960s in various analog formats and its resurgence in the era of digital cinema, linking the 1960s to the 2000s. Chapter 1 focused mainly on militant Third Cinema, while chapter 2 explored art house Second Cinema, even as those simple divisions were problematized. In this current chapter I turn to films that can only be described as primarily, although not exclusively, experimental, in the sense that their main interest is form and the limits of the cinematic medium itself, while other concerns become secondary. If the two previous chapters explored the confluence of politics and intermedial aesthetics in transnational cinema, this chapter is about media nostalgia and about diaspora.

The media nostalgia, which is in part the product of digitization and the obsolescence of certain analog formats, especially celluloid and magnetic video, has resulted in a recent turn toward reclaiming "vintage" media and equipment (Super 8 cameras, celluloid film, Moviolas, etc.) and/or the stubborn persistence of their aesthetics and effects in a digital format. The question of diaspora addressed in the chapter centers on two cities, Buenos Aires and Barcelona. Their selection is not a coincidence or an arbitrary choice: these cities are arguably the two metropoles in the Spanish-speaking world that have generated the most robust exchange of experimental cinema and video art since the 1960s, with decades of mutual influence in these experimental forms of visual media, as I will show. Some of this lengthy tradition we already saw when discussing the cinema of Helena Lumbreras, who was both a Barcelona-based filmmaker and also one whose work turned to Spain and beyond in its internationalist militancy and emulation of Latin American Third Cinema. The same continuity can also be seen in our discussion of the Barcelona School (EdB) in chapter 2, again establishing Spain's second city as the center of experimental and art house cinema in the peninsula, in this case by studying its close affiliation with Cinema Novo. Now we turn to the equally proximate ties between Buenos Aires and the Catalan capital.

The preeminence of these transatlantic urban connections will crystallize as we examine the work of several accomplished, although relatively unknown, Argentine filmmakers who have lived in both capitals or spent considerable time in transit between them. The flow of filmmakers, films, and videos between the two cities has been a constant factor that intensified significantly after the Argentine financial crisis of 2001 but existed prior to that date. For example, a 2008 video art exhibit in Buenos Aires at the MAMBA (Museo de Arte Moderno de Buenos Aires) dedicated exclusively to major Argentine experimental video artists was titled, precisely, "Argentinos en el exterior" [Argentines outside of the country], and out of the seven artists featured, four had relocated to Barcelona (including Gustavo Caprín, whose work we will study in some detail), whereas the rest were based in various other European cities. For historical and linguistic reasons, Spain is the primary destination for Argentine expats (artists or not), with almost three hundred thousand currently residing in the country, after several waves that began in the 1960s during the military regimes and intensified after the 2001 economic crisis. Many with Spanish roots acquired dual citizenship, a process facilitated by the 2007 Law of Historical Memory. Although Madrid also has a significant number of Argentine residents, Barcelona has by far the largest number of any urban center in the country (approximately fifteen thousand). The city has become a preferred destination for experimental filmmakers, video artists, and other visual artists due mainly to its thriving art scene, its lengthy history of cutting-edge avant-garde art, and its many venues for experimental cinema.

Many of these filmmakers bring a sense of nostalgia for the disappearance of old formats, a nostalgia that is also bound up with the experience of self-exile and with the anxiety of integrating into their new cultural milieu. At the same time, the links between filmmakers and video artists living in foreign lands and those that stayed in Argentina remain vibrant and have fostered many a transatlantic exchange of ideas, dialogue, projects, videos, and films. In this chapter I will focus on two specific instances of this transnational phenomenon. In the first part, I will examine the surprising resurgence of the Super 8 format, as well as its digital afterlife, by analyzing the relationship between the films of established Argentine experimental cineastes, such as Narcisa Hirsch and Claudio Caldini, with those of Daniela Cugliandolo, a relatively unknown Argentine filmmaker who relocated to Barcelona. Cugliandolo is representative of other young filmmakers who emigrated to Spain and have explored affective spaces of diaspora through obsolete media that are both in danger of disappearing and paradoxically experiencing a limited resurgence.

Maintaining the focus on media and diaspora, the second part of the chapter turns its attention to a different format altogether, to 1980s analog video, that is, video art recorded on video cassettes with camcorders. I will study how the nostalgia for film and video can be traced in the epistolary video exchanges between two filmmakers who for several years sent each other short weekly video letters, back and forth between Buenos Aires and Barcelona. These filmmakers eventually created a broader transatlantic epistolary video project that was screened at several major museums and galleries worldwide and involved a total of four cineastes living in three different nations (Argentina, Uruguay, and Spain). The two Argentine filmmakers that were the original creative force behind this epistolary video exchange are Andrés Denegri (living in Buenos Aires) and his colleague Gustavo Caprín (living in Barcelona). Their project was titled *This Is Just to Say* (*TIJTS*), named after the first verse of a William Carlos William's poem—and like the subject of that poem, the videos they exchanged focused on the quotidian, on little details, on future projects, on family and friends. The video exchanges represented a transatlantic conversation between two filmmakers who are separated by distance but who bridged that distance through their video and other media. In short, both parts of this chapter have a common thread that will bring us to questions of exile, nationality, and media relations, and the persistence of these elements as filmmakers and video artists and their works are uprooted and translated into other formats and places. I will begin with an inquiry into celluloid, the chronologically older medium, and later turn to video.

Intermediality and Hispano-Argentine Experimental Film: Subverting Media, Transgressing Borders with Super 8

In 2010 the MALBA (Museo de Arte Latinoamericano de Buenos Aires) held a retrospective of 1960s and '70s Super 8 films by Argentine filmmakers Claudio Caldini and Narcisa Hirsch, in what seemed like an anachronistic and nostalgic look to a past technology and long forgotten cineastes. To the contrary, as I will argue, this recuperation of an old format is highly significant for our historical moment (the digital era) and not reducible to mere nostalgia—although nostalgia has a significant part to play in its resurgence. Paradoxically, given the format's celluloid-based medium specificity, the rebirth of Super 8 proves critical for understanding the dissolution of the concept of medium brought on by an increasingly intermedial and digital approach to the arts, a dissolution that is closely connected with the current status of experimental film as diasporic and post-national.

Janus-like, Super 8 simultaneously partakes of the transnational and digital present and recalls the national and analog past. Charles Acland, echoing the sociologist Stuart Tannock, notes that nostalgia functions as a kind of "contemporary structure of feeling," and looking to past technologies such as Super 8 or analog video also represents "the search for historical continuity lodged in nostalgic gestures," a search that reflects the need to identify or heal some "historical rupture" (xiv). In Argentina's case, this "rupture" may be read as the disruption caused by dictatorship and exile or by the recent economic crisis and diaspora. Materially speaking, it may also be viewed as the rupture signified by the passing of celluloid and arrival of the digital. Nostalgia for film is affiliated with a sense about the loss of artisanal practices in the twenty-first century, of the disappearing organic link between celluloid indexicality and the world around us. There are significant questions about "medium" to be considered here, especially relevant for the passing of such "old formats" and as debated in contemporary scholarship by the likes of David N. Rodowick, Philip Rosen, Mary Ann

Doane, Laura U. Marks, and various other critics involved in the "death" of cinema polemics of the early 2000s—some of which I briefly revisit in the chapter. Additionally, I suggest that despite obvious generational differences, both 1960s and today's filmmakers address the experience of loss and nostalgia (for celluloid, for the homeland) through films that deploy "impure" media and overlapping temporalities. By exploring concepts such as exile, time, and memory, these films investigate, for instance, how a sense of "pastness" might be produced, archived, and even falsified by combining Super 8 and digital technology, making the format a repository for real and imagined memories.[2]

Critics often imagine experimental cinema as a non–culturally specific, elitist practice, one that is obsessed with the purity of film as a medium. While partially accurate, this portrayal misses both how experimental film constantly changes and renegotiates its borders to address specific cultural problems and how it becomes hybrid, absorbing a variety of media (analog and digital). Just as contemporary experimental film becomes more intermedial, it also incorporates cross-cultural, transnational influences while still retaining traces of the national. In this first half of the chapter, I focus on Argentine filmmakers by following a genealogy connecting two different time periods and two distant cities: Buenos Aires in the 1960s and '70s and Barcelona today. As I stated above, the choice of these two cities is not arbitrary but has to do with their status as prominent centers for the creation and circulation of experimental filmmaking within the Hispanic world, as centers that mutually influence each other's cultural production. Although the Argentine diaspora has spread widely, Barcelona, on account of its public support for art house and experimental film, through the Centre de Cultura Contemporània de Barcelona (CCCB) [Center for Contemporary Culture in Barcelona] and other venues, has been especially attractive for its filmmakers (La Ferla, "Entrevista").[3] Beyond the many films and filmmakers uniting these distant cities, there is also a compelling conceptual reason behind their selection, since Buenos Aires and Barcelona have experienced analogous events in their recent histories, events that have had parallel repercussions for their film industries. Both cities are in countries that endured dictatorial regimes, difficult transitions to democracy, and more recently, severe economic crises resulting in diaspora. Such events have left traces, thematically and formally, in the films we consider.[4] It is the case that diaspora filmmakers such as Daniela Cugliandolo, whose films I shall discuss, and Gustavo Caprín, whose videos I will later analyze, have adopted transnational identities as Hispano-Argentines. As Vives-González argues, the Argentine government itself promotes "a [shared] transnational space with its citizens in Spain," a virtual imagined community (232).

Super 8 has been garnering the attention of artists and critics precisely because it is a format well-suited to bridge multiple temporalities and geographies. Once considered as being "purely" analog, Super 8, much like analog video, has become complexly intertwined with the digital and gone online. Yet for all this utopian celebration, Super 8 is also the ultimate symbol of obsolescence: it is a low-cost format that allows for no celluloid copies. Since there is no real negative and no way to easily make additional prints, its survival requires its transfer to digital, a sort of diasporic displacement of one medium into another.[5] To project Super 8 means to degrade the original celluloid, bringing it closer with each projection to its ultimate disappearance (hence its natural valence as a metaphor for memory, which also fades with the passage of time).[6] Fittingly, Super 8 has made its comeback by incorporating other media (analog and digital) and artistic modalities: painting, dance, and music, among others. Super 8 is the ideal paradigm to study how experimental film deploys intermediality in the post-national era, blurring media distinctions and global borders.

To frame my discussion about the interplay between intermediality, memory, and transnationality around a concrete example, I begin by examining Daniela Cugliandolo's three-minute short film *Esto no es un recuerdo* (2006) [This Is Not a Memory]. Cugliandolo is one of several filmmakers who, displaced by Argentina's 2001 economic recession, moved to Spain and joined its amateur Super 8 scene. Her movie exemplifies how the material specificity of Super 8 film has been vital for establishing symbolic associations with a form of historical "authenticity" that is no longer dependent on celluloid itself and can now be induced through digital means. As we shall see, her digitized Super 8 footage creates a new kind of indexicality based on hybridity, proving that there are "levels of hybridity in the register of the digital image . . . [and] such hybridities confuse the initiating opposition between digital and indexical" (Rosen, *Change Mummified* 303). Cugliandolo's repurposing of Super 8 shows that the digital is not conceptually opposed to the analog and indexical but might be imbricated with both. By functioning like an externalized, unreliable, and deterritorialized memory, Super 8 also shows how memory might become highly mediated, multilayered, and reconfigured in a transnational context. Super 8 films today have shifted from the immediate concerns of the 1960s regarding militancy and transnational revolution to no less immediate issues about remembrance and forgetting, displacement and exile, in the aftermath of the 1970s and '80s authoritarian rule and the economic debacle of the

2000s, a debacle also attributed in great part to the neoliberal policies pursued during the Argentine military dictatorship and continued during democratic governance.

Questions of historicity (of media, of nation) imply a genealogy. In the next section of the chapter, I perform an exercise in media archeology in order to trace a genealogy of experimental filmmaking in Argentina, that is, I "excavat[e] the past in order to understand the present and the future" (Parikka 2). Turning to Super 8's putative founding moment in Argentina, I analyze *Come Out* (1971), a nine-minute short by the recently rediscovered filmmaker Narcisa Hirsch, to show how it anticipated, and perhaps inspired, intermedial works by contemporary filmmakers such as Cugliandolo.

Finally, returning to the present and before shifting my attention to video, I will bookend the first half of the chapter by analyzing Cugliandolo's five-minute black-and-white film *pneurosis* (2001), a work that further exemplifies the resurgence of the Super 8 format and its pursuit of a post-medium aesthetic linked to the post-national condition (which paradoxically always includes a negotiation with the national), that is, to transnational flows of films and filmmakers. Although Cugliandolo's filmmaking is to a certain degree deterritorialized, transnational, and hybrid, it also retains a strong link to "memories" of the national, activated through a particular use of Super 8 material. In fact, contemporary experimental films of the Argentine diaspora, regardless of their media makeup, are hybrid "in their intentional crossing and the problematization of various borders, such as those between video and film, fiction and nonfiction, narrative and nonnarrative, social and psychic, autobiographical and national" (Naficy 21–22). As with intermediality, exile is a hybrid and fluid state that privileges the mixing of categories, the multiplication of nationalities and allegiances, and the proliferation of artistic exchanges. In spite of the variety of individual projects, I will also argue that the genre and material hybridity shared among today's Super 8 filmmakers, while reliant on newfound artistic collaborations and a transplanted setting, remain partially rooted to earlier Argentine experimental films, which later movies often emulate, cite, and transform.

Fabricating Memories:
Esto no es un recuerdo Is and Is Not a Memory

Cugliandolo, now living in Barcelona, emigrated from Buenos Aires in the aftermath of the 2001 crisis and is in many ways representative of other Argentine filmmakers residing in Spain: highly mobile, in touch with their home country, and fully inscribed in a transatlantic scene. Her films, shot in Buenos Aires and Barcelona, exemplify how digital postproduction has revitalized Super 8, as she unites the intimate spontaneity of small-gauge film with the seamless fluidity of digital video, providing yet another variant of how intermediality has brought together chronologically disparate media and art practices.[7] Cugliandolo is at the forefront of what Argentine film critic Jorge La Ferla describes as "the innovative use of video and digital as part of the process of composition," enacting "a creative practice that involves the filmic, the videographic, and the photochemical, from preproduction to the final transfer, always taking into account the expository possibilities that each of these has to offer" ("Argentine Cinema" 184).

In her films, Super 8 often becomes the symbol for an external prosthetic memory whose obsolescence is precisely the mark of its intimate connection to human processes of remembering and forgetting. But the title of *Esto no es un recuerdo*, the first short I will discuss, suggests that film is really something other than memory, neither a projection of real subjective interiority nor a fragile snapshot of an objective past. Instead, her film is presented as a fabrication, a false home movie, a competent forgery whose aesthetic mode of production achieves the visual quality of 1970s Super 8 but was created in the recent past, employing both analog and digital tools. It does not represent a reconstructed memory of Cugliandolo's childhood in Argentina but a manufactured memory of an imagined Barcelona childhood, exposing a tension between transnational identity and the (fading) persistence of the national, between real and imagined.

By adopting a hybrid materiality, Cugliandolo's work challenges claims of the radical novelty of the digital image *and* those positioning celluloid as outdated and irrelevant. Philip Rosen has maintained that the traditional opposition between digital and analog is overly simplistic:

> Theorists of the indexical image such as Bazin and Barthes fixated on light sensitive chemicals as the key mediating materiality between an object and its depiction of the image. With photography and film as the usual examples, these are said to give an image its quality of a trace, imprint or mold (Bazin) for the spectator. The basis of the digital image, on the other hand, is usually described as a configuration of numbers in binary sets, numerical operations, algorithms. Theorists of the digital image must emphasize the idea that numbers are something like *its*

ground, its mediating "materiality." (*Change Mummified* 305, emphasis in original)

This opposition between the indexical-analog and the numerical-digital is the type of binarism that Cugliandolo undermines with her digitally enhanced Super 8 films. Her movies retain a trace of their celluloid past and thereby restore to the digital the lost connection between world and image that was claimed as "the very currency of the indexical" (Rosen, *Change Mummified* 306).

And yet, despite claims of hybridity, Cugliandolo's films enact a struggle to unite digital and analog, displaying a tension that characterizes digital cinema that otherwise remediates, includes, imitates, or evokes its celluloid past. On the one hand, through her choice of filming in Super 8, she maintains a focus on the material specificity of celluloid and the self-reflexive quality of film as a technical support with unique material constraints, as theorized by André Bazin, Roland Barthes, Rosalind Krauss, and Mary Ann Doane (among others). On the other, through her manipulation of her source material in digital postproduction, she pursues an intermedial approach that suggests a convergence in which all is subsumed under the digital, as conceptualized by David Thorburn and Henry Jenkins.[8] This results in a reconfiguration of "medium" that is not perforce a contradiction, once we begin to think of the digital's capacity to invoke a historicity of media, as it becomes capable of performing its own form of media archeology and unearths a multimedia palimpsest (composed of multiple analog and digital "layers").

As Jussi Parikka defines it, media archeology is precisely the way to "investigate the new media cultures through past new media, often with an emphasis on the forgotten, the quirky, the nonobvious apparatuses, practices and inventions" (2). Similarly, Cugliandolo uses digital technologies to imitate the material specificity of Super 8 film, to produce a "Super 8 effect" that signifies the "affect" typically associated with the graininess, faded color, and degraded quality previously bound to Super 8 film's specific medium. In her short *Esto* this effect even stimulates (and simulates) a kind of family nostalgia, remembrance, and yearning for a past that never was. Thus, an uneasy convergence occurs as celluloid (analog) and digital components are integrated, but the meaning of the Super 8 effect relies on a media history that uncovers why such stylistic phenomena carry with them specific fields of affect and how such hybrid forms maintain or even "fabricate" an indexical connection to the profilmic event. In turn, the notion that this stylistic filter involves history and nostalgia relates to the transnational and to diaspora: Argentine artists in exile invoke Super 8 through its digital "rebirth," to convey the historical displacement of political and economic exile and also to restore a genealogical memory of Argentine experimental film, creating an evanescent family portrait. This connection between the intermedial and the transnational is key to understanding how Argentine experimental film relates to the obsolescence of the cinematic medium and to its own fragile condition of post-nationality, diaspora, and exile.

How does this film enact its radical hybridity? By overlaying media: *Esto* is a digitally captured and post-edited *projection* of a Super 8 film. In this case, the Super 8 original, the material Cugliandolo filmed and edited directly in her Super 8 camera, was projected onto a screen and then filmed (again) with a digital camera. The traces of this process are clearly visible in the digital final product. The Super 8 projection changes location in relation to the darkened digital screen that envelops it, at times claiming more or less of the overall space, metaphorically reflecting the ebb and flow processes of memory and its fading. The process also adds a ghostly "flicker" effect, as the Super 8 projected at eighteen frames per second produces distortions when captured by the nonmatching speed of the digital video camera. There is also a subtle yet uncanny disjunct between the grainy quality of the celluloid and the smooth quality of the HD video. In addition, the foregrounding of the digital camera's presence through its movement echoes the artificial constructedness of adult memories when recollecting, indeed rewriting real or imagined childhood events, just as the digital captures, reedits, reconstructs, and refashions the source celluloid footage. The film taps into real and imagined nostalgia, false memories, and a sense of "impure" and "radical historicity without stable points and end" (Rosen, *Change Mummified* 15).[9]

The short film's opening scene shows an adult woman (sporting childlike pigtails) chasing pigeons in Barcelona's Plaza Catalunya (see fig. 3.1).[10] The washed-out images evoke a sense of childhood memories and seek to produce a nostalgic reverie, of time past, of geographical displacement. It is precisely the uncertain and blurred mechanisms of memory that this lyrical sequence performs, as Cugliandolo draws on techniques such as filming the unfocused, blurred shadow of the running protagonist. The image evokes a sense of a long ago past, of childhood, but also gestures to the forgotten history of Argentine small-gauge cinema, by citing a sequence from Claudio Caldini's Super 8 film *Heliography* (1993) where the filmmaker captured his flickering shadow while riding a bicycle. Cugliandolo's nervous camera

Figure 3.1. *Esto no es un recuerdo* (2006) playing with pigeons in Plaza Catalunya (00:28). *Source: Esto no es un recuerdo* (2006). Dir. Daniela Cugliandolo.

mimics the protagonist's own energy. The camera shifts from first-person shots from the girl's perspective to rhythmic jump cuts shot from a distance. The protagonist skips backward playfully and holds up different toys in a stop-action sequence, recalling early trick films by Méliès that disrupted linear temporality (see fig. 3.2). The suspension of temporality has everything to do with how analog and digital are annealed in a film that is ultimately about the obsolescence of the material, of memory, and of the national, but also about the persistence of these categories, now transformed into new modes of being.

The interplay between the celluloid footage and the in-and-out tracking movements of the digital camera recording the Super 8 projection creates a sense of rhythm that is closely synced with the oneiric soundtrack. The small-gauge footage functions as the substratum on which digitality is overlaid. Thus Super 8's warm colors, intimacy, tactility, and sense of indexicality are transferred onto the new medium, imprinting a memory of celluloid onto digital cinema. Media multilayering echoes the complexities

Figure 3.2. *Esto no es un recuerdo* (2006) stop-action sequence with toys (00:53). Source: *Esto no es un recuerdo* (2006). Dir. Daniela Cugliandolo.

of memory itself, imbricated with affective mechanisms and spectator interpellation, as our sensorial memories become interwoven with the filmic text. "As we watch a film," proclaimed the North American filmmaker Maya Deren, "the continuous act of recognition in which we are involved is like a strip of memory unrolling beneath the images of the film itself, to form the invisible underlayer of an implicit double exposure" (Sitney 37).[11] Super 8 functions as the affective underlayer that *Esto no es un recuerdo* desires to access, expose, and reveal (with the double meaning of uncovering and *revelar*, Spanish for "to develop").

Cugliandolo's film clearly uncovers and develops how cinema induces a sense of personal memory through ordinary everyday experiences, what Akira Mizuta Lippit calls "a mechanical nostalgia of the mundane, a mnemic dimension of everyday life" (57); a private micro-history that attempts to capture the ephemerality of lived experience as it passes, an always already nostalgic desire to film life's fleetingness—connected to the perceived fleetingness of celluloid itself. In her film, Cugliandolo presents the role of home movies as the production of a manufactured truth meant as external supplement to our equally fictionalized physical memories, endowing home movies with an uncanny, un-homely feel. The "faux" home movie—like the faux found footage, or faux surveillance footage exploited by horror movies like *The Blair Witch Project* (1999) or the more recent *Paranormal Activity* (2007), or the cell phone horror films I examine in chapter 4—is a genre unto itself, much like the faux Super 8 aesthetic reproduced by artificially "degrading" the quality of digital video through the use of postproduction techniques. This tendency is exemplified by the existence of a "Super 8" app for filming with the iPhone that mimics the aesthetic of small-gauge, down to the jerkiness and the grainy, scratched, and dirtied surface, similar to the filters Instagram applies to photographs to make them appear faded and "historical" or iPhone apps like Kanon Vintage Film Camera or Huji Cam (its respective tag lines "Just Like the Year 1998" and "Analog Feeling"), which also make digital photographs resemble film. Super 8 has long been used in contemporary films "as home movie footage and/or to evoke pastness" (Thomas). In this film, however, Cugliandolo enlists a real Super 8 camera to generate a false pastness, challenging the belief that Super 8 is able to capture reality (more) objectively (than digital), and casting doubt on absolute notions of authenticity or originality, even while positing a "digital indexicality" (Rosen, *Change Mummified* 307).[12] Indeed, the digital camera arguably retains many "explicitly indexical functions" of the photochemical apparatus, including its "indexical import as a light-sensing device" (Rosen, *Change Mummified* 308).

But if "material" objectivity is questioned by Cugliandolo's film, so is the subjective experience of the spectator. In her *Home Movies and Other Necessary Fictions* (1999) Michelle Citron argues, "[T]he meaning of home movies is in constant flux. This is due, in part, to the fact that we provide a second track, either stories or memories, at the moment of viewing" (Lebow 213). Cugliandolo simultaneously engages and casts doubt on the reliability of our own memories, that is, the second track the spectator provides to her movie. *Esto* mobilizes the nostalgia associated with the aesthetic of Super 8 home movies but problematizes its authenticity by presenting a constructed memory of childhood, reenacted by an adult who merely simulates being a child.[13] Granted, the mobilization of nostalgia is not the only thing at work, for as Thomas astutely observes, "There are some specifics to the trajectory of Super 8 as a non-amateur format that cannot simply be subsumed to general nostalgia or dead technology fetishism." That trajectory involves a shift from the popular "home movie" uses of Super 8 to its rebirth as an artistic and experimental gauge more at "home" in the gallery, or online, than in the family residence—a space now occupied by cell phone videos, the predominant portable format. Such a form (digital faux Super 8) is being used, as I stated, to evoke history, memory, and pastness through the manipulation of style effects, by imitating the characteristics of aged celluloid film. This technique responds to Rosen's concept of "digital mimicry," which he defines as the capacity of the digital to imitate "preexisting compositional forms," including Super 8 film but also any celluloid film, analog video, and any format that can be simulated with digital after effects (*Change Mummified* 309).

Remarkably, despite its status as an art film, Cugliandolo's piece blurs the distinction between the amateur and the "professional," and its footage still evokes the home movie aesthetic. Such aesthetic is achieved, for example, by giving the appearance of unedited, chronological, "as is" filming and by including "flash frames, over and under-exposure, swish pans, variable focus, lack of establishing shots, jump cuts, hand-held camera, abrupt changes in time and place, inconsistent characters and no apparent character development, unusual camera angles and movements, and a minimal narrative line" (Erens 16–17). *Esto* deliberately employs these "amateur" features (here, experimental), as well as much editing and sound/image postproduction. For instance, the silent Super 8 footage is synced with an enigmatic musical track that reinforces the sensation of the fleetingness of the (manufactured) past. The sound editing stimulates private recollections, which interact with a filmed memory that never was but tints everything with affective charge. The electronic sounds are played in a minor key, inducing a mournful sense of loss, of time's passage, of fading memories, of being far from home. This affect might be considered as somewhat counterfeit, based on false social and kinship relations, for we do not recognize the film's character as related to us and we cannot derive any real sense of family or familiarity from this "home movie." Nevertheless, it is quite possible that spectators may tap into a kind of general family mood, the product of their own identification with the home movie genre. And, quite possibly, even a faux home movie such as *Esto* may induce a recalling of events from the spectator's own memory, triggered in part by the aesthetic effects of Super 8.

In his experimental "home movie" *Lost Lost Lost* (1975) Jonas Mekas demonstrated that the home movie aesthetic holds a special meaning for those in exile, like himself and Cugliandolo. In that film Mekas poignantly chronicles the life of Lithuanians exiled in New York City after World War II, as a self-reflexive meditation on the process of filmmaking itself, so that the exploration of "filmic approaches punctuate the larger narrative" (McDonald, "Lost" 23). For Cugliandolo, that larger narrative, glimpsed through the technical devices she deploys (i.e., the Super 8 aesthetic "style" as a trigger for affective nostalgia), is a narrative of Argentine diaspora linked to a history of exile that also recalls earlier work by Hirsch, Caldini, Honik, and other filmmakers displaced, exiled, or marginalized during the dictatorship.

Having seen a concrete example of the potential of Super 8 and digital hybrid films, and before introducing the work of Narcisa Hirsch (and later returning to Cugliandolo), I will investigate some further theoretical considerations regarding Super 8's return and its significance for the "intermedial" and transnational nature of experimental cinema, thus touching on some points already considered in the context of militant and art house filmmaking by previous chapters.

Reflections on Experimental Film, Super 8, and Intermediality

Radically heterogeneous, films that bypass narrative and focus on form are sometimes labeled "experimental." These films often self-reflexively explore their materiality, including the celluloid substrate and its properties as well as the recording and projecting apparatus. Lately, such explorations have extended to the use of digital cameras and postproduction and the combination of analog and digital processes, as I have indicated. Prior to digital's arrival, experimental filmmakers acted upon the celluloid material not just by exposing it to light but also through means that did not require a camera: painting, cutting, scratching, and adhering substances onto the emulsion (e.g., moth wings and flower petals in Stan Brakhage's *Mothlight* [1963]), or even burning it (e.g., Owen Land's *Bardo Follies* [1967]). Beyond investigating the substrate material, filmmakers experimented with filming, editing, and projection techniques to expand and blur the medium's limits, indeed marking a fluidity that often undermined essentialist and materially based notions of independent, singular media.[14] Today, as intermedial practices proliferate, a notion of medium exclusively linked to base material and its formal effects becomes difficult to sustain once those materials are mixed, as with Super 8 film that is later digitized yet maintains some of the effects of celluloid in its afterlife. Digital allows for a "falsification" of celluloid aesthetics, but it also has a degraded aesthetic of its own, achieved through the manipulation of glitches, pixilation, and other forms of digital degradation, making obsolescence itself an aesthetic style that can be rendered across media boundaries but can retain stylistic markers of historical media. These considerations suggest a modified understanding of medium that substitutes the centrality of the material base with a variety of stylistic effects (e.g., the historical look of Super 8 or the pixilation of digital), and that, in the words of media theorist Doron Galili, "allows the examination of media hybridization and convergence without [entirely] sacrificing a positive notion of specificity. If . . . the boundaries between media are fluid, then the appearance of each new technology also introduces multiple possibilities of combinations and overlaps with all other media" (208).

Today, projects freely migrate between analog and digital, since work filmed on celluloid is often transcribed to digital and then archived online. Less frequently, digital high-definition (HD) video is transferred to celluloid, as happens with some commercial cinema (and as was typical prior to theater conversion in 2013). Or to complicate matters, a film like Denis Villeneuve's *Dune* (2021) was shot with digital, transferred to 35 mm, and then the celluloid was rescanned back to digital: the filmmaker stated the original digital was too "crisp," the celluloid too "nostalgic" for a sci-fi film, and the final version combined and altered both sets of effects to get it just right (Mendelovich).[15] While problematizing Greenbergian notions of "purity" and authenticity, these types of migration arguably expand cinema's possibilities for viewership and long-term survival (in that sense medium migration parallels the economically driven immigration of the filmmakers themselves). Admittedly, this migration from one medium to another, from celluloid to digital, does not always guarantee archival success or improved audiovisual lifespan, and preservation experts point out that digital also has serious issues when it comes to long-term survival—some even argue that digital obsolescence is in fact a worse problem than degrading film stock. Inevitably as death, bits also decay ("bit rot"), data becomes corrupt, read-errors proliferate as time passes, and digital storage can be unreliable and also become obsolete as new versions of storage tape and devices are continuously developed, rendering previous ones unusable and driving up the cost of the preservation process. Moreover, storage in the film industry relies on Linear Tape-Open (LTO) technology as a cost-effective way to archive, but those tapes have at most a thirty-year lifespan, which then requires an additional migration to new tapes and formats. As the recuperation and reassembly of Fritz Lang's *Metropolis* demonstrated, celluloid is capable of surviving under the right circumstances (perfect temperature and humidity). What this impossible dream of "eternal storage" underscores is precisely the importance of a "hybrid" approach to preservation, one that allows for a multiplicity of methods and approaches, as the search for an eventual "ideal" solution, the archive that will never degrade, continues. The mixed nature and impure approach to archival practices, drawing on LTO, cloud storage, blockchain, celluloid, and other "obsolete" formats, aligns well with my argument about the increasingly intermedial and border crossing aspects of contemporary audiovisual culture.[16]

Intermediality, therefore, signals an "impure" cinema, in the form of digital-analog hybrids and mixed-media experiments, as Nagib and Jerslev theorize in *Impure Cinema: Intermedial and Intercultural Approaches to Film*, a point we discussed in previous chapters. For them, "there is no denying the difficulty in establishing clear borders between neighboring arts and media, in particular those heavily reliant on ever-evolving technologies, resulting in the constructedness of any attempt to define 'film as film'" (xxi). This intermediality and media convergence have facilitated the transnational flows of cinematic experiments, now easily uploadable to the web. Consequently, both filmmaking and spectatorship are becoming increasingly global, as artists interact through video dialogues across vast geographical distances and virtual, transcontinental filmmaker communities proliferate online. And just as emerging intermedial and hybrid cinematic practices have retained traces from their materially grounded past, the new transnational networks of artists retain, even after their relocations and migrations, ongoing vibrant links with their national origins. At the crossroads between transnational artistic and medial networks, filmmakers like Cugliandolo still stylize their work to evoke a history of nation and past media. Their work is transforming experimental film, as Naficy suggests, into a hybridized border crossing in which media and cultural limits become entirely porous (32). Experimental cinema is intermedial, intercultural, and diasporic.

Now, at the very moment of celluloid's impending disappearance, much avant-garde work on Super 8 film focuses on its potential to "merge" (at least partially) with the digital. The success of its return, evident since the early 2000s, can be seen in the proliferation of Super 8 festivals and the sales of secondhand Super 8 cameras on websites such as eBay (a similar trend is taking place with still photo cameras). As further proof of what the Kodak CEO called an "analog renaissance," during the 2016 Consumer Electronics Show that company announced the anticipated release of a new hybrid Super 8/digital camera that combined filming with celluloid and digital-based features (Sax).[17] Kodak also announced its "Super 8 Revival Initiative," promoting "a range of cameras, film development services, [digital] post production tools and more." The new hybrid camera, according to filmmaker J. J. Abrams, "appears to be the perfect bridge between the efficiency of the digital world and the warmth and quality of analog" (Mamiit). No doubt, Super 8 has an immediate quality about it, a closeness to the human body from which it appears to extend "naturally" on account of its smaller format, its connection to home movies, the portability of its cameras, its capacity for in-camera editing (a practice favored by Cugliandolo), and the haunting warmth of its colors. Like other photographic media, Super 8 can also claim indexical properties that, as Rosen argues, persist after digitalization as a remnant "digital indexicality." Thomas observes, however, that these qualities alone do not explain the resilient return of Super 8, since "there has been no reported Renaissances of 9.5mm or 8mm, though, as long term home movie formats, they must loom large in the memories of many, and their particular look evokes pastness as surely as any two-color process." Super 8's affordability, ease of use, and aesthetic potential gave it an edge for survival, and now, with the added malleability of digital postproduction, ushered its rebirth as an expanded hybrid format.

The return of Super 8 entailed rediscovering long forgotten filmmakers (*superocheros* in Spanish) who acquired a mythical status as underground figures, time travelers, or revenants at the crossroads of old and new, at the heart of a "unique experience of using a medium that was long seen as the newest of aesthetic technologies and the cutting edge of cultural expression but [which] is now becoming the anachronistic embodiment of a passing era," making their films a "reflection and reconsideration about relationships between pasts and futures" (Skoller xxx). A fascination with uncanny temporalities coupled with increased attention to "residual media" has resulted in a (relative) proliferation of international events reframing Super 8 historically but also presenting it as a born-again, digitally transferred practice. At key events such as the 2010 Caldini and Hirsch MALBA retrospective, the filmmakers themselves were on display, becoming projectionists for their works in the spectator-filled screening room (DiTella 18). The hands-on nature of projecting Super 8, with its glitches and impromptu manual repairs, was vital for the viewing experience, a distant cry from the invisibility of the projectionist and the projection apparatus in commercial cinema and, admittedly, in hybrid digitized Super 8.[18]

As stated earlier, the turn to the intermedial coincides with a postnational outlook inherent in hybrid approaches to film, as Super 8 brings international practitioners together through festivals, blogs, and social media, resulting in mutual stylistic and technical influences. The ease with which artists use Super 8 cameras and upload their films online after digital post-production has facilitated its circulation and transnational appeal and diminished the presence of obvious national elements. Nevertheless, the national persists in the transnational, and so-called post-national films should be critically read with that in mind. To do so, I will contextualize Cugliandolo's transnational films in Super 8 practices rooted in 1960s Buenos Aires but also adapted to 2000s Barcelona. This move will illustrate two fundamental aspects of my argument: first, by examining a representative Argentine film by Hirsch, I show that the Super 8 format was always already intermedial and vital to the transnational ebbs and flows of experimental filmmaking; second, by looking at one more film by Cugliandolo, I demonstrate how Argentine filmmakers in the diaspora echo their predecessors by imprinting their digital Super 8 films with a persistent "memory" of celluloid and of the national.

The Birth of Super 8 in Argentina: The Buenos Aires Underground (1960s–1970s)

In the 1960s, a group of Super 8 filmmakers came together under the patronage of the prestigious Goethe Institute in Buenos Aires.[19] Coalescing around luminaires Narcisa Hirsch and Claudio Caldini, the group also included Marie-Louise Alemann, Jorge Honik, his siblings Alberto and Laura Honik, Hugo Arias, Laura Abel, Juan José Mugni, Adrián Tubio, Horacio Valleregio, Juan Villola, Eduardo Pla, and Silvestre Byrón. These Argentines learned from the latest North American and European structural films by the likes of Michael Snow, Ernie Gehr, Hollis Frampton, Paul Sharits, and Peter Kubelka. They drew inspiration from New York New Wave's emphasis on individual expression and technique as seen in the cinema of John Cassavetes, Stanley Kubrick, Martin Scorsese, and Brian De Palma, while rejecting how the Americans subordinated formal elements to narration and character development. The Argentines had greater affinity with the New York underground, emulating Jonas Mekas's home movie aesthetic, Stan Brakhage's painterly manipulation of celluloid, Shirley Clarke's abstract dance films (a foremost influence for Caldini), Maya Deren's psychodramas (critical for Hirsch), Andy Warhol's long-take anti-films, and Lionel Rogosin's neorealist docu-fictions, all well known to the Buenos Aires group. The *superocheros* also learned hands-on from the German filmmaker Werner Nekes, who, like Jonas Mekas, taught Super 8 workshops in Buenos Aires in the 1970s (Alonso, "The Buenos Aires Underground"; Wolkowicz; Rist, *Historical* 241–42).

Known as the Grupo Cine Experimental Argentino, or Grupo Goethe, the *superocheros* began creating their own abstract, structuralist films. Their formalism drew harsh criticism from militant filmmakers such as Fernando "Pino" Solanas and Octavio Getino (Cine Liberación), who's combative *La hora de los hornos*, as we saw in chapter 1, relied on a Soviet-style montage of poverty, violence, injustice, and a dogmatic voice-over calling for armed revolution. Although there was some minor overlap between the two groups, on the whole the militant filmmakers viewed the experimentalists as bourgeois dilettantes, uncommitted to the struggle of their times, or worse, as silently complicit with the military regime.[20] While understandable given the polarized atmosphere, this was an unfairly harsh judgment. It is true that Alemann and Hirsch had connections in the government like many bourgeois families in Buenos Aires, but they did not ideologically support the dictatorship (DiTella 79). It is true that they selected a neutral stance, ostensibly leaving politics out of their films. Working in a climate of political repression the Goethe Group chose a different route: to contest antiquated aesthetic values and institutionalized forms of art.[21] Without reaching the level of dissent espoused by art cinemas like Cinema Novo, the Grupo Goethe's experimentalism represented a countercultural force against the military dictatorship (indirectly) and the hegemony of the established cinema industry (directly). Silvestre Byrón argues that without openly challenging the regime, they were still "exponiéndose al autoritarismo dominante. Aquellas imágenes, contestatarias y plenas de ese irracionalismo amoral, iban reñidas con las recomendaciones del 'ser nacional'" [exposing themselves to the dominant authoritarianism. Those images, contestatory and replete with amoral irrationalism, were in opposition to the government's idea of national identity].[22] Studying the films of the Grupo Goethe provides a genealogical link useful to grasp contemporary Super 8 films of the Argentine diaspora; the origins of its intermediality, concern with transnationalism, and fascination with memory, as well as its understanding of the politics of form, were already manifest in the earlier period. The best entry point into the Grupo Goethe's films is through one of its leading filmmakers, Narcisa Hirsch.

Narcisa Hirsch's *Come Out* (1971)

Intermedial approaches defined Hirsch's career from its outset. She began as a painter and performance artist but became a filmmaker after meeting

Mekas in New York in 1967, and later when the Lithuanian-American presented his films in Buenos Aires (Torres 88). In New York, a hub for experimental cinema, Hirsch became acquainted with films by Deren and other legends, attending screenings at the MoMA and at the Millennium Film Workshop (Szperling 74). She returned to Buenos Aires with prints of structuralist works—among them Snow's *Wavelength* (1967)—and soon began making her own films (Rist, *Historical* 241–42). During the '70s and '80s Hirsch filmed with Super 8 and 16 mm, eventually moved on to video, and recently began working with digitized Super 8 footage; hence, Hirsch exemplifies the increasingly intermedial transformation of experimental film throughout these decades. As Andrea Giunta asserts, her heterogeneous style displays characteristics from structural film (its precision and self-reflexivity) but also from psychodrama (its depth and psychological intensity) (9).

Inspired by Snow's structuralist masterpiece, *Wavelength* (1967), Hirsch filmed *Come Out* in 1971, making one of her most abstract works (Giunta 9). According to Giunta, Hirsch's films are patently structural and control with obsessive precision "the audiovisual, temporal and narrative composition" (4). In *Visionary Film*, Sitney describes structural film as "static, epistemologically oriented films in which duration and structure determine, rather than follow, content" (27). Structural film tends toward abstraction: the camera is often fixed (though not always), there are rarely human figures, and, following a methodical approach, it explores a limited number of variables to investigate its own material nature (analog, digital, or hybrid). Structural film proceeds in an almost scientific manner, for example, through the exploration of a protracted zoom in *Wavelength*, or the search for duration and changing rates of image velocity in *Serene Velocity* (Ernie Gehr, 1970), or the analysis of the fragile nature of both film and memory in *Print Generation* (J. J. Murphy, 1974). As Sitney demonstrates, in these works, "the shape of the whole film is predetermined and simplified, and it is that shape which is the primal impression of the film" (348). Structural films, so calculated, objective and minimalist, contrast with the lyrical or mythopoetic films exemplified by Deren's psychodrama *Meshes*, or Brakhage and Anger's films, which are visually exuberant and deeply subjective works. Hirsch drew on both filmic influences (structuralism and psychodrama), and other ones, including Fluxus films and performances. Hirsch's own understanding of the materiality of film was closer to the Fluxus position, unconcerned with medium purity, deploying an intermediality that freely mixed different media (using various stock sources, painting, and scratching the celluloid, later adding video and now, digital footage). As we shall see, Hirsch was also a precursor to

Cugliandolo and other contemporary filmmakers in how she simulates one medium with another.

Hirsch's *Come Out* (see fig. 3.3) fulfills many of Sitney's criteria for structural film; it is divided into two main sequences, each comprised of a single fixed camera shot. The first is a very long take that starts as a blurred image and gradually becomes focused, revealing a record player's needle placed on a rotating record; this record will also be, after significant remediation, the film's "original" sound source. The second sequence is a much shorter shot showing the record viewed from above, in a static zenithal shot. As the record stops rotating, its title, also the film's title, becomes legible: "Come Out." The film is described by Trerotola as "a formalist view of the cinematic language that conjugates accident and geometry from the complexity of the possibilities of audio and image. . . . *Come Out* at the same time dismounts [*sic*] and reinforces the compositive concept of a sound piece of the same title by Steve Reich." In Hirsch's *Come Out* the music and voices are at first perfectly audible while the image is blurred, but then the sound goes gradually out of phase until the repeating words "come out"

Figure 3.3. *Come Out* (1971) a film by Narcisa Hirsch (08:25). *Source: Come Out* (1971). Dir. Narcisa Hirsch.

become unrecognizable, even as the image sharpens into focus. The reverse disjunction between sound and image is both a structuring and a destabilizing or defamiliarizing element: structuring because such disjunction follows opposing but predictable and meticulously (metrically) controlled patterns, destabilizing because this device is not used for narrative purposes but as a scientific exercise to test the medium's constraints and the potential to go beyond them.

Come Out, however, exceeds abstract experimentation and flirts with representation. This fact underscores a reality: even at its most scientific, structural film always contains an element of the poetic; even at its most abstract, theme, metaphor, and content shine through. Despite her claim that the piece is not political, Hirsch's deliberate choice of the soundtrack by minimalist composer Steve Reich is highly significant. Reich's original lyrics sample a disturbing sentence: "I had to, like, open the bruise up, and let some of the bruise blood come out to show them." Reich remixes the fragment "come out to show them" into a progressively layered sound collage. The original sentence was spoken by Daniel Hamm, a young African American who, along with other youths, was arrested and savagely beaten by New York City police after being wrongly accused of the murder of a grocer during the 1964 Harlem riots, at the height of the civil rights struggle (Perone 72–73).[23] Reich, commissioned by the civil rights movement to create a musical piece that exposed police brutality, produced the soundtrack that Hirsch adds to her experimental film. The piece was both powerful and controversial on account of its avant-garde stance vis-à-vis a political incident (for a detailed analysis of Reich's piece, see Gopinath). Reich recorded Hamm's statement on two audio channels, which at the start of the recording play in unison. As they shift out of phase with each other, the sound begins to reverberate, producing a hypnotic, trance-like effect, described by Reich as "a controlled chaos" in which the words are no longer recognizable (Perone 72). Most significantly, Reich's countercultural music with its reference to racial violence and police brutality in the United States also distantly resonates with the violence Argentina was experiencing during the Dirty War at the hands of police and military forces; this is where the film's translatability and transnational significance resides. Admittedly, Hirsch's formalist handling of source material (like Reich's) renders referentiality as secondary and elliptical.[24] But perhaps more interesting to the argument about intermediality and the transnational flows of art, this piece, through its recourse to aesthetics and the (fragmented) memory of a past event, represents the appropriation and repurposing of one analog medium (the vinyl record) by another (celluloid film) and years later, by its rebirth through digital video. The fraught intersection of politics and intermedial aesthetics is achieved through a transnational shift, in this case from New York to Buenos Aires, or in Cugliandolo's work as we saw, from Buenos Aires to Barcelona.

These intermedial and national shifts do not necessarily result in either the film's depoliticization or its disconnect from the indexical referents. As a result of Hirsch's refusal to pursue narrative (even if she includes it as a veiled subtext), there is an ethics or politics of the image at work here. This politics has to do with both its defamiliarizing potential and a denial to yield to master narratives, which nevertheless accepts and maintains a link (even if asynchronous) to the material, corporeal reality outside the film (arguably, to suffering, repression, and the body as the site for resistance). More to the point, Hirsch situates the image's charge in the very process of layering media. Such layering reaches remarkable levels of complexity, in the kinds of media that are mixed *and* the technologies that are deployed and (re)produced: whether a (diegetic) sound recording (itself repurposed from an already processed fragment of Hamm's tape-recorded "confession") and a filmic image or the (now) vintage technologies of record player, tape recorder and small-gauge film, or different types of images superimposed onto each other. In recent films Hirsch has embraced the layering effect she can achieve with digital manipulation of her 1960s and 1970s Super 8 and 16 mm films. New techniques, such as digitizing Super 8 and posting her films online provide greater visibility for previous work. Hirsch now screens her old films, often in a multiple projection format, projecting a Super 8 or 16 mm image onto a larger video projection of the same film. This palimpsest can be read as a metaphor for her own rebirth in the digital age and as recognition of Super 8 and 16 mm film's digital afterlife.

Patently, Super 8 and other outmoded formats have been digitally repurposed by filmmakers such as Cugliandolo and Hirsch not just to provide a stand in for pastness and historical memory that counters celluloid's putative obsolescence but also to question media boundaries and notions of medium purity, authenticity, or originality. This technological palimpsest is best read, deciphered, and decoded through media archeology approaches, whether academic or artistic, that reposition cinema in an intermedial context. Exemplified by Friedrich Kittler, Wofgang Ernst, Siegfried Zielinski, Jussi Parikka, Erkki Huhtamo, Tom Gunning, Matthew Kirschenbaum, Thomas Elsaesser, and others, such approaches "add unexpected genealogies to our contemporary visual culture and serve to defamiliarize the cinema, and thus to refresh our awareness of it. They can put in crisis habitual classifications and categories, such as text, work or author, rather than put the digital forward as a surreptitious (and even more deterministic) new teleology" (Elsaesser, "The New Film History" 89).

Transnational Super 8 in the Post-Medium Age: From Buenos Aires to Barcelona (and Back Again)

Today, Buenos Aires remains a preeminent center for independent and small-gauge cinema, as reflected in the existence of collectives such as the Club del Súper 8 led by Paulo Pécora and the proliferation of festivals such as the Buenos Aires Festival Internacional de Cine Independiente (BAFICI) or its counterpart in Mar del Plata (MARFICI), the Bienal de la Imagen en Movimiento (BIM), and multiple events sponsored by the University of Buenos Aires Rojas Cultural Center. Young Argentine filmmakers working with Super 8, among other formats, include Jorge La Ferla, Pablo Marín, Ernesto Baca, Hernán Khourián (who studied in Barcelona), Rubén Guzmán, Gonzalo Egurza, Andrés Denegri, Javier Olivera, Macarena Gagliardi Cordiviola, Azune Losana (born in Mexico), Pablo Mazzolo, Leandro Listorti, Tomas Dota, Mario Bocchichio, Benjamin Ellenberger, Gustavo Galuppo, and Sergio Subero, to name the more prominent of a younger generation. Most reside in Buenos Aires (Olivera in Montevideo) but travel to Spain to participate in festivals; there is a vibrant exchange between both countries' experimental film circles and many cultural, linguistic, and historical affinities.

In the aftermath of the 2001 Argentine financial crisis, several filmmakers, including some Buenos Aires *superocheros*, relocated to Barcelona, where experimental film still receives support from institutions such as the CCCB, the MACBA, and the Filmoteca de Catalunya.[25] Thanks to curatorial efforts by filmmaker-promoters such as Albert Alcoz, Antoni Pinent, and others, Barcelona has become a prime destination for Latin American experimental cineastes to showcase their work.[26] Along with Hispano-Argentine filmmakers residing in Barcelona, such as Daniela Cugliandolo, Florencia Alberti, Gustavo Caprín, Iván Marino, and Sol Prado, there are others (such as Gonzalo Egurza), who while not living in Spain travel there frequently. Attesting to these cross-national and trans-temporal alliances, in March 2015 Egurza curated a program of Argentine films at the Zumzeig theater (in Barcelona), featuring 1960s Super 8 films by Jorge Honik and hybrid analog-digital films by Egurza himself. Moreover, collectives such as Barcelona's Crater-Lab have sponsored filmmaker-in-residence stays for Argentine artists as part of their mission to "impulsar la creación de un cine artesanal en soporte fílmico y facilitar las condiciones para realizarlo de manera independiente" [promote the creation of an artisanal filmmaking that uses celluloid and facilitate its independent status]. Although these initiatives don't always specifically target artists from Argentina, there is a unique connection between the Barcelona and Buenos Aires independent film scene precisely because both cities have been at the forefront of Super 8's most recent intermedial return (in its digitized format), and on account of the transnational flows of films and filmmakers already discussed. The transatlantic exchange is founded precisely on the mobility of experimental genres across both national boundaries and media and on the willingness of filmmakers to share their expertise with others, both at home and abroad. Next, I examine one last film by Cugliandolo, adding yet another link to this transnational genealogy of diasporic experimental cinema traceable to 1960s Argentina.

Cugliandolo's *pneurosis* (2001): Between Hitchcock and Méliès, Snow and Deren

In most of her work, Cugliandolo traverses an ambiguous territory, neither fully narrative nor completely experimental, analogous to her in-between national status (at once Argentine and Spanish but also a mix of both, a transnational subject). In her movies, she typically retains a hint of anecdote, although her ultimate purpose is experimenting with different filmic materials and techniques (analog, digital, and hybrid) and challenging spectators' perceptions. As we saw, in *Esto no es un recuerdo* Cugliandolo recaptures Hirsch's interest in memory and time's passage, evoking a nostalgic—yet undeniably fabricated—home movie aesthetic through its digitized Super 8. In *pneurosis*, Cugliandolo deploys digitally enhanced Super 8 footage again, in this case to explore the interplay between subjective and objective perspective. These key works in her trajectory distinctly show that contemporary avant-garde film practice, by becoming self-reflexive about questions of its materiality (broadly understood as a medium, its traces, effects and affects), has brought into focus a transitional stage in experimental media that places high value on hybridizing photochemical film with digital video. This turn to hybrid film has in turn ignited a dialogue about the future of past cinematic technologies and, as we have seen, repositioned Super 8 (and to a lesser extent 16 mm) as a "newly" refurbished format. For young filmmakers, Super 8 functions as a "residual medium" evoking a "retrospective sensibility" associated with the "rediscovery of vintage artifacts and styles" (Acland xiv). By now it should be self-evident that, regardless of whether one accepts intermediality or insists on the outdated specificity of media, these considerations are becoming strictly theoretical in light of a hybrid, contemporary film praxis. Simply put, artists and filmmakers are constantly mixing and repurposing materials and are not troubled by any breach of medium purity. Fortunately, celluloid film's swan song (if that is what the Super 8 revival signals) will not announce the death of cinema; quite the contrary, as Rodowick and other critics assert, it signifies only its transformation, its remediation.

The catalog of the 2008 Cambridge Super 8 Film Festival describes *pneurosis* as "the feminine enigma in the nude. Ordinary objects in the bathroom, at the service of the character's obsessions" (12). Cugliandolo's film functions as a symbolic narrative rooted in the mundane and set in a familiar space. It is centered on the performance of the nude body, highlighting how contemporary Super 8 practice distances itself from the more abstract tendencies of American structuralist film but maintains some of its characteristics, including an interest in filmic materiality and documenting its own technological process. The film, depicting a woman's (strange) bath rituals, is formally structured through a chain of visual and auditory distortions that generate its surrealist overtones. The film *pneurosis* is paradigmatic of Cugliandolo's work in that it only sketches out the most tenuous of narratives, choreographing it to explore a series of plastic visual effects and synchronizing it to a pulsating techno-trance soundtrack.

Playfully winking at the Argentine obsession with psychoanalysis, *pneurosis* resonates with the fragmented logic of a dream, or of mental instability, bringing to mind Jean-Louis Baudry's marvelous description of the cinema as an artificial psychosis (310–11). In addition to its structuralist component, *pneurosis* might also be categorized as a "trance film," a genre with origins in oneiric movies such as Deren's *Meshes* (a film influential for Hirsch, as mentioned), which also explores inner subjectivity; or earlier to Luis Buñuel and Salvador Dalí's 1929 surrealist tour de force *Un chien andalou*; or closer to Buenos Aires, Horacio Coppola's lesser-known 1933 short film *Traum* (Dream). All of these films share what Sitney describes as the structure of a "dream unfolded within shifting perspectives" (15), issuing a challenge to spatiotemporal conventions. Of course, Cugliandolo's film is firmly situated between its psychodrama and structuralist tendencies. That is to say, beneath any appearance of irrationality, *pneurosis* is motivated by a fastidiously rigorous exploration of its own cinematic materiality (of digitally processed Super 8) and is obsessed with light, surface, and texture.

Set in a dilapidated bathroom, the film starts with a rapid montage of disconcerting shots: an upside-down cutout silhouette of a woman, a white screen, a plain tile wall, and the female protagonist swallowing an unknown pill. This opening offers a sample of the illusionistic stop-action that follows, while referencing Alice's trip to Wonderland. The camera then quickly pans around the bathroom and refocuses on the sink, where the title and credits appear. Then, inviting us down the rabbit hole into a journey of inner subjectivity, the camera approaches for an extreme close-up of the drainpipe and spirals in, as if to metaphorically enter the character's psyche, in an eerie citation of the legendary drain shot in *Psycho*'s shower scene. The spectator does not easily identify with the character since neither the camera movement nor the framing assume a fully subjective point of view. Instead, a certain tension is maintained between the psychic subjectivity induced through distortion effects and a more distanced camera position, as the film fluidly oscillates between first- and third-person perspectives; between formalist structuralism and the dreamlike, sexualized psychodrama; between objectivity and subjectivity. We are, for example, treated to optical tricks, which reflect the woman's mental states, achieved through a combination of rapid editing, jump cuts, and shifting in and out of focus. Molding her foamy hair into impossible shapes through analog stop-action filming, Cugliandolo's childlike play renders tribute to Méliès and to what Gunning brilliantly dubbed the early "cinema of attractions," and through the distortions suggests a kind of psychedelic trip (see fig. 3.4).

Besides the analog stop-motion tricks (edited in-camera), Cugliandolo uses digital technology to achieve a defamiliarizing effect, morphing the woman's face so that one of her eyes becomes a rhomboidal shape, eventually dissolving through a graphic match into a metal spigot, suggesting the blurring boundaries between organic and inorganic, and also digital and analog (see fig. 3.5). Although at times it is difficult to separate effects achieved through mechanical means (reflections through spoons, glasses, prisms) from digital filters, distortions, and so on, that is precisely the point—analog and digital effects become indistinguishable and are at the service of an aesthetic that subsumes all to the trance-like marvelous beauty of the film.

Other tricks are equally mesmerizing and reflective on film history, media theory, and material archeology. For example, when the protagonist looks through a toilet paper roll, in a mirroring of Cugliandolo's own act

Figure 3.4. *pneurosis* (2001) and the aesthetic of attraction (01:08). *Source: pneurosis* (2001). Dir. Daniela Cugliandolo.

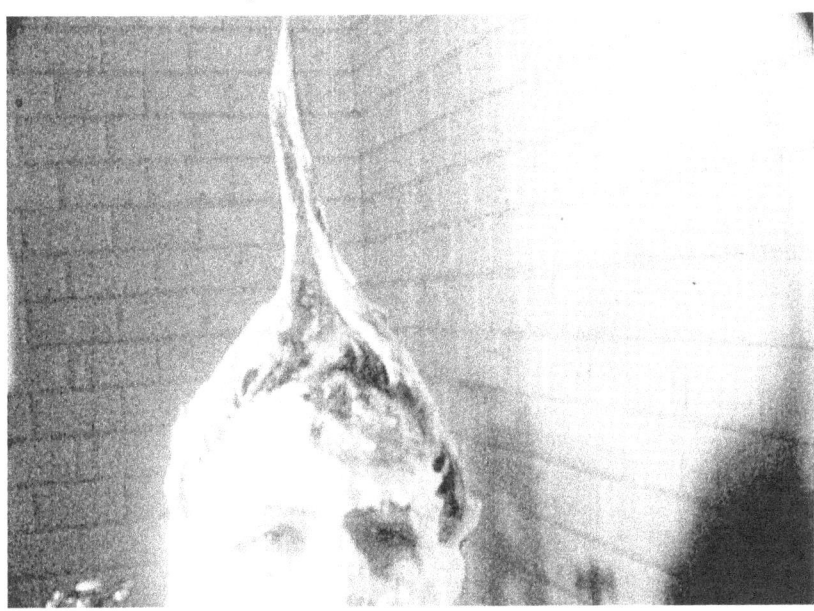

Figure 3.5. *pneurosis* (2001) and digital postproduction effects (04:31). *Source: pneurosis* (2001). Dir. Daniela Cugliandolo.

of filming, which doubles as an intertextual visual parody of Dziga Vertov's revolutionary Kino-Eye symbol (*Kinoglaz*)—displaying an eye reflected inside a camera lens, signifying the superior capabilities of the camera, its position between science and art, and its amalgamation of organic and inorganic vision. Such playful irreverence continues, as any semblance of a routine bath has been defamiliarized through an exploration of devices that skirt the ontological divide between analog and digital, making it impracticable (and irrelevant) to know which effects are achieved through analog lens distortions and which with computer editing or by combining both. This hybrid technological Wonderland turns space and time upside down, for instance when Cugliandolo, through a trick superimposition, places the bidet on a wall. Then a series of increasingly overexposed frames "drown" the woman in light as the overexposure spreads through the filmic negative, foregrounding the remains of the celluloid past that persist in the digital, yet another meta-cultural comment about the postmodern recycling of past technologies.

Still mimicking the influence of a drug-induced pneurosis, a multishot sequence shows the character gripped by obsessive-compulsive behavior as she washes and smells her hands over and over. The rapid montage and repetition of movements recall the obsessive repetitions, spatial gaps, and temporal ellipsis that characterize dreams or hallucinations, and indeed the intermittent nature of cinema itself, as if penetrating the flickering realm, the very memory of an art that is already—imagine that—130 years of age, our beloved shadow-play. The film ends by uncannily replaying its key sequences in reverse, deconstructing temporal flow, turning time back to the era of Super 8. The film's fragmentation and vertiginous use of montage counters digital cinema's visual seamlessness by thematizing the stuttering, intermittent, and at times neurotic action of the Super 8 projector, so prone to breaking, stopping, and even bursting into flames. Serving as a tribute to Caldini and Hirsch's generation, the resulting ontological ambiguity demonstrates that digital video encompasses a persistent analog afterimage that is also intertwined with memories of the (national) past. Despite *pneurosis*'s suggestive psychoanalytic overtones and its rendition of cinema as a neurotic multimedia mashup, filled with slippages, abrupt jumps, in-between spaces, and narrative discontinuities, what matters for Cugliandolo is creating a visual experience that projects a certain phantasmagoric affective mood but resists definitive interpretation. It haunts, but does not clarify its message. No doubt, inherent to the aesthetic deployed by Cugliandolo is the sensation of historicity triggered by her use of past technologies, since "alongside the material entwinement of the old and the new is a particular experience and understanding of the passing of time and historical change" (Acland xvii), an experience that, as we saw with *Esto no es un recuerdo*, is closely linked to (fading) memories (of celluloid), of childhood, of the national, and of history itself, cinematic and otherwise.

Argentine Video Art and Diasporic Dialogues in *This Is Just to Say* (2012–2016)

In the aftermath of Super 8 came analog video, soon thereafter followed by digital video. Both analog video and Super 8 had their origin in the home movie; they were initially home media, created in the home and viewed in the home, with both formats accentuating closeness, intimacy. A fundamental difference, of course, is that in Super 8 (like all celluloid) the light comes from behind the viewer, the image is projected onto the screen, whereas in video the image itself is the source of light, and this is a fundamental distinction that ultimately determines that any Super 8 effect is only an approximation to the actual experience of film. That said, in the transmedia spirit of our time, melding film and video through processes like superimposed projections (such as Hirsch's and Cugliandolo's), rephotographic methods that scan each Super 8 frame individually, digital manipulation or filters, is becoming increasingly frequent.

We have considered how Argentine artists such as Cugliandolo, Hirsch, and Caldini have recuperated an outdated format, Super 8, to investigate issues related to diaspora, memory, nostalgia, and national belonging. But Super 8 is not the only obsolete format that has received attention from experimental filmmakers, as many have also returned to analog video for film projects, freely mixing it with Super 8 and 16 mm formats, as well as digital video.[27] In 2012 two established Argentine artists, one living in Buenos Aires (Andrés Denegri) and the other in Barcelona (Gustavo Caprín), began a collaborative project entitled *This Is Just to Say* (*TIJTS*). The concept for the art project was predicated on establishing an epistolary weekly exchange of videos that would represent an intimate artistic dialogue between the two filmmakers and friends. Filmed in both public and private spaces, the subject matter for the videos was bound by a loose set of "rules" and the results were radically heterogeneous, ranging from completely nonrepresentational abstract pieces, to casually registered quotidian events (people crossing a street, lounging on a balcony, packing for a trip, celebrating an event), to lengthy static camera shots of urban and rural landscapes, to actual epistolary video essays or diary-like entries. In short, the back-and-forth dialogue between the two artists included an assorted arrangement of both carefully constructed and impromptu videos that resisted categorization and coalesced into a chaotic quilt of materials as varied as

> postales, cartas, confesiones, retratos, autorretratos, paisajes, pasajes autobiográficos, registros caseros, delicadas puestas en escena, imprevistos testimonios, grabaciones espontáneas, pequeñas acciones performáticas y bellas imágenes inútiles, que se articulan en el pulso de un íntimo diario personal narrado a un amigo. ("Medios Audiovisuales")

> [postcards, letters, confessions, portraits, self-portraits, landscapes, autobiographical fragments, household recordings, subtle staging(s), unexpected testimonies, spontaneous recordings, small performative actions, and beautiful useless images, all of it beating with the pulse of an intimate personal diary narrated to a close friend.]

Eventually, these artistic videos were archived online, on a website created for the project by the filmmakers. This was not an afterthought, rather for the critic Emilio Bernini it was a driving force behind the project, precisely to explore the possibilities of the combination of the aesthetic possibilities of video (whether analog or digital) and the capacity for the internet to make archiving, and more critically, distribution and viewing possible across the globe almost instantly:

> [U]no de los motivos de la serie es estético, y también tecnológico: intercambiar como cartas los propios videos tiene algo novedoso; y a la vez es algo posible solo con el medio del video y la internet: la duración de las series que pueden extenderse por años no sería posible sin dudas en el cine. ("[No] Serialidad")

> [One of the reasons for creating the series is aesthetic, and also technological: exchanging the videos as letters is innovative, and at the same time it is only possible with the video format and the internet. Series that go on for years are not feasible for movie theaters, for example.]

In addition to the aesthetic considerations of the project, of its desire to explore the materiality of video and its afterlife on the web, there is undoubtedly a powerful affective component to *TIJTS* that stems from its epistolary nature, with a nostalgic sense of "home" and transnational displacement deeply rooted in a country that was, after all, a country of immigrants. According to Andrés Denegri, this affective element found in the videos can be traced to his desire to maintain a link with someone, another Argentine, who had left his homeland as part of the diaspora: "En mi caso este intercambio epistolar tiene como base uno de los motores originales del género, el deseo de mantenerse vinculado a una persona querida" ("[No] Serialidad") [In my case, this epistolary exchange held at its core one of the original driving impulses of that genre, the desire to remain linked to a loved one]. As Denegri explains, key to this intense affective exchange is the idea of the quotidian, of a shared intimacy and immediacy of the little things, even across time and distance: "Al contarle los detalles valiosos de mi cotidianidad y al recibir los suyos con cierta periodicidad, la vida de ambos se entrecruza; a la distancia la vida del otro está presente en la mía, tanto cuando recorro sus relatos como en el acto de narrarle los míos ("[No] Serialidad") [When I tell him (Caprín) the worthwhile details of my daily life, and upon receiving his with some frequency, our lives become imbricated; even at a distance the life of the other is present in mine, as much when I follow his stories as when I narrate my own].

After the first edition of the project, which lasted two years and resulted in fifty-nine epistolary videos, the scope was expanded to include additional filmmakers. Later installments or editions of *TIJTS* (in 2014 and 2016) included the collaboration of two more artists, Javier Olivera, an Argentine who immigrated to Montevideo (Uruguay), and Gustavo Galuppo, who resides in Rosario (Argentina). The video dialogues in the latter two editions were between Gustavo Galuppo and Gustavo Caprín, and also between Andrés Denegri and Javier Olivera. Counting the three installments or editions there are 189 videos, each one every bit as revealing as the next. At its conclusion in 2016 the entire project was archived online, at http://thisisjusttosay.net. Given the sheer magnitude of the project, I will focus here on only two of the videos, more specifically from the epistolary exchange between Denegri and Caprín. Although I tried to select paradigmatic examples, the entire videography needs to be carefully studied in the future. While every video in the series is sui generis and richly complex, through these two selected ones we might extrapolate a general understanding about the project as a whole.

To grasp the significance of *TIJTS* it is useful to first place the art of these filmmakers in contextual perspective. Andrés Denegri (1975–) works mainly on film, video, photography, and installation art. Like many contemporary experimental filmmakers, Denegri freely mixes media including Super 8, 16 mm, and analog and digital video, often exploring the materiality of obsolete media and equipment, including old formats and vintage cameras and projectors. In the catalog from "Máquinas de lo sensible" [Machines of the Sensible], a 2020 retrospective about Denegri's work organized and promoted by the Buenos Aires–based Rolf Art Gallery, we read the following press release description of the filmmaker's conceptual framework and his nuanced conceptualization about the heterogeneous materiality and nature of the cinematic event:

> La recuperación y manipulación del aparato cinematográfico, más la apropiación y recuperación de archivos fílmicos, su nuevo registro digital y el retorno al soporte fotoquímico, se mezclan y culminan en la proyección fílmica y en la exhibición de su maquinaria en forma de instalación. El despliegue del aparato, el correr de la película, el sinfín, el haz de luz que sale de los proyectores y la imagen resultante es un proceso de combinatoria entre medios. ("Máquinas de lo sensible")

> [The recovery and manipulation of the cinematic apparatus, added to the appropriation and recuperation of filmic archives, of their new digital register, and a return to the photochemical base, all of these are intermixed and culminate in the filmic projection and in the exhibition of its machinery through the form of installation art. The showcasing of the apparatus and its resulting image is a process that combines media.]

What this description of Denegri's modus operandi reveals is that the focus of his work is squarely on the hybridity of visual media, on the complexity of combining and intertwining a plurality of media sources and the "sensible machines" that produce them in order to create work that skirts the line between experimental cinema, photography, sculpture, and installation art, indeed bridging the gap between cinema and contemporary visual/installation art. Moreover, Denegri's work builds on a lengthy tradition of "expanded cinema," that is, those efforts that have sought to take cinema beyond its limited projection onto the movie theater screen (or the television screen) and have instead produced myriad alternative spaces and cinematic technologies (in galleries and museums, on building facades, in sculptural and 3D spaces, on bodies). Denegri boldly goes further with these hybrid projects than even most forms of contemporary experimental cinema, which are still mainly created for projection on a flat screen, tethered in many ways to traditional projection, viewing, and distribution. Without wholly abandoning a nostalgia for projection, Denegri moves beyond it. Jorge La Ferla, the noted Argentine experimental cinema critic, declares that Denegri's work is groundbreaking precisely in the ways it joins past and present media with the apparatuses that project them, stating that "la recuperación y manipulación de imágenes del pasado y la combinatoria de soportes culminan en la proyección fílmica y la exhibición de la maquinaria, un todo propuesto como instalación" (La Ferla, *Cine de Exposición* 5–6) [the recovery and manipulation of images from the past and the combination of different (media) supports culminate in the act of filmic projection and in the exhibition of the necessary machinery, all of it proposed as part of an installation piece]. Admittedly, *TIJTS*, unlike other works by Denegri, is not a project meant to be seen on anything other than a flat screen or screens. But *TIJTS* had a rich variety in its forms of distribution, as it was shown in galleries and museums as a set of installation videos; it was part of programs that included the presence of the filmmakers and encouraged public discussion, and it found an enduring afterlife on the internet. Additionally, through its enactment of an intermedial and transatlantic sensitivity, this video dialogue between two filmmakers sought to disrupt the boundaries of more "standard" forms of filmmaking, anchored to specific media, nations, and ideas.

In great part, the hybridity and intermediality we have been considering as constitutive characteristics of contemporary experimental cinema have been reaffirmed by the shift away from cinema screens and toward alternative exhibition spaces, and it was further impelled as the preeminence of celluloid gave way to analog video, and most recently to digital video. We might recall Hirsch's projections of *Come Out*, for instance, when she transferred the original Super 8 onto digital. La Ferla comments precisely on how this transition from analog to digital, but also from movie theaters to alternative spaces (galleries, street walls, museums), has irrevocably altered the material complexity of experimental cinema today. In the estimation of this scholar, "[L]a entrada del cine a los espacios expositivos de arte se produce tardíamente y suele ser a través de su transferencia al video y la informática" (*Cine de Exposición* 11) [The entry of cinema into art's exhibition spaces is a late development and it happened after film's transfer to video and the arrival of computers]. While this material transformation might in part stem from the lack of physical capabilities in art exhibition spaces to project celluloid (with some notable exceptions), La Ferla explains that the phenomenon also echoes the shift away from "film" that happened in cinema theaters in the 2000s, contributing to shifting definitions of the "cinematic": "Es el caso de las muestras que incluyen al cine, pero que se presentan como instalaciones de video o proyecciones en formato digital, donde la materialidad del cine está ausente. Por su parte, las salas de cine están dejando de proyectar cine y, subrepticiamente, ofrecen los soportes digitales y las proyecciones de base de datos como cine" (*Cine de Exposición* 11) [That is what happens in exhibitions that include "cinema" but are presenting it in video installations or as digital projections, so the materiality of film is absent. Additionally, movie theaters are no longer projecting (celluloid) film, and, surreptitiously, present digital media and database projections as if they were, in fact, film].

While I am not interested in rehashing arguments about the passing of celluloid (even as film survives in its newer formats) that have already been addressed by many scholars, perhaps most notably by David N. Rodowick in *The Virtual Life of Film* (2007), what is most relevant here is to recognize that for Denegri and other contemporary experimental cineastes and video artists the end of the predominance of celluloid is not problematic at all. They remain committed to including multiple formats in their work, even if eventually all those formats are subsumed under the digital once their works are transferred to digital video and archived in online databases. According to La Ferla, there were two indispensable technologies that incentivized the increasingly hybrid nature of cinema: first, the development of handheld recording equipment (Super 8, analog video, and digital video cameras), and second, the possibility to upload and manipulate video files with computers. He traces the original experiments with these technologies to 1960s and '70s avant-garde cinema, asserting that "las primeras experiencias de creación de films provenientes de imágenes asistidas por una computadora se remontan a mediados de los años 60, la misma época de la aparición del video portátil y el Súper 8. La paulatina entrada contemporánea del cine al ámbito del museo con carácter de exposición se fue materializando en su transferencia electrónica y digital" (La Ferla, *Cine de Exposición* 22) [the first films that used computer-assisted images date to the mid-'60s, the same period when portable video and Super 8 made their appearance. Cinema's gradual irruption into museums for exhibition purposes became possible after its electronic and digital transfer]. There is little doubt that Denegri, who sees himself as heir to this experimental tradition (like Caprín and Cugliandolo), has also put into practice the heterogeneous combination of media in his own videos.[28]

Having placed Denegri's work in historical context, it is also necessary to explain a few details about his interlocutor in the epistolary project, Gustavo Caprín. Although quite active in the video and installation art scene, Caprín makes his living as a web designer based in Barcelona (Spain). The Argentine expat was trained as a painter and filmmaker in Buenos Aires and later pursued graduate studies in digital art in Barcelona, where he has resided since 2001. Caprín is part of an artistic diaspora that left Argentina chiefly for economic and professional advancement reasons rather than political ones, although motivations for exile can be entangled. Many artists arrived with very strong foundations and were able to adapt quickly. Argentine video art really took off in the late 1980s and early 1990s, even as many filmmakers and video artists, Caprín among them, left the country to find their fortunes elsewhere, mostly in the United States or Europe (López Mato et al. 11–12). Unlike Narcisa Hirsch's generation, who were propelled into exile by the repressive political situation, these video artists sought opportunities to expand their art and study or work abroad as economic adversity at home made their careers increasingly difficult, as we discussed in Cugliandolo's case. As Tamara López explains, there is an imperative toward self-imposed exile, "[E]n muchos casos, se hace necesario salir del país, incluso de manera definitiva. Artistas fundamentales como Marcelo Mercado, Charly Nijensohn, o Iván Marino, y luego Sebastián Díaz Morales o Gustavo Caprín, encuentran hoy en Europa el contexto adecuado para su trabajo constituyendo una diáspora que, afortunadamente, todavía guarda una relación estrecha con nuestro país" (12) [In many cases, it was necessary to leave the country, even definitively. Fundamental artists such as Marcello Mercado, Charly Nijensohn, or Iván Marino, and later Sebastián Díaz Morales and Gustavo Caprín, found in Europe the appropriate context for their work and became part of a diaspora that, fortunately, still maintains close ties with our country (Argentina)].[29]

Argentine video art critic Graciela Taquini frames the situation that has led Caprín and others to seek fortune elsewhere in similar terms, qualifying the phenomenon as a veritable Argentine video artist diaspora:

> Muchos artistas jóvenes emprenden una diáspora con el fin de aprovechar los privilegios—y sufrir los sacrificios—de vivir en el Primer Mundo. Charly Nijensohn, Miguel Rothschild y Marcelo Mercado en Alemania, Iván Marino, Gustavo Caprín y Andrea

Nacach en Barcelona y Sebastián Díaz Morales—artista no muy conocido en el medio argentino—en Holanda circulan en ese establishment. Otros, como Gabriela Golder, desarrollan actividades en la Argentina con largos períodos en el exterior. (46)

[Many young artists go into the diaspora to be able to take advantage of the privilege—and to suffer the sacrifices—of living in the First World. Charly Nijensohn, Miguel Rothschild and Marcello Mercado in Germany, Iván Marino, Gustavo Caprín and Andrea Nacach in Barcelona, and Sebastián Díaz Morales—an artist not well known in Argentina—in the Netherlands. Others, such as Gabriela Golder, work in Argentina but spend lengthy periods outside of the country.]

Undoubtedly nomadism, exile, and a certain nostalgia for home are aspects of daily experience that often find an echo in these artists' work. To cite one relevant example, Caprín's participation in the video correspondence with Denegri in *TIJTS* becomes a reassertion of the need to maintain affective and professional links with the homeland, even as it underscores the reality and distance of self-imposed exile. Interestingly, another intergenerational link is established between the younger generation with their experience of self-imposed exile and the previous one, their parents' generation, whose exile was often not voluntary, both generations now sharing a nomadic, uprooted existence. Javier Olivera, also part *TIJTS* (with Caprín, Denegri, and Galuppo), notes an association between the experience of exile and the artistic process. For example, the process of exile and displacement was determinant in the choice of materials assembled for his latest film *La extraña: Notas sobre el (auto) exilio* (2019) [The Stranger: Notes about (Self) Exile], a documentary that also incorporates extensive video footage from *TIJTS*. What Olivera says about his film applies equally to Denegri and Caprín's hybrid videomaking. Olivera begins by describing the multiplicity of materials he included in *La extraña*: "[L]a película está construida con materiales que van desde planos en full HD, transfers de Súper 8, video DV, tomas con celulares de baja calidad, dos películas argentinas en blanco y negro, una entrevista de la TV española, etc." (Portela) [The film *The Stranger* is assembled with materials that range from full HD shots, transfers from Super 8, digital video, shots made with low-quality cell phones, two Argentine black-and-white movies, a Spanish television interview, etc.]. Then the filmmaker goes on to establish how his "poor quality" film contrasts with commercial productions, stating, "[D]igamos que es un elogio al Lo FI, y esto sí es un gesto estético muy evidente, casi contestando la proliferación de una imagen anabolizada, hiper-retocada, en 4K u 8K del cine de Hollywood" [Let us say that the film is a tribute to lo-fi, and an obvious aesthetic gesture that challenges the proliferation of those anabolic and hyper processed images in 4K or 8K that can be seen in Hollywood cinema]. Finally, Olivera links the obsolescence and degradation of the old formats with the idea of exile: "a mí me interesa la belleza de la degradación y en ese sentido, los distintos formatos y su degradación por haber sido 'exiliados' de sus orígenes, generan unas texturas que para mí son muy expresivas" (Portela) [I am interested in the beauty of degradation, and, along these lines, the various degraded formats that have been "exiled" from their origins and generate certain textures that I find particularly expressive].

In other words, the complexity of exile and diaspora—the thick layering of the subject, the multiple national identities, the transnational perspective—results in a richer, if more ambivalent and "messy," roughly textured lived experience, which is in turn reflected in the artwork generated by these artists and the materials gathered together from the detritus of this uprootedness. Thus, lo-fi and messiness is held in contrast to the seamless portrait of commercial North American cinema. The recourse to lo-fi and "impure" images that I referred to when addressing cell phone cinema has long held a certain cultural cache in video art circles. Media theorist Hito Steyerl, in her article "In Defense of the Poor Image," traces the genealogy of the contemporary digital "poor image" to 1960s imperfect cinema and defines it thus, in ways that echo the *desgaste* (degradation) of exile: "The poor image is a copy in motion. Its quality is bad, its resolution substandard. As it accelerates, it deteriorates. It is a ghost of an image, a preview, a thumbnail, an errant idea, an itinerant image distributed for free, squeezed through slow digital connections, compressed, reproduced, ripped, remixed, as well as copied and pasted into other channels of distribution." Degradation, low aesthetic quality, and the inevitable mix and remix of various source files blend into one final digitized poor video so that, as Steyerl argues, "the poor image is no longer about the real thing—the originary original. Instead, it is about *its own real conditions of existence*: about swarm circulation, digital dispersion, fractured and flexible temporalities. It is about defiance and appropriation just as it is about conformism and exploitation" (my emphasis).

It is evident that neither Olivera nor Caprín, who also uses a variety of media sources in his video art, are concerned with any notions of medium purity when it comes to producing their films, but rather they ascribe to Steyerl's conception of poor images. As a powerful source of self-assertion this ethos of the "poor image" also taps into the recognition by many media practitioners and theorists that although everything has been subsumed in some respects by the all-engulfing digital, by the pixel, that does not necessarily entail the erasure of non-digital source materials and their texture, their granularity, their imperfections. Digitized films made from a heterogeneous assembly of formats do not merely experience media convergence and assimilation but rather embody a condition of the intermedial in which the analog materials persist, even if they do not do so in their previous form; what remains, rather than a single homogeneous file, retains a collage-like quality in which the aesthetic and style of the old format casts an afterimage (as argued in the case of Super 8). Intermediality entails the continuation or seepage of the "old media" aesthetics into the space of the digital.

Just as Rodowick claimed in his classic text on the passing of celluloid, *The Virtual Life of Film*, arguing that the cinematic will endure in a new form, we can extrapolate this "remainder" idea to video, to other disappearing media that experience a digital afterlife, even if what remains is (mostly) stylistic. As Rodowick saw this, "Our audiovisual culture remains 'cinematic' in the sense that the most popular forms of digital media long to recreate and intensify cinematic effects of framing, editing, dynamic point of view, and mobile framing" (133). Regardless, the acknowledgment of the remainder does not mean we should not also accept a degree of loss or transformation. "Alternatively, as befits a medium whose inputs and outputs are discontinuous, transcoding is a one-way street; the perpetuation of cinematic algorithms in the deep structure of digital programming means the disappearance of film, and the rebirth of cinema in the form of programmable algorithms" (Rodowick 133). Within digital culture, as Rodowick sees it, the cinema has lost its special status as the preeminent way to treat moving images, but that does not negate the profound influence the cinema has had in shaping that same digital culture, including its aesthetics: "The idea of cinema persists as a way of modeling time-based spatial forms with computers, but cinema is only one of myriad functions that computers can simulate or model. . . . Our audiovisual culture is currently a digital culture, but with a cinematic look. And cinema, too, is increasingly just another element of digital culture" (133). In the intermedial cinema being created today, digital culture absorbs, contains, transforms, and incorporates other media, even as those media retain many of their aesthetic markers. As Thomas Elsaesser argues in *Film History as Media Archeology*, "[N]o medium replaces another or simply supersedes the previous one. Today, cinema, television, and digital media exist side by side, feeding off each other and increasingly interdependent, to be sure, but also still clearly distinct and even hierarchically placed in terms of cultural prestige, economic function, and spectatorial pleasures" (88).

Moreover, the cinematic image, and even more so the degraded cinematic image, whether it is degrading celluloid or pixelated digital footage or even the imitation of decomposing celluloid through digital effects, can be associated with exile, as we have seen with Cugliandolo's cinema. The association of exile with intermedial approaches to experimental cinema is well established not only theoretically (as we have seen) but also as an artistic practice. This association immediately recalls *Lost, Lost, Lost* by Jonas Mekas, a diary film detailing the Lithuanian filmmaker's 1949 arrival to New York and his experiences as a displaced refugee trying to make that North American metropolis his new home (the resonances with Caprín and Cugliandolo abound). Mekas's emotive, if imperfect, film also depicts the struggles of Lithuanians trying to resignify their identity as Lithuanian-American, as something in between, hybrid, neither Lithuanian nor fully American, an "impure" composite forged of the melding of blurry memories, faded photographs, and washed-out Super 8 home movies. Indeed, this in-between-ness is also present in contemporary exile cinema and video by Caprín, Denegri, and others, often expressed both in terms of content and in relation to media materials. Experiments with media often parallel a questioning of the very concept of national identity and entail a refocusing toward issues of subjective or personal identity, with the body as a "territory" that replaces the lost homeland, as the site where elements from the previous and new homes uneasily merge—again, similarly to the highly hybrid process of the evolving exile identity. While the videos created for *TIJTS* are much more episodic and less narrative than Mekas's film, the exile experience still pervades many of them.

In Caprín's case, although his videos do not directly reference exile like Olivera's, they tend to create a sense of unease or out-of-jointed-ness that recalls the displacement of exile. Caprín focuses on artifacts and inanimate objects rather than people, as well as producing perceptual games that disorient the viewer as to what is on-screen. For Rodrigo Alonso the way Caprín selects and stages his objects—often banal objects taken out of context, such as empty bottles, hammers—is meant to emphasize an experience of disconnection. As the Argentine critic argues, Caprín works in familiar surroundings and conducting small "performance actions." Referencing Caprín's

2002 video art piece *How to Build a House*, Alonso explains that Caprín's performed actions grant the lead role to the objects that he manipulates, rendering them with a strong expressive force—the objects are the protagonists. Other elements characterize his style, so that "empleando una cámara sensible a la oscuridad y trabajando en entornos de escasa luz, [Caprín] consigue una imagen monocroma, verdosa, que se ha constituido prácticamente en una marca autoral. Otro punto importante en sus piezas son los encuadres, que fomentan continuas confusiones y desajustes perceptivos" (Alonso, "Estéticas" 57) [using a light-sensitive camera that can film in the dark, and working in poorly lit spaces, he achieves a monochromatic, greenish image, which has almost become his artistic trademark. The way he uses framing encourages constant confusion and perceptive disconnects].

Having discussed Denegri's and Caprín's work in general terms and broad strokes, we can analyze some of the videos from their *TIJTS* exchange. I will examine the videos through the lens of exile and diaspora, while tracing their deliberate aesthetic of poor images and a marked tendency toward intermedial collage that borrows from older film, video, and installation arts.

This Is Just to Say: The Videos Themselves

Filmed in a variety of formats, among the video exchanges between Caprín and Denegri some were created with Super 8 and later transferred to digital, others were made using obsolete forms of analog video, others yet, directly filmed in digital video. The final "product," although the videos are part of an ongoing, unfinished "process," was rendered into digital video files so it could be uploaded and viewed on digital devices, first by its intended recipients (Denegri or Caprín) and eventually, by a wider internet audience. The videos were linked to by several public sites—while *TIJTS* has its own website where all the videos can be viewed, many were also uploaded to the video streaming platform Vimeo by their creators, as well as promoted on Facebook and other social media sites. As *TIJTS* gained visibility and garnered critical attention, the videos began to be projected in museums and galleries and in some instances included as installation pieces. It is on account of their dynamic capacity to transform, adapt, and cross boundaries as they traverse a variety of media spaces that these works bridge the public and the private spheres. Argentine film scholar Emilio Bernini observes:

> [V]ideos que componen el proyecto supusieron una conversación a la vez pública y privada. Privada, porque, de acuerdo a la lógica

del intercambio epistolar, los videos buscaron articular una relación de intimidad y cotidianeidad. Pública, en la medida en que el soporte para esa conversación no fue sólo el de las imágenes de video, sino también el del dispositivo al cual esas imágenes fueron regularmente cargadas. ("[No] Serialidad")

[The videos that compose the project constitute a conversation that is both public and private. Private, because in accordance with the logic of epistolary exchanges, the videos attempt to articulate an intimate and quotidian relationship. Public, insofar as the media for that conversation entailed not only the video images, but also the venue to which these images were uploaded [via the internet.]

That interplay between the public and the private is present not only in the way the *TIJTS* project was conceptualized but also in the content of each individual video. The back-and-forth motion between personal and public is evident in the first video I will examine, a video that reworks and deconstructs "analytically" (but also affectively) a fragment from a home movie by a lesser-known Iberian experimental filmmaker José Val del Omar (1904–1982, Granada to Madrid). This particular Val del Omar home movie was being screened in Buenos Aires as a museum installation when Andrés Denegri, captivated by it, proceeded to film it with his personal camera from various angles. The scene that fascinated Denegri captures an intimate moment between two individuals, a kiss between Val del Omar and his wife. The other intimate moment taking place, of course, is between three cineastes who are connecting through this particular scene, in this case Denegri and Val del Omar, and indirectly also Caprín. The kiss sequence is extracted from a longer home movie, *Película familiar* (1936–1938) [Family Movie]. Denegri films the kiss scene surreptitiously in the museum with his small personal camera, to finally send it (albeit transformed) as his video "letter" to Caprín in Barcelona. The images travel from the personal and intimate family scene to the public sphere of the museum and back to the intimate (Caprín's inbox) and eventually to the public sphere once again (as the video we are viewing online). This oscillating to and from public and private finds a parallel in transatlantic ocean crossings, as the same familial images, taken in Spain in 1938 in the midst of a fratricide war, have traveled to Buenos Aires, in a country living a difficult transition to democracy, only to then return once again to Spain as a letter from one Argentine to his self-exiled friend—with each oceanic traversal a new layer of affect imprinted on the film as memento mori. The material base for the images has likewise suffered many reversals and transformations: as the 16 mm film taken by Val del Omar, which displays the ravages of time as celluloid degrades, is in turn captured by Denegri's pocket digital camera and then transferred to digital video, to eventually be uploaded and "transformed" into an internet video file and uploaded to a website to be streamed. A deeper dive into Denegri's video will be instructive and help to sort out the complexities of material, translation, time, and memory that he manipulates.

Denegri's video is titled *This Is Just to Say I—Nro 21: (Projects: 02—The Kiss)*. The serial title denotes that this belongs to one of several videos in which Denegri shares an idea for a potential project with Caprín. The video is 3:49 minutes in duration, and although it is captured with a video camera, it records fragments from Val del Omar's 16 mm home movie *Película familiar*, with roughly eighty years separating the "original" and its "copy," to use those highly unstable terms. The Iberian cineaste's eight-minute family portrait is in its own right a fascinating work that skirts the public and private spheres, the intimate and the collective. Shot in Granada during the Spanish Civil War, the film reflects quotidian moments in Val del Omar's family life, even as the presence of the ongoing tragedy can be surmised, a subtext tangibly present for anyone aware of Spanish history. The specific thirty-second fragment "remixed" by Denegri also blurs the public-private divide, as it records an embrace between the Iberian filmmaker and his wife Maria Luisa Santos, a tender instant between them. Filmed in black and white so long ago (and tinted with a blueish hue), the silence of the film is itself somewhat uncanny and points to death, or to emptiness, and at any rate it intensifies the experience of viewing the fragment. Denegri adds to this effect by capturing the sound of the museum's projector in his recording. The short kiss sequence was excised from the longer home movie by Val del Omar and subsequently titled "La Mayor Transferencia (El Beso)" (1938) [The Greatest Transference [The Kiss)].

Selected by Denegri as the base for his video experiment, the silent kiss scene was, as I stated, part of the longer amateur home movie that registered a portrait of Val del Omar's family life, of his wife, his children, and the family home in Granada. Much of the film is unremarkable in that it focuses on the quotidian, on recording his children as they play, interact, and mostly look self-consciously at the camera. There is a concerted and deliberate focus, both in Val del Omar's original "family film" and amplified by Denegri's video, on capturing the way the subjects stare directly at the objective. Shots carefully frame facial expressions and body gestures, and in the kiss sequence the camera seems to linger and draw out the intensity of the lovers' embrace (see figs. 3.6 and 3.7). The kiss, in fact, becomes the

Figure 3.6. *This Is Just to Say I—Nro 21: (Projects: 02—The Kiss)* (2012). Denegri returns to Val del Omar's kiss sequence (02:43). *Source: This Is Just to Say I—Nro 21: (Projects: 02—The Kiss)* (2012). Dir. Andrés Denegri.

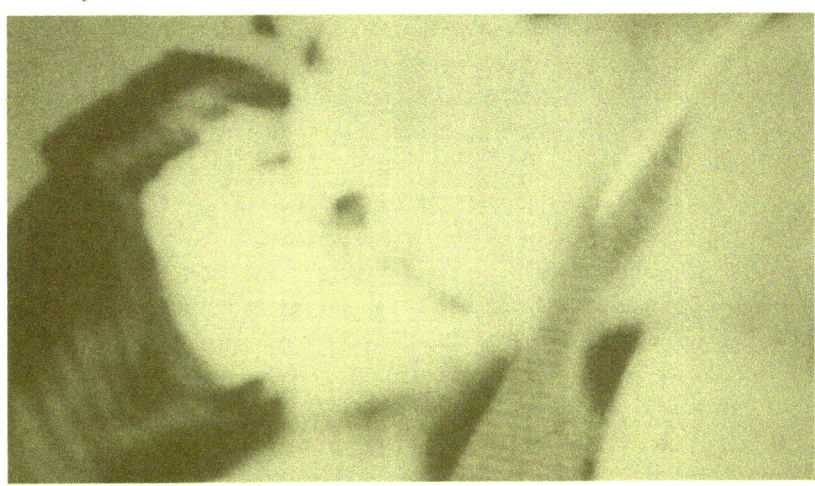

Figure 3.7. *This Is Just to Say III—Nro 6: Oh, the Golden Days of Video Making I* (2016). Bars and tone (00:01). *Source: This Is Just to Say III—Nro 6: Oh, the Golden Days of Video Making I* (2016). Dir. Gustavo Carpin.

obsessive focus for Denegri's video, the action he repeats and deconstructs from multiple angles and distances. The kiss itself, relatively rare in Spanish early cinema, may remind viewers of an even older cinematic work, Edison's film depicting the first on-screen kiss (*The Kiss*, 1896). Denegri's video also mobilizes the affective-symbolic intensity of Barthes's *punctum* (as developed in his 1980 text *Camera Lucida*), a photographic phenomenon that provokes a subjective but often overwhelming and arresting awareness of death (and of life as well). The video's power, following Barthes, lies in its mix of banal domesticity (*studium*) and profound transcendence (*punctum*), made more poignant with the knowledge that everyone depicted on-screen, seemingly so passionately alive, has long been gone from this world—what appears to be happening in the immediate present and so intensely alive is in fact quite dead, long past, and (almost) forgotten. Seen in this light, Denegri's melancholic video is undoubtedly also, or perhaps primarily, a meditation on the history of cinema, on media obsolescence, on the materiality of film and its passing, on exile, on the evanescence of the moment and the passage of time, and on death as the final and inevitable exile (see fig. 3.6).

Denegri opens his video with a darkened screen that allows the spectator to become immersed in the encompassing whirling, clicking, and humming sound of an old movie projector. The video, itself an exercise in media archeology and intermedial layering, demonstrates Denegri's predilection to incorporating older filmic technologies and machines. Not only does he reproduce or capture the sound from a vintage projector, but he recovers and appropriates Val del Omar's forgotten home movie, now "reborn" as a digital project that examines film's historicity. Situated in the present, Denegri attempts to reconstruct the past, to tap into Val del Omar's subjective experience—but the Argentine's video will also oscillate between subjectivity and objectivity. After a few seconds the dark screen gives way to a simple white typeface intertitle. The title shot follows the same format in all the videos in the *TIJTS* series, providing the name of the project (*This Is Just to Say*), the subtitle of the specific video "*Nro 21: (Projects: 02—The Kiss)*," followed by other relevant information that qualify it as an epistolary video, a correspondence sent from a specific time and place: "From: Andrés, To: Gustavo, Where: Buenos Aires, Argentina, Date: 31/03/2012." A montage sequence immediately follows this title. The shots record the projected images from Val del Omar's 1938 film. As I stated, these images are taken by Denegri with a pocket camera from different angles and varying proximity, changing the focus and the framing and arguably intensifying the emotional impact of the images. The sequence of shots includes a close-up of María Luisa Santos's face, followed by a fade to black, then an extreme but out of focus close-up of her expression and also of José Val del Omar's face as they approach each other. Both Santos and Val del Omar stare intently at the camera, as if looking at the spectator through the passage of time, or they might be looking at the person filming (possibly a family member or friend), followed by another fade to black. Building on the collage-like quality of his video, Denegri overlays an email fragment onto the images of the kiss scene. Dated January 28, 2012 (two months prior to the video), the email text reads: "Hablando de proyectos, te comenté lo de Val del Omar?" [Speaking of projects, did I tell you about Val del Omar?]. The brief email extract is meant to bring Caprín into the dialogue, to include him in the interest toward the evocative Val del Omar scene. Then the video contains some blurry black-and-white street images from Granada, also taken from "family portrait." This is followed by the beginning of the affective segment, a brief first teaser or glimpse of the kiss sequence, at the precise moment when the couple are, somewhat awkwardly, physically approaching each other. By overlaying more email text over the original 16 mm footage Denegri once again demonstrates his willingness to mix media that are temporally distant, layering the 1938 celluloid material he captured at the museum, in other words the footage taken by his pocket video camera (and in that process transformed into video), and the email messages transcribed from his digital media and overlaid on the final video. After another fade to black, followed by more street scenes, we return to another reprise of "the kiss." Overlaid onto images of the couple's embrace, we can read an email fragment that states Denegri's motivation to film the Val del Omar kiss sequence:

> Encontré tanta belleza en este autorretrato amoroso realizado en una toma doble que tuve que, de manera oculta e ilegal, registrarlo, con mi camarita pocket, varias veces, y en distintos encuadres. Mi intención es mostrarle estas imágenes a algunas personas, mayoritariamente gente vinculada al cine y al arte, y conversar con ellas sobre esta filmación. El audio de esas conversaciones será grabado y conformará la base de un video (o una instalación), cuya imagen será una repetición insistente de la filmación de Val del Omar.
>
> [I found so much beauty in this lover's self-portrait created with a double take that I had to record it, surreptitiously and illegally, with my small pocket camera, several times and with multiple framing angles. My intent is to show these images to people linked to the world of cinema and the arts and speak with them about this film. I will record the audio of these conversations and that will be the basis for a video (or an installation piece), whose images will be an insistent repetition of Val del Omar's movie.]

Denegri proposes to transform Val del Omar's 16 mm original by making it the basis for a meditation on the cinema as a medium, through an open dialogue with other film and art experts, critics, and practitioners. Ultimately, he completes a version of this project: the video we are viewing. Although somewhat different from the project he proposes in his email, this video still centers on the kiss sequence and it involves a dialogue with Caprín, other film practitioners, and the cinephile viewers of his work. Denegri's analytical interest in the Val del Omar sequence is also inextricably associated with his emotional and subjective fascination with the beauty of the fragment, hence his desire to insistently return to it, again and again. It is the insistence of returning to its *punctum*, as Denegri attempts to capture the elusive nature of the 16 mm film's indexicality, its link to the *hic et nunc* and to the flesh and blood individuals seen in those flickering images, an effort to register its nowness, its aliveness (an aliveness that as Barthes demonstrates refers also to death and mourning). But in this case that indexicality, or an appearance of it, has been transferred, transformed, to a different medium, to digital video. In fact, many of the videos in *TIJTS* share this dual nature: on the one hand they seem like mere "objective" registers of the quotidian, analytic, and dispassionate; on the other hand, they are powerfully lyrical captures of images that suggest something like transcendence, mysticism, poetry. Our suspicions about the tension between science and poetry, technology and art, are confirmed by Denegri's video. As the couple embraces and kisses, the screen once again fades to black. The following frames display some white text against the dark background, words taken from an online conversation dated one week prior: "Y reafirmo: G es in científico loco; A es un poeta melancólico. Hasta la próxima, J." [And I reaffirm: G is a mad scientist; A is a melancholic poet. Until next time, J.]. Denegri includes this email written by Javier Olivera (J), which identifies Gustavo Caprín (G) as the "mad scientist" and Andrés Denegri (A) as the melancholic poet, recognizing that these experimental videos are at once "science" and "poetry." The comment also inserts Olivera into the community of filmmakers that are conversing with this piece of media archeology. Denegri's video closes with a final repetition of the Val del Omar kiss scene. This time the original double take is seen in its entirety without interruptions, a direct quote from the 16 mm version, allowing the viewer to take in the couple's complicitous rapport, their intimate glances, their (visible) laughter, and their inaudible whispers, the scene culminating in the embrace and kiss followed by a final fade to black. The scene's intensity is punctuated by the silence of the film, the ambient noises in the gallery where Denegri is illegally filming, and the loud whirring and clicking noises from the projector.

But a question remains: Why does this Argentine experimental filmmaker select an Iberian avant-garde cineaste for his video art and consider it for a potential "project" that he did not carry out (unless we consider this very video to be that actual project)? Why precisely Val del Omar? Perhaps in part this is a fortuitous coincidence—Denegri saw the fragment while visiting an exhibit and was captivated by the images. But the Argentine artist is also a film scholar as well as an experimental filmmaker and he was undoubtedly aware of the affinities between Val del Omar's and his own work. Denegri is identifying Val del Omar as a precursor and model in a genealogy of experimental filmmakers that dates to the early years of the medium. He is also considering the Iberian filmmaker as a transatlantic kindred spirit and—much like his younger colleague Caprín may see Denegri—as an artistic mentor and influence. There are several factors that elucidate this strong affective and professional affiliation between the long-deceased Val del Omar and Denegri (beyond Denegri's personal obsession with Val del Omar's films). Like Denegri, Val del Omar was a polymath, equally vested in the technical and scientific aspects of the cinema as he was in its aesthetic, artistic, and poetic dimension. Val del Omar set up a laboratory to research film-related technologies, the PLAT (Picto-Luminic-Audio-Tactile) Lab, where he invented various kinds of lenses and audio equipment, experimenting with a variety of audiovisual media. Like Denegri, Val del Omar was fascinated by the nuts and bolts of the cinematic machinery, modifying projectors and tinkering with their moving parts, in short treating the filmic apparatus as if it were a mobile mechanical sculpture of sorts, much like Denegri does in his art installations. Val del Omar was an experimenter in the field of images and materials—he worked with 16 mm, with Super 8 (in the 1970s), and with a variety of other media, including photography and photo collage, painting, and even poetry. A contemporary and friend of Federico García Lorca (also from Granada), María Zambrano, Luis Cernuda, Luis Buñuel, Florián Rey, Carlos Velo, and other luminaries of the Spanish Republic, Val del Omar, like other members of the losing side, suffered an internal exile when that grand experiment of political and artistic freedom came to an abrupt end with the Spanish Civil War and the long dictatorship that followed. Val del Omar was captured by Francoist troops in 1939 and forced to join their ranks to produce propaganda, an unfortunate situation that must have caused great conflict for him (but ensured his survival). Although their stories may be set in different times and places, Val del Omar's life and work has resonances for someone like Denegri, who belongs to the generation of the sons and daughters of those who experienced Videla's military junta and the last Argentine dictatorship. By sharing, through the video epistle, Val del Omar's film fragment with his friend Caprín, Denegri places the question of film, diaspora, and exile front and center in their epistolary project.

The second video I would like to discuss, dated May 4, 2016, is from a later edition of the *TIJTS* project (season III), titled *This Is Just to Say III—Nro 6: Oh, the Golden Days of Video Making I*.[30] This video "letter" is addressed from Gustavo Caprín to Andrés Denegri, from Barcelona to Buenos Aires. It is part of a subseries of six videos (predictably labeled one through six) created by Caprín that are all subtitled *Oh, the Golden Days of Video Making*. Fittingly, the Argentine expat recorded them with his vintage Betacam video camera, although as with most of his work the videos were subsequently digitized. The digitization of old formats, as I have discussed at length, is an inevitable process required to transform the films or videos into files that can be transferred and manipulated digitally. From that practical need to digitize analog video, it follows that questions about the obsolescence of the video format are inherent to Caprín's work. Interestingly, that sense of fleetingness or fragility was always present in magnetic tapes, even when they were new, as Lucas Hilderbrand observes in his book-length study on the subject, *Inherent Vice* (2009): "When videotape was new, video recordings—whether networks' timeshifted programming, conceptual video art and ephemeral happenings, radical collectives' feedback sessions, even home viewers' timeshifting—were often not intended to last" (12). Of course, as the author underlines, videos were a "technology of duplication" that increased capabilities for amateur video reproduction and archiving (71–72). In that sense, videotapes became a kind of memory or semipermanent record of personal and cultural histories. Caprín's videos also promote reflection on what is gained, lost, or changed through the process of digital transfer, reproducibility, and archiving, and at the same time these works also reflect a nostalgia for the fading materiality of an "old" medium. This nostalgia for bygone technology is becoming commonplace in contemporary culture, and much like we saw with Super 8, there are now apps for smartphones that simulate the aesthetic of analog video (such as the *Retro VHS Old School Video* app created by Venn Interactive).

Mariela Cantú, an Argentine video artist, academic, and analog video preservationist, has written about the "passing" of the analog video format in ways that echo Rodowick's writings about the passing of celluloid. While Cantú is assured of the afterlife of magnetic video in a digitized or digital form, she bemoans the tradeoffs of giving up the analog video as a material substrate—as the digital subsumes all cultural products under its regime of zeros and ones. Cantú theorizes about the sense of loss provoked by analog video's obsolescence—a sense of loss that paradoxically fuels the obsessive desire to transfer everything to digital in order to preserve the analog past. She speaks about the strange layering of temporalities, the play between past and present that occurs when an analog file is digitized, understanding this process not as creating a mere "copy" of the past medium but as a kind of interpretation of past events. Thus for Cantú, "[E]sta necesidad de actualización permanente es la que genera esa sensación de obsolescencia, incluso en obras que no superan unos pocos años de realización, creando una historia de un modo llamativamente vertiginoso. Pero un poco a contracorriente de esa percepción, me parece más interesante concebir a la digitalización como una interpretación (posible, cuestionable, reemplazable) del pasado, antes que como un presente irrefrenable y eterno" ("Archivos y video" 98) [This constant need to bring everything up to date (to digitize everything) is what is generating the sensation of obsolescence, even in works that were only created a few years ago, generating a sense of historicity with vertiginous speed. But somewhat counter to that perception, I believe it is more interesting to think of digitization as an interpretation of the (possible, questionable, replaceable) past, rather than understanding the process as creating an unstoppable and eternal present]. Cantú's understanding of the digital as an intermediate phase of sorts, one that is permeated by the vestiges of the past but is equally prone to disappearing and obsolescence, counters notions of the digital as some ultimate format or process, monolithic, homogenous, and inalterable, and mitigates the threat of convergence. She continues, "[E]ntendido de esa manera, el universo de lo digitalizado pone en evidencia su carácter heterogéneo, pues estamos todavía lejos de haber alcanzado una uniformidad digital, a pesar de que este medio parece haber siempre deseado borrar las diferencias entre soportes anteriores al convertir todo a ceros y unos" (98) [From this perspective, the universe of all things digitized displays its heterogenous nature, since we are still far from obtaining a uniform digitized world, even though digital media always appeared to erase medium differences by converting everything into zeros and ones].

For the Argentine critic, then, despite the loss of certain material qualities in the process of digitization, some trace of the analog persists, whether in the heterogenous temporality of the analog-digital transfer or in the ways that the analog aesthetic persists after transfer, forging a hybrid and intermedial object. Let us examine how Caprín himself investigates the qualities of video and video transfer to digital in his work. The video in question is only 01:49, and it depicts the assembly of a set of Legos of different colors (but uniform size), in keeping with the filmmaker's interest in instruction manuals, do-it-yourself (DIY) technical projects, and step-by-step processes of assembly. The film opens with a static image that recalls old televisions, VCRs, and other magnetic media devices from the 1980s (see fig. 3.9). It is a well-recognized standard test pattern, a set of color bars used to verify color settings prior to a viewing.[31] In short, these color bars were used to calibrate the television so that image quality would be optimal. In addition to the color bars presented visually, an audio tone was emitted from the videotape at the same time, thus the phrase "bars and tone."[32]

The bars and tone opening in Caprín's video seems at once standard and expected (for analog videos) and, from a functional standpoint, completely unnecessary since this is a digital video transfer, which does not require adjustment. It is without a doubt a deliberate aesthetic choice that reminds the viewer of the lost materiality of analog video, suggests technical processes that interest the artist (color and sound adjustments), and displays the heterogeneity and complex temporality of the piece, layering the preeminent media of the 1980s and its digital reincarnation. The opening frames declare this video as a piece of media archeology that bridges contemporary visual media mechanisms and past analog media nostalgia, systematicity, and poetics. In short, Caprín keeps the color bars at the outset of his video as a mark (trace) of the analog "origin" or "original" that persists even after digitization—the bars could have been edited out, but they remain as a reminder/remainder/remnant/revenant of, or swan song for, the disappearing VHS and Betamax formats. Through this nostalgic maneuver *Oh, the Golden Days of Video Making* establishes an epistolary dialogue with Denegri's videos about that other passing format, celluloid film. While not a direct response to Denegri's Val del Omar tribute piece (there are many other videos exchanged in between), Caprín is aware that this discourse on media archeology is a strong undercurrent in the *TIJTS* project.

This interest in the materiality of old formats is not new for Caprín. In his video art projects, he records with Betamax tapes and an old Betacam, a system that was replaced by the lower quality but more affordable VHS format by the mid-'80s, although Betamax remained the standard for professional video making and broadcasting for a long time (surprisingly,

Sony continued manufacturing Betamax tapes until 2016). First introduced in 1975, and with a heyday in the 1980s and '90s, both Betamax and VHS had become almost completely obsolete by the early 2000s, replaced by digital video for mainstream applications. A significant number of artists and filmmakers, however, continued to film with the Betamax format. Many artists are attracted to its specific aesthetic qualities despite the increasing difficulty of acquiring equipment given the disappearance of most manufacturers of analog devices (decks, video cassettes, etc.). The obsolescence of the equipment is coupled with the decay of magnetic media over time. This decay is materially different but reminiscent of the degradation suffered by film, and although Beta and VHS tapes are not as volatile as celluloid, magnetic tapes do breakdown over time. Sadly, material decay is responsible for the loss of countless home movies, experimental films, documentaries, and DIY cinema, despite growing efforts to digitize such "lesser" genres. As such, both Beta and VHS also signify a kind of death: of a medium, of an era, and of a particular cultural understanding of cinema and video art. But as of late these formats also signify a rebirth, triggered by their cache as "retro" novelties for younger artists and also for older ones who seek to recapture those "golden days of video making" as well as a certain analog video "texture." Seeking this texture either through recourse to actual analog video tools or by simulating it with digital apps, artists have sometimes returned to the analog video format, a phenomenon not unlike the one involving the (also limited) rebirth of Super 8. The texture or trace of the analog video therefore survives in its new digital format, a point that several theorists (Philip Rosen, Jonathan Rozenkrantz, Mariela Cantú) have also made about celluloid and that, as we have seen, would seem to dilute or even negate theories of absolute convergence.

Case in point, media theorist Jonathan Rozenkrantz argues that analog video that has been digitized is not an example of seamless uniformity, but rather presents "a hybrid image that remains irreducible to processes of simulation" (48–49). The stubborn permanence of the analog, peeking through, reassures Rozenkrantz of an enduring element of the real, one he posits in rather poetic terms: "Here and there, something of the referent remains. There is an analog intervention in the production process that grants these works their particular texture. A virtual trace of an actual VHS image—a digitized grain of analog realness—allowing the perceptive eye to sense that it is not simply looking at a digital after effect" (48–49). Disputing other theorists, such as Laura U. Marks, who sustain that digital video is wholly unconcerned with its own materiality or its analog origins (whether digitized analog video or digitized celluloid), Rozenkrantz instead maintains that instances of analog nostalgia prove that "the aesthetics of remanence . . . remains haunted by a very real analog ghost" (48–49). That ghost, trace, mark, remnant, or leftover signal from the analog may be converted to zeros and ones but manages to carry through in the new format as a type of "indexicality" that does not directly point to an origin but transmits its reverberations. The shift from photochemical or magnetic media to computational ones, at least from the standpoint of the viewer, need not significantly change the viewing experience.

As I stated above, Caprín's go-to recording device is the Betacam SP, a higher resolution video camera developed in the early 1980s (the SP stands for "superior performance"). Naturally, despite its higher quality, this professional-level camcorder still produces videos that appear quite dated when compared with the smoother (some would claim "seamless," but that ignores the capacity for digital images to glitch) quality of HD digital videos. Instead, Caprín's videos can be "jumpy" and blurry, the lighting is deliberately insufficient, and the videotapes are quite possibly old or even reused, but at any rate decayed. Caprín "enhances" the aesthetic of poor quality by recording with inadequate light, resulting in green or blue hues and washed-out tones. The substandard aesthetic of these visual images is carried through to video's digital afterlife as a badge of its material origins.

There is also something quite mechanistic and repetitive about the way Caprín's video progresses. After the initial bars and tone, the film proper opens with a disorienting shot as the handheld camera shakes unsteadily, unable to focus, while a buzzing sound reinforces the video's low-grade quality. The rapid motion of the camera and the extreme close-up to an unidentified shape make it impossible to process what we are seeing. Gradually the camera motions become steadier, and the image comes into sharper focus, finally revealing the object (see fig. 3.8).

In the center of the frame, we see an assembly of blue Legos, arranged more or less in a square shape with a few of the pieces raised above the others, forming an irregular stairstep pattern. The way the 3D Lego block sculpture is arranged and filmed remits to isometric engineering drawings and schematics, and Caprín rotates the shape through multiple positions so we can see it from various angles and facets. The filmmaker is off camera but holds the camcorder with one hand and the Lego structure with the other so that we can, at times, actually see his hand. His voice-over narration is strictly procedural, providing a description of the various items and of how he is assembling them: "estas son las piezas azules . . . el ascendente

Figure 3.8. *This Is Just to Say III—Nro 6: Oh, the Golden Days of Video Making I* (2016). Lego structure assembly, out of focus (00:29). Source: *This Is Just to Say III—Nro 6: Oh, the Golden Days of Video Making I* (2016). Dir. Gustavo Carpín.

y descendiente, o la escala" [these are the blue pieces . . . the ascending and descending, or the scale]. The reference is not without ambiguity; it could allude to a musical scale or to an architectural set of steps since either could resemble the steplike arrangement of the blue Legos, or it could be a reference to something altogether different (an instrument, a range of values, an apparatus or mechanism), or to nothing at all. What matters to the filmmaker is the process of systematically filming and assembling the Legos and how the two (filming and assembling) may be interconnected. Next, Caprín sets the camera on the table to offer a static/stable but off-kilter shot, as he lists the next step in the assembly process in monotone, "vamos a agregar ahora una pieza amarilla, y una roja más" [we are now going to add a yellow and a red piece]. There is something very matter-of-fact in the way Caprín dryly communicates his assembly instructions, suggesting something like an algorithmic process combined with the knowledge of object geometry or the instructions provided to assemble some piece of furniture or machinery. At the same time, the camera movements are less than precise; there is not

228 | Expanding Cinemas

a highly structured or carefully planned out set of camera orientations, movements, or perspectives of the Lego assembly, rather there is a set of gestural motions that suggest a casual and spontaneous filming process, one with serendipitous and contingent effects. This embrace of spontaneity and inclusion of contingent elements is evident at certain moments, for example when Caprín must remove some unsightly plastic bags that were on top of the table that he is using as a surface or base to film the Lego assembly. There is a contrast between these two components of his video making, the systematic and the spontaneous, and this contrast itself seems to be a commentary on the hybridity of the analog-digital assembly present in the filmmaker's work. There is, he seems to suggest, space for the contingent, the unplanned, and the chaotic even within digital image-making (or in digital capture of analog video). Beneath its mechanistic surface there is also child's play in the Lego assembly process.

When he adds the two brightly colored pieces to the blue base, Caprín is also creating an abstract sculpture or geometrical composition, reminiscent of both modern and contemporary art practices that tend toward minimalism (see fig. 3.9). The composition is equally suggestive of generative art,

Figure 3.9. *This Is Just to Say III—Nro 6: Oh, the Golden Days of Video Making I* (2016). Lego structure or contemporary art? (00:43). Source: *This Is Just to Say III—Nro 6: Oh, the Golden Days of Video Making I* (2016). Dir. Gustavo Carpin.

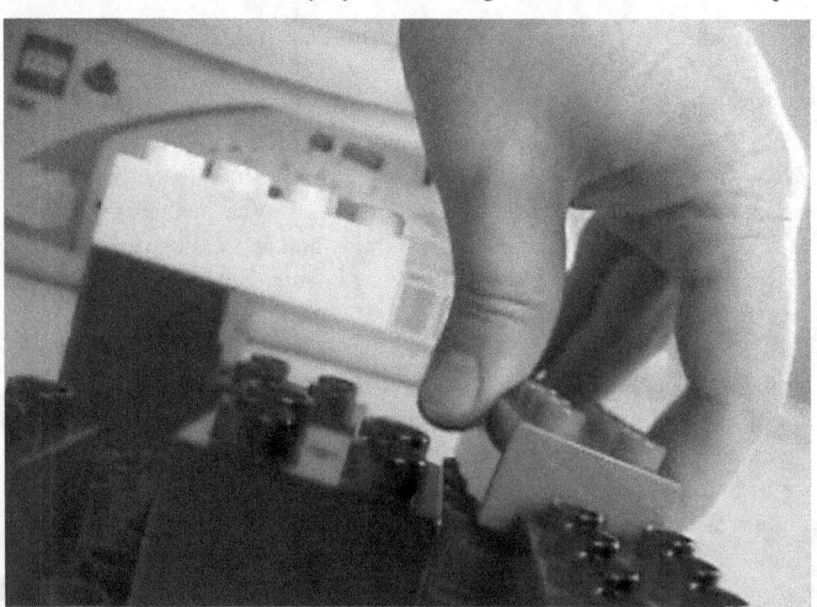

an aesthetic practice that seeks to find the precarious balance between order and chaos, between the expected and the contingent, between control and relinquishment. In generative art, by programming a set of deterministic instructions and constraining algorithms, artists use computers to achieve surprisingly unexpected designs. For generative artists, the autonomous system (the computer, or the program) makes design "decisions" that were traditionally in the purview of the artist so that the creative act is in part demystified as it becomes a "process." For Caprín, his video pieces are all about the mixing of disciplines (scientific and artistic), the mixing of materials (analog and digital), the mixing of processes (deterministic and random). By definition, his videos are intermedial, transnational, and transdisciplinary, and they reveal themselves through a logical, step-by-step, assembly-like process.

After placing these two colorful pieces, Caprín removes some objects from the table that cluttered the background of the image, discarding unnecessary material and packaging as in any assembly process that requires a clear work surface: he discards the box of Legos and several unsightly plastic bags. Caprín then slides a small blackboard behind the Lego structure with the word "bird" written in English. This irruption of the natural world (or its verbal representation) is an unexpected turn, an event escaping the logic of the assembly algorithm. Of course, it is not a bird but its linguistic sign, and by association it conjures up Magritte's experiments in writing words on his canvasses to explore the nature of signs and their referents—in one such painting (among many), *La clef des songes* (1953) [The Key to Dreams], Magritte paints a water pitcher on a surface that resembles a blackboard and underneath labels it "the bird" using the same type of didactive cursive white (chalk-like) lettering as Caprín. While Caprín may be referencing the disconnect between words and objects (Foucault) or between words and seeing (John Berger), he may also be strictly providing a linguistic representation of a bird. The frame around the blackboard might suggest a window, one through which a "bird" is visible, even though the video avoids registering an actual bird, as that would be superfluous to the point, which is the process or algorithm being assembled. Naturally, the word may be intended as a label for the Lego sculpture, as if to suggest the abstract arrangement of Legos is, in some way, supposed to resemble a bird. After removing the blackboard, Caprín narrates his following actions in detail: "sostengo el micrófono con la mano derecha, y con la izquierda voy a hacer la toma desde arriba" [I hold the microphone with my right hand and with the left I will film the shot from above]. We realize, of course, that the filmmaker is not only narrating the assembly of the Legos but providing a secondary track with a step-by-step how-to video about making a video, or even how to duplicate this particular video. The exercise is a meta-reflection on the procedural nature of experimental filmmaking. The long take of the Legos from a zenithal position is also striking, as the yellow and red pieces make for a dramatic contrast with the less distinguishable blue base. Just as the video we are viewing is assembled from different "takes" (different angles, positions, etc.) although with a single continuous shot, Caprín has built the assemblage from assorted Lego blocks. Both are illustrative of a step-by-step process, inextricably linked, an assembly that takes place in space and over time, sequentially, metrically. It is a mini-installation piece, and when the video is played in a gallery (as with various *TIJTS* videos exhibited in Buenos Aires at the Centro Cultural Recoleta and MACBA, or Tabakalera in San Sebastián) as part of an installation, as the spectator can walk around and view it from different perspectives and in relation to other videos from the series, the association between the built space, the video and its content becomes discernible. It becomes, in essence, one of various building blocks that form a greater assembly, or one more letter in an epistolary anthology. Then, unexpectedly, the video cuts abruptly to a black screen that displays its title, date, and other technical information about the video, following the standard format for all *TIJTS* pieces. The assembly (of the Lego, of the video, of the instruction manual), and the video itself, are now complete. Much like Denegri's video, the "finished" product is at once an idea for a project, a work in progress or a process in itself, and also the final piece, the "finished" work.

This video is articulated in relation to Caprín's other work, which, in the words of the artist, generally seeks to create a "visual language that explores the operation of certain systems and incorporates procedures from other disciplines and fields of knowledge" ("How to Build").[33] As I stated above, the filmmaker is more interested in the process of creating the video than in the final product. He manipulates various materials (the Legos, the blackboard, analog and digital video) and records how those materials behave under different pressures and circumstances. The constructivist approach to the video itself—its step-by-step filmmaking, the narration of those steps, their logical sequence—the use of the "construction" Legos and their primary colors, the more or less systematic camera movement, and the minimalist editing suggest the aesthetic of an instructional manual or a DIY repair video. Caprín tends to use common objects in his art, in this case the Legos, a work table, a blackboard, the Lego box, and some plastic bags. The construction and filming of the Legos is conducted as an exercise meant to investigate not only the material nature of the pieces (how they assemble, their geometric specificity, their combination possibilities, their aesthetic properties including shape and color scheme) but even more so the material nature of video itself. What is striking about the short video is that despite, or because of, the low quality of the image and lighting and the loose (minimalist) filming and editing style, the creation of the work is deliberate, calculated, and methodical. The execution of Caprín's videos might seem haphazard at first, but on closer inspection it is revealed to be suggestively choreographed. The video piece is at once systematic and chaotic, rigid and loose. Every item is deliberately placed, every effect is considered (whether the effects are controlled or seemingly "fortuitous"), every change is measured. Movements are explained, labeled, and carried out with precision, although the precision is not obsessive, allowing space for the contingent and unexpected to irrupt or facilitating such irruptions. Beyond Caprín's voice and the humming of the video camera, the only other noises are distant and unrecognizable ambient sounds—the absence of other sounds. Special effects or music eliminates any possibility to mistake this video piece as anything other than a technical manual or perhaps a lab experiment, as a schematic provided for the viewer to assemble their own Lego structure or their own video piece. In some respects, the dispassionate nature of the exercise contrasts with Denegri's video that we previously analyzed, which is deeply affective from the standpoint of the content of the images even as it pays tribute to Val del Omar's own scientific interest in the cinema.

As a counterpoint to Denegri's video, Caprín's meditation on the nature of video as a format seems to be primarily mechanistic, despite the deceptively emotive quality of the film's subtitle, *Oh, the Golden Days of Video Making*. Perhaps the intensity of the piece is provided by the stark contrast between the nostalgia for analog video (it is there, beneath its surface and in its subtitle) and the distanced subject matter. Both videos (Denegri's and Caprín's) do share an affinity and interest in the passage of old media and in the way these media are put together. Both videos are "projects" that were never quite completed, although both are themselves the projects they reference. Although these two videos are not in direct dialogue with each other (they were not "adjacent" or close in time within the series), they nevertheless partake of the same interests. They attest that the freedom of content choice for the *TIJTS* project was absolute. This leeway is not unexpected since Denegri and Caprín were on a similar wavelength when it came to their epistolary video exchange and the rules they followed.

According to Caprín, "[N]os propusimos que fuera con la mayor libertad: no nos mantuvimos fieles ni a estilos ni convenciones ni a nada salvo la sensibilidad puntual de lo que queríamos contar: algo que nos había pasado durante el día, una idea para un proyecto, o la contestación (a veces en espejo) de lo que nuestro interlocutor nos había dicho" ("[No] Serialidad") [We decided that (content decisions) would follow the greatest freedom: we were not faithful to any style, nor to any conventions or anything else, except for the sensibility of what we wanted to tell: something that had happened that day, an idea for a project, or the reply (sometimes a mirrored response) of something our interlocutor had told us].

Affinities between the two works, so distinct on the surface, also abound. Like Denegri's, this video is eminently heterogeneous, impure, intermedial. The digital version arguably retains the trace from its analog video "original," although admittedly its putative originality is suspect. The video could possibly be a copy of a copy—a recreation in digital video rather than a capture of the first analog video. In reality, there is no way to know whether the video's analog effects were postproduced. In fact, Cantú has theorized about the difficulty of establishing anything close to an idea of an "original" when it comes to video, a format that she believes is characterized by its impurity, its contamination and heterogeneity, indeed by its disconnect from the concept of a "first copy" or original. This heterogeneity is linked to the video's many formats, argues Cantú, "[S]i bien podríamos colocarlo bajo el paraguas de la imagen electrónica, es difícil pensar al video por fuera de la multiplicidad de sus formatos (cintas de 2 pulgadas, de 1 pulgada, Betamax, U-Matic, VHS, Hi-8, Betacam, mini DV, DVCAM, Betacam digital o Digi Beta, D I, D II o el CG, el DVD, la HDD, etc.), así como de la necesaria mudanza de soportes para asegurar su supervivencia" ("Archivos y videos" 97–98) [Although we could simply categorize video under the umbrella of the electronic image, it is difficult to understand video without considering its multiple formats (2" tape, 1" tape, Betamax, U-Matic, VHS, Hi-8, Betacam, mini DV, DVCAM, digital Betacam or Digi Beta, D I, D II or CG, DVD, HDD, etc.), as well as the transfer of its support base to various other materials or formats as needed to guarantee its survival]. The difference between video and other material formats that have a clear-cut original lies, for Cantú, in the virtual impossibility to find that first version—although perhaps that concept of "original" or "first version" does not even matter. She argues that even within the confines of preservation work, restoration techniques generally do insist on working with originals for certain objects, for example in painting or sculpture, because they are singular works. But even in the case of film and photography, says Cantú, preservationists still prefer to work with the negatives, and these negative reproducible images are the closest thing to an original. However, as she stipulates, this fetish toward the original all but vanishes with video since its survival has been linked precisely to the absence of any original. According to the Argentine preservationist, "[S]i bien tuvo que existir una primera copia en el momento de creación, su circulación y por lo tanto su existencia (dos coordenadas que al tratarse de un medio técnicamente reproducible aparecen prácticamente asociadas), han sido definidas por la imposibilidad de rastrear aquella copia primera, en pos de la multiplicación y la difusión" ("Archivos y videos" 97–98) [Even though there must have been a first copy when a video was created, its circulation and its existence (two coordinates that are associated with each other in the case of technically reproducible media) have been defined by the impossibility to track down that initial copy, after its multiplication and diffusion].

Beyond its import for preservation, forensics, and archival work, it is video's capacity for proliferating copies and disconnect from an "original," its distance from a potential first copy, that renders this analog format as the ideal candidate for its transfer to digital, a transfer that should not presuppose the same kind of "loss" or sense of angst as that provoked by the transfer of a celluloid film to digital with its concomitant loss of indexicality. Additionally, there is always the need for an intermedial process at stake when an artist chooses to record using a camcorder, since analog video can (for the most part) only be edited in-camera, which means it will be necessary to digitize the footage for any sort of extensive editing to take place. This is also the case for those artists who work with Super 8 today, since most do not edit the celluloid strip directly but only during postproduction after the film has been digitized. Direct editing (the kind that was once done using Moviolas and editing tables) has now been replaced by digital editing using commercial software, making the process more accessible and less arcane. Most artists transfer their analog videos to digital for editing, circulation, and distribution reasons, that is to say for practical reasons. In-camera editing is typically linear (starts at the beginning of the video) and requires significant planning on the part of the filmmaker prior to recording, while computer editing is nonlinear (can edit at any point of the recording, shuffle parts around at will) and provides flexibility to make changes during postproduction. So for filmmakers like Caprín, the affordances of a hybrid approach (film with Betacam, edit with a digital computer) tap into the best of both worlds—they achieve the aesthetic they desire (in this case a 1980s-video look) and they can manipulate files with ease and digitally touch up the final product.

For Caprín, as well as Denegri and the other participants in what is, after all, a group project, perhaps the fundamental component of this intermedial video archive is the collaborative and dialogical aspect. In the exchange of video "letters" the artists reinforce the ties that bind them, despite the distance and their new countries (for those that migrated). They are first and foremost video artists, but they also share a national origin in Argentina and a cohesive outlook as global artists who produce work in the diaspora, or in its shadow for those who stayed behind. The artists sustain that *TIJTS* is principally a collaborative effort, so although each video has an author with a distinct authorial style and voice, it is only when viewed in its totality that the project begins to signify. If the essence of this experimental video project is its collaborative nature and its epistolary format, its material characteristics are defined by its impurity, by the commingling of formats. Denegri establishes a genealogy between Super 8, video, and finally the internet as technological developments that have enabled filming the quotidian, recuperation of the experience of knowing an "other" through daily contact and dialogue, even at a distance and asynchronously—akin to written correspondence in the past. All these formats have facilitated immediacy and proximity, even across vast distances and oceans. But it is the space provided most recently by the internet for archiving, distributing, and exhibiting the videos that makes for a technological development that is radically innovative and renders possible the public access to this otherwise intimate dialogue. Denegri observes that video is not the medium itself but rather a tool, whereas the internet is the medium: "las cartas solo se vuelven públicas a través de su edición en libros; si nosotros simplemente nos enviáramos videos, uno al otro, no se constituiría esta obra permanentemente accesible a todos que es *This Is Just to Say*. Parece que el soporte es el video, pero en este caso el video es sólo la tinta, el papel del libro que hace de *This Is Just to Say* una obra es Internet" [letters only become public once they are edited in books; if all we had done was exchange videos amongst ourselves, *This Is Just to Say* would not be the open and accessible work that it is. It seems like the medium is the video format, but in this case the video is only like the ink, whereas the paper that makes this project an actual artwork is internet itself].

So, for Denegri and Caprín, even more critical than having the videos projected in museums or displayed as installation pieces, their eventual endpoint is exhibition and distribution through the internet. It is the internet that magnifies their geographical dimension, that allows the project to become truly transatlantic and collaborative. Like his friend and collaborator, Caprín also elaborates on this point about the importance of group work across media and national boundaries as he attempts to define the quintessence of the *TIJTS* video collection in terms of avant-garde collage:

> [L]a primera visión es una proliferación de estilos, juergas, cantos, mugidos y esquivadas varias. Podría ser algo como: collage, pastiche, potpurrí. . . . Es como cuando de chico te metías todos los dulces en la boca y los mezclabas, o cuando pintabas y mezclabas los colores . . . a ver qué pasaba. El referente plástico sin duda es el collage más auténtico, clásico y descalabrado: un Kurt Schwitters. Por momentos veías que había un caos total, reinaba la desconexión. . . . Pero al siguiente mensaje todo se aclaraba, había sido solo una pequeña digresión. El único factor de unidad lo ponen las etiquetitas: el "autor," el día, el lugar, el "destinatario," etc. Y pongo comillas ya que, como acertadamente comenta Emilio [Bernini], no se trata sino de una obra grupal. ("[No] Serialidad")
>
> [The first vision of the project shows a proliferation of styles, parties, songs, bellowing and digressions. It might be something like collage, pastiche, potpourri. It is like when, as a child, you would mix a bunch of different candy in your mouth, or when you would draw, mixing all the different colors . . . just to see what would happen. The nearest visual arts referent is the most authentic, classical, and insane collage: the work of Kurt Schwitters. At times you could sense a complete chaos, a total disconnect. . . . But in the next message everything became clear, the previous one had just been a little digression. The only unifying component is the labels: the "author," the day, the place, the "recipient," etc. And I use quotation marks because, as Emilio Bernini argues, this is a collective work.]

And like any conversation, dialogue, or group project that is founded on small, "unimportant" events, on a conversation between distant friends across an ocean, subject matter are little objects, daily happenings, shared memories from the past, little things that do not rise to any epic heights. It is quotidian history rather than more "heroic" history-making or narrating.

It is a less totalizing perspective than the dogmatism of the militant period, a perspective that has turned its back on grand narratives, to be sure, but is no less dynamic or aesthetically daring in its relentless exploration of medium, identity, and origins. Denegri and Caprín's generation, to which Cugliandolo also belongs, does not wish for rigid ideological positions or battles, the kind that their parents' generation engaged in. It is precisely in this familial light, through a transatlantic aesthetics of the everyday and the intimate, that this profoundly hybrid project was presented at the MACBA (Museo de Arte Contemporáneo de Buenos Aires) in 2014, when the museum's blog stated that the videos narrated "una historia íntima, de estar en casa, trabajar en el estudio, pasear en familia y de andar solo. No hay guerras mundiales, ni fechas, ni batallas, sólo la película de súper 8 que uno encontró, los inventos estrafalarios que nunca se concretan, el paisaje tras la ventana del nuevo hogar, el mecanismo de la persiana de aquel estudio, esa arqueología ordinaria que uno comparte con los que lo acompañan" [an intimate history, about being at home, working at the studio. Strolling with family and going on solitary walks. There are no world wars, no significant dates, no battles, only the Super 8 film that the artist found, the strange inventions that were never built, the landscape behind the window of a new home, the mechanism for the blinds in that studio, that ordinary archeology that one shares with those who are living with us]. As if to underscore the transatlantic nature of the project, another MACBA, this time the Museu d'Art Contemporani de Barcelona (which shares the same initials as its counterpart in Buenos Aires) also screened some of the films from *TIJTS* in 2014, a tale of two MACBAs and two (later four) artists.

What we can conclude about the work of these two filmmakers and video artists Andrés Denegri (still in Buenos Aires) and Gustavo Caprín (resettled permanently in Barcelona) is that despite the distance that separates them, they share a set or artistic interests and aesthetic affinities that place them at the forefront of a diaspora of visual artists that increasingly advocates for hybrid approaches to filmmaking, regardless of formats used. Specifically looking at *TIJTS*, the filmmakers understand these videos as a layering of past and present temporalities, memories, images, and media. Like Val del Omar's kiss, remixing the archive of cinematic and video art results, for them, in affective palimpsests, in works that layer their referentiality, like those early avant-garde collages by cubist and constructivist artists like Schwitters, Picasso, Braque, and Gris. Indeed, collage culture is at the root of contemporary digital culture, which has always incorporated, copied, reclaimed, and remediated previous media forms.

Concluding Remarks:
Intermediality as Film and Video's Affective Afterlife

Writing in *Cinema Journal* about the intermediality noticeably present in Latin American art practices, the late Ana M. López called for a recalibration of the critical apparatus to account for a "contemporary mediascape [that] is a complex mix of traditional media and increasingly more visible processes of convergence, transmediality, and intermediality; clearly, this is an area in which a recognition of the mutual permeability of media must be enacted and addressed" (140). What López proposed, in effect, is new research that would focus on media relations, redirecting critical attention to an ever-changing field of media experimentation. Undoubtedly part of that focus involves adopting media archeology approaches that can theorize how so-called residual media (Super 8, analog video, etc.) have gained a new viability through their hybrid coupling with digital technologies. What we now have in terms of creative media is an amalgam no longer easily reduced to either digital or analog but closer to interdependent alternatives that appropriate and heterogeneously incorporate what is desired from past media à la carte according to the sought-after aesthetic. Intermediality, broadly understood, extends beyond materials and methods and into venues of production, archival and reposting.

This is not to claim that some filmmakers do not still insist on the concept of media "purity," of the perfect symbiosis between a format and its material base. These filmmakers, who do exist, mourn the passing of celluloid, or in some cases of analog video or any number of other formats that have been deemed obsolete by consumers' tastes and market forces—at least until they are reclaimed and recuperated under a nostalgic drive or "tucked" into an emerging format. Critics Alejandra Torres and Clara Garavelli, in their analysis of the contemporary experimental film scene in Argentina and its diaspora, make that very point. For them, filmmakers who insist on medium specificity have taken an oppositional stance toward video art, understanding the hybrid tendencies germane to that format as departing from "originary" cinema. Setting the stage, Torres and Garavelli explain that in recent years there has been a renewed interest in experimental cinema in Argentina. Consecrated artists such as Claudio Caldini and Narcisa Hirsch successfully screen and promote experimental film. Younger filmmakers, committed to their love of celluloid, have returned to Super 8 and 16 mm. While most filmmakers also work in digital or combine various formats, and the distinction between film and experimental video is becoming rather obsolete, some filmmakers remain adamant about maintaining these distinctions. Thus, argue Torres and Garavelli, this reduced group of filmmakers "se inclinan hacia un tratamiento material de las imágenes con una nostalgia y reivindicación de los proyectores y cámaras antiguas en 8, 16 e incluso 35 mm, [y] abogan por una pureza de la imagen fílmica. Intentan así acercarse a un estado primigenio del cine, insistiendo en separar a sus producciones de los circuitos correspondientes al video experimental" (10–11) [remain anchored in approaching the materiality of images with nostalgia and insistence on the relevance of old cameras and projectors, whether in 8, 16, or 35 mm, advocating for the purity of the filmic image. They would seek a return to an originary state of the cinema, differentiating and distancing their work from that of experimental video altogether].

None of the cineastes I examined here take this oppositional stance against video but freely incorporate all formats. As Torres and Garavelli indicate in their study of the contemporary experimental scene, at this juncture most filmmakers hold a fervently hybrid understanding of the terms "film" and "video," terms that are often interchanged as they no longer necessarily retain a physical anchor to the media that used to host them (celluloid strips, magnetic tapes, etc.). Both celluloid and analog video have entered a transmedial stage in which their afterlife is fully digital (virtual), even as it retains (aesthetic) traces of past media. In any case, the question of media origins may be moot for practitioners, given that "si bien el soporte video es abandonado en pos de una comprensión transmedial de las obras" (11) [although video as a format has been abandoned in favor of a transmedial understanding of the works], a plurality of contemporary visual artists show little interest in circumscribing their work to only one field, one medium, or one format.

No doubt, experimental filmmakers (and videographers) still consider the venue where their films are screened as a critical component of their conceptual meaning. At the same time, they are also increasingly cognizant of the limitations associated with what once constituted the privileged loci for projection: movie theaters, museums, galleries, nightclubs, and festivals. As we saw with Cugliandolo's films and with the *TIJTS* video project, these filmmakers now explore digital platforms for display and archival, such as YouTube and Vimeo, which perforce require digitizing and media convergence. As I hope to have shown, such convergence need not signal the erasure of past media, as their traces and memories are ingrained (or inpixilated) within "digital indexicality" and as memories or affective recollections triggered by simulated effects. The renaissance of Super 8, as exemplified by Cugliandolo's films, and the (limited) return of analog video, as seen in Denegri and Caprín's work, signal a shift from purist notions of celluloid or analog video toward media integration, tapping into the possibilities that digital capture and editing offer. It does not signal film or video's imminent death, but rather their afterlife, their extension into new digital forms of experimental practice. Such practice insists on retaining a lingering trace of celluloid cinema and its craft (a hint of the old "aura," a touch of affect); similarly, it retains a hint of that quality that made analog video the defining format of the 1980s and '90s, for a generation that reached adulthood watching and making VHS tapes. The internet, in this sense, has become "the terrain on which sentimental attachments, vernacular knowledges and a multitude of other relationships to the material culture are magnified and given coherence," the place where film and video have consolidated their intermedial—and perhaps affective—afterlife (Straw 3). Moreover, one might argue, following Walter Benjamin's line, that the new technology has facilitated access (and decreased distance) to these films and video pieces, with an interesting democratizing effect: it is easier to create, access, view, and exchange experimental cinema and video art than ever before (that said, the number of artists in these genres remains small). A paradox ensues, since, as I intimated elsewhere in this essay, part of the politics of the experimental aesthetic is its capacity to induce estrangement and to defamiliarize, disrupting habits and causing us to see the world "anew." The internet, on the other hand, tends to bring us closer, to refamiliarize us, and to bridge distances and gaps, to restore a sense of "homeliness." If the experimental becomes mainstream, or at least easily available, we may ask: Will it lose its potential to effect change? I do not think this move online necessarily represents a significant co-optation or compromise for experimental cinema or for video art, at least not any more so than its presence in museums and galleries. Even online, these experimental forms retain their status as "rare" genres capable of shocking and defamiliarizing viewers (and yes, of boring them as well) and as constantly reinventing themselves as forms, ever more hybrid. And even online, experimental formats remain relatively marginal, only viewed by a few filmmakers and fans. While the internet has facilitated access, it has done so only for a self-selected group, for those already interested in these extreme forms of visual art. In that sense the relative political strength or weakness of experimental cinema and video art remains as elusive as it does for most other experimental genres.

There is no denying that the internet has become a sort of home in the diaspora, a place where the local and global are bridged, where filmic memories might be archived, where video dialogues can be maintained, and where a new community of Argentine filmmakers, regardless of where they actually live (self-exiled, migrants, nomadic, diasporic, or settled in some place they call home), can gather and playfully reinterpret what those labels (Argentine, filmmaker) mean in an increasingly post-national, post-medium age, as they listen to the fading mechanical sound of the Super 8 projector, now digitally reproduced.

Chapter 4

Cell Phone Cinema and Amateur Genre Film in the Luso-Hispanic Atlantic

Introduction: Cell Phone Filmmaking

In previous chapters we have considered the ties between Latin American and Iberian militant cinema in the 1960s (chapter 1), the transatlantic associations between Brazilian and Spanish art cinema in the following decades of the late 1960s and '70s (chapter 2), and the emergence of a transatlantic experimental cinema of the Argentine diaspora, bridging the late 1960s and the 2000s, in the context of nostalgia for disappearing analog media (chapter 3).[1] In the current chapter I analyze how yet another seismic shift in cinematic medium and technology has been adapted (and adopted) on both sides of the Atlantic. I am referring to the new possibilities for filming with a pocket-sized device that is within the reach of almost anyone, the cellular phone. The democratizing potential facilitated by this communication technology is borne out by the fact that by 2019 there were over eight billion mobile phones worldwide, just surpassing the global population (Shilina-Conte 34). While production of moving images with a cell phone or a digital single-lens reflex (DSLR) camera does not automatically equate with the creation of interesting, relevant, or worthwhile works, from among the vastly increased numbers some decidedly rise to the task. It is therefore not an exaggeration to say that the cell phone has shifted the paradigm for not only fiction, documentary, and experimental cinema but also home movies (including a radical turn to the selfie-film and an expanding obsession with social media videos). The cell phone has also revolutionized citizen journalism, placing cameras into virtually all hands and allowing for the documenting of everything from police brutality (Darnella Frazier's citizen video of George Floyd's murder in 2021) to natural disasters (the countless videos documenting Hurricane Ian in 2022) and political unrest (selfie videos by rioters storming the US Capitol on January 6, 2021, or anonymous videos documenting protests against draconian COVID-19 measures in China during fall 2022), to name some salient examples.

While there could be some hesitation in considering all material shot with cell phones as "cinema" proper, especially if we consider the term's historic association with certain conventions, a specific industry, and affiliated institutions, the word here is meant to also extend to work by amateurs and hobbyists or to forms like vlogs, web series, micro-movies, eyewitness reportage, and other audiovisual materials that may or may not have a narrative function. Understood in this encompassing way, in fact, the term brings us back to the definition of cinema as moving images. And it reminds us that, insofar as some of these formats and experiments are "replacing" (or perhaps transforming, even enriching) the traditional cinema, they represent its future or some of its possible futures. Bazin made precisely this same argument when stipulating that what is proper in moving image production (and what is "cinema") is what the audience or the spectator decides it is through their viewing choices, or as the French critic succinctly puts it in *What Is Cinema?*, "[W]e must say of the cinema that its existence precedes its essence" (71).

Although the focus of this chapter is narrative cell phone cinema, there is a powerful association between the transnational citizen journalism and activism facilitated by cell phones with the work we saw in chapters 1 and 2 (militant cinema and art house, both close allies of Third Cinema), or even with the technological adaptation of new handheld formats from past decades (Super 8 and analog video cameras) as we saw in chapter 3. Tanya Shilina-Conte adroitly outlines these connections as well as the eminently transnational and intermedial nature of the format, claiming that "by virtue of its pocket-ability, the widespread coverage of cellular networks, and the affordances of anonymous clandestine filming, the camera phone has travelled with migrants across international borders and also become an indispensable tool for citizens documenting uprisings in authoritarian countries. From this perspective, phone footage cinema has evolved into a successor of Third Cinema, or 'an imperfect cinema,' combining revolutionary participation with its own spectatorship" (35). While the fictional films I will study are not anonymous and stake no claims toward revolutionary participation or politics, they are radical in their own right—formally, conceptually, and in terms of the accessibility and democratization they represent for global filmmaking.

An Overview of Cell Phone Cinema as a Medium

Cell phone cinema is an emergent phenomenon, or more accurately, one that has already fully emerged but continues to rapidly evolve. The format is ideally suited for independent filmmakers in the Global South, although it is being embraced everywhere as a discrete, portable form of making cinema quickly and cheaply. Cell phones are being used to make every type of film, whether documentary, fiction, or hybrid genres, in addition to its widespread use in news media and for social purposes. Although it has been characterized as a "mode of minor cinema" (Wilson, "Film Festival Participation" 289), filmmakers of the ilk of Christopher Nolan, Michel Gondry, and Steven Soderbergh are referring to the cell phone as the new Super 8 in its capacity to reinvent film practices. Certainly, the sheer production of cell phone video is vast in terms of volume. Considering both amateur and professional works, the numbers easily outstrip other audio-visual media. According to industry sources up to seventy-five percent of global video consumption is played on mobile phones, and many of those videos are also created with cell phones, often leading to a reframing (or reorienting) of the screen, away from "landscape" to the "vertical" format, and creating a separate subcategory of vertical cinema (Kegishyan). With easy-to-use technology and low production costs, as well as open and free or relatively cheap distribution via online streaming, cell phone cinema has arguably democratized access to filmmaking for many who cannot afford costly cameras and have no access to the world of professional cinema. It is true that certain challenges remain, including that good material might end up lost amidst the glut of overproduction. Given reduced attention spans online, these kinds of cell phone cinema mainly garner the attention of cinephiles who are interested in these types of experimental or amateur products. On the other hand, as I discuss, many of the better works find a wider audience through participation in festivals (online and offline) and dedicated websites. Some of the films even go viral, although not to the extent that other less artful, at times comical, cheaply thrilling, or outrageous videos might, but that is perfectly acceptable given their niche nature. In that sense, these cell phone films acquire views in the thousands or hundreds of thousands, rather than the millions, and have less spectators than commercial cinematography, a case similar to the status of Super 8 and other amateur and alternative formats.

There may even be an inverse relationship or trade-off when it comes to these formats between wider distribution (i.e., going viral) and striving for aesthetic value. Even as alternative production and distribution avenues liberate filmmakers from the constraints of the mainstream industry, they limit artistic potential and marginalize these films, now labeled as the work of amateurs by the established industry. For instance, according to Gavin Wilson, this corpus is considered by the mainstream industry as a "transient, marginal or minor cinema" (*Cell/ular Cinema* 89). On account of this marginalization "phone films face difficulties in appropriating the industrial and economic/commercial benefits that are often enjoyed by mainstream cinema, placing them fundamentally in a delegitimized position" (Wilson, "Film Festival Participation" 289). Since the "birth" of cell phone cinema in the early 2000s, filmmakers favoring this format have wrestled with a troublesome paradox. Many enthusiastically embrace a low-budget, transgressive, and independent filmmaking while desiring and striving for higher production quality in the hopes to eventually compete with commercial cinema. Efforts to reconcile these seemingly clashing tendencies have profound repercussions on the content and aesthetics of cell phone films. On the surface, they appear rough. These hybrid works are made close to the body and typically combine digital and analog elements. Many have a post-digital aesthetic displaying glitches, digital errors, flickering, pixilation, and other visual distortions, either deliberate, contingent, or as a function of lo-fi technology. But these works also show considerable postproduction and attention to cinematography, as we shall see.

In this chapter I define the main features of global cell phone cinema, presenting a broad overview of the format. Then, turning to Latin America and Spain, I examine four paradigmatic cell phone horror flicks, a genre with a significant presence in mobile filmmaking since its inception. Although this turn to genre film may seem as a departure from previous chapters, cell phone cinema can, regardless of its subject, be considered as a kind of "experimental" format, sharing aspects with home movies and early Super 8 practices while maintaining connections to citizen journalism and even documentary film. As part of my analysis, I raise many critical questions about this format: Are these films part of a transatlantic globalized cinema, as they appear to be? How do the different functions and affordances of the phone (text, voice, image) and its functionality as a minicomputer (with access to social media, GPS, music, video, etc.) enhance and complicate the device's inherent intermediality? Might this format change the game—from a cinema made and distributed by the commercial industry to self-produced films created by autodidacts and distributed freely online? Is online self-distribution a prerequisite for the global, intermedial, and materially "impure" nature of the films? Finally, will these cell phone films also be co-opted by market forces and lose their do-it-yourself (DIY) quality? Whatever might be the future of this format, the independent film landscape has already been radically altered by this technology.

The Cell Phone Flick: Basic Facts

Luis Felipe Cardona's ninety-second short *Checklist* (Colombia, 2004) was among the first generation of fiction films made with a cell phone in Latin America and Spain, and in fact globally, since the first cell phones equipped with video cameras only became available in 2003.[2] First-generation phone cameras could only record short videos (ten to fifteen seconds). This encouraged the creation of micro-narratives as well as repeating loops to create the appearance of a longer film (and anticipating the ten-second duration of TikTok videos when the app was initially launched in 2018). Both camera quality and video length improved drastically over a few short years. By 2009, Apple released its first phone with video capabilities, the iPhone 3GS, which rivaled the video quality of existing high-definition (HD) cameras. Today's videos are a distant cry from pioneering efforts. *Checklist*, as one of the first films shot on a cell phone, was a precursor to contemporary global cell phone cinema, a first, halting step.

The film's plot is humorous if somewhat banal. *Checklist* narrates the story of an absent-minded man who, after attempting several times to leave his house one morning, keeps having to return to collect items he has forgotten—his watch, his wallet, his Walkman (the latter a wink to retro technologies). Tired of his forgetfulness, the protagonist finally taps a virtual display window that is also visible on the spectator's own screen. The text superimposed on the video mimics early cell phone displays and offers a checklist menu of the items the man needs (see fig. 4.1). In the film's comical yet bizarre conclusion, the protagonist can be seen walking down the street, naked from the waist down. The joke is that he thought he had "checked" everything (keys, wallet, Walkman, etc.), but he forgot to put on his pants because they were not on the checklist. With this visual gag Cardona cautions against our overdependence on technology, suggesting

Figure 4.1. Early Latin American cell phone fiction film, *Checklist* (2004) (01:11). Source: *Checklist* (2004). Dir. Luis Felipe Cardona.

that digital gadgetry cannot solve human failings, a message paradoxically delivered with the (then) latest cell phone model. Thus, from the outset of the modality of cell phone filmmaking we see a certain cautious ambivalence attuned to the benefits and dangers of technology.

The film, awarded the first prize in the micro-movie division of the 2004 Berlin Short Film Festival, embodies various other contradictions evidenced by cell phone cinema from its inception. For instance, Cardona—an outsider to the mainstream movie industry—argues that commercial production and distribution "en la realidad latinoamericana, es un hobby caro e inútil" (Marín, "Felipe Cardona") [within the Latin American reality, is an expensive and useless hobby]. Yet although Cardona claims to be hacking into the mainstream industry by using cell phones and self-distributing his films, he gladly accepts corporate sponsorship and works toward commercial quality standards (Marín). *Checklist* was made possible by the German Siemens mobile phone company, which donated the phone, organized the festival, and awarded Cardona a three-thousand-euro prize. Likewise, although the film displays a rough, pixelated aesthetic and low definition typical of "glitchy" early cell phone videos (not a deliberate choice), it also uses professional postproduction techniques including split screens, double exposures, and a sophisticated image and sound montage. *Checklist* therefore functions as both a viral humor video and as a self-reflexive film about the interpenetration of cell phone technology with contemporary life. As I will show, the contradictory attitudes and uses of technology present in *Checklist* are inherent and even constitutive of this latest cinematic format, the cell phone film.

Filmed exclusively or partially with mobile phones, cell phone cinema, despite being around since the early 2000s, is still new enough to be classified as "emergent."[3] Given the format's reliance on alternative distribution (often underground, viral, and online), as well as its lo-fi production quality, cell phone filmmakers are often considered "amateurs" by their mainstream peers. At times, filmmakers accept this marginalization by deliberately adopting styles and genres that are on the fringe of mainstream cinema, including a marked tendency toward horror and sci-fi. There seems to be a special affinity between cell phone films and horror, based on the genre's proclivity toward found footage and surveillance feeds, which share an aesthetic of immediacy and "authenticity" with phone-produced videos.

This illusion of the real, the immediate, the authentic and unedited, and even the unmediated is fabricated in part by the raw look of cell phone cinema. I am referring to its low-grade, unpolished texture, especially in its early years, today achieved through apps and postproduction glitching. Immediacy is also enhanced by the device's portability. The portability and adaptability of the cell phone as an audiovisual technology has also had a positive impact on creative freedom, facilitating independence from traditional methods of production and circulation, and at times endowing the films with a disruptive potential, as they are less likely to be beholden to commercial interests. I would suggest, however, that this seemingly antithetical position toward commercial cinema has always wavered, and as the capabilities of cell phones have improved, mobile phone cinema has begun to approximate its mainstream counterpart in terms of its aesthetics, production, and distribution. Nevertheless, as Wilson observes, sweeping claims about cell phone films often miss the modality's wondrous heterogeneity, so that the "scholar searches for typicality in phone films at her or his peril. Whether distributed and seen online or in a film festival environment, phone films vary widely in their subject matter, narrative concerns and stylistic treatment" ("Film Festival Participation" 289). With that caveat in mind, we can still define certain aesthetic concerns, trends, and commonalities that emerge across mobile films, even as we recognize their amazing heterogeneity.

Cell phone films are almost invariably transnational on various levels, as filmmakers target international festivals and share their work in public websites with global audiences. The movies themselves are often the product of cross-cultural themes and international collaborations, and even local productions can be seen globally once uploaded to the web. Films created by Latin American or Spanish producers tend to share a common language and cultural affinities, even as they also differ in local accents (when in Spanish) or levels of English proficiency (when in English). As might be expected, given the predominance of English online and that filmmakers aspire for global diffusion, a significant number of films are in English, or at the very least closed-captioned once they are uploaded.

When it comes to genre cell phone films, globalizing tendencies seem to be amplified. Iberian and Latin American horror films are marked by mutual influence and also emulate their Hollywood counterparts. This mark of transnationalism within Iberian and Latin American film has also been prominent in commercial cinema since the 1990s (in mainstream, non–cell phone films), exemplified in films by acclaimed international auteurs such as Guillermo del Toro, Alfonso Cuarón, Juan José Campanella, Pedro Almodóvar, Alejandro Amenabar, and a long list of other arguably post-national directors. But transnationalist tendencies are equally present in the considerably less glamorous, underground DIY productions of cell phone cinema, including its horror subgenre. In addition to the horror genre's robust local presence in small theater venues and its promotion at the national and local level throughout Latin America, according to Risner, "a transnational horror cinema culture is composed of horror and genre film festivals, DVD distribution companies, legal and illegal streaming sites, and websites that cover horror and genre cinema" ("The Reach" 117). Strong affinities and stylistic commonalities notwithstanding, I am not arguing for the existence of a flattened mobile cinema that is the same across the Atlantic or even within each country or region, as national elements and local particularities persist. For Chris Perriam, Isabel Santaolalla, and Peter Evans it would be critical malpractice "to indicate an unproblematic, idealizing and seamless sameness across nations and industries. . . . [Cinematic transnationalism] is not necessarily a breaking free of the boundaries and binds of the national construct" (4). In other words, transnationalism coexists with regional specificity.

In contrast with commercial cinema (firmly ensconced within an established industry), in cell phone features the tension between transnational and local elements is further complicated by its status, uneasily wavering between amateur and (semi)professional—a duality discernible in Cardona's *Checklist*. Those filmmakers who consciously engage in cell phone movies (as opposed to simply using the phone to record for personal use), whether they consider themselves amateur, professional, or in between, wrestle with those contradictory tendencies and identities. On the one hand, some make films that are rough and independent, transgressive, and free from creative constraints; on the other, some strive for a higher production quality and have commercial aspirations. Some filmmakers try to do both, uneasily straddling DIY and commercial impulses. Efforts to reconcile these tensions have had repercussions on the content and aesthetics of cell phone films, as the format's boundaries are negotiated.

In the following pages I delineate some of the contours of cell phone cinema, a format that remains mostly unexplored to date, at least from a cultural studies perspective. I will first frame cell phone cinema as a transnational phenomenon, broadly defining its main features and briefly describing its historical development. But the subject of this chapter is the subset of works that are created by filmmakers that retain some affiliation with either Spain or Latin America, even if their films have a much broader reach. More specifically, I will analyze three movies from Latin America and one from Spain that exemplify the evolution of the cell phone horror genre, paying close attention to formal aesthetics, content choices, and modes of distribution. Each film represents a distinct moment within the technological development of cell phones and responds to the affordances brought about by those technical changes. At the same time, even as we delineate specific elements linked to the national origin of the films, we can observe considerable similarities in approach, partly due to adherence to genre conventions but also stemming from the exchanges and mutual influence made possible by (transnational) internet distribution. Simply put, cell phone filmmakers are viewing and learning from each other's work across regions and languages, as well as emulating established mainstream global cinemas (Hollywood included). I focus on horror because, as mentioned above, it is a prominent genre within Latin American and Iberian cell phone movies, often favored by neophyte filmmakers experimenting with genre.

This penchant toward horror and related subgenres reflects not only the affinity of horror with cell phone aesthetics but also its broader popularity in the region, underscoring Gustavo Subero's point that "Latin American filmic production since the turn of the twenty-first century clearly evidences a resurgence of horror films" (xxiii). The genre has served in the continent as a way to deal (through metaphor and allegory) with a set of anxieties, from political, drug, and gender violence to economic inequality, immigration, environmental crisis, and the ever-present fraught relationship with the wealthy and domineering neighbor to the north, as well as issues of local import. In Argentina alone, according to Carina Rodríguez, "una década (a partir del año 2000) bastó para poblar la producción nacional con casi 100 largometrajes [de terror]" (13) [a decade, beginning in the year 2000, sufficed to populate national cinema with almost one hundred horror films].

Despite the genre's undeniable popularity, directors creating horror films are often obligated to seek ingenious ways to self-fund, produce, and exhibit their work. This is in part because traditional screening venues and access to funds from national institutes have been in short supply for genre films in Latin America and, somewhat less so, in Spain. For example, in Argentina, horror films have historically received scant funding from the Instituto Nacional de Cine y Artes Audiovisuales (INCAA) and have had limited access to the circuit of national cinemas, forcing filmmakers to find "different exhibition spaces for horror movies such as film festivals and organized screenings at cultural centers. Otherwise . . . national horror films in Argentina are viewed privately through Internet downloading or purchased as DVDs at informal street markets" (Risner, "This City" 25). Horror cinema has faced similar challenges in other Southern Cone nations, even though the genre is on the rise within youth culture. According to Jonathan Risner, there has been "an increase in the public and the private exhibition of Chilean horror films," but in general much activity occurs online, as the country's horror filmmakers seek to interface with and establish "ties to a larger transnational horror cinema culture" ("The Reach" 116). Similar obstacles throughout the continent are met with online solutions. Even in Mexico, where the genre has fared better in terms of its commercial viability (both in cinema and television showings), horror remains marginal in relation to other genres, so that "while audiences enjoyed these delirious tales and box offices gorged on the receipts, the majority of film historians and critics openly denounced the recycled plot lines, genre mashups, and financial straightjackets under which they [horror filmmakers] had to operate" (Cinema Tropical).

When it comes to providing hard statistics about the number of films made with cell phones in the region, regardless of genre, there is at present no reliable sources. That said, while there is currently no media distribution research or reception studies focused specifically on cell phone cinema production in Latin America, there is anecdotal evidence that points to the growing popularity of horror and sci-fi. In my own research I identified seventy-four films from Spain and Latin America made with cell phones by searching video streaming sites and film festival websites; from those, sixteen films could be categorized as horror, twenty-one percent of this random sampling. The turn to low-budget genre production, improvised filming, and alternative screening venues has been facilitated by the cell phone format and by online streaming, but there are also the aforementioned aesthetic reasons as to why the horror genre "fits" with mobile devices.[4]

Cell Phone Cinema as a Post-Digital Hybrid and Intermedial Format

The proliferation of cell phone filmmaking responds to changes in the ways images are produced and consumed in the post-digital era, that is, in the twenty-first century. If the digital represented a shift away from the analog and the material, the recent post-digital turn seeks to rehumanize aesthetic practices, making them more accessible and portable, to bring them closer to the body, closer to intimate spaces. Cell phones facilitate this closeness and are allowing almost anyone to create and disseminate their own videos, in an era when intimacy is habitually produced and performed online. Viewing practices are shifting from the big screen to small portable screens that function as extensions of ourselves. Cell phone films are primarily seen on mobile phones, tablets, and laptops and only occasionally in movie theaters. Theater viewership, which minimally counters the general trend toward smaller screens, is only made possible by niche cell phone film festivals such as SmartFilm in Colombia.[5]

These heterogeneous viewing practices are paralleled by a multiplication of communication technologies with video and audio recording tools, ranging from early phones with poor cameras and microphones, characterized by low pixel capabilities, dating from the early to mid-2000s (but still used at times for various reasons), to the very latest Android and iPhone models capable of HD video capture and outfitted with special lenses (telephoto, anamorphic, etc.), stabilizing tripods and shoulder rigs, and assorted phone cages (for better handling), not to mention the use of drones with their own designated cameras or phone attachments. Today, high-quality material can be edited on a computer or directly on the cell phone with specialized apps and enhanced with postproduction effects that blur distinctions between professional and amateur work. Soon phones will have the kind of filmmaking capability only dreamed of by first-generation cell phone filmmakers working during the initial development of the technology, in the early 2000s.

The sheer heterogeneity of source footage assures that cell phone video is eminently intermedial, even when those media are mostly processed through a digital format. Understanding "medium" broadly as we have been throughout this text, one can see how despite the final "convergence" into a single digital file, aspects from each contributing material medium remain in the final product. Cell phone films combine footage from a variety of phones, as each generation and phone type offers different aesthetic possibilities, from rough, blurry pixilation to high definition. Other movies edit digital and analog materials together to create hybrid formats (much as we saw in the work by Cugliandolo and Hirsch, although they did not use cell phones but rather professional digital cameras). Post-digital practices in film and video strive to restore a sense of materiality, of tangible texture, to digital work, often through approaches that avoid high fidelity and high definition, in a response to the sameness imposed by the process of digital convergence. David Berry and Michael Dieter characterize the post-digital as "a hybridized approach towards the digital and non-digital, finding characteristics of one within the other, deliberately mixing up processes of making things discrete, calculable, indexed and automated in unorthodox ways" (6). Naturally, in the Global South post-digitality is also linked to access; simply stated, independent filmmakers often use whatever materials are available, regardless of format or medium, quilting them together in original ways. The materials and media available to cell phone filmmakers are also accompanied by a plethora of communication channels and formats that can be included in the body of the film, such as texting, phone calls, email, social media and dating messaging, video calls, and other apps and functions.

The filmmakers are orchestrating the cell phone's many functions within the finished videos so that the screen becomes a palimpsest of the latest digital phenomena overlaid onto a more or less conventional storyline. The presence of all these forms of communication within phone movies also reinforces the idea of global connectedness, of transnationalism, especially possible when there is a shared language, whether Spanish or more commonly, English. Reflecting the transnationalism of the medium and its filmmakers, storylines are often themselves associated with mobility and border crossings, as cell phone films are set in cars, buses, trains, planes, and even elevators, and characters are constantly on the move. The films are viewed on a variety of screens, including on cell phones, which are the ultimate in movable venues not tethered to a specific location but intimately close to the individual viewer and therefore closely embedded in everyday life. Currently the phone's geolocative capabilities allow the device to suggest the viewing of specific videos (based not only on preference and viewing histories but on location and assumed language), so that the cell phone movie can be tailored in highly specific and individualized ways. This individualization on the one hand allows for the establishment of viewing communities that share like-minded interests, but on the other, it can atomize the potential viewership for films. Multitasking may take place when viewing on mobile screens, resulting in distracted viewing practices, which may in turn influence the kinds of films that are prioritized (action and horror, for instance, possibly require less attention than other genres, such as documentary, art films, or even suspense thrillers).

Finally, there have been films that are specifically designed for or released via mobile apps, such as *Haunting Melissa* (Neal Edelstein, 2013), an episodic film for viewing on iPhone/iPad that changes each time it is viewed, adding new auditory and visual elements through the use of so-called dynamic story elements, prerecorded fragments that are added in response to spectator choices so that the narration is not wholly fixed. This sort of interactivity is reaching new levels in horror, almost blending into the video game genre, with interactive horror flicks such as the (gimmicky) German movie *Last Call* (Christian Mielmann, 2010), promoted as "the first interactive horror film." Although *Last Call* was not shot with cell phones, it employed them: during the theatrical performance viewers who had preregistered their numbers might receive a call on their cell phone, as the lead actress would ask them for suggestions regarding her situation (the chosen viewer could then select among a set of options and trigger an associated prefilmed outcome).

Just as cell phone films mix various formats and media, they are the end product of a hybrid collaboration of sorts, between the filmmaker's body (supposedly analog/organic yet closely attached to its cell phone prosthesis) and the camera (digital/inorganic) through which he or she views the world. Actors, who like the filmmakers are intuitively familiar with cell phones, also develop some "post-human" characteristics and respond synergistically to its motion during filming, more attuned to this proximal device than to the distant cameras used in conventional filmmaking. From the standpoint of a spectator viewing these cell phone films, it may be difficult to separate the movements of the actor from those of the cell phone itself, making the small, close-to-the-body technology starkly different from the detached and mechanized camera of commercial cinematography, which needs specialized operators and highly trained actors, floor markings, clapboards, and other cumbersome paraphernalia in order to regulate the action. To be sure, such close proximity also reveals disconnects between analog and digital (body and phone), exposing dysfunctions and incompatibilities that occasionally become the subject of the movies themselves. As we saw in Cardona's *Checklist* these films don't always espouse a seamless integration between technology and its human users but may critique the shortcomings of such couplings (zombie films often enact fears of a postapocalyptic, post-human condition in which the enmeshed nature of organic and inorganic is considered through a dystopian lens). Other scenarios in cell phone films are less dramatic but remain cautious about the encroachment of technology into our lives and bodies. According to Roger Odin, many cell phone films represent the "small events related to the mobile [failures] in everyday life: no answer, connection problems, misunderstanding (this is not the right number), loss of the mobile" (163–64). In contrast with these technophobic examples, other films become self-obsessed with the technical possibilities of the device, demonstrating a tendency to fetishize technology associated with the early years of any new format, an avant-gardist obsession with the new.

As discussed, when cell phone cinema gains in popularity, it exposes an inherent paradox: even while insisting on its marginal position in relation to traditional cinematic institutions and venues, this modality has made significant inroads into commercial distribution. Some films have been quite successful commercially, for example *Tangerine* (Sean Baker, 2015, shot on iPhone 5), which premiered at Sundance, or Isabel Coixet's collective documentary *Spain in a Day* (2016, original title in English) made from thousands of shared mobile phone videos, also screened theatrically. Nevertheless, most cell phone filmmakers seem to want to distance themselves from mainstream cinema, whether by choice or just as a defensive reaction to their lack of access to established commercial circuits. This was certainly the case in early cell phone cinema, which displayed noncommercial characteristics such as its low-budget self-funded production, brevity, and an aesthetic quality that Caroline Bassett defines as only "good enough" (149) and that, following Wilson, I associate with a post-digital aesthetic that revels in glitches and errors. Precisely because of its openness to fresh perspectives and experimentation, as well as its DIY attitude, cell phone cinema is presumed to offer an alternative to Hollywood and other mainstream commercial cinemas (and promoted as such). Cell phone films, however, also borrow from and appropriate—not always critically—elements from Hollywood genres and from other popular culture, including television commercials, music videos, and home movies; indeed, the equivalent of "home movies" today are invariably shot on a cell phone. Perhaps it was inevasible, however, that as cell phone films began to achieve higher quality and longer duration, the filmmakers' anti-commercial stance softened and even disappeared altogether.

Cell Phone Cinema as a Global, Transnational, and Collective Phenomenon

In Latin America, as in much of the Global South, obtaining access to high-quality digital cameras or to 35 mm equipment can be difficult without economic and institutional support—especially in countries that do not have the long filmmaking tradition one finds in Argentina, Brazil, Mexico, and Cuba. While in Spain such access to technology has been less challenging, the effects of the global financial crisis in the first decade of the twenty-first century also drove many aspiring Spanish filmmakers to seek the use of affordable filmmaking equipment and distribution mechanisms. For that reason, and especially in India, Asia, and Latin America, cell phone cinema has spread considerably in terms of volume and popularity and, according to Roger Odin, has also "assumed remarkable proportions in Africa" (162). In many countries of the Global South, especially in places where mainstream media are under rigid state controls, cell phone cinema is often allied and enmeshed with activist journalism. During the Arab Spring in countries where journalists were unable to do their work, citizens decided to narrate their own stories and document events using their cell phones. As Chad Elias observes, "[O]ne of the most significant aspects of the wave of protests and uprisings that began in Syria in 2011 was the use of the cell phone camera as a tool of documentation, political activism, and creative expression." During the 2022 Iranian protests for women's rights, smartphones allowed protesters to organize, communicate, and film events, although the phone's geolocative functions also facilitated the government's surveillance of the citizenry, as security services increasingly rely on location data and spyware.

The cell phone film has also become a staple at international film festivals. In Europe and North America, cell phone film festivals proliferate, with signature events in Barcelona (Cinephone International Smartphone Short Film Festival), Lisbon (Super 9 Mobile Film Fest), and San Diego (International Mobile Film Festival), to name just some examples. These are transnational festivals that accept entries from all countries; the films are easily submitted online, and winning movies are screened on-site and later shared on festival websites. Although the films are often still categorized with national labels, these markers are increasingly hyphenated and more difficult to assign as filmmakers, crews, actors, and the films themselves become increasingly globalized. The festival exhibition model garners an initial limited in-person audience (typically through a large-screen experience) but later gains additional diffusion through online viewing (on smaller, individual portable screens).

Despite its evident growth, it is difficult to ascertain the exact quantity of cell phone films in actual numbers (that research remains necessary but is out of this book's scope). There are currently no statistical studies tracking cell phone cinema production. That includes research specifically focused on cell phone films accounting for number of releases, video site views or downloads, number of sold copies (in the rare cases where DVDs exist), box office sales (since outside of festivals, commercial screening is highly unusual), or other data typically available for mainstream cinema. There is, as mentioned, some anecdotal information about the recent rise of cell phone films. Jan Simons links the increase in cell phone filmic production to the 2005 launching of YouTube and the advent of 3G cell phones equipped with video cameras. According to Simons, "[A]lthough figures are hard to come by, DIY movies, many of which are made with cameras built-in to mobile devices or computers, seem to constitute the bulk of YouTube's supply" (95). To arrive at precise numbers, it would be necessary to determine what "counts" or constitutes a cell phone film, involving complex considerations of whether to include ad hoc films posted online by individual YouTubers, for example, or whether to limit the number to films with some kind of "fictional" intention—many "narrative" vlogs and day-in-the-life videos would fall in a liminal space. Odin provides some statistical detail regarding one specific country in Africa. He singles out Nigeria's Nollywood as a leading case of the growth of cell phone cinema in the Global South. Nollywood is a global producer of B movies, turning out over one thousand films per year, most shot on inexpensive DSLR cameras or cell phones, and employing an improvisational home movie aesthetic. These are not art films but movies inspired by West African popular culture as well as mainstream Hollywood cinema (Mahir and Austen 1–8). Gerard Goggin studies a thriving DIY film industry in South Africa, a country that produced a pioneering full-feature cell phone film, *SMS Sugar Man* (Aryan Kaganof, 2008). *SMS Sugar Man* was deemed "good enough" to prompt talk of its transfer to 35 mm for theater release (Goggin 98). While Latin America and Spain have not adopted the cell phone film on a

Nollywood scale, the practice has burgeoned in the last decade, especially in the Southern Cone and Spain where a majority of the phone film festivals are held—although, as mentioned, these are transnational festivals open to international entries.

As should be expected, each global region relates differently to dominant Hollywood and European cinematic styles, just as production quality and degrees of professionalism vary widely. Case in point, the technical quality of cell phone cinema from Asian countries—predominantly South Korea and Japan, but also China—is remarkably high by any measures (technical quality, narrative sophistication, cinematography, etc.), as seen in films like Park Chan-wook's *Night Fishing* (2011), awarded a Berlin Golden Bear for short features and shot on an iPhone 4. The Korean filmmaker also produced another short horror-action masterpiece, this one with the iPhone 13 Pro, entitled *Life Is But a Dream* (2022), created in partnership with Apple and therefore fully lodged within the non-amateur arena. Similarly commercialized and shot with the same phone model, Chinese filmmaker Zhang Meng's *Chinese New Year: The Comeback* (2022) equally pushes the boundaries of what is possible in terms of cinematography. *Chinese New Year* was part of Apple's "Shot on iPhone" campaign, like Damien Chazelle's *The Stunt Double* (2020), and as such the films function in part as advertisements for the products they are shot with, rendering any claims to amateurism or marginality difficult to maintain.

The bulk of cell phone films, however, still remain noncommercial and privilege "dramatic content driven by narrative concerns over proficiency in technical aspects of filmmaking" (Wilson, "Film Festivals" 3). This emphasis on content over form can be attributed in part to the (still) early stage of the format's development and the neophyte status of many cell phone filmmakers. The lack of professional training can unfetter filmmakers to experiment with style without preconceptions about what counts as "proper" cinematic language, unburdened by the demands of a production company, budgets, or commercial viability, encouraging them to revel in their "amateur" status, as conceived through its Latin etymology: *amator*, "lover," one motivated by passion rather than pecuniary interest. Cell phone films can hearken to the style and DIY spirit of garage cinema, which, according to Denilson Lopes, "seeks to create an alternative dramaturgy and staging based on reduced production costs by using digital supports and by relying on alternative distribution outlets based on an increased use of festivals, exhibitions, and cineclubs rather than the large distribution networks which have a reduced number of film releases and are dominated by North American blockbusters"

(295). Developed in the early 2000s, "garage cinema" (*cinema de garagem*) is a specifically Brazilian type of artisanal, independent, and postindustrial filmmaking that arose in the wake of Y2K fears as anti-globalization sentiments spread worldwide. The style, influenced by vlogs, video games, reality TV, and other alternative audiovisual media, overlaps aesthetically with cell phone films (Lima and Ikeda). As with garage cinema, phone films access distribution through online streaming or via participation in phone film festivals. Unlike the typically low-grade garage cinema, however, Latin American and Iberian cell phone films range in quality from lo-fi to hi-fi. The lo-fi "look" can be a deliberate choice or the result of a particular phone's limitations. Hi-fi films made with 4K and even 5K ultra HD phone cameras approximate what a professional camera would produce and are even used to shoot commercials and music videos. The arrival in the second decade of the 2000s of 5G (fifth-generation global mobile network) technology has further increased upload and download speed regardless of resolution quality and is already available in most major Latin American metropolitan areas. Yet in smaller cities and rural areas filmmakers still work with older systems and less reliable connectivity. The coexistence of disparate technological capabilities, speeds, and training results in a rich variety of mobile films. Alternating between gritty and slick, cell phone cinema is being created by self-taught novices and seasoned professionals alike.

Regarding the heterogeneous assortment of cell phone films and underscoring their multigeneric and intermedial nature, Odin stipulates that "productions use every kind of short form, and are characterized by a strong hybrid tendency—a mixture of documentary and fiction, documentary and video art, animation and digital art, diary and experimental cinema, of sex, gore, trash and politics" (159). This variety includes genre films from horror and sci-fi, seemingly favored by novice filmmakers, to comedies and detective noir. There are serial "mobisoaps" and "mobisodes," mini-episodes only a few minutes long that are commercial spinoffs from TV series, as well as full-length web series.[6] To cite one Latin American example, *Chateo, luego existo* (David Fernando López Castillo, 2016) [I Chat, Therefore I Exist] is a Colombian web series distributed through YouTube, with up to 250,000 views per episode, for a total of ten episodes in its only season. Filmed with a cell phone, *Chateo* presents the characters' interactions exclusively through virtual modalities—social media, video chatting, YouTube vlogs, phone calls, and texting. At times, the series imitates the appearance of an iPhone screen so that spectators feel they are watching on a cell phone, and the series also mimics laptop screens and generally adopts an internet aesthetic.

Latin American and Iberian Cell Phone Films: Four Case Studies

In the following sections I analyze four cell phone films—three Latin American and one Spanish—to broadly show how the format has developed across the region as well as to explore transatlantic affinities. I deliberately chose horror, a popular genre in amateur formats that, as mentioned, has a significant presence and special affinity with cell phone film aesthetics. Restricting the analysis to one genre facilitates the comparisons across time and national boundaries in what is otherwise a vast corpus. Hailing from four different nations (Argentina, Colombia, Chile, Spain), these four films display shared genre conventions and exemplify contradictions inherent to mobile phone filmmaking: the oscillation between amateurism and professionalism, between low-grade and polished products, between defiance and acquiescence to commercial necessities. In addition, these particular films represent distinct stages in the aesthetics, production, and distribution of cell phone cinema. The Latin American films include a first-generation phone film titled *Rojo en el bosque sangriento* (Tetsuo Lumière, Argentina, 2006), a horror musical short created with a more advanced model iPhone titled *Sangre y levadura* (Juan Carlos Mazo, Colombia, 2016), and a found footage horror feature shot with three cell phone cameras and released to commercial screens, *09 La película* (Javier Aguirrezábal, Chile, 2014). The final work I examine is *iMedium* (Alfonso García Lopez, Spain, 2018), a sci-fi horror film shot with an iPhone that projects the darker side of cell phone technologies toward a disturbingly dystopian near future.[7] Although these four films could be seen as representing different developmental stages, suggesting a kind of technological teleology or causality (from lower quality and limited capabilities to increasingly better films), many of the same material frictions and aesthetic tensions reappear in each work, undermining notions of techno-determinism that would posit the latter films as objectively "better" (although they might be technically more complex and use more recent phones with better cameras).

These films can also be described as inherently intermedial and post-digital in that they challenge divisions between material and virtual, between continuous and discrete, the very distinctions on which the digital was based. The films illustrate that the post-digital is also characterized by a reintroduction of the human element in the shape of flaws and contingencies, inserted into the supposed seamlessness of digital cinema: "To signal the human failure element, post-digital cinema produces data-moshing, glitch art anti-aesthetics" (Hayward 107). The cell phone's status as a prosthetic extension of the filmmaker renders the experience of making and viewing these films more immediate, closer to the body, hence facilitating a rehumanized post-digital experience as spectators' bodies also become intercorporeally linked and phenomenologically extended "into" the narratives.

Case 1: A First-Generation Argentine Cell Phone Movie

Completed in 2006 and therefore a first-generation cell phone film, *Rojo en el bosque sangriento* is a comedic horror movie that cleverly doubles as a meta-reflection on low-budget filmmaking. The film provides insight into the initial period of cell phone filmmaking, a period marked by a DIY attitude, by a collaborative spirit among practitioners, and by the ingenuity needed to work with the very limited affordances of early phone cameras. The apparent rejection of commercialism displayed by these early films, however, is compromised in later works. *Rojo* was produced and directed by Tetsuo Lumière—the pseudonym of a self-taught underground filmmaker and somewhat mysterious figure. Truly independent, *Rojo* received no funding from official institutions such as the INCAA. Since the 1990s Lumière has filmed with VHS cameras, digital photo cameras, and cell phones. Despite many hardships, including being homeless during the crisis of the 2000s, Lumière has created over forty shorts and three feature-length sci-fi and horror films, all on shoestring budgets. Although his rough-around-the-edges films are by no means burdened by technical perfection, Lumière, an avowed cinephile, displays a degree of sophistication and cinematic knowledge. His style is layered with references to silent film (he adopted his pseudonym Lumière as a tribute to early cinema), to sci-fi and horror classics, and to Japanese underground film (hence the "Tetsuo," a reference to the eponymous 1989 Japanese cyberpunk horror film by Shinya Tsukamoto). Lumière belongs to a Buenos Aires–based cult cinema scene that screens and distributes films mainly through independent festivals, such as the Buenos Aires Rojo Sangre or the Sitges Horror Film Festival, or by uploading their work to free online platforms.

Rojo's narrative is humorously self-reflexive about its status as a film created with a format antithetical to commercial cinema. The film opens with a long static shot of an empty beach, the lo-fi pixelated image displayed in washed-out grays and greens, the sound of crashing waves partially garbled by low-quality audio—typical shortcomings for first-generation low-resolution cell phone video. The initial frame is intended ironically, a "wide" landscape establishing shot meant to capture the grandiose seascape vista and set the scene but only manages to produce a grayish, degraded, and barely discernible image. Katie MacEntee explains that prior to HD cameras, cell phone films displayed "low resolution video and a distinct blurry, choppy aesthetic" (4). Over time, the camera phone's technical limitations became aligned with a rough aesthetic that was seen as both inevitable and as a positive quality linked to a proof of authenticity, as if we were watching life unfolding and not a scripted film. Even after cameras improved, this low-resolution look became generally associated with digital video, so "the kind of aesthetic discerned in the mobile screen can also be observed in some other forms of digital media. There is a well-established digital aesthetic that valorizes 'good enough' quality as an aesthetic: Less is often more (the hacker ethic has this aesthetic, as does much tactical media, as does the popular turn to retro-gaming)" (Bassett 150). As low resolution has given way to much higher definition in recent years, "pixelated images due to low-resolution cameras—so iconic in the beginning—have become a conscious choice" (Botella).

Also making the most of his low-resolution camera, Lumière relies on visual and aural noise to disrupt any expectation of a seamless signal, making the spectator aware of the cell phone film's flaws, contingencies, and limitations. Perhaps the lo-fi aesthetic also counters the tendency toward techno-fetishism seen in (for example) ultra-high-resolution films sponsored by Apple's "Shot on iPhone" campaign and its attendant commodity worship driven by the social exchange value we ascribe to new tech. Cell phones might be necessary tools for the budget filmmaker, Lumière seems to suggest, but they can be treacherous and unreliable and indicative of a hyper-materialism in twenty-first-century brand culture. Lumière's film, however, exudes its garage aesthetic and lacks libidinal attachment to its still-clunky phone technology (with its non-graphical interface, mechanical press buttons, small display screen, and poor resolution). The degraded image provides his film an appearance recalling found footage classics such as *The Blair Witch Project* (Daniel Myrick and Eduardo Sánchez, 1999) or *Paranormal Activity* (Oren Peli, 2007) and closely associated with surveillance camera footage, an aesthetic very much in vogue in the first decade of the 2000s (see fig. 4.2). As Marc Olmsted argues, like their filmic found footage predecessors cell phone horror films are self-reflexive about their own recording function and adopt the aesthetic constraints of video capture and surveillance devices.

Underscoring the link between cellular technology and surveillance has been a trend in cell phone cinema since its inception, especially in the horror genres. This is not surprising given the affinity of the cell phone

Figure 4.2. Opening establishing shot from *Rojo en el bosque sangriento* (00:26). Source: *Rojo en el bosque sangriento* (2006). Dir. Tetsuo Lumière.

film medium with found video material, with home movies, and with the potential to upload supposedly found videos to self-publishing websites such as YouTube, where the fiction-reality binary can be destabilized by the fabricated appearance of reality: the grainier the image, the more real it seems to some. This contemporary horror penchant toward surveillance and grainy reality aesthetics has continued in the second decade of the 2000s as millennial filmmakers developed an interest in social media–related narratives using not so much phones but webcams. The use of laptop webcams has been ubiquitous for the vlog horror subgenre, with films such as *Followed* (Antoine Le, 2018), the faux-documentary *Death of a Vlogger* (Graham Hughes, 2019), or arguably the first in this modality, *Vlog* (Joshua Butler, 2008)—works that display disturbing levels of extreme violence, supernatural thrills, and an unapologetically glitchy aesthetic.

Rojo opens with a static camera framing a tranquil ocean scene, suddenly disrupted when a woman darts across the foreground. Her fast movement destabilizes the image, leaving a glitchy, pixelated trace in her wake. The unexpected appearance of a barely discernible figure gliding by is a horror genre staple. Seconds later, a man runs in pursuit through the same static scene. Lumière then abandons this static framing—more appropriate for large commercial cameras—turning to his small, lightweight phone's maneuverability to dynamically capture the chase. Enhancing a sense of spontaneity and immediacy, the phone camera's video quality also adds to the ominous sense of looming threat. This effect is the product of the blurred and shaky fast-moving images and the camera's position in close physical proximity to the bodies of the actors. All these characteristics fabricate a (low-grade) real-life feel that has been exploited by filmmakers to increase affective reactions by spectators. The gestural expressivity allowed by a handheld phone camera contributes to the illusion of real-time-ness, even when the videos are several years old. *Rojo* plays with this illusion of immediacy. As the chase proceeds through a wooded area, several point-of-view shots alternate from the woman's perspective to her pursuer's in a classic slasher film "stalk shot." The phone, held close to the characters' bodies, only allows for blurred and fragmented images, denying the scene the totality provided by establishing shots and traditional static shot/reverse-shot sequences. In this sense, the cell phone has brought about a new cinematic aesthetic that is by now quite familiar and associated with mobile media viral videos, YouTube vlogging, and so on. The use of point of view is critical in *Rojo* since it allows the spectator to identify with the victimized woman and heightens the sensation of fear as the stalker approaches. The proximity of the cell phone to bodies conveniently obscures the off-screen space, fueling paranoid fear of what lurks beyond our visual field. Thus, while the opening long shot fills the spectator with foreboding about an unseen threat, the close-up shots during the chase place spectators on-screen with the victim as she hides, is discovered, and flees again. The tension reaches a climax once the woman is cornered by her assailant. Extreme facial close-ups of the victim and aggressor alternate in rapid montage as tension mounts to a fever pitch. Then the woman screams loudly as the man raises a knife, his arm frozen in midair.

Up to this point Lumière has not departed from slasher genre expectations, but now the plot, style, and tone shift to offer a humorous meta-reflection about cell phone filmmaking. More broadly, the film also comments on the difficulties faced by Latin American underground filmmakers. The unexpected ringing of a cell phone—presumably the same cell phone being used to film—jarringly interrupts the narrative flow. Two of the phone's functions, communication and recording, are placed in conflict but also brought into alignment. At first it appears that the irruption of the call represents an extradiegetic element, but soon it is reabsorbed and subsumed into a meta-narrative about the cinema. Shattering the fictional narrative, the next shot after the ring tone reveals the cell phone that was supposedly being used to film the movie (see fig. 4.3).

Figure 4.3. A meta-reflexive moment as the phone rings in *Rojo en el bosque sangriento* (01:50). *Source: Rojo en el bosque sangriento* (2006). Dir. Tetsuo Lumière.

In practice, at this point the actual filming has already switched to a second (unseen) phone that remains outside the frame. This second phone serves to create a higher level of fiction (we now have a story within a story), but it also problematizes the divide between fiction and reality, or fictional and documentary narrative. What follows is a self-reflexive turn toward a hybrid autofictional or autobiographical mode. A "fictional" director answers the call, played by the real filmmaker Lumière, now in character and on-screen holding the cell phone. The shift in tone from horror to comedy is evident: the call is from a producer named Esteban Espilbergo, a humorously Hispanicized version of Steven Spielberg and a dig at Hollywood. Espilbergo informs Lumière that he is willing to produce the movie the latter is currently making (the one we are viewing) but suggests making it less violent and adequate for family viewing. On one level, this is a critique against the demands placed on directors to conform content to mainstream sensibilities. But the segment also contains a dose of self-derisive humor. Simply put, it is inconceivable for Lumière that a marginal underground filmmaker would be asked to—or even wish to—enter the commercial arena. No major studio producer would fund a DIY cell phone film by an unknown amateur, such a "big break" seemed preposterous and would, at any rate, represent a selling out on the filmmaker's part. Consequently, the fictional director informs Espilbergo that he is already producing his own film and prefers submitting it to a festival rather than seeking mainstream distribution. *Rojo* did in fact premiere at the very modest CeluFilmFest (Argentina, 2007), the first cellular film festival in Buenos Aires, a lightly attended local event. The fictional director abruptly terminates the call by informing Espilbergo about a practical concern for cell phone filmmaking: he is running out of battery and needs the remaining minutes to finish his movie. Lumière therefore contrasts mainstream films that can afford lengthy production schedules and expensive equipment but are bound by restrictions of marketability with budget-constrained but thematically freer garage productions like his. Despite this apparent rejection of commercialism, however, one must wonder what transpires once an actual call from a mainstream producer reaches an underground filmmaker. As we shall see with the other films I discuss, it is not unusual for cell phone filmmakers to wish to reach broader audiences and screen their work in commercial venues, and this has become increasingly possible in recent years as the quality of cell phones has improved and amateur audiovisual culture has become more sophisticated.

Then, in another faux "behind the scenes"–type sequence, while preparing to resume the murder scene Lumière spreads fake blood (from ketchup packets) on the actress's face, emphasizing again the film's low-budget status. After the action resumes, the ringing phone interrupts it a second time, reminding viewers again that this film was not shot with expensive equipment but with a cell phone that, like the amateur filmmaker, has other functions. As the credits roll, we hear the director in voice-over as he apologizes to his irate mother for having borrowed her phone, exemplifying how nonprofessional filmmakers often depend on relatives and friends to back their movies and careers (this is the case in terms of not only providing financial assistance but also serving as actors and crew, much like one would expect from home movies and artisanal productions). These constraints can paradoxically also become strengths, since as Wilson observes, "[C]ell cinema filmmakers appear to be attracted to the working methods and aesthetic sensibility associated with low budget, guerrilla filmmaking, unfettered by the conventions and expense incurred in using traditional film production apparatus" (*Cell/ular Cinema* xi). But while this carefree amateurism was the norm during the initial years, once phone cameras improved and professionally trained filmmakers began to make cell phone films (or amateurs learned professional-level skills), there was a marked shift toward commercializing the format, requiring larger budgets, professional actors, and in some cases theatrical and DVD distribution to secure profits. This period also marked a move toward greater transnationalism as filmmakers sought to make their films appealing to global festivals and a broad internet audience. Today, there is a gamut of cell phone films ranging from the polished work sponsored by large transnational companies or produced by studios to the makeshift home videos supported by local funding, and everything in between.

Case 2: A Musical Thriller from Colombia

Whereas *Rojo* is a first-generation cell phone movie made with a low-resolution camera and dating from 2006, the 2016 horror musical *Sangre y levadura* belongs to a second wave of films created with technically superior Androids and iPhones (in this case the iPhone 6s Plus, which at the time was the latest model). Accordingly, *Sangre y levadura* marks an aesthetic shift from the glitch and "good enough" of earlier works to a sleeker HD video. The film's glossy aesthetics were inseparable from its obvious commercial aspirations, discernible in the recruitment of professional actors and the design of elaborate sets departing from the amateur style favored by *Rojo*. Such aspirations aside, the film occupies an intermediate position, neither fully professional nor entirely homemade and underground. *Sangre* is situated somewhere between the first film we analyzed and the one that follows, in a sliding scale of their relative entanglement with the mainstream film industry.

Much like its earlier predecessors, this film may be more polished but still prioritizes the cell phone camera's capabilities of flexibility, mobility, and ease of use, leading to what David Bordwell qualifies as an "intensified continuity" editing style that can be allied with a post-digital aesthetic (16–28). While Bordwell traces intensified continuity back to the video era of home VHS, and even earlier to the 1960s, this style has only gained in currency with the digital era, as the editing pace of sequences quickens, the camera becomes hyper-mobile, and shots are increasingly shorter. The critic argues that contemporary digital cinema has not wholly eliminated Hollywood continuity, adapting the classical style instead to account for digital tools and changing spectator sensibilities. As Bordwell describes it, contemporary use of intensified continuity recruits closer framing in dialogue scenes, uses a free ranging camera, and adapts to smaller screens, which (given their small display) favor close-up shots rather than panoramic takes or establishing shots.[8] This description maps onto cell phone cinema's predilection for close-to-the-body framing and small-screen spectatorship. Andreas Treske confirms that "video on mobile phones already automatically engages the viewer with closer action and more details than landscapes. The video recording device in the observer's hand is shaky; it concentrates on aspects of the moment and might switch between changes in positioning of the observer/recordist" (103). For Wilson, the proximity of the cell phone to the body and the dynamic close-up shots endows these films with an "ambulatory" style. The appearance of the ambulatory style stems from the walking motion of the person filming with the cell phone, and Wilson argues that the visual illusion of movement enhances spectators' sense of embodiment:

> Representations of movement on-screen, foregrounded in the visual aesthetic of a phone film, contribute to the viewer's identification with the sensation of perceived movement. The nature of the perceived appearance of ambulation stimulates the viewer's identification with the filmmaker as the character apparently experiencing ambulatory movement while the image was recorded. The nature of the filmmaker's walking motion introduces an additional character into the cast for the film, the ideological presence of the filmmaker. Therefore, ambulatory motion connotes additional meanings such as agility, instability, haste or indecision, and a physical connection between the hand and screen of the mobile phone camera. ("Film Festival Participation" 291)

To this same point, Jakob Nielsen has stated that the motion of cell phones allows for a kind of focalization that associates "the movement of the camera with the viewpoints of characters or entities in the story world" (26). That means one can potentially discern the individuated handheld camera work as representing a particular character—and even more so if the phone is held by the specific actor playing that character rather than by a filmmaker who "plays" various parts or adopts a neutral camera point of view. Thus both the intensified continuity aesthetic and cell phone cinema's inherently close framing style respond to new spectatorship patterns, as films are increasingly viewed on computers, tablets, and cell phones rather than cinema screens. Even when films are presented at festivals, it is the online afterlife that ensures greater viewership. That said, both enhanced continuity and the ambulatory dimension of cell phone films can be deemphasized if a filmmaker chooses to work against the small-screen aesthetic. For example, the cell phone can be stabilized to eliminate the sensation of movement (perhaps dissociating the camera from a character's point of view), and the latest generation of cell phones deploy cameras that can powerfully capture landscape shots with excellent resolution. Nevertheless, as the majority of the films are still viewed on smaller screens these choices seem to operate against the grain of the more suitable aesthetics of the close-up, an aesthetics that holds for mobile cinema transnationally.

Sangre y levadura was an entry in Smart Films 2016, an annual festival originally held in Bogotá that is sponsored by various Colombian publicity and technology companies as well as several cultural institutions. The festival is meant as a transnational enterprise, and as of 2022, in addition to its eight editions in Colombia, the festival has been held five times in Mexico and three in Paraguay. Although the festival has mainly featured films from amateur and semiprofessional filmmakers, it has also elicited contributions by recognizable names such as Oliver Stone (United States), Robert Rodríguez (United States-Mexico), and Fernando Trueba (Spain). Smart Films accepts entries from any country but primarily screens high-quality cell phone films from throughout Latin America and Spain. The festival had a remarkable 1,016 submissions in 2016 alone,—and has continued growing.[9] *Sangre*, that year's overall winner, was shot by a transnational professional crew and performed by actors who had TV soap opera credits across the region. Regardless, cast and crew—mostly friends of the filmmaker—worked for free to accommodate a limited budget.[10] The director, Juan Carlos Mazo, is an independent filmmaker with musical theater experience in Colombia and Ecuador. Despite its small budget, *Sangre* looks decidedly polished in comparison with Tetsuo Lumière's DIY underground movie.

Taking the format to a markedly intermedial level, Mazo's film promiscuously amalgamates aspects from a heterogeneous mix of intertextual sources, including but not limited to surrealist art, Antonin Artaud's Theater of Cruelty, musical thrillers of the ilk of Steven Sondheim's *Sweeney Todd* (1979), German expressionist film, the cinema of Tim Burton, and the bizarre art films of Alejandro Jodorowsky. Displaying considerable technical mastery with the cell phone camera, Mazo stages the entire film as a single five-minute take with no cuts. The use of a single take intensifies an immersive, suspenseful viewing experience, since excessive cutting or editing can be distracting (*Making of Sangre*). Single take scenes, challenging with larger cameras and crews, are quite feasible with a maneuverable cell phone and minimal personnel, eliminating the need to cut the action to reposition actors, props, or filmmaking equipment. Given the economy of working with a digital format, the crew rehearsed the five-minute film multiple times so it could be perfectly executed during real-time filming. Once filming began, the single take was repeated until the desired quality was obtained with little additional cost.

This film, like other transnational cell phone productions, was made possible by the integration of human and technical creativity: the cell phone camera's capacity to record and process a variety of media (for communication, creation, performance, surveillance, documentation) and the willingness of the crew to experiment with new techniques and to work pro bono. The latter point is important; since these actors felt that they were part of a special project, they were willing to share their labor in ways that evoke the underground ethos displayed by first-generation cell phone films, which were often staffed by friends and family. As I stated earlier, *Sangre* negotiates an in-between space, neither fully professional/commercial nor completely amateur/independent, a space that many transnational cell phone films inhabit.

For instance, although most cell phone movies film in existing ad hoc spaces to reduce costs, *Sangre* had a specific set design that was justified in terms of the film's link to theater. Given the director and crew's transnational background in theater and daytime television—formats that consistently rely on set designs—they opted for an elaborate interior space. *Sangre* is set in a postapocalyptic bread factory that is populated by zombie-like employees, all of this requiring considerable wardrobe, makeup, and lighting effects. The lugubrious atmosphere and decayed institutional decor—poorly lit, claustrophobic rooms with dirty tile walls—evokes horror film settings such as mental asylums, prisons, and seedy hotels, partaking of a transnational zombie apocalypse sensibility that favors small enclosed interior spaces and responds to twenty-first-century fears about humanity's reduction to "bare life" under global capitalism and its many attendant crises (economic inequality, refugees, wars, terrorism, and out-of-control technology).

The film's plot is as somber and oppressive as the setting. The action opens when the bread factory supervisor struts into a dimly lit room to inspect his ragged staff, who, like him, look more like inmates than bakers, more dead than alive. Initially identified only by numbers (like depersonalized prisoners) the staff act and resemble undead beings: moving stiffly in unnatural jerks, flour-covered faces pasty white, darkly encircled eyes sunken and shifty, and uniforms filthy and torn. One of the women employees, clearly sick (perhaps affected by radiation poisoning? By a pandemic virus? By contaminated food and water?), barely holds her trickling vomit (see fig. 4.4).

The supervisor then breaks into song. The shrill tone of the melody contrasts with its upbeat lyrics: "las tres de la mañana y ya va a empezar un nuevo día, que felicidad" (00:10) [three in the morning and a new day is about to begin, such joy]. The careful script and rehearsed delivery marks yet another departure from first-generation cell phone films, which favored spontaneous dialogues. In those early days, the underworked scripts were well matched to a carefree point-and-shoot filming style, often with a single phone. This short is closer to musical theater, where attention to lyrics, rhyme, meter, and choreography matters greatly. The script and its delivery reinforce the film's central conflict, boss versus employees, as reflected in the sycophantic, monotone, and insincere response from the bakers: "Muy buenos días, señor supervisor, nos reportamos a tiempo y con honor, muy bendecidos por trabajar aquí, trabajo digno y ganas de servir" (00:20–30) [Good morning, mister supervisor, here we are honorably on time, blessed to work here, with a dignified job and our will to serve]. Nonplussed by their sarcasm, the supervisor counters their ironic reply with an ominous threat:

Figure 4.4. Inspecting the ghoulish bakers in *Sangre y levadura* (01:22). Source: *Sangre y levadura* (2018). Dir. Juan Carlos Mazo.

Hay empleados en el lote 43–57 que aun no han entendido las normas. Que no conocen el método. Que no reconocen la autoridad. La empresa y yo, su supervisor, esperamos que este comportamiento sea corregido a la brevedad. De lo contrario, me veré en la obligación de hacer algunos . . . recortes. (01:00–12)

[There are employees in the 43–57 batch who have not grasped the rules. Who do not know the method. Who do not recognize authority. The company and I, your supervisor, hope that this behavior will be remedied in brief. Otherwise, I will be obligated to make some . . . cuts]

The performance is top-notch for a relatively low-cost cell phone film. The acting and choreography are as meticulous as the set design and script. The actors' movements are theatrically expressive, gestural, and syncopated with the sound score, providing a nervous energy to this musical thriller. Such histrionic and physical acting is in turn tightly cropped by the up-close cell phone framing. Body-centered acting, typical in post-digital cinema as theorized by Bordwell, is propitiated by the phone camera and could be said to recall the "gestural quality of text messaging" (Bassett 149). The actors are in sync with the movements of the cell phone camera, as the entire single shot becomes a complex choreography with little room for errors. No doubt, we see in this film a blend between skill sets and techniques that originate in commercial cinema and those that hail from cell phone cinema's body-centered spontaneity. This integration is distant from *Rojo*'s opposition to commercial influence and its rough homemade style. And yet, both share the same transnational approach to distribution, disseminated through streaming platforms like YouTube and social media sites that are free of charge (but may have advertising). While most filmmakers assert their intellectual property over their work, which is almost never anonymous (unlike citizen reportage in conflict zones, as Shilina-Conte has shown), they do not demand direct payment for viewing.

Mazo constructs the scene to take advantage of the cell phone's capacity to achieve maximum proximity to the actors. Such proximity is necessitated by the difficulty of the cell phone camera to smoothly zoom in or out, unless it is outfitted with specialized apps. In the absence of such apps, the cameraperson holding the phone must approximate the subject as closely as needed. Today, the shaky handheld aesthetic of older cell phones can be all but eliminated with image stabilizing rigs and apps. *Sangre* uses these devices to maintain spontaneity while avoiding the disorienting viewing experience of found footage films like the aforementioned *The Blair Witch Project*, also present in Lumière's *Rojo*. The camera can be held close to the filmmaker's body, encouraging a total body approach to filming, but remain steady, providing a carefully controlled proximity between cameraperson and subject. In the opening scene Mazo rotates the cellphone camera smoothly around the supervisor, adjusting its height and tilt so that the angle remains low and off-kilter, expressionistically distorting the character's physical appearance to make him look towering, intimidating, yet also dangerously unstable. After a few seconds, a head-on angle is reestablished and the framing tracks from one employee to the next as the supervisor delivers his speech, recording their reactions of dread and revulsion (see fig. 4.5).

In the next scene (which flows from the first one with no cuts), the phone tracks two characters, María and Ana, with a shot that weaves through the factory's labyrinthine hallways. Since the phone has no cables, no extraneous sound equipment, no dollies or bulky tripods, it is free to roam and capture the narrow spaces as desired. By disregarding Hollywood continuity norms such as the 180-degree rule, Mazo creates unusual choreographies that intensify the scene's growing tension: actors scurrying about, rapid shifts from one character to the next, disorienting angles, and blurred shadows darting across the visual field, techniques that are staples of the hor-

Figure 4.5. Employees react to supervisor's speech (00:56). *Source: Sangre y levadura* (2018). Dir. Juan Carlos Mazo.

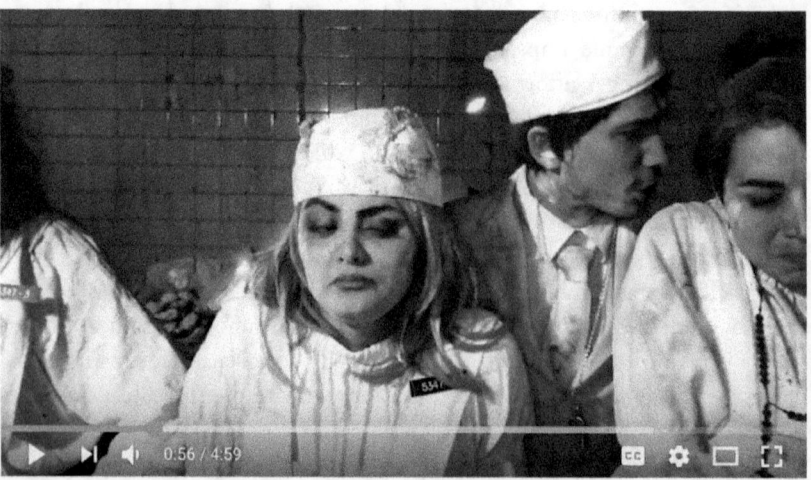

ror genre. Novice filmmakers frequently neglect filming and editing norms because they lack cinematographic training, but Mazo, who has studied film, decides when to violate continuity rules and when to uphold them, and the cell phone's mobility enhances that flexibility. With its destabilizing visual approach, *Sangre* adopts Bordwell's intensified continuity style, creating an immersive atmosphere that confuses spatial relations but also provides a sense of "being there," a sensation of presence and proximity characteristic of cell phone narratives.

Mazo's tight framing, mostly medium and close-up shots, is also warranted by the dark setting, which makes distance shots difficult to resolve, but this composition further amplifies the claustrophobia and complements the unhinged behavior of the characters. The unease is underscored with off-kilter angles, rapid pans, and the constantly shifting narrative focalization as characters quickly enter and exit the frame. The lighting itself, which approximates studio low-key illumination with its high-contrast chiaroscuros, was achieved with modest means. The main light source was a fluorescent ring set up around the iPhone to prevent shadows when shooting close-ups in the dimly lit space. Given the constant motion of the camera phone throughout the single-shot film, standard studio-type light setups were not feasible. Elaborate lights would have been costly and difficult to conceal out of frame. The close framing, energetic tone, and rapidly moving camera work also conform to Bordwell's intensified continuity style. Steven Shaviro, reflecting on twenty-first-century cinema, has coined the term "postcontinuity" to describe a style that is analogous to Bordwell's intensified continuity. For Shaviro, postcontinuity, which characterizes most digital cinema today (and is particularly evident in mobile phone films), is a framing and editing style in which "a preoccupation with immediate effects trumps any concern for broader continuity—whether on the immediate shot-by-shot level, or on that of the overall narrative" (123). What Bordwell and Shaviro are getting at is that digital cinema, of which cell phone films are a large subset in terms of volume, has subordinated visual continuity rules and the spectator's sense of orientation vis-à-vis the screen space to achieving a (sometimes dizzying) effect of the real, the bodily, and the immediate.

Despite its preoccupation for immediacy, this particular film enacts a tension between the hyperrealist tendency of cell phone footage and the theatricality of its acting and set design. This tension is also played out through the influence of the film's various media and genres—theater, music, visual arts, and TV soap operas, all of them rendering the work as spectacularly intermedial. In an interview, Mazo stated that his short was also inherently theatrical because it was adapted from an earlier fifteen-minute micro-theater piece (*En las mañanas*). The final result, I would suggest, is a hybrid work, between musical theater and film, that stages a conflict between the contrived theatricality of the acting and the hyperreal immediacy that results from the unobtrusive closeness of cell phone filming, between the realistically depicted cruelty of the characters and the defamiliarizing effect of their singing. This defamiliarizing effect will climax dramatically as the plot spirals out of control and finally unravels with a shocking denouement.

First, we discover that the employee named María is pregnant. Her co-worker Ana recommends an abortion and asks who the child's father is, but María remains stubbornly silent for unknown reasons. Elsewhere in the bread factory, the supervisor is lecherously chasing after Magdalena, another employee. Cornering her, he forces Magdalena into a sexual act, which remains partly off-camera (he is framed from the waist up, she is presumably below). Again, the cell phone allows filming the chase scene without the need for expensive dolly shots. The fluorescent lighting intensifies the lurid atmosphere and the close framing seeks to place the spectator uncomfortably "there" during the rape. When another employee discovers the assault, the supervisor breaks the man's neck in a grotesque display of graphic violence. The convulsive rapidity of the events and exaggerated nature of the gestures and bloody violence retains an air of Artaud's Theater of Cruelty, shocking viewers and, ideally, propelling them into the scene. Returning to the plot, María has revealed to her co-workers that the same supervisor left her pregnant during a similar rape incident. Seeking revenge, the employees revolt against the supervisor and throw him into the oven—quite possibly Mazo's tribute to *Sweeney Todd*. As the film ends, the camera tracks out to show a distressed María killing herself and her unborn child by plunging a knife into her belly.

We have discovered striking differences between *Sangre y levadura* and *Rojo en el bosque sangriento*. While the first film—edited on the phone with minimal cutting—espoused a rough aesthetic and relied on amateur techniques, the second approaches the polished look of commercial cinema and draws on multiple peripheral devices, including stabilizers, a phone light rig, and the latest computer-based postproduction tools. At the same time, core tenets of cell phone cinema such as its close-to-the-body approach, its DIY and do-it-with-others (DIWO) attitude, and its commitment to low cost persist in both films, emerging as common attributes of transnational cell phone cinema (indeed we shall see these attributes generally hold for the Chilean and Spanish films we will consider next). Finally, both works demonstrate an indie ethos that embraces democratizing and egalitarian approaches to filmmaking and distribution methods, although perhaps to different degrees. As will be apparent in the next case, in order to acquire further commercial viability cell phone cinema has to make additional concessions in terms of production and marketing strategies, but it does so at the risk of losing its underground and amateur status, of "selling out." More critically, even when the leap is made toward fully professionalized filmmaking, results are far from guaranteed, suggesting that the format might be better suited to the low-cost online distribution that characterized its early years.

CASE 3: A CELL PHONE FOUND FOOTAGE TRIPTYCH FROM CHILE

The technical know-how displayed by *Sangre* is taken to yet another level in *09 La película*, a film that places the cell phone directly in its title, since "09" is the prefix used to call cell phones in Chile. By self-reflexively foregrounding the cell phone as a recording tool and as the film's driving narrative device, *09* signals the pervasiveness of cell phone culture in contemporary Latin America and its filmmaking potential, as well as hinting at the vague threat represented by technological horror (when devices go awry). Besides being a film made with cell phones, *09* captures the cultural changes cell phones have had in the continent, especially regarding the ability to document, to communicate, and, no less important for this film, to entertain. Unlike the other films I discussed, this one was built around a national advertising and promotion campaign. The film *09* was tactically advertised as the first feature film made with cell phones, which was patently false (actually quite a few films have made similar claims) but an excellent marketing strategy meant to appeal to younger audiences. The film also proved the ease with which cell phone cinema blends with twenty-first-century forms of popular culture, in this case with found footage horror—although it is necessary to also point out that the origins of found footage lie with experimental and documentary cinema, with the repurposing of archival sources that we saw in the chapters dedicated to militant cinema (Hardcastle 108–09).[11] The alliance with this youth-favorite genre and the aggressive marketing campaign propelled *09* into mainstream cinemas, although it only managed to secure a short run at a limited number of screens. The film therefore found itself at the margins of a mainstream industry that it deliberately courted, getting tantalizingly closer to it than the previous two films. In fact, acclaimed Chilean filmmaker Pablo Larraín's production company, Fábula, provided funding for this movie. Perhaps due to a miscalculation (as better commercial results were expected), the filmmakers never tapped into the amateur or festival film scenes. Instead, they were adamant about creating a mainstream commercial feature and restricted access to their film beyond its original screening run to ensure robust theater attendance and a potential DVD deal that never materialized. Without a DVD distributor, and not available online like most cell phone films, *09* had limited dissemination and is now almost impossible to view, underscoring one of the drawbacks of not fully embracing the DIY ethos that encourages sharing the films online to broaden viewership, which, arguably, is a core tenet of the democratizing logic behind cell phone cinema's existence (along with free access, broad distribution, etc.).

Despite its failed commercial ambitions, *09* succeeded in developing various technical innovations that furthered the cell phone cinema format. The film experimented by enlisting three Samsung Galaxy S2 cellular phones—one for each of its lead actresses, who doubled as camerapeople. Despite its commercial status and professional cast, the choice of not having designated camerapeople allowed *09* to masquerade as a selfie-film, a film made by true amateurs. Following a *Rashomon*-like nonlinear plot, each of the three main characters documents events from a different perspective, each filming with their own phone. To fully grasp the action, the spectator has to reorder all three narrative threads, which are presented sequentially so that with each additional perspective we approximate a complete picture, but only at the end do we possess all the information. This multiphone approach allows for various filming styles so each point of view corresponds to a particular character—some are more restrained (slower and deliberate camera motion), others more risqué (quicker pans, swishes, etc.). The spectator can also determine who is filming or whose point of view is on display through other means—who is in the frame (and who is not), audio cues, and the direction of movement, all of these elements generating a kind of embodied sympathy between character and spectator. Miche Dreiling has theorized this character focalization aspect of cell phone films, declaring that its effect is that "the viewpoints of the characters—and by extension, their characterizations in the film—become distinct. To the viewer, this cultivates a deep sense of familiarity with the characters. This is deeper than the familiarity engendered by a typical film because rather than getting to know a person by watching them move on screen, we are being moved by the person—our very gaze directed by them, as if we are seeing the world through their eyes" (180). In all cases, regardless of whose point of view is favored, filming becomes shakier, more frantic, and less focused as events begin to unravel and tension mounts within the narrative.

Despite its unusual plot structure, the story is fairly typical of the horror genre. Three college friends (Carolina, Andrea, and Florencia) are spending the weekend at Carolina's parents' secluded vacation home to celebrate her birthday, and as predicted from genre expectations, the parents are away. During their stay the women find out from news reports that a couple has been murdered in the woods nearby and that the police are asking locals to remain locked in their homes until the culprits are apprehended. Since Carolina has to complete a project for her journalism class, the three friends unwisely decide to use their phones to document the unfolding events (a wink at the citizen journalism I previously mentioned). Although at the outset they do not expect anything to happen (it is a kind of game), they are soon proven wrong. Armed with their cell phones, the friends record the increasingly tense atmosphere and threatening happenings that occur in the home and its environs. These include strangers arriving and pleading for help as they flee from unseen assailants, unexpected and terrifying noises and manifestations of the supernatural, and eventually several violent deaths. Other events linked to character development complement the main plot, including interpersonal rivalries between the women, Carolina's drug addiction, and parent-child conflicts.

Reflecting a *cinéma vérité* aesthetic, the editing does not seem to significantly clean up the rough filming style of the three protagonists, at least on its surface. This rough appearance, however, is partly a deliberate effect. The actresses received training on using the phone so it would look spontaneous (but not dizzyingly so), and there was considerable postproduction of the raw material. Additionally, the seemingly unrehearsed dialogue also reinforces a sense of immediacy and authenticity even though it was fully scripted. In a fascinating turn, then, this film has been scripted and edited to mimic an amateur cell phone film, although its conditions of production are almost wholly professional. Authenticity is courted and produced through technical means. The appearance of authenticity, however, is not strictly determined by the use of cell phones and the ensuing aesthetic but also generally aligns with the contemporary horror genre itself. According to Xavier Aldana, "twenty-first century horror films have been given a documentary treatment that, in some cases, intrinsically shapes their structures and narratives" (123). In *09* a documentary treatment is particularly noticeable in scenes that place little emphasis on the quality of the filming, instead favoring the capture of a supposedly unmediated reality. This effect is achieved, for example, by foregrounding the presence of the cell phones as neutral, objective tools that record and archive real-time events without altering them; thus, we see footage from a phone that fell on the floor, strange angles as phones are held while running, and so forth. This suggestion of an unmediated reality is at odds with the subjective point-of-view perspective offered by the individual segments filmed by each of the protagonists and previously discussed. Despite the conflict between objective and subjective camera use, a deliberately roughened style acts as a certification of reality, precisely because it diverges from the polished aesthetic of fictional Hollywood cinema and is closer to surveillance footage, home videos, and citizen reportage, all supposedly neutral observational modes (see fig. 4.6).

Not surprisingly, *09*'s director, Javier Aguirrezábal, cites as inspiration independent horror films such as *The Blair Witch Project*, the Spanish franchise *[REC]* (Jaume Balagueró and Paco Plaza, 2007), and the Uruguayan film *La casa muda* (*Silent House*, Gustavo Hernández, 2010), all of them works that simulate an unmediated reality through "found" footage.[12] Created with micro-budgets and nonprofessional recording equipment (video cameras, photo cameras, cell phones) these works depend on handheld filming, display a glitch aesthetic, and purport to have been filmed by amateurs, typically the protagonists themselves. These same protagonists play up the fact that they are not actors but normal people recording real-time events

Figure 4.6. Meta-reflexive shot captures the filming process in *09*. YouTube trailer (00:43). *Source: 09 La película* (2014). Dir. Javier Aguirrezábal.

from their lives. Found footage films, regardless of camera type, display "a number of common stylistic traits and a shared preoccupation with the mediation of real events and the ubiquity of violence in the media" (Aldana 124). Fixated on the objects that mediate them (cameras, cell phones), these films constantly justify the presence of recording equipment within the narrative. They also contrive to explain the existence of the recorded material—the supposedly found footage that is conflated with the film we are viewing—with dubious explanations such as the making of a documentary in *The Blair Witch Project* or a class project in *09*. These efforts by the diegetic filmmakers constitute what Anne Hardcastle describes as having the "perfunctory role" in setting up the required suspension of disbelief, but in addition "form part of a sophisticated construction of viewer positioning(s) created through film style, documentary codes, and direct address to and about the camera" (108).

Other efforts to pass these films as real found footage include playing "with the possibility of the real death of some of its characters" (Aldana 123). While every film genre attempts to immerse spectators in their narrative fantasy, these particular horror films rely on the titillating ambiguity, experienced to varying degrees by spectators, of whether there has been a crossover between the real and the fictional worlds. In many cases the image of death provided by found footage is one that results from a simulated self-mediation—selfie-films taken by the actors (posing as real individuals) recording situations that lead to their demise, which often happens offscreen (but may be heard). This particular subjective mode of address (a pseudo-testimonial) is one that speaks to contemporary viewers and might lead to greater affective investment in the narrative because it mirrors their own social media practices of self-construction and their own use of selfies and selfie videos. In addition, it taps into what Hardcastle identifies as a documentary-like ethos, as the use of self-referential point-of-view camera work also "borrows from documentary practices and magnifies the native strategies of horror film by drawing on combined tools for producing a 'realistic' encounter with terrifying events that ultimately intertwines emotional and cognitive experiences in cinema" (109).

The recourse of *09* to found footage is evident, quoting directly from techniques used by *Blair Witch*, the "textbook example of the immersive and unsettling effects that may be achieved by using hand-held cameras—from rustling twigs to shadow play and the famous close-up confessional sequence" (Aldana 122). In *Blair Witch*, one shot became iconic: the selfie close-up showing a terrified and hyperventilating Heather (one of the disappeared fictional filmmakers), expressing regret at how things turned out. The instantly recognizable image was also used for the publicity materials, including trailers, posters, and the official website. Aguirrezábal includes a similar confessional scene at the close of *09* and emulates the *Blair Witch* marketing strategy. As Carolina breaks down under the stress of the horrific events, she looks straight into the phone in extreme close-up and expresses regret at what has taken place (see fig. 4.7). It is the image of impending death I referred to, one premised on the subjective testimonial point of view. As with *Blair Witch*, the image of a tearfully terrified Carolina was repurposed for *09*'s website and publicity posters. It is worth noting that this is the only film of the three discussed that had a publicity strategy complete with promotional trailers, posters, and television appearances by actors and crew leading to the premiere; in that sense any pretense to amateurism, despite the deliberate found footage aesthetic, was merely a marketing device.

Confessional scenes, whether in the film or in promotional materials, enhance the illusion that we are witnessing documented real-life events. Accordingly, Aguirrezábal argues that *09* is a hyperrealist film, since its spontaneous filming style and found footage storyline parallel the way youth use cell phone video for documenting purposes and for social media posting. The film's documentary-like approach collapses extra and intradiegetic

Figure 4.7. Carolina's confessional: a classic transnational found footage shot. YouTube trailer (02:00). *Source: 09 La película* (2014). Dir. Javier Aguirrezábal.

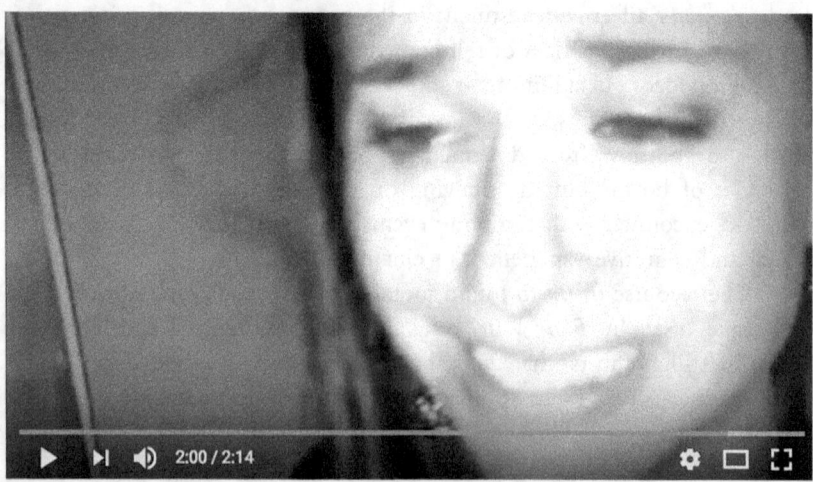

elements; the protagonists handle the camera phones themselves so that spectators might, under the film's suggestive spell, slide into the belief that they are seeing what the characters saw and filmed, rather than a postproduced version. The filmmakers go to great lengths to maintain the fiction of immediacy and reality that facilitates, at least momentarily, this suspension of disbelief.

Since the movie was filmed over one weekend in a nonstop action sequence—a single shot—it acquired an additional reality effect, the illusion that screen time and real time are identical. To enhance this hyperrealism by attempting a unity of time and space, at no time during the weekend of filming were any members of the crew (besides the actors) present on the set—which was an actual house, not a built set. Because all three actresses were constantly moving and filming, there was no extraneous crew, and no off-screen space crowded with film cameras or technical props. This was also the case in the other films discussed, but in *09*, absent *Rojo*'s self-derisive amateur style and *Sangre*'s theatricality, the absence of crew and confinement of the actors in the house during filming additionally enhances the illusion of witnessing real events. Minimizing film set paraphernalia allows actors to enter the fantasy more fully and reinforces the fiction that what spectators see is a recording of something that actually happened. The film was edited by using portions from the action captured by each of the three phones, although no explanation is provided within the narrative about who was responsible for such editing. Additional sound and lighting equipment was discretely situated so it did not disturb the realism of the scenes for the actors, and by extension, for the spectators.

As mentioned, this film represents an elaborate attempt to simulate the capture of an "unmediated" real-time happening, which spectators see only after the event has already taken place, like reviewing surveillance footage. What *09* demonstrates is that cell phone cinema not only retains elements of a surveillance aesthetic, but, quite paradoxically, it also embodies the twenty-first-century idea that everything is being filmed, that immediate reality itself can only be interpreted through filmed experience and through what we can view on our phones, tablets, and computers. According to Kevin Wetmore, the "instantaneous quality" of contemporary horror films stems from "the increasing presence in public platforms of 'terrorist-made, internet dispersed videos of real torture' . . . [which are] responsible for the ubiquity of the pseudo-documentary / found footage horror film" (qtd. in Aldana 123). The immediacy and proximity of the cell phone as a device that is intimately aligned with our bodily experiences reinforces the (falsified) sense of the real and further enmeshes or sutures spectators with the events depicted on-screen.

As with all these efforts to enhance filmic realism, this film also adopts a cell phone glitch aesthetic. Although made with the latest Galaxies, digital imperfections were kept or added in postproduction to increase the authenticity factor. Unlike the previous films we analyzed, however, *09* was intended as a commercial product, edited with commercial software and financed by a Chilean television channel and a cell phone carrier. It was shown on large cinema screens and only available through this distribution method and through some limited online pay sites. It is, unlike the other films, difficult to access, although a two-minute video trailer was uploaded to YouTube for marketing purposes, and the "making of" is available online. Therefore, *09* functions more like a traditional commercial film in its promotion and distribution networks than as an independent low-budget cell phone production. But while *09* could signal the beginning of the end for amateurism and free access to cell phone cinema, the reality is that, for now, the vast majority of films are still low budget and freely available online. The film's commercial failure might signal that the lanes for cell phone filmmaking within established commercial circuits are few and narrowly restricted.

Case 4: *iMedium*, Haunted Apps, and the Iberian Horror Cell Phone Film

Cell phone cinema production in Spain, as in Latin America, has achieved remarkable levels of quality in the last decade, with outstanding filmmakers such as Conrad Mess and Alfonso García Lopez. While my focus in this section will be primarily on García's short film *iMedium* (2016), I want to briefly mention Mess as someone whose work represents an antithetical approach in its search for increasing sleekness and near-commercial glossiness. Although both García and Mess embody the tension between commercialization and amateurism examined in prior films, their movies are counterpoints to each other in various ways and are therefore useful in delimiting the contours of Iberian cell phone filmmaking. That said, both of these filmmakers display the sort of profoundly transnational outlook on their craft that has been highlighted throughout this book and can also be said to characterize the horror genre at-large. Indeed, as Jorge Marí cogently advocates for in his edited volume *Tracing the Borders of Spanish Horror Cinema and Television* (2017), contemporary Spanish horror cinema lends itself to transnational analysis on multiple levels, including the international or unidentifiable location of the films, the fact that many are shot in English rather than Spanish, the international scope of the intended audience, and the transnational nature of the cast and crews, so that these movies make us recognize that "not only the concept of national cinema falls into scrutiny but also that of the nation itself" (5).

Mess (a pseudonym for Luis Mieses, Zaragoza 1974) has created several award-winning shorts such as his gothic horror film *The Other Side* (2013), a veritable masterpiece shot entirely with an iPhone 5 and financed through crowdfunding. Mieses/Mess has achieved relative notoriety in Spain's short film circuits for the quasi-commercial quality of his films, all of them shot exclusively with iPhones. He also won an award at the 2014 International Mobile Film Festival in San Diego for his film *The Fixer* (2013), which gave him an opportunity to establish contact with the global cell phone film scene. Despite a late start in life and lack of formal training, he has flirted with the possibility of entering the commercial film industry and reportedly received interest from Hollywood producers (although these have not materialized, perhaps a sign that cell phone filmmaking remains outside the established industry).

Editing with easy-to-use programs such as Adobe Premiere and adding sleek visual effects in postproduction, in *The Other Side* Mieses carefully crafted elaborate settings rendered in dark, brooding tones that resonated with fans of gothic horror. His attention to detail and systematic approach—he works from fully written scripts, storyboarding, and costume design and follows up with impeccable editing—diminishes the gap between professional and amateur, prompting Wilson to assert that Mieses's movies "assume what might be regarded as the legitimizing sheen of commercial production values, foregrounding stylistic tropes familiar from mainstream cinema" (*Film Festivals* 290). Tapping into both mainstream and genre conventions (in a decidedly transnational style, but with a noticeable if anachronistic flourish of German expressionism), this Spanish filmmaker's movies are unusual in that they do not engage thematically with the technological culture of the moment, that is to say, at the level of content. Mieses seems to be somewhat atypical when compared to other filmmakers working with mobile phones in that he is not interested in including depictions of contemporary technology or social media in his films, but he is more interested in showcasing the familiar tropes of genre cinema (noir, gothic, psychological thriller). This somewhat paradoxical disavowal of emergent technologies (which are very much used in the process of making and editing the films) is nonetheless an exception, rather than the rule, in most cell phone films.

As we have seen in previous examples, much of mobile cinema is self-reflexive and prone to commenting on the sociocultural shifts represented by cell phone technologies and the parallel phenomenon of social media also inextricably linked to our phones and to our increasingly mediated lives.

Moreover, striving for higher production values and expressing an interest in the commercial film industry, as in Mieses's case, is not always considered as a positive trend by critics and filmmakers, even when it results in polished films. Wilson is one detractor of these increasingly glossy stylistics. He argues that one of the problems with the seamless commercial aesthetic seen in Mieses's films is that by attaining such high definition and visual quality, the movies become distanced from the specificity of the mobile phone as a (hybrid) medium, so that "in removing themselves ever more from their phone film origins, these films abrogate their relationship with the technology that spawned them. The medium used becomes almost coincidental, appearing to have little bearing on what the spectator is eventually presented with. It could be argued that their cinematic pleasures are those of reassuring familiarity, embodying a mode of address that reformulates a kind of legitimization borrowed from commercial cinema" ("Film Festival Participation" 290). It would seem that Wilson is advocating for maintaining a specifically roughened mobile phone aesthetic in order for a cell phone film to remain "authentic" to its origins and medium. While I would not go quite so far in this insistence for a kind of medium specificity, I do concur that there is merit in the mobile aesthetic of the "good enough," an aesthetic that, as I observed earlier, relies on some of the limitations of first-generation mobile media (pixilation, blurriness, closeness to the body), instituting these as an indexical marker of the cell phone itself. Such an aesthetic, whether obtained "authentically" (by using older devices) or deliberately fabricated, allows viewers to perceive the film as if seen through a phone, thereby bringing attention not just to the content but to the movie's (almost) artisanal production and editing process, and indirectly to its democratizing message that anyone could make a film if they wish to do so.

That is why films such as *Rojo*, or even *09* (despite its commercial aspirations), retain a strong link to the technology that created them in contrast to Mieses's distanced cinematic style. It is also why a DIY approach evokes the "minor" cinema aesthetic such technology is associated with, displaying an evident self-reflexivity and what Wilson dubs the mode's "ambulatory" qualities, akin to the previously described concept of close-to-the-body filmmaking. As a reminder of our previous discussion, Wilson describes this "ambulatory discourse" as an embodied association between the phone, the filmmaker (and actors), and, through the film's aesthetic experience, the spectators. As he describes it, the camera work "takes on or infers the rhythmic motion of human ambulation; movement in sync with the filmmaker's walking as the image is being recorded" ("Film Festival Participation" 291). This aesthetic of movement, the ambulatory style, has repercussions that go beyond its "look" and affect the meaning and content of the films: "in this way, the process of a given film's mode of production significantly affects its resulting visual aesthetic . . . [and succeeds in] communicating codified meanings of forward momentum, progress toward a destination, of time passing" (291).

In their commercial-like seamlessness (their serenely static framing, well-balanced shots, and studied lighting), Mieses's films become detached from those ambulatory qualities and disconnected, perhaps even alienated, from the sensations of immediacy, presence, and movement sought after by other cell phone filmmakers. Naturally, many of these aesthetic affinities between mobility and cell phone films stem inherently from the material nature of the phone itself, as Wilson astutely observes, since "the mobile phone's lightness and maneuverability is mirrored in how subject matter is treated [in the films]. Camerawork and visual style indicate qualities of fluidity, imprecision, improvisation of shot construction, and a looseness of composition and framing, further concretizing the phone film's visual aesthetic as one of delegitimizing the normative cinematography of commercial filmmaking" ("Film Festival Participation" 293–94). This improvisational quality is counter to Mieses's obsessive scripting and storyboarding, as well as to his carefully composed cinematography and meticulous postproduction.

Something similar could be said about Mieses choice of narrative topics, firmly grounded in the cinematic mainstream, and his predisposition toward Hollywood-esque stylistics, which are at odds with the philosophy and praxis displayed by many other cell phone cineastes and also do not quite seem aligned with contemporary social media culture and the prevalence of screens, immediacy, and a spontaneous point-and-record aesthetic. Indeed, while Mieses in his film *The Other Side* turns for inspiration to the predigital (celluloid) past, to the age of Victorian monsters and vampires, it is more typical for contemporary mobile cinema horror to focus on the immediate present or the near future and on the role technology plays in its intersection with the darker side of fantasy; the bulk of such films seek to morosely expose the negative transformation of contemporary society in the presence of new technologies.

286 | Expanding Cinemas

Having established Mieses's work as atypical but indicative of one trend in cell cinema, I would now shift attention to a self-referential film that is more representative of the panorama of mobile cinema, *iMedium* (2018), a horror short by Alfonso García Lopez (Madrid, 1974) and scriptwriter Vicente Rubio (Tarragona, 1975). Much of what I discussed above regarding the self-reflexivity about the dangers posed by technology as seen in contemporary cell phone horror is exemplified by *iMedium*'s promotional poster, which depicts the cell technology itself as a bloody and uncanny device haunting our communication channels (see fig. 4.8).[13]

Figure 4.8. *iMedium* promotional poster: the haunting of our cell phone technology. *Source:* Public domain.

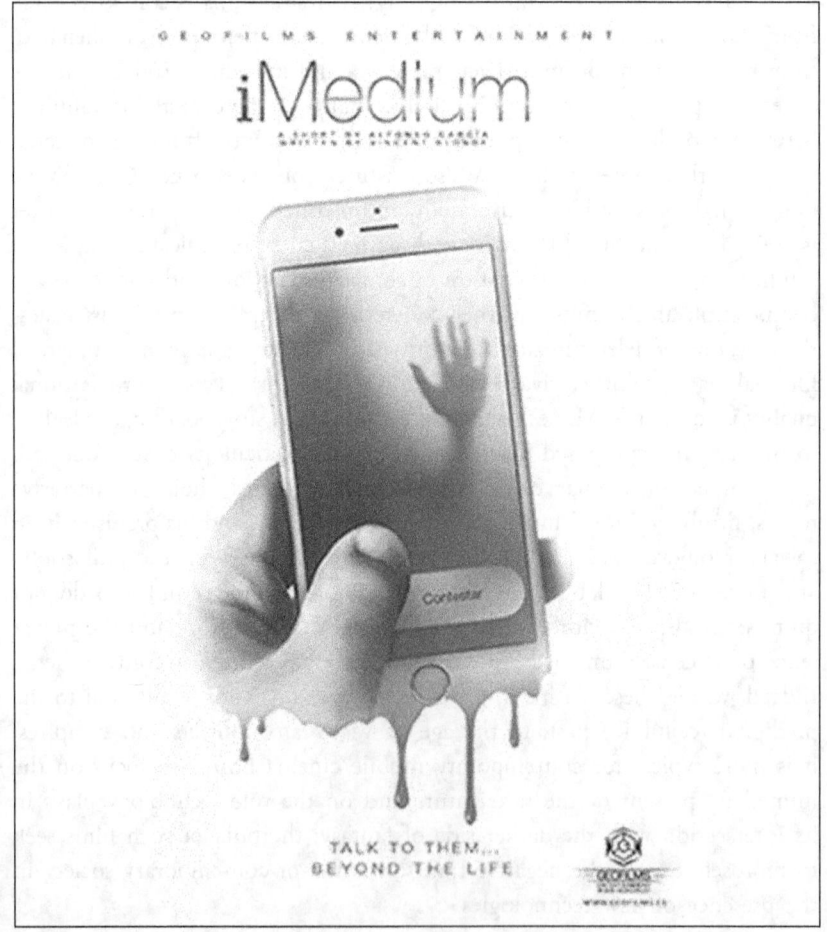

The penchant for self-examination displayed by horror films about technology has led critic Kimberley Jackson to refer to these works as a type of meta-horror, defining the current state of the horror genre by "its sense of being at an end, its increasing self-awareness, and its concern with the relationship between media and message" (2). *iMedium* self-reflexively signals its imbrication with smartphones from its title onward, with the conspicuous lowercase "i" that denotes the Apple branding scheme. I am referring to the copyrighted and trademarked letter "i" that points most obviously to the internet, perhaps to imagination (inspiration, inventiveness, innovation), but also to the highly individualistic ("I," irresponsible, inert, indolent) culture the megacompany is targeting by eliciting and demanding a cult-like loyalty to its brand. The symbolic "i" also alludes to its near monopoly hold over the tech industry, as the "i" prefix has become synonymous with the very latest gadgets and the sleekest designs, but also with unrestrained corporate interest. In effect, Apple, the world's first trillion-dollar company, has an economy greater than many small nations and the wherewithal to shape media culture in its own image—hence the pervasive and seemingly infinitely specular multiplication of the "i" (iMac, iPod, iBook, iPhone, iPad, iCloud, iOS, etc.). In a fascinating turn toward technological skepticism, if not resistance, García's film seems to sabotage the notion of sleek perfection associated with the Apple brand, even as it recognizes our slavish devotion to the same. The unspoken irony is that García makes this implicit critique even as he uses an iPhone to create and present his negative appraisal of out-of-control technology, which is a recurring theme in all his films. Thus, the very critique embodies within itself the impossibility of escaping the commercialization of everything, even the afterlife.

A brief synopsis of the plot is helpful to disentangle some of these ideas. The six-minute short is shot in a first-person point of view as with other selfie-horror flicks. The film opens with an initial screen of the *iMedium* phone app loading (see fig. 4.9), immediately followed by an extreme close-up of the middle-aged protagonist Luz peering into her phone camera and accessing this fictional application that allows users to connect with dead loved ones.

To be more precise, the film dizzyingly alternates between several types of subjectivity: Luz's first-person subjective point of view; a second point of view that seems to be located behind (or within) the phone screen and we can presume is from the (ghostly) perspective of Alicia, Luz's dead daughter; and occasional objective point of view shots not associated with any of the characters or motivated by the cell phone, so they function as "cheat" shots

Figure 4.9. *iMedium* the application (00:13). *Source: iMedium* (2016). Dirs. Alfonso García and Vincent Blonde.

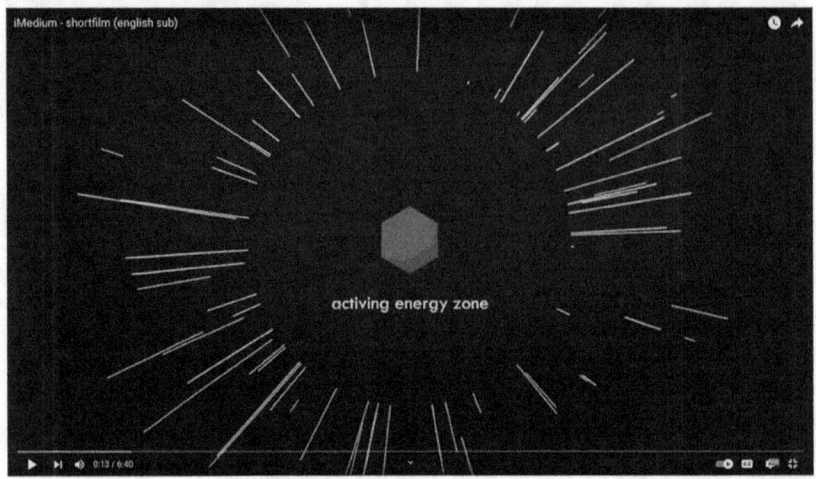

used to provide additional information. In the opening scene, a distraught Luz is searching for her daughter Alicia, who has been missing for some days. Fearing the worst, she accesses the *iMedium* app in order to establish contact with the beyond, as advertised by the soothingly robotic female voice from the app. The uncanny voice, almost human (but not quite), taps into a well-established filmic trope that genders horrifying technologies as female. A frantically terrified Luz finally establishes a connection with her daughter through the app, thus realizing she must be dead. In this scene, as in most of the film, the framing is jumpy and partly out of focus, with fragmented, off-kilter, and extreme close-ups of Luz's panicked face alternating with brief glimpses of her dark surroundings, presumably her late daughter's bedroom. This loose camera work escalates the tense atmosphere and denies a clear view of what is happening on-screen. We never see Alicia's face since we are not shown the phone screen except when the app is loading, also adding to a feeling of strangeness and anxiety. Through the app, Luz asks Alicia what happened to her, and the girl begins to tell her she was abducted in a car, but then she breaks off in screams as she relives the trauma. By this point Luz is emotionally overwrought, and the camera work has become as unsteadily frantic as her behavior. It is then that her husband enters the room and attempts to calm her down, telling Luz that he wants to take her to the hospital—suggesting that she is suffering a breakdown and might be dangerous to herself and others. Substantiating this suspicion, the next shots show Luz, now covered in blood from having cut herself off-screen, threatening her husband with the knife and then fleeing her home. The still dizzying camera captures her as she drives off to find Alicia, dead or alive. Alicia's voice and directions, a kind of haunted GPS operating through the *iMedium* app, lead Luz to a secluded area in the city's outskirts. There, in a shallow grave, she finally finds her daughter's body. Alicia, still speaking through the app from beyond, accuses her father of having abused her sexually and then murdered her. Arriving at the grisly scene, Luz's husband is confronted by his horrified wife. After a struggle and in keeping with the slasher genre, he kills and buries Luz next to Alicia. The film closes morbidly as the husband is accessing the app to establish contact with Luz, presumably to ask for forgiveness, a conclusion that provides circularity to the work that started and ended with the activation of the phone app (and thereby implicating the technology in the horrors the audience has witnessed).

Beyond its gruesome narrative content, *iMedium* can be described as a skillfully accomplished short that nevertheless maintains a roughened surface style. The film was produced by the filmmaker's company, Geofilms Entertainment, which he co-owns with the scriptwriter Vicente Rubio—curiously, like Mieses/Mess, Rubio also employs an Anglo pseudonym Vincent Blonde.[14] Not a newcomer to amateur film, García is the director of several award-winning sci-fi and horror cell phone shorts, including *La boca del león* (2013) [The Lion's Mouth], *Sector Zero 4* (2014), *The Cloud* (2015), *Alien Inside* (2015), *Money* (2016), and *Ruta 360* (2017). He works for the Spanish television industry and is also well-known in the short film festival circuit in Spain, where he has won the cell phone film category at the prestigious Sitges Film Festival. Unlike Mieses, however, García seems (for now) to be content to work on the short film format and to remain at the margins of the commercial film industry, perhaps in part because his work for television pays the bills.

García has been a fixture at international festivals, often winning in the category of cell phone films. Some of the festivals where he has presented his work include the long-established fantasy and horror festival Mórbido in Mexico City (in existence since 2007) and the acclaimed International Sitges Film Festival near Barcelona, which was founded in 1967 and is arguably the oldest genre festival in the world. International genre festivals like Mórbido and Sitges increasingly have large sections dedicated to shorts and sometimes exclusively to cell phone films.[15] Sitges sponsored for a few years a subsection dedicated to mobile phones that was humorously named Phonetastic Sitges

Mobile Film Festival. This subsection was eventually discontinued—now all films are subsumed under the short film section, possibly an admission to the improved quality of cell phone films and consequently to the increasing difficulty in determining if a movie was made with a mobile apparatus or with an HD camera, which has arguably rendered the distinction somewhat moot. In these festivals Iberian and Latin American cell phone films compete side by side, often in the same categories, without distinction of country of origin, providing the festivals with a decidedly transnational outlook. While the potential spectatorship for shorts within cinema (big-screen) viewership remains low, and few of the films featured in the category of cell cinema make it to commercial screens beyond the festival circuit, online viewership is ever expanding. García and Rubio's movies have been prominently featured in various online sites, including in their YouTube Geofilms channel, which provides a broad (and free) distribution venue.[16] García understands the future of micro-movie cell phone cinema to be located in the shift toward small-screen production, distribution, and viewing, admitting an inability to compete with commercial feature-length cinema on its own terms:

> Creo que el futuro del cine con Smartphone esta sobre todo en internet y en las propias pantallas de los Smartphones. Competir en la gran pantalla con películas rodadas en cine digital es una batalla casi perdida, pero esas películas tendrán que pasar por pantalla pequeña tarde o temprano y ahí es donde la distancia entre los formatos se reduce, y el poder del Smartphone tiene infinitas posibilidades. Será igual de respetable hacer una película con móvil que con 35 mm, siempre y cuando tengas algo que contar. (Cabrera)

> [I believe that the future of smartphone films is located on the internet and with smartphone screens. Competing on the big screen against films shot with HD cameras is a lost battle, but those films will have to go to the small screen sooner or later, and that is where the distance between formats is decreased, and the potential of smartphone cinema reveals infinite possibilities. Soon, it will be just as respectable to film a movie with a cell phone as with 35 mm, as long as it has a story to tell.]

The films by this Spanish duo (García and Rubio) share much, aesthetically and thematically, with the Latin American movies we have already discussed, underscoring the transnational characteristics of the cell phone modality and the horror genre. Almost all of García's films combine sci-fi and horror, integrating the device of the cell phone and related technologies within the storyline itself, at times either as the apparatus that is conspicuously filming what is happening (in a kind of "live streaming" version of found footage) or as the technology that precipitates the terrifying events. The prominence of the cell phone, presented almost like an additional actor or even as the protagonist, can be traced to García's earliest films *La boca del león* and *Sector Zero 4*. It could be said of all his movies that the cell phone is both the technology used for filming and an intradiegetic device within the narrative that often motivates the action, taking center stage much like in *Rojo en el bosque sangriento* or *09*. And similarly to *Sangre y levadura*, despite an increasing professionalization in the use of mainstream cinematic techniques, García's films retain a playful DIY attitude and a low-budget approach. For instance, García typically rigs the cell phone with auxiliary devices that approximate its standards closer to commercial cinema but also expose the experimental and precarious assemblage he is working with. The filmmaker attaches special lenses, stabilizers, batteries, lights, and sound equipment, using common household items such as duct tape or screws to attach these makeshift recording peripherals to the cell phone and to create a Franken-camera, which he sometimes fastens to rollerskates to facilitate traveling shots ("Monográfico").[17]

Returning to *iMedium*, it is apparent that the movie's strong point is its narrative concept and how closely its storyline ties with its decidedly mobile, shifting, and almost low-grade aesthetic, with constant changes of location, perspective, and lighting. *iMedium* explores the sinister idea of a mobile phone app that can connect us directly with the dead, or preferably, with *our* dead. The film can therefore be fully ascribed to the subgenre of techno-horror, broadly defined as "those artworks exploring the potentially disquieting negotiations humans enter into with our tools, machines and social structures" (Powell 22). Bringing an "app" into the narrative foregrounds another function of cellular phones we had not yet seen in the films I examined earlier, one that investigates the computing power of programs created specifically for use with smartphone technologies and their capacity to go awry. Rather than focusing strictly on the communicative component of a cell phone—the ability to speak via sound, or sound and image, through video calls using apps such as *WhatsApp* or *FaceTime*—the film also interrogates the cultural anxiety that revolves around social media platforms and networked technology, conforming to a variety of the subgenre that Teresa Lobos has termed "social media horror," seen in films such as *Open Windows* (2014) or *Unfriended* (2014). Viewers' quotidian familiarity and use of social media platforms and apps that, according to Lobos, are considered as an extension of personal virtual space, render the horror as more real, immediate, and intrusive than even the (traditional) found footage films previously discussed.

Lobos makes a solid case that a new filmic form is emerging in which the bulk of the action "takes place on computers through social media." These films reflect critically upon a contemporary anxiety triggered by the intrusion of new technology in the social sphere, exploring concerns related to cyberbullying and cybercrime, teen suicide, the loss of privacy, threats to the democratic order, the proliferation of online pornography, and digital gaming addiction, to name but a few of the dangers one can encounter online. Another insidious and troubling aspect of mobile apps is that they are often targeted to increase productivity and efficiency in a 24/7 connected world, raising concerns about self-exploitation and workaholism, relinquishment of personal privacy, pervasive tracking, and other issues related to surveillance stemming from the apps' geolocative capabilities, all of these fears adding to a growing paranoia about out-of-control technology. Concerns about the intrusive nature of apps are also fodder for thematic exploration in cell phone horror films, which have focused on the mobile dimension associated with these apps, enhancing the sensation of an evil that is unescapable since it is, quite literally, in our pockets or even prosthetically attached to us.

It now seems difficult to fathom that mobile apps were not available in early-generation cell phones, at least not in their present, easy-to-use one-click form. Apps did not become ubiquitous until the mid-2000s, when they became fully commercial (although often free) and easily distributed through platforms such as the Apple App Store or Google Play. The idea of centering a horror film around an app is not original to *iMedium*, since the Dutch full-length feature film *App* (2013) by director Bobby Boermans (Eindhoven, Netherlands, 1981) played with a similar concept. In the Dutch thriller, *Iris* is an app in the female protagonist's cell phone that functions much like *Siri*, as a personal assistant or AI interface and purveyor of information for the user. Predictably, as the film progresses, *Iris* becomes sentient and increasingly malevolent, thus emulating a long tradition of uncanny technology-gone-bad cinema and echoing such classic computer villains as the Hal-9000 unit in *2001: A Space Odyssey* (Stanley Kubrick, 1968), or the earliest gendered and evilest cyborg of them all, Hel from Fritz Lang's *Metropolis* (1927). These works, in addition to their tendency to gender evil as female, are "tapping into a variety of horrific plots involving robots [or machines] run amok—including stories of transcendence, sentience and regeneration" (Powell 22). What becomes clear in the most recent deployment of horrifying (cell phone) technologies, however, is that they are not a mere symptom of Luddite technophobia, but rather, as David Powell argues, "a form of creeping pervasive dread born of symbiotic uncertainty in our relationship to technology and our shifting perceptions of what it means to be human" (23). The fear of devices acquiring sentience is closely allied to our dread of losing our "humanity," however that may be defined. Arguably, our cellular phones, like our social media practices, are increasingly taking over our lives and displacing in-person human interaction, a phenomenon that has been called the "social displacement hypothesis," a highly contested theory. This threat of increasing technologically induced social isolation has been met, in some cases, with a turn toward mindfulness, efforts to decrease screen time, and pressure to limit social media practices.

In addition to mobilizing these anxieties, films like *iMedium* foreground the phone's ubiquitous proximity to our bodies and our virtual existence in social media, almost from birth to death. The Dutch film *App* has an additional trick, however, which is that, when viewed at the movie theater (or later, in DVD format), semi-personalized messages (supposedly from *Iris*) synchronized with the film were sent to the spectators who had previously downloaded the app designed for this purpose. This clever gimmick served to recruit a second interactive screen meant to further enhance the film experience and increase the sensation of horror and the immediacy of the evil presence, now reaching into the spectator's own pocket and speaking to them individually, prompting the sense that "apps blur boundaries between cinematic and spectatorial space by imagining the user's mobile device as infected by the same malevolent spirits plaguing the characters in the films onscreen" (Svensson and Hassoun 171). As with social media horror in general, these cell phone films wish to elicit a sensation of vulnerability linked to the proximity of the device to our bodies, and in some cases, to our minds. Furthermore, it can be argued that for those who viewed *App* in the theater—with the addition of the second screen, the phone with the downloaded app—the movie became an expanded cinema experience, one that stretched the boundaries of the medium, spilling over into spaces beyond the traditional theater screen. That proximity enhanced the experience of terror, creating "an immersive, corporeal experience enabling the user to engage a film with a heightened sense of intimacy and immediate physical danger" (Svensson and Hassoun 179). The use of second screen strategies such as these has been widely documented for television by critics such as Guy Finley, who explains that in certain programs consumers "engage in relevant content on a second device while simultaneously watching something on the first screen" (Finley, qtd. in Svensson and Hassoun 171). Alexander Svensson and Dan Hassoun have observed a similar phenomenon with cinematic second screens (whether seen in theaters or DVD format), including options like the possibility to view a film while simultaneously posting messages to a dedicated Facebook page, or accessing one-time-use streaming commentary for a movie, or engaging with more interactive and participatory alternatives that "create enhanced and immersive experiences by synchronizing the user's mobile screens with the home TV set [or theater screen] playing the movie" (171).[18]

The short *iMedium* does not reach *App*'s level of technical sophistication and cannot *strictus sensu* be considered as expanded cinema, although with the addition of a Facebook page that promotes the (fictional) *iMedium* app as if it were a real application, one might argue the filmmakers have broadened the universe of the film beyond its original cinematic space or its online uploaded version. In a sense these expanded intermedial practices disrupt the linearity of the film by introducing paratextual materials that the viewer can choose to interact with or recall before, during, or after seeing the short.[19] In addition to whatever goal the paratextual material may fulfill in terms of enhancing the viewing experience, including by adding a social dimension (with the Facebook page), it also serves additional purposes that stem from the multiple media that are engaged. In the Facebook page one can view several promotional videos for the fake app, including a realistic-looking advertisement and some faux reaction videos of people speaking with their dead loved ones.

While some of this "extra" material may function as a marketing ploy to engage interest for those who have not seen the film, it also serves as a thinly veiled critique of a troubling aspect of Spain's audiovisual culture. I am referring to the proliferation of psychic mediums, fortune tellers, and card readers in the Iberian mediascape, most conspicuously seen in television but also present in radio and the internet, preying on gullible spectators. Such mediatic mediums also have a technological (material) correlative in certain devices marketed for their capacity to establish connections with the beyond. While the app featured in the film does not (yet) exist, the filmmaker may have based it on "spirit box" apps that are already commercially available. "Spirit boxes" are technological devices that purportedly can detect paranormal activity and typically include assorted scientific and pseudoscientific gadgets: electromagnetic field (EMF) readers, temperature sensors, magnetometers, photographic and sound equipment, and other tools used to "record" the spirit world; one can purchase these devices easily on Amazon, for example. Mobile apps have also been programmed to recreate some of these spirit-detecting tools for use in cell phones, including the *Ghost Hunting Tool*, *Ghost Radar*, and *Real Ghost Detector* apps, all available through the App Store. Amalgamating all these spiritualist tendencies and devices, *iMedium* connects with that thread of communicating with the dead through a phone app and spins it into a terrifying story that exposes the risks entailed by uncanny technologies and their ofttimes exploitative nature, as yet another tenebrous outshoot of the dark web.

What we might conclude from this fairly representative techno-horror short is that cell phone genre cinema shares some qualities with experimental film, for instance its tendency to investigate its own materiality, a move reminiscent of feature films by such cult directors as David Cronenberg and Alejandro Jodorowsky. In reality, these films are neither pure entertainment nor mostly experimental but often encode a relevant critical message. What *iMedium* and other films like it suggest through their experimental self-reflexivity is that the horrible is not a distant threat but might be concealed beneath our ordinary, everyday cell technology, immediately adjacent to ourselves, perhaps even within our bodies. Hidden in this film, whether intentionally or not, is a critique of our rampant individualism, our growing isolation, the commodification of personal relations, and even of the self, perhaps exacerbated by the rapid development of digital technologies. Such troubling commodification of the human subject is on display in social media practices, from the intrusiveness of social and messaging apps to the self-absorbed obsession with selfie videos and the contrived manufacture of a virtual self for public consumption online.

In these techno-horror films, cell phone communications become disrupted, apps malfunction, and subservience to technology often leads to self-destruction. Internet and social media technologies, along with cell phones, are presented not as linking us together and bringing us into closer contact but as destabilizing and alienating tools that dehumanize us, pushing us toward greater anonymity and loneliness rather than collectivity. As phone apps such as *iMedium* become haunted, rather than connecting us with a spiritual beyond or with each other, these "cursed" technologies seem to result in death, despair, and isolation, underscoring the irony of our affective separation from each other in a virtually interconnected yet artificial reality.

Therefore, these transnational cell phone films oscillate between the optimism of creating with a malleable device, one that allows for greater intimacy and immediacy between filmmaker and subject filmed, and a sense of the dangers such technologies may represent as they replace other forms of interpersonal associations. Between the delightfully immersive sensory and visceral fright and the critical stance about technology's potential to destruct/disrupt our lives, in our postmodern late capitalist societies these films best reflect contemporary angst and confusion about our technology. By expanding the possibilities for viewing the films and occasionally adding additional screens, the films also seem to encourage greater immersion within the narrative. In that sense, and despite the somewhat dystopic perspective they sometimes take, these films increase viewing pleasure, so that according to Svensson and Hassoun, their focus on "bodily sensation and multiple modes of spectatorial experience gels quite nicely with the proposed attributes and benefits of second screen technologies, such as haptic engagement, deepened immersion, decreased passivity, and (particularly within the home) increased mobility" (181). Which is to say, in addition to channeling our hopes and fears, cell phone cinema is also a potent form of entertainment within easy reach of transnational audiences.

The Future(s) of Cell Phone Cinema in Latin America and Spain

As these films show, cell phone cinema raises utopian expectations of access and distribution for all, of media democratization, and of unleashed creative potential, but it also reflects dystopian concerns about surveillance, criminality, and technological determinism. The films themselves are changing, from their rough origins as self-produced works that depended on alternative distribution and displayed an aesthetic of the "good enough" to more recent works that favor mainstream distribution venues and aim for finished styles that approach the expectations of commercial cinema. At the same time resistance is growing against this drive toward cinematic commercialism, as some directors assert their amateur status and its attendant rough aesthetic as a badge of authenticity, claiming that to be the legitimate look of mobile cinema. It is unclear whether the shift toward greater commercialization will become widespread, or if the opposite tendency will prevail, or, more likely, the two will coexist and allow for different levels of professionalism. Currently, only a handful of phone films reach theater release or DVD distribution, while the majority remain anchored in the DIY or DIWO (do-it-with-others) modes of production. Although most films are forced to make do with limited budgets, this lack of resources has arguably been liberating for many directors since, as Wheeler Dixon suggests, it frees the filmmaker "from the obligation to please market researchers and massive audiences" (1). In sum, it remains to be seen whether market pressures will curtail the formal freedom and spontaneous approach these films have displayed to date, or whether cell phone filmmaking will remain mostly an underground amateur practice.

The full potential of cell phone cinema also remains unknown. To date, the format has helped to revitalize amateur filmmaking in Latin America and Spain, providing a new tool for fiction, documentary, experimental, animation, and other uncategorized types of filmmaking. At a time when mainstream Spanish-language cinema has become transnational and is discarding some of its national characteristics to tap into international festivals and global markets, cell phone cinema still maintains some ties to local cultural practices (smaller film festivals, cult viewership, home projections), even as, in the best cases, it refashions established genres such as horror or science fiction. Not all films are successful in being innovative; some, like *09*, are mostly imitative of established formats and genres, failing to take full advantage of the possibilities offered by the cell phone camera or by online distribution platforms. Others, such as *iMedium*, seek to expand beyond a single screen and redefine the idea of cinematic space. Cell phone cinema therefore balances a set of transnational and local features, negotiating them at the level of form, by deliberately promoting or rejecting a roughened cell phone style, and at the level of content, by returning time and again to questions related to the emergence of cell phones as documentation devices, to the presence of surveillance technologies, and to the precarious status of amateur filmmakers.

This chapter laid out preliminary observations about the still very young cell phone fiction cinema in Latin America and the Iberian Peninsula. Further work is needed to study these films and this new format, to understand its role within the greater Luso-Hispanic Atlantic cinematic corpus, and to determine whether it will lead to greater inclusion and democratization, or to increased surveillance, commodification and exploitation. Are we witnessing a cinematic format that will change the game from wholesale distribution and commercial cinema made by film school professionals to self-produced films created by autodidacts and distributed freely online? Or will these films be co-opted by market forces? Whatever the future of the format, the independent film landscape has already been profoundly altered by cell phone technologies, eminently intermedial and transnational in nature.

Chapter 5

Expanded and Immersive Cinema

VR, AR, and MR Film in Latin America, Latinx US, and Spain

Introduction: The Emergence of Virtual Reality

While the films I examine in this section are not typically "experimental" from the standpoint of their content (although they sometimes can be), they are so from the standpoint of the technologies and platforms they rely on, which are still in an early phase of their development. In that sense these works, imperfect as they are, can be said to usher in a still immature but promising new modality of the cinematic. Admittedly, after its exponential growth in the early 2000s, cinematic virtual reality (VR) is in a (temporary) production lull, at least as I write this in 2024. This slowdown is most likely triggered by the somewhat prohibitive cost of VR headsets and the dearth of sufficient content to encourage their purchase by consumers. The lack of mass sales in turn results in lagging investments in VR technologies after an initial boom circa 2015 (Lomas). Many of the troubles affecting VR stem from the inflated expectations set during the technology's initial years, including the assumption that VR would attain mainstream acceptance within a short time frame in the way other technologies, such as cell phones and tablets, managed to do. Instead, VR has been closer to a niche technology of interest to a reduced demography of (mainly white and male) enthusiasts, rather than a broader, inclusive, more accessible phenomenon (Lomas). Moreover, the hardware itself still has room for improvement, especially in terms of addressing various technical problems such as "latency," defined as the time lag between the movement of a tracked object and its corresponding movement as seen on a graphical output screen—a problem that affects interactive and gaming VR more than its cinematic VR counterpart but persists nonetheless. There are signs, however, that VR is making significant inroads in the arts, with the inclusion of expanded reality (XR) in its many variants in installation and museum spaces, with the buzz sparked around Facebook's "metaverse," and with the growth of social VR platforms such as VRChat, RecRoom, Somnium, AltSpace, or BigScreen, which allows for group film viewing in a VR space. All signs indicate a renewed and vigorous interest from filmmakers, creators, and investors alike toward broadening the cinematic experience to include virtual and augmented reality, at least in principle if not (yet) in widespread practice.

We might envision the pandemic and "post"-pandemic era (2020 onward) as signaling a third wave of VR, the first wave having taken place in the 1990s and the second between 2010 and 2015. The quarantine and isolation stemming from COVID-19 protocols fueled a resurgent interest in VR as a way to both isolate at home and find community online. As of forecasts in 2024, revenues from AR and VR technologies are expected to grow by 9 to 10 percent annually over the next decade, with the United States and China as the leading producers and consumers in this sector. Despite its resurgence, the survival of VR technology and of VR and other XR cinema is not assured. For some critics, these technologies amount to little more than gimmicky variants on video gaming that will have little impact on cinema as an art form. Many of the criticisms leveled against VR film formats echo concerns expressed about early cinema, when the medium was fundamentally understood not as art but as a spectacle aligned with the circus and other so-called lowbrow attractions. With time, expanded cinema and its VR and augmented reality (AR) variants may find greater acceptance as a bona fide art form, and that may depend on the availability of transformative VR experiences such as the ones I examine in this chapter.

Intermedial Virtual Reality, Immersion, and Interactivity

This chapter, therefore, investigates a shift in screen media as a subset of cinematic works, following the impetus of other expanded new media technologies that explore synthetic environments (XR, VR, AR, MR)[1] as cinema strives to abandon its bidimensional nature, escaping the frame, blurring the boundary between the on-screen and real space and acquiring an increasingly immersive nature. The chapter reflects both on the technical and aesthetic novelty of VR cinema and on what the spectator experiences when "viewing" these intermedial works. Arguably, part of that spectatorial experience that sets VR apart involves a sense of immersion. Of course, film has always been cognitively immersive (as one becomes engrossed by the narrative), but what I am referring to is the capacity of virtual and augmented reality to create the illusion that the spectator is physically on scene, transcending time and space (or at least momentarily forgetting the mediated aspect of the experience) to inhabit the same locus as the characters of the narrative. Indeed, some narratives place the spectator as a participant (through strategies such as first-person point of view, direct address by fictional characters, the capacity to affect narrative outcomes, etc.). In other cases, the spectator is akin to a free-flowing agent, invisible to the other characters but able to "explore" the narrative space within certain preprogrammed constraints. In VR films, from a cinematic standpoint the filmmaker often gives up some control in terms of predetermining the spectator's point of view, as the latter can shift about to see from different angles and locations, at times even alternating between first- and third-person perspective, so that XR, AR, and VR cinema can be said to be pluriperspectival.

Regardless of the perspective shifts that VR works can provide, they generally aim for an "immersive" experience. According to Witmer and Singer, immersion is "a psychological state characterized by perceiving oneself to be enveloped by, included in, and interacting with an environment that provides a continuous stream of stimuli and experiences" (227). The sense of "being there" triggered by immersion is called "presence" and can vary greatly for different spectator-participants depending on their level of engagement with XR, so presence is quite subjective. Presence can also relate to the position taken by the spectator vis-à-vis the way they are included in the narrative itself, as a function of how they are written into or interpellated by the creative piece. According to Kath Dooley, "the VR viewer is 'present' in a more active sense, as either an observer/witness situated within the *mise en scène* of the work or a protagonist who is directly addressed and involved in the unfolding drama" ("Virtual Reality" 98). Dooley makes a detailed case for how these new formats are changing and demanding a new kind of screen grammar, one that is not yet fully developed but will alter "narrative structure, audience acclimation and the directing of viewer attention" ("Storytelling" 161). Thinking about spectatorial response to VR also brings us to the question of "interactivity," the capacity of the viewer to interact or have a direct effect on the narrative's development, which in the case of video games can be quite high. For cinematic projects, interactivity can vary greatly—from a minimal level in projects such as Robert Rodriguez's 2018 VR film *The Limit* to a much higher degree of participation in Alejandro González Iñárritu's award-winning 2017 VR installation *Carne y Arena*, which I mentioned in the introduction. The same can be said for the degree of viewer choice, which in cinematic VR projects can be limited to looking around to see the full 360-degree space, but in the more extreme interactive storytelling (which at times approaches story-driven video games) might include greater freedoms to move about (not just looking but traversing the space) as well as changing the outcome of the narrative itself based on a set of choices.

Opinions vary on what might be the more effective mechanism for storytelling. On the one hand, proponents of what John Mateer calls "cinematic virtual reality" advocate for limiting the viewer's level of control to just being able to look around and alter their viewpoint, rather than to effect actual changes in the narrative—that means the cinematic experience follows a preset single path, reminiscent of mainstream cinema (Mateer 14–25). For Dooley, the illusion of greater interactivity can be falsified, since "[a] strategic VR writer can create the illusion of choice when in fact they are creating a series of audio and visual cues that result in a preconceived narrative experience" ("Storytelling" 170). On the other hand, according to Witmer and Singer, a combination of immersion and interactivity can enhance the sensation of presence for the filmic spectator-participant (225–40). The fact that this illusion of "presence" is seen as one of VR's selling points would suggest that cinematic VR should strive for a degree of interactivity superior to cinema, even at the cost of simplifying story and character development. Thomas Elsaesser has astutely observed that even in the best cases this interactivity remains somewhat of an illusion, especially in narrative works (non-games), so that "what commonly passes for interactivity in narratives is strictly speaking hyperselectivity. The aim is to program an architecture of multiple choices presented from a pre-arranged menu, and leading to different paths, which among themselves have certain nodal points. When these are carefully or cunningly devised, they can give the illusion of freedom of response" ("Pushing" 303). Nevertheless, in terms of "presence," cinematic VR does not approach the levels attained by social VR platforms such as Facebook's recently released Horizon Worlds or the more established VRChat or Somnium, as illustrated by Joe Hunting's highly self-reflexive VR documentary *We Met in Virtual Reality* (2022), which takes place entirely in VRChat and follows several individuals who during the COVID-19 pandemic established relationships and alternate lives wholly within VR chat spaces; most appropriately, the documentary is "filmed" within these spaces through the use of a virtual camera. The sense of presence for the characters of this film became so intense that their VR lives seemed to them more real than their real-world ones.

Most VR films, however, tend to be less immersive and are linear in nature. Cinematic VR has a predetermined duration and the viewer's choices are usually limited to choosing a viewing angle or perspective, that is, to determining where (and from where) they direct their gaze at any given point in the narrative. This freedom to let one's gaze wander, paradoxically, presents a challenge for filmmakers who struggle in motivating spectators to look "in appropriate directions at appropriate times" (Mateer 17). Films tend to be short, typically ranging between five and twenty minutes in duration, as longer ones can cause discomfort and dizziness for the headset wearer. VR films are at times presented without editing cuts, in a continuous or near continuous real-time single shot narrative where screen time equals viewing time. When transitions and editing cuts are used, they are motivated by the narrative and used to smooth over abrupt story changes, for instance a fade to black if a character falls asleep or is knocked out.

Although VR cinema is relatively new, there have been several high-profile projects by renowned filmmakers. Adding to the VR hype, recent films have addressed VR subject matter without actually using the technology. As an example, we could cite Steven Spielberg's *Ready Player One* (2018), based on Ernest Cline's eponymous novel, which is not really a VR film from the standpoint of the spectator, but rather a film about VR that used some VR technology for several animated sequences; notably, it is also one of the first films to critically reflect on both the dangers and benefits of an immersive and at times escapist alternate reality that separates our bodies from their physical environment. "Striking Vipers," the first episode of *Black Mirror*'s fifth season, is another high-visibility work exploring the potential for complete immersion and perception within a VR game, as well as posing ethical questions about gender and sexuality vis-à-vis avatars and virtual bodies. Without being actual VR cinema projects *Ready Player One* and "Striking Vipers" brought the idea of VR and VR cinema to public consciousness.

Other projects can be defined as VR cinema, but they often combine various media. I already mentioned Iñárritu's *Carne y Arena*, part VR cinema and part art installation, and will later analyze it in detail. George Lucas's Lucasfilms teamed with the production company The Void to create the (interactive) VR cinematic experience *Star Wars: Secrets of the Empire* (2018), which is an intermedial hybrid combining game, installation, and VR cinema. Other notable projects include the aforementioned action film *The Limit* by Robert Rodriguez and the immersive documentaries by Nonny de la Peña, such as *Border Stories* (2019). Nonny de la Peña is an ardent proponent of VR's potential to activate empathetic responses from the audience and has dedicated herself to promoting the ethical uses of VR cinema. Many of these projects by Latin American, Iberian, and Latinx filmmakers have been showcased at festivals such as Sundance (in the Experimental New Frontier category), for example the short, animated VR film *Battlescar: Punk Was Invented by Girls* (2019) starring Rosario Dawson, set in the 1970s New York City punk scene with a Puerto Rican American lead character and a decidedly feminist stance. *Spheres: Songs of Spacetime* (2018), narrated by Jessica Chastain, originally premiered at Sundance and is now a three-part VR documentary series that takes the viewer on a journey through the sights and sounds of space, originally screened in festivals, later purchased by distributor City Lights for a six-figure deal (the largest to date for a VR production) and now available through Oculus. What all these projects reveal is that despite its precarious position as an emerging medium, VR is making fledgling inroads into mainstream media.

Historical Antecedents and State of the Technology

The technological antecedents of VR and other forms of XR can be traced back to nineteenth-century optical devices, chief among them the stereoscope but also the panoramic painting and other Victorian-era experiments in vision. These objects, seen as curiosities, became forms of home entertainment for the bourgeois public. Assorted devices (stereoscope, magic lantern, etc.) shared an affinity with the more established visual and audiovisual narrative technologies of phonography, photography, and film but also brought together other media. The optical toys borrowed freely from painting (panorama), performance, vaudeville, and the circus, and they interplayed with the architectural spaces where they were displayed: theaters, exhibition halls, private homes. Critics such as Miriam Ross, John Mateer, and Francisco Julián Martínez Cano observe that over time cinematic technology has sought to approximate Bazin's concept of "total cinema," moving toward a kind of multisensorial and intermedial experience that desires to be indistinguishable from the real world, in other words, approximates a fantasy of complete perceptual realism. This supposedly seamless integration of real and virtual, incidentally, was anticipated by the pioneer researcher who created the first VR headset, Ivan E. Sutherland, who in his seminal 1965 essay "The Ultimate Display" wrote about the thrilling but also frightening possibilities of the medium: "The ultimate display would, of course, be a room within which the computer can control the existence of matter. A chair displayed in such a room would be good enough to sit in. Handcuffs displayed in such a room would be confining, and a bullet displayed in such a room would be fatal. With appropriate programming such a display could literally be the Wonderland into which Alice walked" (508).

So VR follows in the footsteps of the cinema and its inventions, which arguably progressed toward increasing levels of realism. Since the arrival of cinema in 1895, other film technologies followed, including synchronized sound, color, Dolby sound, 3D, widescreen, IMAX, CGI effects, and now expanded cinematic reality (VR, AR, 360-cinema, 4D cinema, etc.). Much as their predecessors, VR, AR, and mixed reality (MR) are profoundly intermedial, often combining computer graphics and artificial environments with real-life material filmed with 360-degree cameras, text overlays, and so on. Intermediality is perhaps most apparent in projects that integrate VR within installation art (e.g., Iñárritu's *Carne y Arena*), but it is present to various degrees in most VR work. In addition to being intermedial, VR projects also amalgamate several technologies: cinematic (using cameras, sound equipment, etc.), computing (computers, headsets, monitors, hand controllers), and traditional "technologies" associated with video gaming, theater, sculpture, painting, and so on.

When situating VR in a line of past immersive technologies, researchers should avoid teleological thinking, such as envisioning a technically predetermined journey from cinema toward immersive VR. According to Miriam Ross:

> VR is commonly assumed to represent the final stage of total cinema where VR will provide an advanced, and even perhaps indistinguishable, replication of the external world. Integral to this formulation is a paradigm in which contemporary VR systems are always somewhat latent, on the cusp of reaching the state of total cinema. Their present-tense ontology is effaced by future-thinking discourse that is continuously in the process of ideating how the next technological advances in audiovisual media will fully realize VR's potential. ("Simulation" 1708)

Rather than such linear techno-determinism, it is more productive to consider VR as yet another intermedial technology that could evolve in a variety of ways, is impossible to anticipate, and could even disappear altogether.

A look at the actual VR hardware is useful to better understand both theoretical implications and the difficulties in promoting VR as an aesthetic and cultural modality. VR technologies have been around for limited research, military, and industrial use since the 1960s, but they have only been commercially available since 2015–2016 and are becoming more affordable for the general public (Mateer 15; Ross "Virtual Reality's," 299). VR technology comprises a wide range of devices, including headsets (or head-mounted displays [HMDs]), such as the cheapest Google Cardboard (introduced in 2017) and other viewers that work in tandem with one's cell phone (a basic and low-cost mobile VR), to more expensive stand-alone headsets (HTC Vive, Oculus, VR Samsung Gear, Playstation VR, Microsoft Windows Mixed Reality, Meta Quest, etc.) that may also include hand controllers, data-gloves, and other peripherals aimed at enhancing immersivity and interactivity. There are also mobile devices with positional tracking to account for and respond to the user's motion and fixed displays that can also track head movement. The more sophisticated the VR device, the more movement it can track—in some cases only rotation (as the head turns various ways), in other cases rotation and translation, which enables an exact locating of the viewer in 3D space, and in the case of the Teslasuit, providing full-body tracking and sensory feedback as well as simulated (virtual) tactile and haptic experiences. The inclusion of artificial intelligence (AI) in VR content design has added a whole new level, allowing for the "experience" to be tailored to individual users with real-time language processing, resulting in an increase of realism and engagement, for instance, in VR narratives. Personalized interactions and real-life adaptions make each VR experience unique; at the same time, existing biases within the data sets used to train AI systems and the possibility for increased surveillance are some potential concerns. I examine the specific uses of AI for the cinema industry in some detail in the book's coda, but much work is needed in this new area of research.

There are also many venues to experience VR. While in the early days most people consumed VR primarily at festivals or installation spaces—or in special university-based CAVE (Computer Assisted Virtual Environment) or AGAVE (Access Grid Augmented Virtual Environment) environments—most VR has now shifted away from the gallery or lab to the private home. Today, films and other VR products can be downloaded onto headsets or streamed directly on phones or HMDs, although the more high-tech experiences may still require being at a specialized movie theater, festival venue, or installation space. There are now various web platforms dedicated to creating and selling or sharing VR content, among them Jaunt VR, a start-up later acquired by Oculus that offers hundreds of cinematic VR works, or gaming platforms such as Steam and countless apps and services such as Within VR, The Daily 360, or various YouTube VR channels.

VR films, therefore, can be experienced either as part of an audience that is supposed to feel holographically present in a common story world—as in apps like Bigscreen VR, which allows multiple users to share a single VR environment—or as a sole spectator. The idea of a shared VR experience seems promising, although wearing a headset tends to have an isolating effect and it is unclear whether the interaction between virtual avatars diminishes societal isolation. For those who crave simulating a communal experience, platforms and apps like Bigscreen VR and CineVR (a mix between a film screening and a social media app designed by Paris-based Cinémur) create a multiuser 3D virtual theater in which one can view films with a limited number of other users (from a handful to twenty or thirty, depending on the service), on demand, including private rooms and special events—all of it virtual.

Virtual Reality as Intermedia

The question of media mixing (intermediality) that has been central to experimental cinema (and this book) is also integral to XR formats. It can be argued that virtual and augmented reality functions as an extension of the type of intermediality we have been discussing in other chapters, especially if we are open to considering various forms of media mixing, rehashing, layering, and adapting as instances of "inter" or in-between media. Intermediality can be appreciated in the gamut of rendering techniques used by VR—from digital animation to the video capture of images from real life (or the overlay of both in AR) to the use of tangible materials in some installations. The mix of virtual and material elements is aligned with a tradition of media mixing as seen since the 1960s in Latin America and elsewhere. Incorporating assorted media and materials within VR and AR can intensify the sense of presence already discussed. Examples include the intent to provide tactile experiences through the use of hand controllers (through vibration or by their simulation of grasping and touching), the enveloping surround-sound provided by HMDs, or haptic sensations provided by specialized wearable devices such as the full-body Teslasuit or the "haptic revolver" that "renders touch contact, pressure, shear forces, textures, and shapes using a rotating wheel beneath the index finger" (Whitmire et al.). While many of these approaches rely on digital technology, other VR projects rely on analog ones (using materials such as sand, mimicking wind, etc.). The sensation of "reality" in VR is therefore achieved through an amalgamation of media and materials that trigger various sensations (visual, auditory, tactile, olfactory, etc.).

Admittedly, much of VR's sensory input effects have digital, abstract, and numerical origins rather than material ones. But as Elsaesser suggests, although VR is mainly anchored in abstract data and digital processes, in VR "several different perceptual–sensory registers and cognitive systems [are] employed to render the composite 'effect' of reality" ("Pushing" 299). This assortment of registers and experiences, however, does not render a unified and seamless whole, according to the critic, but a patchwork of uneven sensations: "Together, their combination does not make for one continuous 'field,' such as we encounter it in everyday perception" (299). Instead, what we have is something closer to a patchwork intermedial collage, to "the amalgamation of heteroclite elements in a geometrically constructed, homogeneous space" (299).

Thus, as is the nature of the intermedial artwork, VR assembles digital and material elements and perceptual, cognitive, and imaginary processes in complex ways that surpass the characteristics and possibilities of any one particular medium. And while the dissolving border between reality and fantasy craved by VR enthusiasts may never be fully achieved—and has dystopian potential should it ever be—our way of interacting with these collage-like manufactured worlds will (paradoxically) become increasingly seamless and device-free, the interface ever so transparent. So argues Elsaesser, suggesting that "VR as immersive experience will develop in ways rather similar to the newer 3D technologies: making the prosthetics (head-mounted display, 3D glasses) less and less obtrusive, if not disappear altogether. In all other respects, VR would come to be seen as a sub-category of 'augmented reality'—the exposure to and interaction with any information-rich environment, whose 'reality' is 'augmented' by data, accessible or retrievable by an appropriate technology (e.g., smart glasses, smartphones) that serves as a perceptual–experiential interface" ("Pushing" 302).

Astonishingly, much of the conversation about intermediality as it relates to VR had been anticipated by none other than Sergei Eisenstein.

In "Stereoscopic Films," his relatively understudied final essay written in 1948 (immediately before his passing), Eisenstein reacted to Aleksandr Andriyevsky's 3D film *Robinson Crusoe* (1947). Andriyevsky's experimental movie, which predated Hollywood's forays into 3D cinema by several years, garnered considerable excitement from other filmmakers and audiences alike. In his essay Eisenstein praised *stereokino* (stereoscopic cinema, VR's immediate predecessor) for its capacity to unite the film, its characters, and audience into a kind of organic whole. We could infer that for the Soviet filmmaker, who was a believer in cinema's intermedia relationship to other arts, *stereokino* represented an intense intermedial experience that drew the audience into the plane of the moving images. Eisenstein also thought of stereoscopic cinema as being inextricably interconnected to theater and other arts, but also comprising "absolutely new arts, unheard-of forms and dimensions ranging far beyond the scope of the traditional theatre, traditional sculpture and traditional . . . cinema" (Zone 190). Eisenstein's belief in the intermedial nature of the cinema itself was projected onto this new "cinematic" format, and at its center he placed the sensory experience of the spectator, who could now (imaginatively and also perceptually) "enter" the depth of the screen or, alternatively, commune with a 3D image that escaped the confines of the flat screen and penetrated the space occupied by the audience. So enveloped the spectator becomes one more organic medium in the whole that is being created.

Arguably, something similar occurs with cinematic MR and AR when the virtual is overlaid onto the real world so that the cinematic is extended into 3D physical space, as Eisenstein anticipated. Regarding AR, Elsaesser also highlights the importance of the coexistence between virtual and real, "where the virtual is defined not in terms of illusion, but rather as a mediated form of presence of something elsewhere in either time or space or both" ("Pushing" 298). Technologically enhanced multisensory experiences (360-vision, stereoscopic audio, proprioception, tactility and hapticity, smell) thus bring an added dimension to the concept of intermediality, taking it beyond the simple mixing of media into a layering of media and materials within multiple time and space. MR represents a kaleidoscopic type of presence that does not delete the self into an imaginary world or propose a seamless utopia of wholeness; rather, these projects are an amalgamation and collage-like assemblage of digital and material, virtual and real, a space in which the user-viewer retains a distributed embodiment that allows for inhabiting and negotiating various "realities" at once. In the latest MR technologies such as Microsoft HoloLens, the HMD scans the actual real space and incorporates the virtual "holographic" projections into the world of the viewer-participant—the program can scan the physical space and conform the narrative objects to it. For instance, in the interactive detective narrative *Fragments* (2016), clues to a murder can be "hidden" behind real objects in the spectator's living room, and the virtual objects are obscured by physical ones so that the two sets of objects really begin to comingle, although in a fragmentary way (hence the title of the work).

The Emergence and Viability of VR in Latin America and Spain

Interest in VR cinematic narratives in Latin America and Spain has grown in recent years. Although film festivals dedicated exclusively to VR cinema are a mere handful (and only two are well established, VR Fest MX in Mexico and XRAR in Argentina), a burgeoning number of events are including an XR section, fueling interest by content creators and the tech community to invest (some) time, effort, and money into VR projects (Jurado Martin 140–42). What these cinematic narratives offer is the possibility to fashion content that is region-specific since, when it comes to VR, "while the hardware is universal, there will ultimately be a need for content in Spanish or Portuguese and some content will need to eventually have cultural fluency" (Hackl). Still, most content creators are independent filmmakers struggling to find a commercially viable product and larger audiences. Financing options in Latin America are often limited to self-funding, crowdfunding, or community funding. Despite such difficulties, software creators and hardware manufacturers alike are broadening their focus to the Spanish-speaking markets (along with other non-English markets, notably in Asia), promoting VR at major trade shows, conferences, and festivals throughout the region. Such promotional efforts are targeted to a broad range of potential customers, from major industry groups to individual VR users. At times the promotion for content goes hand in hand with the development and introduction of the latest hardware technologies.

Case in point, in 2019, at the Mobile World Congress in Barcelona, with great fanfare Microsoft introduced their improved MR headset HoloLens 2, with the promise of its capacity to achieve a seamless integration between the digital and physical world in potential applications from medicine to archeology, education, and entertainment. According to company executives the device represents a revolutionary MR HMD for a world where computing is becoming dematerialized, diffused through an intangible "ether" (the cloud, wireless, meshes, virtual spaces) rather than hardwired and anchored to specific material objects (cables, computers, phones, headsets). Yet the tech world's fantasy of frictionless integration between physical and virtual elides material barriers and dystopian possibilities, among them the device's prohibitive cost, the unresolved technical challenges for VR and MR in the Global South, and the increasing militarization of VR worldwide, including applications in drone surveillance and border control (Slater-Robins).[2] Many of these issues, in particular those related to borders, immigration, and surveillance, are of particular interest to Latin American and Iberian VR developers. The militarization of XR and its claims to resolve world problems suggest both dystopian and utopian scenarios for VR's not too distant future.[3]

Along positive lines, some developers and researchers have made claims about VR's capacity to increase empathy, an idea that I will examine later in the context of de la Peña and Iñárritu's works. There is also a hope that VR can bring attention to immigration and refugee crises, inequality, and other problems that plague the Global South. Celine Tricart's award-winning VR narrative *The Key* (2019) is a prime example of socially driven VR cinema, a poignant narrative about refugees that drinks deeply from the well of Latin American magical realism. Several interesting projects have been created in Latin America and Spain that, through their use of narrative and recourse to intermediality, disrupt what Ross calls the "integral image utopia" that was the ultimate desire of Bazin's total cinema fantasy, a dream of total immersion also predicted by VR pioneer Ivan Sutherland in the 1960s ("Simulation" 1710). These socially conscious works undermine the assumption of a universal spectator (who is free from gender, ethnic, racial, and ability markers) that characterized the first wave of VR in the early 2000s, shifting focus toward embodied forms of viewership and to inhabit the experience of the Other (immigrant, racial or ethnic minority, etc.). Although most VR programs presume an able-bodied user, or at least require certain levels of mobility, some of these works from the Global South also consider the implications of disability. Here I might mention two works from Argentina, the VR series *Metro Veinte* (*Four Feet High*, 2018), which explores the coming-of-age experiences of a wheelchair-using teenage girl, or the animated film *Pájaros de papel* (2021), whose lead character is a visually impaired boy.[4] The issue of VR and accessibility as it relates to mobility, vision, hearing and other types of different ability remains a work in progress, with some VR games and narratives making efforts toward greater inclusivity, but still a long path ahead (Stoner). Similarly, while most contemporary VR cinema is created in English (and later dubbed into Spanish), some of these works allow for other linguistic and cultural identity positions, somewhat mitigating VR's dominant Anglocentrism.

When it comes to XR in all its formats, the question of national origin becomes even more difficult to ascertain than with other audiovisual media we have already discussed (experimental cinema, cell phone films, etc.). Since the majority of venues for distribution of VR cinema are Internet platforms and apps (such as Oculus VR, YouTube VR, Littlestar, Within, Discovery VR), it is the works' online existence rather than the geographical location of creators and spectators that defines these pieces not as merely transatlantic (in the case of collaborations across the ocean) but as transnational and globalized. Where in twenty-first-century cinema we see multination transnational co-productions, in VR projects that globalization is amplified, with production companies, VR firms, distributors, directors, technical staff, and actors located throughout the globe, working remotely in teams that may never meet in the flesh. The growing centrality of transnational collaborations in the XR and VR cinema industries is also linked to the popularity and successful dissemination of these types of media at both local and global levels. At this point, both transnationality and intermediality become constitutive of VR works, with the possible exception of locally based VR journalism. In addition, there is another subset of XR projects that are location-based and use geolocative technology, projects that are designated as location-based experiences rather than as cinema. Despite the medium's intensified transnationalism, I have focused in my case studies on works that retain elements that still anchor them to a locale, either through thematic or aesthetic concerns, through the national origin of their primary creators or on account of the language and cultural referents in the piece.

Where is VR taking hold in the Spanish-speaking world? For one, in the United States (with Spanish-language Latinx VR projects), including along the US-Mexico border. Within the Luso-Hispanic Atlantic, the major creators of immersive reality products (mostly VR and AR) are in Spain, Argentina, Brazil, Colombia, and Mexico and are in small, private sector start-up firms (with less than ten employees) or in university settings (Kay).[5] Regarding transatlantic partnerships, there are efforts underway to establish collaborative VR projects between Latin American and Spanish universities (Kay).

Who are the content creators that are the backbone for these VR firms and projects in Latin America and Spain? Typically, they are young developers in their twenties and thirties (mostly male), and many come from film or tech backgrounds. Many, such as Nicolás Alcalá, can be considered "transnational" subjects—Alcalá is both Spanish and Argentine and currently lives in Los Angeles. His company (Future Lighthouse), which closed in 2019 due to financial difficulties, was a start-up based in both Madrid and Los Angeles. He provides an example for the obstacles encountered by small firms to secure funding, develop VR projects, and finally monetize them. Alcalá's work was focused on cinematic VR aimed at a broad audience and mostly in English. His firm created a significant eighteen projects in a three-year span, including several award winners at the Venice International Film festival's VR section. *Tomorrow: The Evolution of Language* (2016) is representative of the short films created by Alcalá, a visionary work that, perhaps overoptimistically, argues for VR as the ultimate technology for fostering empathy. Despite the start-up's best efforts, the company folded because it was not able to make its VR work financially viable. Forming a tight-knit and relatively small international community, content creators often know each other or have collaborated in the same projects. Another VR creator from Spain, Madrid native James A. Castillo, worked on Alcalá's animated VR film *Melita* (2017). Castillo, in turn, is the creator of a sophisticated VR cinematic narrative *Madrid Noir* (2021), an animated detective noir that I will delve into in detail in the case study section.

It is unclear whether VR will overcome the challenge of financial viability. Currently Latin American governments are not supporting or developing XR in any significant way. Most support comes from private organizations, such as Collective of Digital Artists in Virtual and Augmented Reality, who offer grants and prizes to Latin American artists. There are some signs of change, however. In Argentina industry groups have coalesced together to form the Asociación de la Industria de Tecnologías Inmersivas Argentinas, and in Mexico XR has garnered some institutional support through the Instituto Mexicano de Realidades Mixtas. In Colombia the Asociación Colombiana de Realidades Inmersivas y Emergentes has successfully funded projects and promoted screenings. In Spain there has been a more robust amount of private industry funding and possible collaborations with other European Union countries. The challenge remains, however, to fund projects and create cinematic content and ultimately find the viewers for those projects. These economic and technological pressures undoubtedly influence the way the works themselves are created, promoted, and distributed, generating a strong tendency to seek the broadest possible public, lean into universal narratives, and make content mainly in English.

In the next sections I will perform a deep dive into various projects, balancing close readings with broader theoretical speculations about the nature of VR as an intermedial global cultural phenomenon. I will consider the ways these directors represent a set of mutual interconnections and influences, and the affinities and divergences between the Iberian and Latin American works. I have chosen four case studies from various locations that address Spanish-related VR content to get a sense for geographic variation and to better understand the way VR may develop in the future. I selected two animation films, one from Spain and one from Argentina, and two pieces related to immigration and social justice, one by Mexican director Alejandro González Iñárritu and one by Latinx journalist Nonny de la Peña.

Animated Virtual Reality Cinema: *Madrid Noir* and *Pájaros de papel*

In November 2021 the loosely organized international trade body for all things XR, the Academy of International Extended Reality hosted its fifth annual VR Awards. Most appropriately the awards ceremony was held virtually in AltspaceVR, a platform for live virtual events, and simultaneously broadcast via YouTube and Twitch. Two interactive VR films won big: taking first place in Best VR Film of 2021 was *Pájaros de papel* and Best VR Experience was *Madrid Noir*.[6] Significantly, both are works by Hispanic filmmakers (although they may self-identify as Spanish or Argentine first and foremost), the Spanish-born James Castillo for *Madrid Noir* and the Argentines Germán Heller and Federico Carlini for *Pájaros de papel*. Despite competing in separate categories (film vs. experience) both projects fall squarely within the interactive cinematic VR format; that is, both are narrative forms that demand a degree of input from the spectator. Indeed, they share many other characteristics. In each case the role of the spectator is relatively minimal, especially when compared with video games. For both works the narrative remains primarily in third-person and the spectator's actions do not change the story outcome or select from multiple endings. When discussing interactivity in VR, Elsaesser argues that it is often more a perception than a reality, similar to how it functions in any kind of narration, so that interactivity depends on the skill of the storytelling, "the ability to suggest an open future at every point of the narrative, while having planned or 'programmed' the progress and the resolution in advance" ("Pushing" 304). That said, there are moments in both films where the spectator is interpellated directly or can take certain actions (take photographs, open boxes, create visual designs in the 3D space, etc.). Whether the narrative flow continues unimpeded or comes to a halt, it can be argued that these interludes introduce a kind of multiperspectivism, while allowing "the viewer-as-user to 'enter' into and explore 'pockets' of the narrative world, which are not exactly parallel universes, yet have a high degree of autonomy, while nonetheless belonging thematically or in their visual or aural motifs to the underlying story world" (305).

As I suggested earlier, interactivity often seems to intersect with intermediality in these works. In the opportunities for interaction in both *Madrid Noir* and *Pájaros de papel* the user-viewer partakes of an intermedial intervention into the VR work, whether the taking of photographs (within the narrative), the drawing with light or making music, or some other task that involves a reference or even direct use of other media, or more accurately, the simulation of other media within the digital VR space. In that instance the recourse to the intermedial directly empowers, embodies, and involves the spectators into the narrative action, suturing them in and arguably vesting the experience with greater affect. Let us examine both works in some detail to see what they are about and what effects they provoke in spectators.

Madrid Noir as Transnational Intermedia VR Animation

A detective noir set in 1930s and 1950s Madrid, *Madrid Noir* premiered at New York's 2021 Tribeca Film Festival, but the project originated as the modest animated VR pilot *Madrid Noir: Prologue* (2018). Following an incremental funding strategy, the filmmakers pitched the full-length version to producers by screening their five-minute pilot at film festivals. In 2021, after making the festival rounds and gathering awards, the forty-five-minute full-length *Madrid Noir* achieved a "permanent" venue through the Oculus Quest platform, much like *Pájaros de papel*, which followed a parallel development trajectory.

For both *Madrid Noir* and *Pájaros de papel*, achieving financial viability in a limited VR market meant that the filmmaker-designers balanced local subject matter centered on Spain and Argentina with broader issues directed at a global audience. *Madrid Noir* walks a line between its somewhat exoticized Spanish elements and vague historical referents and presenting a story universal enough to be easily understood by a primarily Anglocentric audience. The director, Castillo, explains how Spanish cultural content seeps through, albeit in a generic and depoliticized fashion:

> Myself and a lot of the other members of the team are Spanish, so there are little winks and references to local things that we like, from store fronts to signs, etc. If I was to highlight one

> particular thing, it would be the posters. The story takes place in 1935, just before the Spanish Civil War. We were mindful not to hammer down the politics of the conflict too hard, but we wanted to make sure that we presented a Spain that was politically divided. If you pay attention to the posters you see in the streets, those are all based on real posters of real political parties that were active back then. ("*Madrid Noir* Delivers")

The transnational quality of the film therefore reflects the cross-cultural identity and personal experience of the filmmaker, James Castillo (a Spanish national), the writer Lawrence Bennett (British), and a crew of designers and animators (from assorted continents and nations). Castillo, like Alcalá and other young VR filmmakers, embodies the privileged transnational subject (in contrast with economic migrants), moving through and residing in various countries and developing a sense of both intensely urban and "global" belonging. Born and raised in Madrid, the son of an Irish mother and a Cuban father, Castillo relocated to the United States as an adolescent to live with Cuban American relatives in Miami, and more recently has settled in London as a freelance director. Castillo welcomes his transnational and immigrant identity as a strength: "My family was one defined by immigration. Both of my parents left their countries very young; one running away from a communist takeover, and the other following her ex-pat Irish family" (Sylvan).

Such an unmoored life experience leads to an identity that is, for better or worse, resistant to strong identification with any single nation-state, as the filmmaker claims a rich multicultural heritage. For Castillo. having a family with Spanish, Chinese, Mexican, Irish, and Cuban American aunts, uncles, and cousins "made it hard to fully understand the idea of nationalism because [they] refused to choose a flag or to set roots anywhere" (Sylvan). Inevitably, the sense of (a somewhat diffuse) multiculturalism and dislocation also informs his film, which is set in a stylized Madrid in the past but also closes in an idealized and depoliticized Havana. Moreover, despite his claims to immigrant status, it is Castillo's privileged middle-class mobility that facilitates his international professional career, providing opportunities that may have been difficult to obtain in Spain (the same could be said about many Latin American VR creators who share similar transient multinational lifestyles). Castillo, for instance, has worked in various capacities within the Spanish, British, and American film industries, participating in prominent projects such as Guillermo del Toro's *Tales of Arcadia* (2016–2020), an animated Netflix series spun into a film and other transmedia projects (Sylvan). As Castillo asserts, there is a diaspora of technical talent from Spain and Latin America working on VR animation projects worldwide ("James Castillo [Director]"), although this new diaspora is less driven by radical politics and more by the search for successful professional careers.

Let us examine the work, *Madrid Noir*, in greater detail. The plot is relatively straightforward. The piece opens in the 1950s in the interior of a Madrid apartment. The protagonist Lola is a twenty-something woman, but the spectator doubles as an unnamed character or player in this first-person narrative. As an active player the spectator can see their virtual hands and move around the space (with limitations), with a degree of interactivity. Lola is in the apartment to pack her missing uncle Manolo's effects. In the process, Lola discovers clues to Manolo's mysterious disappearance years earlier. Some of the clues, in fact, are discovered by the spectator-player, as part of the interactivity allows for opening desk drawers, boxes, and filing cabinets. This allows the spectator-player to find several items that will later gain relevance in the narrative. As in any whodunit, clues are a literary device that engage the spectator into a degree of participation, making this an ideal format for a VR experience. Literary detective fiction already functions as a game or puzzle between author and reader, or perhaps between fictional detective and reader. In *Madrid Noir* this mechanism is amplified by the sensation of immersion into the space and the participation in clue-finding, weaving the spectator-player into the narrative as Lola's active collaborator. The narrative also provides "dead time" that allows for the spectator (in the role of player) to explore the space, look for items, get different views, and so on. Occasionally these temporal lapses are prompted at Lola's behest, for instance when she suggests the spectator should investigate a box. Finding certain items triggers the narrative flow to continue. For example, when the spectator-player encounters the uncle's bowtie in a drawer, Lola says, "Don't be fooled by the cheesy bowtie." Discovering clues also evokes Lola's memories from when she was a little girl and stayed with her uncle in this same apartment, one year before the outbreak of the Spanish Civil War.

As Lola remembers the past, the space initially fades to black and then returns to the apartment again. Now Lola is there as a little girl, although the voice-over narration remains her adult self. The story unfolds as little Lola begins to suspect something is amiss with her beloved uncle and trails after Manolo in his nightly perambulations through the city. The spectator, in first-person point of view, also follows the child Lola as she snoops on her uncle's interactions with various shady characters, but the information is filtered through a child's uncomprehending perspective. At one point it seems as if Manolo is involved in someone's murder. This section of the film ends when Lola's uncle discovers she has been tailing him and sends her packing, back to her mother. Then the story returns to "present-day" 1950s Madrid, back with the adult Lola at the same apartment. The denouement of the piece occurs when Lola, with the help from the spectator-player, discovers a hidden letter that her uncle had left for her in which he explained his activities: he was an undercover police detective that infiltrated a Madrid organized crime gang and eventually disarticulated it, but then he had to disappear for his own protection. As Lola examines one final clue, a recently dated anonymous postcard from Havana, she determines Manolo may be hiding in Cuba. In a transnational twist, the piece closes in tropical Havana (see fig. 5.1), as Lola expectantly waits for someone, presumably her long-lost uncle, to open a door somewhere in the Cuban capital, but the screen fades to black without a clear resolution.

The piece, in addition to its technical virtues, is also quite conscious about media, intermediality, and transnationalism, highlighting these concerns within the narrative itself. *Madrid Noir* consciously associates VR to its intermedial past by including elements from literature, cinema, theater (and interactive theater), photography, video games, and music (zarzuelas), among other media.[7] References to other media serve a couple of purposes in *Madrid Noir*. On the one hand, such references render tribute to the precursors of a younger medium (VR), a medium that is still developing its

Figure 5.1. Lola arrives to La Habana in *Madrid Noir*. Source: *Madrid Noir* (2021). Dir. James Castillo.

own language. References and uses of older media also allows for the borrowing and adaptation of techniques and narrative devices into VR—using cinematic transitions, literary genre, theatrical sets, and so on. On the other hand, references to past media increase the potential for interactivity for the spectator-player, and hence, of immersion and presence. I already pointed out the obvious reference to the (highly interactive) literary detective genre, as well as its cinematic counterpart noir film. *Madrid Noir* borrows devices from both, from the mechanism of establishing clues to propel the narrative forward to the cinematic way in which "scenes" transition into each other through fades to black.

In addition to borrowing from literary techniques and from cinematic language, the piece is profoundly theatrical, beginning with its basic structure: *Madrid Noir* is divided into two main acts (Madrid 1930, Madrid 1950), uses set and prop design, and mimics stage illumination (moving spotlights, mood lighting, etc.). Interestingly, the spectator-player triggers the start of these acts by inserting a reel into a projector by using the invisible avatar's virtual hands, so that VR cinema and theater are inextricably associated. The menu sequence simulates an old-time 2D movie screen, the kind often seen in silent-era movie theaters. Each act includes several distinct sets, the action wandering through various locations, including the apartment and different parts of the city. As in a real set, although the film takes full advantage of the 3D nature of VR, there are certain areas that appear flat and others that the spectator cannot access (backstage). At times spectators are allowed to see the changing between sets, as walls descend and furniture moves about. Items in the narrative have a distinct feel of set props, adding to the theatrical style of the story. Moreover, a spotlight is used at certain moments in the narrative to focus the spectator's attention on a particular part of the space. This has a theatrical effect (that arguably detracts from some realism) but also resolves a problem in VR cinema, the possibility that the viewer misses the main area of the action while looking elsewhere.

References to media abound. Photography, for example, plays a prominent role, both within the narrative (Lola is an amateur photographer) and as an intermedia inserted in the story in various ways (historical references, to provide clues, etc.). In one instance the spectator-player can take photographs with a camera within the VR narrative. In a reference to the history of photography the camera can even toggle between a contemporary digital one or an old analog model. The spectator holds the camera in first-person point of view, and as they bring it close to their face, they can see through the viewfinder, snapping photos and gathering evidence of suspicious activities (see fig. 5.2). The virtual viewfinder allows for framing, focusing, and taking the picture just like in real life. Taking "virtual" photos with a virtual camera within a VR story is quite self-reflexive about the nature of reality, as it presents a simulacrum within a simulacrum.

As the photograph is taken, the image replaces the "real," the virtual duplicates the material object, and the 2D image replaces the simulated 3D effect of VR.[8] Later in the narrative the camera turns up (it had been discarded after this initial sequence), and the player helps Lola to develop the photos inside a makeshift darkroom. The process of development, hanging the photos to dry, watching the image appear—hailing back to predigital cameras—adds to the archeological media layering. And the information revealed by the negatives is critical to solving the mystery of Manolo's disappearance. As the spectator-player shakes one of the undeveloped photos, the final clue appears, revealing that Lola's uncle may be in Cuba.

Madrid Noir also has a multilayered soundscape. Woven into the audio there is a musical collage, from thematic noir tones to echoes of traditional Iberian music like the zarzuela to Jazz and Cuban music. Thus, the score of this cinematic VR is as transnational as its cast and plotline. The narration is mainly in English but at certain times Lola switches into Spanish briefly

Figure 5.2. Photography as intermedia (*Madrid Noir*). Source: *Madrid Noir* (2021). Dir. James Castillo.

(e.g., when she is speaking with her mother on the phone), adding to the global flavor.

In addition to supporting the narrative and enriching the viewing experience, by layering older media and familiar artistic formats such as theater and photography *Madrid Noir* eases the irruption of the "new" so the spectator will not be overwhelmed by the uncanniness of VR. That familiarity provided by this media genealogy does not detract from the emergence of "newness" in the piece, the sense that the experience is something distinctly other than film, photography, or literature, triggering different effects and relying on new mechanisms even as some of the visual language is adapted from past media. Some of the differences are worth noting, however. Where the cinema relied on distance and a detached spectator, VR seeks proximity, a spectator surrounded by the action and at times even participating in it. Where the cinema desired a seamless narrative with few interruptions to the flow of the storyline, VR often stops the narrative progression with prompts and tasks for the spectator-player. Where the cinema and photography frame the scene, as this story reminds us, here VR breaks the frame and provides volume, a space to be explored. There is a sense of immediacy, of real-time events unfolding, the simulation of presence that hinges in many ways on the degree to which the spectator becomes a player.

Pájaros de papel: Synesthetic Visions in Interactive VR Animation

If *Madrid Noir* uses intermediality to recall a history of past technologies and augment the sensation of presence (while ostensibly telling a detective story), *Pájaros de papel* (parts 1 and 2) seeks to combine various media to transport the user to an evocative oneiric space where empathy becomes possible through music. In fact, *Pájaros de papel* is thematically and formally organized around its musical score and the user's capacity to interact with it. The piece seeks to also remove one layer of mediation by enabling direct hand-tracking technology, rather than using the controllers as in most video games and VR cinema. The controllers already seek to provide a sense of "presence," visualizing hand positions based on the pressing of buttons as if the virtual hands were one's own flesh and blood hands. This sense of presence can also be encouraged through other means—for instance *Madrid Noir* allows the viewer to select hand skin tone, a gesture toward inclusivity but also one meant to improve user identification with the simulated hand.

But moving beyond controllers to directly use one's hands as in *Pájaros de papel* intensifies the experience of embodiment within the narrative. Hands are our primary tool for gesturing, grasping objects, sensing our environment (along with vision and hearing), and even enhancing communication and the ability to relate to virtual characters or avatars. In *Pájaros de papel* there are profoundly interactive moments when viewers can use their hands to create swirls of light that are syncopated to the music, so the experience becomes one of conducting or improvising with the musical score. The hand (touch) is therefore connected to the music (hearing) and to the visuals produced by hand motion (sight) in a synesthetic ballet.

In this immersive VR film, sound, rather than sight, is central—although the visual elements are also quite arresting. But this allegorical piece is premised precisely on the possibility of darkness and silence to unexpectedly irrupt into a world of light and sound. The musical score was arranged by French composer and sound artist Cyrille Marchesseau (who had worked with the film's director Germán Heller on several projects). Indeed, music and sound are key to immersion in any cinematic VR, but not every film or video maximizes its possibilities. Audio cues can be used to direct the attention of the viewer, but also to envelop them in a simulated audioscape. A realistic audio experience enhances the visual VR and mimics what hearing is like in the real world. Headsets with head tracking and audio location can respond to the user's head movements (as well as hand ones), and this in turn reinforces the sensation of immersion. Likewise, localization and distance can be pinpointed with the use of sound cues, using loudness, attenuation, reverberation, and other techniques. As VR systems become more sophisticated and latency decreases (the delay between user action and response from the system), the sensation of "being there" becomes more pronounced. Audio also increases the sense of participation and presence, which *Pájaros de papel* uses to great effect. Ultimately, and not entirely unlike what happens with literature, film, and other narrative forms, the medium itself begins to disappear as one is taken into the story, except in this case the experience can occur in first-person point of view as well as third (the user follows along with Toto's story but also intervenes from a first-person perspective).

Pájaros de papel was directed by 3DAR founder Germán Heller and its art director Federico Carlini, both Argentines with lengthy experience in the Argentine film and animation industries. The company, founded in Buenos Aires, has gone global with several offices worldwide, including one in California. As with Castillo's multinational crew, Heller's team includes members working remotely throughout Latin America, including several animation artists in Chile. A global firm, 3DAR targets its services mostly to clients in the United States and Europe ("Creating and Managing VR"). Prior to *Pájaros de papel* the 3DAR team had created another award-winning VR animation film, *Ojos sombríos* (*Gloomy Eyes*, 2019), also set in a world without light. Like *Pájaros de papel*, *Ojos sombríos* won various awards and was eventually financed by Oculus and its parent company Facebook (now Meta). *Pájaros de papel*, following the same model as *Ojos sombríos* and *Madrid Noir*, was first piloted and promoted at festivals such as Venice VR before it was fully developed and eventually acquired by Oculus for broader distribution, as content for its headset (Pietrobon, "The World").

Although the emphasis in this VR film is on experience rather than story, on the music and the contemplative mood it evokes or generates, there is still a thin plot, or the outline of one. Ostensibly set in Buenos Aires, *Pájaros de papel* tells the story of Toto (whose voice in the English version is played by British actor Archie Yates), a visually impaired little boy who walks with a cane and has a talent for music. While this character plays into the ableist stereotype of the blind's natural affinity to music, the question of disability is beside the point within the loose narrative, which is instead about the loss of inspiration. I therefore leave a critical reading of this work's misrepresentation of visual impairment and blindness for a future article (see fig. 5.3). By Heller's own admission the central takeaway of the story is how music can serve as a channel to awaken emotion and

Figure 5.3. *Pájaros de papel* has a narrative focus on music, disability, and inspiration. *Source: Pájaros de papel* (2020). Dirs. Germán Heller and Federico Carlini.

empathy ("Explore the Worlds"). The boy is an orphan (perhaps a veiled reference to the 1970s Dirty War and the orphans of the disappeared) who lives with his grandmother and his sister. He is also close to his grandfather, who is estranged from Toto's grandmother and lives elsewhere in the same town. Early in the narrative Toto's sister is kidnapped (disappeared) by a dark force who takes her to the world of shadows. Toto's grandfather, Robert (voiced by Edward Norton), is a musician who has lost his inspiration and has caged some mysterious luminescent paper birds in his cellar. These birds are a metaphorical stand-in for inspiration itself, but they also serve as go-betweens, linking the world of tangible reality and a dark shadow world that looms threatening but remains vaguely undefined. While there may be some political allegory alluding to Argentina here, the storyline is directed toward a more universal and globally consumable notion of good versus evil. Toto's grandmother, an Italian immigrant to Buenos Aires, is the family's caregiver. Toto, as the protagonist, will need to rescue his sister from the world of the shadows, restore inspiration to his grandfather, and facilitate the viewer-user's experience of learning to manipulate the music of the piece.

The music itself is quite eclectic, with markedly Argentine tones—Toto (a Sicilian nickname for Salvatore or Antonio) plays the bandoneon, an iconic instrument in the world of tango. Indeed, several moments of the film involve tango, including a piece by Astor Piazolla originally recorded by Argentine bandoneon composer Juan José (Juanjo) Mosalini while in political exile in Paris in the 1970s. While the many references to Argentina, and more specifically Buenos Aires, are obvious, the more oblique ones to the dark years of the dictatorship are buried in allegorical fog and mostly decipherable for local viewers only—the disappearance of the sister, the dark forces swirling around the city, the feeling of oppression, melancholia, and exile. The film also gestures to the history of Italian Argentine immigration—Toto's grandmother listens to her radio in Italian, and the clothing the boy wears is a direct reference to 1920s immigrant's attire—as is the bandoneon itself, brought by German and Italian immigrants to Argentina in the nineteenth century. Other musical influences in the film include American jazz and contemporary digital music, so that the soundscape in *Pájaros de papel* is even more layered than in *Madrid Noir*.

But the music, in addition to setting the film's melancholy tone and the evocative atmosphere, also serves to enlist the user's active participation. Rather than being a passive witness to the narrative, the user (or spectator-player) must interact with it at several key points. In one scene, as Toto plays the bandoneon in the solitary predawn hours, users can produce light effects by moving their hands in unison with the music. As the light envelops the 3D space surrounding character and user alike, the sense of immersion is magnified. The capacity of the user to control these light streams and to sync them to the music begins to shift the narrative toward something closer to an improvisational performance, a collaboration between the preprogrammed music and a light show, which changes with every individual viewing. This moment also begins to define "the common ground that might exist between narratives and games" (Elsaesser, "Pushing" 306). Similar interactive events occur in other scenes in which the spectator intervenes by adding to the visual effects in ways that enhance the musical experience. While the spectator is still bound by the constraints of the program—the light show can only do what is within its programmed parameters, and the narrative eventually begins to flow again—this is still a powerful moment for interactivity as well as multimediality.

Music and its absence also serve to underscore more terrifying scenes, for example the moment when Toto's sister disappears or, rather, is abducted by a mysterious shadow (a moment with some historical resonance for Argentine viewers). Immediately before the kidnapping we hear a haunting song by Brazilian vocalist Nicole Salmi, and then the music abruptly stops. Then Toto's voice-over narration describes how the "Great Shadow" came and took his sister away "to the other side." The narrative thread is gossamer-like, tenuous, and lacking in particulars. What matters is the sensory experience, which at times becomes intensely lyrical and in this scene is tinged with foreboding. In another allegorical scene, Toto muses, "The invisible, is silence. The home for all the great musicians from the past. One day, it will be my home too." It is unclear if he is referring to literal silence, to the loss of inspiration, or perhaps to death, immigration, or even to blindness as a kind of silence. The vagueness of the narrative is in keeping with the fractalization of VR narratives and the ways they distribute agency between characters and users (spectators). *Pájaros de papel* is like a musical score; its structure relies on the repetition of phrases, musical and verbal, on recursivity, on pattern. After Toto's enigmatic words, a melancholic tune begins to play, and the viewer can again manipulate streams of bluish light to create patterns and designs with their hands. The blue patterns are in keeping with the sad music so that the visual and aural media work in tandem. The story allows for four interludes of immersive and interactive play where the user directly intervenes.

Another key narrative scene takes place inside a jazz club several decades in the past, prior to Toto's birth. The viewer has the distinct sensation of witnessing a live jam session; indeed the music is a prerecorded performance by a jazz quartet. The scene's ambiance envelops the spectator, whose perspective is as if seated at a table just behind Toto's grandfather, who is at that point a younger man. While the user has no direct interaction here—they are merely a witness to the jazz performance and to the conversation—the feeling of being present is intense. In this scene Toto's grandfather, a professional musician, reveals that he has lost his inspiration. Later we find out that in an unsuccessful effort to regain it, he caged the strange paper birds that are the (literal) source of inspiration, but he remains unable to compose. Soon thereafter, after another fade to black, the narrative shifts forward, returning to Toto's time. In this new sequence the spectator sees how Toto rescues his sister from the world of silence and shadows, restoring a sense of harmony.

Throughout its duration the narrative remains allegorical and enigmatic, gesturing toward the need to restore some sort of balance in the world. Disability is only acknowledged in vague terms, as when Toto's grandmother asserts that "the blind hear better. They dream deeper." While this assertion is problematic in its ableist connotations, it touches on the story's point about the centrality of sound and music and their link to the oneiric realm. In the film's grand finale, Toto rescues his grandfather from the shadows as well as from his own descent into despair, further reestablishing a sense of harmony. The paper birds are also freed, and thus inspiration returns.

As the final upbeat musical piece begins to play, the viewer is again able to create a light show with their hands. The voice-over narration emphasizes the importance of this joint creation, stating, "It is my composition. It is my masterpiece. But it is also yours. You were my inspiration. It is by playing together that we start to create something." What follows this invitation to collaborate varies with each individual user. If the user actively engages, they can sway their hands to co-create an aesthetic spectacle of streaming light beams. The image, reactive to the movement of the user, who is in turn reactive to the musical sounds, creates a real-time jazz improvisation, a collaborative interaction between human user and program (machine).

The interactive sequences in *Pájaros de papel* combine various orchestral sounds, percussion, string instruments, voice, and the soulful bandoneon. As with any improvisational scheme, there is a balance between the preprogrammed composition and allowing the user to introduce certain variations within it. While *Pájaros de papel* creates a compelling sense of 3D space through sound and uses multidirectional recordings that facilitate a sensation of being surrounded by the music, it does not recruit the absolute maximum possibilities offered by dynamic binaural recording—that is, recording that both responds to the user's head movement and originates in different locations in the 3D space (see fig. 5.4)—possibly because this would have made the project more costly and difficult to implement for the commercial headsets. That said, *Pájaros de papel* achieves what its director set out to do, which was to create an intermedial, immersive, and interactive composition of "sensory landscapes," one in which the music "connects everything to our memories and emotions" (Pietrobon, "Interview").

Immersive Immigration Experiences for Empathy: *Use of Force* and *Carne y Arena*

There has been a proliferation of 3D and 360-degree immersive journalism in Spain and Latin America since the mid-2000s, as journalists recruit novel formats to offset the declining interest in print journalism and as traditional television and radio newscasting comes under pressure from Internet-based media. In Spain, for instance, there were over 150 works of *periodismo immersivo* [immersive journalism] in the two-year period from 2015 to 2017, including a range of formats from 360-degree video to VR, AR, and MR projects. Although immersive journalism recently lost some steam due to its somewhat onerous production and distribution methods, it is entering

Figure 5.4. *Pájaros de papel*, interactivity, synesthesia, and musical improvisation. *Source: Pájaros de papel* (2020). Dirs. Germán Heller and Federico Carlini.

what could be described as a "second wave" at the turn of the 2020s. Immersive journalism seeks to provide the spectator with fact-based first-person experiences of global and local current events and nonfiction narratives with the hopes of mobilizing empathy and, ideally, effect long term social change. Unlike the two animated fiction works I just examined, immersive journalism pieces do not necessarily require a headset. They can be viewed like any other video from a mobile device or PC and are often uploaded to free online platforms such as YouTube VR or the *New York Times* VR app.[9] The spectator, however, can still navigate through the video and look around in 360 degrees, either with the cursor or mouse or by simply moving the mobile device around to view the scene from all directions. Admittedly the degree of "interactivity" is typically low for this genre, since most immersive journalism projects are one-directional linear narratives filmed with a single 360-degree camera. In contrast with VR animation pieces like *Madrid Noir* or *Pájaros de papel*, in immersive journalism the viewer can opt to examine different parts of the filmed environment but cannot change the flow of the narrative. That said, and specifically regarding documentary or journalistic 360-degree videos, even this limited interactivity allows the spectator to engage with the surroundings and obtain a broader perspective and context for the social issue under scrutiny (Gracia and Damas 77–78).

Although most immersive journalism uses actual video filmed in 360-degrees, some projects have substantially greater technological investment, using animation and digital environments to reenact events, to imagine fictional counterfactual scenarios, or to allow the spectators to interact and participate in the action, bringing these projects closer to a gaming or interactive VR experience. In some instances, animation is combined with real-life audio recordings, or vice versa, creating mixed experiences that creatively expand the boundaries of traditional reportage. When using animation rather than captured footage, the question of photorealism might be beside the point, as "the sense of presence in the story is more important in creating authenticity" (Sirkkunen et al. 16). The use of animation to recreate events is critical to both pieces I examine here.

In Latin America, younger media consumers are increasingly seeking immersive journalism, and media outlets in Mexico, Argentina, Brazil, and Chile regularly post VR and 360-degree videos on their websites as well as on social network sites such as Facebook and YouTube (López Linares). Despite increased interest, immersive journalism remains a daunting proposition in the region. Plagued by poor connectivity and low server capacity, journalists struggle to introduce these new formats for storytelling, since "the challenge of integrating 360 videos into the newsrooms of Latin American media adds to the challenge of overcoming the economic and technological barriers of the region. In a time when media companies cut more staff than they hire, it becomes more difficult to boost innovations like immersive videos and Virtual Reality" (López Linares). Reflecting the region's material challenges, research into the topic of immersive journalism is also lagging when it comes to Latin America. As the authors of the first edited volume on immersive journalism observe, "[A]lthough we are seeing the presence of immersive journalism in every continent . . . there is a limited understanding of practices and case studies in Latin America and Asia" (Gynnild et al., "Introduction" 6). No doubt there have been several prominent immersive journalism projects created in the Spanish-speaking world, many exploring the issue of migration and immigration. One example is the 360-degree documentary *Cruzar* [Crossing] (2020), directed by the Ecuadorian Juan Pablo Urgilés, which exposes the plight of Venezuelans who leave their country for other Latin American nations or the United States by first crossing the border between Venezuela and Colombia. The film locates the viewer in the proximity of a migrant named Arianna, accompanying her from her home in Venezuela to her destination in Ecuador, so that the spectator becomes a witness and companion in one migrant's arduous journey.

While 360-degree videos, which only require a special camera, may be the most accessible and affordable format for immersive journalism, more elaborate formats purportedly intensify spectatorial engagement. Next, I examine two thematically related and yet quite distinct projects that viscerally lay bare the question of immigration through a more embodied approach to immersive VR journalism. Arguably, both works extend the boundaries of mainstream journalism. They do so by adopting reenactment and fictionalization techniques and by seeking to "embody" the spectator in the precarious position of victimized migrants with the intent to elicit empathy and spark social change. And both pieces are transnational in that they deploy US and Mexican resources and crews to examine abuses linked to the US-Mexico border. The first work, *Use of Force*, is an early VR experience from 2013 created by the pioneering Latinx journalist Nonny de la Peña. The second, *Carne y Arena*, is a VR installation by Mexican filmmaker Alejandro González Iñárritu. In both cases VR, intermediality, and immersion are mobilized to appeal to the viewer's social consciousness.

Use of Force as Empathy or Distancing VR Documentary Animation

Use of Force is arguably one of the pioneering VR projects created for immersive journalism. The five-minute piece is based on a tragic incident that took place at the San Ysidro port of entry at the US-Mexico border. It involved the 2010 deadly tasing and beating of undocumented Mexican immigrant and longtime San Diego resident Anastasio Hernández Rojas at the hands of Border Patrol officers. Hernández Rojas had been deported that same year and was apprehended as he attempted to cross back into the United States to reunite with his family. After an initial tussle and once he was already on the ground and handcuffed, the Border Patrol tased him, beat him with batons, and kicked him, eventually causing his death. Several witnesses captured the incident with cell phone videos. The Border Patrol confiscated bystander cell phones and destroyed the videos to cover up the incident but missed two videos that later became the basis for the VR project. The San Diego coroner's office classified Hernández Rojas's death as a homicide, but charges against the responsible officers were initially dismissed (as of 2022, over a decade later, the family still awaits justice).

VR journalist Nonny de la Peña was inspired by the grainy surviving video footage to create an immersive experience in which the user becomes one of the event's direct witnesses, entering the first-person point of view with the aid of a headset. The piece is an animated graphic representation of the event but includes the actual audio from that night's cell phone recording. The original *Use of Force* screening was at the 2014 Tribeca Film festival, and subsequently it was seen at other high-profile festival venues. The experience as originally designed required single users to put on the headset without being told what they were going to experience. Unable to directly intervene in the action but forced to watch the recreated beating, spectator-witnesses reported being faced by conflicting emotions—horror, guilt, remorse, helplessness, and so on. At the same time, the participants were given a "virtual" cell phone with which they could document sixty seconds of the event as evidence, transforming them from passive witnesses into active participants documenting the atrocity, or as concerned citizens gathering evidence for a future trial. The intent was that the brutality and horror of the piece also might trigger an empathetic reaction from users, creating a better informed and engaged public. According to de la Peña, "With the diminishing number of people reading newspapers and watching television news, it seems clear that using new technologies to tell nonfiction stories is crucial to an informed democracy" (Kemmerle).

Nonny de la Peña first became involved with VR at the EventLab, a think tank affiliated with the University of Barcelona and the Institución Catalana de Investigación y de Estudios Avanzados [Catalan Institute for Research and Advanced Studies]. EventLab conducts research on the societal impact of VR and its practical applications in a variety of fields, under its directors Mel Slater and Mavi Sánchez-Vives. At EventLab, de la Peña learned the concept of first-person embodiment, or how to make the spectator inhabit the skin of her documentary subjects. She outlines the idea in her 2010 article "Immersive Journalism: Immersive Virtual Reality for the First-Person Experience of News," where she argues, "The fundamental idea of immersive journalism is to allow the participant, typically represented as a digital avatar, to actually enter a virtually recreated scenario representing the news story. The sense of presence obtained through an immersive system (whether a Cave or head-tracked head-mounted displays [HMD] and online virtual worlds) . . . [this experience] affords the participant unprecedented access to the sights and sounds, and possibly feelings and emotions, that accompany the news" (292). The two models de la Peña considers are for the viewer to enter the narrative either as a witness to the events (playing themselves, an external observer) or as a subject within the narrative, even as the victim. For *Use of Force* she chose the witness model, while in other projects she has opted for the victim, for example in *Gone Gitmo* (2007) she places the viewer's avatar in the body of a Guantanamo Bay detainee, in a VR cell. In every instance, de la Peña advocates persuasively that the empathetic possibilities of immersive journalism through VR depend precisely on placing the spectator in the midst of the event in question, "transferring people's sensation of place to a space where a credible action is taking place that they perceive as really happening, and where, most importantly, it is their very body involved in this action" (de la Peña et al. 299–300).

Let us examine how *Use of Force* might function as a motor to elicit empathy by bringing users to the tragic event and rendering them as active witnesses (see fig. 5.5). Although similar claims about empathy have been made for film and written accounts, researchers argue that VR can intensify the viewer's emotional connection through presence. VR storytelling can place the user in the shoes of the victim, or in those of the perpetrator of a crime or abuse, but in this project the user is an observer who must decide where they stand—both in terms of their physical location and

Figure 5.5. *Use of Force*, empathy or distance? *Source: Use of Force* (2013). Dir. Nonny de la Peña.

what actions to take. The only possible action allowed by the program is to bear witness and document the homicide in progress, since the avatar cannot interfere. Filmmakers like de la Peña and Chris Milk (director of the 2015 VR documentary about Syrian refugees *Clouds over Sidra*) insist that VR cinema renders users more empathetic, allowing them to experience what it is like to be the Other (Milk, "How Virtual"; Constine). Of course, this "experience" takes place from a position of safety and for only a brief time, so the impact can be limited, and the effect, if any, of VR on empathy remains controversial. While it is difficult to measure empathy empirically, "[several] studies consistently pointed to an uptick in empathic behavior following the VR experience" (Palmer). Still, preliminary research remains inconclusive, with some findings pointing toward increased engagement and emotional response to real-life events, while other studies suggest spatial immersion in VR can also lead to lessened attention and difficulty in following a story as it unfolds (Barreda-Ángeles 155). Setting aside the question of empathy, cinematic VR nonetheless engages with viewers on various levels, cognitively, affectively, and even physically.

In *Use of Force*, when the user first puts on the headset there is no introduction or credit sequence as there are in other cinematic VR narratives. As in real life, one just finds oneself in a situation with no paratexts or expectations and may be initially disoriented. Yet, although no context is provided, the sheer brutality of the scene and the powerlessness of the victim makes it clear that this particular use of force could not be justified under any conceivable circumstance. Arguably, having more information could substantiate this judgment for the user, but it might also eliminate the impact of arriving at the same conclusion through the sheer intensity of the experience. Users find their avatars standing in a nighttime virtual space depicting a street, opposite the fenced parking lot of the Border Patrol facility at the San Ysidro border crossing. There are some ambient sounds including crickets and voices, not fully distinct. Users are outside a fence with no direct entry to the scene. They cannot cross the fence to approach the area where the action is taking place, but they can walk around and view the action from multiple perspectives, including from a walkway above. Other virtual bystanders surround the user, some pointing their cell phone cameras toward the parking lot and thus modeling the "witnessing" behavior. One of these programmed bystanders is a replica of a woman who documented the real incident and was later motion-captured in the lab to recreate her involvement for the VR experience—we might say she was included as an embodied witness and as a link between the past event and its virtual reenactment. In the lot we see a couple of patrol cars and a dozen officers, some standing by and others surrounding someone who lays on the ground. The scene is poorly lit, but we can clearly see three or four policemen kicking and beating a man who is handcuffed and writhing on the ground. He is pleading with the officers and screaming in pain as some beat him repeatedly while the others watch.

The violent attack escalates and drags on for a seemingly eternal five minutes (the same duration as the real event), and anecdotally the user-witnesses seem to have a visceral reaction to the VR experience. The digitally animated reenactment is both realistic and disturbingly graphic, and the images are synced with the audio from the witness phone footage. The participants can walk around and use their virtual cell phones to record, as happened in the original event. In documented showings of the VR experience, it has been noted that users often feel compelled to say something, even as they realize the event is not "real." Their shocked comments intermingle and echo the real audio in which one can audibly hear "He is not resisting," "Are you getting this?," "Oh my God," and "Why are you using excessive force?" among other bystander comments.

This intermingling of recorded audio and real-time reaction by users also blurs the line between past event and present experience, further intensifying the episode. In many ways, this VR recreation is more impactful than the cell phone video still available on YouTube. While the original video footage was grainy and mostly undiscernible (but sinister), the animated 3D recreation is painfully detailed, and the feeling of presence is intense, especially when the user can feel embodied in the scene and is actively moving around and recording the action. The act of recording may mitigate the user's sense of impotence and restore agency, not to the victim but to the act of witnessing. Moreover, according to Kellie Marin, by "recording" the event as part of the VR experience, users can begin to reverse "immigration surveillance practices by enabling participants to watch back virtually" and by focusing on the migrant experience and its inhumane dimension rather than on legal or political justifications for border enforcement and militarization (41). By using the virtual cell phones, "participants can turn the surveillant eye back on the authorities to capture their violations and imagine themselves as resistant actors to dominant surveillance practices" (Marin 42).

There can be little doubt the intensification of the experience also has to do with a kind of layering of media—combining the VR environment and graphics, the audio recovered from the original cell phone files, and the material circumstances of the viewing itself—at an art installation, at a film festival, at a museum, or even in a private home. Thus in MR some media are mixed or combined, while others are layered onto reality itself, to a degree disrupting the separation of media/representation and actual life. Every one of these material, medial, and individual circumstances of viewing make for a wide array of reactions. Again, as in other VR projects, the flesh and blood participants also become enmeshed with the digital media, through their embodied avatars and through their dual embodiedness.

Midway through the *Use of Force* simulation, users are transported to a different perspective, now a look from above, standing on a pedestrian bridge that overlooks the yard. This provides another perspective on the scene from a bird's-eye view, mimicking, as Marin points out, surveillance cameras (51). But this vantage point proves equally frustrating in that bystander comments cannot make the brutality stop. Near the end of the VR experience, we see one of the officers tase Rojas and drag him into a transport vehicle, unconscious. As the scene fades, we hear one of the bystanders asking, "Where are you taking him?"

The powerful effect *Use of Force* has on viewers may partly reside in the claustrophobic nature of the event and its recreation, limited as it is to the enclosed yard, roughly five minutes in duration, so that the sheer concentration of the experience makes it ideal for VR, as de la Peña indicates: "[VR is] particularly suited to certain kinds of stories, where one significant event takes place in a defined space" (Garling). The possibility to walk around and record the event as it unfolds is also key to its impact. If during the real event at the San Ysidro port it was the presence of cell phones that allowed the documenting and eventual reporting of the atrocity committed, the VR experience uses technology to address the anti-immigration attitudes that made this tragedy possible in the first place. According to Marin, "[O]ne way to challenge narratives that emerge out of tracking, documenting, and circulating rhetorics about the 'problem' with illegal immigration and control is by using technologies to level the asymmetrical relationship that mutes immigrants' experiences" (43). Although the impact of VR as "empathy machine" on any individual user cannot be directly measured, the existence of VR projects like this one serves as a countermeasure to alter the hostile dynamic toward Latin American immigration in the United States and elsewhere. The project deploys both its intermedial layering and its immersive sense of presence to ask questions about transnational immigrant and refugee rights and the limits and limitations of border militarization and enforcement.

Carne y Arena: Immigration, Immersion, and Interactivity in Documentary VR Cinema

To gain further perspective on how intermedia and MR works can expose transnational migration and border issues, we shift focus from the work of de la Peña, a US-based Latinx journalist-filmmaker, to a VR installation by a renown Mexican filmmaker. Created in 2017, Alejandro González Iñárritu's *Carne y Arena* was inspired by real-life events at the border and informed by the filmmaker's previous movie *Babel*, and also draws heavily on Nonny de la Peña's work, including *Use of Force* (Miranda). In this imaginative and acutely intermedial MR installation, the Mexican filmmaker expands the VR medium to include the spectators' material surroundings (the soil they walk on, the air they feel, the items they carry) in addition to their virtual environment, thus creating an amalgam of the real and the virtual.[10]

It is unfeasible to categorize *Carne y Arena* in terms of any single media or genre because the piece promiscuously mixes various media and genres. Directed by Iñárritu and co-produced with the VR firm ILMxLab (a division of Lucasfilms), *Carne y Arena* is best described as expanded cinema, a work that combines installation art, VR or MR cinema, 360-video, immersive journalism, interactive theater, and performance. This cinematic VR project was a labor of love, motivated by a desire to push technical boundaries but also bring attention to a social justice issue. Iñárritu maintains that he had no expectations for making a profit, bringing the project closer to art-activism than to commercial cinema or VR. In the same vein, the filmmaker sustains that the project subordinates its technological dimension to the story's human elements, with the goal of fostering understanding across borders and nationalities by engaging viewer empathy. Echoing Iñárritu, Catherine Leen sees this goal as aligning with the sanguine expectations placed on VR, since "the enhanced technological capacities of VR in recent years mean that it has often been championed as a medium that can communicate across nations and ethnicities and offer new possibilities for understanding and exchange" (42).

Carne y Arena also serves as a counterexample to certain types of detached VR experiences that extract entertainment from violence (e.g., first-person point of view shooter VR). Iñárritu's installation has received both significant praise and also some deserved criticism. In Mexico, for instance, the cost of entry (three hundred pesos or fifteen dollars) priced the installation out of reach for many (Leen 47). While Iñárritu arguably did not wish for the piece to become a commodified museum work, *Carne y Arena* has been shown mainly at elite institutions (Cannes Film Festival, Milan's Fondazione Prada, the Los Angeles Contemporary Museum of Art, Dallas's Nasher Sculpture Center). Charges levied against the work's elitism have gone hand in hand with critiques against how it trivializes the politics of immigration or how it spectacularizes violence. Leen cogently suggests that these criticisms reductively focus on the VR middle section to the exclusion of the remainder of the installation, failing to understand how every component informs and contextualizes the spectator's affective and cognitive response (47). Considered wholistically, *Carne y Arena* becomes an enriching experience.

The ironic paradox of creating a VR piece to highlight problems in the physical world is not lost on Iñárritu. The complete title of the work, *Carne y Arena: Virtually Present, Physically Invisible*, foregrounds the very invisibility that, sadly, constitutes the undocumented migrant's reality. Although the piece is firmly focused on the US-Mexico border, Iñárritu is also calling attention to a global problem, the displacement and migration of large numbers of people for economic and political reasons, whether to the United States, Europe, or elsewhere. As he has done throughout his career (in films such as *Babel* and *Biutiful*), the Mexican cineaste deliberately links concerns about Mexican and Central and Latin American immigration more broadly to parallel situations in Spain and Europe, underscoring the interconnectedness of these issues globally and pointing out that these dislocations typically transcend national boundaries and demand global solutions. Iñárritu's work has long been associated with transnationalism, including his participation in multiple transatlantic co-productions between Spain and Mexico (*Biutiful*), but also his endeavors directing US independent productions (*21 Grams*) and his preference for transnational megastars such as Javier Bardem (Spain) and Gael García Bernal (Mexico). As Dolores Tierney argues, Iñárritu has provided alternative models for creating and producing film, financing globally but maintaining an anchor in Latin America, as "a Mexican filmmaker, working on productions outside of his native country but still working with his early collaborators and a largely Mexican and Latin American creative team: Mexican cinematographer Rodrigo Prieto [or with Mexican cinematographer Emmanuel Lubezki in *Carne y Arena*], Mexican production designer Brigitte Broch, Argentine composer Gustavo Santaolalla and Mexican screenwriter Guillermo Arriaga" (5). To his credit, Iñárritu's creative focus has remained on themes that have global reach but retain a particular concern for Mexico and Central America, such as immigration, narcotrafficking, dislocation, poverty, and labor exploitation. By taking these familiar themes to VR, the filmmaker wished to tap into immersion as a form of (political) involvement for the spectator. To increase the sense of immersion Iñárritu draws on the power of an intermedial installation that activates all the senses (using sand, wind, sound, 3D images, etc.). According to Tierney, the recourse to a multimedia installation dovetails with the filmmaker's renewed interest in a transnational pro-immigrant politics: "Iñárritu's self-identification as a political figure connected to his national group and a pan-continental identity was solidified by his next work, *Carne y Arena*, a VR art installation reproducing the migrant refugee experience which has been circulating globally" (6).

There are various antecedents to *Carne y Arena* that predate even *Use of Force*, comprising a first wave of VR narratives from the late 1980s and early 1990s, at a time when a fledgling VR field was the purview of gaming industry research or university-based scientific and military applications. Projects such as *Angels* (1989) by Nicole Stenger and *Dancing with the Virtual Dervish* (1994) by Diane Gromala and Yacov Sharir investigated the potential for embodied experiences and immersion through VR and multimedia. *Placeholder* (1992) was another groundbreaking narrative intermedia piece that combined installation art and VR, a clear precursor to *Carne y Arena*. Directed by Brenda Laurel and Rachel Strickland, *Placeholder* recreated several natural environments in 3D VR, adding also spatialized sound and speech, as well as animated characters. The virtual "natural" space could be visited concurrently by two participants using HMDs. The level of interaction was unprecedented for the early 1990s: participants could walk in the virtual space, interact with other participants, and use their hands to move virtual objects. The piece had a decidedly experimental art bent, and rather than realism (mimetic imitation of nature) it sought for its users to identify with a sense of place and with the natural world. In the words of the project directors:

> One of our objectives with *Placeholder* was to experiment with capturing actual places—in the attitude of landscape painting traditions or documentary cinema, for example—using video and audio recorded on location as the raw material for constructing the virtual environment. It must be emphasized that we were not concerned with achieving a high degree of sensory realism—something bristling with polygons and MIPs [Mood Induction Procedures] that might induce a perfect audiovisual delusion of sticking your head in the "real" waterfall. No, it gets more slippery than that. What we have really set out to capture or reproduce is just the simplest "sense of place." (Laurel et al.)

I shall return to how the question of "sensory realism" was resolved in *Carne y Arena* later, as the decision to render animated figures rather than film actual people was a technical necessity, but any loss of realism was offset by the high definition of the animation and the multiplicity of sensory stimuli achieved through a layering of media.

Another direct antecedent to Iñárritu's VR piece includes Lawrence Paul Yuxweluptun's *Inherent Rights, Vision Rights* (1992), an installation that exposed white settler colonialism by placing viewers' avatars inside an indigenous longhouse during a (virtual) ceremony, forcing the spectator-participants to assume their positionality (as intruders) vis-à-vis the sacred indigenous space. As with Iñárritu's piece, the users are confronted by ethical dilemmas through the immersive experience and ideally improve their cultural awareness. More recent works include the numerous journalism projects by Nonny de la Peña, such as her installation *Project Syria* (2014) shown at the Victoria and Albert Museum, a piece that locates the user virtually in a Syrian refugee camp. Like *Carne y Arena*, all these projects fundamentally sought to engage with spectators affectively by placing them in situations that bolstered awareness of alterity, literally in the other's moccasins.

Carne y Arena's stated objective is to generate empathy and support for the plight of those undocumented immigrants who are forced by dire conditions to face death as they cross various international borders in Central America, the Sonoran Desert, and the US-Mexico wall, and enter the United States hoping for a better life. Most migrants hail from Mexico or Central America, some even further away, as proof of complex transnational refugee flows, a point showcased in Iñárritu's piece. One challenge to immerse spectators into VR is the difficulty in bridging the distance between real and virtual, or the knowledge that what one is experiencing is not "real" outside of the constructed virtual space. Iñárritu's installation seeks to disrupt the spectator's sensation of double situatedness, or what Ross calls a "double embodiment"—the sense of being at once within the illusion and at a safe locale, in their chair at home or at a theater ("Simulation" 1715). This mental leap is achieved by preparing the spectator in several ways prior to entering the virtual experience proper—transforming the spectator into a receptive participant. The exhibit elicits this sympathetic viewer by providing contextual information about the crossing experience through printed and video material in the preexhibit area, and again after the VR experience is over, but also by placing material objects recovered at the border in key areas. Thus, the tripartite installation is bookended by physical experiences (an introductory vestibule and a "debriefing" gallery space at egress), with the VR experience situated in the middle, facilitating reflection before and after the more visceral VR segment, but also blending the real with the virtual to somewhat mitigate the feeling of "double situatedness."

In the VR section, as the barefoot spectator enters (through a small door) a large strange and darkened space that is entirely dedicated to the illusion itself, they begin to experience the real world receding (akin to entering a cathedral). As the intermedial layering is increased and more materials and sensations are included—the sand underfoot (real), the wind (real but simulated with large fans and through sound effects), the noise of helicopters and sirens (surround audio from actual sources)—the illusion begins to fuse with the real sensorium, and the spectator becomes fully immersed. We might consider the piece as MR, given its annealing of material and virtual elements, delineating a format that blurs "the boundaries between performance, spectatorship, and real and virtual environments, and piloted interactive VR technology and hybrid environments that merge 360 video with real-time three-dimensional computer graphics" (Cegys and Weijdom

81). The large radius of movement allowed by the space augments the reality level, as does the interactive sophistication of the installation. Current technologies that foment realism include "advanced locomotive systems, such as omnidirectional treadmills and footwear, and AI driven interactive character design" (Ross, "Simulation" 1717). However, Ross adds that "the limitations of these current technologies mean the viewer is almost always aware of certain constrictions on their movement and their inability to fully interact with the virtual world" (1717). Even within these limitations and the predominance of the visual, Ross argues that *Carne y Arena* surpasses other screen media (film, television, Internet-based media) by engaging with a multisensorium. As he sees it, "even when 'expanded' VR works provide extra sensory input such as actual sand-covered floors and dusty backpacks in Iñárritu's *Carne y Arena* . . . the content delivered by the HMD determines how the user feels present in the virtual world" ("Virtual Reality's" 298). But, argues Ross, the power of the visual coupled with the auditory and the sense that the action is not limited within a frame intensify presence, so that "within this context, the optical illusion plays a significant role in creating an enhanced multisensory experience that builds upon the synesthetic qualities evident in much screen media . . . but with new implications for how we might 'feel' our way through diegetic space now that distance from the screen is seemingly dissolved" (298).

As I mentioned, one factor that perhaps detracts from the reality effect and immersive possibilities is the decision to use computer-generated (animated) versions of the actual migrants—their motion captured using bodysuits and transferred to the animation—rather than actual 3D images of the migrants themselves (as with 360-degree film). The use of filmed 3D material that one could walk around remains technically impractical, especially since the mobile spectator needs to see everything from multiple perspectives, whereas in 3D cinema the spectator can only see from the camera's 360-degree perspective. In *Carne y Arena* the computer images can be continuously rendered in real time as the spectator moves about, which is impossible with filmed images. The use of performance capture somewhat mitigates the lessened naturalism of the rendered migrants, since their movement and gestures were directly recorded, the faces and expressions of the animated characters were carefully modeled after real migrants, and their actions were based on the stories they recalled.

A detailed analysis of the sequence of events that constitute *Carne y Arena* clarifies how the centrality of intermediality and the ways "onboarding" (entering the VR space) and "offboarding" (exiting the VR space) can enhance reality effects and verisimilitude. The piece has been defined by

Iñárritu himself as a tripartite installation or a three-act "play," divided into physical, virtual, and intellectual segments, each relying on various media and each combining real and virtual elements (Martínez Cano 171).

I experienced *Carne y Arena* on April 2, 2022, in Dallas, at the Nasher Sculpture Center, one of the last venues where it was shown (the last was at the Omaha Kaneko Art Museum later the same year), more than four years after it premiered and was awarded a Special Achievement Oscar for best VR cinema, a discretionary award the Academy grants on very rare occasions for "especially deserving" projects.[11] What follows are my reactions and critical observations after visiting the Dallas installation.

The so-called onboarding or lead-up to the virtual reality piece begins as one arrives at the installation site. This first preparatory segment provides basic knowledge that will aid the participant to decode the "visceral" part of the piece, but also begins to set a somber mood. Outside the entrance to the pavilion hosting *Carne y Arena*'s Dallas exhibition (located in the 1936 Texas Centennial Exposition grounds), we are greeted by a large poster of a red, luminescent heart superimposed on a landscape of the desert, somewhere in the southwest of the United States or the north of Mexico (see fig. 5.6). This heart is presented as a cartographic metaphor for the border and

Figure 5.6. *Carne y Arena*. The author in front of Dallas exhibit. *Source*: Photo by author, April 2022.

for the cleft identity of the immigrant and the exile. Divided by a dashed line indicating the frontier, one side of the heart is marked with the word "U.S.," the other, "T.H.E.M." For Leen, "the image of the heart reinforces the idea of a shared humanity that transcends borders," but the line also marks a painful division (44). The implicit message suggests the artificiality of a border that injuriously separates a space that is organically whole, just as a heart cannot be severed without damage or death for the organism. Thus, even before entering the hall, the spectator can begin to reflect on the inhumanity of borders that arbitrarily separate us from our neighbors.

Entering a cavernous hangar-like space (subdivided into various smaller areas), I am greeted by staff members. At the outset I am directed to leave all valuables, including jacket and cell phone, in a small locker, then proceed to sign a waiver acknowledging that the extreme realism of the VR experience can lead to a variety of issues, including nausea, vertigo, seizures, and also emotional and physical discomfort. The darkness of the space and dire warnings in the waiver set a mood of apprehension, one that will dovetail with the immigrant journey the spectator is about to experience. D'Aloia has astutely observed that these initial requisites also "inform the mental and physical disposition of the visitor, like preliminary rites: the waiver as acknowledging awareness, the coat check room as stripping, and the passage through various spaces and waiting outside as an introduction."

Still in the foyer, there is a segment of corrugated metal border fence on display and a plaque in English and Spanish explaining that the wall hails from Arizona and the type is known as landing mat, recycled from helicopter touchdown pads dating to the Vietnam War. The wall piece also enacts a thinly veiled critique against the Trump administration's efforts to extend the border wall, so that from the outset a link is established between militarization, war, and the border. After a brief wait, I was allowed to proceed through the remaining rooms. In an initial small space, I read the artist's statement and learned various bits of information about what led Iñárritu to create the project and the ethnographic process he followed to document the migrants' journey. In the statement he asserts that he wanted the migrants' stories to be more than a statistic, "but would instead be seen, felt, heard and experienced."

After reading the statement, I proceeded through a metal door into another enclosed space labeled "Depósitio" [deposit] as if for objects, or cadavers, or even inmates. Crossing that door, one enters a more sensory-based part of the installation, although we are not yet in the VR segment. It is an antiseptic white metallic space, a small, windowless room that feels like an institutional space or the interior of a storage container, illuminated by harsh neon and with no decor save for some barren steel benches. Here and there one can see worn and mismatched shoes and clothing strewn about, clearly the discarded belongings of migrants (see fig. 5.7). A sign confirms that the items "were found in the Arizona desert" where "over 10,000 migrants have died attempting to cross." These worn out, dirty objects represent a direct link to reality, and I am tempted to touch them. Iñárritu repeatedly emphasizes tactility and its connection to lived experience: "You are touching the life of a person through an object" (Miranda).

The room is cold and inhospitable, the barren walls evoke the uncomfortably cold holding cells (*hieleras*) used by Border Patrol to temporarily detain migrants as they await processing (Miranda). A dark mood—oppressive, somber, funerary—is pervasive. Through a loudspeaker I hear a disembodied voice that states, "Put your shoes and socks in the locker," also reiterated by a bilingual sign above said locker. After placing my footwear in a small metal locker, a flashing red light and jarringly loud siren ushers me into the next room. This new space is significantly vast, pitch black, very

Figure 5.7. *Carne y Arena* material signs of immigrant tragedies. *Source*: Photo by author, April 2022.

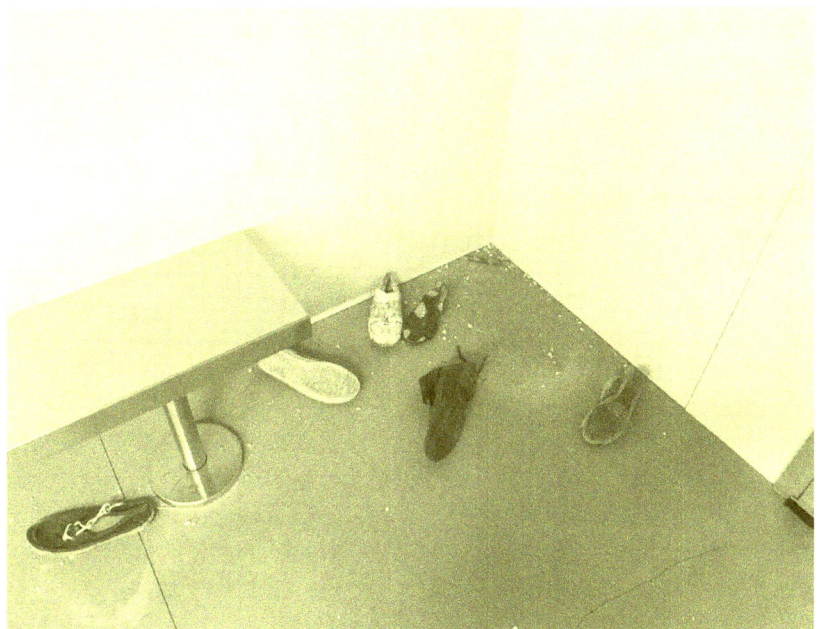

cold. A red-orange band of light all along the wall eerily slices the space in two. Only one participant is allowed into the space, although there are two other rooms like it within the exhibit. I walk in barefoot, feeling the rough sand, dirt, and gravelly surface, as well as a cold wind-like effect created by fans. In the center of the room, there are two attendants with assorted equipment. They provide me with a backpack, an Oculus Rift headset, and headphones. The attendants sternly tell me that I can wander anywhere in the VR space, but if I stray too close to the walls, they guide me back. While even a gentle tug within the VR experience can be disorienting and dislodge a participant from the immersive sense of presence, this is a reminder about the physical and technological limits of the medium and the persistence of double embodiment, the sensation of being both in the virtual space and in the physical world as well.

Now begins the intense experiential segment, meant to trigger a feeling of closeness or empathy with the subjects depicted. Once the VR headset is donned, the first awareness is that of being in a sparsely vegetated desert in the predawn hours. The stark landscape was captured by the cinematographer in the Sonoran Desert—it is a digital composite of 360-degree video and VR. As I cross this expanse, alone, I can hear audio of the wind and crunching sand, feeling its texture beneath my bare feet. Then a group of migrants appears from the scrub, speaking in hushed tones in Spanish. Their figures, though highly naturalistic, are recognizable as animated avatars modeled on real individuals. The scenes that follow are a reenactment assembled from the journeys of migrants interviewed by Iñárritu, distilled into a single composite experience.

The migrants are mainly women, children, and older individuals. An injured woman begs to turn back and is ordered by the coyote to keep moving. After a short while, the wind begins to increase both in the VR space (where sand is flying, as is everyone's hair), and in the real space (where powerful fans are kicking up actual dust). Suddenly, blinding search lights bathe the scene. The deafening sound of a low-flying helicopter surrounds our location, its threatening rotors intensifying the windstorm (physically felt from the powerful fan blasts). Fully engulfed by sound, a feeling of presence overwhelms me, proving that "the sensory disturbance that the visitor experiences through the carefully calibrated sound leads to a lack of a sense of security and feelings of vulnerability" (Leen 46).

Several Border Patrol cars quickly converge on the exposed group, including the participant (me). Significant confusion ensues amidst a cacophony of languages. The officers, wielding weapons and attack dogs, forcefully demand that the group kneel. In the chaos, a man, perhaps the coyote, is shot while attempting to flee. The experience becomes so intense that, reportedly, participants often kneel alongside the virtual migrants. Indeed "there are reports of a myriad reactions to the piece, with some visitors hiding behind the guards, others trying to help the migrants, and still others falling to their knees" (Leen 46). The officers then handcuff and gruffly question the group about their identity and about the coyote's whereabouts. Other officers interrogate some unaccompanied minors. Positionality for the participant can shift between that of an uncomfortable witness, a detached observer, and a fellow traveler with the migrants (my own experience was in flux between these throughout the piece). There is also a degree of spectacle to *Carne y Arena*, as one might momentarily revel in its technical and aesthetic achievement and forget its origin in real suffering.

At this point the scene fades suddenly to a different space. The migrants are sitting around a long table sharing a meal. Then, in another shift the table transforms into a raft crammed with people. The rough waters eventually toss several migrants overboard. Is this a reference to crossing the Rio Grande, or the Suchate river that separates Guatemala and Mexico? Or is it the Mediterranean, a common site for many migrant tragedies? Given Iñárritu's desire to tap into the universal angst of migration, it may stand in for all water crossings. The oneiric scenes of the meal and boat tragedy speak to the sorrow of leaving family and the perils of traversing borders, humanizing the migrants for the spectator-participant.

This melancholic and somewhat phantasmagoric interlude makes the sudden return to the action-packed desert scene even more jarring. Suddenly, I am back under the harsh helicopter light as the migrants are roughly interrogated. The ghostly trace of a human heart briefly appears in the sky, its red tissue beating. It is the image from the poster, only imperceptibly visible for an instant, a subliminal reminder of our common humanity. Amidst the scene's mounting tension, I (the participant) am also unexpectedly thrust into the position of a migrant, confronted by a screaming officer who points his weapon and demands that I place my hands in the air. In this uncanny turn, the virtual officer seems to be aiming his gun directly at me, looking into my eyes from only a few paces away. Shifting location seems to elicit a response from the trooper, who seemingly moves along with me. After a few climactic seconds, as the confrontation begins to feel unbearable, everything fades again. It is dawn, the participant is alone in the desert, the migrants are gone. There is a small yellow towel hanging on a mesquite tree, and beneath it, some white shoes—this is a reference to a real-life story Iñárritu heard about a woman who was left behind after breaking her ankle in the desert. Her little son gave her the towel to protect her from the dust. When she was found weeks later, only the towel and shoes remained, everything else was bones (Miranda). The reference is only available after doing research on the piece, but Iñárritu includes it nonetheless as a tribute. After a few moments the staff takes the VR helmet off and that concludes this component of the experience. Although it only lasted seven minutes, it seemed longer.

After collecting shoes and personal items, and shaking the sand off my feet, I enter another darkened space. This is the "offboarding" component of the program, the section where reflection, analysis, and reckoning should take place. Here embodiment is replaced, in other words, by cognition. In this final room the only source of light is provided by screens placed in nine wall niches. Each screen contains an HD video image of one of the migrants from the VR film (one screen has two), and one has a Border Patrol officer. All the videos are static close-ups of faces, the only imperceptible movement an occasional blink. At certain intervals, the image blurs and a text narrating each harrowing trek appears superimposed on the migrants' faces (see fig. 5.8). The silent migrants look directly at the viewer, their

Figure 5.8. HD video testimonial by migrants. *Source*: Photo by author, April 2022.

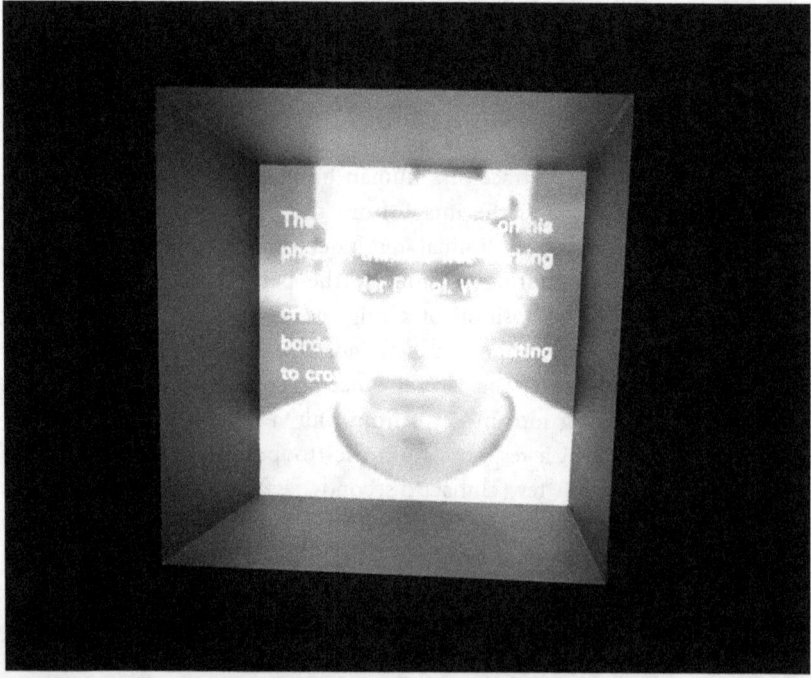

stoic expressions filmed precisely on November 6, 2016, the day Trump was elected (Leen 45). These faces and stories are meant as *testimonios*, first-person accounts of a gut-wrenching journey, its causes and effects. For Leen, they are "a testimony of extreme hardship and suffering but also of endurance and remarkable courage" (47). Each of the migrants individuated by name (Lina, Carmen, Manuel, Luis, Amaru, Selena, Francisco, Yoni, Jessica) as well as the Border Patrol officer (John). The stories shed retroactive light on the VR experience, clarifying why some spoke English while others did not, why some spoke only Mayan language, why some children were unaccompanied by adults, and what their previous journeys had been like. Their stories are compelling and, sadly, familiar.

Underscoring the transnational aspect of cross-border migration, the migrants hail from Mexico, Guatemala, El Salvador, and Honduras. The suffering portrayed in migrants' faces and by the details of their lives through these video portraits proves more stirring for some participants than the VR segment. Lina, a woman in her fifties, left Guatemala in the 1990s after her husband was killed during the long Civil War. After a dangerous crossing she reached Los Angeles and became a domestic worker, saving money to bring her children to the United States. It took her twenty years to save enough to reunite with her youngest child, by then already twenty-three (Ohanesian). Another migrant, Carmen, speaks about pretending to be a lesbian to avoid being raped by the police who apprehended her. Other stories are equally poignant, making the participant wonder what sort of nation would deny entry to individuals who have endured so much. John, a Border Patrol officer in his sixties, asserts that nobody could lack empathy toward those crossing the border, yet he does not see the connection between his job and the unyielding political stance that would refuse compassionate entry for even dire refugee cases.

There is admittedly a conflict between claims of transnationalism and globalism at the heart of Iñárritu's filmmaking, and that constitute the essence of his intermedial projects, and the very concrete experience of a national border, a physical obstruction that is porous only for those who possess significant socioeconomic privilege. Nevertheless, the experience of borders as barriers is itself a global phenomenon: whether a Syrian or Ukrainian refugee fleeing war, a Moroccan or sub-Saharan migrant seeking economic opportunity, or a Central American fleeing violence and poverty, the barriers they encounter, manmade and natural, represent the same contradiction between global connectivity and economic disparity. Iñárritu's VR installation aims to undermine the rigidity of such borders, to break down some of their defenses and make their crossing an experience that can be, to some degree, shared by those who are on the privileged side of the line (and arguably by increasing awareness, arriving at pro-immigrant political action). The border as a dashed line separating "U.S." from "T.H.E.M." (to cite the exhibition poster) begins to dematerialize as we recognize the commonality of all human experience, but also as we learn to empathize with the particular circumstances of the dispossessed. It is the potential for that reflection to occur (perhaps even in those who hold power) that the radicality of this piece resides—more so than in its technical or aesthetic achievements.

Necessarily (given these lofty goals), the VR segment of the installation is firmly based on real-life experiences, and the people depicted are actual migrants. Iñárritu met them and conducted interviews at Casa Libre, a migrant shelter in downtown Los Angeles. The process of creating the exhibit constituted a reenactment: Iñárritu first rehearsed with the migrants in a theater workshop and later on set while filming in the Sonoran Desert. The migrants played themselves, or a version of themselves, wearing the same clothes they used during their crossing and repeating similar actions (Leen 39). The commingling of media (intermediality) is key to the entire exhibit, including the VR segment—which is really MR, if we account for the sand, the wind, and other physical materials—echoing what Paul Cegys and Joris Weijdom write about a similar VR piece, "Virtual Reality technology can be harnessed by a mixed reality performance design, which includes both the material and virtual environment, creating a complex stratigraphy of intermedial textures and visual dramaturgies that coexist inside, outside and in between perceptual realities" (81). Iñárritu relies on intermediality to accentuate realism, and as a result he hopes to foster empathy. *Carne y Arena*, according to the filmmaker, was conceptualized as a "multi-layered, tripartite work" drawing on "part theater, part documentary, and part-physical installation, it's a virtual installation—it's many different arts combined" (Iñárritu qtd. in Leen 39).

But whether MR or VR can trigger empathetic responses to a greater degree than other media (or at all) remains an open question.[12] As D'Aloia puts it, Iñárritu's intent is "to experiment with VR technology in order to explore the human condition in an attempt to break the dictatorship of the frame, within which things are just observed, and claim the space to allow the visitor to go through a direct experience walking in the immigrants' feet, under their skin, and into their hearts." Undoubtedly, for some spectators this experience achieves the presence and affect necessary to immerse them in the event and convert them into participants of sorts. D'Aloia describes how the installation generates presence, "largely based on the virtual presence of a physically invisible spectator, who is nonetheless engaged corporeally and affectively through simulations and haptic means. In *Carne y Arena*, the subject's separation from real space is compelling, and there is a strong sense of presence through which the work places the visitor in the midst of distant events" (D'Aloia). For this critic, not only the VR section but the installation's onboarding and offboarding components, from the signing of the waiver to the final testimonials, forge a powerful experience that "radicalizes the potential for engagement" (D'Aloia). Other critics qualify the piece as "profoundly affecting," both visually and aurally (Leen 46). By transcending the cinematic frame, according to D'Aloia, the spectator becomes an actor in a "scenic-performative space similar to that of a theater." Similarly, Cegys and Weijdom observe that these types of installation MR works create a "profound sense of embodiment, and intermedial performance design, [which] can expand the field of scenography and imbue the performative act with new relations between creator(s) and experiencer(s)" (98). There are, however, shortcomings in the piece for D'Aloia and other critics. While the immersion effect is powerfully achieved, there is negligible actual interaction—the participant is neither seen by the virtual migrants nor able to affect the outcome or participate in any significant way beyond observing. Even the climax, when the participant is directly addressed by the Border Patrol officer, is in reality a clever trick, not a real instance of interactivity. It is an illusion that the avatar can see or respond to prevent our escape.

The main mode of the piece therefore remains spectatorial, according to D'Aloia, with spectators becoming "powerless witnesses" rather than active participants. Additionally, the fact that the spectator can see neither their virtual feet nor hands (unlike in some other games or cinematic VR experiences) triggers "a paradoxical conflict between tactile stimulation and visual perception." This conflict might precipitate the VR double embodiment discussed earlier, the sense of being both there (presence) and also elsewhere (in the "real" physical world). The inclusion of tactile (haptic) strategies like sand and wind effects enlists presence, but the invisibility of the participant and the lack of interaction counters it, resulting in a disembodied observer of the events, or one that oscillates between presence and absence.

The seesawing between presence and distance is illustrated by the aforementioned moment when, at the end of the VR segment, the spectator is directly interpellated by the Border Patrol officer, and the sense of "safe" distance, at least for a few moments, vanishes. Then spectators become integrated, embodied, and present—becoming participants who, as anecdotally reported, will follow the officer's orders and raise their hands. But the illusion vanishes quickly, leaving the participant stranded between the real and the virtual. While the debate about the work's empathetic potential may not have a definitive resolution (perhaps it is a subjective matter), when taken as a whole the installation successfully communicates its pro-immigrant message. According to Leen, *Carne y Arena* is "an activist work that calls into question the persistently negative portrayal of migrants by offering an alternative reality based on the migrants' own lived experiences and suturing the audience into this traumatic world" (52).

For some spectators, a reaction of empathy (or a cognitive realization rather than an emotional response, or a combination of both) materializes with the reflection that takes place in the last section, when confronted with the nearly static cinematic portraits of the migrants and their superimposed stories. I concur with D'Aloia's suggestion that, while "the concreteness of somatic perception in itself is by no means a precondition for empathy," it is the nonvirtual testimonial images and text that consolidate "[the] immediate experience with the acquisition of a memory that is now truly shared." These same offboarding experiences, images, explanatory text, and contextual information allow for an intellectual engagement with the material that goes beyond any strictly emotional or empathetic reaction. Seen from that vantage, VR is a continuation of other expanded cinema experiments that already suggest their capacity to trigger empathy based on their aesthetic and thematic construction, rather than the material characteristics of their medium. Similarly, VR is the endpoint of a lengthy media history in which the frame has constantly come into question, been broken and stretched, taken to the streets, and altogether dispensed with, as we saw in the intermedial experiments of the Argentine Grupo Goethe or the work of the video artists we examined in previous chapters (similar efforts were undertaken by painters, photographers, etc.). As various critics opined, VR's relative success does not entail the replacement or "death" of cinema but suggests that the two media will coexist, comingle, and at times hybridize in films that may, for example, insert VR sequences within a more traditional flat screen experience to punctuate that portion of a work. And we shall see more MR installation cinema, where material and virtual media will be used to create a hybrid reality. The technical skill and resources these projects will demand shall also ensure future transnational collaborations and themes, many of them between Spain and Latin America.

Coda

Future Trends in Experimental Cinema and Audiovisual Technology across the Luso-Hispanic Atlantic

Introduction: New Trends for a New Era?

In his comprehensive study about contemporary Mexican cinema, *Screening Neoliberalism*, Ignacio Sánchez Prado reasonably concludes that "twenty-first century Mexican film is no longer a vehicle for the expression of the national, or a form of culture that may be used for the cultural and social democratization of the country" (226).[1] I find myself energetically agreeing with the first half of Sánchez Prado's assertion, at least if we think of the "national" exclusively in terms of what it has signified until the onset of the twenty-first century. I would extend that statement to include other national cinemas from throughout the Luso-Hispanic Atlantic that are also losing their "national" specificity. As to the second part of Sánchez Prado's assertion, I am less fatalistic about the inexorable dwindling of avenues for democratization found in this particular cultural form, at least when it comes to its emerging and less industry-driven variants such as cell phone cinema, amateur video, and other formats cropping up in social media platforms such as YouTube or TikTok. I have a similar hopeful outlook toward low-budget films screened in local and online festivals that still celebrate a DIY approach to making movies and harbor interests that do not merely reduce to profit. These amateur cultural forms still hold the promise of greater access, promote certain democratic perspectives, and, arguably, infuse film with a modicum of diversity and inclusion in terms of what is represented and who is doing the representing. I am not so naive as to ignore the less desirable aspects to these projects and processes and recognize that views on "the democratizing potential of the Internet" can be fueled by "utopic desire" (Hudson and Zimmermann 61). There is no denying the reality of the corporatization of the Internet, its manipulation by bad actors, the proliferation of surveillance, deep fakes, inequality, and so on. But it is also certain that the new digital media formats with their ease of production and the mobility of cell phone cameras have shifted us away from large industrial cinema's single perspective and toward appreciating "the complexities of life's meanings from multiple points of view and perspectives" (Hudson and Zimmermann 134–35).

Similarly, some virtual reality (VR) cinema projects, although certainly not all, place citizen journalism and social issues front and center, and although VR headsets are still cost-prohibitive, there are signs that access to this format is expanding in Latin America and Spain. By the same token, neoliberal interests are also tapping into this potentially lucrative expanded reality market as the metaverse becomes a tangible fact across the Luso-Hispanic Atlantic, exemplified by the activity of US-based tech multinationals such as Meta (erstwhile Facebook), or the less-known NVIDIA Corporation, a global leader in software, artificial intelligence (AI), and gaming design. These and other profit-driven corporations are investing in education programs in the region to foment future AI development as well as initiatives that could lead to greater participation in VR, augmented reality (AR), and mixed reality (MR) across the region. Driven by self-interest, they are doing so in light of projections for a four hundred percent increase over the next decade for the VR market in Latin America, with Mexico and Brazil leading the way with the fastest growth and adoption of these novel "cinematic" technologies (Contreras). While these global corporations' intentions are transparently financial and self-promotional, there might be a glimmer of hope as they partner with higher education institutions and think tanks throughout the Luso-Hispanic Atlantic, including the Institute for Research on Internet and Society in Rio de Janeiro, the C-Minds Eon Resilience Lab in Mexico City, or the University of San Andrés in Buenos Aires, as well as various nonprofit organizations such as the Immersive Learning Research Network in Ecuador. Such joint research offers the possibility for a partial redirection of tech work toward education, philanthropy, and the public good. These tech companies' stated objectives in the region are fomenting grassroots projects and sparking creative potential in the development of immersive technologies, as well as democratizing access to the metaverse (Contreras). Although the entanglement of neoliberal tech giants with the field of education is concerning for various reasons, including the way that these emerging technologies will likely exacerbate existing divides along class, gender, racial, and ethnic lines, some benefits might be derived from these types of public-private partnerships as well.

The initial VR development programs being pursued through partnerships between universities and research institutes with the backing of major corporations are being touted as following a "technology for humanity" approach that places human rights and ethics at the center of their plans to develop VR, AR, and AI projects throughout the region. While it is necessary to be guardedly skeptical about these corporations' intent to deliver on such lofty goals (given that they are primarily profit-driven), and to become aware of the myriad ways the metaverse will amplify and reproduce the very neoliberal practices and mechanisms that have been ubiquitous in the physical world, there is a potential that expanded reality (including AR, VR, and MR) and AI might improve lives and increase connections among disparate groups and nationalities.

Regardless of their beneficial and/or detrimental effects, these technologies represent a shift away from the national and toward transnational and even fully deterritorialized exchanges of people, experiences, and information. Increasingly the virtual spaces promoted through VR and AR are divorced from the nation-state, populated by avatars, and gathering individuals who share common interests and affinities rather than identifying primarily through national origin. Instead, nationality, or more likely the multiple nationalities held by the many transnational subjects working in the technology sector, whether voluntary expats, immigrants, or displaced individuals, becomes one of the less visible affiliations driving these group formations and alliances. At the same time, creators and artists still retain their links to the physical world and experience a sense of belonging to a local and even to a (diffuse) national culture, as we saw in the works I analyzed in chapter 5, so that the local, the national, and the transnational remain constantly shifting dimensions in these cultural products, as they are in the fluid identities of their creators.

Next, I would like to examine some of the more salient experimental cinematic technologies, those that are most likely to become prominent across the Luso-Hispanic Atlantic in the coming decades and that will accentuate the increasingly intermedial and transnational character of the arts in the region—these might be the cinema of tomorrow, in other words. Likewise, the purpose of this coda is to conclude the book by providing a succinct glimpse into these formats that I did not have an opportunity to examine in greater depth in the preceding pages but that I believe complete the panorama of new cinematic formats taking hold across the Luso-Hispanic Atlantic. I selected four emerging video technologies: 360-degree cinema (an economic version of VR I briefly mentioned in chapter 5), machinima and other computer-generated imagery (CGI)-animated films, TikTok cinematic work (as exemplary of short online video platforms), and finally AI-generated video and film. This is just a sampling among various new forms and formats that are becoming available to moving image creators in Latin America and Spain, but it suffices to indicate the expanding creativity and hybridity we can find throughout the region's audiovisual arts in the twenty-first century.

360-Degree Cinema

Speaking directly to the local challenges to implement the latest cinematic technologies in the region, cost is most often the principal limiting factor. This is the case, for example, when it comes to complex VR cinema projects such as the ones I examined earlier in this book, which require sophisticated animation, large teams of programmers and designers, and expensive equipment, as well as considerable initial investment. But there have been other successful options to create a "poor" version of VR, which can be associated with the lengthy "make do" history of cinema in Latin America and with a tradition that has evolved from Third Cinema's "imperfect cinema" to the Brazilian "aesthetics of hunger" to the "good enough" aesthetics of cell phone cinema and so on. I am referring to 360-degree cinema, which has been considerably easier to implement across the region thanks to the development of special and relatively affordable cameras for surround filming. Not surprisingly, 360-degree cinema has been particularly favored by a recent variant of social issue immersive journalism that places a high premium on immediacy, and the format has begun to make its presence felt at smaller film festivals and via online distribution. Directed by the young Ecuadorian filmmaker Juan Pablo Urgilés using 360-degree technology, *Cruzar* (*On the Other Side*, also *Cross*, 2020) is a prime example of this type of work, which I briefly mentioned in chapter 5. *Cruzar* was co-funded by the United Nations High Commissioner for Refugees (UNHCR) and the European Union with the purpose of raising awareness about migrants and refugees from throughout Latin America, and to justify maintaining emergency assistance funding levels (UNHCR). This collaboration between multiple Latin American countries (Venezuela, Ecuador, Colombia) and the European

Union illustrates the by now familiar transnationalism of immersive cinema, while highlighting the potential of these projects to also bring attention to local and regional issues such as the Venezuelan migrant crisis—local issues that at the same time affect multiple nations and have a resonance for similar problems across the globe. *Cruzar*, for example, documents the story of an economic migrant named Arianna who leaves Venezuela and traverses the Colombian territory to eventually reach Ecuador in order to pursue her dreams of accessing educational opportunities and building a better life. These are the dreams of economic migrants anywhere, making the movie simultaneously of local (Venezuela), regional (Ecuador, Venezuela, Colombia), and global relevance. To grant them voice and agency in the filmmaking process, several of the featured migrants were incorporated into the film crew as assistants, advisers, and even co-decision-makers with the team of professional filmmakers. As I discussed in chapter 5 with Nonny de la Peña's and Alejandro González Iñárritu's VR projects, this film also seeks to access a presumed reserve of spectatorial empathy by bringing to the attention of audiences the travails of migrants, refugees, asylum seekers, and, more broadly, the displaced. As with VR, the enveloping nature of the 360-degree experience arguably intensifies the sense of being "there" and in that way seeks to better engage viewer affect. Proponents of these projects believe that the empathetic potential exists whether the work is experienced with a headset or through a more accessible but decidedly less immersive method, such as via a cell phone video that allows users to manually rotate the image and see it from various viewpoints. Critics counter that the multiperspectivism and capacity to navigate distracts viewers from the center of the narrative action in the films, considering their 360-vision a gimmicky liability rather than an asset. In truth, while these pieces encourage a different kind of viewing that allows greater freedom, the attention still seems drawn to the main action, and the rest of the enveloping scenario becomes a backdrop. It also encourages multiple viewings because one wishes to catch details missed during the first experience.

Other 360-degree films, such as the Cuban production *Bembé* (2017) by filmmakers Patricia Díaz and Marcos Louit, are aimed at raising awareness about Afro-Cuban heritage and traditions by portraying Yoruba rituals such as *bembé* that combine percussion music, dance, and trance practices. *Bembé* is an observational documentary meant for both internal and external consumption, rescuing neglected island traditions but also promoting its culture for tourism purposes—and arguably as a distraction from some of the island's troubling political and economic issues. Projects such as *Cruzar* and *Bembé* illustrate a format that is still in development and unsure of its place, as these immersive movies and technologies explore various arenas, from educational programs to journalism to business and profit-driven enterprises to pure entertainment, and even to activist and consciousness-raising projects that seek to have a greater humanitarian impact on society and align with what used to be the exclusive purview of social documentary filmmaking.

In addition to pursuing these industry- and academic-driven efforts at 360-(VR)-cinema and emerging formats like cell phone movies, filmmakers throughout the Luso-Hispanic Atlantic have also been working with other new formats, as spectators become more actively engaged and intrigued by interactive "experiences" rather than static viewing practices associated with traditional film viewership. The increasingly obsolete darkened theater screening is a collective experience of a bygone era, as theorized by Raymond Bellour and others. As interest in new technologies of display and their playful dimension grows, narratives become more gamified, which can entail greater immersion, and, in the eyes of some, might facilitate a participatory experience. This immersive storytelling approach to VR sets up a contrast between the idea of "experimental" as it applies to the technologies themselves, still in a developmental phase, and "experimental" as it applies to radical forms, content, and ideas (as works acquire a certain avant-garde and politically progressive valence). While these immersive cinematic technologies might be at the edge of what's possible in terms of hardware, they often embrace a typically commercial and traditionalist angle to narrative content. Thus immersive technologies are being introduced to narrative storytelling for the primary purpose of enveloping spectators in the story world, to create the sense of being there in ways that are expected to be significantly more engaging than classical flat-screen cinema. But they do so by creating conventional narratives that follow standard linear trajectories and do not necessarily represent a progressive stance (formally or politically). There is, however, a value to their status as emerging technologies; that is to say, their newness makes them "experimental" at this point in time, and their potential for contestation remains in flux—they can disrupt existing expectations and open new avenues for the cinematic arts even if they do not actively seek contestation. What is apparent is that spectators seek a greater degree of agency and participation in their access to contemporary audiovisual technology, beyond the role of mere consumers or passive viewership. In the next section, I will examine various animated formats that have gathered momentum in the Luso-Hispanic Atlantic region and that illustrate both the potential to integrate local concerns into the works and the possibility for users to become co-creators and claim some agency in the filmmaking process.

Machinima and Other CGI-Animated Cinema

Animated films have had a presence in Latin America since at least the Argentine film *El Apóstol* (1917) [The Apostle], a stop-motion political satire animated with cutout figures, by early pioneers Quirino Cristiani and Federico Valle, a film that has regrettably disappeared. In Spain, the oldest recorded case is the also lost animated short with the politically incorrect title *El apache de Londres* (1915) [The London Apache], from an unknown filmmaker (Tirado 145). Much has changed in the interim in the region's animated cinema. The contemporary scene includes notable recent works by acclaimed filmmakers, such as Guillermo del Toro's stop-motion Academy Award–winning *Pinocchio* (2022), which enlists 3D-printed puppets or a more traditional 2D-animated co-production between Chile and Brazil, *Nahuel y el libro mágico* (*Nahuel and the Magic Book*, 2020) by Chilean filmmaker German Acuña (Del Toro's film was also a transnational effort with the work completed mainly in Mexico and the United States, and Acuña's movie also included scenes in the Mapuche language). While these are both exemplary works in contemporary animation from the Luso-Hispanic Atlantic, I am interested in identifying more obscure animation formats that approximate the experimental DIY, amateur, and edgier works I have considered elsewhere in this book, works that inhabit the intersection of multiple media forms, for example at the nexus between cinema, new media arts, and video gaming. Machinima is one such experimental modality that has been trending since the late 1990s not only across the Luso-Hispanic Atlantic but also in North America, Europe, and Asia. It could still gather additional momentum in terms of production, visibility, and popularity in the future, although admittedly it could just as likely fizzle out of existence. The term "machinima" is a techno-neologism combining the words "machine," "animation," and "cinema," and it identifies a modality that is a precursor to AI cinema in the sense that the filmmaker manipulates a video game's AI-controlled responsive behavior to achieve desired effects.

Machinima can be broadly described as 2D or 3D computer-animated narratives that are influenced by popular formats such as video games, comics, and Japanese anime, as well as partaking of fan culture. In some respects, machinima is a variant of fan fiction since it creates new and original stories by relying on existing universes, characters, and plots borrowed typically from existing video games. The machinima format is typically created by video capture of video game frames, or by filming from within video game engines (in-game footage) or with other CGI methods and subsequently edited with standard video editing tools and structured along narrative lines to fashion original online animated cinema. True to their DIY ethos, machinima are most often distributed via dedicated and highly popular YouTube channels but also through other user-generated content platforms such as Vimeo, Twitch, Daily Motion, and Newgrounds.[2] The simplest and cheapest way to create a machinima is within the reach of almost anyone. It involves playing a video game, screen capturing segments from the gameplay (by selecting multiple viewpoints from within the game or, more primitively, by capturing the player action with a rudimentary screen recorder), and then editing the recorded material using software and adding voice-over, other sound, and additional effects to fashion a new narrative from the fragments—a truly intermedial process. The format therefore has a close affiliation not only with video game and anime fan culture but also with experimental found footage cinema and home movies. The format anticipates the creative potential now ushered by AI-assisted or AI-generated cinema, as we shall see in this coda.

Machinima also places an unusual cinematic medium within the reach of those amateur filmmakers willing to experiment with this modality, introducing video gamers, new media artists, and social media video makers to its aesthetic and messaging potential. On a more sophisticated level, users who have programming knowledge can hack into or modify (also known as "modding") the game space to create additional narrative scenes and visual effects. The process is subversive in the sense that it breaks rules and programming expectations; it takes a proprietary video game, or creates an imitation of one, and upends the game's intended purpose. As Danny Kringiel sees it, "[W]hen turned into a machinima film or a mod, games are diverted from their original purpose—the player no longer follows the developer's carefully prefabricated gameplay structures. Instead, she empowers herself to transform the game, to play creatively with its underlying structures, rules, and mimetic elements" (263).

In addition to highlighting the profound intermediality of these approaches to filmmaking, these machinima projects are often composed of transnational teams, either amateur fans or experienced programmers who want to "bend" their favorite games into stand-alone stories. The machinima projects further illustrate the increasing gamification (or ludification) of cinematic narratives and the emphasis on interactivity, immersion, and participation that we saw with VR and other emerging formats. This phenomenon is a global one, and multidirectional: as cinema becomes more game-like, video games become increasingly more cinematic and narrative. Whether games become movies, or like movies, and movies become games, or like games, all these emerging formats are increasingly intermedial, transmedial, and transnational. As Henry Lowood and Michael Nitsche argue, "[M]any machinima pieces are global co-productions, influenced and watched by players from many different countries and distributed via Web sites and networked file servers. Thus, even as its roots in the self-referential fan culture of digital games must be acknowledged, the growth and anticipated evolution of machinima are connected to its cultural and technical accessibility beyond game culture" (viii). Machinima have also gained a modest degree of mainstream visibility and even acceptability as art institutions such as the Whitney Museum of Art in New York or the Museum of Interactive Cinema in Milan have held exhibits dedicated to the modality and festivals have promoted the format since the early 2000s, including the New York (2008), Milan (2022), and Oberhausen (2023) machinima festivals, among others. Carlos A. Scolari and Damián Fraticelli reflect on the capacity for machinima, and indeed video games more broadly, to cross borders and insert themselves in transnational circuits with relative ease. They stipulate that video games are the cultural products that have undergone the least modifications when moving across cultures. As they observe, one plays the exact same version of *Doom* or *Tetris*, and in the same way, whether in Buenos Aires, Madrid, or Tokyo. Their hypothesis is that video games trigger "regímenes espectatoriales y de interacción que ya han tenido éxito en su expansión cultural: el cine (especialmente de animación) y las experiencias de interacción persona-ordenador que generan los distintos programas" (206) [spectatorial and interactive regimes that have already been successful in other types of cultural expansion: animation cinema and the human-computer interactions that are generated by various software].

No doubt, many films today include CGI for the purpose of special effects as a routine aspect of postproduction, but machinima specifically create (or use previously created) virtual worlds and environments (a prime example would be massive multiplayer environments such as *Second Life* or sandbox-type game spaces such as *Minecraft*), user-designed characters, and video game landscapes (natural and artificial) in order to render a kind of film through the use of avatar-actors. I suggest that machinima is a hybrid format located somewhere between narrative video games and animated film, between interactive theater and avant-garde video. In more complex works, computer algorithms, and increasingly AI, can be involved in generating fractal landscapes (which mimic natural ones with surprising accuracy) and architectural spaces (based on 3D models) that can be used for the settings of these types of films. More often, amateur filmmakers (or as they sometimes call themselves "machinimators") record fragments of a movie or an entire film in preexisting video game worlds or virtual environments, using avatars as the actors (through a sort of digital puppetry) and later dubbing in actor voices and mashing other elements into the video and audio files (music, fragments from other films, live footage from drones and surveillance cameras, etc.).

Essentially, in machinima the filmmaker or machinimator can direct a film in a virtual world that is already designed or programmed, using the animated actors or avatars, and can do so at a low cost so that this format is available for anyone with the technical knowledge and access to a computer. During the "filming" process the machinimator captures a real-time game sequence from within the virtual environment to build a piecemeal narrative that will be later assembled and reorganized with a video editor. Many existing games have responsive AI-driven environments that allow for customizing avatars and changing illumination and points of view, allowing for a range of camera shots and scenarios. Dialogue is typically added afterward, either scripted or spontaneously, and elements can be brought in during editing from a variety of other digital and analog sources. For instance, in some sophisticated platforms, character animation can be created by tracking the movement of real actors and scenes from other audiovisual media can be "mashed" seamlessly into the final film.

The earlies machinima date back to the early 1990s, with one of the original precursors being *Diary of a Camper* (1996), created by an anonymous group of gamers, a primitive example of the modality that used video capture from the first-person shooter game *Quake* (1996). Perhaps one of the more recognizable examples of the use of machinima in the United States is when the animated series *South Park* recycled recorded footage from the multiplayer online role-playing game *World of Warcraft* (2004) in their popular episode "Make Love, Not Warcraft" (2006). In that episode the directors incorporated scenes filmed during the actual playing of the game into their classic 2D animation show and made the video game capture integral to the storyline: the animated characters were in fact supposed to be playing the game, so each one had an avatar in the game space. A more recent example, which received over six million views on YouTube and was first live streamed on Twitch by its creator "wayneradiotv" and his friends-collaborators, is the nine-episode series *Half-Life VR but the AI Is Self-Aware* (2020) based on the game *Half-Life* (1998), which combined a VR environment with improvisational theater techniques to create a hilarious storyline that explored the concept of a self-aware gaming AI. Other machinima works are decidedly less known and much closer to the DIY spirit that characterizes the genre. This is the case for the narrative action story *Wrath of the Tarot Kings* (2022), created by Dustin Bell, possibly a pseudonym or handle for its unidentified machinimator. This work is fully assembled with footage from the action-adventure video game *Red Dead Redemption 2* (2018). This particular piece has been influential for other machinimators, having been viewed by other creators globally, including by many generating Spanish-language works. Remarkably more interesting from an avant-garde standpoint, and hailing from the Philippines, Frederick C. Borromeo's wholly experimental, nonnarrative *Distortion* (2023) bears mention. *Distortion* is a movie that uses *RPG Maker* to self-reflect on questions of aesthetics and the artistic limitations of video games, making it a meta work about machinima itself. Another interesting piece is a film by renowned postconceptual artist Cory Arcangel titled *Super Mario Movie* (2005), which hacks the old Nintendo game to reflect on the passing of old games, on the nostalgia and obsolescence of the video game format. Of course, for each of these experimental and self-reflexive pieces there are many that are quite unimaginative and seem tethered to narratives that are wholly derivative from the games they are repurposing—stories that focus on action or violence and set up difficult to follow plotlines. Roger Ebert, writing a piece on machinima in the year 2000, during the modality's early days, anticipated its advantages and shortcomings: "The key elements in Machinima are low cost and artistic freedom. These movies do not require actors, set designers, cinematographers, caterers, best boys, or key grips. They can be made by one person sitting at a computer. This is revolutionary. But my guess is that the films themselves will not be as revolutionary as the techniques used to make them—that out of those basements and bedrooms will come not cinematic art but elaborations on the themes of video games" (Ebert).

While Ebert's point applies to a significant portion of machinima, some works still stand out as worthy of critical consideration. Several notable examples from the Luso-Hispanic Atlantic include the political thriller *Vlogger* (2011), by Catalan filmmaker Ricard Gras, a movie that combines footage from the gaming (virtual) world, specifically from the *Half-Life* first-person shooter video game, with actual webcam footage and other media inserts, edited into a feature-length film, or his earlier *Breakout Game Mod* (2009), which is an abstract exploration of the original game *Breakout* (Atari, 1976) with a mashup of electronic music evocative of early games in the background. Another inventive Latin American creator (or team of creators) who goes by the name of Nooby Crazy (and Nooby Studios) is likely Mexico-based, unsurprising since that country has one of the most thriving gamer cultures in the region. Nooby Crazy filmed a machinima entitled *Omicron* (2023), loosely framed around the pandemic and the corona virus variant by the same name, using the video game first-person shooter platform *Halo Reach* (2010). As is often the case, the exact identity of the machinimators or team of creators is not reliably knowable, although some clues are provided in the film and through allied websites. The group's name (Nooby Crazy) is a reference to "Noob," a slang term used by *Minecraft* fans to describe an inexperienced player or "newbie." Both their use of gamer-specific terminology and their commentary in YouTube and on their webpage leave little doubt about the close association between the creation of machinima and video game fan culture. While the actual location of the creators of *Omicron* cannot be determined with absolute certainty, specific comments on their Facebook page, which are in both English and Spanish, as well as the *chilango* Mexico City slang they deploy, suggest the possibility that at least some are located in the Mexican capital, a possibility reinforced by the fact that the announcements they make when releasing new works are referred to as being in "Mexico time."

Regardless of their content the point could be made that machinima are, by their very nature, transgressive and marginally "illegal," especially when their creators, who often wish to remain anonymous, do not seek permission from video game makers for the appropriation of their material, thereby entering a gray area in terms of copyright infringement (again, this anticipates some of the issues that are now emerging in relation to AI-generated art). Playing into that attitude of transgression, the format has appealed to many artists who wish to explore controversial current events related to anything from ongoing wars and conflicts (Syria, Ukraine, etc.) to gender representation in video games, to social inequalities, to various conspiracy theories, to name just a few of their chosen subjects. As we saw, other artists have focused on creating abstract films, and many machinima makers are focused on fashioning a new type of narrative cinema, working well within the constraints this form represents. As Matt Turner suggests,

"[M]aking distinctions between 'popular-machinima' and 'artists-machinima' isn't necessarily productive: not all the above makers would describe themselves as artists, and to deny artistic value to the machinima being made online would be doing it a disservice." Regardless of their artistic potential and cultural value, machinima have emerged as a popular underground form of cinematic creation, one that embraces an intermedial ethos informed by video game, comic book, and music culture and has enjoyed popularity with the younger demographics across the Luso-Hispanic Atlantic.

Many of these machinima are also in conversation with mainstream animation. But the two modalities have very different goals, publics, and access to resources. In sharp contrast with the underground scene specific to the cinematic subvariant that is machinima, there have been some highly successful CGI-animated films created by mainstream filmmakers from the region, such as José Juan Campanella's 2013 *Metegol* (distributed as *Underdogs* in the US), an Argentine-Iberian co-production. At the cost of twenty-one million dollars, *Metegol* was among the most expensive films from the Luso-Hispanic Atlantic region to date, receiving theatrical releases worldwide and netting impressive profits. On the other hand, other works had more modest financial success but garnered international recognition for their artistic value, such as the Chilean short *Historia de un oso* (*Bear Story*, 2014), a poignant allegorical tale about the 1973 military coup and its aftermath directed by Gabriel Osorio, a movie that received many accolades at festivals and even won an Oscar for its animation. Osorio's film exemplified the hybrid nature of some of these works by combining 2D and 3D CGI, as well as stop-motion and analog animation techniques in its production. According to Oslavia Danaé Linares Martínez, these CGI-animated films and machinima works from the Luso-Hispanic Atlantic represent a complex balance of cultural influences and territorial allegiances, uneasily managing regional and transnational pressures:

> Digital technologies have come to coalesce national and regional animations with globalization, disrupting established production modes, making them more susceptible to cultural trends like MTV, Japanese anime, and social media. This has bound them to the technological dominance of U.S.-based online platforms . . . but also favored a sense of a regional cohesion that is exemplified by regional online animation networks and culturally related multinational audiences. These associations have also expanded beyond the region and in some ways globalized

the visual culture of Latin American online viewers. Moreover, this globalizing trend goes on par with that of animation production in the world. (11)

Regardless of how we consider animation and its capacity to engender greater access to filmmaking, especially in the case of DIY efforts like machinima, the fact is that the region has achieved significant global successes and increased visibility for its creators, amateur and professional alike. The spirit that moves those creating low-budget underground machinima in anonymity might be closer to the ethos of the cell phone filmmakers I discussed in previous chapters, certainly in terms of the low-cost methods of production and distribution through social media platforms. In some cases, at least in terms of skirting questions of illegality, copyright infringement, and anti-establishment content, these amateur machinimators might even be said to approach the militant work of the 1960s, although without the political conviction or single-minded purpose of those utopian years, and at much lower stakes. But in contrast with these obscure underground machinima, films like Del Toro's *Pinocchio* or Campanella's *Metegol* respond to a commercial drive that has also fully tapped into transnational festival circuits and streaming services and propelled the region's animation onto the global stage. I now turn to yet another emerging modality, one created exclusively for the platform TikTok, that is closer to the DIY spirit of irreverent filmmaking and video game appropriation.

The Short Form Video: TikTok Cinema

In many ways TikTok stands in for various other social media/cell phone editing apps that do similar things with short form audiovisual content (including Funimate, Instagram Reels, Likee, Huddles, Triller, Cheez, Firework, Snapchat, etc.), as well as those no longer in existence like Vine. Short form videos last from a few seconds to a few minutes, require minimal or no editing, and are a preferred format for Gen Z and younger creators and consumers of audiovisual material—and given the ease with which these videos are created and instantly uploaded, there is often little difference in the function of making videos and consuming the videos created by others. Similarly, the possibility for collective work has grown, as many of these platforms have collaborative tools that facilitate group editing and video creation. The existence of many among these apps is motivated by content creators' desire to generate profits, and, primarily, for the corporations that own the platforms to capitalize on such profit models. Of course, YouTube remains a preeminent video sharing platform but does not usually favor the short form videos or the vertical format. Instead, with no length restrictions, YouTube typically houses longer videos and even the kinds of higher quality festival fare that I shared in chapter 4 (and Vimeo is even more aligned with professional filmmakers). When it comes to these other short form platforms, while they might cater to slightly different users (teens, celebrities, fashion vloggers, influencers, etc.), their basic functions—their "functionality" in the lingo of the medium—are similar: making and storing short looping videos, providing easy editing and effects, and the addition of music. The formats operate with content algorithms that promote addictive behavior, as well as ways to monetize or at least the promise and illusion of monetization. In fact, we could consider most of these platforms as genealogical descendants of other short online video formats, such as the aminated GIFs that populated the early web, early flash-based animations, or video memes, along with other first-generation Internet cultural phenomena. It is instructive to examine TikTok, arguably the most popular and successful among these short form video sharing platforms, as a stand-in for the others and as a useful indicator for future trends.

As of late, TikTok has come into increased global scrutiny by virtue of its ownership by a Chinese corporation and through the efforts of various countries to ban its use. The platform has alarmed Western governments who are concerned about privacy issues and, more acutely, fear the company's potential manipulation by the Chinese Communist Party. Regardless, TikTok has had a remarkable impact in the video making world, especially in the amateur video arena. The company has grown exponentially with more than eight hundred million users, a number that does not include Douyin subscribers (the company's Chinese branch, both owned by the Chinese tech company ByteDance), and with over one billion app downloads by 2020. Statistics show that by 2022 there were 136 million TikTok users in Latin America alone, making it one of the most rapid growth regions for the platform globally. While the United States remains the leading country in terms of TikTok usage (113 million), Brazil is in third place (82 million) and Mexico in fourth (56 million), with Spain further down the list (9 million) (Bianchi). What is evident is that usage of the platform is in the midst of a vertiginous global expansion phase, and the countries of the Luso-Hispanic Atlantic are at the forefront of this growth phenomenon.

Initially launched in 2016 as a music video creation and sharing application, TikTok has morphed beyond its original functionality as users explore various innovative ways to create with the format, making videos lasting in duration from three seconds and up to ten minutes, while also tapping into the social media dimension of the application by sharing, promoting, and commenting on other users' posts. The ease with which one can assemble short looping videos has led to the proliferation of micro-movies, DIY music videos, amateur performances, comedy skits, rant videos, and an astounding and self-reinventing variety of user-generated content. Simple to use editing features and the capability of doing all editing directly on the phone with results that can, in the best of cases, rival commercial cinematic postproduction has further bolstered the popularity of the app and platform. Its features include the capacity to speed up or slow down video files to match sound, introduce filters to alter the image, sample sound and images from various sources (including the popular lip-sync features), and share across multiple other platforms. TikTok's popularity, especially with Gen Z (born approximately from the mid to late 1990s through the early 2010s), is having an impact on the mainstream film industry and shaping the expectations of younger audiences, who look for viewing experiences tailored to their interests and with an interactive potential. According to Mackenzie Scott, "[F]ilmmakers like [Alfonso] Cuarón are dipping their toes into the TikTok pool, and some [new directors] are even leveraging this platform to launch their professional careers."

Within the many videos housed by TikTok, there is a subset that could be described as the platform's cinematic variant. With a proliferation of hashtags (groupings of videos under similar content) such as #filmmakers, #youngfilmmakers, #cinematography, #film, #movie, #filmmakersoftiktok, #doplife, and #filmmakerlife, or in the Spanish-speaking world #pelicula, #cine, and countless others, there is also an increasing presence of both short films and instructions on how to become a filmmaker available on TikTok. Short films are sometimes divided into parts (to be able to create a longer work) or left as short pieces with minimalist narratives that often privilege comedy, slapstick, and body-centered humor.

There is a broad variety of genres, however, and under these hashtags one can find a heterogeneous and chaotic mix of videos that sometimes use repurposed film fragments or mash-ups to create new fiction works. There are also film reviews, film technique instruction videos, home made films, self-referential pieces (selfie-films), and countless other types of audiovisual works, some entirely uncategorizable. These films align formally and content-wise with what is being called "vertical cinema" or vertical movies, that is, movies shot with cell phones and meant to be viewed on cell phones (format with aspect ratio 9:16). Vertical cinema is closely allied to the subject I explored in chapter 4 (cell phone films), although those films were primarily shot using a "landscape" orientation and did not, overall, fully embrace their vertical possibilities. There is, however, significant crossover with younger filmmakers working in DIY methods and self-distributing on platforms like YouTube, who also rely on TikTok for promotion, distribution, and community-building.

TikTok videos are predominantly, if not entirely, vertical, and the platform is a logical distribution method for amateur filmmakers who wish to experiment with the emerging vertical format. Similarly, vertical videos are also common in Instagram and Snapchat, further facilitating multiplatform video sharing. While some notable filmmakers, including Damien Chazelle (best known for his Academy Award–winning 2016 film *La La Land*), have shot short films in the vertical format (Chazelle's 2020 short *The Stunt Double* is one of the finest examples to date), amateur films are at the forefront of testing the limits of the vertical screen. These filmmakers are implementing techniques to elicit the most cinematic benefit of the vertical orientation of the frame, for example by arranging the action from top to bottom or vice versa, rather than side to side as with conventional cinema. Some compositions and storylines are better suited for the vertical format—narratives that want to emphasize verticality for some reason, such as urban stories illustrating the enclosure or claustrophobia one feels in crowded downtown scenarios or narratives that focus on a single human character or on isolated figures. Other stories, involving expansive landscapes or large groups of individuals, may be less served by a vertical frame. It is also the case that the mise-en-scène needs to adapt to the phone screen aspect ratio so that sets and props take full advantage of the format when they approximate this same verticality. Similarly, the use of space, whether on-screen space or off-screen space, is distinct for these movies as well. Sound design is lagging and limited by the capabilities of the phone, or the headphones, so there is less use of surround features or special effects that would not be appreciable in the vertical format. I would like to examine a few examples of the types of video and/or cinema one can encounter specifically in TikTok by focusing on work that has been created by/for users from across the Luso-Hispanic Atlantic region. However, as was the case with cell phone movies more broadly, it is at times very difficult to ascertain the origin of a film or of the filmmaker if the works are not credited or if users post under handles rather than their actual names—and in fact, at times the anonymity seems to be the point, as it frees the creator from self-censorship.

The "landscape" of vertical cinema (pun intended) contains both DIY examples and major corporate interests, all of them attempting to capture the attention of millions of TikTok users. Diamond Films Latin America, the largest independent film distribution company in Latin America, distributes approximately thirty major mainstream feature-length films each year, both US productions for consumption in Latin America and the Iberian Peninsula and films from the region filmed in Spanish, and less often Portuguese, that are distributed throughout the Luso-Hispanic Atlantic. As part of its effort to reach younger audiences, Diamond Films has also entered the selfie-film space by supporting the creation of content specific for TikTok and other phone cinema–friendly platforms. The company is likewise behind the drive to promote TikTok video making in Latin America and Spain, as well as using the social media app to promote the more conventional films it distributes, at times creating vertical trailers or short promotional videos for its large screen format cinema. Part of Latin America's Telefilms Group, Diamond Films expanded to the other side of the Atlantic, forming Diamond Films España in 2016, so the company now has three distinct branches, a Latin American division, one located exclusively in Brazil, and the Spanish subsidiary. The company uploads to its TikTok page videos by content creators from across multiple Spanish-speaking nations, including many from Argentina, Mexico, Brazil, and Spain.

TikTok has amplified the presence of Latin American and Iberian media influencers and industry specialists who comment on the cinema of the region. The Mexican filmmaker-producer Pepe González (TikTok handle @pepegg33), who has a considerable 360,000 followers on TikTok and a significant presence on Twitter (now X) and Instagram as well, is an entertainment industry insider who has created a sizable archive of TikTok videos that could be described as "meta" TikToks, covering topics ranging from the art of video making to film reviews and a wide variety of other advertising and industry related-content. A professional video maker, Pepe González has also created many TikTok videos about filmmaking as an art form, discussing cinematographic techniques and his own process of video creation.[3] He is, in many ways, representative of the semiprofessional young filmmaker who maintains a foothold in both mainstream cinema and the DIY online space, aware of the potential of emerging formats to amplify the reach of his mainstream work.

Some other film and video makers have been able to increase their visibility through participation in a handful of festivals and events that featured TikTok prominently. Principal among these events, the Vertical Cinema Festival, organized by TikTok in 2020, included users/creators from Mexico, Colombia, Chile, Argentina, and Peru and cataloged videos under three main genres and hashtags: narrative shorts (#FilTokFicción), documentary pieces (#FilmTokDocumental), and music videos (#FilTokmusical).[4] Among the more notable and higher production quality fiction works one finds Mexican actor Pepe Valdivieso's short *Ansiedad* (2020) [Anxiety].[5] Valdivieso is an actor who has had relatively minor roles in Mexican film and television but has gathered a large following for his TikTok videos and maintains a visible presence in other social media platforms. His video *Ansiedad* is representative of most work in this developing format, neither fully professional nor completely amateur. It is a one-minute circular narrative that features a protagonist who confronts his identical double, a kind of materialization of his self-doubt and anxiety. His double is also a relentlessly critical voice that tells him everything he does turns out poorly. Despite being short, the video is nevertheless attentive to mise-en-scène, editing, and other filmmaking elements. The protagonist and his doppelganger are dressed in stark opposition (the critical and negative persona completely in black, the "true" self in bright colors) and the short does a superb job establishing this simple but effective narrative line, which gets a point across about mental anxiety and the destructive nature of self-criticism, aligning it with self-help affirmation videos. The film ends in the place it began, which makes for an interesting endless narrative loop as it begins to play again, and again (taking formal advantage of a standard TikTok feature).

As I stated above, there is a significant number of videos that are comedic in nature. The video *El 2020 tuvo un guía diferente* (2020) [The Year 2020 Had a Different Guide] is a humorous creation by Argentine Pablo Bruschi, an actor, comedian, YouTuber, and creator across various social media platforms who has an astounding nine million followers on TikTok. It is precisely this capacity to go viral and gather large numbers of followers that makes the platform attractive to those who may not have other avenues to showcase their work and who may also seek to monetize it by taking advantage of its algorithm—although that potentially favors a turn toward sensationalist works that become click-bait. Bruschi's videos, however, are typically reminiscent of stand-up routines and not particularly concerned with cinematography or a film-school aesthetics. This is to be expected, as he is not a trained filmmaker but mainly a comic and actor. The videos tend to feature him in the center of the screen (selfie-style) as he engages in various antics and uses props and costumes to enhance the comedic effect. In this particular video he enacts a dialogue between God, Jesus, and the Devil—all parts he plays himself, with different costumes and props. The simple story details how, when God leaves on vacation for the year, he delegates to the Devil custody of Earth with disastrous results

(Jesus, apparently, is too busy playing video games). In the highly irreverent video Bruschi references major negative stories from that year's news and current events, including the COVID-19 pandemic and the death of basketball star Kobe Bryant, among other global-level disasters. While the aim of the video is primarily to entertain and promote the videographer's stand-up career, there is also some care to present a relatively polished video with significant editing cuts and a scripted narrative, and an underlying social critique about the state of world governance.

Not all films are narrative fiction, comedic, or strictly anecdotal. There are some content creators engaging in semi-experimental works as well. For instance, *¿Estamos solos?* (2020) [Are We Alone?] is a semi-abstract Spanish-language video by Dani Ferdinow, a creator whose country of origin or location is difficult to ascertain with any precision (as is the case with many videos) but whose montage editing and manipulation of filters and other distortion tools is reminiscent of the 1960s avant-garde. In this video, the subject is centered on the narrator's philosophical musings about the nature of reality, our place within the cosmos, and the possibility of extraterrestrial life. While displaying both abstract and heavily distorted images, a voice-over asks whether we are truly alone in the universe and what the experience of "reality" signifies. The images offered through a dizzyingly rapid montage include close-ups of an eye, sketches depicting strange looking humanoids taken from cave paintings, and grainy photographs of UFOs, all interspersed with various abstract images and distorted footage of the night sky. The quality of the piece resides in the balance between its aesthetic composition (the deliberate montage or collage of assorted images taken from the web), the superimposition of the thoughtful and self-reflecting voice-over, and the added extradiegetic music, as well as the experimental tonality of the work.[6]

Not all films produced for TikTok are strictly amateur work either. In April 2022, TikTok initiated the #TikTokShortFilm Competition as part of a partnership with the Cannes Festival, to foment the next generation of young filmmakers. In the competition, awards were given for the best film, best editing, best script, and so on. Legitimating the platform as a venue or laboratory for upcoming filmmakers and video artists, the grand prize winner was awarded a not insignificant 10,000-euro purse. As I complete this book in 2024, the second year of the competition is underway, indicating a potential for the modality's long-term permanence as a viable medium for filmmaking. Winners are chosen from among the forty most viewed videos, so that TikTok users have a voice in the selection process, even if this means that some promising videos get disqualified by virtue of not having enough views. The 2022 winning video, hailing from Japan, was a three-minute short titled *Kitte kitte iino?* [Okay to Cut Trees?] by Mabuta Motoki (@lang_pictures), a film that explores environmental concerns through the eyes and the painstakingly exacting work of an artisan woodworker. Shortly thereafter, TikTok also partnered with the San Sebastián film festival in Spain. In September 2022, the festival created a TikTok account (@sansebastianfes), which focused on Spanish-language videos, although most of the channel was oriented toward promoting the festival and including brief interviews with celebrities, filmmakers, and other personalities, rather than showcasing TikTok films per se. Other initiatives within TikTok that focus on film and are oriented to beginning filmmakers include the channel @TikTokShortFilmFestival, which housed a festival that provided awards of up to one thousand dollars for the best film uploaded to the venue. It is evident that the "vertical format" is here to stay, although its most promising work may well remain firmly anchored in the DIY amateur scene rather than in efforts at cross-promotion by the established film industry.

That said, TikTok as a company is working to gain additional visibility and respectability for its content by working with other media and film industry partners. For example, in 2019 Netflix joined Adobe and TikTok to initiate a contest of micro-movies created in and for the platform and grouped the works under the banner "Great Untold" story. While most of these films are ephemeral by nature, as well as transient, mobile, and wholly fragmented (short, schematic episodic, and sometimes mere vignettes), it is evident that these types of "cinematic" TikToks have a high appeal for the younger audiences in the Luso-Hispanic Atlantic, just as they do for other global youth. On the flipside, the possibility of sharing these videos and micro-movies instantly and having them go "viral" also generates pressure to make their content commercially driven and to include product placements and outright advertisement even within their short duration (a problem exacerbated by the active pursuit by brands for inclusion in the work of creators in these platforms with the promise of corporate patronage). There are also the added tendencies to binge-watch videos, often coupled with the attention deficit and mindless scrolling that leads to fragmentary and inattentive viewing practices, all of which favors, and perhaps even encourages, shorter formats and a "distracted" spectator.

In general, the TikTok cinema format offers accessibility and the potential for new stories for the Luso-Hispanic Atlantic. Creators produce videos in many different styles and genres, leaning into minimal dialogue but highly charged visual storytelling. As stated by the company in a post in its own platform's newsroom, "[W]ith only a few seconds and limited equipment, they [TikTok creators] can build scenes with multiple camera shots and actors all while sitting alone in their room. Other users take their camera on the go and frame everyday life in a way that draws the eye in and helps us look at life in a unique way. These creators (extremely short-filmmakers) help inspire a community of artistic individuals to create the cinematic side of TikTok" ("The Cinematic Side"). On a darker front, the possibility of addiction to short, low-quality videos, as facilitated by an endless scrolling that the platform incentivizes, coupled with the frivolity of most TikTok content, threatens to drown out the more transgressive and rare cinematic work that one can find within the vast majority of mediocre videos cluttering the platform. Going forward it will be useful to have some content curation so that such remarkable pieces can rise above the rest of the video archive and the Spanish-language filmmakers doing interesting work can also gain additional global visibility.

AI-Generated Cinema

AI's capacity to generate art across various media and artistic disciplines—from music and literature to the visual arts—has increased exponentially after the latest developments in super computing, artificial neural networks, machine learning, computer vision, and natural language processing, to name just a few of the numerous "deep learning" technologies transforming our world, for better and worse.[7] This controversial technological revolution is impacting film and video as well, as AI-generated content permeates every aspect of the industry from script writing to pre- and postproduction and, increasingly, filmmaking itself. AI-assisted projects can be controversial because they raise unsettled issues, including the nature of authorship and authenticity, the rightful ownership of original material scraped by AI from the Internet, and the loss of human jobs. Other concerns include AI's potential to aggravate systematic bias in representation (by magnifying existing cultural bias), or its threat to meaning-making as the purview of human intelligence—that is, its challenge to the belief that storytelling is precisely what makes us human. These debates are a reprise of what was once argued about older technologies as they emerged, photography, for example, or even the cinema itself provoked much hand-wringing. These now enshrined technologies were seen as methods of mechanical reproduction that displaced the human-based techniques found in painting, replacing artists with mere technicians, stripping art's aura. These arguments have lost their force over time, but there is a difference once human agency itself is partly or entirely eliminated from the process of image selection and creation, once the artistic process is reduced to issuing textual prompts to a machine that then generates the actual objet d'art. While examining these concerns in depth goes beyond my scope, I acknowledge that AI needs to be adopted with ethics in mind rather than released to the world without care, as seems to be happening. In addition, AI and AI-generated culture must be critically appraised from a variety of disciplines to gauge both its beneficial and deleterious effects. Whether or not such a culture exists, and will continue to grow exponentially, is really no longer up for debate. The question now becomes, How might we address these artifacts as critics, and how will they transform our region of interest—the Luso-Hispanic Atlantic?

Putting aside these legitimate concerns about AI for now, I wish to focus on the ways the technology is already altering film and video in the region. The impact of AI has been tremendous in the world of painting, illustration, and the visual arts in general, and is already acutely felt in cinema and video production. Although AI has been used in film for decades—in assistance generating scripts, in various preproduction tasks, in audio mixing, in dubbing, in postproduction editing including modifying lighting and color effects, in advertising and sales forecasting, and in a variety of other "tedious," time-consuming processes—it has not been adopted wholesale for the creation of entire films, in the creative component of filmmaking, except for a handful of exceptions. As powerful text-to-video tools are developed that can generate 4K moving images either based on text descriptions or by transforming source videos, generating increasingly complex movies with AI is becoming a reality. Currently one can, for example, take an existing video and run it through an AI tool and prompt it to recreate the work in the style of a particular filmmaker's aesthetic, even adding sound—and although the quality of the final product is still underwhelmingly rudimentary (featuring overly stylized images, poor consistency or continuity in movement, image instabilities, morphing and distortions, simplistic backgrounds, etc.), it is rapidly improving so that soon AI films will achieve photorealistic levels and become indistinguishable from non-AI-generated cinema.

The point is that while these sorts of experiments are much easier to conduct with still images, film and video processed by AI is already quite feasible. There are many tools available to even amateur cineastes to experiment with AI cinema, and their early works make for fascinating case studies.[8] In this section I will briefly mention just a few of these attempts at creating AI films, beginning with a couple of global projects and then focusing on the Luso-Hispanic Atlantic more specifically. Of course, it must be understood that, as I write this in February 2024, a fully AI-generated film is not just yet within reach of filmmakers, that is, one in which an entire feature-length movie is generated based on prompts by a user or filmmaker—but this will almost surely be a reality by the time the book reaches print. What is possible presently is the use of AI to facilitate filmmaking, or make possible the transfer of images and videos, even text, into partial AI cinematic experiments. These experiments are compelling, not because of their current aesthetic or narrative value but on account of the possibilities they suggest for cinema in the region in future years.

It is also quite self-evident that these AI projects exemplify both of the main axes that have structured my argument throughout this book, the transnational and the intermedial. That is, that these AI-assisted films are created in eminently transnational conditions by filmmakers and teams that work across multiple national boundaries, with funding from various global sources, and with audiences that are located across the digital expanse. These AI projects are also inherently intermedial, as text is transformed into images and videos, as materials from various sources are mined and aggregated or mashed together, as music and voice is overlaid onto the final products. Furthermore, AI can intensify and personalize the intermedial nature of contemporary arts, that is, target a specific use of images, sound, text, and video for a particular user depending on their preferences. Thinking along post-humanist lines, we might even consider the co-operative human-to-machine interactions that create these works as a kind of intermediality, or perhaps a cyborg-like assembly of flesh and machine, an analog and digital hybridization. The kind of interactivity and immersion I discussed in relation to VR cinema can be enhanced using AI, including the recruitment of chatbots embedded within cinematic narratives to elicit viewer interaction, perhaps to modify the ending of the films, or to bring other forms of media into works that will be in a permanent state of flux or becoming. We might envision, for example, a tailorized on-demand web series that responds to the user's personal experience and desires, or an interactive and immersive AI-generated VR environment that mimics reality almost perfectly, with either of these possibilities suggesting hopeful and dystopian scenarios. The combinations are endless in terms of the transnational connections and the intermedial variations facilitated by AI's intervention into the cinema.

The following works are transnational precursors that serve as referents for other films from the Luso-Hispanic region. These films demonstrate that we are still at the beginning stage of what may be possible. The 2022 short *The Crow* by the Irish computer artist Glen Marshall is arguably the first AI-generated film to have won a major award, claiming the Jury Prize at Cannes. Marshall used a work he found on the Internet as the base material for his AI-animated short. He transferred this original film, frame by frame, by running the mp4 file through a neural network and natural language processor called CLIP (Contrastive Language–Image Pretraining) designed by OpenAI, the same company that created the ChatGPT bot. By using CLIP Marshall transformed the original video, providing it with a different aesthetic look, but the similarities between both works raise concerns about copyright. The base video was Duncan MacDowel's short *Painted* (2012), depicting a contemporary performance featuring dancer and choreographer Dorothy Sakaly. Sakaly's dance is staged in the crumbling ruins of a building that is being overrun by vegetation. Imitating a crow's movements, Sakaly makes this decomposing industrial setting her own, reclaiming it for the natural world. This narrative concept, nature reclaiming the artificial, is reversed in the AI work.[9] *The Crow* takes this stylized imitation of a bird's movement performed by a human and converts it into the animated image of a somewhat anthropomorphic "dancing" crow. The metaphor of metamorphosis presented in *Painted* is therefore reductively literalized in *The Crow*. Instead of the natural world symbiotically occupying an artificially built environment, Marshall generates an artificial process that is coding or masking over a human performance. By transforming *Painted* with some basic commands and minimal postproduction, Marshall arguably appropriated the previous labor by the dancer, or by the filmmaker and crew, offering no compensation.

The question of originality and authenticity, as well as concerns about artists' rights, loom large here. What are the rights of the filmmaker and artists who created the source video? What is the actual creativity displayed by *The Crow*, given the automated nature of the process? In *The Crow*, the process of transferring the source video to AI-generated animation responded to Marshall's prompt to adapt each frame to show the "painting of a crow in a desolate landscape" (Macaulay). Fed through the AI program, every frame of the original film was reinterpreted as the painting of a crow in a stark, empty landscape, so that Marshall's movie could be mapped one to one onto the video capture of the human performance in *Painted*. Although Marshall credited the original material he transformed, the project still serves as an example of the boundaries AI-generated films can cross in terms of copyright infringement and lack of originality. Some of these concerns could be mitigated simply by creating an original source file to transform through the AI, rather than relying on material found online. As with most new technology, the question of ethics is often complex and demands careful consideration, requiring the kind of critical reflection that unfortunately seems to lag with the unrestrained rush to adopt the tools themselves.

I would like to highlight another intriguing cinematic AI, the social media series *Salt* (2022–) still under production. *Salt* is being promoted as the first work created "entirely" by AI, although such claims for firstness regarding emerging technologies are often hyperbolic. Fabian Stelzer, a German technology businessman, created *Salt* using commercial AI programs such as Midjourney and DALLI-E. Stelzer deployed AI software to mine the Internet for retro sci-fi images and then edited them as frames in his film, later adding sound and voice-over with an AI voice generator (Kan). The series is therefore "shot" in a dystopian 1970s science fiction lo-fi style, combining images selected for having this particular aesthetic and then applying filters to render the images more graphically cohesive when assembled into "scenes." To compensate for the sensation that we are viewing a set of thematically linked but independent still images, the filmmaker avails himself of postproduction effects like moving the camera along the images, zooming, or tracking along them to create a certain flow (the so-called Ken Burns effect). The series, still evolving, is a loose narrative about salt mining in outer space, as a group of space explorers discover a planet consisting mostly of that substance—appropriately, the film's minimalist script is generated with ChatGPT. Currently there are only a few short scenes available for viewing on X, erstwhile Twitter.

These two-minute clips are highly reminiscent of Chris Marker's sci-fi experimental short *La Jetée* (1962) in that they are also primarily composed of still images with voice-over narration. *Salt* may never be completed and, unlike Marker's film, does not presume a philosophical inquiry into time and memory or a meta-reflection on temporality and duration in the cinematic medium. But there are some similarities in the aesthetic of both works as they use similar pans, zooms, dissolves, and editing techniques to make the still frames come alive. These sparks of animation were central to Marker's film. In Stelzer's case the illusion of movement is a stratagem that helps elide the fact that these are just static images processed through an AI. In Marker's film there is a single, short live-action filmed sequence, when a woman blinks almost imperceptibly, but that instant encapsulates *La Jetée*'s self-referentiality—the shutting of her eyelid a direct reference to the gap between frames, a reference to the camera-eye or Kino-Eye in Vertov's cinematography, and a reference to the very flicker of celluloid film as projected in analog. It is at once a recognition of the continuity of human life, its analog quality, and the discontinuity of the cinema, its fragmentation—its segmentation into frames, or today, into digital pixels.

The challenge for AI cinema creators resides precisely on how to produce actual moving images through AI software and assemble them into a meaningful narrative, into a continuous whole, rather than just producing visually stunning but incoherent and fragmentary works. In AI video this is a problem called "frame" or "temporal" inconsistency, that is, the difficulty of generating a particular aesthetic and maintaining it from frame to frame without the presence of distortion effects—for example objects that appear, disappear, or change shape unpredictably between frames, triggering disconcerting effects and a kind of "flicker" curiously reminiscent of early cinematic experiments. Even using still images, narrative cohesion remains a challenge. While the decadent sci-fi look in *Salt* aesthetically unifies the images into a semi-cohesive project, overall the effort remains fragmentary and incomplete. For example, to make this project more collaborative, Stelzer released it via Twitter (X) in short pieces, allowing users to suggest and vote on various potential narrative paths. The story develops along a "choose your own adventure" structure, and while this strategy—reminiscent of the comments section in YouTube—may have engaged viewers, it also made for a more disjointed narrative.

Several other global efforts at birthing AI cinema are yielding results that remain unsatisfying in terms of visual and narrative quality but suggest an evolution of cinematic AI toward increased feasibility, aesthetic value, and creative potential.[10] Various imaginative projects point toward a reconceptualizing of sci-fi and fantasy genres, and some entail imitating a particular filmmaker's vision in an extension of fan culture practices. This applies, for instance, to Johnny Darrell's use of the AI Midjourney to reimagine the 1982 sci-fi classic *Tron* through the lens of Chilean filmmaker Alejandro Jodorowski's cinematic style, creating a set of stills that stunningly combine both of those influences as a new hybrid.[11] The emphasis, and quite possibly AI's best contribution to the cinema, lies in exploring worlds and artworks that never existed but are nonetheless possible and can now be materialized through supercomputing.

Allow me to transition from a faux-Jodorowski film to some actual AI efforts in the Spanish-speaking world. Across the Luso-Hispanic Atlantic there are some halting and exploratory works of AI-assisted cinema and video. One example involves a transatlantic collaborative effort between

Colombia and Spain. Jorge Caballero's Colombian production company Gusano Films has worked with Barcelona's Pompeu Fabra University on AI and interactive media projects. Caballero and his fellow documentary filmmaker, the Catalan Anna Giralt Gris, have been jointly developing a web series called *Artificio* (2020–) [Artifice]. This documentary-style web series explores the possibilities for AI interventions into various art forms, including (but not only) the cinema. While not overly reliant on the technology, AI tools are used to generate some of the script and voice-over in the series. *Artificio* also includes AI-generated graphics and the series documents examples of AI applications in the arts. At an embryonic stage, the project has to date only released a trailer, so it remains to be seen whether it will lead somewhere promising. Caballero and Giralt expanded the web series concept to a broader initiative also called *Artificio*, which organizes workshops and encourages applied research on how to democratize access to AI while guarding against its drawbacks (Caballero and Giralt Gris). A certain discomfiture and uncertainty in terms of what to do with AI is illustrative of other "seed" (initial, exploratory) efforts from throughout the region, as artists learn to apply this new technology.[12]

To mention one final example of the potentially groundbreaking nature of transnational AI research and development, I will close by highlighting a team composed of two Chilean software designer-artists (Cristóbal Valenzuela Barrera and Alejandro Matamala Ortiz) and their Greek computer scientist colleague (Anastasis Germanidis). Their jointly owned New York–based company has created RunwayML, a software platform that enlists machine learning to generate and edit video projects. This powerful tool is leading to the next generation of AI-assisted films and videos, as artists use it to create mind-bending special effects with text-based prompts. The creators of this software claim, somewhat hyperbolically, that RunwayML can "turn any image, video clip or text prompt into a compelling piece of film." While these tools are in development and not widely available, or their use can require a steep learning curve, they are being gradually adopted by amateurs and professionals of the audiovisual industry. AI-assisted, modified, or generated videos are appearing on YouTube and other social media platforms. These Chilean designers are also vested in expanding the use of AI throughout the Luso-Hispanic Atlantic and have been promoting their software throughout Latin America and Spain. Their company sponsored the so-called first AI Film Festival, which took place in New York from February to March 2023.[13]

The velocity with which these tools are developed and almost immediately adopted by content creators is dizzying, so that by the time this book comes out in print we will be closer to the seminal moment when an AI will generate an entire film with minimal or even no human input (prompt-and-go). The implications of this potentially self-generating cinema are broad, and if a Hal-9000 scenario in which the machines take over seems a bit far-fetched, other disquieting possibilities loom larger, not just in terms of human displacement but also in relation to ethical concerns and questions about the disappearing role of the artist and filmmaker. Many of these issues are already present in Latin America and Spain, where, for example, voice actors who dub foreign films in Spanish are being substituted by AI algorithms that can do the "same" but cheaply—although never as accurately. The algorithms have been trained by processing the very human voices they are duplicating, so that voice actors are training AI to replace human intellectual work, to take their jobs—often their voices are being used for this "training" without their consent. Recalling decades of neocolonial exploitation and foreign investment and extraction of resources in the continent, most of the companies doing the AI dubbing are not Latin American or even from Spanish-speaking countries but scattered globally to maximize profits (Cholakian and Iglesia). Thus, the anticipated bonanza of the brave new world emerging around AI and its wondrous possibilities is simultaneously dampened by a lack of foresight regarding the imminent dangers such unrestrained capabilities can bring to humanity, especially to nations vulnerable to exploitation across the region. AI-generated and AI-assisted cinema is just one dimension of the impact this technology will have and that film critics need to understand even as the technology continues to evolve. Critics need to weigh the real effects of this technology, considering all positions between a techno-utopianism that only fathoms opportunities and a more pessimistic outlook that reflects solely on the impending demise of filmmakers, actors, and writers. More to our point, we need to gauge how the Luso-Hispanic Atlantic might respond to this new format, and with what specific works and strategies.

The Intermedial and Transnational Character of Emerging Cinemas and Networked Media Video

Intermediality, as we have seen throughout this study, is central to many of these cinematic experiments, from work created with cell phones that must adapt to different expectations and inhabit a space close to the body or VR works that also seek an embodied experience, to AI cinema and its scrapping of the accumulated layers of Internet art and accumulated knowledge from across all disciplines, to earlier militant, art house, and experimental movies that were always attuned to questions of materiality and of incorporating assorted materials within audiovisual platforms. Intermediality in the case of VR acquires an added dimension, the way user bodies themselves begin to cross media boundaries, as VR participants are virtually transported inside the experience of others, even if only partially. In that sense the crossing of the spectator (or user's) body from our "physical" space into the virtual one represents the ultimate form of media transgression. Something similar might be said of AI's amalgamation of human and machine knowledge (perhaps consciousness), as cinematic works become a reflection of both of these processes annealed. The story of the intermedial in Luso-Hispanic Atlantic film and video is a story of adaptation to difficult conditions of production, so that including and working with found footage, collaging materials clipped from newspapers and other print analog sources, and adopting an aesthetic of the "good enough" have become signatures of experimental movie-making in this region. All these factors reinforce the assertion by film theorist Philip Rosen that "cinema's specificity is to be not specific" ("Impurity to Historicity" 12). Regarding the profound transformation of both the cinema and the concept of medium, theorists have redefined and broadened what they signify by "medium specificity" to allow for both digital convergence and new experiments such as AI, VR, and cell phone filmmaking and viewing, as well as other as yet unimagined emerging formats. For instance, Erika Balsom in her introduction to *Exhibiting Cinema in Contemporary Art* (2013) declares:

> The contemporary moment is not simply one of convergence, but also one that sees an unleashing of multiple medium specificities that disperse the notion of cinema across varied conceptual and material spaces. Ideas of what the cinema might be are now articulated in numerous and incompatible forums, ranging from Hollywood's increasing efforts to combat online bootlegging through campaigns that emphasize the giganticism of the multiplex screen to partnerships with mobile telephone companies (now rebranding themselves as providers of "multimedia devices") to deliver content on tiny, handheld gadgets. (15)

Yet, as we saw in the work of Narcisa Hirsch, Daniela Cugliandolo, Andrés Denegri, and Gustavo Caprín, the presence of Super 8 and analog video images within contemporary film practices makes possible new interpretations of old images and older media aesthetics. All of these images and media are now archived in the cloud, so they have become a repository for continuous repurposing by filmmakers, whether human or artificial. Such constant material changes have been a reality since the very initial years of the cinema, and certainly, as I showed throughout the book, since the explosive experimenting of the 1960s. This continuous expansion of the cinema happened as militant filmmakers like Lumbreras, Solanas, or Álvarez equated experimenting and interrogating the notion of pure, discrete media with the radical politics they espoused; further expansion occurred when art filmmakers like Rocha and the EdB sought to crystallize new approaches to filmic representation and to allow their radical aesthetics to broaden the minds and attitudes of spectators. In both instances, the practice of expanding cinema (formally and materially) also functioned as a socially transformative act.

It is no less a reality that all the works I have examined throughout this book evaded simple identification in terms of their nations of origin. Filmmaking is increasingly a cross-border activity, whether amateur or professional, and filmmakers' sense of national belonging has become wonderfully complex in an era when relocation through travel, exile, diaspora, and economic displacement shapes and reframes everyone's lives. Ever more so, individual artists and institutions, as well as production companies, are becoming independent of individual nation-states. There are also more filmmakers creating in DIY fashion without relying on traditional venues and forms of production and distribution, accessing global audiences by relying on direct digital distribution of their work. Relations across multiple countries are forged based on shared affinities and interests, and diasporic cineastes maintain links to multiple countries. Conversations are forged across the Luso-Hispanic Atlantic, as we saw in the epistolary videos between Denegri and Caprín, for instance, or much earlier, in the exchanges between Latin American and Iberian filmmakers during the 1960s. The content and nature of cinema across the region reflects both its transnational and intermedial tendencies, as national identities are replaced by other forms of affiliation for many characters, as the films center on topics related to movement and mobility, and as the presence of digital media becomes central to the stories being told. Concerns about the power of technology to separate us are also present in narratives, for example in the horror cell phone films I examined. Similarly, the emergence of AI cinema has raised questions about the ethics of human-computer collaborations in filmmaking, and films will soon reflect these pressing concerns. Borders, media, and bodies have become gradually more porous, as the Luso-Hispanic Atlantic becomes increasingly more diffuse as a region, including not only Latin America, the Iberian Peninsula, and other Spanish- and Portuguese-speaking nations but also communities that identify with the region throughout the globe. The changes that transnationalism and intermedial practices across the Luso-Hispanic Atlantic will bring to cinematic culture in coming years are wholly unpredictable but will undoubtedly be exhilarating and will foment innovative forms of experimental, documentary, and fiction cinema for the foreseeable future, as the cinema continues to expand beyond any material and geographic boundary or limitation.

Notes

Introduction

1. All translations from the Spanish and Portuguese are my own, unless otherwise noted.

2. I analyze *Carne y Arena* in detail in chapter 5.

3. Although I experienced this eye-opening VR installation at the Nasher Sculpture Center, *Carne y Arena* toured multiple global sites so that the exhibit itself functioned as a metaphor for transnational migration.

4. It is not my intention to equate the dangerous and life-altering experience of border crossing with the aesthetic act of transgressing media borders, even if the latter functions with political intent. They are not the same, and the stakes are vastly different. My point is that there are affinities, even material affinities, between these two acts, which are worth exploring if and when questions of intermediality and transnationalism intertwine.

5. Youngblood's book has also been reappraised in several other recent volumes, for example Alan L. Rees's edited collection *Expanded Cinema: Art, Performance, Film* (2011), a work that looks even further back to early abstract cinema and continues on to the early 2000s, examining the influence of happenings, performance, video art, sonic festivals, and other forms of cinema that move beyond the single screen and conventional spectatorship. Similarly, Janine Marchessault and Susan Lord's *Fluid Screens, Expanded Cinema* (2007) studies "a range of moving-image technologies that are encompassed by the phenomenology of the cinema" and seeks to think through the expansion of the frame outward, from a decidedly global perspective (7). Finally, pushing the concept of "expansion" even further along, and aligned with the latest technological developments, Federico Biggio argues in an article in *NECSUS European Journal of Media Studies* that, today, the cinema is not only intermedial as Youngblood stipulated but also informational, so that it will lead

to a "cognitive augmentation process by means of artificial intelligence and computational technologies" (175). Others have written on this subject, for example Riccardo Venturi offers a brief comparative recounting on the idea of "expanded cinema" as seen in both the United States and Europe in his article "Rethinking the Expanded Cinema."

6. See, for instance, Jonas Mekas, "On the Expanding Eye," *Village Voice*, 6 Feb. 1964, or "More on Expanded Cinema: Emshwiller, Stern, Ken Jacobs, Ken Dewey," *Village Voice*, 2 Dec. 1965; Stan VanDerBeek, "'Culture: Intercom' and Expanded Cinema: A Proposal and Manifesto," *Film Culture*, vol. 40, Spring 1966, pp. 15–18; Carolee Schneemann, "Expanded Cinema: Free Form Recollections of New York," International Underground Film Festival, London, 1970. For a complete list of primary and secondary bibliography, see "Expanded Cinema" at https://monoskop.org/Expanded_cinema.

7. While the New Latin American Cinema of the 1960s did achieve notoriety and respect, thanks to the international visibility of filmmakers like Glauber Rocha (foremost director in Brazil's Cinema Novo), Pino Solanas and Octavio Getino (as representatives of the militant cinema of the Argentine Cine Liberación), or Julio García Espinosa and Santiago Álvarez (originators of Cuba's "imperfect cinema"), or, barely studied but just as relevant, the indigenous cinema of Jorge Sanjinés's Ukamau group in Bolivia, much less attention has been paid to work that did not conform exactly to North American and European expectations of "guerrilla" cinema or did not reach the level of festival distribution enjoyed by films such as *La hora de los hornos* or *La battala de Chile* (*The Battle of Chile*, Patricio Guzmán, 1975–1979). I am referring to lesser-known militant films such as Helena Lumbreras's *El campo para el hombre* (*Field for Men*, 1973), but also to the abstract and structural films by the likes of Claudio Caldini or Narcisa Hirsch (Argentina), or even to understudied works by well-known filmmakers, such as Rocha's *Cabeças cortadas*.

8. The book begins its journey in the 1960s for a reason. There is a before and after the 1959 Cuban Revolution in the political, social, and cultural imaginary of the Luso-Hispanic Atlantic, a change that is reflected especially by the emergence of a vibrant experimental, documentary, and militant cinema at that time, as exemplified by the revolutionary New Latin American Cinema that erupted onto the scene and showed how experimental art and militancy could be placed at the service of political projects. The cinema was seen as a medium that could mobilize the masses, a realization also embraced by fascism in the 1930s and '40s. Through that mass mobilization appeal, many believed that the cinema could provide the necessary ignition for a systemic global change. That revolutionary spark also marks a shift away from a cinema of literary adaptation, comedies, and historical dramas and toward a vibrant era of experimentalism throughout Latin America and, to various degrees, worldwide. Thus 1959 is a logical dividing line to examine noncommercial filmmaking, even as there were various examples of innovative form dating from pre-

vious periods, most notably during the historical avant-garde with works by pioneers such as Mario Peixoto (Brazil), Horacio Coppola (Argentina), Segundo de Chomón (Spain), or Luis Buñuel (Spain/Mexico) to name some outstanding examples. But these luminaries were notable exceptions in an otherwise mostly commercial film landscape in the Luso-Hispanic Atlantic in those early years.

9. In a fascinating discussion about the ways in which the "digital" has disarticulated our previous paradigms, Benoît Turquety discusses how the division between professional and amateur, always a shaky proposition, no longer holds water today, as the roles of creator, editor, distributor, and archivist become enmeshed and the very notion of *spectatorship* morphs into something different: "Today most devices that can play moving pictures and sounds (such as computers, phones, tablets, etc.) can also make and distribute them. Images are made to be shared, each one calling for a response, their circulation constituting the very foundation of social networks such as Instagram, Snapchat, or Flickr. This irruption of digital culture into film studies seems to have upset the discipline, blurring its contours and cracking its foundation, precisely because the concept of the 'spectator' has become inappropriate to describe the diversity of contemporary relationships to moving images. The paradigm has been exposed and in the same gesture put under critical pressure" (29).

10. For an excellent overview and first approximation to the experimental cinema of Latin America and Spain, a catalog to an exhibition by the same name, see Jesse Lerner and Luciano Piazza's *Ism, Ism, Ism/Ismo, Ismo, Ismo: Experimental Cinema in Latin America* (2017).

11. Case in point, while González Iñárritu's main body of work is decidedly commercial and has been instrumental in ushering in a new era of transnational filmmaking that began with his first global hit and directorial debut, *Amores perros* (*Love's a Bitch,* 2000), instead *Carne y Arena* was decidedly experimental from the standpoint of its innovative technology and lacked the sort of commercial intent and appeal displayed by the filmmaker's previous oeuvre. But it still falls somewhere in between in the spectrum of commercially successful versus underground and marginal.

12. I have not coined the term "Luso-Hispanic Atlantic," which has already appeared in prominent works of cultural criticism, for example in the volume *Figurative Inquisitions: Conversion, Torture, and Truth in the Luso-Hispanic Atlantic* (2014) edited by Erin Graff Zivin.

13. Of course, Nagib and Jerslev borrow the term "impure cinema" from Bazin's 1951 article "Pour un cinéma impur: Défense de l'adaptation," later translated as "In Defense of Mixed Cinema." In this text Bazin advocates in favor of literary adaptations to the cinema.

14. A word about the formatting of film titles throughout the book: for the first mention of a foreign film, I provided its original title in italics, and then, if known, the English release title (also in italics, and inside a parenthesis). If, to

the best of my knowledge, there was no translated release title, I provide my own translation in brackets to indicate it is a translation rather than a release title. All subsequent mentions of a film use the original title or an abbreviated version.

15. Among the first group of general texts there are many fine works, such as Deborah Shaw's *Contemporary Latin American Cinema: Breaking into the Global Market* (2007), Stephen Hart's *A Companion to Latin American Film* (2004), John King's now-canonical *Magical Reels: A History of Cinema in Latin America* (2000), Zuzana Pick's *The New Latin American Cinema: A Continental Project* (1993), Julianne Burton's *The Social Documentary in Latin America* (1990), Gabriel Teshome's comprehensive classic about global Third Cinema (including Latin America) *Third Cinema in the Third World: The Aesthetics of Liberation* (1982), Vinicius Navarro and Juan Carlos Rodríguez's *New Documentaries in Latin America* (2014), and the much needed *Indigeneity in Latin American Cinema* (2022) by Milton Fernando Gonzalez Rodriguez, to name but a few of the well-established and some newer volumes in the field.

16. Earlier texts, however, bypass the transnational dimension, including *The Cuban Image: Cinema and Cultural Politics in Cuba* (1985) by Michael Chanan, which concentrates on the production from that island-nation, as well as works that examine the New Argentine Cinema, such as Gonzalo Aguilar's *Otros mundos: Ensayo sobre el nuevo cine argentino* (2006) [Other Worlds: Essay About the New Argentine Cinema], or Jeffrey Middents's examination of the specialized film press in *Writing National Cinema: Film Journals and Film Culture in Peru* (2009).

17. This observation is not meant to criticize these texts for what they do not do, that is simply not their chosen area of inquiry. My point is that there is a space left vacant in the research to which I wish to contribute.

18. One book that does take on the horror genre is Jonathan Risner's *Blood Circuits: Contemporary Argentine Horror Cinema* (2018), which studies the international dimension of horror film circuits and nevertheless manages to examine the Argentine case in great depth.

19. See Tamara Falicov, "Programa Ibermedia: Co-production and the Cultural Politics of Constructing an Ibero-American Audiovisual Space," *Spectator*, vol. 27. no. 2, Fall 2007. See also her chapter "Ibero-Latin American Co-productions: Transnational Cinema, Spain's Public Relations Venture, or Both?," in Stephanie Dennison's *Contemporary Hispanic Cinema*, pp. 67–88.

20. There are other critical texts written in Spanish about experimental cinema, but most have not focused on Latin America and Spain (or not exclusively). An example is Albert Alcoz's *Radicales libres: 50 películas esenciales del cine experimental* (2019) [Free Radicals: 50 Essential Films of Experimental Cinema], which analyzes fifty "canonical" works of mainly Anglo-American experimental cinema, with a handful of European exceptions and only one Latin American film by Fernando Birri. Alcoz does include five films from Spain, one each by Luis Buñuel, Salvador Dalí, Iván Zulueta, José Val del Omar, and Pere Portabella.

21. While my own text also includes some narrative cinema with experimental tendencies, as well as amateur films that dabble with subgenres such as horror and sci-fi, or works whose experimental nature is mostly present through their use of new media, I do depart from Tompkins's approach in that I also analyze more extreme experimental genres that have rarely been included in any cinema histories to date.

22. Various conversations and even collaborations transpired between filmmakers from both groups (most saliently involving Glauber Rocha), and both "schools" were also in close contact with other emerging art house cinemas, such as the French New Wave and Italian neorealism, or the British and the Czech New Waves.

23. Often this diaspora reconnects us to the past, to the 1960s and to the forced exile that resulted from political unrest in Latin America and Spain. A second wave of exiles—in this case fleeing the many global economic crises of the twenty-first century—has also resulted in exchanges (to and from, and sometimes back again) across the Luso-Hispanic Atlantic. These exchanges are tinged with media nostalgia, a nostalgia aligned with homesickness and a sense of loss. This kind of affective reaction, that is nostalgia, etymologically from the Greek *nostos* (return) and *algos* (pain), is a reaction that reflects the pain or yearning for a return that is often impossible. The same displaced filmmakers weave into their filmmaking their yearning for lost or replaced media, which is a mourning symptomatic of the passing and obsolescence of analog formats in the era of digital media (perhaps best exemplified with celluloid film and magnetic video, but also other formats such as vinyl, audiocassette tapes, and so forth).

24. As some of its practitioners see it, VR is qualitatively different from cinema, in ways that are diametrically opposed to cell phone filmmaking, for instance. If cell phones made the screen much smaller (but mobile and closer to our body), VR has enlarged the screen space to envelop our senses in 360-degrees, radically expanding the frame. This has fomented the illusion that the spectator has transcended spatiotemporal laws to be physically present within the narrative space. That presence, I would argue, can vary radically, from that of a mere detached observer to an active participant in the narrative. VR narratives court intermediality to intensify engagement and presence—as the viewer, or user, is enveloped by the story world they are often surrounded by many art forms and sensory inputs, including music, dance, architecture (VR emphasizes the architectural and 3D of its "screen" as well as the sense of space, proprioception, movement), and other forms that are either evoked or directly used as the viewer "transits" through the virtual space.

25. The complexity and specialization of developing VR has had an opposite effect to that seen in cell phone cinema in terms of democratization and immediate distribution. Here, a small cadre of specialists, typically young and necessarily tech savvy, have connected globally to work on projects across national borders. VR development teams are scattered through various nations, challenging any easy categorization in terms of national origin. Developers move around from country to country, and funding is also typically raised from multiple countries (often

collaborations between the United States, Spain, and those Latin American nations at the forefront of this technological medium, such as Argentina, Brazil, Chile, and Mexico).

Chapter 1

1. Some preliminary and partial material from this chapter was previously published in the *Studies in Spanish and Latin American Cinemas* journal and is reproduced here with the permission of the editors. See Eduardo Ledesma, "Helena Lumbreras' *Field for Men* (1973): Midway between Latin American Third Cinema and the Barcelona School," *Studies in Spanish and Latin American Cinemas*, vol. 11, no. 3, Fall 2014, 271–88.

2. These filmmakers created influential works on insurgency, such as *Roma città aperta* (1945) [Rome Open City] by Rosellini, and decolonization, such as *La battaglia di Algeri* (1966) [The Battle of Algiers] by Gillo Pontecorvo, who was not trained at the Centro but learned hands-on working as an assistant to Dutch filmmaker Joris Ivens. For a full list of international students who attended the Centro, see Flavia Laviosa et al.

3. As briefly mentioned in the introduction, and as we discuss in the next chapter in great detail, Lúcia Nagib and Anne Jerslev have also written extensively about similar "impure" approaches to film, editing a volume with the title *Impure Cinema* in 2014.

4. The cinema of the French New Wave made its impact on Solanas primarily through Jean Luc Godard's films. Solanas and Godard knew each other and often acknowledged a mutual affinity in style and political objectives, despite vast differences in the conditions of their militancies within dictatorial Argentina and democratic France.

5. For extensive coverage of intermediality in visual poetry and related experimental writing practices, see my book *Radical Poetry: Aesthetics, Politics, Technology and the Ibero-American Avant-Gardes 1900–2015* (2017).

6. Oscar Masotta was an Argentine Marxist writer, Lacanian psychoanalyst, and artist who was affiliated with the Torcuato di Tella Institute and the 1960s Argentine avant-garde. He left Argentina in exile for Barcelona in 1974 and was heavily involved in clandestine militancy both in Argentina and Spain.

7. By Third Cinema I refer not only to the prominent Argentine Third Cinema but also to other interrelated aesthetic-political film practices such as Cuba's "imperfect cinema," Brazil's "Cinema Novo" (which might also be categorized as closer to art cinema) and other militant cinemas loosely classified in the 1960s under the rubric of the New Latin American Cinema. Fernando Solanas and Octavio Getino, seemingly more precise in their categorization, starkly differentiated Third Cinema from First Cinema (Hollywood) and Second Cinema (European art cinema).

8. For more on Ivens, *The Spanish Earth* and some of the Dutch auteur's filmmaking techniques, especially the practice of reenactment, see my article "Staging the Spanish Civil War: History and Reenactment in Joris Ivens' *The Spanish Earth* (1937)," *Bulletin of Spanish Visual Studies*, vol. 4, no. 1, 2020, pp. 1–32.

9. There was a brief interlude of censorship liberalization, which lasted from 1963 to 1969, under Manuel Fraga Iribarne's oversight as minister of information and tourism, and José María García Escudero's directorship of the ministry's film section (D'Lugo, "Catalan" 138). For a full account of film censorship under Franco, see Román Gubern and Domènec Font's *Un cine para el cadalso: 40 años de censura cinematográfica en España* (1973) [Film for the Gallows: 40 Years of Cinematic Censorship in Spain], or Font's *Del azul al verde: el cine español bajo el franquismo* (1976) [From Blue to Green: Spanish Cinema Under Francoism]. For a broader perspective on censorship, see Gubern's *La censura: Función política y ordenamiento jurídico bajo el franquismo (1936–1975)* (1981) [Censorship: Political Function and Legislative Organization under Francoism] (1936–1975)].

10. The title is borrowed from a verse in "A una España joven" ["To a Young Spain"] (1915), a poem by Antonio Machado.

11. Julianne Burton stipulates that "to the eyes of a growing number of Latin Americans, behind Hollywood's 'pure entertainment' mask, there's an agent of cultural and political domination lurking" ("The Hour" 34).

12. In an intriguing echo NCE filmmaker Basilio Martín Patino later used "Los cuatro generales" for his experimental collage documentary *Caudillo* (1974), a film that forms part of a trilogy about the Spanish Civil War and its brutal aftermath; Patino's film is also an indictment against Franco (the eponymous Caudillo) and his prominent role in Spain's fratricidal war and lengthy dictatorship.

13. This translation is a modified version from Camí-Vela's own translation of the film script ("Between" 257–58).

14. Interestingly, the original photograph was not taken in Asturias (although it does belong to that greater conflict) but in Brañosera (Palencia), on Oct. 8, 1934. A source for the original photograph, published in the *Illustrated Daily Courier*, can be found in the archive Narodowe Archiwum Cyfrowe in Poland.

Chapter 2

1. Some preliminary and partial material from this chapter was previously published in the *Journal of Spanish Cultural Studies* and is reproduced here with the permission of the editors. See Eduardo Ledesma, "Intermediality and Spanish Experimental Cinema: Text and Image Interactions in the Lyrical Films of the Barcelona School," *Journal of Spanish Cultural Studies* vol. 14, no. 3, Fall 2013, 254–74. As widely documented, many of the integrands of the EdB, even those who were members of the Catalan bourgeoisie, did not strongly identify as Catalan,

with the possible exceptions of Pere Portabella and Ricardo Bofill. Some were from other parts of the Peninsula, including the Portuguese-born Nunes.

2. Rocha was a thorn in the dictatorship's side for many years but began to shift toward a more ambiguous political position and ultimately made dubious declarations in support of the generals in the mid to late 1970s, once they had pledged to move toward democracy. This ideological change, however, was highly controversial and led many in the left to speculate that Rocha was becoming psychologically unhinged (Shaw and Dennison 85–86).

3. In 1973 Augusto Martínez Torres and Manuel Pérez Estremera would go on to publish a volume about the New Latin American Cinema, entitled *Nuevo cine latinoamericano* that dedicated its longest chapter to Cinema Novo (Elena 236).

4. Despite this stark difference in terms of hierarchical structure and division of labor, there were significant contacts between Lumbreras's collective and the EdB, including through Llorenç Soler, who collaborated with both.

5. The term "intermediality" can be traced to its earlier version, "intermedia," defined by Fluxus artist-theorist Dick Higgins in 1966 as a space between media and between disciplines (Blom 65). To date, the lion's share of research on intermediality hails from Germany, with prominent work by Ulrich Weisstein, Werner Wolf, Jürgen Müller, Jens Schröter, and Irina Rajewsky, among others. On ideology and intermediality, see Schröter's essay "The Politics of Intermediality." In the United States there is relevant foundational work by Jay Bolter and David Grusin (*Remediation*, 2000) and Henry Jenkins (*Convergence Culture*, 2006). Canada houses the Centre for Research into Intermediality at the University of Montreal, comprising thirty researchers from McGill University, the University of Ottawa, the University of Amsterdam, and the University of Paris III.

6. Rajewsky understands this as a spectrum that spans from "mere contiguity of two or more material manifestations of different media to a 'genuine' integration, an integration which in its most pure form would privilege none of its constitutive elements" (52).

7. Intermedial is distinct from related terms describing media relations, such as intertextuality (references between two or more verbal texts), transmediality (the transfer of the same narrative from one medium to another), remediation (as defined by Bolter and Grusin, the incorporation of "old" media, such as radio, television, print journalism, into "new" digital media), hypermedia, or indeed multimedia (Rajewsky).

8. A couple of contemporary sources on this subject include John R. Corbin's article "The Myth of Primitive Spain," or various sections in the 1990 book-length study by the Department of the Army and the Library of Congress, *Spain: A Country Study* (see pp. 68, 79, 124, 138). In that text, the DoA's assessment is as negative as it seems biased and/or inaccurate: "On this scale, Spain, with a score of 122 for the 1979–80 period, ranked thirty-seventh out of 107 countries, quite far behind most

other West European countries and comparable to several advanced Third World states, such as Mexico and Argentina" (124); in other sections, the DoA describes Spain's pre-democracy economy as the worst in Western Europe and the nation is categorized as "underdeveloped" (138).

9. Through a series of unexpected historical turns and profiting from his unscrupulous political savvy, in 1985 Sarney became the first president of democratic Brazil and governed during one of the most politically corrupt and inefficient administrations in that country's history.

10. These vastly different musical styles are interspersed throughout the film, for example: bossa nova (51:00), rock 'n' roll (1:02:00), opera (1:13:00), and so on.

11. Not to confuse Aranda's *Fata Morgana* with the Werner Herzog film by the same name, released in 1971, about mirages in the Saharan Desert.

12. *Film Ideal*, a partisan periodical closely allied with the EdB (like *Fotogramas*), dedicated an article in 1969 to Godard's synthesis of form and ideological critique, as well as pointing out the ways the filmmaker integrated current political concerns in his work, as elements for critique: "el arreglo de cuentas con la sociedad industrial y de consumo emprendido por Godard . . . consiste en integrar la Guerra [del Vietnam] en su propia obra" [the settling of scores with industrial and consumerist society enacted by Godard . . . consists of integrating the (Vietnam War) in his own filmmaking] (Molist et al. 126).

13. Muñoz Suay was a fascinating individual who held almost every possible role within the film industry, from director (as second-in-command to Berlanga in *Bienvenido, Mr. Marshall* [*Welcome, Mr. Marshall!*] and to Patino in *Nueve Cartas a Berta* [*Nine Letters to Berta*]), to script writer, to producer of numerous films (among them Buñuel's *Viridiana*, but also most of the EdB's work), to producer and script writer for Rocha's film and other creative and supportive functions.

14. I am referring to metalepsis in the narratological sense (see Genette), as a transgression or contamination between different ontological narrative levels or story worlds, or indeed, between the real and the fictional worlds.

15. The caveat is that intentions aside, the association between form and politics often has unforeseen results. History has shown that an aesthetically radical avant-garde can be at any end of the political spectrum.

16. As James observes, Mulvey had made her insightful critique of Hollywood cinema in her 1973 essay for the journal *Screen*, "Visual Pleasures and Narrative Cinema," a seminal article that ushered in feminist film theory.

17. The NCE originated from the 1955 Salamanca meeting of filmmakers (Luis Berlanga, Juan Antonio Bardem, Carlos Saura, Basilio Martín Patino, and others) who desired to overhaul Iberian cinema by improving technical quality and turning to social issues. A politically daring filmmaking by the NCE and the EdB was made possible by a lessening of censorship attributed to Manuel Fraga's role at the helm of the Ministry of Information and Tourism and José María Escudero's

directorship of cinematography. The regime's interest in improving Spain's image abroad resulted in increased state sponsorship of films considered to be "of quality," permitting a larger pool of filmmakers to access funds.

18. The influence of Guy Debord's particular use of dialectical montage (his recourse to repurposed and pirated images, news clippings, and photographs as well as overlaid text frames, irregular rhythms, and syncopated cutting) can be seen in the EdB's aesthetic and ideological filmmaking methodology, especially in the case of Nunes and Esteva, and to a lesser extent by the school's other cineastes. Situationism, the spark behind the May 1968 upheavals, weighed heavily on the EdB's own critique of the society of consumption, a critique that was complicated by its ambivalent relationship to the Barcelona elite that in many ways supported their projects.

19. Similar uses of fashion models in avant-garde films can be seen in Jean Luc Godard's *Une femme mariée* (*A Married Woman*, 1964), Jacques Demy's *Model Shop* (1969), Michelangelo Antonioni's *Blow-Up* (1966), or closer to home, NCE Carlos Saura's surrealist-inspired *Peppermint Frappé* (1967), whose opening sequence rhythmically edits photographs of models clipped from international fashion magazines.

20. Ironically, 1968 was also declared the International Year for Human Rights by the United Nations despite the dismal conditions of human rights around the world that year.

21. Fèlix Fanés, one of the few critics to make reference to the use of different media by Portabella (along with Marsh and Rosalind Galt), states, "Far from the specificity of the cinema, (Portabella's) process incorporates other expressive media, developing like a hybrid composed of different materials" (Fanés 475, my translation).

22. Portabella had employed this identical numerical structure in *No compteu amb els dits* (1967), in which he includes twenty-eight sequences. Since this short film was finished one year earlier than *Nocturno 29*, it is obvious that the number of sequences also corresponds to the years under Franco.

23. Rabal had also acted for Buñuel in *Nazarín* (1959) and other films and for the EdB in Jacinto Esteva's 1968 *Después del diluvio* [After the Flood], and the Spanish star was becoming increasingly involved in art house and experimental cinema circles.

24. Albert Elduque reports that there was an early Rocha script for a similar film entitled *O testamento de Don Quixote* [Don Quixote's Will] ("O touro" 455–65).

25. Clémenti, who was quite well-known in the 1960s, had a similar role in Pasolini's *Porcile* (*Pigsty*, 1969), played the devil in Buñuel's surrealist film *La Voie lactée* (*The Milky Way*, 1969), and also had a leading part in *Belle de Jour* (1967).

26. There is an interesting documentary about the film, entitled *El viaje Glauber* (2014) [The Glauber Journey], which examines the production, reception, and historical context, as well as some thoughtful analysis. It was created as part of the Universitat Autònoma de Barcelona's year-long course in creative documentary, the Máster en Documental Creativo, by Fermín Sales, Cristina Algarra, Estel la

Muñiz, Davani Varillas, and Víctor Sanz. The film is available on YouTube, www.youtube.com/watch?app=desktop&v=iogjsTCZmHI.

27. In another scene the soundtrack is a flamenco mass, a fusion genre that brings together popular music (flamenco) with classical music and religious mysticism, as well as dance. Flamenco itself is a crossover musical style that combines guitar and percussion, as well as singers and dancers, often of gypsy descent.

Chapter 3

1. Some preliminary and partial material from this chapter was previously published in the *Revista Hispánica Moderna* and is reproduced here with the permission of the editors. See Eduardo Ledesma, "Intermediality and Hispano-Argentine Experimental Film: Subverting Media, Transgressing Borders with Super 8," *Revista Hispánica Moderna*, vol. 70, no. 2, Dec. 2017, 117–41.

2. Although this chapter focuses on the Argentine *superocheros* primarily, there was a thriving amateur scene in various other Latin American countries at this time, including Venezuela and Mexico. Speaking to the transnational networks of collaboration among Super 8 practitioners in their introduction to *Global Perspectives on Amateur Film Histories and Cultures* (2020), Masha Salazkina and Enrique Fibla-Gutiérrez state, "[A]mateur filmmaking shaped local film cultures through its participation in institutions such as film societies and clubs, specialized publications and archives (both formal and informal), and different forms of oppositional media and artistic experimentation. Many of these initiatives extended internationally through festivals, symposia, and other regular exchanges, creating networks which are yet to be fully accounted for and often placing their centers in unexpected locations" (15). Some additional chapters in this excellent volume that deal with Super 8 from the Luso-Hispanic Atlantic include Jesse Lerner on the Mexican Super 8 movement's connection to the student protests and counterculture of the 1960s, "Super 8 in Mexico"; Pablo La Parra-Pérez on the subversive deployment of Super 8 during that same period by Galician amateur filmmakers under Francoism, "The Wind from the South: Experiences of Substandard Filmmaking in Galicia in the 1970s"; and Isabel Arredondo's exploration of the Super 8 festival scene in Venezuela in "Early International Super 8 Film Festivals: The Case of Caracas 1976–1980."

3. The CCCB has long promoted experimental and documentary film.

4. There has also historically been, according to Vives, a preferential treatment toward Argentines and other Latin Americans in Spanish immigration law, based on a shared cultural identity and linguistic affinity. Unfortunately, possibly because of Spain's own ongoing crisis since 2008, some of these special privileges are being gradually rescinded (232).

5. In reality, Super 8 could produce negatives and be used to generate copies, although this was not typically done, in fact it was quite rare. The majority of Super

8 used a reversal stock destined primarily for home projection, and as reversal film it produced a positive image, instead of negatives and prints. (That said, there was a Super 8 negative stock that existed and could have been used to create positive prints, just as reversal stocks existed for other gauges, so there is nothing inherently impossible about a Super 8 negative.) In contrast, most large celluloid formats (like 35 mm) used a negative film that later had to be processed into positive prints that could be projected. Super 8 was easy to use since cartridges could be inserted into the camera without the need to thread the celluloid. Moreover, Super 8 went from being silent to gaining sound capability in 1973.

6. In fact, Super 8 did disappear from the 1980s until the late 1990s, as film stock dwindled and laboratories stopped developing 8 mm film, replaced by video (VHS), which in turn has been replaced by digital video.

7. Distinctly meta-filmic and intertextual, Cugliandolo's films also quote, parody, and critically deconstruct her 1960s precursors, from Argentine Super 8 filmmakers (Narcisa Hirsch, Claudio Caldini, and Jorge Honik) to the North American postwar avant-garde (Maya Deren, Jonas Mekas, and Stan Brakhage) and even established art cinema auteurs (Federico Fellini, François Truffaut, and Alfred Hitchcock).

8. On the side of medium specificity, see for example, André Bazin's *What Is Cinema?* (2005), Roland Barthes's *Camera Lucida* (1981), Mary Ann Doane's article "The Indexical and the Concept of Medium Specificity" (2007), or Rosalind Krauss's essay "Two Moments from the Post-medium Condition" (2006). For arguments in favor of convergence, see David Thorburn and Henry Jenkins's *Rethinking Media Change* (2003).

9. The film recalls a sense of loss evocatively described by Rodowick in his elegy to celluloid: "as film disappears into an aesthetic universe constructed from digital intermediates and images combining computer synthesis and capture, and while I continue to feel engaged by many contemporary movies, I still have a deep sense, which is very hard to describe or qualify, of time lost" (164).

10. The actress is Mariana Chiesa Mateos, a visual artist born in La Plata (Argentina) in 1967, who subsequently emigrated to Barcelona in 1997, and after working there as an artist for years, finally moved again to Bologna, Italy, in 2008. The original Super 8 footage dates back to 2002.

11. Maya Deren and Alexander Hammid's 1943 short film *Meshes in the Afternoon* had a profound influence on Argentine experimental filmmakers, including Hirsch and Cugliandolo (see Szperling). Albert Alcoz also sees an influence from Deren on the work of David Lynch, especially evident in the 2001 film *Mulholland Drive* (61).

12. Among the arguments put forth to disarticulate the exclusive link of indexicality to the analog image, Rosen mentions the deployment of surveillance cameras and other mechanisms that are ontologically digital but whose indexicality (link to a pro-digital event) is accepted. Other examples include ultrasounds, x-rays,

and other images in which the "origin," historicity, or even authenticity would not be questioned.

13. Regarding nostalgia, see Dominik Schrey's "Analogue Nostalgia and the Aesthetics of Digital Remediation."

14. Filmmakers expand the "filmic" medium (digital and analog) by assembling complex projection loops and using multiple screens simultaneously, superimposing film upon film to create intermedial viewing experiences.

15. The picture I suggest here regarding the back and forth between analog and digital is even more complex if we consider the period between the early 2000s, when digital capture became gradually standardized in the industry, and approximately 2013, the year when movie theaters made their final and large-scale transition to digital projection, as 90 percent of screens globally converted. During that ten-to-fifteen-year period it was necessary for almost every film shot in digital to be printed to celluloid to enable its projection in theaters that lacked the capability to work with digital. Moreover, during this time, even those films that had been shot in celluloid underwent digital postproduction and then necessitated conversion to celluloid again so they could be projected in the majority of theaters that did not (yet) have digital projection. This meant that most films underwent an opposite lifecycle to that experienced by *Dune*, from analog to digital and then back to analog again. Today, the only theaters that retain a capability to project 35 mm celluloid features are art house or small-town theaters that never made the conversion, or more likely they can project in both analog and digital. The list of analog film exhibitors dwindles with each passing year, so the documenting of these last theaters to work with celluloid is in itself an exercise in nostalgia and a tribute to film's passing. Even fewer venues can still project 70 mm, although this author had the enriching experience of viewing Alfonso Cuarón's *Roma* (2018) projected in its full 70 mm glory at the Music Box Theater in Chicago.

16. As archivist and preservation specialist, David Walsh wonders, "Maybe there is a point in choosing a few iconic films from our collection and putting them in a dry cave in a format that is easily deciphered and unlikely to decay too rapidly. What would that be? 35mm black and white motion picture film on polyester stock perhaps?" (37). For an in-depth reflection on film preservation and digital data loss, read his excellent article "Eternal Digital Storage: The Impossible Dream."

17. The camera includes "a foldout LCD viewfinder and a computerized menu where light, exposure, and other variables can be controlled, and the audio will be simultaneously recorded onto a digital memory card, for later editing. This hybridized model extends to post-production as well: shoot your film and drop it in the mail, and Kodak processes it into negatives that you can display via a projector, digitally scans the footage, and uploads it to a cloud-based service where you can download and share it" (Sax). According to a Toronto manufacturer of film stock, "[D]emand for film has more than doubled over the past two years—especially for Super 8 stock" (Sax).

18. Argentina's 1960s underground filmmaker Claudio Caldini praises Super 8's potential to liberate filmmaking by making it more affordable, accessible, and flexible than larger formats (16 and 35 mm) (*Experimental Films* 29). Given its fragile material, Super 8's reliance on the "original" print has been necessarily replaced by the multiplicity it gains once digitized. This reproducibility marks a shift away from the uniqueness of the work of art that would have been, for Walter Benjamin, democratizing, even as it fuels nostalgia for film's lost aura. In today's intermedial environment, analog and digital are combined to redefine "the limits of both," creating "film-digital hybrids" that "evoke both the digital in the filmic apparatus or the filmic in the digital algorithms" (Kim 31–32).

19. The underground scene coalesced around the Goethe Institute, the Instituto DiTella (until its closure in 1971) as the "apagón cultural" intensified during the dictatorship, the interdisciplinary arts center Centro de Arte y Comunicación [Center for Art and Communication], and the Escuela Panamericana de Arte (Caldini and Marín, *Experimental Films* 32–33).

20. Some cases of overlap included Gerardo Vallejo, a member of Cine Liberación and cameraman for *Manzanas* (1966) [Apples], a happening by Hirsch; Raimundo Gleyzer, member of the militant Cine de la Base, later disappeared by the dictatorship, who worked on *Marabunta* (1967), a performance by Hirsch; Tomás Sinovcic, a friend of Caldini's, who began with experimental and turned to political film (he founded Contra-Cine), disappearing in 1974 (Rist 241–42).

21. The Goethe Group also had some links with the Super 8 filmmakers of UNCIPAR (Unión de Cineastas de Paso Reducido) [Union of Small Gauge Filmmakers]—"paso reducido" meaning either 8 or 16 mm small-gauge cinema. Formed in 1972, UNCIPAR filmmakers created short fiction films but aspired to full features and commercial success (Andermann 11; Torres 90; Caldini and Marín, *Experimental Films* 32–33).

22. This countercultural, anti-hegemonic position was an irritant for the authoritarian system, even if it did not directly challenge it. As David Oubiña documents, "[D]uring the years of the dictatorships the last vestiges of the industry were dismantled, films were censored, and filmmakers were persecuted, exiled and even murdered" (38). In the 1970s several of the Grupo Goethe filmmakers left Argentina or retreated to rural parts of the country, in either self-imposed or forced exile, some under pressure from the military regime and others because of their unwillingness to join the militant left. Caldini and Honik, for example, spent time in Spain.

23. Reich has received some critique about his potential appropriation of African American speech and culture (even for the appropriation of Black music), perhaps not without credit in light of some racist remarks he purportedly made in the 1970s. For considerations about this subject, see Sumanth Gopinath's chapter "The Problem of the Political in Steve Reich's *Come Out*" in *Sound Commitments: Avant-Garde Music and the Sixties.*

24. Recalling Snow's 1967 *Wavelength*, a pseudo murder mystery in which any hint of plot is wholly subservient to formal experimentation (an off-screen "murder"

of sorts occurs midway through the film, almost imperceptibly, the victim played by Hollis Frampton. The minimalist suggestion of narrative was meant as more of an inside joke among filmmakers).

25. There are also virtual Super 8 communities, including one on Facebook called "Super 8 Barcelona Community," as well as other virtual gathering points such as the websites www.super8-spain.com and www.super8.es.

26. For example, the CCCB exhibition "Cine a contracorriente: Latinoamérica y España. Diálogos, confluencias, divergencias en los últimos 80 años" (2010) [Film Against the Grain: Latin America and Spain. Dialog, Confluence and Divergence in the Past Eighty Years] was critical in fostering the dialogue between Latin American and Iberian cineastes, as was "Super 8: Little Big format" (2009) at the same venue.

27. Andrés Denegri, Sergio Subero, Gustavo Galuppo, Pablo Marín, Gustavo Caprín, Gabriela Golder, Jorge La Ferla, and Hernán Khourian are just some of the names associated with the newest generation of experimental film and video artists in Argentina.

28. Some of Denegri's work can be seen at the Rolf Art Gallery (Buenos Aires), rolfart.com.ar/artists/andres-denegri/.

29. There have been several important exhibitions in recent years focused on the concept of diaspora and/or exile. To name just one, the Argentine curator and scholar Rodrigo Alonso organized "Estudio Abierto" [Open Studio] in 2005, an event that foregrounded video installation art by three exiled video artists: Gustavo Caprín, Charly Nijensohn, and Gabriela Golder. Golder's piece was in fact titled *Diáspora* (García, "El video" 88).

30. Caprín's video can be viewed on Vimeo at vimeo.com/161616619?fb-clid=IwAR1Yjw0_IYs-U5I9GR6dtmFa9REBKh107r5gEJxfJ48yP0v4A1oEj44aOqw.

31. More specifically, the chart represents the "SD SMPTE" color bars; the initials stand for Standard-Definition Society of Motion Picture and Television Engineers, the organization that established the color bars in the 1970s to be the North American video standard.

32. The purpose of the bars and tone was to serve as a reference or target for the calibration of color and audio levels issued by the videotape recording during transmission. Comparing the image and sound to the known standard provided video engineers with an indication of how a National Television Standards Committee (NTSC) video signal may have been altered by recording or transmission and what adjustments needed to be made to bring its appearance back to specification.

33. Caprín's video "How to Build a House" can be viewed at www.hamaca-online.net/titles/how-to-build-a-house/.

Chapter 4

1. Some preliminary and partial material from this chapter was previously published in the *Revista de Estudios Hispánicos* and is reproduced here with the per-

mission of the editors. See Eduardo Ledesma, "Cell Phone Cinema: Latin American Horror Flicks in the Post-digital Age," *Revista de Estudios Hispánicos*, vol. 53, no. 3, Oct. 2019, 821–54.

2. The first films were shot with the Nokia 3660, 6600, and 7600; the Sony Ericsson Z1010; and the Siemens U15.

3. I use terms "cell phone" and "mobile phone" interchangeably. Although mobile phone is common in Europe and cell phone is in use predominantly in the United States, both terms are analogous in Spanish to *teléfono celular* (in Latin America) or *teléfono móvil* (in Spain).

4. Links between horror and phone technology have been exploited in many films, from the disembodied voice (*Scream*, 1996), to the cursed phone number (*End Call*, 2008), to internet transmissions from the dead (*Pulse*, 2008) or evil electronic signals (*Cell*, 2016).

5. Some festivals are sponsored by brands (Apple, Nokia), others are independent events that encourage burgeoning filmmakers who lack access to traditional formats and film institutions (film schools, professional studios, larger festivals).

6. One example is *24: Conspiracy*, a low-budget version of the TV series *24*, released by Verizon in 2005 in twenty-four one-minute episodes.

7. Another interesting possibility with cell phones is to create collective films using footage from multiple individuals. Acclaimed Iberian filmmaker Isabel Coixet edited a collective anthology documentary entitled *Spain in a Day* (2016). Coixet's film was inspired by Kevin Macdonald's *Life in a Day* (2011) and has been followed by other "crowd-sourced" films such as *Voicemails from Strangers* (Gregory Austin McConnell, 2019), and these films may indeed suggest a turn to collaborative filmmaking among strangers.

8. Bordwell is not the only critic to observe the radically changing nature of post-digital cinema. Shane Denson and Julia Leyda make a similar point in the introduction to their *Post-Cinema: Theorizing 21st-Century Film* (2016), arguing for a new episteme in "post-millennial film and other media, one that is evident in new formal strategies, radically changed conditions of viewing, and new ways in which films address their spectators. Contemporary films, from blockbusters to independents and the auteurist avant-garde, use digital cameras and editing technologies, incorporating the aesthetics of gaming, webcams, surveillance video, social media, and smartphones, to name a few. As a result of these developments and reconfgurations, the aesthetic boundaries between art house film and blockbuster have become increasingly blurred as the mechanisms and perspectives of classical continuity are formally and materially challenged by a post-cinematic media regime" (4).

9. It is also the first large-scale cellular phone film festival in Latin America, similar in its approach to exhibition and financing as well-established predecessors such as Pocket Films festival in Paris (2004 until 2010) or Mobile Film Festival in Hong Kong (in its ninth edition).

10. The best-known actress in the group is Yuri Vargas (Ana), who has theater, film, and television experience in Colombia, but also Majida Issa (María), an

actress who had a role in the acclaimed soap *El clon* (released in English as *The Clone*, 2010, a remake of the influential Brazilian series *O Clone*, 2001), or Juana del Rio (Magdalena) and Juan Pablo Urrego (the supervisor), who have acted in Colombian *telenovelas*.

11. In her discussion of found footage horror cinema in Spain, Anne E. Hardcastle observes, "Found footage horror films frequently mimic the appearance of archival, actuality, or home-made pieces in their use of less professional equipment or media, 'amateur' filming techniques, and even visual or audio degradations and imperfections associated with age or casual (in some cases violent) treatment of the footage or equipment)" (109).

12. Certainly, we could provide a long list of examples in the found footage genre coming from the Luso-Hispanic world. For example, Alejandro Amenábar's now classic *Tesis* (*Thesis*, 1996) comes to mind as a precursor, as do Carles Torrens's *Emergo* (released in English as *Apartment 143*, 2011) and Barreda Luna's *Atroz* (*Atrocious*, 2010), to name some obvious examples.

13. As a curious aside, it is notable that despite the prevalence of English in these films from Spain and Latin America, there are still a significant number of instances in which the nonnative speaker elements come through—for example in the poster's tagline, "Talk to them . . . beyond the life" [*sic*], a straight calque (loan translation) from "más allá de la vida."

14. An English subtitled version of *iMedium* can be seen on YouTube at www.youtube.com/watch?v=C5Dfqv8QVHw. See the Facebook page for Geofilms Entertainment here: www.facebook.com/geofilmsentertainment/?eid=ARDuMCVJ_ 1c_XtDDka5qiYvmrU6KjqmTacuv8aGhQxJb7wvW-GSzP_ODUeIZ4ZqKfn1oGw GV0nqo9GOw.

15. Their film *iMedium* garnered several awards and competed in many festivals, including PIFFF in Paris, Tenebra Film Fest in Mexico, A Night of Horror Festival in Australia, the Miami Fear Fest, and the Sacramento Horror Film Festival, as well as the Fantasia Internacional Film Festival in Montreal.

16. See the Geofilms channel at www.youtube.com/channel/UC8Qb85J1 cQ7enDBMqBUK6Gw.

17. For example, García explains that for one of his films, *Sector Zero 4*, "he utilizado una óptica gran angular. El iPhone pegado con cinta americana a una antorcha de LED que a su vez hace de sujeción. Una batería externa para iPhone. Un micro direccional conectado a un grabador Tascam" (Cabrera) [I used a wide angle lens. The iPhone attached with duct tape to an LED light that also doubles as a support. An external iPhone battery. A directional microphone connected to a Tascam recorder].

18. Even more ambitious than the Dutch feature *App*, the J-horror film *Sadako 3D 2* (2013), a sequel to the now classic film *Ringu* (*The Ring*, Hideo Nakata, 1998), pulls out all the stops by both making the feature 3D and adding a free app that provides various vibrations, sounds, lights, images, and other special effects for spectators' mobile phone screens.

19. The Facebook page with the fake app can be seen at www.facebook.com/imediumapp/videos/17740012819482225/.

Chapter 5

1. According to VR designer Kaitlyn Irvine, "Extended Reality (XR) refers to all real-and-virtual environments generated by computer technology and wearables. The 'X' in XR is a variable that can stand for any letter. VR encompasses all immersive experiences. These could be created using purely real-world content (360 video), purely synthetic content (Computer Generated), or a hybrid of both. Augmented Reality (AR) is an overlay of computer-generated content on the real world that can superficially interact with the environment in real-time. With AR, there is no occlusion between CG content and the real-world. Mixed Reality (MR) is an overlay of synthetic content that is anchored to and interacts with objects in the real world—in real time. Mixed Reality experiences exhibit occlusion, in that the computer-generated objects are visibly obscured by objects in the physical environment" ("A Definitive Guide").

2. An expensive device costing up to five thousand dollars, HoloLens has had fewer cinematic and narrative applications than other more affordable HMDs in the market, although it has been successfully integrated into the business, manufacturing, and medical industries, and, disturbingly but unsurprisingly, been highly sought-after by the United States military, which signed a twenty-two-billion-dollar contract to adapt HoloLens for the theater of war (Slater-Robins).

3. This militarization extends even to the realm of video gaming and cinematic narratives, in the form of first-person point of view shooter type games and also of increasing violent VR horror and war narratives.

4. While the focus of my reading is not the disability studies angle of this work, there is plenty that can be said on the subject of the flawed representation of visual impairment and blindness. This piece is not exempt of ableism and misunderstandings about the capabilities of those differently abled. For a lengthy and productive discussion on this subject I recommend David Bolt's *The Metanarrative of Blindness* (2013), Georgina Kleege's *Sight Unseen* (1999), or, Martin Jay's *Downcast Eyes: The Denigration of Vision in Twentieth-Century French Thought* (1993). For an example of films that treat the subject of blindness from a nuanced and non-ableist perspective, read my 2022 article in *Disability Studies Quarterly*, "Blind Cinema: Reframing Visual Impairment in *Shadow Girl* (Chile 2016)."

5. In Argentina, for example, approximately ninety percent of the works being developed can be categorized as VR, with the rest in other modalities (AR, MR).

6. Another Hispanic nominee was the La Caixa sponsored work *Symphony: A Journey into the Heart of Music* (2020), which was directed by Igor Cortadellas.

7. As Castillo points out, "Sobre todo de películas policiacas, pero también en Videojuegos, e incluso en zarzuelas. Si hay algo que he intentado hacer en mi

corta carrera es empujar las narrativas de género dentro del ámbito de la animación, tengo una relación cercana con el cine de los años 40 y 50, películas como *Perdición* de Billy Wilder o *EL tercer hombre* de Carol Reed han sido fundamentales para definir la estética del proyecto" ("James Castillo [Director]") [Especially detective films, but also videogames, and even zarzuelas. In my short career I have pushed genre narratives into animation cinema, I am closely aligned with the cinema of the 1940s and 50s, films such as *Double Indemnity* by Billy Wilder or *The Third Man* by Carol Reed have been key to the aesthetics of my project].

8. Photography (as a 2D art) is not the only media cited by *Madrid Noir*. Stereoscopic (3D) photography was a predecessor of both the cinema and VR, a format already hailed for its immersive capacity in its nineteenth-century heyday.

9. In addition to the *New York Times* several other major newspapers have started to create immersive journalism in 360 and VR, including the BBC, *The Guardian*, and *USA Today*, among others (Barreda-Ángeles et al. 154).

10. Alejandro Gonzalez Iñárritu acknowledged when accepting the Oscar for *Carne y Arena* in 2017 that his initial experience with VR was Nonny de la Peña's *Hunger in Los Angeles* in 2012, which was a direct inspiration for his own VR experiments.

11. In addition to its premiere in the seventieth Cannes Festival (2017), and its showing in Dallas, the installation has been seen at various high art institutions including the Prada Foundation in Milan, the Los Angeles County Museum of Art, the Philips Collection in Washington, DC, and at Centro Cultural Universitario, Tlatelolco, Mexico City, to name but a few.

12. For a detailed outline of the criticisms levied against VR cinema by various critics, see Leen's in-depth discussion on the subject ("Visceral Reality" 43).

Coda

1. Some preliminary and partial material from this chapter was previously published in *FORMA: A Journal of Latin American Criticism and Theory* and is reproduced here with the permission of the editors. See Eduardo Ledesma, "Do Androids Dream of Electric Llamas? AI Generated Cinema in Latin America," *FORMA: A Journal of Latin American Criticism and Theory*, vol. 3, no. 1, 2023, 77–105.

2. The term machinima should not be conflated with the popular YouTube gaming channel "Machinima," which housed many of these types of videos, or the company Machinima Inc. later purchased by Warner Bros. and finally by AT&T. The now defunct multiplatform Machinima Inc. operated from 2000 through 2019 and its YouTube channel peaked at eighteen million subscribers and was the most viewed YouTube channel worldwide in 2013 with two billion views (Onanuga). AT&T shut down the channel in an effort to consolidate its operations, to the chagrin of its millions of subscribers.

3. Pepe Gonzalez's films can be seen on TikTok at www.tiktok.com/@pepegg33?lang=en.

4. The fiction category videos can be found at www.tiktok.com/tag/filmtokficci%C3%B3n?lang=en.

5. Valdivieso's *Ansiedad* can be viewed at www.tiktok.com/@pepinovaldivieso/video/6863077310552132865?lang=en.

6. Ferdinow's video can be seen at www.tiktok.com/@ferdinow/video/6864179202426424578?lang=en.

7. Among the more distressing effects we should consider the disruptive impact AI will have on academia and, more specifically, on the language disciplines. While this is not a concern explored in this book, see my article "Critical AI Studies and the Foreign Language Disciplines: What Is to Be Done?" *PMLA*, vol. 139, no. 3, forthcoming 2024.

8. Meta's Make-A-Video is one such easy-to-use tool, so that with a text prompt and some basic parameters the AI can generate an acceptable video on virtually any subject. Google's Imagen Video is another such tool, which has gained notoriety through the generation of short videos, including one showing a Teddy bear washing the dishes or another depicting an elephant walking under water while wearing a birthday hat, all of these quaint works created entirely by the AI with just some simple human text prompts. Other tools such as DreamFusion can even generate 3D images from text description.

9. Set inside a crumbling abandoned building, the source video's dancer was clad in a tattered black shawl and performed a routine that imitated, in stylized fashion, the movements of a crow. Marshall borrowed the concept and adapted it to the prompts he fed the AI software (Hahn).

10. One such project currently being developed in Finland is an AI tool called Cine-AI, designed to generate cinematographic scenes specific for video game narratives, using characters, scenarios, and parameters extracted from the games themselves—bringing to mind our previous discussion on machinima.

11. These images are currently available at the following website: https://www.djfood.org/fantasy-jodorowsky-tron-visualisations-by-johnny-darrell/.

12. As Caballero and Giralt Gris state on the website for the *Artificio* project (artificio.gusano.org/en/home/#).

13. The first AI film festival, held in New York City on March 2023, has this website: aiff.runwayml.com/.

Works Cited

21 Grams. Directed by Alejandro González Iñárritu, performances by Sean Penn, Naomi Watts, Charlotte Gainsbourg, Danny Huston and Benicio del Toro, Focus Features, 2003.

Acland, Charles R. Introduction. *Residual Media*, edited by Charles Acland, U of Minnesota P, 2007, pp. xiii–xxvii.

Aguilar, Gonzalo. *Otros mundos: Ensayo sobre el nuevo cine argentino*. Arcos, 2006.

Aguilera Skvirsky, Salomé. *The Ethnic Turn: Studies in Political Cinema from Brazil and the United States, 1960–2002*. 2009. U of Pittsburgh, PhD dissertation.

Aguirrezábal, Javier, director. *09 La película*. Fábula, 2014.

———. *Trailer 09 La película*. Fábula, 2014. *YouTube*, uploaded by Canal Trece, 17 Feb. 2014, www.youtube.com/watch?v=ACyTXyEBEYQ.

Aguirrezábal, Javier, and Felipe Segura. *Making of 09 La película*. Ywanna Films and TV, 2014. *Vimeo*, uploaded by Ywanna Films, 15 Mar. 2014, vimeo.com/89213729.

Alcoz, Albert. *Radicales libres: 50 películas esenciales del cine experimental*. Universitat Oberta de Catalunya, 2019.

Aldana, Xavier. "Reel Evil: A Critical Reassessment of Found Footage Horror." *Gothic Studies*, vol. 17, no. 2, 2015, pp. 122–35.

Alonso, Rodrigo. "The Buenos Aires Underground." *Jornadas de homenaje: Los primeros cien años del cine en Argentina. Facultad de Filosofía y Letras*. Universidad de Buenos Aires, 1997, www.roalonso.net/es/arte_y_tec/underground.php. Unpublished conference paper.

———. "Estéticas. Poéticas. Prácticas." *Historia crítica del video argentino*, edited by Jorge La Ferla, Malba–Fundación Costantini y Museo de Arte Latinoamericano de Buenos Aires, 2008, pp. 49–62.

Álvarez, Santiago, director. *Ciclón*. ICAIC, 1963.

———. *LBJ*. ICAIC, 1968.

———. *Now!* ICAIC, 1965.

Amago, Samuel. *Spanish Cinema in the Global Context: Film on Film*. Routledge, 2013.

Andermann, Jens. *New Argentine Cinema*. I. B. Tauris, 2012.

Angels, created by Nicole Stenger, SGI and Waterfront Technologies, 1989.
Aranda, Vicente, director. *Fata Morgana*. Films Internacionales, 1965.
Arnau Roselló, Roberto. *La guerrilla del celuloide: Resistencia estética y militancia política en el cine español (1967–1982)*. 2006. Jaume I U, Castellón, PhD dissertation.
———. "Los colectivos cinematográficos en la España tardofranquista militancias, transgresiones y resistencias." *DOC On-line: Revista Digital de Cinema Documentário*, no. 15, 2013, pp. 293–318.
Arredondo, Isabel. "Early International Super 8 Film Festivals: The Case of Caracas 1976–1980." *Global Perspectives on Amateur Film Histories and Cultures*, edited by Masha Salazkina and Enrique Fibla-Gutiérrez, Indiana UP, 2020, pp. 278–95.
Aubert, Jean-Paul. *L'École de Barcelone: Un cinéma d'avant-garde en Espagne*. Paris: L'Harmattan, 2009.
———. *Seremos Mallarmé. La Escuela de Barcelona: Una apuesta modernista*. Madrid: Hispanoscope, 2016.
Avellar, José Carlos. *Glauber Rocha*. Madrid: Cátedra / Filmoteca Española, 2002.
———. "ImagiNation." *Cinema Comparat/ive*, vol. 4, no. 9, 2016, pp. 71–79.
Baker, Sean, director. *Tangerine*. Magnolia Pictures, 2015.
Balagueró, Jaume, and Paco Plaza, directors. *Rec*. Castelao Producciones, Filmax, 2007.
Balsom, Erika. "Introduction: The Othered Cinema." *Exhibiting Cinema in Contemporary Art*, Amsterdam UP, 2013, pp. 9–26.
Barreda-Ángeles, Miguel, et al. "Virtual Reality Storytelling as a Double-Edged Sword: Immersive Presentation of Nonfiction 360°-Video Is Associated with Impaired Cognitive Information Processing." *Communication Monographs*, vol. 88, no. 2, 2021, pp. 154–73.
Bassett, Caroline. "Is This Not a Screen? Notes on the Mobile Phone and Cinema." *Transmedia Frictions: The Digital, the Arts, and the Humanities*, edited by Marsha Kinder and Tara McPherson, U of California P, 2014, pp. 147–60.
Battlescar: Punk Was Invented by Girls, directed by Martin Allais and Nico Casavecchia, performance by Rosario Dawson, ARTE, Atlas V, and Ryot Films, 2019.
Baudry, Jean-Louis. "The Apparatus: Metapsychological Approaches to the Impression of Reality in Cinema." *Narrative, Apparatus, Ideology: A Film Theory Reader*, edited by Philip Rosen, Columbia UP, 1986, pp. 286–318.
Barthes, Roland. *Camera Lucida: Reflections on Photography*. Translated by Richard Howard. Hill and Wang, 1981.
Bazin, André. "In Defense of Mixed Cinema." *What Is Cinema, Vol. 1*, edited and translated by Hugh Gray, U of California P, pp. 53–75.
Beaver, Frank E. *A Dictionary of Film Terms*. Peter Lang, 2007.
Beiras, Xosé Manuel. *O atraso económico de Galiza*. Galaxia, 1972.
Benítez de Gracia, María José, and Susana Herrera Damas. "Análisis del nivel de inmersión de los reportajes en vídeo en 360° producidos por medios periodísticos españoles." *Comunication and Society*, vol. 32, no. 2, 2019, pp. 77–95.

Bentes, Ivana, editor. *Glauber Rocha: Cartas ao mundo*. São Paulo: Companhia das Letras, 1997.

Bentley, Bernard P. E. *A Companion to Spanish Cinema*. Tamesis, 2008.

Bernini, Emilio, editor. "(No) Serialidad, video e internet. En torno a *This Is Just to Say*." *Kilómetro 111: Ensayos sobre cine*, no. 14–15, 22 Jun. 2019, kilometro111cine.com.ar/no-serialidad-video-e-internet/.

Bernstein, Emma. "Medium Specificity." 2011. *The Chicago School of Media Theory*, WordPress, lucian.uchicago.edu/blogs/mediatheory/keywords/medium-specificity/.

Berry, David, and Michael Dieter. "Thinking Post-Digital Aesthetics: Art, Computation and Design." *Postdigital Aesthetics: Art, Computation and Design*, edited by David Berry and Michael Dieter, Palgrave Macmillan, 2015, pp. 1–11.

Berry, Marsha, and Max Schleser. *Mobile Media Making in an Age of Smartphones*. Palgrave, 2014.

Besas, Peter. *Behind the Spanish Lens: Spanish Cinema Under Fascism and Democracy*. Arden P, 1985.

Bianchi, Tiago. "TikTok in Latin America: Statistics & Facts." *Statista*, July 2022, www.statista.com/topics/9670/tiktok-in-latin-america/#topicOverview.

Biggio, Federico. "Augmented Consciousness: Artificial Gazes Fifty Years after Gene Youngblood's *Expanded Cinema*." *NECSUS European Journal of Media Studies*, vol. 9, no. 1, Spring 2020, pp. 173–92.

Biondi, Beniamino. *Fata Morgana: Il cinema catalano e la Scuola di Barcellona*. Piombino: Associazione Culturale Il Floglio, 2011.

Biutiful, directed by Alejandro González Iñárritu, performances by Javier Bardem, Maricel Álvarez, Hanaa Bouchaib, and Guillermo Estrella, Focus Features, 2010.

Blázquez, Elena. "Helena Lumbreras et le Colectivo de Cine de Clase: Une pratique cinématographique militante à la fin du franquisme et durant la transition en Espagne." *Cahiers de civilisation espagnole contemporaine* [online], vol. 24, June 2020, journals.openedition.org/ccec/9627.

Blom, Ina. "Boredom and Oblivion." *Fluxus Reader*, edited by Ken Friedman, John Wiley and Sons, 1998, pp. 63–91.

Bollig, Ben, and David Wood. "Film-Poetry/Poetry-Film in Latin America. Theories and Practices: An Introduction." *Studies in Spanish & Latin American Cinemas*, vol. 11, no. 2, 2014, pp. 115–25.

Bollig, Ben. *Moving Verses: Poetry on Screen in Argentine Cinema*. Liverpool UP, 2021.

Bolt, David. *The Metanarrative of Blindness*. U of Michigan P, 2013.

Bonet, Eigeni, and Manuel Palacio. *Práctica fílmica y vanguardia artística en España 1925–1981*. Madrid: Universidad Complutense, 1983.

Border Stories, directed by Nonny de la Peña, Emblematic Group, 2019.

Bordwell, David. "Intensified Continuity. Visual Style in Contemporary American Film." *Film Quarterly*, vol. 55, no. 3, 2002, pp. 16–28.

Botella, Caridad. "The Aesthetics of Cellphone-Made Films." *Artpulse Magazine*, vol. 4, no. 14, 1 Jan. 2013, artpulsemagazine.com/the-aesthetics-of-cellphone-made-films.

Burch, Noël. "Film's Institutional Mode of Representation and the Soviet Response." *October*, vol. 11, 1979, pp. 77–96.
Burke, Frank. *A Companion to Italian Cinema*. Wiley Blackwell, 2017.
Burton, Julianne. *Cinema and Social Change in Latin America: Conversations with Filmmakers*. U of Texas P, 1986.
———. "The Hour of the Embers: The Current Situation in Latin American Cinema." *Film Quarterly*, vol. 30, no. 1, 1976, pp. 33–34.
———. "The Old and the New: Latin American Cinema at the (Last?) Pesaro Festival." *Jump Cut*, no. 9, 1975, pp. 33–35, www.ejumpcut.org/archive/onlinessays/JC09folder/PesaroReport.html.
———. "Revolutionary Cuban Cinema." *Jump Cut*, no. 19, Dec. 1978, pp. 17–20, www.ejumpcut.org/archive/onlinessays/JC19folder/CubanFilmIntro.html.
Byrón, Silvestre. "Arte y Rebelión." *La regón central*. Pablo Marín, blogger, 8 July 2006, laregioncentral.blogspot.com.ar/2006/07/arte-y-rebelin-por-silvestre-byrn-eaf.html.
Caballero, Jorge, and Anna Giralt Gris. *Artificio* (webpage), 2021, artificio.gusano.org/en/home/.
Cabral da Costa, Wagner. "O *Maranhão* será *Terra em Transe*? História, política e ficção num documentário de Glauber Rocha." *Proj. História PUC-São Paulo*, vol. 29, no. 2, Dec. 2004, pp. 447–75, file:///Users/eduardoledesma/Downloads/9976-Texto%20do%20artigo-24758-1-10-20120622%20(2).pdf.
Cabrera, Javier. "Alfonso García: 'Tan respetable es hacer una película con móvil como con 35 mm.'" *El taller audiovisual*, eltalleraudiovisual.com/alfonso-garcia-entrevista/.
Caldini, Claudio, and Pablo Marín. *Experimental Films 1975–1982*. Antennae Collection, 2012. Blu Ray and two booklets.
Cambridge Super 8 Film Festival Catalog. 2008. www.cambridge-super8.org/wp-content/uploads/2009/11/CS8Programme2008Booklet.pdf.
Camí-Vela, M. "Between Hope and Disillusion: The Militant Cinema of Helena Lumbreras." *Plan Rosebud: On Images, Sites and Politics of Memory*, edited by María Ruido, Xunta de Galicia/Centro Gallego de Arte Contemporáneo, 2009, pp. 251–62.
———. "Entre la esperanza y el desencanto. El cine militante de Helena Lumbreras." *Plan Rosebud: Sobre imágenes, lugares y políticas de memoria*, edited by María Ruído, Xunta de Galicia/Centro Gallego de Arte Contemporáneo, 2009, pp. 543–54.
Cantú, Mariela. "Archivos y video: No lo hemos comprendido todo." *Cuaderno 52*, vol. 15, no. 52, May 2015, pp. 95–106.
Caprín, Gustavo. "How to Build a House." *Hamaca: Moving Image Platform*, www.hamacaonline.net/titles/how-to-build-a-house/.
Cardona, Luis Felipe, director. *Checklist*. 4GP, 2004. *YouTube*, uploaded by movilfilmfest, 16 May 2009, www.youtube.com/watch?v=7s8dMt_p53U.

Cardoso, Mauricio. *O cinema tricontinental de Glauber Rocha: Política, estética e revolução (1969–1974)*. 2007. U of São Paulo, PhD dissertation, teses.usp.br/teses/disponiveis/8/8138/tde-12022008-110659/publico/TESE_MAURICIO_CARDOSO.pdf.

Carlini, Federico, and Germán Heller, directors/creators. *Pájaros de papel*, produced by 3DAR, 2019.

Carne y Arena (Virtually Present, Physically Invisible), directed by Alejandro González Iñárritu, Lucasfilms, 2017.

Casas, Quim. "Entrevista con Pere Portabella: El estilo del productor y la reflexión del director." *Los Nuevos Cines en España: Ilusiones y desencantos de los años sesenta*, edited by Carlos F. Heredero and José Enrique Monterde, Filmoteca Española, 2003, pp. 333–42.

Castillo, James, director/creator. *Madrid Noir*, 2021.

Castillo, Luciano. "Apostillas a propósito de *Now!*" *La Jirimilla, Revista de cultura Cubana*, 29 Aug. to 4 Sept. 2015, www.epoca2.lajiribilla.cu/articulo/11058/apostillas-a-proposito-de-now.

Cegys, Paul, and Joris Weijdom. "Mixing Realities: Reflections on Presence and Embodiment in Intermedial Performance Design of *Blue Hour VR*." *Theater and Performance Design*, vol. 6, no. 1–2, 2020, pp. 81–101.

Cerdán, Josetxo, and Miguel Fernández Labayen. "Introduction: Digital Changes in Latin American Cinemas." *Journal of Latin American Cultural Studies*, vol. 28, no. 4, 2019, pp. 493–502.

Cerdán, Josetxo, et al. "Censorship, Film Studios and Production Companies." *A Companion to Spanish Cinema*, edited by Jo Labanyi and Tatjana Pavlović, Wiley Blackwell, 2015, pp. 391–433.

Chan-wook, Park, director. *Night Fishing*. Moho Films, 2011. *Vimeo*, uploaded by iPhone Film Festival, 27 Dec. 2014, vimeo.com/115480849.

Chanan, Michael. *The Cuban Image: Cinema and Cultural Politics in Cuba*. BFI, 1985.

———. "New Cinemas in Latin America." *The Oxford History of World Cinema*, edited by Geoffrey Nowell-Smith, Oxford UP, 1996, pp. 740–50.

Choi, Eunha. "*The Hour of the Furnaces*: Collaborative Cinema's Fragmentary Form." *Dissidences*, vol. 7, no. 12, 2016, pp. 1–30, digitalcommons.bowdoin.edu/dissidences/vol7/iss12/2/.

Cholakian, Lucía, and Facundo Iglesia. "Voice Actors Are Training the AI That Will Replace Them." *Rest of World*, Feb. 2023, restofworld.org/2023/ai-voice-acting/.

Cinema Tropical. "The Academy Museum Presents a Series on Mexican Horror Cinema." 3 Oct. 2022, www.cinematropical.com/cinema-tropical/the-academy-museum-presents-a-film-series-on-mexican-horror-cinema.

"The Cinematic Side of TikTok." *TikTok*, 12 Mar. 2020, newsroom.tiktok.com/en-us/the-cinematic-side-of-tiktok.

Citron, Michelle. *Home Movies and Other Necessary Fictions*. U of Minnesota P, 1999.

Clouds over Sidra. Directed by Chris Milk and Gabo Arora, United Nations / Samsung, 2015.
Come Out. Directed by Narcisa Hirsch, Mq2*, 2013. DVD.
Constine, Josh. "Virtual Reality, the Empathy Machine." *TechCrunch*, 1 Feb. 2015, techcrunch.com/2015/02/01/what-it-feels-like/.
Contreras, Santiago. "The Growth Potential of the Metaverse in Latin America." *Dailycoin*, 23 Sept. 2022, dailycoin.com/the-growth-potential-of-the-metaverse-in-latin-america/.
Corbin, John R. "The Myth of Primitive Spain." *Anthropology Today*, vol. 5, no. 4, Aug. 1989, pp. 15–17.
Cox, Anna. "New 'Cinema of Attractions'? The Barcelona School's Exhibitionist Loops." *Hispanic Review*, vol. 78, no. 4, Autumn 2010, pp. 529–49. Project Muse.
Crater-Lab. "Experimental Cinema." 2014, expcinema.org/site/en/directory/crater-lab.
"Creating and Managing VR Experiences with Germán Heller." *DistantJob Podcasts*, 30 Aug. 2019, distantjob.com/blog/podcasts/creating-and-managing-vr-experiences-with-german-heller/.
Cruzar. Directed by Juan Pablo Urgilés, performances by Agny González, Antonella González, and Luis Velázquez, Imán / Transmedia, 2020.
D'Aloia, Adriano. "Virtually Present, Physically Invisible: Virtual Reality Immersion and Emersion in Alejandro González Iñárritu's *Carne y Arena*." *Senses of Cinema*, no. 87, June 2018, www.sensesofcinema.com/2018/feature-articles/virtually-present-physically-invisible-virtual-reality-immersion-and-emersion-in-alejandro-gonzalez-inarritus-carne-y-arena/#fnref-34428-14.
D'Argenio, Maria Chiara. "A Poetic Cine Urgente: Experimentalism and Revolution in Santiago Álvarez's Documentary Films." *Studies in Spanish & Latin American Cinemas*, vol. 11, no. 2, Jun 2014, pp. 127–45.
Dancing with the Virtual Dervish. Created by Diane Gromala and Yacov Sharir, performance by Sharir Dance Company, 1994.
de la Peña, Nonny, et al. "Immersive Journalism: Immersive Virtual Reality for the First-Person Experience of News." *Presence: Teleoperators and Virtual Environments*, vol. 19, no. 4, 2010, pp. 291–301.
de la Puente, Maximiliano Ignacio. "El aporte de Joris Ivens al cine documental latinoamericano." *RevistaTierra en Trance. Reflexiones sobre cine latinoamericano*, May/June 2010, tierraentrance.miradas.net/2010/05/ensayos/el-aporte-de-joris-ivens-al-cine-documental-latinoamericano.html.
del Valle Dávila, Ignacio. "Crear dos, tres . . . muchos collages, es la consigna. El collage en el documental latinoamericano de descolonización cultural." *Cinémas d'Amérique latine*, no. 21, 2013, pp. 42–55.
Denegri, Andrés, Gustavo Caprín, Javier Olivera, and Gustavo Galuppo, directors. *This Is Just to Say* (2012–2018). 189 videos, https://thisisjusttosay.net/.
Dennison, Stephanie. *Contemporary Hispanic Cinema: Interrogating the Transnational in Spanish and Latin American Film*. Boydell & Brewer, 2013.

---. "National, Transnational, and Post-national: Issues in Contemporary Film-making in the Hispanic World." *Contemporary Hispanic Cinema: Interrogating the Transnational in Spanish and Latin American Film*. Boydell & Brewer, 2013, pp. 1–24.
Denson, Shane, and Julia Leyda. "Perspectives on Post-Cinema: An Introduction." *Post-Cinema: Theorizing 21st-Century Film*, edited by Shane Denson and Julia Leyda, Reframe Books, 2016.
Department of the Army. *Spain: A Country Study*. Area Handbook Series. Federal Research Division of the Library of Congress, DA Pam, 1990.
DiTella, Andrés. *Hachazos*. Caja Negra, 2011.
Dixon, Wheeler. Introduction. *Experimental Cinema: The Film Reader*, edited by Wheeler Dixon and Gwendolyn Foster, Routledge, 2002, pp. 1–16.
Doane, Mary Ann. "The Indexical and the Concept of Medium Specificity." *Differences: A Journal of Feminist Cultural Studies*, vol. 18, no. 1, 2007, pp. 128–52.
Dooley, Kath. "Storytelling with Virtual Reality in 360-degrees: A New Screen Grammar." *Studies in Australasian Cinema*, vol. 11, no. 3, Nov. 2017, pp. 161–71.
---. "Virtual Reality: Moving Beyond a Cinema of Attractions." *Screen Education*, no. 98, Mar. 2018, pp. 97–103.
D'Lugo, Marvin. "Across the Hispanic Atlantic: Cinema and its Symbolic Relocations." *Studies in Hispanic Cinemas,* vol. 5, no. 1–2, July 2009, pp. 3–7.
---. "Catalan Cinema: Historical Experience and Cinematic Practice." *Quarterly Review of Film and Video*, vol. 13, no. 1–3, 1991, pp. 131–46.
---. *Guide to Spanish Cinema*. Greenwood Press, 1997.
Dreiling Miche. "Rear-facing Camera: Cell Phone Cinematography in *Midnight Traveler* (Hassan Fazili, 2019)." *Frames Cinema Journal*, vol. 18, June 2021, pp. 177–88.
Ebert, Roger. "The Ghost in the Machinima: Will the Use of Video Game Technology to Make Movies Result in Art or Kitsch?" *Yahoo Internet Life*, Ziff Davis, 1 June 2000, web.archive.org/web/20010405112906/http://www.zdnet.com:80/yil/stories/features/0,9539,2572985,00.html.
Eisenstein, Sergei. "Stereoscopic Films." *Notes of a Film Director*. Translated by X. Danko, Foreign Languages Publishing House, 1948, pp. 129–37.
Elduque, Albert. "Hunger and Rotten Flesh: Cinema Novo, Pasolini, Eisenstein." *[In]Transition: Journal of Videographic Film & Moving Image Studies*, vol. 3, no. 3, 2016, mediacommons.org/intransition/2016/hunger-and-rotten-flesh.
---. "O touro fica: Anotações sobre *O Testamento de Dom Quixote*." *REBECA—Revista Brasileira de Estudos de Cinema e Audiovisual*, vol. 4, no. 1, March 2015, pp. 455–65, rebeca.socine.org.br/1/article/view/354/161.
Elena, Alberto. "La sombra del cangaceiro: El cine brasileño y la crítica española." *Archivos de la filmoteca: Revista de estudios históricos sobre la imagen*, no. 36, 2000, pp. 228–41.

Elena, Alberto, and Mariano Mestman. "Para un observador lejano. El documental latinoamericano en España." *Cine documental en América Latina*, edited by Paulo Antonio Paranaguá, Cátedra, 2003, pp. 79–92.

Elias, Chad. "Emergency Cinema and the Dignified Image: Cell Phone Activism and Filmmaking in Syria." *Film Quarterly*, vol. 71, no. 1, Fall 2017, 14 Sept. 2017, filmquarterly.org/2017/09/14/emergency-cinema-and-the-dignified-image-cell-phone-activism-and-filmmaking-in-syria/.

Elsaesser, Thomas. "National, Transnational, and Intermedial Perspectives in Post-2008 European Cinema 1." *Contemporary European Cinema: Crisis Narratives and Narratives in Crisis*, edited by Betty Kaklamanidou and Ana Corbalán, Routledge, 2018, pp. 20–36.

———. "The New Film History as Media Archeology." *Cinémas: Journal of Film Studies*, vol. 4, no. 2–3, 2004, pp. 75–117.

———. "Pushing the Contradictions of the Digital: 'Virtual Reality' and 'Interactive Narrative' as Oxymorons between Narrative and Gaming." *New Review of Film and Television Studies*, vol. 12, no. 3, 2014, pp. 295–311.

Erens, Patricia. "The Galler Home Movies: A Case Study." *Home Movies and Amateur Filmmaking*, special issue of *Journal of Film and Video*, vol. 38, no. ¾, Summer–Fall 1986, pp. 15–24.

Esto no es un recuerdo. Directed by Daniela Cugliandolo, courtesy of filmmaker, 2006. MP4.

"Expanded Cinema." 6 Dec. 2023. *Monoskp* (wiki). monoskop.org/Expanded_cinema.

"Explore the Worlds of Darkness and Music in *Paper Birds*." *Meta*. Meta Quest Blog, 15 Jan. 2021, www.latest.oculus.com/blog/explore-the-worlds-of-darkness-and-music-in-paper-birds-on-the-quest-platform/?locale=es_ES.

Expósito, Marcelo, editor. *Historias sin argumento: El cine de Pere Portabella*. Valencia: Ediciones de la Mirada. Barcelona: Museu d'Art Contemporani de Barcelona, 2001.

Fanés, Fèlix. *Pere Portabella: Avantguarda, cinema, política*. Barcelona: Pòrtic, Filmoteca de Catalunya, 2008.

Faulkner, Sally. *A Cinema of Contradiction: Spanish Film in the 1960s*. Edinburgh UP, 2006.

———. "New Spanish Cinema in the 1960s: Interviews with Antxón Eceiza and Julio Diamante." *Studies in Hispanic Cinemas*, vol. 2, no. 3, 2005, pp. 205–16.

Fernández Labayen, Miguel, and Xosé Prieto Souto. "Film Workshops in Spain: Oppositional Practices, Alternative Film Cultures and the Transition to Democracy." *Studies in European Cinema*, vol. 8, no. 3, 2011, pp. 227–42.

———. "A Network of Affinities: Helena Lumbreras's Collective Films and Social Struggle." *Modern Language Review*, vol. 11, part 2, 2017, pp. 397–412.

Fernández-Santos, Ángel. "La mirada encendida: Escritos sobre cine." Random House, 2014.

Fisher, Austin, and Iain R. Smith. "Transnational Cinemas: A Critical Roundtable." *Frames Cinema Journal*, no. 9, framescinemajournal.com/article/transnational-cinemas-a-critical-roundtable/#lmazdon. Accessed 1 Apr. 2023.

Font, Domènec. *Del azul al verde: El cine español bajo el franquismo*. Editorial Avance, 1976.

Fragments. Created by David Dedeine, Asobo Studios, 2016.

Fuentes, Francisco, and Noemí Vera. "Transcontinental Shakespeare: Macbeth and Tyranny in Glauber Rocha's *Severed Heads*." *Shakespeare and Tyranny: Regimes of Reading in Europe and Beyond*, edited by Keith Gregor, Cambridge Scholars Publishing, 2014, pp. 259–76.

Gabilondo, Joseba. "The Hispanic Atlantic." *Arizona Journal of Hispanic Cultural Studies*, vol. 5, 2001, pp. 91–113.

Galili, Doron. "Television from Afar: Arnheim's Understanding of Media." *Arnheim for Film and Media Studies*, edited by Scott Higgins, Routledge, 2011, pp. 195–212.

Galt, Rosalind. "Impossible Narratives: The Barcelona School and the European Avant-Gardes." *Hispanic Review*, vol. 78, no. 4, 2010, pp. 491–511.

———. "Mapping Catalonia in 1967: The Barcelona School in Global Context." *Senses of Cinema*, vol. 41, 2006, pp. 1–15.

———. "Missed Encounters: Reading, *Catalanitat*, the Barcelona School." *Screen*, vol. 48, no. 2, 2007, pp. 193–210.

García, Ana Claudia. "El video en el espacio: un nuevo espacio de sentido. Video, esculturas, objetos e instalaciones." *Historia crítica del video argentino*, edited by Jorge La Ferla, Malba–Fundación Costantini y Museo de Arte Latinoamericano de Buenos Aires, 2008, pp. 67–90.

García Borrero, Juan Antonio. "Santiago Álvarez." *Cine documental en América Latina*, edited by Paulo Antonio Paranaguá, Cátedra, 2005, pp. 156–63.

García Espinosa, Julio. "For an Imperfect Cinema." Translated by Julianne Burton. *New Latin American Cinema, Vol. 1*, edited by Michael T. Martin, Wayne State UP, 1997, pp. 71–82.

———. "Por un cine imperfecto." *A cuarenta años de 'Por un cine imperfecto' de Julio García Espinosa: Selección de textos*, Ediciones ICAIC, Instituto Cubano del Arte e Industria Cinematográficos, 2009, pp. 9–23.

García Garzón, Juan Ignacio. *Paco Rabal, aquí, un amigo*. Madrid: Alagaba, 2004.

García Márquez, Eligio. *Tras las claves de Melquíades: Historia de Cien años de soledad*. Norma, 2001.

García-Merás, Lydia. "El cine de la disidencia. La producción militante antifranquista (1967–1981)." *Desacuerdos. Sobre arte, políticas y esfera pública en el Estado español. Cine y video*. MACBA / Arteleku, *UNIA arte y pensamiento*, n. 4, 2007.

Garibotto, Verónica, and Antonio Gómez. "Historical Stasis: Solanas and the Restoration of Political Film after the 2001 Argentine Crisis." *Studies in Hispanic Cinemas*, vol. 6, no. 2, 2009, pp. 125–38.

Garling, Caleb. "Virtual Reality, Empathy and the Next Journalism." *Wired*, 3 Nov. 2015, www.wired.com/brandlab/2015/11/nonny-de-la-pena-virtual-reality-empathy-and-the-next-journalism/.

Gatti, José. "Anamnese de *Cabeças cortadas*." *Crítica Cultural*, vol. 4, no. 1, 2009, pp. 109–26, portaldeperiodicos.animaeducacao.com.br/index.php/Critica_Cultural/article/view/6328/3826.

Gazelas, Aristides. *An Introduction to World Cinema*. McFarland, 2000.

Genette, Gérard. *Narrative Discourse: An Essay on Method*. Translated by Jane E. Lewin. Cornell UP, 1980.

Getino, Octavio. "El cine como hecho político." *Cine, cultura y descolonización*, edited by Fernando Solanas and Octavio Getino, Siglo XXI, 1973, pp. 125–70.

———. "The Cinema as Political Fact." *Third Text*, vol. 25, no. 1, 2011, pp. 41–53.

Giunta, Andrea. "Narcisa Hirsch. Portraits." *alter / nativas*, vol. 1, 2013, pp. 1–19, 30 Apr. 2015, www.alternativas.osu.edu/en/issues/autumn-2013/debates/giunta.html.

Goggin, Gerard. *Global Mobile Media*. Routledge, 2011.

Gómez Viñas, Xan. "El campo para el hombre." *Blogs & Docs. revista on line dedicada a la no ficción*, Apr. 2011, www.blogsandocs.com/?p=685.

Gone Gitmo. Directed by Nonny de la Peña and Peggy Weil, Annenberg School of Communication and Journalism, 2007.

González Iñárritu, Alejandro, director/creator. *Amores Perros*. Zeta Entertainment, Alta Vista Films, 2000.

———. *Carne y Arena: Virtually Present, Physically Invisible*. Lucas Films ILMxLAB, 2017.

Gopinath, Sumanth. "The Problem of the Political in Steve Reich's *Come Out*." *Sound Commitments: Avant-Garde Music and the Sixties*, edited by Robert Adlington, Oxford UP, 2009, doi.org/10.1093/acprof:oso/9780195336641.003.0007.

Gras, Ricard. "Machinima, el Hollywood de los videojuegos." *Meristattion*, 15 Jan. 2018, as.com/meristation/2006/10/02/reportajes/1159787700_036767.html.

Greenberg, Clement. "Towards a New Lacoon." *Art in Theory, 1900–2000: An Anthology of Changing Ideas*, edited by Charles Harrison and Paul Wood, Blackwell, 2003, pp. 554–60.

Grusin, Richard, and Jay David Bolter. *Remediation: Understanding New Media*. MIT P, 2000.

Gubern, Román. *La censura: Función política y ordenamiento jurídico bajo el franquismo (1936–1975)*. Ediciones Península, 1981.

———. *Viaje de ida*. Editorial Anagrama, 1997.

Gubern, Román, and Domènec Font. *Un cine para el cadalso: 40 años de censura cinematográfica en España*. Editorial Euros, 1973.

Guevara, Ernesto. "Crear dos, tres . . . muchos Viet-Nam, es la consigna. Mensaje a la Tricontinental." *Tricontinental*, special issue, 16 Apr. 1967. Reprinted in *Paradigma*, vol. 1, no. 1, Feb. 2013, www.cheguevaralibros.com/uploads/5906216.pdf.

Gutierrez, Maria. "'Uma viagem borgeana pela obra de shakespeare': *Cabezas cortadas*, filme de ditador e esperpento de Glauber." *Revista de Crítica Literaria Latinoamericana*, vol. 37, no. 73, 2011, pp. 95–115.

Gynnild, Astrid, et al. "Introduction: What Is Immersive Journalism?" *Immersive Journalism as Storytelling: Ethics, Production and Design*, edited by Turo Uskali et al., Routledge, 2021, pp. 13–24.

Hackl, Kathy. "Mexico Celebrates First VR Festival in Latin America." *VR SCOUT*, 13 Sept. 2016, vrscout.com/news/mexico-celebrates-first-vr-festival-latin-america/.

Hahn, Cory. "News Media and Historiography in Brazilian Cinema." *Brazil: Media from the Country of the Future,* edited by Laura Robinson et al., Emerald Publishing, 2017, pp. 19–36, books.emeraldinsight.com/resources/pdfs/chapters/9781786357861-TYPE23-NR2.pdf.

Hahn, Silke. "Artificial Imagination: Art No Human Eye Has Ever Seen—About *The Crow*." *Heise Online*, 9 Apr. 2022, www.heise.de/hintergrund/Artificial-Imagination-Art-that-no-human-eye-has-seen-before-about-The-Crow-7252721.html.

Hansen, Miriam B. *Cinema and Experience*. U of California P, 2012.

Hardcastle, Anne E. "Why They Film: The Camera and Viewer Address in Found Footage Horror Films from Spain." *Tracing the Borders of Spanish Horror Cinema and Television*, edited by Jorge Marí, Routledge, 2017, pp. 108–23.

Hayward, Susan. *Cinema Studies: The Key Concepts*. 4th ed., Routledge, 2013.

Herkman, Juna. "Introduction: Intermediality as Theory and Methodology." *Intermediality and Media Change*, edited by Juha Herkman et al., Tampere UP, 2012, pp. 10–28.

Hernández, Gustavo, director. *La casa muda*. Tokio Films, 2010.

Herrera, Júlio. "Entrevista a Juan Carlos Mazo y Yury Vargas." *En las mañanas con Uno*. Canal Uno, Colombia. *YouTube*, uploaded by En las mañanas con Uno, 21 Sep. 2016, www.youtube.com/watch?v=bpAE1fS6yEM.

Higginbotham, Virginia. *Spanish Film Under Franco*. U of Texas P, 1988.

Higgins, Dick. "Intermedia." *Something Else Newsletter*, vol. 1, no. 1, 1966, pp. 1–4.

Hilderbrand, Lucas. *Inherent Vice: Bootleg Histories of Videotape and Copyright*. Duke UP, 2009.

Hudson, Dale, and Patricia R. Zimmermann. *Thinking Through Digital Media: Transnational Environments and Locative Places*. Palgrave, 2015.

Hunger in Los Angeles. Directed by Nonny de la Peña, Virtual Pyedog, 2012.

Inherent Rights, Vision Rights. Created by Lawrence Paul Yuxweluptun, 1992.

Irvine, Kaitlyn. "A Definitive Guide to Navigating the Landscape of Extended Reality." *Viget*, 31 Oct. 2017, www.viget.com/articles/xr-vr-ar-mr-whats-the-difference/.

Jackson, Kimberley. *Technology, Monstrosity, and Reproduction in Twenty-First Century Horror.* Palgrave, 2013.

Jacobson, Brian R. "The 'Imponderable Fluidity' of Modernity: Georges Méliès and the Architectural Origins of Cinema." *Early Popular Visual Culture*, vol. 8, no. 2, pp. 189–207.

"James Castillo (Director): 'Si estás buscando un ejemplo de porqué la realidad virtual merece tener un espacio dentro de la cultura audiovisual, deberías ver *Madrid Noir*.'" *The Citizen*, 17 June 2021, thecitizen.es/cultura/james-castillo-entv.

James, David. *Allegories of Cinema: American Film in the Sixties.* Princeton UP, 1989.

———. *The Most Typical Avant-Garde: History and Geography of Minor Cinemas in Los Angeles.* U of California P, 2005.

Jay, Martin. *Downcast Eyes: The Denigration of Vision in Twentieth-Century French Thought.* U of California P, 1993.

Jenkins, Henry. *Convergence Culture: Where Old and New Media Collide.* NYU P, 2006.

Johnson, Randall, and Robert Stam. *Brazilian Cinema.* Columbia UP, 1995.

Juan-Navarro, Santiago. "Intermedialidad y auto-representación en el documental cubano de vanguardia: el caso de Nicolás Guillén Landrián." *Tropelías: Revista de teoría de la literatura y literatura comparada*, no. 27, 2017, pp. 91–109.

Jurado Martin, Montserrat. "Aproximación a los certámenes cinematográficos de realidad virtual, aumentada e inmersiva en América Latina." *Comunicación y Medios*, no. 42, 2020, pp. 134–45.

Kaganof, Aryan, director. *SMS Sugar Man.* African Noise Foundation, 2008.

Kan, Michael. "The Footage in this Sci-Fi Movie Project Comes from AI-Generated Images." *PC Magazine*, 1 Sept. 2022, www.pcmag.com/news/the-footage-in-this-sci-fi-movie-project-comes-from-ai-generated-images.

Kay, Jeremy. "LatAm VR Creators in TRENDS Call for Collaboration." *ScreenDaily*, 12 Dec. 2017, www.screendaily.com/news/latam-vr-creators-in-trends-call-for-collaboration-exclusive/5124973.article.

Kegishyan, Irina. "Mobile Video Statistics." *Yans Media*, 2022, www.yansmedia.com/blog/mobile-video-statistics.

Kemmerle, Karen. "*Use of Force* Incorporates Virtual Reality to Achieve a Unique Impact." *Tribeca*, 16 Apr. 2014, tribecafilm.com/news/use-of-force-nonny-de-la-pena-interview-storyscapes.

The Key. Directed by Celine Tricart, performance by Alia Shawkat, Lucid Dreams Productions, 2019.

Kim, Jihoon. "Bruce Elder's Film-Digital Hybrids and Materialist Historiography." *Millennium Film Journal*, vol. 56, Fall 2012, pp. 30–40.

Kinder, Marsha. *Blood Cinema: The Reconstruction of National Identity in Spain.* U of California P, 1993.

———. *Refiguring Spain: Cinema, Media, Representation.* Duke UP, 1997.

King, John. *Magical Reels: A History of Cinema in Latin America.* Verso, 1990.

Kleege, Georgina. *Sight Unseen.* Yale UP, 1999.

Knabb, Ken, editor. *Situationist International Anthology.* Bureau of Public Secrets, 2006.

Kringiel, Danny. "Machinima and Modding: Pedagogic Means for Enhancing Computer Game Literacy." *The Machinima Reader*, edited by Henry Lowood and Michael Nitsche, 2011, online edition, MIT P Scholarship Online, 22 Aug. 2013, doi.org/10.7551/mitpress/9780262015332.003.0008.

La Ferla, Jorge. "Argentine Cinema: A State of Affairs." *The Film Edge: Contemporary Filmmaking in Latin America*, edited by Eduardo A. Russo, Teseo, 2010, pp. 173–98.

———. *Cine de Exposición. Instalaciones Fílmicas de Andrés Denegri*. Installation Catalog. Espacio de Arte Fundación OSDE, 2013.

———. "Entrevista con Jorge La Ferla: El video argentino y su tradición cinematográfica." *Cinéfagos.net*, 2005, www.cinefagos.net/index.php?option=com_content&view=article&id=696:entrevista-con-jorge-la-ferla&catid=82&Itemid=64.

La Parra-Pérez, Pablo. "The Wind from the South: Experiences of Substandard Filmmaking in Galicia in the 1970s." *Global Perspectives on Amateur Film Histories and Cultures*, edited by Masha Salazkina and Enrique Fibla-Gutiérrez, Indiana UP, 2020, pp. 171–89.

Laurel, Brenda, et al. "*Placeholder*: Landscape and Narrative in Virtual Environments." Placeholder Virtual Reality Project, 1994, tauzero.com/Brenda_Laurel/Placeholder/CGQ_Placeholder.html.

Laviosa, Flavia, et al. "International Students at the *Centro Sperimentale di Cinematografia* in Rome: 1935–2020: A History to be Written." *Journal of Italian Cinema & Media Studies*, vol. 9, no. 2, pp. 175–209.

Lebow, Alisa. *The Cinema of Me: The Self and Subjectivity in First Person Documentary*. Wallflower P, 2012.

Ledesma, Eduardo. "Blind Cinema: Reframing Visual Impairment in *Shadow Girl* (Chile 2016)." *Disability Studies Quarterly*, vol. 42, no. 1, Winter 2022.

———. "Cell Phone Cinema: Latin American Horror Flicks in the Post-digital Age." *Revista de Estudios Hispánicos*, vol. 53, no. 3, Oct. 2019, pp. 821–54.

———. "Critical AI Studies and the Foreign Language Disciplines: What Is to Be Done?" *PMLA*, vol. 139, no. 3, forthcoming 2024.

———. "Do Androids Dream of Electric Llamas? AI Generated Cinema in Latin America." *FORMA: A Journal of Latin American Criticism and Theory*, vol. 3, no. 1, 2023, pp. 77–105.

———. "Helena Lumbreras' *Field for Men* (1973): Midway between Latin American Third Cinema and the Barcelona School." *Studies in Spanish and Latin American Cinemas*, vol. 11, no. 3, Fall 2014, pp. 271–88.

———. "Intermediality and Hispano-Argentine Experimental Film: Subverting Media, Transgressing Borders with Super 8." *Revista Hispánica Moderna*, vol. 70, no. 2, Dec. 2017, pp. 117–41.

———. "Intermediality and Spanish Experimental Cinema: Text and Image Interactions in the Lyrical Films of the Barcelona School." *Journal of Spanish Cultural Studies*, vol. 14, no. 3, Fall 2013, pp. 254–74.

———. *Radical Poetry: Aesthetics, Politics, Technology and the Ibero-American Avant-Gardes 1900–2015*. State U of NY P, 2017.

———. "Staging the Spanish Civil War: History and Reenactment in Joris Ivens' *The Spanish Earth* (1937)." *Bulletin of Spanish Visual Studies*, vol. 4, no. 1, 2020, pp. 1–32.

Leen, Catherine. "Visceral Reality in Alejandro González Iñárritu's *Carne y Arena / Virtually Present, Physically Invisible* (2017)." *Studies in Spanish & Latin American Cinemas*, vol. 18, no. 1, 2021, pp. 37–55.

Lerner, Jesse. "Super 8 in Mexico." *Global Perspectives on Amateur Film Histories and Cultures*, edited by Masha Salazkina and Enrique Fibla-Gutiérrez, Indiana UP, 2020, pp. 190–205.

Lerner, Jesse, and Luciano Piazza. *Ism, Ism, Ism / Ismo, Ismo, Ismo Experimental Cinema in Latin America*. U of California P, 2017.

Lesage, Julia. "Godard and Gorin's Left Politics, 1967–1972." *Jump Cut: A Review of Contemporary Media*, vol. 28, Apr. 1983, pp. 51–58, www.ejumpcut.org/archive/onlinessays/JC28folder/GodardGorinPolitics.html.

Liehm, Mira. *Passion and Defiance: Film in Italy from 1942 to the Present*. U of California P, 1986.

Lima, Dellani, and Marcelo Ikeda. *Cinema de garagem: Um inventário afetivo sobre o jovem cinema brasileiro do século XXI*. Suburbana, 2011.

Linares, Andrés. *El cine militante*. Castellote, 1976.

Linares Martínez, Oslavia Danaé. "Latin American Online Animation: General Overview of its Contextual Conditions and Analysis of its Formal Traits." 2019. Concordia U, master's thesis, spectrum.library.concordia.ca/id/eprint/985799/1/Linares_MA_F2019.pdf.

The Limit. Directed by Robert Rodríguez, performances by Michelle Rodríguez, Robert Avila, and Norman Reedus, STX Entertainment's VR Studio, 2018.

Lisa, Mariano. *La Claqueta*: "Helena Lumbreras—Mariano Lisa—Colectivo de Cine de Clase—Cine Fórum la Claqueta." *YouTube*, uploaded by carlmelchor, 25 Nov. 2018, www.youtube.com/watch?v=Alu5zJ_jW-M.

———. "Re: preguntas sobre el cine de Helena y tuyo." Email from Mariano Lisa. Received by Eduardo Ledesma, 18 Feb. 2019.

———. "Rico cine pobre: *El campo para el hombre* (Colectivo Cine de Clase)." Unpublished document, Oct. 2014, martirom.cat/wp-content/uploads/2018/12/105-El-campo-para-el-hombre-CCC.pdf.

Lobos, Teresa. "Screened Terror and Networked Fear: Unfriended, Horror, and the Digital Age." *Off Screen*, vol. 19, no. 4, Apr. 2015, offscreen.com/view/horror-and-the-digital-age.

Lomas, Natasha. "This VR Cycle Is Dead." *TechCrunch*, 26 Aug. 2017, techcrunch.com/2017/08/26/this-vr-cycle-is-dead/.

Lopes, Denilson. "*Alumbramento*, Friendship, and Failure: New Filmmaking in Brazil in the Twenty-First Century." Translated by Stephen Hart. *A Companion to*

Latin American Cinema, edited by Maria Delgado et al., Wiley-Blackwell, 2017, pp. 294–306.

López, Ana M. "Calling for Intermediality: Latin American Mediascapes." *Cinema Journal*, vol. 54, no. 1, Fall 2014, pp. 135–41.

López-Quiñones, Antonio Gómez. "Transatlantic Film Studies in the Age of Neoliberalism: Towards a Postnational Cinema?" *Transatlantic Studies*, edited by Cecilia Enjuto-Rangel et al., Liverpool UP, 2019.

López Linares, César. "Virtual Reality and 360 Video Still Not Profitable in Latin American Journalism, but They Are Attracting New Audiences." *LatAm Journalism Review*, vol. 11, Jan. 2017, latamjournalismreview.org/articles/virtual-reality-and-360-video-still-not-profitable-in-latin-american-journalism-but-they-are-attracting-new-audiences/.

López Mato, Tamara, et al. *Técnica: Video*. Olmos Ediciones, 2009.

Losada, Matt. *The Projected Nation: Argentina Cinema and the Social Margins*. State U of NY P 2018.

Lowood, Henry, and Michael Nitsche. Introduction. *The Machinima Reader*, edited by Henry Lowood and Michael Nitsche, 2011, online edition, MIT P Scholarship Online, 22 Aug. 2013, doi.org/10.7551/mitpress/9780262015332.003.0008.

Lumbreras, Helena, director. *El campo para el hombre*. Colectivo Cine de Clase, 1973.

Lumière, Tetsuo, director. *Rojo en el bosque sangriento*. TL Short, 2006. *Vimeo*, uploaded by Tetsuo Lumière, 18 Feb. 2015, vimeo.com/119971397.

Lusnich, Ana Laura, et al., editors. *Pantallas transnacionales: El cine Argentino y Mexicano del período clásico*. Ediciones Imago Mundi, 2017.

Macaulay, Thomas. "How an Award-Winning AI Film Was Brought to Life by Text-to-Video Generation." *TNW*, 26 Aug. 2022, thenextweb.com/news/text-to-image-generator-creates-award-winning-ai-film-the-crow.

MACBA. "Blog del Departamento Audiovisual del Museo de Arte Contemporáneo de Buenos Aires." audiovisualmacba.wordpress.com/actividades-2/399-2/. Accessed 15 May 2023.

MacEntee, Katie, et al. "What's a CellPhilm? An Introduction." *What's a Cellphilm? Integrating Mobile Phone Technology into Participatory Visual Research and Activism*, edited by Katie MacEntee et al., Sense Publishers, 2016, pp. 1–18.

Mack, Jonathan. "Finding Borderland: Intermediality in the Films of Marc Forster." *Cinema Journal*, vol. 56, no. 3, 2017, pp. 24–46.

Madrid Noir. Directed by James A. Castillo, performances by Godeliv Van Den Brandt and Fernando Guillén Cuervo, Atlas V, No Ghost, 2021.

"*Madrid Noir* Delivers Moody Mystery on the Oculus Quest Platform." Oculus Blog, July 2021, www.oculus.com/blog/madrid-noir-delivers-moody-mystery-on-the-oculus-quest-platform/?locale=sv_SE.

Mahir, Saul, and Ralph Austen. Introduction. *Viewing African Cinema in the Twenty-First Century: Art Films and the Nollywood Video Revolution*, edited by Saul Mahir and Ralph Austen, Ohio UP, 2010, pp. 1–8.

Mamiit, Aaron. "Kodak Brings Nostalgia with Super 8 Digital Camera That Can Record on Film." *Tech Times*, 6 Jan. 2016, www.techtimes.com/articles/121888/20160106/kodak-brings-nostalgia-with-super-8-digital-camera-that-can-record-on-film.htm.

"Máquinas de lo sensible—Andrés Denegri." *Rolf Gallery, Gacetilla de prensa*. Exhibition press release. Dec. 2019–Jan.y 2020. www.rolfart.com.ar/wp-content/uploads/2019/11/Rolf-Art-Exhibitions-Andre%CC%81s-Denegri-Maquinas-de-lo-sensible-Gacetilla-de-prensa-ES.pdf.

Marchessault, Janine, and Susan Lord, editors. *Fluid Screens, Expanded Cinema*. U of Toronto P, 2008.

Mariani, Andrea. "The Cineguf Years: Amateur Cinema and the Shaping of a Film Avant-Garde in Fascist Italy (1934–1943)." *Film History*, vol. 30, no. 1, 2018, pp. 30–57.

Marí, Jorge. Introduction. *Tracing the Borders of Spanish Horror Cinema and Television*, edited by Jorge Marí, Routledge, 2017, pp. 1–12.

Marín, Diana. "Felipe Cardona, el video maker." *Pasa la voz*. Blog. Universidad Javeriana, Colombia, Oct. 2009, revistapasalavoz.blogspot.com/2009/10/felipe-cardona-el-video-maker.html.

Marin, Kellie. "Pseudo-Sousveillance: (Re)imagining Immigration Narratives and Surveillance Practices by Experiencing *Use of Force*." *Screen Bodies*, vol. 4, no. 2, Winter 2019, pp. 39–58.

Marín, Pablo. "Spiritual Constructions: On Claudio Caldini's Films." *Experimental Films 1975–1982*. Antennae Collection, 2012. Blu Ray and two booklets.

Marks, Laura U. *The Skin of the Film: Intercultural Cinema, Embodiment, and the Senses*. Duke UP, 2000.

Marsh, Leslie. *Branding Brazil: Transforming Citizenship on Screen*. Rutgers UP, 2021.

Marsh, Steven. "The Legacies of Pere Portabella: Between Heritage and Inheritance." *Hispanic Review*, vol. 78, no. 4, Autumn 2010, 551–67. Project Muse.

———. *Spanish Cinema Against Itself: Cosmopolitanism, Experimentation, Militancy*. Indiana UP, 2020.

Martí Rom, José María. "Breve historia acerca del cine marginal." *Cinema 2002*, vol. 38, 1978, pp. 56–60.

Martin-Jones, David. "Transnational Allegory/Transnational History: Se sei vivo spara/Django Kill . . . If You Live, Shoot!" *Transnational Cinemas*, vol. 2, no. 2, Mar. 2012, pp. 179–95.

Martínez Cano, Francisco Julián. "Impresiones sobre *Carne y Arena*: Crítica cinematorgáfica y realidad virtual." *Miguel Hernández Communication Journal*, vol. 9, no. 1, 2018, pp. 161–90.

Martínez Torres, Augusto. *Buñuel y sus discípulos*. Huerga and Fierro, 2005.

———. *Glauber Rocha y Cabezas cortadas*. Anagrama, 1970.

Martínez Torres, Augusto, and Manuel Pérez Estremera. *Nuevo cine latinoamericano*. Anagrama, 1973.

Marx, Karl. *Critique of the Gotha Program*. 1875. Wildside Press, 2008.
Mateer, John. "Directing for Cinematic Virtual Reality: How the Traditional Film Director's Craft Applies to Immersive Environments and Notions of Presence." *Journal of Media Practice*, vol. 18, no. 1, 2017, pp. 14–25.
Matuskova, Magdalena. *Cuban Cinema in a Global Context: The Impact of Eastern European Cinema on the Cuban Film Industry in the 1960s*. 2017. U of California at Los Angeles, PhD dissertation, escholarship.org/content/qt6vg1k3p8/qt6vg1k3p8_noSplash_c42e74d09c5eba0a227e3b16fd369dbd.pdf.
Mazo, Juan Carlos, director. *Making of Sangre y levadura*. La Jácara Mojiganga, 2016. *YouTube*, uploaded by SmartFilms, 1 Aug. 2016, https://www.youtube.com/watch?v=-aOba8C8Pd0.
———. *Sangre y levadura*. La Jácara Mojiganga, 2016. *YouTube*, uploaded by SmartFilms, 14 July 2016, https://www.youtube.com/watch?v=esF-hTT3jdQ.
McDonald, Scott. "Avant-Garde Film: Cinema as Discourse." *Journal of Film and Video*, vol. 40, no. 2, Spring 1988, pp. 33–42.
———. *Avant-Garde Film: Motion Studies*. Cambridge UP, 1993.
———. "Lost Lost Lost over *Lost Lost Lost*." *Cinema Journal*, vol. 25, no. 2, Winter 1986, pp. 20–34.
———. *Screen Writings*. U of California P, 1993.
McKee, Robert Irwin, and Maricruz Castro Ricalde, editors. *Global Mexican Cinema: Its Golden Age*. Palgrave MacMillan, 2013.
McLuhan, Marshall. *Understanding Media: The Extensions of Man*. MIT P, 1994.
Méchoulan, Éric. "Le temps des illusions perdues." *Intermédialités*, no. 1, Spring 2003, pp. 9–27.
"Medios Audiovisuales en el Arte Contemporaneo." *Fundación Proa*, 6 Nov. 2006, proa.org/proanoticias/2019/06/11/medios-audiovisuales-en-el-arte-contemporaneo/?fbclid=IwAR3RaaMaYSIZJZVPqDWULoi7GjbOZkgDI-vtCvau44A-00myQ1E-1GVMDvIo.
Mekas, Jonas. "On the Expanding Eye." *Village Voice*, 6 Feb. 1964.
———. "More on Expanded Cinema: Emshwiller, Stern, Ken Jacobs, Ken Dewey." *Village Voice*, 2 Dec. 1965.
Melita. Directed by Nicolás Alcalá, performances by Julie Maisey, Megan Jones, Jonathan Mellor, and Jessica Preddy, Future Lighthouse, 2017.
Mendelovich, Yossy. "*Dune* Was Shot on ALEXA LF, Transferred to 35mm Film, Then Scanned Back to Digital." *Y. M. Cinema Magazine*, 3 Dec. 2021, ymcinema.com/2021/12/03/dune-was-shot-on-alexa-lf-transferred-to-35mm-film-then-scanned-back-to-digital/.
Mestman, Mariano. "Third Cinema / Militant Cinema: At the Origins of the Argentinian Experience (1968–1971)." *Third Text*, vol. 25, no. 1, 2011, pp. 29–40.
Metro Veinte. Directed by María Belén Poncio, performances by Delfina Diaz Gavier and Cristobal Lopez Baena, Ezequiel Lenardon / Detona Cultura, 2018. VR series.

Middents, Jeffrey. *Writing National Cinema: Film Journals and Film Culture in Peru.* Dartmouth College P, 2009.

Mieses, Luis (Conrad Mess), director. *The Fixer.* 1 May 2012. *YouTube,* uploaded by International Mobile Film Festival, www.youtube.com/watch?v=cDnYcopmBc0.

Milk, Chris. "How Virtual Reality Can Create the Ultimate Empathy Machine" [Video]. TED Conferences, Vancouver, BC, 22 Apr. 2015, www.ted.com/talks/chris_milk_how_virtual_reality_can_create_the_ultimate_empathy_machine?language=en.

Miranda, Carolina. "How a Migrant Woman's Death Influenced Alejandro Iñárritu's Oscar-Winning VR Project *Carne y Arena.*" *Los Angeles Times,* 28 Nov. 2017, www.latimes.com/entertainment/arts/miranda/la-et-cam-alejandro-inarritu-lacma-20171127-htmlstory.html.

Mizuta Lippit, Akira. *Ex-cinema: From a Theory of Experimental Film and Video.* U of California P, 2012.

Molist, Segismundo, et al. "Semana Internacional del Cine en Color." *Film Ideal: Revista Cinematográfica Mensual,* vol. 108, 1969, pp. 125–50.

"Monográfico de Geofilms." *Tarambana,* 15 Feb. 2017, www.tarambana.net/espectaculos/monografico-de-geofilms/.

Mourenza, Daniel. "Segon capítol de l'Escola de Barcelona." *el Queixal,* vol. 48, Dec. 2008, p. 10.

Müller, Jürgen E. "Intermediality and Media Historiography in the Digital Era." Translated by Miriam Sentner. *Acta Univ. Sapientiae, Film And Media Studies. The International Scientific Journal of Sapientia,* vol. 2, 2010, pp. 15–38, www.acta.sapientia.ro/acta-film/C2/film2-2.pdf.

Mulvey, Laura. "Visual Pleasure and Narrative Cinema." *Screen,* vol. 16, no. 3, Autumn 1975, pp. 6–18.

Murphy, Jill, and Laura Rascaroli, editors. *Theorizing Film Through Contemporary Art: Expanding Cinema.* Amsterdam UP, 2020.

Murray, Janet. *Hamlet on the Holodeck: The Future of Narrative in Cyberspace.* MIT P, 1998.

Myrick, Daniel, and Eduardo Sánchez, directors. *The Blair Witch Project.* Haxan Films, 1999.

Naficy, Hamid. *An Accented Cinema: Exilic and Diasporic Filmmaking.* Princeton UP, 2001.

Nagib, Lúcia. "An Intermedial Reading of Glauber Rocha's Cosmogony." *Towards an Intermedial History of Brazilian Cinema,* edited by Lúcia Nagib, Edinburgh UP, 2022, pp. 323–44.

———. "The Politics of Impurity." *Impure Cinema: Intermedial and Intercultural Approaches to Film,* edited by Lúcia Nagib and Anne Jerslev, Tauris, 2014, pp. 21–40.

———. Preface and acknowledgments. *On Cinema: Glauber Rocha,* edited by Ismael Xavier, I. B. Taurus, 2019, pp. x–xiv.

Nagib, Lúcia, and Anne Jerslev. Introduction. *Impure Cinema: Intermedial and Intercultural Approaches to Film*, edited by Lúcia Nagib and Anne Jerslev, Tauris, 2014, pp. xviii–xxxi.

Nagib, Lúcia, and Stefan Solomon. "Intermediality in Brazilian Cinema: The Case of Tropicália." *Screen*, vol. 60, no. 1, Spring 2019, pp. 122–27.

Nagib, Lúcia, et al., editors. *Towards an Intermedial History of Brazilian Cinema*. Edinburgh Studies in Film and Intermediality. Edinburgh UP, 2022.

Nadal-Melsió, Sara. "Editor's Preface. The Invisible Tradition: Avant-Garde Catalan Cinema Under Late Francoism." *Hispanic Review*, vol. 78, no. 4, Autumn 2010, pp. 465–68.

Nielsen, Jakob I. "Five Functions of Camera Movement in Narrative Cinema." *Transnational Cinematography Studies*, edited by Lindsay Coleman et al., Lexington Books, 2017.

Nunes, José María, director. *Sexperiencias*. Filmscontacto, 1968.

Odin, Roger. "Spectator, Film and the Mobile Phone." *Audiences: Defining and Researching Screen Entertainment Reception*, edited by Ian Christie. Amsterdam UP, 2012, pp. 155–69.

Ohanesian, Liz. "The Virtual Terror of Border Crossing: Iñárritu's *Carne y Arena*." *KCET* (radio), 15 Aug. 2017, https://www.kcet.org/shows/artbound/the-virtual-terror-of-border-crossing-inarritus-carne-y-arena.

Ojos Sombríos. Directed by Fernando Maldonado and Jorge Tereso, performance by Colin Ferrell, ARTE, 3DAR, and Atlas V, 2019.

Oliver, Juan José. "Entrevista con Vicente Aranda." *Film Ideal: Revista Cinematográfica Mensual*, no. 208, 1968, pp. 76–80.

Olmsted, Marc. "The Paranormal Activity of 'Reality' Horror: The Selfie, the Self-Reflexive and the Legacy of Michael Snow." *Otherzine*, no. 32, Spring 2017, www.othercinema.com/otherzine/the-paranormal-activity-of-reality-horror-the-selfie-the-self-reflexive-and-the-legacy-of-michael-snow/.

Onanuga, Tola. "The Collapse of Machinima Is a Stark Warning to YouTube Creators." *Wired Business*, 27 Jan. 2019, www.wired.co.uk/article/machinima-youtube.

Oubiña, David. "Building at the Margins: Trajectories of New Independent Cinema in Latin America." *The Film Edge: Contemporary Filmmaking in Latin America*, edited by Eduardo A. Russo, Teseo, 2010, pp. 33–46.

Pájaros de Papel (part 1 and 2). Directed by German Heller and Federico Carlini, performances by Edward Norton, Archie Yates, and Joss Stone, 3DVR and Baobab Studios, 2021.

Palmer, Alex. "Can Virtual Reality Teach Empathy?" *Discover Magazine*, 28 July 2021, www.discovermagazine.com/technology/can-virtual-reality-teach-empathy.

Paranaguá, Paulo Antonio. "Orígenes, evolución y problemas." *Cine documental en América Latina*, edited by Paulo Antonio, Paranaguá, 2003.

Parikka, Jussi. *What Is Media Archeology?* Polity Press, 2012.

Peli, Oren, director. *Paranormal Activity*. Blumhouse Productions, 2007.

Pereira da Silva, Humberto. *Glauber Rocha: Cinema, estética e revolução*. Paco, 2016.
Perone, James. *American History through Music: Music of the Counterculture Era*. Greenwood P, 2004.
Perriam, Chris, et al. "The Transnational in Iberian and Latin American Cinemas: Editors' Introduction." *Hispanic Research Journal*, vol. 8, no. 1, Feb. 2007, pp. 3–9.
Pethő, Ágnes. *Cinema and Intermediality*. Cambridge Scholars Publishing, 2011.
Pierre, Sylvie. *Glauber Rocha*. Cahiers du cinéma, Paris, 1987.
———. *Glauber Rocha: Textos e entrevistas com Glauber Rocha*, translated by Eleonora Bottmann. Campinas, São Paulo: Papyrus Editora, 1996.
Pietrobon, Agnese. "Interview with German Heller." *XRMust*, 6 Sept. 2021, www.xrmust.com/xrmagazine/german-heller-paper-birds/.
———. "The World of *Paper Birds*: When Memories Get Physical." *Storytelling in VR, AR, 360*, 8 Dec. 2020, vrgeschichten.de/en/paper-birds.
Placeholder. Created by Brenda Laurel and Rachel Strickland, Interval Research Corporation, 1992.
Pneurosis. Directed by Daniela Cugliandolo, courtesy of filmmaker, 2006. MP4.
Portabella, Pere. "Pere Portabella about Joan Brossa." *Pere Portabella*, 2000, pereportabella.com/en/archive_post/2000-writing-pere-portabella-about-joan-brossa/.
———, director. *Nocturno 29*. Films 59, 1968.
Portela, Alejandra. "#DocBuenosAires 2018: Entrevista a Javier Olivera por *La extraña*." *Leedor*, 19 Oct. 2018, leedor.com/2018/10/19/docbuenosaires-2018-entrevista-a-javier-olivera-por-la-extrana/.
Powell, Daniel. *Horror Culture in the New Millennium: Digital Dissonance and Technohorror*. Lexington Books, 2019.
Project Syria. Created by Nonny de la Peña, MxR Studio, USC School of Cinematic Arts, Vangelis Lympouridis, World Economic Forum, 2014.
Rajewsky, Irina O. "Border Talks: The Problematic Status of Media Borders in the Current Debate about Intermediality." *Media Borders, Multimodality and Intermediality*, edited by Lars Ellestrōm, Palgrave, 2010, pp. 51–68.
———. "Intermediality, Intertextuality, and Remediation: A Literary Perspective on Intermediality." *Intermédialités / Intermediality*, no. 6, 2005, pp. 43–64.
Ready Player One. Directed by Steven Spielberg, performances by Tye Sheridan and Olivia Cooke, Warner Brothers, 2018.
Rees, Alan, Duncan White, Steven Ball, and David Curtis, editors. *Expanded Cinema: Art, Performance, Film*. Tate Publishing, 2011.
Renan, Sheldon. *An Introduction to the American Underground Film*, Dutton, 1967.
Riambau, Esteve. *La producció cinematogràfica a Catalunya, 1962–1969*. 1995. Universitat Autonoma de Barcelona, PhD dissertation.
Riambau, Esteve, and Casimiro Torreiro. *Temps era temps: El cinema de l'Escola de Barcelona i el seu entorn*. Generalitat de Catalunya, Deptarament de Cultura, 1993.

Risner, Jonathan. "'This City Is Killing Me': The Circulation of Argentine Horror Cinema and Buenos Aires in Pablo Parés and Daniel de la Vega's *Jennifer's Shadow* (2004) and De la Vega's *Death Knows Your Name* (2007)." *Studies in Hispanic Cinema*, vol. 7, no. 1, 2011, pp. 23–34.

———. "The Reach of Genre: The Emergence of Chilean Horror Cinema." *Chilean Cinema in the Twenty-First-Century World*, edited by Vania Barraza and Carl Fischer, Wayne State UP, 2020, pp. 107–28, zoboko.com/text/vgjjmjv3/chilean-cinema-in-the-twenty-first-century-world/13.

Rist, Peter H. "Agit-prop Cuban style" *Offscreen*, vol. 11, no. 3, Mar. 2007, offscreen.com/view/agit_prop_cuban_style.

———. *Historical Dictionary of South American Cinema*. Rowman and Littlefield, 2014.

Robinson Crusoe. Directed by Aleksandr Andriyevsky, performances by Pavel Kadochnikov, Yuri Lyubimov, and Aleksandr Smiranin, 1947.

Rocha, Glauber. "The Aesthetics of Hunger." Translated by Burnes Hollyman, edited by Michael Chanan. *Twenty-Five Years of New Latin American Cinema*, London: BFI, 1983, pp. 13–14.

———. "Cinema Novo and the Dialectics of Popular Culture." *Cinema and Social Change in Latin America: Conversations with Filmmakers*, edited by Julianne Burton, U of Texas P, 1986, pp. 105–13.

———. *Mostra Glauber por Glauber*. Catalogo, edited by João Luiz Vieira. Embrafilme, 1985.

———. *On Cinema: Glauber Rocha*, edited by Ismail Xavier, I. B. Taurus, 2019.

———. "The Tricontinental Filmmaker: That Is Called Dawn." *Brazilian Cinema*, edited by Randall Johnson and Robert Stam, Columbia UP, 1995, pp. 76–80.

Rocha, Glauber, director. *Cabeças cortadas*. Mapa Filmes and Filmscontacto, 1970.

———. *Terra em transe*. Mapa Filmes, 1967.

Rocha, Glauber, Manuel Asín and Daniel Pitarch Fernández "Impreciso, difuso, bárbaro: Montaje de citas sobre *Cabezas cortadas* de Glauber Rocha." *Concreta: Sobre creación y teoría de la imagen*, no. 12, 2018, pp. 54–67.

Rodowick, David. *The Virtual Life of Film*. Harvard UP, 2007.

Rodríguez, Carina. *El cine de terror en Argentina: Producción, distribución, exhibición y mercado*. Bernal: Universidad Nacional de Quilmes, 2014.

Rosen, Philip. *Change Mummified: Cinema, Historicity, Theory*. U of Minnesota P, 2001.

———. "From Impurity to Historicity." *Impure Cinema: Intermedial and Intercultural Approaches to Film*, edited by Lúcia Nagib and Anne Jerslev, I. B. Taurus, 2015, pp. 3–20.

Ross, Miriam. "Simulation and Flesh: Total Cinema, Virtual Reality and 1930s Science Fiction." *Textual Practice*, vol. 35, no. 10, 2021, pp. 1707–23.

———. "Virtual Reality's New Synesthetic Possibilities." *Television & New Media*, vol. 21, no. 3, 2020, pp. 297–314.

Rozenkrantz, Jonathan. "Analogue Video in the Age of Retrospectacle: Aesthetics, Technology, Subculture." *Alphaville: Journal of Film and Screen Media*, no. 12, Winter 2016, pp. 39–58, www.alphavillejournal.com/Issue12/ArticleRozenkratz.pdf.

Rozsa, Irene, and Masha Salazkina. "Dissonances in 1970s European and Latin American Political Film Discourse: The Aristarco–García Espinosa Debate." *Canadian Journal of Film Studies*, vol. 24, no. 2, 2015, pp. 66–81.

RunwayML. 2023, runwayml.com/.

Ruoff, Jeffrey. "Home Movies of the Avant-Garde: Jonas Mekas and the New York Art World." *To Free the Cinema: Jonas Mekas and the New York Underground*, edited by David James, Princeton UP, 1992, pp. 294–312.

Salazkina, Masha. "Moscow-Rome-Havana: A Film Theory Road Map." *October*, no. 139, Winter 2011, pp. 97–116.

———. "Soviet-Italian Cinematic Exchanges, 1920s to 1950s: From Early Soviet Film Theory to Neorealism." *Global Neorealism: The Transnational History of a Film Style*, edited by Saverio Giovacchini and Robert Sklar, U of Mississippi P, 2012, pp. 37–51.

Salazkina, Masha, and Enrique Fibla-Gutiérrez, editors. "Introduction: Global Perspectives on Amateur Film Histories and Cultures." *Global Perspectives on Amateur Film Histories and Cultures*, Indiana UP, 2020, pp. 1–26.

Sales, Fermín, et al., directors. *El viaje Glauber* (2014) [The Glauber Journey]. Universitat Autònoma de Barcelon, Máster en Documental Creativo. *YouTube*, uploaded by UAB, www.youtube.com/watch?app=desktop&v=iogjsTCZmHI.

Sánchez Prado, Ignacio. *Screening Neoliberalism: Transforming Mexican Cinema, 1988–2012*. Vanderbilt UP, 2014.

Sanderson, John. *Sed de más: La cinematografía internacional de Francisco Rabal*. Universidad de Valencia, 2014.

Sax, David. "Kodak's Old School Response to Disruption." *The New Yorker*, 27 Jan. 2016. Web. 30 Mar. 2016, www.newyorker.com/business/currency/kodak-and-the-analog-response-to-disruption.

Saxton, Libby. *No Power without an Image: Icons Between Photography and Film*. Edinburgh UP, 2020.

Schelling, Vivian, editor. *Through the Kaleidoscope: The Experience of Modernity in Latin America*. Verso, 2000.

Schrey, Dominik. "Analogue Nostalgia and the Aesthetics of Digital remediation." *Media and Nostalgia: Yearning for the Past, Present and Future*, edited by Katharina Niemeyer, Palgrave, 2014, pp. 27–39.

Schröter, Jens. "The Politics of Intermediality." *Acta Univ. Sapientiae, Film and Media Studies. The International Scientific Journal of Sapientia*, no. 2, 2010, pp. 107–24, www.acta.sapientia.ro/acta-film/C2/film2-6.pdf.

Scolari, Carlos A., and Damián Fraticelli. "Enunciar la interacción: Las reseñas y anticipos de videojuegos." *Homo Videoludens 2.0. De Pacman a la gamification*.

Col·lecció Transmedia XXI, edited by Carlos Scolari, Laboratori de Mitjans Interactius, Universitat de Barcelona, 2013, pp. 205–22.

Scott, Mackenzie. "TikTok Video Ideas: A Guide for Filmmakers." *Soundstripe*, 3 Jan. 2022, www.soundstripe.com/blogs/tiktok-video-ideas-a-guide-for-filmmakers.

Serna, Laura Isabel. *Making Cinelandia: American Films and Mexican Film Culture before the Golden Age*. Duke UP, 2014.

Shaviro, Stephen. *Post-Cinematic Affect*. CPI Anthony Rowe, 2009.

Shaw, Lisa, and Stephanie Dennison. *Brazilian National Cinema*. Routledge, 2007.

Shiel, Mark. *Italian Neorealism: Rebuilding the Cinematic City*. Wallflower Press, 2006.

Shilina-Conte, Tanya. "Phone Footage and the Social Media Image as Global Anonymous Cinema: Ana Nyma's (Anonyme) *Fragments of a Revolution* (2011) and Peter Snowdon's *The Uprising* (2013)." *Frames Cinema Journal*, vol. 18, Summer 2021, pp. 29–68.

Shohat, Ella, and Robert Stam. *Unthinking Eurocentrism: Multiculturalism and the Media*. Routledge, 1994.

Simons, Jan. "Between iPhone and YouTube: Movies on the Move." *Video Vortex Reader II: Moving Images Beyond YouTube*, edited by Geert Loving and Rachel Somers, Amsterdam: Institute of Network Cultures, 2011, pp. 95–107.

Sirkkunen, Esa, et al. "Exploring the Immersive Journalism Landscape." *Immersive Journalism as Storytelling: Ethics, Production and Design*, edited by Turo Uskali et al., Routledge, 2021, pp. 13–24.

Sitney, P. Adams. *Visionary Film: The American Avant-Garde, 1943–2000*. Oxford UP, 2002.

Skoller, Jeffrey. *Shadows, Specters, Shards: Making History in Avant-Garde Film*. U of Minnesota P, 2005.

Slater-Robins, Max. "The Death of HoloLens May Have Been Greatly Exaggerated." *Techradar*, 7 Feb. 2022, www.techradar.com/news/the-death-of-hololens-may-have-been-greatly-exaggerated-microsoft-says.

Solanas, Fernando, and Octavio Getino. "Hacia un Tercer Cine. Octubre 1969." *Cine, cultura y descolonización*, edited by Fernando E. Solanas and Octavio Getino, Siglo XXI, 1973, pp. 55–92.

———. "Towards a Third Cinema." Translated by Julianne Burton. *New Latin American Cinema, Vol. 1*, edited by M. T. Martin, Wayne State UP, 1997, pp. 33–58.

———, directors. *La hora de los hornos*. Grupo Cine Liberación, 1968.

Solomon, Stefan. "'The Cloak of Technicolor': Intermedial Colour in *Antônio das Mortes*." *Screen*, vol. 60, no. 1, Spring 2019, pp. 137–47.

Spheres: Songs of Spacetime. Created by Eliza McNitt, performances by Jessica Chastain, Millie Bobby Brown, and Patti Smith, Protozoa Pictures and Atlas V, 2018.

Stam, Robert. "*Land in Anguish* Revolutionary Lessons." *Jump Cut*, no. 10–11, 1976, pp. 49–51. https://www.ejumpcut.org/archive/onlinessays/JC10-11folder/TerraTranseStam.html.

———. "Palimpsest Aesthetics: A Meditation on Hybridity and Garbage." *Performing Hybridity*, edited by May Joseph and Jennifer Natalya Fink, U of Minnesota P, 1999.

———. "The Two Avant-Gardes: Solanas and Getino's *The Hour of the Furnaces*." *Documenting the Documentary: Close Readings of Documentary Film and Video*, edited by Barry Keith Grant and Jeannette Sloniowski. Wayne State UP, 2014, pp. 271–86.

———. *Tropical Multiculturalism: A Comparative History of Race in Brazilian Cinema and Culture*. Duke UP, 1997.

Star Wars: Secrets of the Empire. Created by David Goyer and George Lucas, ILMxLAB and The Void, 2018.

Steyerl, Hito. "In Defense of the Poor Image." *e-flux Journal*, no. 10, Nov. 2009, www.e-flux.com/journal/10/61362/in-defense-of-the-poor-image/.

Stone, Rob. *Spanish Cinema*. Harlow: Longman, 2001.

Stoner, Grant. "VR Is Here to Stay. It's Time to Make It Accessible." *Wired*, 1 Mar. 2022, www.wired.com/story/virtual-reality-accessibility-disabilities/.

Straw, Will. "Embedded Memories." *Residual Media*, edited by Charles Acland, U of Minnesota P, 2007, pp. 3–15.

"Striking Vipers." *Black Mirror*, created by Owen Harris, season 5, episode 1, performances by Anthony Mackie, Yahya Abdul-Mateen II, and Nicole Beharie, distributed by Netflix, 2019.

Subero, Gustavo. *Gender and Sexuality in Latin American Horror Cinema: Embodiments of Evil*. Palgrave MacMillan, 2016.

Sutherland, Ivan E. "The Ultimate Display." *Information Processing*. Proceedings of 1965 IFIP Congress, vol. 1, 1965, pp. 506–08.

Svensson, Alexander, and Dan Hassoun. "'Scream into Your Phone': Second Screen Horror and Controlled Interactivity." *Participations: Journal of Audience and Reception Studies*, vol. 13, no. 1, May 2016, pp. 170–92.

Sylvan, Edward. "Director James A. Castillo of *Madrid Noir*: 5 Things I Wish Someone Told Me When I First Became a Filmmaker." *Authority Magazine*, 9 Aug. 2021, medium.com/authority-magazine/director-james-a-castillo-of-madrid-noir-5-things-i-wish-someone-told-me-when-i-first-became-a-a410dceae422.

Symphony: A Journey into the Heart of Music. Directed by Igor Cortadellas, performances by Gustavo Dudamel and the Mahler Chamber Orchestra, La Caixa Foundation, 2020.

Szperling, Silvina. "Ritual in Transfigured Time: Narcisa Hirsch, Sufi Poetry, Ecstatic Dances, and the Female Gaze." *International Journal of Screendance*, vol. 3, Fall 2013, pp. 72–84.

Taquini, Graciela. "Tiempos del video argentino." *Historia crítica del video argentino*, edited by Jorge La Ferla, Malba–Fundación Costantini y Museo de Arte Latinoamericano de Buenos Aires, 2008, pp. 25–47.

Thomas, Peter. "Anywhere but the Home: The Promiscuous Afterlife of Super 8." *M/C Journal*, vol. 12, no. 3, July 2009, journal.media-culture.org.au/index.php/mcjournal/article/view/164.

Tierney, Dolores. "Shifting Conceptions of Alejandro González Iñárritu: Interpreting the Auteur." *Studies in Spanish and Latin American Cinemas*, vol. 18, no. 1, 2021, pp. 3–8.

Tirado, Gonzalo. "Los filmes de animación en los cines del Madrid de entreguerras (1916–1939)." *Hispania Nova*, no. 19, 2021, pp. 141–65.

Tomorrow: The Evolution of Language. Directed by Nicolás Alcalá, Future Lighthouse, 2016.

Tompkins, Cynthia. *Experimental Latin American Cinema: History and Aesthetics*. U of Texas P, 2013.

Torrell, Josep. "Nocturno 29: La primera película política del estado español." *Los Nuevos Cines en España: Ilusiones y desencantos de los años sesenta*, edited by Carlos F. Heredero and José Enrique Monterde, Filmoteca Española, 2003, pp. 449–54.

Torres, Alejandra. "Seeing (Oneself) Looking into the Camera: An Interview with Narcisa Hirsch." *International Journal of Screendance*, vol. 3, Fall 2013, pp. 85–100.

Torres, Alejandra, and Clara Garavelli. "¿Qué es lo experimental del cine y video experimental argentino?" *Imagofagia*, no. 9, 2014, pp. 1–29.

Townsend, Christopher. "From the Periphery to the Interstices: Avant-Garde Film, Medium Specificity and Intermediality, 1970–2015." *Cinematic Intermediality: Theory and Practice*, edited by Kim Knowles and Marion Schmid, Edinburgh UP, 2021, pp. 73–87.

Trerotola, Diego. "Filme von Narcisa Hirsch / Films by Narcisa Hirsch." Viennale Program, Vienna International Film Festival, Oct.–Nov. 2015, www.viennale.at/en/films/filme-von-narcisa-hirsch-programm-1.

Treske, Andreas. *Video Theory: Online Video Aesthetics or the Afterlife of Video*. Transcript-Verlag, 2015.

Tsukamoto, Shinya, director. *Tetsuo: The Iron Man*. Self-produced, 1989.

Turner, Matt. "Art within the Machine: How Machinima Turns the Camera on Videogames." *BFI*, 2 Apr. 2019, www2.bfi.org.uk/news-opinion/sight-sound-magazine/features/machinima-videogames-cinema-art.

Turquety, Benoît. "Understanding (Amateur) Cinema: Epistemology and Technology." *Global Perspectives on Amateur Film Histories and Cultures*, edited by Masha Salazkina and Enrique Fibla-Gutiérrez, Indiana UP, 2020, pp. 27–42.

UNHCR (United Nations High Commissioner for Refugees). "UNHCR and the European Union Launch 360-degree Interactive Film on Venezuelan Displacement in Ecuador." *UNHCR Global Website*, 24 Mar. 2022, www.unhcr.org/news/announcements/unhcr-and-european-union-launch-360-degree-interactive-film-venezuelan.

Use of Force. Directed by Nonny de la Peña, Tribeca Film Institute New Media Fund, 2013.

Valencia, Andrés, director. *Chateo, luego existo*. Valencia Producciones, 2016. Web series.

VanDerBeek, Stan. "'Culture: Intercom' and Expanded Cinema: A Proposal and Manifesto," *Film Culture*, no. 40, Spring 1966, pp. 15–18.

Venturi, Riccardo. "Rethinking the Expanded Cinema," translated by Simon Pleasance, *Critique d'Art: Actualité internationale de la littérature critique sur l'art contemporain*, no. 45, Nov. 2015, www.journals.openedition.org/critiquedart/19157.

Vilarós, Teresa M. "Barcelona come piedras: La impolítica mirada de Jacinto Esteva y Joaquim Jordà en *Dante no es uúnicamente severo*." *Hispanic Review*, no. 78, vol. 4, Autumn 2010, pp. 513–28.

———. "Cine y literatura en la España de los sesenta: Testimonio de un primer proceso de desideologización." *Literatura española y cine*, edited by Norberto Mínguez Arranz, Editorial Complutense, 2002, pp. 193–207.

Vilaseca, David. "Deleuze and the Barcelona School: Time in Vicente Aranda's *Fata Morgana* (1965)." *Spanishness in the Spanish Novel and Cinema of the 20th–21st Century*, edited by Cristina Sánchez-Conejero, Cambridge Scholars, 2007, pp. 19–30.

———. *Queer Events: Post-Deconstructive Subjectivities in Spanish Writing and Film, 1960s to 1990s*. Liverpool UP, 2011.

Villazana, Libia. "Redefining Transnational Cinema." *Contemporary Hispanic Cinema*, edited by Stephanie Dennison, Cambridge UP, 2013, pp. 25–46.

Vives-González, Luna. "Insiders or Outsiders? Argentine Immigrants in Spain." *Citizenship Studies*, vol. 15, no. 2, 2011, pp. 227–45.

Walley, Jonathan. *Cinema Expanded: Avant-Garde Film in the Age of Intermedia*. Oxford UP, 2020.

Walsh, David. "Eternal Digital Storage: The Impossible Dream." *Journal of Film Preservation*, no. 108, Apr. 2023, pp. 33–38.

Ward, Julie. "Caminar en zapatos migrantes: La lógica fronteriza de la instalación de realidad virtual *Carne y Arena* de Alejandro González Iñárritu." *Investigación Teatral: Revista de artes escénicas y performatividad*, vol. 12, no. 20, 2021, pp. 50–68.

Wayne, Mike. *Political Film: The Dialectics of Third Cinema*. Pluto Press, 2001.

We Meet in Virtual Reality. Directed by Joe Hunting, independently produced, 2022.

Whitmire, Eric, et al. "Haptic Revolver: Touch, Shear, Texture, and Shape Rendering on a Reconfgurable Virtual Reality Controller." *Proceedings of the 2018 CHI Conference on Human Factors in Computing Systems* (ACM 2018). Montréal, Apr. 2018, ACM, ubicomplab.cs.washington.edu/pdfs/hapticrevolver.pdf.

Williams, Bruce. "In the Heat of the Factory." *Marxism and Film Activism: Screening Alternative Worlds*, edited by Ewa Mazierska and Lars Kristensen, Berghahn Books, 2015.

Williams, Mark. "Rewriting Media History: Intermedial Borders." *Convergence Media History*, edited by Janet Staiger and Sabine Hake, Routledge, 2009.

Wilson, Gavin. *Cell/ular Cinema: Individuated Production, Public Sharing and Mobile Phone Film Exhibition.* 2015. U of Leeds, PhD dissertation, etheses.whiterose.ac.uk/8475/.

———. "Film Festivals for Mobile Cinema: Vehicles for Segyehwa in South Korean Moving Image Culture." *Cultural Translation and East Asia: Creativity, Film, Literature and Religion*, special issue of *JOMEC Journal*, no. 6, 2014, pp. 1–13.

———. "Film Festival Participation and Identity Formation: Non-professional Creativity and the Pleasures of Mobile Phone Filmmaking." *Discourses of (De)Legitimization: Participatory Culture in Digital Contexts*, pp. 288–304.

Wilson, Kristi M. "Ecce Homo Novus: Snapshots, the 'New Man,' and Iconic Montage in the Work of Santiago Álvarez." *Social Identities*, vol. 19, no. 3/4, 2013, pp. 410–22.

Witmer, Bob G., and Michael J. Singer, "Measuring Presence in Virtual Environments: A Presence Questionnaire." *Presence*, vol. 7, no. 3, 1998, pp. 225–40.

Wolkowicz, Paula. "Escenas del under porteño. Experimentación y vanguardia en el cine argentino de los años 60 y 70." *Imagofagia*, vol. 9, Apr. 2014, www.asaeca.org/imagofagia/sitio/index.php?option=com_content&view=article&id=402%3Aescenas-del-under-porteno-experimentacion-y-vanguardia-en-el-cine-argentino-de-los-anos-60-y-70&catid=54%3Anumero-9&Itemid=169.

Xavier, Ismail. *Allegories of Underdevelopment: Aesthetics and Politics in Modern Brazilian Cinema.* U of Minnesota P, 1997.

———. "Glauber Rocha: Crítico y cineaste." *La Fuga*. 30 Apr. 2015, www.lafuga.cl/glauber-rocha-critico-y-cineasta/457.

Youngblood, Gene. *Expanded Cinema*. E.P. Dutton, 1970.

———. Introduction to the fiftieth anniversary edition. *Expanded Cinema, fiftieth anniversary edition*. Fordham UP, 2020, pp. xiii–xxxii.

Zimmerman, Patricia. *Reel Families: A Social History of Amateur Film*. Indiana UP, 1995.

Zone, Ray. *Stereoscopic Cinema and the Origins of 3D Film, 1838–1952*. UP of Kentucky, 2007.

Index

ableism, 311–312, 323, 326
Abrams, J. J., 190
Abstract Expressionism, 130
abstraction, 118–119, 193–195
  iconicity and, 82, *83*, 84–85
absurdism, 105–106, 129–130, 158–159
Academy of International Extended Reality, 314
"accented cinema," 21, 36, 40
An Accented Cinema (Naficy), 21
Access Grid Augmented Virtual Environment (AGAVE), 306–307
accessibility, 239, 254–255, 352–353, 355, 360, 378
  of cell phone cinema, 251, 296
  internet archiving and, 54, 204, 207–208, 214–215, 234–235, 238–240
  of 360-degree videos, 329
  VR issues with, 4, 299, 311–312
Acland, Charles, 176
Acuña, German, 357
addiction, addictive behavior and, 292, 365, 372
Adobe, 283, 371
Adorno, Theodor, 131
advertisements, 150–151, 371
  cell phone cinema and, 257, 261, 275, 279–280

Fata Morgana drawing on, 128–129, 131–133, 138–139
aesthetics, 6, 13, 202–205, 211–212, 233–234, 381
  AI and, 373–378
  analog, 222–225
  avant-garde, 55, 126
  cell phone films, 244–251, *246*, 254, 258–263, *262*, 265–293, *270*, *272*, *278*, *280*
  cinéma vérité, 277
  EdB, 125–128
  experimental, 97–98, 239
  of the "good enough," 254, 296, 380
  home movie, 186, 191, 198
  of hunger, 90, 96–97, 354
  intermedial, 104, 173, 195–196, 200
  memory and, 195–196
  militant cinema, 53–54, 63–67, 70, 72–73, 82–83
  mobile, 16, 284
  modernism, 122
  of montage, 81–82
  obsolescence as, 187–188, 225
  post-digital, 244, 254, 266
  post-medium, 179
  radical, 10, 381
  realist, 65–66

431

aesthetics *(continued)*
   Super 8, 174, 183–190, 198–199
   Third Cinema, 53, 66
   transatlantic, 236
   video game, 361
   VR cinema, 301
"An Aesthetics of Dreams," Rocha, 101, 160
"An Aesthetics of Hunger" ("Eztetyka da Fome") (Rocha), 90, 95–96
affect, 2, 175, 181–184, 202, 217–218
   intermediality and, 237–240
   nostalgia and, 205
Afro-Cuban heritage, 355–356
AGAVE. *See* Access Grid Augmented Virtual Environment
L'Âge d'or, 92, 153, 166–167
agency, 325, 334, 355–357, 373
agit-prop, 35, 44, 75, 85–86
Aguilera Skvirsky, Salomé, 159
Aguirrezábal, Javier, 278, 280
AI. *See* artificial intelligence
Aisemberg, Alicia, 24
Alcalá, Nicolás, 312–313, 316
Alcoz, Albert, 386n20, 394n11
Aldana, Xavier, 277
Alemann, Marie-Louise, 191–192
Allá en el Rancho Grande, 165
Allegories of Underdevelopment (Xavier), 100
Almendros, Néstor, 57
Alonso, Rodrigo, 213–214
AltSpace, 300, 314
Álvarez, Santiago, 33, 55, 65, 75–76, 137, 384n7
   ICAIC films by, 41–49
   Lumbreras impacted by, 44–45, 48, 56, 67–68
   montage by, 47–48, 51, 68
Alves, Castro, 112
Amago, Sam, 25

amateur films, 11, 17, 24, 351, 367, 385n9, 387n21, 393n2
   cell phone films and, 29, 242–244, 247–249, 257, 259, 265–266, 274, 296–297
   home movies as, 26, 216–221, *217*
   machinima and, 358, 360
   reproduction capabilities for, 222
   Super 8 and, 186
   TikTok cinema as, 367–370
Amaya, Antonio, 162–163
ambulatory style in cell phone films, 267–268, 284–285
Amenábar, Alejandro, 17
Amores perros, 385n11
anachronism, 155, 163, 190
analog films and formats, 381–382, 387n23, 395n15. *See also* obsolescence
   analog video, 203–214
   digital *vs.*, 180–181
   indexicality and, 176–178, 180–183, 220, 233, 394n12
   nostalgia for, 173–177, 241
   preservation of, 222–223
   transmedial stage for, 238
Andrade, Oswald de, 104
Andriyevsky, Aleksandr, 309
Android phones, 251, 266, 276
Anémic cinéma, 118–119
Angels, 337
Anger, Kenneth, 193
Anglocentrism, 312, 315
animation, 375
   machinima and, 357–364
   stop-motion, 183, *184*, 200, 357, 363
   VR, 314–327, *318*, *320*, *323*, *327*, 338–350
anonymity, 60, 78, 271, 295, 367
Ansiedad, 369

anti-commercialism, 120, 254–255
anti-establishment stances, 10–11, 66, 87, 364
Antônio das Mortes (*O dragão da maldade contrao santo guerreiro*), 95, 158
Antonioni, Michelangelo, 51, 131, 392n19
Antropofagia, 104
El apache de Londres, 357
El Apóstol, 357
App, 292–294, 399n18
Apple, 245, 257, 261, 287. *See also* iPhone
appropriation, 362, 396n23
AR. *See* augmented reality
Arab Spring, 255
Aranda, Vicente, 28, 57, 125, 135–136, 391n11. See also *Fata morgana*
  emigration to Venezuela by, 128–129
Arcangel, Cory, 361
Argentina, 30, 357, 393n4. *See also* Buenos Aires; Cine Liberación
  cell phone cinema, 260–266, *262, 264*
  diaspora from, 177, 179, 187, 191–192, 203–214, 236, 241
  dictatorial, 60, 174, 176–179, 192, 222, 324, 338n4, 396n22, 396nn19–20
  Dirty War, 195, 324
  economic crisis, 174, 176–180
  expats in Spain from, 28–29, 174–175, 178–180, 203, 209–214
  experimental cinema from, 174–175, 177, 179–182, 191–193, 203–214
  Grupo Goethe, 10, 28–29, 191–192, 350, 396nn21–22
  horror genre in, 250, 386n18

INCAA, 250, 260
Super 8 filmmakers in, 191–237, *194, 201, 217, 227, 228*, 393n3, 394n7, 396n18
superocheros from, 190–192, 197, 393n2
Third Cinema, 37, 388n7
VR cinema from, 310–316, 321–327, *323, 327*, 400n5
Arredondo, Isabel, 393n2
Arriaga, Guillermo, 337
art cinema, art house cinema and, 10, 50, 67, 85, 93–95, 394n7. *See also* avant-garde
  EdB, 101
  as oppositional cinema, 87–89
  TIJTS as, 175–176, 203–236, *217, 226, 228*
Artaud, Antonin, 268, 274
artificial intelligence (AI), AI cinema and, 282n5, 352, 354, 372–380, 402nn7–10
  experimental cinema and, 30–31
  machinima as a precursor to, 357
  VR and, 306
Artificio, 378
Asociación Colombiana de Realidades Inmersivas y Emergentes, 313
Asociación de la Industria de Tecnologías Inmersivas Argentinas, 313
Asturian Revolution (1934), 80, *80*
Aubert, Jean Paul, 170–171
audiences. *See* spectators
audiovisual cultures, 212–213 189, 265, 294
augmented reality (AR), 300–301, 305, 307–309, 352–353, 400n1
authenticity, 188, 247, 261, 277, 296
  AI and, 372, 375
  Super 8 film and, 178, 185, 196

authoritarianism, 30, 52–53, 178–179, 192. *See also* dictatorships
in Brazil, 88, 97–100
avant-garde, avant-garde films and, 49, 57, 208, 359–360, 392n19, 394n7
aesthetics, 55, 126
by Aranda, 129
collage in, 235
European, 43–44, 53, 66, 85
expanded cinema and, 7–8, 11–13
intermediality and, 43–44, 93–95, 118–119
Italian, 34
by Rocha, 95–96
Super 8, 189
Surrealist, 143–145
Avellar, José Carlos, 160, 168

Babel, 335
Bakhtin, Mikhail, 42
Balsom, Erika, 380
Banco do Estado do Maranhão, 99
Barbaro, Umberto, 35
Barcelona, Spain, 174–175, 177, 191, 196–198, 203–214, 236
Barcelona School. *See* Escuela de Barcelona (EdB)
Bardem, Juan Antonio, 57, 125–126, 337
Barrera, Cristóbal Valenzuela, 378
Barthes, Roland, 42, 180, 217–218
Bassett, Caroline, 254
La batalla de Chile. Tercera parte, 66
La battaglia di Algeri, 388n2
La battala de Chile, 384n7
Battlescar: Punk Was Invented by Girls, 304
Baudry, Jean-Louis, 199
Bazin, André, 180, 242, 304–305, 311, 385n13
on "impure cinema," 115–116

Beiras, Xosé Manuel, 70–71
Bell, Dustin, 361
Bellour, Raymond, 356
belonging, national, 203, 381
Bembé, 355–356
Ben-Barka, Souheil, 36
Benjamin, Walter, 81–82, 239, 396n18
Bennett, Lawrence, 316
Berlanga, Luis García, 57
Berlin Short Film Festival, 246
Bernal, Gael García, 17, 337
Bernini, Emilio, 204, 214–215
Berry, David, 252
Berry, Marsha, 26
Betacam, 222, 224, 226
Betamax, 224–225
Bienvenido, Mr. Marshall, 126
Biggio, Federico, 383n5
BigScreen, 300, 307
Bilbatúa, Miguel, 49
Biondi, Beniamino, 90
Birri, Fernando, 36–37
Black Mirror (series), 303
The Blair Witch Project, 185, 261, 272, 278–280
Blázquez, Elena, 40, 51
blindness, 323, *323*, 326, 400n4
Blood Cinema (Kinder), 122
Blood Circuits (Risner), 386n18
Blow-Up, 392n19
La boca del león, 289, 291
Boermans, Bobby, 292
Bofill, Ricardo, 129, 389n1
Bolex cameras, 62
Bollig, Ben, 22, 24, 113
border crossing, 2, 6, 189, 252, 333–350, 383n4
Border Stories, 304
Bordwell, David, 266–267, 271, 273, 398n8
Borromeo, Frederick C., 361
Brakhage, Stan, 113, 191, 193

Branco, Castello, 88
Branding Brazil (Marsh), 24
Brazil, 19–20, 95, 111, 357, 365. *See also* Cinema Novo
   "aesthetics of hunger" in, 90, 96–97, 354
   authoritarianism in, 88, 97–100
   censorship in, 97–100, 152–153, 170
   exile from, 89, 97–98, 151–152, 167–168
   garage cinema from, 257–258
   military rule in, 28, 88–89, 97–104, 122–123
Breakout (video game), 362
Breakout Game Mod, 362
Brillante porvenir, 129
Broch, Brigitte, 337
Brossa, Joan, 133, 141, 143–146, 148, 150
Bruschi, Pablo, 369–370
Bryant, Kobe, 370
budget. *See* costs, budgets and
Buenos Aires, Argentina, 174, 177, 196–198, 203–214, 236
   Buenos Aires Underground, 191–192
Buñuel, Luis, 51–52, 73, 199, 384n8, 392n23
   L'Âge d'or by, 92–93 153, 155, 166
   Un chien andalou by, 118–119
   Rocha and, 105–106, 152–154, 159
Burch, Noël, 65
Burton, Julianne, 37–38, 75, 96–97, 166–167, 389n11
Byrón, Silvestre, 192

Caballero, Jorge, 378
Cabeças cortadas, 28, 89, 105, 170–172, 384n7
   intermediality of, 161–169, *165*
   as a Rocha and EdB collaboration, 92–93, 117–118, 151–161
   surrealism in, 92, 152–158, 166
Cabral da Costa, Wagner, 99–100
Cahiers du Cinéma (journal), 89–90
Caldini, Claudio, 175, 190, 202, 384n7
   Super 8 film and, 176, 182–183, 396n18
Camarades, 41
Cambridge Super 8 Film Festival, 199
cameras, 182–183, 189–190, 194, 255
   DSLR, 241, 256
   handheld, 35, 37, 62, 101–102, 168, 226, 267
   for 360-degree cinema, 305, 329, 354
   virtual, 302–303, 320
El camino hacia la muerte del viejo Reales, 60
Campanella, José Juan, 363–364
El campo para el hombre, 49–54, 61, 66–69, 384n7
   financing, 62–65
   iconicity in, 82, *83*, 84–85
   intermedial and hybrid strategies in, 70–73, *74*, 75–78
   intertextuality in, 78–82, *79*, *80*
Canciones para después de una guerra, 125
Cannes Festival, 3, 370–371, 375
Cantú, Mariela, 222–223, 232
Capa, Robert, 69
capitalism, 10, 49, 52, 65–66, 68–69, 79, 296
   division of labor and, 124, 135
   Fata Morgana addressing, 131
   financing and, 120
   Nunes addressing, 141
   Rocha on, 96
   techno-capitalism, 134–135

Caprin, Gustavo, 29, 175–176, 203–214, 221–222, 238–239, 380–381
  digital video utilized transfer by, 224–236, *227*, *228*
Cardona, Luis Felipe, 245–246, 254
La carga, 79, *79*
Carlini, Federico, 314, 322–323
Carne y Arena, 5, 302, 329, *341*, 383n3, 401nn10–11
  migrants and refugees in, 1–4, 30, 335–350, *343*, *346*
Carrero Blanco, Luis, 58, 62
La casa muda, 278
Casas, Ramón, 79, *79*
Castillo, James, 314–316, 400n7
Catalan, 389n1
"Catalan Cinema's Radical Years, 1968–1978" (MoMA exhibit), 54
Catalan Socialist Party, 62
Catholicism, 71–73, 101–102, 114, 151
Caudillo, 389n12
CAVEs. *See* Computer Assisted Virtual Environments
La Caza, 125–126
CCCB. *See* Centre de Cultura Contemporània de Barcelona
Cegys, Paul, 348–349
cell phone cinema, *246*, 352, 387nn24–25, 398n9, 398nn3–7, 399nn17–28
  advertisements and, 257, 261, 275, 279–280
  aesthetics and, 182–183, 187–188, 244–251, *246*, 254, 258–263, *262*, 265–293, *270*, *272*, *278*, *280*, 354
  amateur films and, 29, 242–244, 247–249, 257, 259, 265–266, 274, 296–297
  ambulatory style in, 267–268, 284–285
  as collective phenomenon, 255–258
  costs of, 243–244, 251, 254, 257–258, 260, 268–269, 274, 278, 291, 296–297
  democratization and, 29, 241, 243, 296–297
  distribution for, 243–244, 257–258, 260, 271, 274–275, 282, 290, 296
  in film festivals, 246–248, 251, 255–257, 265, 267–268, 276, 289–290
  found footage in, 247, 259, 261–262, 275–282, *278*, 279–281, *280*, 399n11
  horror, 29, 244, 247–250, 257, 266–275, 282–296, *286*, *288*, 381
  immediacy in, 262–263, 271–274, 277, 281–282, 295–296
  intermediality of, 251–255, 259–260, 273–274, 294, 379–380
  Latin American and Iberian, 244–246, *246*, 259–297, *262*, *264*, *270*, *272*, *278*, *280*, *286*, *288*
  spectators for, 26, 243–244, 253, 266–268, 279, 282–283, 290, 293
  TikTok cinema as, 351, 364–372
  transnationalism of, 241–242, 247–250, 252, 255–259, 266, 268, 295–297
  on YouTube, 256, 258, 261–263, 271, 282, 290
celluloid formats, 178, 208, 376–377, 393n5, 394n9, 395n15. *See also specific formats*
  medium specificity and, 27
  nostalgia for, 174–177, 184–186, 188
  photography and, 19

Rodowick on, 222–223
transmedial stage of, 238
CeluFilmFest, 265
censorship, 46, 48, 140–141, 158, 367, 396n22
　in Brazil, 97–100, 152–153, 170
　EdB addressing, 123–124
　self, 88–89, 367
　in Spain, 52–53, 56–58, 126–127, 389n9, 391n17
Center for Contemporary Culture Tabakalera, 54
Centre de Cultura Contemporània de Barcelona (CCCB), 177, 393n3
Centro Documentazione Cinemae Lotta di Classe, 38
Centro Sperimentale di Cinematografia, 33–38, 45, 49–52, 388n2
Cerdán, Josetxo, 24
CGI. *See* computer generated images
Chanan, Michael, 98
Chastain, Jessica, 304
chatbots, 374–376
Chateo, luego existo, 258
ChatGPT, 375–376
Chazelle, Damien, 257, 367
Checklist, 245–247, *246*, 248, 254
Un chien andalou, 118–119, 149, 166–167, 199
Chile, 51, 357
　horror cell phone cinema from, 250, 275–282, *278*, *280*
China, 257, 300, 365
Chinese New Year, 257
Choi, Eunha, 82
Chomón, Segundo de, 118, 384n8
Ciclón, 48–49
El cielo gira, 128
Cine Cubano (periodical), 48
Cine de la Base, 396n20

Cine Liberación, 36–37, 40–41, 396n20
　militant cinema of, 61, 63–64, 66–67, 90, 384n7
El cine militante (Linares), 40
cinema. *See specific topics*
Cinema Expanded (Walley), 7–8
Cinema Journal, 237
Cinema Novo, 10, 46, 174, 192, 384n7, 388n7, 390n3
　aesthetics of, 97, 101–103
　Aguilera Skvirsky on, 159
　EdB and, 27–28, 87–93, 101–103, 117–120
　musical intertexts used by, 91
　Nagib on, 161
　Rocha and, 27–28, 95–98
Cinema Nuovo (magazine), 37–38
cinéma vérité aesthetic, 277
cinemanovistas, 89–90, 93, 103
CineVR, 307
citizen journalism, 241–242, 244, 277, 352
Citron, Michelle, 185
Clarke, Shirley, 191
La clef des songes, 229
Clémenti, Pierre, 155, 392n25
Cline, Ernest, 303
Coixet, Isabel, 254, 398n7
Cold War, 129
Colectivo Cine de Clase (Class Film Collective), 54–56, 64–65, 77–78, 90
　Escaned on, 85–86
　formation and ideology of, 58–61
collaborative, epistolary videos as, 175–176, 203–236, 381
Collective of Digital Artists in Virtual and Augmented Reality, 313
Colombia, 313, 329, 355, 377–378
　cell phone cinema from, 251, 266–275, *270*, *272*

colonialism, 92–93, 97, 338
  Rocha addressing, 106–107, 113–114, 154, 160
Come Out, 179, 192–197, *194*
comic books, *129*, 129–130, 132–133, 137–138
commercial filmmaking, 5–6, 13, 248–249, 384n8, 385n11
  cell phone cinema compared to, 253–255
  Latin American resistance to, 9–10
commercialism, 10, 13, 131, 134, 150, 169, 260, 265–266, 296
commodification, 123, 124, 127, 295, 297
Computer Assisted Virtual Environments (CAVEs), 306–307
computer generated images (CGI), 339–340, 400n1
  machinima and, 354, 357–364, 401n2
En Construcción, 128
constructivism, 11, 122, 230, 236
consumerism, 123–124, 128–129, 131–135, 139, 151
Contemporary Hispanic Cinema (Dennison), 18, 24
Coppola, Horacio, 199, 384n8
copyright infringement, 362, 364, 375–376
Cortadellas, Igor, 400n6
costs, budgets and, 11, 35, 188, 363. See also financing, funding and
  cell phone cinema related, 243–244, 251, 254, 257–258, 260, 268–269, 274, 278, 291, 296–297
  machinima related, 360–361, 364
  Super 8, 178, 190
  VR cinema related, 299, 311, 352, 354
counter-cinemas, 12–13, 22–23, 50–54, 192
  of EdB, 57, 93
  of Rocha, 159–160
counterculture, countercultural forces and, 94–95, 127, 192
COVID-19 pandemic, 1, 362, 370
  VR and, 300, 302–303
Cristiani, Quirino, 357
Critique de la separation, 129–130
Cronenberg, David, 295
cross-cultural identities, 15, 316
The Crow, 375
Cruz, Penélope, 17
Cruzar, 329, 354–356
Cuarón, Alfonso, 24, 366, 395n15
Cuarterolo, Andrea, 24
Cuba, 39, 46, 355–356
  Cuban Revolution, 9–10, 27, 35, 45, 51, 137, 384n8
cubism, 118–119
Cugliandolo, Daniela, 28, 175, 209, 252, 380–381, 394n7, 394n11
  Esto no es un recuerdo, 178–187, *183*, *184*
  Hirsch and, 193–194, 196
  pneurosis by, 29, 179, 198–200, *201*, 202–203
  renaissance of Super 8 and, 238–239
  transnationalism of, 191
Cura, Domingo, 68–69

Dadaism, 130, 133, 145–146, 153
Dalí, Salvador, 145–146, 152–155, 166–167, 199
DALL-E, 376
D'Aloia, Adriano, 348–350
Dancing with the Virtual Dervish, 337
Dante no es únicamente severo, 105
D'Argenio, Maria Chiara, 44
Darín, Ricardo, 17
Darrell, Johnny, 377
Dawson, Rosario, 304
Death of a Vlogger, 262

"death" of cinema, 176–177, 199, 350
deaths, 1, 30, 156, 274, 330, 343,
    345–346
  of Carrero Blanco, 58, 62
  of Guevara, 68–70
  in *Terra em transe*, 110–111
Debord, Guy, 129–130, 392n18
decolonialism, decolonization and, 36,
    40, 53, 96–97
defamiliarization, 128, 139, 144, 195–
    197, 200, 202, 239, 274
dematerialization, 310–311, 348
democratization, 10, 239, 351–352
  of access to AI, 378
  cell phone cinema and, 29, 241,
    243, 296–297
Demy, Jacques, 392n19
Denegri, Andrés, 29, 175–176, 203–
    222, 231–232, 234–239, 380–381
Dennison, Stephanie, 18, 24
Denson, Shane, 398n8
Deren, Maya, 184, 191, 193, 199,
    394n11
detective genre, literary, 317–319
deterritorialization, 21, 178–179, 353
Deus e o diabo na terra do sol, 95, 105,
    144
Día de muertos, 125
dialectical montage, 44, 47, 85, 392n18
Diamond Films Latin America, 367–
    368
Diary of a Camper, 360
diaspora, 173, 176, 203–214, 316–
    317, 387n23
  Argentine, 177, 179, 187, 191–192,
    203–214, 236, 241
  exile and, 222
Díaz, Patricia, 355–356
dictatorships, 27, 142
  in Argentina, 60, 174, 176–179,
    192, 222, 324, 338n4, 396n22,
    396nn19–20

Rocha addressing, 92–93, 99–101,
    107–108, 151–161
  in Spain, 56, 170, 177, 221, 389n9,
    389n12, 390n2
Diegues, Carlos, 157–158, 161
Dieter, Michael, 252
digital afterlife, 175, 196, 212, 223,
    226, 238–240
digital capture, 182, 228, 239, 360,
    395n15
digital convergence, 252, 380
digital films and formats, 352–353,
    379–382, 385n9, 394n6, 394n12.
    See also cell phone cinema
  AI cinema and, 282n5, 372–379,
    402nn7–10
  hybridization of, 198–199, 203–214
  machinima and, 357–364, 401n2
  nostalgia for analog media and,
    173–177, 241
  post-digital cinema following,
    259–260
  postproduction and, 180–181, 190–
    191, 200, *201*, 359–360, 395n15
  Super 8 and, 178, 180–184
  360-Degree Cinema, 354–357
  TIJTS hybridizing, 203–215
  TikTok cinema and, 351, 364–372
digital indexicality, 185, 190, 238
digital postproduction, 180–181, 190–
    191, *201*, 395n15
digital projections, 208, 395n15
digital single-lens reflex (DSLR)
    cameras, 241, 256
digitization, digital capture and, 182,
    228, 395n15
  materiality and, 222–224, 239–240
  Super 8 film, 175, 187–191, 193,
    196, 198, 207, 233–234
Dirty War (Argentina), 195, 324
disability, 311, 323, *323*, 326, 400n4
Distortion, 361

distribution, 246, 255
  alternative forms of, 10, 207, 211, 214–215, 234–235
  of cell phone cinema, 243–244, 257–258, 260, 271, 274–275, 282, 290, 296
  commercial, 6, 254
  DVD, 248, 266, 296
  self, 245–246, 262, 367
Ditirambo, 127
divisions of labor, 60–61, 76, 124, 135, 390n4
Dixon, Wheeler, 297
DIY films, 225, 256, 265, 268, 274–275, 291. *See also* cell phone cinema
Doane, Mary Ann, 94, 181
documentaries, documentary film and, 5–6, 23–24, 128, 160, 210, 244, 254
  Bembé, 355–356
  British documentary movement and, 37
  ethnographic, 2, 51–52, 73
  militant cinema as, 37–41, 45–46, 48–54, 57–58, 60, 85
  realism, 35, 103–104
  VR, 304
Dooley, Kath, 301–302
double embodiment, 339, 344, 349
double exposures, 184, 246
double situatedness, 339
Dreiling, Miche, 276
DSLR. *See* digital single-lens reflex
dual citizenship, 174–175
dubbing, 360
  AI, 373, 379
Duchamp, Marcel, 118–119
Dune, 188, 395n15
duration, 364–372
  of cell phone films, 245
  of VR cinema, 303

dystopia, 259, 296, 308, 311, 374, 376

Ebert, Roger, 361
Ecuador, 355
EdB. *See* Escuela de Barcelona
education, 352–353, 355
Eisenstein, Sergei, 43–44, 77–78, 85, 117, 308–309
Elduque, Albert, 392n24
Elias, Chad, 255
Elsaesser, Thomas, 15–18, 212–213, 302, 308–309
embodied experiences, 1–2, 311, 329–334, 337–338, 379–380
  in cell phone films, 267, 284–285
  double, 339, 344, 349
Emerson Collective, 3
empathy, 30, 327–328, 355
  VR cinema eliciting, 4–5, 304, 311, 313, 321, 329–336, 339, 348–350
The End, 120
English language, 248, 252, 282–283, 311–313, 320–321, 399nn13–14
Enlightenment, 93
epistolary videos, 175–176, 203–236, 381
Escaned, Mariano Lisa, 48, 50–55, 59, 62–63, 72–73
  on Colectivo Cine de Clase, 85–86
Escorel, Eduardo, 157–158
Escudero, José María García, 389n9, 391n17
Escuela de Barcelona (EdB) (Barcelona School), 56–58, 174, 389n1, 390n4, 391n12, 391n17, 392n18
  Cabeças cortadas and, 92–93, 117–118, 151–161
  Cinema Novo and, 27–28, 87–93, 101–103, 117–120
  Fata Morgana and, 91, 128–135, *129*, *132*

intermediality of, 91, 119–120, 128–131, *129*
Lumbreras and, 67, 85
NCE compared to, 125–128, 170
Nocturno 29 and, 92, 143–151, *145, 147*
poetry used by, 125, 133, 143–151, *146*
responding to Francoism, 88–89, 91–92, 123–124, 127–128
Sexperiencias and, 91, 136–143, *138, 140*
Escuela Documental de Santa Fe, 36–37
Escuela Oficial de Cinematografía, 59
España 68, 60, 69
¿Estamos solos?, 370
Esteva, Jacinto, 57, 105, 157, 392n23
Esto no es un recuerdo, 29, 179–187, *183, 184*, 198, 202–203
estrangement, 77, 139, 239
ethics, 169–172, 303, 338
  AI and, 373, 375–376, 379, 381–382
  VR and, 304, 306
ethnographic documentary, 2, 51–52, 73
L'étoile de mer, 118–119
Europe, European cinema and, 35, 40, 209, 255–257, 323, 336–337
  avant-garde, 43–44, 53, 66, 85
  Cuban film industry and, 48
  European Union, 313, 354–355
  imperialism in, 96
European Union, 313, 354–355
Evans, Peter, 248
EventLab (think tank), 331
Exhibiting Cinema in Contemporary Art (Balsom), 380
exile, 178–179, 182, 186–187, 324, 341–342, 388n6
  from Brazil, 89, 97–98, 151–152, 167–168
  forced, 61, 123, 387n23, 396n22
  internal, 221–222
  nostalgia and, 175–176, 210
  obsolescence linked with, 211, 213
  to Paris, 159
  of Perón, 58–59
  self-imposed, 97–98, 209–210
  "voluntary," 97, 151–152
expanded cinema, 1–2, 6–13, 23, 27, 206–207
Expanded Cinema (Youngblood'), 6–7, 383n5
experiences, cinematic, 2, 300, 302–304
experimental cinema, 2–3, 11, 13, 24, 173, 241, 338, 358, 385n11, 386n20
  aesthetics, 97–98, 239
  AI, 30–31
  Argentine, 174–175, 177, 179–182, 191–193, 203–214
  in Barcelona, 174–175, 177
  of El campo para el hombre, 65–70
  of Grupo Goethe, 10, 28–29, 191–192, 350, 396nn21–22
  Hispano-Argentine, 28–29, 176–187, *183, 184*
  hybridity and, 177, 198–199
  Iberian, 215–221, *217*
  intermediality and, 6–7, 12, 91, 104–118, *109, 115*, 169–172, 187–191, 237–238
  Super 8, 187–192
Experimental Latin American Cinema (Tompkins), 25, 34, 37, 45, 387n21
Extended Reality (XR), 3, 300–301, 311–313, 352–353, 400n1
La extraña, 210–211
"Eztetyka da Fome" (Rocha), 90, 95–97. *See also* "An Aesthetics of Hunger"

Facebook, 214, 300, 302, 323, 328, 352–353, 362. *See also* Meta
Fages, Pere I., 158–159
Falicov, Tamara, 25
fan fiction, 357–358
Fanés, Fèlix, 150, 392n21
fascism, 34, 58–59, 70, 122–123, 384n8
  Adorno on, 131
  in Spain, 134–135, 151
fashion models, high fashion and, 130–131, 134, 140–141, 392n19
Fata Morgana, 28, 57, 91–92, *129*, 130, *132*, 134, 391n11
  drawing on advertisements, 128–129, 131–133, 138–139
  script written by Suárez for, 127
Fellini, Federico, 59
Une femme mariée, 392n19
Ferdinow, Dani, 370
Fernández Labayen, Miguel, 24, 64
Fernández Santos, Ángel, 90
fetishism, 122, 134, 185, 233, 254, 261
Fibla-Gutiérrez, Enrique, 26, 393n2
film festivals, 351, 354, 359, 364, 378, 398n5, 398n9, 402n13. *See also specific film festivals*
  Brazilian filmmakers in, 96–97, 105
  cell phone cinema in, 246–248, 251, 255–257, 265, 267–268, 276, 289–290
  militant documentaries in, 48–49, 51, 57–58
  Super 8, 198
  VR cinema and, 310, 314–315, 323, 330
Film History as Media Archeology (Elsaesser), 212–213
Film Ideal (periodical), 89, 391n12
Filmoteca de Catalunya's Conservation and Restoration Center, 54

financing, funding and, 120, 250, 282, 374. *See also* costs, budgets and
  for 360-degree cinema, 354
  for *El campo para el hombre*, 62–65
  NCE, 126–127
  for *Terra em transe*, 99
  VR cinema, 310, 313, 315
Finley, Guy, 293–294
First Cinema, 39, 388n7. *See also* Hollywood cinema
first-person point of view, 183, *183*, 200, 287, 301, 322, 327–328, 330–331
The Fixer, 283
Fluid Screens, Expanded Cinema (Marchessault, Lord), 383n5
Fluxus, 93, 119–123, 133, 193, 390n5
Followed, 262
forced exile, 61, 123, 387n23, 396n22
foreign investment, 127, 379
formalism, 194–195, 200
found-footage, 358, 380
  cell phone cinema and, 247, 259, 261–262, 275–282, *278*, 279–281, *280*, 399n11
Fraga, Manuel, 391n17
Fragments, 310
Frampton, Hollis, 76, 396n24
France, 159, 388n4
  French New Wave, 28, 37, 46, 50, 90, 120, 388n4
Francoism, Francoist Spain and, 28, 57, 70, 135, 221–222, 389n12, 393n2
  Bardem addressing, 125–126
  El campo para el hombre under, 50–52, 64–65
  EdB responding to, 88–89, 91–92, 123–124, 127–128
  film censorship under, 56–58, 389n9
  La hora de los hornos under, 39–40
  Kinder on, 122

Madrid Noir set in, 30
NCE addressing, 126
Portabella addressing, 146–147
Fraticelli, Damián, 359
French New Wave, 28, 37, 46, 50, 90, 120, 388n4

Gabara, Rachel, 35
Gabilondo, Joseba, 13
Galili, Doron, 188
Galt, Rosalind, 52–53, 67, 120, 124–125, 127–128, 133
  on *Sexperiencias*, 139–140
  on surrealism, 153
Galuppo, Gustavo, 205
gamification, 356, 358–359
garage cinema (*cinema de garage*m), 257–258
Garavelli, Clara, 237–238
García Espinosa, Julio, 45–46, 63, 76, 384n7
García López, Alfonso, 282, 286–287, 289–291, 399n17
García Márquez, Gabriel, 45, 155, 160
gender, 54–55, 199–200, 292–293, 299
  counterculture on, 94
  "impure cinema" and, 116
generative art, 228–229
Geofilms Entertainment, 289
geolocative technology, 252–253, 255, 312
Germanidis, Anastasis, 378
Getino, Octavio, 21, 33, 37, 39, 192, 384n7, 388n7
  Lumbreras and, 51, 55
  militant cinema defined by, 66–67
Gil, Gilberto, 104
Giunta, Andrea, 193
Gleyzer, Raimundo, 396n20
global audiences, 247–248, 381
Global Mexican Cinema (Irwin, Ricalde), 25

Global North, 8–10, 12
Global Perspectives on Amateur Film Histories and Cultures (Salazkina, Fibla), 26, 393n2
Global South, 243, 255–256, 311
globalization, 15–16, 248, 312, 347, 363–364
Godard, Jean Luc, 38, 89, 98, 101, 329n19, 388n4, 391n12
  counter-cinema of, 120
Goethe Institute, 191, 396n19
Goggin, Gerard, 256
Gone Gitmo, 331
González, Pepe, 368
González Iñárritu, Alejandro, 17, 24, 30, 385n11
  Carne y Arena by, 1–5, 302, 314, 329, 335–350, 355, 401n10
Google, 306, 402n8
Goulart, João, 88, 99
Granada, Spain, 215–219
Gras, Ricard, 361–362
Grau, Jorge, 57
Greenberg, Clement, 122
Gris, Anna Giralt, 378
Gromala, Diane, 337
Grupo Goethe (Grupo Cine Experimental Argentino), 10, 28–29, 191–192, 350, 396nn21–22
Guantanamo Bay, 331
Guatemala, 347
Gubern, Román, 39, 129
Guerin, José Luis, 128
Guerra, Ruy, 90
Guevara, Alfredo, 52
Guevara, Che, 68–70
Guillén Landrián, Nicolás (Nicolasito), 48, 61
Gusano Films, 378
Gutiérrez Alea, Tomás, 45–47, 81
Guzmán, Patricio, 66

"Hacia un tercer cine" (Solanas, Getino), 39, 46
Haddad, Mousa, 36
Hahn, Cory, 114–115
Half-Life (video game), 360–362
Half-Life VR but the AI Is Self-Aware, 360–361
Halo Reach (video game), 362
Hamm, Daniel, 195
Hammid, Alexander, 394n11
handheld cameras, 35, 37, 62, 101–102, 168, 226, 267
haptic sensations, 307–308, 349
Hardcastle, Anne E., 279, 399n11
Harlem riots (1964), 195
Hassoun, Dan, 294, 296
Haunting Melissa, 253
Havana, Cuba, 316, 318
HD video. *See* high-definition video
head-mounted displays (HMD), VR, 306–311, 326–327, 332–333, 338
Heliography, 182–183
Heller, Germán, 314, 322–324
Hernández, Miguel, 145
Hernández Rojas, Anastasio, 330
Herzog, Werner, 391n11
Higgins, Dick, 44, 120, 123, 390n5
high fashion, 130–131, 134, 140–141, 392n19
high-definition (HD) video, 182, 188, 226, 251, 266, 346, *346*
Hilderbrand, Lucas, 222
Hirsch, Narcisa, 175, 252, 380–381, 384n7, 394n11, 396n20
  Caprín compared to, 209
  Come Out by, 179, 192–197, *194*, 207
  Cugliandolo compared to, 28–29
  Super 8 films and, 176, 190–192, 198
Hispano-Argentine experimental film, 28–29, 176–179
Historia de un oso, 363

historicity, 179, 181–182, 202–203, 218, 223
HMD. *See* head-mounted displays
Hollywood cinema, 9, 256–257, 266, 272, 380, 389n11, 391n16
  "accented cinema" and, 21
  neorealism *vs.*, 57
  realist aesthetics and, 65–66
  Serna on, 24–25
HoloLens, 254, 309–311, 400n2
home movies, 12, 180, 184–185, 190, 203, 215, 358
  aesthetics of, 186, 191, 198
  as amateur films, 26, 216–221, *217*
  nostalgia and, 29
  Zimmerman on, 26
Home Movies and Other Necessary Fictions, 185
La hora de los hornos, 21–22, 37–41, 47, 49, 60, 192, 384n7
  dogmatism of, 101
  police repression and, 68
  populism of, 58–59
  slaughterhouse scene in, 77
horror films, 253, 262, 398n4, 399n11
  Argentine, 250, 386n18
  cell phone cinema and, 29, 244, 247–250, 257, 266–275, 282–296, *286*, *288*, 381
  Mexican, 250, 289
How to Build a House, 213–214
human-computer collaborations, 359, 381
Hunger in Los Angeles, 401n10
Hunting, Joe, 302–303
Las Hurdes (Tierra sin pan), 51–52, 73
hybridity, hybridization and, 4, 178, 339–340, 350, 374, 377, 396n18
  of Argentine diaspora films, 179
  in Brazilian films, 111
  of cell phone cinema, 258, 264
  in Cuban cinema, 36
  of experimental films, 177, 198–199

intermedial, 70–73, *74*, 75–78, 91, 227–228, 303–304
of Lumbreras, 53–54, 70–73, *74*, 75–78
of machinima projects, 359–363
post-digital, 251–255
by Rocha, 104–105, 116
of Super 8 films, 181–182, 187–190, 198–199, *201*, 202
in *TIJTS*, 203–236, *227*, *228*
hyper-materialism, 261
hyperrealism, 273, 280–281
hyper-theatricality, 28, 104

Ibermedia Program, 25
ICAIC. *See* Instituto Cubano del Arte e Industria Cinematográficos
iconicity, 80–81, 82, *83*, 84–85
iconography, 69–70
identities, 14, 94
cross-cultural, 15, 316
cultural, 5, 312, 393n4
immigrant, 213, 316
national, 22, 37, 154, 180, 192, 211, 213, 231, 381
transnational, 29, 177, 180
ILMxLab, 335–336
Imagen Video tool, Google, 402n8
iMedium, 29, 259, 282–297, *286*, *288*, 399n14–15
immediacy, 205, 321, 354
in cell phone cinema, 262–263, 271–274, 277, 281–282, 295–296
immersive journalism (*periodismo immersivo*), 312, *327*, 327–350, *332*, *341*, *343*, *346*, 354, 401n9
"Immersive Journalism" (de la Peña), 331
immersive technologies and experiences, 38, 300–301, 305–306, 317, 322, 352–356
empathy via, 30, 327–337
"imperfect cinema," 63, 211, 354, 384n7, 388n7

imperialism, 9–10, 47, 92, 96, 160
impure cinema, 19–20, 36, 122, 189, 385n13
Bazin on, 115–116
EdB embracing, 95
Francoism undermined by, 135
intermediality and, 91
Lumbreras and, 67–68
Impure Cinema (Nagib, Jerslev), 91, 189
"In Defense of the Poor Image" (Steyerl), 211
INCAA. *See* Instituto Nacional de Cine y Artes Audiovisuales
inclusivity, 297, 311–312, 321–322
independent filmmakers, 11, 29, 243, 252, 310
indexicality, 196, 226, 284
analog formats and, 176–178, 180–183, 220, 233, 394n12
digital, 185, 190, 238
indigeneity, 16, 338, 384n7
Industrial Revolution, 79
Inherent Rights, Vision Rights, 338
Inherent Vice, 222
Instagram, 185, 367, 368
installation art, VR and, 305, 335–350, *343*, *346*
Institució Catalana de Investigación y de Estudios Avanzados, 331
Instituto Cubano del Arte e Industria Cinematográficos (ICAIC), 37, 41–49, 61, 67, 78
Instituto Mexicano de Realidades Mixtas, 313
Instituto Nacional de Cine y Artes Audiovisuales (INCAA), Argentina, 250, 260
intellectual property, 271
interactivity, 359–360, 374
in immersive journalism, 328
in *Pájaros de papel*, 314–315, 321–327, *323*

interactivity *(continued)*
  VR cinema and, 301–302, 314–315, 317, 321–327, *323*
"Intermedia" (Higgins), 44
intermediality, 79–82, 85–86, 390nn5–7, 395n14
  aesthetics and, 104, 173, 195–196, 200
  affect and, 237–240
  art cinema and, 93–95
  avant-garde and, 43–44, 93–95, 118–119
  of *Cabeças cortadas*, 161–170, *165*
  El campo para el hombre and, 70–73, *74*, 75–78
  of cell phone cinema, 251–255, 259–260, 273–274, 294, 379–380
  defined, 42–44, 93
  of EdB, 91, 119–120, 128–131, *129*
  experimental film and, 6–7, 12, 91, 104–118, *109*, *115*, 169–172, 187–191, 237–238
  in *Fata Morgana*, *129*, 129–131, 135
  of Hispano-Argentine experimental film, 176–187, *183*, *184*
  of Lumbreras, 53–55, 70–73, *74*, 75–78
  of machinima projects, 358–363
  in *Nocturno 29*, 143–151, *145*, *147*
  of Rocha, 104–118, *109*, *115*, 161–169, *165*
  in *Sexperiencias*, 137–143, *139*
  in *Terra em transe*, 104–118, *109*, *115*
  text-image interactions as, 28, 91–92, 113, 118–124
  of *TIJTS*, 203–236, *227*, *228*
  transnationality and, 5–11, 14–15, 18–24, 27, 41–49, 315–321, *320*, 374, 379–382
  of VR, 300–305, 307–315, 337–350, 379–380
  Youngblood on, 383n4, 383n5

internal exile, 221–222
International Mobile Film Festival, 283
International Monetary Fund, 75
internet, 295, 312, 327–329, 351–352, 372, 375
  archiving via, 54, 204, 207–208, 214–215, 234–235, 238–240
intertextuality, 42–43, 78–82, *79*, *80*, 155, 161, 165
intradiegetic devices, 161–162, 280–281, 291
An Introduction to the American Underground Film (Renan), 7
iPhone, 245, 251, 253, 257–259, 261, 266, 273, 283
  Super 8 aesthetics and, 185
Iran, 255
Iribarne, Manuel Fraga, 389n9
Iris, 292
Irwin, Robert McKee, 25
Ism, Ism, Ism/Ismo, Ismo, Ismo (Lerner, Piazza), 25
Issa, Majida, 398n10
Italy, 48, 50, 121
  Italian Communist Party, 59
  Italian neorealism, 36, 55, 102, 387n22
  Rome, 33–38, 45, 59, 388n2
Ivens, Joris, 51, 388n2
Izquierdo, Pelayo, *129*, 129–130

Jackson, Kimberley, 287
Jacobson, Brian, 118
James, David, 94–95, 122–124, 391n16
Japan, 257, 260
Jaunt VR, 30
Jenkins, Henry, 181
Jerslev, Anne, 19–23, 91, 189, 385n13
La Jetée, 376–377
Jodorowsky, Alejandro, 268, 294, 377
Johnson, Randall, 109–110
Jordà, Joaquim, 105, 121, 125–127
"Jornadas de Sitges" (1967), 121

Journal of Latin American Cultural Studies, 24
Juan-Navarro, Santiago, 55, 68, 75

Kafka, Franz, 82, 84
Kalatozov, Mikhail, 49
Karmitz, Marin, 41
The Key, 311
Kinder, Marsha, 25, 122, 149
Kino-Eye symbol, 201–202, 376–377
The Kiss, TIJTS, 216–222, *217*
Kitte kitte iino?, 371
Kodak, 189–190, 395n17
Korda, Alberto, 69
Krauss, Rosalind, 171, 181
Kringiel, Danny, 358
Kristeva, Julia, 42

La Ferla, Jorge, 180, 207–208
La Parra-Pérez, Pablo, 393n2
Ladri di biciclette, 51
Lang, Fritz, 188
Larra, Mariano José de, 84
Larrain, Pablo, 275–276
Last Call, 253
latency, 299–300
Latin America. See *specific topics*
Laurel, Brenda, 337–338
Leen, Catherine, 336, 350
Legendary Entertainment, 3
Leipzig Film Festival, 51
Lejos de los árboles, 57
Lenin vivo, 121
Lerner, Jesse, 25–26, 393n2
Leyda, Julia, 398n8
Lichtenstein, Roy, 129–130
Life Is But a Dream, 257
The Limit, 302, 304
Linares, Andrés, 40, 58
Linares Martínez, Oslavia Danaé, 363–364
linear narratives, 65, 294, 303, 328, 352, 356

Linear Tape-Open (LTO) technology, 188–189
Lippit, Akira Mizuta, 184
Llobet Gràcia, Lorenzo, 127–128
Lobos, Teresa, 291–292
location-based experiences, 312
lo-fi aesthetic, 211, 261
Lopes, Denilson, 257
López, Ana M., 237
López, Tamara, 209
López-Quiñones, Antonio Gómez, 24
Lord, Susan, 383n5
Losada, Matt, 24
Lost, Lost, Lost, 186, 213
Louit, Marcos, 355–356
Lowood, Henry, 359
LTO. See Linear Tape-Open technology
Lubezki, Emmanuel, 3, 337
Lucas, George, 303–304
Lumbreras Giménez, Helena, 33, 36, 69, 174, 384n7, 390n4. See also *El campo para el hombre*
  Álvarez impacting, 44–45, 48, 56, 67–68
  Colectivo Cine de Clase and, 54–56, 58–61
  counter-cinemas and, 50–54
  hybridity used by, 53–54, 70–73, *74*, 75–78
  intermediality of, 53–55, 70–73, *74*, 75–78
  montages by, 70–71, 78–82, *79*, 84–85
  realism and, 70–73, *74*, 75–77
  Solanas impacting, 55–56, 77–78
Lumière, Tetsuo, 260–265, 268, 271–272
Lusnich, Ana Laura, 24
Luso-Hispanic Atlantic, 3, 8–10, 13–14, 384n8, 385n12, 393n2. See also *specific countries*

Luso-Hispanic Atlantic *(continued)*
    cell phone cinema from, 244–251,
        256–297, *262*, *264*, *272*, *278*,
        280, *286*, *288*
    emergence of VR in, 310–314
    emerging video technologies in,
        351–382
Lynch, David, 394n11

Macdonald, Kevin, 398n7
MacDonald, Scott, 124
MacDowel, Duncan, 375
MacEntee, Katie, 261
machinima, 354, 357–364, 401n2
Mack, Jonathan, 42
Macunaíma, 157, 161
Madrid Noir, 30, 313, 314–322, *318*, *320*, 401n8
magical realism, 155, 311
magnetic video, 174, 223, 387
Magritte, René, 229
mainstream cinema, 9, 57, 73–74,
        151, 246–247, 302, 368
    cell phone cinema and, 244, 253–
        256, 275–276
    EdB compared to, 128
    09 La película and, 275
    stylistic tropes of, 283, 291
Make-A-Video tool, Meta, 402n8
Makharam, Ababacar Samb, 36
Making Cinelandia (Serna), 24–25
MALBA. *See* Museo de Arte Moderno
    de Buenos Aires
Mañana . . ., 136
Manhatta, 118–119
Manzanas, 396n20
Mapa Films, 105
Marabunta, 396n20
Maranhão 66, 99–100
Marchessault, Janine, 383n5
Marchesseau, Cyrille, 322

Marí, Jorge, 282–283
Marías, Miguel, 90
Marin, Kellie, 334–335
Marker, Chris, 376–377
Marks, Laura U., 22, 225–226
Marsh, Leslie, 24
Marsh, Steven, 94–95, 125, 143–146, 152
Marshall, Glen, 375
Martí, José, 68
Martínez Cano, Francisco Julián, 304
Martínez Torres, Augusto, 89–90, 105, 167, 390n3
Martins, Paulo, 103, 169
Marxism, 33, 49–50, 55, 58–59, 61, 67, 71, 76
    intermediality and, 86
Masotta, Oscar, 388n6
mass media, 3, 44, 95, 117–118, 131, 133–134
    propaganda and, 148–149
Mateer, John, 302, 304
Mateos, Mariana Chiesa, 394n10
materiality, 11, 28, 187–190, 196, 238, 252, 295
    Carne y Arena and, 4–5
    digitization and, 222–224, 239–240
    in *Película familiar*, 215–220, *217*
    structuralism and, 193–194, 199
    in *TIJTS*, 205–220, *217*, 224–237, *227*, *228*
Mazdon, Lucy, 41
Mazo, Juan Carlos, 268–269, 272–274
McLuhan, Marshall, 71
mechanical reproduction, 372–373
media archaeology, 179, 181, 196, 218, 220, 224, 237
media convergence, 171, 189, 212, 238
medium specificity, 8, 20, 36, 178, 187, 211–212, 380
    Álvarez manipulating, 47

avant-garde filmmakers on, 119
celluloid, 27
EdB disregarding, 130
"impure cinema" and, 115–116, 122
Lumbreras and, 50, 53–54
El mégano, 45–46
Mekas, Jonas, 7, 38, 186, 191–193, 213
Méliès, Georges, 118, 183, 200
Melita, 313
Memorias del subdesarrollo, 46, 81
memory, 177–187, 190, 192–193, 198, 202–203, 350
 aesthetics and, 195–196
 Cugliandolo exploring, 29
Meshes in the Afternoon, 193, 199, 394n11
Mess, Conrad, 282–283, 285, 289
Mestman, Mariano, 38–41, 58–59
Meta (company), 352, 402n8
metalepsis, 91, 132, 137–138, *140*, 146, 391n14
meta-reflection, 230, 260, 263, 276
metaverse (Facebook), 300, 352–353
Metegol, 363–364
Metro Veinte (VR series), 311
Metropolis, 188, 292
Metz, Christian, 163
Mexico, 24, 51, 107, 164–165, 310, 313, 337–350, 393n2
 horror films from, 250, 289
 TikTok usage, 365
 US-Mexico border, 1, 13, 312, 329–330, 336, 339
micro-movies, 242, 245–246, 366, 371
Microsoft, 309–311
middle-class, 2, 88, 107, 169–170, 316
Midjourney, 376–377
migrants and refugees, 213, 242, 316
 in *Carne y Arena*, 1–4, 30, 335–350, *343*, *346*

immersive cinema addressing, 311, 354–355
 in *Use of Force*, 30, 329–335, *332*
militant cinema, 9, 62, 174, 275, 381, 384n7, 388n7. See also specific directors; specific groups
 aesthetics and, 53–54, 63–67, 70, 72–73, 82–83
 of Cine Liberación, 61, 63–64, 66–67, 90, 384n7
 compared to *Terra em transe*, 117
 defined, 66–67
 documentaries as, 37–41, 45–46, 48–54, 57–58, 60, 85
 EdB and, 26, 121, 135, 170
 on Grupo Goethe, 192
 La hora de los hornos significant for, 38–41
 Iberian, 27, 33, 38–39, 49–54, 56–61, 65
 transnational, 33–38, 41–49
militarization, 306, 311, 335, 400nn2–3
Milk, Chris, 332
"minor" cinema, 9, 22, 25, 173–176, 243–244, 284
Mirizio, Annalisa, 50
mise en scène, 98, 301, 367, 369
mixed reality (MR), 2, 305, 309–310, 334–336, 339–340, 348, 352, 400n1
mobile aesthetics, 16, 284
mobile apps, 253, 292, 295
*Mobile Media Making in an Age of Smartphone*s (Berry, Schleser), 26
Mobile World Congress, 310–311
Model Shop, 392n19
modernism, 20, 96, 118–119, 122, 138–139, 146–147
monetization, 313, 365, 369

montage, 27, 36–37, 43, 45
   by Álvarez, 47–48, 51, 68
   dialectical, 44, 47, 85, 392n18
   by Lumbreras, 70–71, 78–82, *79*, 84–85
   Soviet-style, 44, 46, 52, 55, 75, 192
Mórbido in Mexico City, 289
Mostra Internazionale del Cinema Nuovo, 37
Moving Verses (Bollig), 22, 24, 113
MR. *See* mixed reality
Muerte al invasor, 45
Muerte de un ciclista, 57, 125–126
Mulholland Drive, 394n11
Müller, Jürgen E., 43, 94
multimedia, multimediality and, 325, 337–350
multiperspectivism, 314–315, 355
multisensory experiences, 19, 304–305, 309, 321–327, *327*, 340
Mulvey, Laura, 126, 391n15
Muñoz Suay, Ricardo, 121, 153, 158
Murphy, Jill, 6
Museo de Arte Moderno de Buenos Aires (MALBA), 174, 176, 190, 236
Museum of Interactive Cinema, 359
musical theater, 268, 270, 274
Mussolini, Benito, 34
Les mystères de Château de Dé, 118–119

Nadal-Melsió, Sara, 44, 49, 134
Naficy, Hamid, 21–22, 36, 40, 110, 189
Nagib, Lúcia, 19–23, 91, 104, 189, 385n13
   on Cinema Novo, 161
   on "impure cinema," 116
   on *Terra em transe*, 110, 112–113
Nahuel y el libro mágico, 357

Nasher Sculpture Center, 1–2, 282n3, 336, 341
national belonging, 203, 381
national cinemas, 1, 8–9, 24, 41, 250, 351
national identities, 22, 37, 154, 180, 192, 211, 213, 231, 381
nationalism, 15–16, 112, 122, 171–172, 316
NCE. *See* Nuevo Cine Español
Nekes, Werner, 191–192
neocolonialism, 65–66, 81, 97, 379
neoliberalism, 24, 36, 352–353
neorealism, 34–38, 45–46, 50–51, 57–58, 102, 129, 160
neosurrealism, 169
Netflix, 316–317, 371
Neto, Torquato, 104
New Hollywood (American New Wave), 66
New Latin American Cinema, 34–36, 40, 46, 101, 384nn7–8, 388n7
New Wave cinema, 191
New York, 54, 186–187, 191–193, 195–196, 213
newspapers, 137–138, *139*, 141–142
Nielsen, Jakob, 267
Nigeria, 256
Night Fishing, 257
Nitsche, Michael, 359
No compteu amb els dits, 146
Noche de vino tinto, 136
Nocturno 29, 28, 57, 67, 92, 143–151, *145*, *147*
NO-DO. *See* Noticiarios y Documentales
Nollywood (Nigeria), 256–257
noncommercial filmmaking, 13, 21–22, 257, 284n8
nonlinearity, 276–277
Nooby Crazy (Nooby Studios), 362

North Africa, 36
nostalgia, 173, 182, 241, 361, 387n23, 395n15, 396n18
  aesthetics and, 225–226
  affect and, 205
  Caprín invoking, 224, 231
  for celluloid formats, 174–177, 184–186, 188
  exile and, 175–176, 210
  home movies and, 29
  obsolescence and, 27, 203, 206, 237
  temporality and, 29, 177, 198
Noticiarios y Documentales (NO-DO), Spain, 53, 65, 70, 132, 148–149, 166
Nouvelle Vague, 106, 119–120, 125
Nova Cançó, 158
Now!, 47, 49, 67–68
Nuestro Cine (journal), 49, 89–90, 158
09 La Película, 29, 259, 275–282, *278*, *280*, 284, 297
Nuevo Cine Español (NCE), 55, 56–58, 102, 391n17
  EdB compared to, 125–128, 170
Nuevo cine latinoamericano (Torres, Estremera), 393n3
Nunes, José María, 28, 57, 67, 125
  Sexperiencias by, 92, 120–121, 136–143, *138*, *140*
NVIDIA Corporation, 352

O testamento de Don Quixote, 392n24
O todos o ninguno, 63–64
obsolescence, 165, 174, 182–183, 196, 211, 222–223
  nostalgia and, 27, 203, 206, 237
  of Super 8, 27, 178, 180, 203
Oculus (Facebook), 304, 307, 323, 344
Odin, Roger, 254–256, 258

Oh, the Golden Days of Video Making, TIJTS, 222–237, *227*, *228*
Oiticica, Hélio, 104, 166
Ojos sombríos, 323
Olivera, Javier, 205, 210–212, 220
Olmsted, Marc, 261
Omicron, 362
Open Windows, 291–292
OpenAI, 375
opera, 116–117
Ortiz, Alejandro Matamala, 378
Osorio, Gabriel, 363
the Other, 13, 311, 332
The Other Side, 283, 285
Oubiña, David, 396n22

Padrós, Antoni, 90, 121
Painted, 375
Pájaros de papel, 30, 311, 314–316, 321–327, *323*, *327*
Pantallas transnacionales (Lusnich, Aisemberg, Cuarterolo), 24
Paranormal Activity, 185, 261
Parikka, Jussi, 181
Park Chan-wook, 257
pasodoble (music), 162–163
Pasolini, Paolo, 50, 60, 98, 101, 113
Patino, Basilio Martín, 125, 389n12
Peixoto, Mario, 384n8
Película familiar, 215–221, *217*
Peña, Nonny de la, 30, 304, 314, 329–335, 338, 355, 401n10
Peppermint Frappé, 131, 392n19
Perdigão, Paulo, 160
Pereira da Silva, Humberto, 152–153
Pérez Estremera, Manuel, 89–90, 393n3
periodismo immersivo. *See* immersive journalism
Perón, Juan, 58–59
Perriam, Chris Perriam, 248

Pesaro Film Festival, 96–97, 105, 113
Pethő, Ágnes, 94
phenomenology, 260, 383n5
PHI Studio, 3
photography, 19, 190, 217–218, 232–233, 372, 401n8
    as intermedia in *Madrid Noir*, 319–321, *320*
    newspaper, 137–138, *138*
    poetry and, 113
    in *Terra em transe*, 114–115, *115*, 137
photorealism, 328, 373
Piazza, Luciano, 25–26
Pinocchio, 357, 364
Placeholder, 337–338
PLAT (Picto-Luminic-Audio-Tactile) Lab, 221
plurivocality, 78
pneurosis, 198–200, *201*, 202–203
poetry, 108–113, *109*, 116
    EdB and, 125, 133, 143–151, *146*
police brutality, 68–69, 77, 79, 159, 195, 241–242
political allegory, 28, 91, 100, 107, 143, 169
    in *Pájaros de papel*, 324–326
Pompeu Fabra University, 378
Pontecorvo, Gillo, 59–60, 388n2
poor images, 211–212, 226
Pop Art, 129–131
popular culture, 120–121, 161–162
    in *Terra em transe*, 111–112
populism, 16, 58–59, 98–104, 114, 122–123
Portabella, Pere, 28, 57, 93, 101, 125, 389n1, 392nn21–22
    addressing Vietnam War, 141
    Nocturno 29, 92
    Rocha and, 105–106
Positif (journal), 89
positionality, 138, 338, 345

post-cinema, 1, 5–6, 10
Post-Cinema (Denson, Leyda), 398n8
postcolonialism, 34–36, 162
post-digital cinema, 27, 398n8
    cell phone cinema as, 251–255, 259–260, 271
post-human, 253–254, 374
post-medium age, 171, 179, 197–198, 240
postmodernity, 88, 134, 202, 296
post-national age, 176, 178–179, 190–191, 240, 248
postproduction, 201, 372, 375–376, 395n17
    cell phone cinema, 247, 283
    digital, 180–181, 190–191, 200, *201*, 359–360, 395n15
post-structuralism, 152
Powell, David, 293
preproduction, 372–373
"presence," VR immersion and, 301–302, 321–322
Prieto, Rodrigo, 337
Print Generation, 193
privacy issues, 365
Project Syria, 338
The Projected Nation (Losada), 24
propaganda, 65, 114, 148–149, 221–222
    Marxist, 98–99
Psycho, 200
psychoanalysis, 152, 163, 199, 202
psychodramas, 193, 200
public-private partnerships, 216, 352–353
punctum, 217–218, 220

Quake (videogame), 360
Queimada, 59–60

Rabal, Francisco, 392n23
racial injustice, 68, 195

Radicales libres (Alcoz), 386n20
Radiotelevisione Italiana, 59
Rajewsky, Irina, 20, 390n6
Rascaroli, Laura, 6
Ray, Man, 118–119
Raza, 70
Ready Player One, 303
realism, 282, 304–305, 338, 340, 342, 348
    avant-garde *vs.*, 34
    of *El campo para el hombre*, 65–70
    documentaries and, 35
    Lumbreras approach to, 70–73, *74*, 75–77
    Rocha destabilizing, 112, 116–117
    Socialist, 49, 70, 125, 149–150
Red Dead Redemption 2, 361
Reel Families (Zimmerman), 26
reenactment, 64, 329, 331–335, *332*, 344, 348
Rees, Alan L., 383n5
Refiguring Spain (Kinder), 25
Reich, Steve, 194–195, 396n23
Renan, Sheldon, 7
representation, 171, 195
    in *Sexperiencias*, 139–140, *140*
representation, filmic, 85, 381
residual media, 190, 199, 237
revolutionary violence, 68–69, 97
Ricalde, Maricruz Castro, 25
Ringu, 399n18
Rio, Juana del, 398n10
Risner, Jonathan, 250, 386n18
Robinson Crusoe, 309
Rocha, Glauber, 87–89, 384n7, 390n2, 392n24
    on aesthetics of hunger, 90, 96–97
    Cinema Novo and, 27–28, 95–98
    EdB collaboration with, 92, 151–161
    exile of, 89, 97, 167–168

intermediality of, 104–118, *109*, *115*, 161–169, *165*
    in *Nuestro Cine*, 90–91
Rodowick, David, 43, 199, 208, 212, 222–223, 394n9
Rodríguez, Carina, 250
Rodriguez, Robert, 302, 304
Rogosin, Lionel, 191
Rojo en el bosque sangriento, 29, 259–266, *262*, *264*, 271–272, 274, 281, 285, 291
Rolf Art Gallery, 206
Roma, 395n15
Roma città aperta, 388n2
Rome, Italy, 33–38, 45, 59, 388n2
Rosellini, Roberto, 35, 38, 388n2
Roselló, Roberto Arnau, 53, 67
Rosen, Philip, 180–181, 185, 190, 380, 394n12
Ross, Miriam, 304–305, 339–340
Rozenkrantz, Jonathan, 225–226
Rubio, Vicente, 286, 289–291
RunwayML, 378
Russian Revolution, 34

Sadako 3D 2, 399n18
Saenz de Heredia, José Luis, 70
Sakaly, Dorothy, 375
Salazkina, Masha, 26, 35–36, 40, 393n2
Salles, Walter, 17
Salmi, Nicole, 325
Salt, 376
San Sebastián film festival, 371
Sánchez Prado, Ignacio, 24, 351
Sánchez-Vives, Mavi, 331
Sanderson, John, 105
Sangre y levadura, 29, 259, 266–275, *270*, *272*, 281, 291
Sanjinés, Jorge, 90, 384n7
Santaolalla, Gustavo, 337
Santaolalla, Isabel, 248

Santos, Carles, 143
Santos, Maria Luisa, 216, *217*, 218–219
Sarney, José, 99–100, 391n9
Sarney Costa, José, 99
Saura, Carlos, 125–126, 131, 392n19
Saxton, Libby, 69
Schleser, Max, 26
Schneemann, Carolee, 7
sci-fi films, 29
  AI, 376–377
  horror and, 259, 291
Scolari, Carlos A., 359
Scott, Mackenzie, 366
Screen (journal), 391n16
screen media, 300, 340
Screening Neoliberalism (Sánchez Prado), 24, 351
Second Cinema, 39, 53, 87, 124, 173, 388n7
  Rocha and, 95–96
  Third Cinema *vs.*, 126, 143, 171
Sector Zero 4, 289, 291, 399n17
self-censorship, 88–89, 367
self-distribution, 245–246, 262, 367
selfie-films, 241, 276, 279–280, 287, 366, 368
self-imposed exile, 97–98, 209–210
self-referentiality, 6, 279, 286, 359, 366, 376–377
self-reflexivity, self-reflexive turn and, 168, 171, 181, 186–187, 198
  in cell phone cinema, 246–247, 260–261, *261*, 264, *264*
  in *Fata Morgana*, 133
  in *Memorias del subdesarrollo*, 46
  in *Terra em transe*, 112–113
  in Third Cinema, 75
sensory experiences, 296, 309, 321–327, *327*, 338, 340–343, 349
Serene Velocity, 193
Serna, Laura Isabel, 24–25

70 mm, 395n15
Sexperiencias, 28, 57, 67, 92, 120–121, 136–143, *138*, *140*
Shakespeare, William, 110, 154, 162, 164
Sharir, Yacov, 337
Sharits, Paul, 76
Shaviro, Steven, 273
Sheeler, Charles, 118–119
Shilina-Conte, Tanya, 242
short form videos, 245, 364–372
Sica, Vittorio De, 35, 51
Simons, Jan, 256
Singer, Michael J., 301–302
single take films, 268–269, 281
Sinovcic, Tomás, 396n20
Sitges Film Festival, 289–290
Sitges Horror Film Festival, 260
Sitney, P. Adams, 124, 193–194, 199
Situationism, 121, 392n18
16 mm, 35, 193, 196, 203, 206, 215–216, 219–221
  Lumbreras using, 62
The Skin of the Film (Marks), 22
slasher genre, 263
Slater, Mel, 331
SmartFilm festival, 251, 268
SMS Sugar Man, 256
Snapchat, 367
Snow, Michael, 76, 193, 397n24
"social displacement hypothesis," 293
social media, 214–215, 271, 291–295, 351, 358, 367–369
  horror, 291–294
socialism, 34–35, 46, 62, 158
Socialist realism, 49, 70, 125, 149–150
Solanas, Fernando "Pino," 33, 45–46, 192, 384n7, 388n4, 388n7
  La hora de los hornos by, 21, 38–41
  influence of Birri on, 36–37
  Lumbreras impacted by, 55–56, 77–78

Soler, Llorenç, 48, 59–60, 390n4
Somnium, 300, 302–303
Sondheim, Steven, 268
soundtracks, musical scores and, 195, 320–327, *327*, 393n27
  for *Cabeças cortadas*, 162
  montage and, 48
South Africa, 256
South Korea, 257
South Park (television show), 360–361
Souto, Prieto, 64
Soviet Union, 27, 125
  Soviet-style montage, 44, 46, 52, 55, 75, 192
Spain, Iberian cinema and, 3, 23–26, 41, 96, 337, 377–378, 390n8, 391n17
  animated films in, 357
  Argentine expats in, 28–29, 174–175, 178–180, 203, 209–214
  Barcelona, 174–175, 177, 191, 196–198, 203–214, 236
  cell phone cinema from, 257–258, 282–297, *286*, *288*
  censorship in, 52–53, 56–58, 126–127, 389n9, 391n17
  dictatorial, 56, 170, 177, 221, 389n9, 389n12, 390n2
  found footage horror cinema in, 399n11
  NO-DO, 53, 65, 70, 132, 148–149, 166
  Spanish Civil War, 51, 69, 133, 148, 216, 221, 289n12, 316–317
  TikTok usage, 365
  transition to democracy, 54–55
  VR cinema from, 30, 312–313, 315–320
Spain in a Day, 254
Spanish Cinema Against Itself (Marsh, S.), 94–95, 125

Spanish Cinema in the Global Context (Amago), 25
Spanish Civil War, 51, 69, 133, 148, 216, 221, 289n12, 316–317
Spanish Communist Party, 57–58
Spanish Journal of Cultural Studies, 49
spectator-participants, 4, 30, 301, 338
spectator-players, 317–321, 324
spectators, 7, 189, 242, 385n9, 398n8
  cell phone film, 26, 243–244, 253, 266–268, 279, 282–283, 290, 293
  empathy and, 355
  global audiences as, 247–248, 381
  immersive technologies and, 356
  militant cinema, 44–45
  nostalgia of, 185
  transnational, 17
  universal, 311
  user-viewer, 30, 309, 315
  VR cinema, 1, 301–302, 314–315, 330–335, 340–345, 348–350
  as witnesses, 330–335, 345, 349
Spheres, 304
Spielberg, Steven, 264, 303
spyware, 255
Stam, Robert, 77, 91, 98, 108–110, 112–113, 116
Star Wars: Secrets of the Empire, 303–304
Steam (gaming platform), 307
Stelzer, Fabian, 376
Stenger, Nicole, 337
stereoscope, stereoscopic cinema and, 304, 309
"Stereoscopic Films" (Eisenstein), 309
Steyerl, Hito, 211–212
stop-motion sequences and animation, 183, *184*, 200, 357, 363
Strand, Paul, 118–119

streaming services and platforms, 1, 243, 251, 258, 360–361, 364. *See also* distribution
Strickland, Rachel, 337–338
structuralism, 95, 152, 193–194, 199–200
  of Rocha, 163–164
Stunt Double, 257
Suárez, Gonzalo, 127
Suay, Muñoz, 391n13
Subero, Gustavo, 249–250
Sundance Film Festival, 254, 304
Super 8 film, 243–244, 380–381, 393n2, 393n5, 394n6, 395n17
  aesthetics, 174, 183–190, 198–199
  from Argentina, 191–237, *194*, *201*, *217*, *227*, *228*, 393n3, 394n7, 396n18
  digitization of, 175, 187–191, 193, 196, 198, 207, 233–234
  experimental films, 8, 187–191
  Hispano-Argentine experimental film, 176–187, *183*, *184*
  intermediality and, 187–196
  militant cinema using, 62
  nostalgia for, 173–177
  in the post-medium age, 197–198
  resurgence of, 175–190, 225, 238–239
  Val del Omar using, 221
Super Mario Movie, 361
superocheros (Super 8 filmmakers), 190–192, 197, 393n2. *See also* Grupo Goethe
surrealism, 73, 97, 105–106, 118–119, 171, 199, 268
  avant garde, 143–145
  in *Cabeças cortadas*, 92, 152–158, 166
  in *Fata Morgana*, 129–130
  in *Terra em transe*, 111

surveillance, 29, 185, 306, 311, 352, 394n12
  cellular technology and, 247, 255, 261–262, 278, 297
  immigration, *332*, 334
Sutherland, Ivan E., 305, 311
Svensson, Alexander, 294, 296
Sweeney Todd, 268, 274
Symphony, 400n6
Syria, 255

Taboada, Javier de, 40
Tales of Arcadia (series), 316–317
Tangerine, 254
Tannock, Stuart, 176
Taquini, Graciela, 209–210
techno-capitalism, 134–135
techno-determinism, 259, 306
techno-horror, 291, 295
technophobia, 254, 293
techno-utopianism, 22, 379
Telefilms Group, 368
temporality, 119, 170, 190, 202–203, 281, 339–340
  in *Madrid Noir*, 317, 321
  nostalgia and, 29, 177, 198
  obsolescence and, 223–224
  single take films and, 268–269
  Super 8 and, 178, 183, 190
  in *Use of Force*, 333–335
Terra em transe (*Entranced Earth, Land in Anguis*h), 28, 95, 97, 98–103, 168
  Cabeças cortadas compared to, 156–158
  intermedial experimentation in, 91, 104–118, *109*, *115*
  populism and, 98–104
Teslasuit, 306–308
text-image interactions, 28, 91–92, 113, 118–124,

text-to-video AI tools, 373–374
Theater of Cruelty, 268, 274
theatricality, 28, 104, 273–274, 281, 319–321
Theorizing Film Through Contemporary Art (Murphy, Rascaroli), 6
Third Cinema, 8–10, 21, 37, 39–41, 173–174, 242, 354, 388n7
  militant documentary and, 50, 52, 85
  realism and, 66
  Rocha and, 95–96, 153
  Second Cinema *vs.*, 126, 143, 171
  self-reflexive agit-prop techniques in, 75
Third World, 39, 47, 53, 92, 96–97, 141, 160
third-person perspectives, 200, 301
35 mm, 188, 255–256, 395n15
This Is Just to Say (*TIJTS*), 29, 175–176, 203–236, *217*, *226*, *228*
Thorburn, David, 181
3D cinema, 309, 327, 340
3D space, 30, 306, 324–327
3DAR, 322–323
360-Degree Cinema, 30–31, 305, 327–329, 339–350, 354–357
Tierney, Dolores, 337
Tierra sin Pan (*Las Hurdes*), 51–52, 73
TIJTS. See *This Is Just to Say*
TikTok cinema, 30–31, 351, 364–372
TikTokShortFilmFestival, 370–371
Tomorrow, 313
Tompkins, Cynthia, 25–26, 37, 387n21
Torcuato di Tella Institute, 388n6
Toro, Guillermo del, 7, 24, 316–317, 357, 364
Torrell, Josep, 143, 147, 149
Torres, Alejandra, 237–238
total cinema, 304–305, 311

Totti, Gianni, 121
"Toward an Imperfect Cinema" (García Espinosa), 46
Townsend, Christopher, 20
Tracing the Borders of Spanish Horror Cinema and Television (Marí), 282–283
transnational migration, 335, 383nn3–4
transnational subjects, 198, 312–313, 316, 353
transnational turn, 8, 18
transnationalism, transnationality and, 312, 353, 357, 375, 377–378, 383n4
  of *Cabeças cortadas*, 151–161
  of cell phone cinema, 241–242, 247–250, 252, 255–259, 266, 268, 295–297
  Hispano-Argentine, 174–187, *183*, *184*
  of *La hora de los hornos*, 38–41
  identities and, 29, 177, 180
  immersive cinema and, 312–313, 354–355
  intermediality and, 5–11, 14–15, 18–24, 27, 41–49, 315–321, *320*, 374, 379–382
  of machinima projects, 358–359, 363–364
  Super 8 practices and, 191, 195–196
  transnational filmmaking and, 2–5, 14–18, 28, 88, 97, 151, 191 393n2, 337, 385n11
  Villazana on, 35–36
  of VR animation, 314–321, *318*, *320*
Trerotola, Diego, 194
Tres cantosa Lenin, 76
Treske, Andreas, 267
Tribeca Film Festival, 315, 330

Tricontinental magazine, 39, 149
tricontinental revolutionary spirit, 36, 38–39, 81, 96, 123, 137, 149
   tricontinental cinema and, 37, 154, 171–172
Tron, 377
Tropicalism, 104, 121–122, 158, 161–169, 171
Trump, Donald, 342 1, 346–347
Turner, Matt, 362–363
Turquety, Benoît, 385n9
Tuset Street, 57
Twitch (platform), 314, 360–361
Twitter (X), 368, 377
2001: A Space Odyssey, 292
El 2020 tuvo un guía diferente, 369–370

Ukamau group, 90, 384n7
"The Ultimate Display" (Sutherland), 305
uncanniness, 182, 185, 190, 216, 288, 295, 321
UNCIPAR. *See* Unión de Cineastas de Paso Reducido
underdevelopment, 96–97, 100, 107, 156, 171, 390n8
underground filmmakers, 53, 59, 190, 260, 263–265, 396n18
Understanding Media (McLuhan), 71
Unfriended, 291–292
UNHCR. *See* United Nations High Commissioner for Refugees
Unidad Móvil Rosario, 41
Unión de Cineastas de Paso Reducido (UNCIPAR), 396n21
United Nations High Commissioner for Refugees (UNHCR), 354
United States, 27, 232, 242, 316, 329–335, 347, 360–364
   Argentine expats in, 209

civil rights movement, 68, 195
imperialism, 9–10, 47
New Wave cinema from, 191
structuralism, 199
TikTok usage in, 365
US-Mexico border, 1, 13, 312, 329–330, 336, 339
VR usage in, 300, 312
Universidad Pompeu Fabra, 128
University of Barcelona, 331
Urgilés, Juan Pablo, 329, 354
Urrego, Juan Pablo, 398n10
Use of Force, 30, 327–335, *332*, 337
user-generated content, 358, 366

Vajnstok, Vladimir, 49
Val del Omar, José, 215–222, *217*, 231, 236
Valdivieso, Pepe, 369
Valle, Federico, 357
Valle Dávila, Ignacio del, 47
Vallejo, Gerardo, 36–37, 396n20
VanDerBeek, Stan, 7
Veloso, Caetano, 104, 158
Venezuela, 329, 355, 393n2
Venice International Film festival, 313
Le vent d'est, 120
Venturi, Riccardo, 383n5
El verdugo, 57
vertical cinema, 243, 366–371
Vertical Cinema Festival, 368–369
Vertov, Dziga, 43, 75–76, 202, 376–377
VHS videos, 224–225, 239, 394n6
Vida en sombras, 127–128
video games, 2, 30–31, 357–363, 400n3, 402n10
   VR and, 299–302, 314
video sharing platforms, 365, 367. *See also* streaming services and platforms

Vietnam War, 51, 139, 141
Vilarós, Teresa, 127
Vilaseca, David, 132
Villazana, Libia, 35–36
Villeneuve, Denis, 188
Vimeo, 214–215, 238
"vintage" media, 28, 174
violence, 262, 274, 279, 288–289, 344–345
   immersive journalism reenacting, 331–335, *332*
   represented in *Sexperiencias*, 139–141, *140*
Viridiana, 93, 149
The Virtual Life of Film, 208, 212
virtual reality (VR), VR cinema and, 352–353, 383n3, 387nn24–25, 400n1, 400n5, 401nn10–11
   animated, 314–327, *318*, *320*, *323*, *327*, 338–350
   double embodiment of, 339, 344, 349
   emergence of, 299–300, 310–314
   empathy and, 4–5, 304, 311, 313, 321, 329–336, 339, 348–350
   HMD for, 306–311, 326–327, 332–333, 338
   immersive journalism and, 327–350, *332*, *341*, *343*, *346*, 401n9
   interactivity and, 301–302, 314–315, 317, 321–327, *323*
   intermediality of, 300–305, 307–315, 337–350, 379–380
   in Latin America and Spain, 310–314
   spectator-participants and, 4, 30, 301, 338
   spectators, 1, 301–302, 314–315, 330–335, 340–345, 348–350
   technological antecedents of, 304–307
   360-Degree Cinema and, 354–357

Visionary Film, 193
visual impairment, 311, 323, *323*, 326, 400n4
"Visual Pleasures and Narrative Cinema" (Mulvey), 391n16
Vives-González, Luna, 177–178, 393n4
Vlog, 262
vlog horror subgenre, 262
Vlogger, 361–362
voice-over narration, 66, 72–73, 226, 265, 317, 325–326, 376
   in *La hora de los hornos*, 81
The Void (production company), 303–304
"voluntary" exile, 97, 151–152
"Vor dem Gesetz" (Kafka), 84
VR. *See* virtual reality
VRChat, 300, 302–303
"Vuelva usted mañana" (de Larra), 84

Walley, Jonathan, 7–8
Walsh, David, 395n16
Ward, Julie, 5
Warhol, Andy, 77, 129–130, 191
Wavelength, 193, 397n24
We Met in Virtual Reality, 302–303
webcams, 262
Weijdom, Joris, 348–349
West Africa, 256
Western rationalism, 93, 97–98, 152
Wetmore, Kevin, 281
What Is Cinema? (Bazin), 242
Whitney Museum of Art, 359
William, William Carlos, 175
Wilson, Gavin, 46–47, 244, 247, 254, 267, 283–284
Witmer, Bob G., 301–302
Wood, David, 113
working-class, 38, 52, 58, 63–64, 136
World of Warcraft (videogame), 360

World War II, 34–35, 121, 186–187
Wrath of the Tarot Kings, 361

Xavier, Ismail, 91, 100, 103
XR. *See* Extended Reality

Youngblood, Gene, 6–7, 23, 383n5
YouTube, 314, 334, 351, 357, 358, 360–362, 365
    archiving via, 54, 238
    cell phone cinema on, 256, 258, 261–263, 271, 282, 290
    YouTube VR, 328
Yuxweluptun, Lawrence Paul, 338

Zavattini, Cesare, 38, 50
Zhang Meng, 257
Zimmerman, Patricia, 26

www.ingramcontent.com/pod-product-compliance
Lightning Source LLC
Chambersburg PA
CBHW070231240426
43673CB00044B/1755